HERITAGE OF MUSIC

VOLUME II
THE ROMANTIC ERA

HERITAGE OF MUSIC

EDITED BY
MICHAEL RAEBURN AND ALAN KENDALL

VOLUME II
THE ROMANTIC ERA

CONSULTANT EDITORS
DENIS MATTHEWS, LUDWIG FINSCHER
AND ROBERT DONINGTON

OXFORD NEW YORK
OXFORD UNIVERSITY PRESS
1989

Oxford University Press, Walton Street, Oxford OX2 6DP

Oxford   New York   Toronto
Delhi   Bombay   Calcutta   Madras   Karachi
Petaling Jaya   Singapore   Hong Kong   Tokyo
Nairobi   Dar es Salaam   Cape Town
Melbourne   Auckland
and associated companies in
Berlin   Ibadan

Oxford is a trade mark of Oxford University Press

Published in the United States
by Oxford University Press

British Library Cataloguing in Publication Data
Heritage of music.
    1. Music—History and criticism   I. Raeburn, Michael,
1940-   .II. Kendall, Alan, 1939-
    780'.903   ML193
ISBN 0–19–520493–X (set)
        0–19–505371–0 (vol.2)

Library of Congress Cataloguing in Publication Data
Main entry under title:
Heritage of music.

    Includes index.
    Contents: 1. Classical music and its origins —
2. Romantic music — 3. Legacy of nineteenth-century
music — [etc.]
    1. Music—History and criticism.   I. Raeburn, Michael,
1940-   . II. Kendall, Alan, 1939-
ML160.H527   1988   780'.9   85-21429
ISBN 0–19–520493–X (set)
        0–19–505371–0 (vol.2)

Title-page illustration: J. G. Schadow,
Marianne Schlegel as Mignon, 1802

Produced by Heritage of Music Ltd

Design and art direction: David Warner
Picture research: Julia Engelhardt, Lisa Agate,
Robert Turnbull, Helen Ottaway
Artwork: Roy Coombs
Translations from German: Derek McCulloch,
Alexander Lieven
Color origination: Scala, Florence

Printed in Hong Kong

CONTENTS

THE AGE OF BEETHOVEN AND SCHUBERT

OTTO BIBA & DENIS MATTHEWS

Opposite: Beethoven's study on the second floor of the Schwarzspanierhaus, a former monastery that had been turned into an apartment house, where the composer lived for the last eighteen months of his life. This lithograph is from a drawing made at the beginning of April 1827, shortly after Beethoven's death.

Haydn, Mozart and Beethoven all spent the greater part of their lives in Vienna. Franz Schubert spent virtually the whole of his life in that city, and his short lifespan, from 1797 to 1828, coincided with a period of great political, economic and social change there. In all probability Haydn in his later years suffered from this unrest, and Beethoven, too, who settled in Vienna in 1792, lived through the same era. However, we find in their lives and works relatively few references to current events. Both Haydn and Beethoven were clearly defined personalities, in the same way that they are unmistakably representatives of the Classical style in music, so one can hardly maintain that they are typical figures of a period of change. By way of contrast, Schubert was born into this transition. He himself was not a political person in the strictest sense of the word, but much of his life, and the course that it took, can only be correctly understood and interpreted if we see him in his historical and social context, and if we accept that he forms part of no fixed tradition, either in his person or in his music. He grew up in a time when everything was in a state of flux.

The Holy Roman Empire, which for generations in the course of its one thousand years of existence had been ruled from Vienna, effectively came to an end during the Napoleonic Wars and legally expired in 1806, when Emperor Franz II formally relinquished his ancient title to Napoleon. Two years earlier, however, the break-up of the old Empire was implicit in Franz's decision to assume the title of *Austrian* Emperor, Austria having hitherto been only an Archduchy. For us today this is merely a fact, but for people living at the time it represented the end of a millennium and the beginning of something completely new. For the first time the German-speaking lands were no longer part of a far-reaching political union, with traditions reaching back to the Middle Ages, and the formality, if only a formality, of an elected Emperor. Now they were divided into the Austrian Empire, the Prussian Kingdom and a whole host of autonomous minor principalities. All these found themselves in a state of war with France under Napoleon, relieved intermittently by short-lived armistices and peace treaties, but at all times either dependent upon or subjugated by him. For a period of two decades political peace and stability gave way to disunity

and war. The fact that Austria was now an Empire, and as such the peer of France and Russia, was the result of an act of patriotic self-assertion. It had no real political meaning until 1815, when the Congress of Vienna compensated for the humiliations and cruel setbacks of the previous years. The old *Reich* had come to an end, and with it the dominance of the Hapsburgs, and Austria and Vienna, over the wider German-speaking area. Instead, the new Empire, ruled by Hapsburg Emperors still with Vienna as their seat, conferred new status and importance upon Bohemia, Moravia, Hungary and neighboring territories to the east, southeast and south, which, together with Austria, formed this new political unit. The Hapsburg Empire had begun its evolution into states of different nationalities and languages. The Hungarians – to name but one example – began to feel themselves to be not only Hapsburg subjects (and happy ones at that), but also *Hungarians*. All this must be considered when one finds, for instance, the sudden emergence of an *all' ungherese* (in Hungarian style) element in music.

Although Vienna remained the imperial seat, even here changes came about that reflected the political developments. The aristocracy of the old Holy Roman Empire went into decline, but their counterparts from Hapsburg territories began to show a new sense of their station and above all a sense of identity tinged with national pride. They kept up appearances as best they could in Vienna, but came to look upon their country seat in the provinces as more than just a financial asset and a summer retreat. These country seats now tended to be converted into the real residential home, with a sense of belonging to that area. And so it was that cultural life began to blossom in the provinces as never before.

In economic terms the aristocracy had lost virtually all the status that it had enjoyed in the mid-eighteenth century. Emperor Joseph II had abolished serfdom in the 1780s and issued new legislation on land tax, so that the financial returns from land were severely diminished. Since 1792, with only short intermissions, Austria had been in wars with France that involved the whole of Europe, and which were ended only by the *Völkerschlacht* (Battle of the Nations) fought near Leipzig in 1813. These wars brought considerable hardship to the people and heavier financial burdens to the aristocracy (and to a lesser extent the Church) than had hitherto been the case. The urge to build became a thing of the past, as did also the private court orchestra. Few titled families were now in a position to maintain even the smallest ensemble of four to six players. Many musicians previously in aristocratic employment became music teachers, took up posts in local administration or entered other professions, and began to play an important role in municipal and public musical life. They had become part of the middle classes, which were also finding a

new identity. Later than had been the case in Britain, for example, these were becoming a politically significant factor – albeit relatively unprotected – exercising a strong economic and cultural influence. What hitherto had been achieved culturally by the aristocracy was now perforce, and in different forms, carried out by the middle classes.

• Economic realities •

The benefits of the old form of patronage appear in the life of Joseph Haydn, who had worked his way up through the echelons of the aristocracy, from Baron Fürnberg via Count Morzin to Prince Esterházy. As Kapellmeister of a court *Kapelle* he enjoyed a high standard of living. The publication of his works spread his fame beyond his home province and brought him commissions from afar. The Prince made no serious limitations upon him, and he was free to negotiate his own terms with publishers. Furthermore, he had an orchestra at his permanent disposal with which he could experiment and try out new material, an advantage that proved crucial not only to the development of his own personal style, but to the evolution of classical music. In 1790 the Prince died, and the vastly expensive private orchestra was disbanded, but in recognition of his service Haydn retained the title of Kapellmeister and continued to be paid by the next Prince, though he retained no musical duties. A few years later Prince Nicolaus II Esterházy engaged musicians again to form a new, much more modest court orchestra, but this was an exception to the general trend.

Opposite: Vienna was chosen as the city in which the victorious allies met to restore order to Europe after the downfall of Napoleon, and what is now known as the Congress of Vienna took place there in 1814-15. Here the dignitaries are shown at the conference table. *Fidelio* was chosen as the opera to mark the opening of the Congress, and the foreign dignitaries made Beethoven a gift of 4,000 silver florins.

Above: Austria was a battlefield for much of the period of the Napoleonic Wars, and the lives of the civilian population were often disrupted. Beethoven, in common with many others, was infuriated both by the inconvenience and the humiliation. Here, occupying French officers are dining off the population in the central Austrian town of Eisenerz in 1801.

Right: In 1812 Napoleon suffered his greatest reverse when his *Grande Armée*, which had hitherto seemed invincible, was totally vanquished by the combination of the burning of Moscow and a retreat through the rigors of a Russian winter.

but the business did not flourish until the early nineteenth century, notably between 1815 and 1830, also the years of Schubert's brief maturity, when he became known primarily as a composer of songs.

• Concerts and salons •

The success of Schubert's widely published songs shows that a composer's attention to a particular medium will inevitably be affected by chance and circumstance. Would Mozart have endowed the clarinet so well if he had not been influenced by the playing of Anton Stadler? Or Haydn have written his last dozen symphonies if he had not been free to travel to London? Would Beethoven have made his far-reaching return to the string quartet in his last years

Ludwig van Beethoven's career shows an even closer connection between political events and their cultural repercussions, which affected not only the terms of service and earning potential of composers, but also the repertoire played and the very nature of music-making. His father was a member of the electoral *Kapelle* in Bonn, and his own earliest musical experiences were with this orchestra. He came to Vienna in 1792 to study at the instigation of Count Ferdinand Ernst Waldstein. His bursary was paid by Elector Maximilian Franz, who lived in Bonn but came from Vienna and was a Hapsburg archduke. In the same year Bonn was caught up in the war, and in 1794 the city was occupied by French troops. This marked the end of the Electorate, and the orchestra was disbanded. Count Waldstein and the last elector both fled to Vienna, the latter dying there in 1801, and the Count in 1823 in total poverty. When, in 1808, Beethoven was given the promise of a yearly stipend from Archduke Rudolph, Prince Lobkowitz and Prince Kinsky to keep him as a freelance composer in Vienna rather than lose him to the court of the new King of Westphalia, Napoleon's brother Jérôme, in Kassel, this was the last major act of patronage by the aristocracy. The fact that the Kinsky and Lobkowitz families were later unable to carry out in full the promise they had made was not due to lack of goodwill on their part; circumstances had simply made such promises impossible to honor.

The new role of the middle classes in musical life was beneficial to composers, though initially not particularly rewarding financially. Beethoven, and later Schubert, learned that it was increasingly the publishing houses that made composing a viable occupation, as the circulation of works became more widespread. Engraving made this possible; however, only those works or types of composition that had the promise of wide appeal were printed. Large-scale orchestral works rarely qualified as such, but appeared in keyboard scores or arrangements for smaller resources. The earliest music publishers in Vienna were set up in the 1770s,

Above: The Viennese music-publishing house of Artaria, founded in 1770 and publishers of Mozart, Haydn and Beethoven, produced this representation of *Das Caroussel*, a horse ballet performed in the Spanish Riding School in Vienna, as part of the celebrations held in the city in 1814 for the meeting of the Congress.

without the incentive of a commission from the music-loving Prince Galitzin? Such reflections are especially relevant to Schubert. He seems to have had little opportunity of hearing his mature orchestral works played – not even the 'Great' C major Symphony – and his various attempts at opera were frustrated by inept libretti and his own lack of stage experience. Songs, piano music and other chamber works were at least assured of a hearing among friends and amateurs, and the informal gatherings known as 'Schubertiades' compensated for the fact that only one official 'concert' of Schubert's music was given during his life. His prolific output of four-hand piano duets, for instance, served a more companionable and accessible medium than the opulent one of two pianos, for which he composed nothing. If some passages in the 'Grand Duo' seem to cry out for the orchestra, the reason is again a practical one. By this time the piano had become the versatile general practitioner of music; most composers made 'short scores' of symphonies in advance, and in due course accepted or produced piano transcriptions as a means of making their works known.

Beginning in the early 1780s, attempts had been made in Vienna to organize public concerts in which the music itself had pride of place. Previously concerts had been put on by composers and virtuoso performers as a means of publicity or a source of income – or as 'benefit' concerts for charitable purposes. The idea that someone other than the musicians should put on a concert and determine the program and performers (always guided, of course, by public taste) was a new one. The initial attempts were generally unsuccessful, largely because the organization of them was difficult and the expense too high. We must remember that at that

Left: The Old University in Vienna, whose main hall was the setting for many of the city's most important concerts, including the 'Kavalierskonzerte.' It was here on 8 December 1813 that Beethoven conducted an orchestral concert during which the *Battle of Victoria* (op.91) and the Seventh Symphony (op.92) were first heard.

Below: A ball in the Grosser Redoutensaal, Vienna. It was here that Beethoven's first orchestral works for Vienna were played – a set of dances composed in 1795. In 1814 his Seventh and Eighth Symphonies (op.92 and op.93) both received performances here.

time Vienna had no concert halls. Either one booked a theater on a free day, or hired rooms that were intended for other purposes, and often attached to restaurants. Furthermore, Vienna had theater orchestras, but no concert orchestra. For concerts an orchestra was generally got together on an *ad hoc* basis, drawn mostly from the original *dilettanti*: trained evening a week for an aristocratic family, or on Sundays and holy days in a church. There was, however, immense interest in music tuition, the ability to play a musical instrument being an accepted part of the upbringing of the young. Some idea of the importance attached to music tuition can be gained from a writer, Joseph Rohrer, who in 1797 observed that 'in every

Above: Steyregg, in Upper Austria, painted in 1835. Schubert spent a week here in the summer of 1825 with his friend the singer Vogl, as guests of Countess Weissenwolf. Schubert wrote of her excellent singing and of her great admiration for his work. She even hinted to him that she would have liked to have his Walter Scott songs dedicated to her.

musicians who did not earn their living from playing. The formation of the Gesellschaft der Musikfreunde (Society of the Friends of Music) in Vienna in 1812 was the first step in consolidating regular public concerts. Concerts organized by composers and performers still took place, but the Society's events were promoted for and by music-lovers; its membership comprised both practicing musicians and 'supporters.' The Society, which still exists today, set up a choir and an orchestra, started a collection of music and instruments, and founded a Conservatory.

Until the establishment of the Conservatory, the teaching of music outside the church and the court had been entirely in the hands of private music teachers. They had to look upon themselves primarily as teachers, though often they were composers trying by this means to increase their incomes, especially since free board and lodging were sometimes offered. Alternatively they were performers who had time to spare, because – for example – they were engaged to play chamber music on one

cultured family there is a fortepiano. Whether or not music features too prominently in the normal middle-class education of young girls is another question.' Things had not changed by Schubert's time, when the *Weiner Zeitung* carried many advertisements for music teachers. In 1819, for example, we read: 'a young man, well-versed in fortepiano and violin, and composing for both instruments, offers to give a few hours teaching in the above instruments and on the guitar, in which thoroughness and a reasonable price are at all times combined. . . .' It is important to note that such tuition often transcended the elementary level and developed into a musical partnership on a paid basis. The opportunities to use or improve one's skill on an instrument were many and varied, extending to the world of the music salon.

The 'salons' were the most important feature of musical life in Vienna between 1790 and 1830. This, too, was a consequence of political changes and historical events. As the 1812 date of the founding of the Gesellschaft indicates,

11

during the Napoleonic Wars large-scale musical events had been hardly feasible. Music was played in more intimate surroundings. And after the Congress of Vienna stringent regulations were enforced by the police to secure law and order and economic recovery. As a result, people preferred to withdraw into their own homes, so as not to give the impression of political or social involvement of any kind. Music-making became an important part of such socializing, and the larger salons were semi-public concerts in private houses. We can describe them as semi-public in that the audience was an important factor in the event, so much so that lack of space meant that people were sometimes crowded out of the drawing-room into side rooms. The audience comprised friends and acquaintances of the family organizing the concert, but in some cases the concerts were open to strangers with an interest in music, and some families issued invitations or entrance tickets. To avoid confusion, each family chose a particular day and an interval of one week or several weeks between each concert. A devotee would know on which day one could attend a particular family's concert. Generally speaking, these 'drawing-rooms' were held only in the six-month winter season; during the summer families moved to their summer houses or organized journeys and excursions, so that musical events such as these were not appropriate.

Right: The Tuchlauben in Vienna with, on the right, the building erected in 1830-1 by the Gesellschaft der Musikfreunde. Since its foundation in 1812, the society had already become a model for the concert societies which were to be the new promoters of music in the nineteenth century. In 1827 Schubert had lodged in the house next door with his friend Schober, and on 26 March 1828 the only known organized concert of his music during his lifetime was given in the old concert hall of the Gesellschaft.

• The Classical masters •

No history of western music can fail to give a lion's share to the overwhelming figure of Beethoven. Yet, taking a retrospective and panoramic view of the Classical period, it seems natural enough to link him with Schubert, although the decision would have surprised many of their contemporaries and immediate successors. Whereas Beethoven became internationally renowned during his lifetime, it took at least half a century for Schubert to be known and valued at anything like his real worth. He was a torch-bearer at Beethoven's funeral, then lived only twenty months more himself. On his tombstone were engraved the touching words of Grillparzer: 'Music has entombed here a rich treasure, but still fairer hopes.' 'Fairer hopes' may be true enough in view of Schubert's death at thirty-one, but did Grillparzer have any idea of the extent of the existing treasure?

Schubert acquired some fame during his lifetime as a composer of songs, and he was loved and admired by his circle of friends, but he was little known to the musical world at large by the time of his tragically early death. An English musical dictionary published in 1827 refers to five Schuberts, but the Franz we remember is not among them. And even when many of his larger-scale works became known, published and performed, they tended to perplex would-be admirers by what Schumann called, with foresight, their 'heavenly length.' Schubert's more relaxed treatment of sonata form, in particular, drew forth unfair but inevitable com-

Above: Ignaz Jahn's Restaurant in the Augarten, where from 1782 seasons of subscription concerts were given, starting at 7 or 8 in the morning, in which both Mozart and, later, Beethoven took part. Beethoven's Second Symphony (op.36) was first heard here in 1804.

We know in principle how important and popular the musical salon was at this time; what we lack almost completely is detailed information, for there were not public advertisements for the salons and no program sheets, although one would love to know just how such events were organized. Memoirs, diaries and letters give us some sketchy insight into the kind of repertoire and the performers. It comes as a surprise, for instance, to read that not only chamber music, piano music and songs were performed, but also concertos and orchestral works as large as symphonies.

parisons with the dramatic and intellectual force of Beethoven, whom he so much revered. Fortunately, posterity has long since learned to admire Schubert for his own unique and complementary qualities: his spaciousness, spontaneity, harmonic magic and unmatched lyrical gifts. His last twenty months alone were marked by an output comparable with the rich outpourings of Mozart's Vienna period. They would have been rewarding enough if they had simply yielded the great String Quintet in C and a handful of songs including 'Der Doppelgänger.' But what of *Winterreise*, the E flat Trio, the Fantasies in C for violin and in F minor for piano duet, the Mass in E flat and the last three piano sonatas? Though the 'Great' Symphony in C is now known to have been written two or three years before, the list for the last months in

Deutsch's catalogue makes astonishing reading, as though the still young composer somehow knew that time was running out.

Whereas Mozart and Haydn became close friends and mutual admirers, Beethoven and Schubert, by a curious irony, scarcely met, the only known occasion being a brief visit Schubert made with some friends to see the ailing Beethoven a week before his death. He had long admired Beethoven from afar, even though in his shyness the actual distance may have been no further than the opposite side of one of Vienna's squares. It can hardly be accidental that we feel the haunting allegretto of Beethoven's Seventh Symphony lurking behind so many of Schubert's works, whether *Rosamunde*, 'Death and the Maiden,' the 'Wanderer' Fantasy or the A flat Variations for four hands. On the other

Below: Bird's-eye view of Vienna within the city walls, as depicted in 1785. We see from this what a compact, and relatively small, place the city was at the time. The buildings of the Hofburg (imperial palace) are at the top left with St Stephen's cathedral below in the center.

hand, Beethoven is said to have recognized the 'divine spark' in the few of Schubert's songs that were shown to him. If the songs have led some writers to proclaim him as a harbinger of Romanticism, Schubert's continuing allegiance to Classical forms in such late works as the C major Quintet, the G major Quartet and the B flat Piano Sonata shows his lasting debt to the past. In fact, Beethoven and Schubert, despite the Romantic overtones in some of their music, might well be claimed as the last truly comprehensive masters of the Classical style.

It is worth considering the implications of the word 'Classical.' The division of musical history into labeled chronological periods has become customary and convenient. We speak automatically of Renaissance, Baroque, Classical and Romantic music and associate the labels with distinct styles and textures, forms and media. Even the untutored layman with a taste for the Baroque will find a common flavor in Monteverdi, Purcell and Bach, despite their differing dates and nationalities. Lovers of Romantic piano music are likely to feel at home in a succession of composers from Chopin to Rachmaninov, while in other media even those arch-opposites, Wagner and Brahms, may be found to have shared a basic harmonic language. Such periods are certainly not watertight compartments; round figures can, how-

Above: J. N. Hummel (1778-1837), who was a pupil of Mozart. An accomplished pianist and a famous composer in his own day, he was for a time considered a serious rival of Beethoven's with the Viennese public. A transitional figure between the Classical and Romantic styles, Hummel took over the outward forms of Mozart's Classicism, lending them an ornamental quality, rather than exploring their essence, as did Beethoven.

Left: A piano made in the early years of the nineteenth century by W. Southwell of Dublin. It exemplifies the ornamental Classicism which was the dominant decorative style of the period.

ever, provide useful landmarks if by chance they coincide with important events. The death of Bach in 1750 may be felt to signify the passing era, even though Handel outlived him, and it has provided historians with a convenient border-line between Baroque and Classical. Eighty years later, in 1830, Berlioz produced his *Symphonie fantastique*, an avant-garde work in its own time, long regarded as symbolizing the most daring spirit of the new Romanticism. Between these dates, 1750 and 1830, fell the life's work of Haydn and the entire lives of Mozart, Beethoven and Schubert. This became by general consent the 'Classical' period, and it is easy to see how it came to be regarded as such by the later Romantics. Tchaikovsky admired Mozart above all others, and Wagner worshiped Beethoven: these were the 'classics' that had stood the test of time, like Goethe and Schiller in the world of poetry.

The term 'Classical' has of course acquired wider musical associations. It covers the age of the string quartet and the symphony, of the growth and stabilization of the orchestra, of the success of the fortepiano and the fading out of the harpsichord continuo, of the advent of public concerts and – especially with Mozart – of the humanization of opera. This all evolved against a changing social background in which freedom of thought and individual liberty began to challenge the traditional hierarchies of society, the dogma of the Church and the authorities of royalty and aristocracy.

The contrasting life-stories of the first great Classical masters, Haydn and Mozart, show the transition at work already. Haydn, born in 1732, enjoyed the patronage of the Esterházy family for most of his creative life, only acquiring real freedom to travel in his sixtieth year. On his first visit to London he heard of the death of Mozart, whose early fame as a prodigy had taken him as a child to more lands than Haydn was to see in his whole life. Yet Mozart was buried in a pauper's grave. His failure to find adequate and regular patronage in his maturity has been partly blamed on his impracticality and his restless temperament, yet posterity will always find it hard to forgive the society of the time for so neglecting one of the greatest geniuses who ever lived. Meanwhile, within months of Mozart's death, the young Beethoven arrived in Vienna, where Franz Schubert was born five years later. Beethoven, who triumphed over physical adversity and fought his battle with the material of music with lone determination, might be called the first great freelance composer of the new order, and though he had his many aristocratic patrons he treated them as equals, and they in turn respected his genius. Schubert, naturally gifted and prolific like Mozart, lived modestly and like him died too young. So the parallels and the contrasts reassert themselves, setting the scene for the chapters which follow.

The musical language that Beethoven inherited – and transformed – owed much to a wide variety of sources: to Haydn and Mozart certainly, but in fact the Classical style, a vague

but unavoidable expression, evolved from a whole amalgam of influences. There were the early Viennese symphonists like Monn and Wagenseil and the experiments of the Mannheim school; the vogue for Italian opera, including the fast–slow–fast plan of the Italian operatic overture, often significantly called *sinfonia*; and the growing preference for the solo concerto instead of the larger groupings of the Baroque *concerto grosso*. There was the demand for tuneful entertainment music, of the kind immortalized in Mozart's *Eine kleine Nachtmusik*. There were rustic and folk elements, especially in Haydn, which found their way into symphonies, quartets and piano sonatas; and the simultaneous emergence of the string quartet and the development of the fortepiano had their own effects on musical textures.

Though it may seem paradoxical, there was also the rediscovery of Bach and the virtues of strict counterpoint. It was this integration of the 'learned' manner that added depth and intellectual strength to the Classical forms. Nor should one overlook the seriously 'expressive' North German style of C. P. E. Bach, and the 'Sturm und Drang' movement that brought intense emotions to the surface in so many minor-key works from the 1770s onwards. As for the 'learned' style, both Haydn and Mozart had studied counterpoint in their youths as a matter of course, but it was not until about 1782 that Baron van Swieten brought manuscript copies

Above: Luigi Cherubini (1760-1842) being inspired by the Muse, in an unfinished portrait by Ingres. Born in Florence, Cherubini settled in Paris in the late 1780s, where he was eventually to become director of the Conservatoire. Beethoven met him when Cherubini visited Vienna in 1806 and admired the monumentality of his music, in particular his serious operas written around the turn of the century. These epitomize the severe French Classicism of the revolutionary period without a trace of Rococo decoration.

Above left: A portrait of Beethoven published in Leipzig by the Bureau de Musique in 1801, not long after he had settled and begun to make his mark in Vienna.

Above center: The program for a concert held on 8 January 1796, in the Kleiner Redoutensaal, Vienna, as a benefit for the singer Maria Bolla. Haydn conducted, and Beethoven was soloist in a piano concerto, possibly the one in B flat (op.19).

Above right: Haydn, who encouraged Beethoven to go to Vienna to have lessons from him, and who gave him much practical help, though his actual teaching had little or no influence on Beethoven's musical development. This portrait dates from 1791.

of Bach's *Forty-eight*, the famous preludes and fugues of *Das Wohltemperierte Klavier*, to Vienna. The young Beethoven was fortunate, since his teacher, Neefe, had introduced him to them from an early age in Bonn. It is a humbling thought, too, to recall that shortly before his death Schubert enrolled for some classes in counterpoint that he never lived to take.

• Sonata form •

Historians have sought other titles for the age in question. It has been called 'the Viennese period,' for although Schubert was the only really great composer of the time to have been born there, Vienna was undoubtedly the lure of others and the most thriving musical center of the late eighteenth century. Another label, 'the age of the sonata,' brings us face to face with the ambiguities of technical terms. The word 'sonata' had long been used to denote a piece to be 'sounded' or 'played,' in contrast to a vocal 'cantata,' but by the time of the Classical period the meanings had become far more specific. The sonata was an extended work, generally in three or four movements, for one or at most two players. Where more players were involved, the title became trio, quartet, quintet and so forth, culminating in the symphony (or 'sinfonia'), which was in essense a sonata for orchestra. Since a desire for formal perfection characterized the Classical approach, the sonata and its parallels became a stronghold of expression and discipline, dominated by the procedure known rather misleadingly as 'sonata form.' It may be felt to be a misnomer for three main reasons; first, because it describes the design of a single movement and not a work as a whole; second, because it is equally applicable

to a quartet or a symphony, to a self-contained overture, or – with certain important modifications – to a concerto movement; and third, because a Classical sonata was not bound to adopt it. A well-known exception is Mozart's Piano Sonata in A, K.331, which consists of a set of variations, a minuet and trio, and a rondo-type finale that is not in normal rondo form either. Yet the principles of sonata form are so all-prevailing that they are worth considering in some detail.

As a means of organizing and developing musical ideas, sonata form became second nature to the Classical composer and dominated large-scale music throughout the Romantic period too. It may be said to have evolved by a process of natural selection, out of which emerged the familiar procedure of exposition, development and recapitulation – infinitely satisfying and flexible. The crux of the matter lay, however, in the essential difference between the exposition and the recapitulation, the former moving to a new key for the 'second subject,' the latter ending firmly in the home key. Everyone who enjoys music must feel the almost gravitational effect of harmonic stability as contrasted with the adventures of key-changes, to be found in the simplest popular tunes as well as the most enduring masterworks.

One reason for the lasting success of sonata form was its provision of a sequence of events with well-defined landmarks and an overall feeling of symmetry, and while a discussion of its evolution and principles is more relevant to the Haydn–Mozart period, it is important to reconsider them in relation to Beethoven and Schubert. They provide, for example, a common denominator for the first movement of such varied works as Beethoven's 'Eroica' Symphony and op.110 Piano Sonata, Schubert's 'Unfinished' Symphony and 'Trout' Quintet, and his solitary Quartettsatz – in fact a single movement for string quartet. The alternative name of 'first-movement form' could, however, mislead. Beethoven's earlier A flat Sonata, op.26, begins, like Mozart's K.331, with a set of variations, whereas all three movements of Mozart's 'Prague' Symphony are in sonata form. Sonata form in itself would appear to be a three-part structure – or even four-part with Beethoven's extended coda, as in the 'Eroica' – yet it must be stressed that it derived from binary and not from ternary form.

In brief, a simple 'binary' piece consists of two halves, the first moving away from the home key to a different one – in technical terms usually the dominant or the relative major – and the second returning home. This was the plan of countless Baroque pieces, whether one-movement sonatas by Domenico Scarlatti or dance-movements from Bach suites; but as time went on composers tended to expand the second 'half,' thereby requiring a more extended re-establishment of the home key for the sake of finality. In fact, part two began to show two distinct phases within itself, exploratory and recapitulatory. This clear evidence of sonata form 'in the making' is illustrated in some of the binary preludes from Book II of Bach's *Forty-eight*, notably those in D major, F minor and B flat, all of which have well-defined points of recapitulation; but since these would hardly have been known to many of the earlier Classical composers, the tendency was obviously more universal. The binary origin also explains the lingering tradition of repeating the development–recapitulation part of sonata-form movements as well as the exposition. The first movement of Beethoven's Piano Sonata in F sharp, op.78, is a late example of this; while the finale of the 'Appassionata'

Sonata, op.57, is unusual in that Beethoven marked the latter part to be repeated – but not the exposition, thus delaying the shattering impact of the coda.

Any discussion of musical forms must face the fact that to some extent every work of art makes its own rules. In the 'Trout' Quintet Schubert wrote the second and fifth movements in two more or less identical halves, suggesting a kind of sonata form without development and with (in this context) an amusingly irresponsible key-scheme. In the first movement of his G major Quartet, on the other hand, his recapitulation abounds in new thoughts, variants and textures. As for the exposition sections of sonata-form movements, the terms first and second 'group' may be preferred to 'subject,' since a series of themes may be involved in each. Yet Haydn sometimes carried one main

Below: The title-page of Beethoven's three sonatas for piano (op.2), which were published by Artaria in Vienna and dedicated to Haydn. The dedication, Beethoven's recognition of gratitude to his teacher, was made at the time Haydn left for his second visit to England, so bringing their association to an end.

Left: Before Haydn left for England, he wrote a letter, dated 23 November 1793, to the Elector of Cologne in support of his 'pupil' Beethoven. In the letter he particularly requested financial help for Beethoven and enclosed several of his compositions, predicting great fame for his 'dear pupil.'

idea through both groups – 'monothematicism' – thereby emphasizing, often with humor, that contrast of key was the prime consideration.

•The formal repertory •

The satisfying architecture and the endless dramatic potential of sonata form did not exclude other structural possibilities. One popular alternative was variation form, especially when its subject was as attractive as Schubert's 'Trout' theme in the fourth movement of the A major Quintet. The art of variation, in the strictly Classical sense, provided its own discipline, depending on the composer's mastery of texture and ornamentation while removing the drama of key-change, except from major to minor or vice versa. It is true that Beethoven wrote a set of piano variations, op.34, that runs round a whole circle of keys, and that Schubert allowed his penultimate variation in the 'Trout' to wander far from home; but these, in the Classical scene, were the exceptions that proved the rule.

Another basic form was the rondo, in which the returns of a main theme are separated by interludes or 'episodes.' It was not the sole property of finales: the adagio of Beethoven's 'Pathétique' Sonata and the funeral march of the

'Eroica' are in rondo form. A cross-influence of sonata form produced the sonata-rondo, much favored by Mozart and Beethoven in their concerto finales, in which the first and third episodes correspond to the exposition and reprise of a second subject or 'group.' Meanwhile the more concise varieties of binary and ternary form found their places in the traditional minuet (or scherzo) and trio; and the predominance of binary form did not prevent Mozart, for example, from introducing simple ternary-shaped themes in the trios of his late E flat and 'Jupiter' Symphonies.

The technique of variation-writing also provided its hybrids: the slow movements of Beethoven's Fifth, Seventh and Ninth Symphonies combine strict variations with episodes or afterthoughts. Haydn had explored the possibilities of 'double' variations on alternating minor and major themes, but in his F minor Andante and Variations for piano he also added a coda of Beethovenian proportions. The 'Theme and Variations' as a self-contained work had been a common enough side-product – both Mozart and Schubert wrote attractive sets for piano duet – but the greatest and longest set to come out of the Classical period was undoubtedly Beethoven's monumental 'Diabelli' Variations, op.120, inspired by a simple waltz-theme and an invitation, which he declined, to contribute a single variation to a composite work. A further discipline, that of counterpoint in varying degrees of strictness, has already been mentioned for its enrichment of Haydn's and Mozart's later works. It could hardly have been foreseen that in his last period Beethoven would rediscover the fugue as a highly personal, expressive and dramatic medium.

Yet, as an antidote to such intellectual concentration, the freer forms, impossible to classify on account of their improvisatory manner, retained their attraction. Beethoven's piano Fantasy, op.77, has all the feeling of a written-down extemporization, while a 'Fantasy' or 'Fantasia' could also involve an introductory cadenza for piano, leading to a series of concerto-like variations with orchestra and a surprising choral finale – as happened with Beethoven's Choral Fantasy, op.80 – or indicate the compression of a four-movement sonata into a continuous whole – as was the case with Schubert's F minor Fantasy for four hands or, on a more expansive scale, his 'Wanderer' Fantasy for piano solo.

• Opera •

Although Schubert's stage works met with almost no success, there is much attractive music locked away in them, quite apart from the well-known *Rosamunde* extracts. There are, for example, exquisite love duets in *Alfonso und Estrella*, based on a libretto by Schober and completed in 1822. Yet it is clear that neither Schubert nor Beethoven inherited Mozart's innate gift for opera. Beethoven's only opera,

Fidelio, though a great masterpiece, is a law unto itself. It has been said that Beethoven, one of the most dramatic of all composers, left opera where he found it; but it may also be claimed that *Fidelio*, like *Die Zauberflöte*, transcends the awkwardness of its hybrid form through the genius and profound humanity of its music. Beethoven considered other operatic projects, including *Faust* and *Macbeth*, but none came to fruition. He had worked on an opera, *Vestas Feuer*, for Schikaneder, the librettist of *Die Zauberflöte*, and he used material from it when he became absorbed in *Fidelio*. *Fidelio*, or *Leonore* in its earlier versions, gave him trouble enough: it was first performed in 1805, then twice rewritten, in 1806 and in 1814. The laborious gestation of many of Beethoven's works is illustrated in his sketchbooks, and those that survive give a fascinating insight into his composing methods, but in the case of *Leonore* and *Fidelio* the completed scores show how the final version involved a tightening-up of the libretto and a critical pruning of the musical content. Even the magnificent third *Leonore* overture, itself a rewriting of the more spacious but less well-proportioned no.2, had to be sacri-

Opposite and above: These three paintings, which span the working lives of Beethoven and Schubert, show the changing currents of Romanticism underlying the culture of the period. The Romantic Classicism of Angelika Kauffmann's painting of *Design and Poetry* (*c.* 1795) gave way to the tragic vision expressed by Caspar David Friedrich's *Woman in front of the Setting Sun* (1818), while by the year of Schubert's death (1828), Erasmus Ritter von Engert's painting of a Viennese garden shows the wistful decorative quality of the bourgeois 'Biedermeier' style.

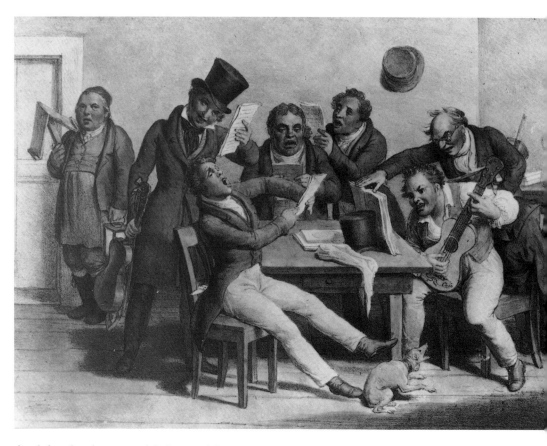

Right: Music-making in the home, as portrayed in this caricature of Schubert's time, in which a male vocal ensemble displays its prowess, accompanied by a guitar.

Below: A coffee cup bearing Schubert's portrait. Made in 1822, it provides remarkable evidence of the young composer's fame in Vienna. The design is taken from a drawing made by Leopold von Kupelwieser the year before, in 1821.

ficed for the shorter and lighter *Fidelio* overture. The dramatic force of symphonic music had become too great and too self-sufficient for the opera house, and Beethoven recognized this.

It is easy to understand the attraction of the *Leonore* subject for Beethoven, with its embodiment of the feminine 'ideal,' in view of his known distaste for the more frivolous plots of *Figaro* and *Don Giovanni.* Stories of rescue and escape had in any case a topical appeal in the days of the French Revolution and the Napoleonic Wars, and Bouilly's original *Léonore* had been based on a true incident of a devoted young wife saving her husband from a tyrant's prison. The removal of the venue to Spain, as with *Figaro,* did not disguise the relevance of the message and the emotions involved. Beethoven's own devotion to this task followed his work on the 'Eroica' Symphony, and it is noteworthy that the finest of his other theater music, *Coriolan* and *Egmont,* should also have been inspired by heroic subjects.

• Inspiration and genius •

It was natural, too, that Beethoven, having triumphed over personal despair at his deafness should have identified himself with the new ideals of individual liberty and dignity. Yet the 'heroic decade,' as his middle period is sometimes called, did not preclude the complementary qualities: the realization of the 'Pastoral' Symphony rests alongside the elemental drama of the Fifth, the persuasive manner of the Fourth Piano Concerto contrasts to the grandeur and brilliance of the 'Emperor.' The sketchbooks, moreover, show fascinating cross-influences even between works of vastly different character. The first movements of the Fifth Symphony and the Fourth Concerto turn a similar rhythmic pattern to their own purposes, and the sketches show that Beethoven worked at them side by side; while *Fidelio* was the surprising beneficiary of an idea rejected from the finale of the concerto – it became instead the orchestral motif in the Prisoners' Chorus.

The sketchbooks of Beethoven are remarkable documents of human endeavor and achievement. They were not, of course, intended for our perusal; they are purely the private record of the workings of Beethoven's mind – the workshop, as it were, in which his compositions were built up the hard way, stone upon stone. Indeed, once we have studied the sketches, the labors of Hercules seem far more credible than the mental effort involved in the creation of, for example, the 'Eroica' from the first rough jottings Beethoven made for it. Even the arresting opening chords, simple as they may seem, were distilled from long and cautious forethought. A mere glance at the sketchbooks leaves an indelible impression: the uncouth, unpromising nature of the earlier thought in the light of the finished article. We cannot avoid being wise after the event. Beethoven, being wise before the event – a rarer form of wisdom – was at first concerned solely with capturing the germ of an idea in no matter how primitive a form. Only then, it seems, could his particular genius set to work. If Carlyle's dictum on genius was right – 'the transcendent capacity for taking trouble' – then Beethoven, from the testimony of the sketches, was the greatest genius music has ever known. The association of his name with human aspirations, struggles and triumphs had an overwhelming influence throughout the Romantic period, affecting such radically different composers as Wagner and Brahms.

Sibelius, in his own youthful studies in Vienna, reflected on the contrast between Beethoven's labors and the supreme natural gifts of Mozart. 'Beethoven,' he wrote, 'did not have the greatest *natural* talent, but he subjected everything he did to the most searching self-criticism and by doing so achieved greatness.' The absence of direct evidence should not, however, mislead the music-lover into assuming that prolific composers were simply passive recipients of some divine impulse, though this romantic notion was aided and abetted by the stories of Handel composing the whole of *Messiah* in three weeks and Mozart his three greatest symphonies in less than two months. In such cases speed is not synonymous with ease, as we learn from Mozart's reference to 'long and wearisome labor' in connection with the quartets he dedicated to Haydn. This brings back the subject of Schubert, whose sheer output in so few years led posterity to regard him, so Percy Scholes maintained, as 'the classic example of "inspiration" as the novelists picture it.' Did he not compose 'Hark, hark, the lark' in a restaurant on the back of a menu card?

Nevertheless, enough material survives to show Schubert's own self-criticism at work. The score of the 'Great' C major Symphony preserves a famous last-minute change of thought over the main subject of the first allegro, where strokes of a penknife turned a commonplace repetition into a purposeful motif. A short-score 'sketch' of the 'Unfinished' is even more revealing, one idea requiring simplification, another needing expansion, and yet another – in the closing bars of the first movement – lacking its vital melodic ingredient.

Modern research has also thrown new light on the chronology of Schubert's works. Whereas nearly all Beethoven's important works were printed during his lifetime and provided with official opus numbers, Schubert's suffered complete confusion through delayed and random publication. Concert programs are still liable to refer to his earliest A minor Piano Sonata (1817) as 'op.164' and his last (1825) as 'op.42,' and even such misleading traditions die hard. In 1951, however, Otto Erich Deutsch produced a new Thematic Catalogue, applying himself to Schubert as Köchel had done to Mozart in the 1860s and, more recently, Hoboken to Haydn. Later researchers may continue to query Deutsch's precise order, but by general consent the 'D' numbers are now as essential for Schubert as 'K' numbers for Mozart. They are, of course, adopted in the present volume.

Above: The Musician's Dream, a drawing of about 1820 by Caspar David Friedrich (1774-1840). Many German Romantic writers saw the musician as the archetypal sensitive artist-hero – an image that reaches its tragic climax in Schubert's *Die Winterreise*. The works of the German painter Friedrich reflect the ideas of the Romantic movement in ways that often provide striking parallels to the musical expression of Beethoven and Schubert.

LUDWIG VAN BEETHOVEN

ALAN KENDALL & BASIL LAM

Opposite: Ludwig van Beethoven (1770-1827), a miniature on ivory, dated 1803, by Christian Horneman.

Although only twenty years elapsed between the death of Bach and the birth of Beethoven, how very different were their worlds, and their conceptions of their mission in life. Temperaments aside, the lives of the two men illustrate vividly the fundamental change in the musician's role in society. If one inserts Mozart, born in 1756, between the two, then the change becomes even more evident. Bach's whole career was spent in the service of institutions of one sort or another and was to varying degrees influenced by the demands of those institutions. Mozart started out in the same way, attempted to free himself, but virtually died in the process. Only Beethoven managed to be independent of the regular patronage of the Church or a princely court. In so doing, he established once and for all the status of the artist in society.

This achievement cannot be overestimated, for its goes hand in hand with the upheavals that took place during his own lifetime, of which the French Revolution became the symbol. Even though it must have seemed, after the Congress of Vienna, that little had been achieved politically and socially and that the *status quo* had been largely restored, in reality there was a very different spirit abroad. The recognition given to Beethoven during the Congress in 1814 was reflected in the fact that *Fidelio* was the first opera given in the presence of the foreign dignitaries on 26 September that year.

Despite being at the center of world events, there is little or no evidence that Beethoven held any views on politics. The significance of *Fidelio*, or *Leonore* in its first version, lay for Beethoven in its subtitle 'Conjugal love.' Of course this had not prevented Beethoven – in common with countless others of his day – from being at first elated and then disillusioned with the phenomenon of Napoleon Bonaparte. The erased dedication of the 'Eroica' Symphony is there for all to see. After that, however, the composer seems to have cared about Napoleon only when the bombardment of Vienna by the French in 1809 forced him to take refuge in a cellar, and earlier that year he had seriously entertained an invitation from Napoleon's brother, Jérôme, to go as Kapellmeister to Kassel in the newly created kingdom of Westphalia.

There were ideals to which Beethoven subscribed, but they proclaim themselves in the music. And the fact that his personal life often fell far short of high ideals seems only to make the expression in the music more intense. He longed, for example, to find love and the delights and solace of a conjugal relationship, but he was unable to form, let alone sustain, such an attachment. He would have loved children of his own, hence the almost hysterical way in which he imposed his guardianship on his nephew.

In terms of earning a living from his work, Beethoven always maintained that he found such a thought distasteful. As he elaborated to the publisher Hoffmeister in 1801, he had an ideal conception of a kind of artistic marketplace to which creative artists brought their output and received in return sufficient for their worldly needs. This did not prevent him, however, from playing one publisher off against another to extort better terms, and indeed being downright dishonest about what he had for sale and what was actually completed.

Finally, ideas about the brotherhood of man should be set in the context of his almost impossible demands on his friends and the way in which frequently he most hurt those best disposed towards him. His distrust and contempt when dealing with servants made it almost impossible to find anyone prepared to work for him. Such, however, was the nature and extent of his genius that subsequent generations have been prepared to accept all this. Beethoven's legacy to mankind consists not only of the works themselves but of the life itself.

Ludwig van Beethoven was born in Bonn on 15 or 16 December 1770. His grandfather, also Ludwig, had moved to Bonn as a young man and in March 1733 became a singer in the court chapel of the Elector of Cologne. His son Johann followed him into electoral service, and at the age of sixteen, in 1756, his engagement at court was confirmed, by which time he had already been carrying out some of the duties. Unfortunately Johann was by no means as talented as his father, and there was never any question of his attaining the rank of Kapellmeister as his father eventually did. In fact, with a family to support and insufficient funds to do so, Johann took to drink, and it was into such a household that Ludwig was born.

When it became apparent that the boy had talent, his father lost no time in exploiting the fact. Ludwig was by no means a child prodigy on the lines of Handel, Haydn or Mozart, of course, but already on 26 March 1778 he was billed for his first concert in Bonn. His father unashamedly gave his age as six, no doubt to make his son's abilities seem more remarkable. We have no record of the success of the venture, either financially or artistically, but, luckily, the experience seems to have made Johann van Beethoven realize that his son was in need of much better tuition than he himself could provide.

Not unnaturally, he looked first to his colleagues on the musical staff at court. There was the court organist, Gilles van den Eeden, but he was by now well advanced in years, having arrived in Bonn before Ludwig's grandfather. There was the tenor, Friedrich Pfeiffer, who came to Bonn for the theater season of 1779 and who is supposed to have given Beethoven some piano lessons. There was also Christian Gottlob Neefe (1748-98), who had come to Bonn with the same company as Pfeiffer in 1779, but who settled there and in 1781 became court organist.

Beethoven himself was in no doubt whatsoever about his debt to Neefe. As he wrote to him in one of his earliest surviving letters: 'Thank you for the advice you have so often given me about progress in my God-given art. If ever I become a great man, you also will have shared in my success.' In Cramer's *Magazin der Musik* of 2 March 1783 Neefe himself announced quite unequivocally that Beethoven would certainly become a second Mozart if he continued as he had begun. He also said that he had encouraged Beethoven to the extent of getting published, in Mannheim, a set of nine variations his pupil had written on a march by Ernst Christoph Dressler. These now bear the designation WoO.63 ('WoO' stands for 'work without opus no.') and were probably composed in 1782. What Neefe also said in the announcement was that Beethoven deserved – and needed – help to enable him to travel. Neefe knew instinctively, as a man who had traveled extensively himself, that Bonn would not provide the scope for the development of Beethoven's talent and that without any doubt his destination should be Vienna.

However, it was not until 1787 that Beethoven set off for Vienna, with the hope of meeting Mozart and taking piano lessons from him. The visit was little short of disaster from almost every point of view. Despite Mozart's reported praise of the young Beethoven, the latter seems to have inspired little real reaction, and he ran critically short of money. He had to borrow funds in Augsburg when he set off on the return journey and came back to find his beloved mother dying and the family finances also in a disastrous state.

Luckily Ludwig still had his court music duties, and by dint of hard work he was able to repair the situation. During this period he gained useful experience playing the viola in the orchestra in the court theatrical season, as well as continuing to play organ and harpsichord. His sight-reading became a matter of admiration, and he gained acquaintance in this way with much of the current German, Italian and French operatic repertory. When he presented one of his early compositions – a funeral cantata – to his grandfather's successor, Andrea Lucchesi, for his comments, the Kapellmeister is said to have handed it back, remarking that, since he did not understand it he could not correct the mistakes. He performed the work, nevertheless, and according to reactions at the first rehearsal, the performers showed 'great astonishment at the originality of the composition.'

• Beethoven and Haydn •

In the closing weeks of 1790 Haydn passed through Bonn on his way to London, and when he returned in July 1792, Beethoven showed

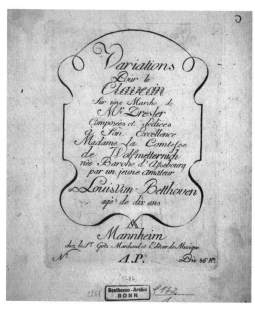

Left: The title-page of the variations on a march by Dressler (WoO.63), which was Beethoven's first published composition, written in 1782. Beethoven was eleven at the time, not ten years old as the title states.

Below: A silhouette of Beethoven at the age of sixteen by Joseph Neesen, one of the earliest portraits that has come down to us.

him one of his compositions, and the great man encouraged him to persevere. In fact, it may well have been decided there and then that Beethoven was to go to Vienna to have lessons from Haydn. Permission had to be sought from the Elector, however, and again there was the question of financing the trip. Eventually Beethoven set out at the beginning of November 1792, destined never to return to Bonn.

By this time, in addition to the Dressler variations, he had composed three piano sonatas (WoO.47), three piano quartets (WoO.36), a *Ritterballet* (WoO.1) for Count Waldstein, and two cantatas, one on the death of Emperor Joseph II and another for the accession of Leopold II. Then there were some songs, as well as a certain amount of chamber music. Even more interesting, perhaps, in view of Beethoven's subsequent development, was a piano concerto (WoO.4) dating from 1784, which survives only in the solo part with reduction of the orchestral tuttis, and fragments of a violin concerto. However, one must bear in mind that Beethoven went to Vienna primarily as a pianist, and it was in particular his extemporizations at the keyboard, which were then very much in vogue, that soon gained him a reputation.

Opposite: Helene von Breuning with her brother and her four children in 1782. The widow of a court councillor, she was a friend and adviser to the young Beethoven, and her house soon became a second home for him, and her son Stefan (*far right*) his good friend.

Presumably Beethoven contacted Haydn fairly soon after his arrival in Vienna. Beethoven recorded in a notebook that the two took chocolate and coffee together on 24 and 29 October 1793, by which time Beethoven must have been in the city for almost a year. In the interval his father had died in the December of 1792, and he had had considerable trouble in ensuring that his salary continued to be paid back in Bonn. Then in July 1793 the house of Artaria had published a set of twelve variations for piano and violin on 'Se vuol ballare' from Mozart's *Le Nozze di Figaro* (WoO.40), which was presumably one of the five works sent with a covering letter from Haydn, and an accompanying one from the young Beethoven himself, to the Elector of Cologne.

In fact Haydn was preparing to go back to England towards the end of 1793, so he wanted to announce that he would not be able to give Beethoven lessons after the end of the year. The five compositions were sent as a testimony to their joint labors, and Haydn took the opportunity of asking that Beethoven be given 1,000 florins for the coming year, since he had lent him 500 out of his own pocket, 'of which not a *kreuzer* was spent unnecessarily.' The reply, which arrived a month later on 23 December, was to the point. The Elector pointed out that four of the five works had been composed in Bonn, and that if Beethoven was simply going to get into debt, then he might as well go home.

Haydn left for England on 19 January 1794, and despite the fact that Beethoven lost the continuing contact with the great man, he may not have been all that sad. In actuality the lessons had not been a great success, and Beethoven had more or less been working with the composer Johann Baptist Schenk behind Haydn's back, using as textbook J. J. Fux's *Gradus ad*

Parnassum. After Haydn's departure Beethoven went to Johann Georg Albrechtsberger for counterpoint and to Salieri for Italian vocal writing.

By October 1794 Beethoven was living in the house of Prince Karl Lichnowsky, a pianist of some talent who had been both pupil and patron of Mozart. Prince Lichnowsky held regular Friday morning music sessions at his house, and in the course of these Beethoven met such excellent professional musicians as the violinist Ignaz Schuppanzigh, the violist Franz Weiss and the cellist Nikolaus Kraft. There was also an excellent amateur cellist, Nikolaus Zmeskall. As a token of thanks to Prince Lichnowsky, Beethoven dedicated several works to him, including the op.1 Trios for piano, violin and cello. The third Trio, in C minor, in particular, already displays the composer's originality, and Haydn, after hearing the first performance, advised his pupil to publish the other two without this one, fearing, perhaps, that its modernity would be misunderstood.

On 16 December 1795 the *Wiener Zeitung* announced that Haydn, recently returned from England, and Beethoven would give a concert in the Redoutensaal of the Hofburg. On the program were three of Haydn's 'Salomon' symphonies and Beethoven's Piano Concerto in B flat, op.19, which had received its first performance earlier in the year, with the composer as soloist, at one of the annual concerts in the Burgtheater in aid of the Tonkünstler-Sozietät. There was further collaboration between Beethoven and Haydn in January 1796, but the following month Beethoven left for Prague with Prince Lichnowsky. He next went to Dresden, where he received a gold snuffbox from the Elector of Saxony for his piano playing,

Above: Prince Karl Lichnowsky (1756-1814), who had been a pupil of Mozart, and whose acquaintance Beethoven soon made on his arrival in Vienna. For a time in the mid-1790s Beethoven lived in his house. The composer dedicated several works to Lichnowsky, including his op.1, a set of three trios for piano, violin and cello.

Left: The opening bars of the Piano Sonata in C minor, op.13, the *Sonate pathétique*, which was dedicated to Prince Karl Lichnowsky. The autograph is lost, and this is the first edition as published by Hoffmeister in Vienna.

26

and then to Berlin, where he played for Frederick William II of Prussia and received another snuffbox, but this one was filled with gold coins. More significantly from the musical point of view, however, was the fact that he met Jean-Pierre Duport, for whom he composed the Cello Sonatas, op.5. These were published by Artaria the following spring (1797), together with the Piano Sonata for four hands, op.6, the Trio for violin, viola and cello, op.3, the String Quintet, op.4 – which was in fact an arrangement of the earlier Wind Octet, op.103 – and a set of piano variations on a Russian dance from *Das Waldmädchen* (WoO.71). There is little doubt that Beethoven's music was now coming to the attention of a wider public, and no longer was he known only as pianist and improviser.

Above: The title-page of Beethoven's 'Pathétique' with its dedication to Prince Lichnowsky. Note the fashionable use of French, and the fact that the work is designated by the publisher as for either harpsichord or pianoforte.

Among the aristocracy Beethoven had extended his acquaintance to Count Moritz Lichnowsky (the Prince's brother), Prince Odescalchi, Prince von Liechtenstein and Prince von Schwarzenberg. It was in the Schwarzenberg Palace in Vienna that Haydn's *Creation* was first given in 1798, and when Beethoven's Septet for violin, viola, clarinet, horn, bassoon, cello and double-bass, op.20, received its first performance there, Beethoven remarked: 'This is my creation.' Beethoven dedicated his set of variations for piano and cello on a theme from Handel's *Judas Maccabaeus* (WoO.45) to Princess Lichnowsky at about this time, so the Schwarzenberg connection did not eclipse his long-standing one with the Lichnowskys.

The year 1797 had in fact been a very productive one in terms of published work, for in addition to the Handel variations mentioned above, Artaria had published the E flat Piano Sonata, op.7, the Serenade for violin, viola and cello, op.8, and the Piano Rondo, op.51 no.1. The song 'Adelaide,' op.46, must also have been written by this time, and there were also the variations for two oboes and cor anglais on 'Là ci darem' from Mozart's *Don Giovanni* (WoO.28), which were heard at a benefit concert in Vienna on 23 December 1797.

The next year was marked by a highly successful visit to Prague, during the course of which Beethoven again played the B flat Piano Concerto. It may have been on that occasion that he used the revised version of the finale, instead of the original rondo (WoO.6), and he may also have given the first performance of the op.15 Piano Concerto in C, usually known as no.1 (despite its earlier opus number, it is in fact a later work than the op.19 concerto). Both concertos were, like those of Hummel and other contemporaries, written for the composer as virtuoso soloist, and they remain close both in form and in the style of their virtuosity to the model of Mozart's last piano concertos, his 'Coronation' Concerto (K.537) in particular. In Beethoven's C major Concerto the powerful first movement is followed by a largo, which includes an extended dialogue between piano and clarinet, and the finale is a fine example of his youthful rumbustious high spirits.

• Early piano sonatas •

Of Beethoven's thirty-two piano sonatas, the first nine were published by the end of 1799, and these works mark a new point in his development as a composer. The piano sonata was by now well established as a form; Clementi had produced a group of sonatas in 1773, and J. L. Dussek was already writing for the instrument in the 1780s; less Classically minded than the austere Clementi, Dussek became a celebrated virtuoso, and both composers must have influenced the young Beethoven to some extent. The sonatas of Mozart and, more important, of Haydn served as models for the deeper qualities of Classical tonality and thematic work, but in the lesser masters he discovered the rhetoric of the instrument.

Beethoven's first set of three sonatas had appeared as his op.2 in 1796. The quiet opening of the very first (reminiscent of the last movement of Mozart's G minor Symphony, no.40) makes it plain that, far from wanting to astonish with sheer virtuosity, Beethoven was anxious not to start his opus with anything that might suggest a challenge to Haydn, to whom the music is dedicated. This opening allegro is lightly scored – much of it is in two parts only – and it is no more ambitious a piece of piano writing than most of C. P. E. Bach. It can in fact be played, with surprisingly convincing effect, on that composer's favorite instrument, the clavichord. But the boy-virtuoso, pride of Bonn's salons, had matured rapidly, and although the C major Sonata (op.2 no.3) betrays an innocent wish to impress with keyboard brilliance, the placing of the F minor work as the first to meet the appraising eye of critic or friend was a clear declaration of serious intent. In his improvisations Beethoven could beat the exponents of mere velocity at their own game, but from the beginning of his career in Vienna he showed he was not available as some aristocrat's status symbol. The *prestissimo* finale of this first sonata demands both agility and power – two characteristic features admired in Beethoven's playing – but the two middle movements make no outward gestures.

If the first sonata belongs in spirit to the Bonn years, the second, from the quiet, but peremptory octaves of its opening to the indolent charm of the final rondo, may perhaps be seen as a self-portrait of the young genius from the provinces who never doubted his ability to conquer Viennese society. Though others had already exploited the rhetorical powers latent in the piano, the first movement of this A major sonata, brilliantly effective in its keyboard textures, offers a wealth of thematic development and contrasts of key. Clementi had written finely serious slow movements, as of course had Haydn and Mozart in their sonatas, but the deep meditative calm of Beethoven's *largo appassionato*, its sustained melody supported by imaginary plucked strings of cellos and basses, introduces a new kind of musical poetry.

The third sonata of op.2 makes more concessions to virtuoso display in its outer movements, but the adagio is full of a touchingly naïve solemnity. In its middle section a dialogue between bass and treble (both for the left hand) gives to the piano new and beautiful tone colors that anticipate the great Romantics half a century later. A device later to become typical of Beethoven makes its first appearance in the scherzo, when the first few notes recur over and over again, each time with new shades of meaning in rhythm and harmony.

The op.7 Sonata in E flat, written towards the end of 1796 soon after Beethoven had completed the cello sonatas for Duport, is a work

of great charm, despite its grand scale, and it later became known as 'Die Verliebte,' the woman in love. Beethoven dedicated it to one of his pupils, Countess Babette Keglevics, an indication of how successfully the unpolished young master had established himself in high Viennese society. It was soon followed by the three string trios of op.9 and another set of piano sonatas, published by Eder of Vienna on 5 July 1798 as op.10. These three works could scarcely be more contrasted: no.1, in C minor, looks back to Mozart's finest sonata (K.457), which is in the same key; no.2, in F, has instead of a slow movement a wonderful allegretto prophetic of Schubert; while no.3, in D, is a 'Grande Sonate,' like op.7, though not so designated by the composer.

The second sonata reaches an unassertive perfection in all three movements, free as it is from the C minor tensions of no.1. But while the opening allegro and central allegretto (in F minor, with a middle section in D flat) are well within the reach of amateurs, Beethoven's disregard for his public is demonstrated by the mock-fugal presto, which is beyond the reach of all but first-rate pianists. In its humorous abrupt contrasts and impatient energy, this makes the other side of another, doubtless unintended, self-portrait. The whole sonata is full of the wit, charm, willfulness and poetry of the young Beethoven, loved by his friends for his generosity and cheerfulness. Op.10 no.3 has a brilliant first movement and a broadly planned slow movement (*largo e mesto* – slow and sad), the only large-scale slow movement in such a somber mood before the huge 'Hammerklavier' Sonata of later years. In contrast with the 'social' unsubversive rondos of op.7 and op.22, the rondo finale of this sonata is the work of one who knows he has a captive audience, to be submitted to the whims of a composer whose inventive resources are limitless. Czerny said it gave some notion of Beethoven's incomparable improvisations.

Below left: Muzio Clementi (1752-1832). Although his fame has rested almost entirely on his piano exercises, Clementi was a fine composer, as his recently rediscovered symphonies show. He was also a piano manufacturer and a music publisher, including a number of Beethoven's works among his firm's publications.

Below: The title-page, in French, of Clementi's *Gradus ad Parnassum*. These exercises for perfecting piano technique were dedicated to Princess Wolkonsky and published by Breitkopf & Härtel in Leipzig. As the title suggests, with the stages or steps (*gradus*) of this tutor, the pianist might hope eventually to arrive at Mount Parnassus, the abode of the Muses of Greek mythology.

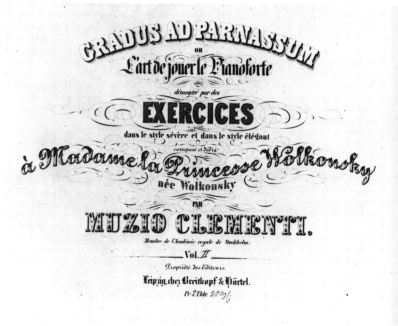

With op.13 we reach one of the most successful of all Beethoven's works in gaining wide celebrity. It was published late in 1799 and within five years an arrangement for string quintet was advertised thus: 'the excellent, universally loved and accepted *Sonate Pathétique* by the famous Beethoven transcribed'. Unlike the popular titles 'Moonlight' and 'Appassionata,' the description 'Pathétique' (impassioned) is original, though whether it was Beethoven's own or a suggestion from the publisher remains uncertain. This was one of a number of compositions – including also op.1 no.3, op.9 no.3 and op.10 no.1 – to give the key of C minor its peculiarly 'Beethovenian' character several years before his masterpiece in this key, the Fifth Symphony.

If op.13 is concerned with the elevated passions, the two delightful sonatas published as op.14 permit nothing to disturb their concentrated but transparent textures. Beethoven composed the E major Sonata with much care, as may be seen from the many pages of sometimes lengthy drafts of its themes and their possible development. It is also written in a most sensitive keyboard style, in which the extreme registers of the somewhat limited piano of the period were finely contrasted. Uniquely among the piano sonatas, he subsequently transcribed the work for string quartet. That Beethoven admired the work of Domenico Scarlatti seems apparent from the brilliant and light-hearted finale to op.14 no.2 in G major.

The 'Pathétique' had been published in 1799 by both Eder and Hoffmeister in Vienna, while Mollo, another Viennese publisher, issued op.14 right at the end of the year, bringing to a close Beethoven's first intensive period of work on the piano sonata form, one of the three forms (the symphony and string quartet, which are discussed in separate chapters below, being the others) for which, using the work of Haydn and Mozart as a starting-point, he established a paradigm that has never been superseded.

•The new century•

One must also assume that work must already have begun on the First Symphony op. 21, during the autumn of 1799, for it had its first performance on 2 April 1800, and the composing, copying, and rehearsing of the parts must have required at least these intervening months.

Above: The Bohemian musician J. L. Dussek (1760-1812), another important pioneer of piano technique and a prolific composer.

Left: The introductory page of *Gradus ad Parnassum* gives notes on the fingering technique used by Clementi in his work.

Above: Anna Louisa Barbara (or Babette, as she was popularly known), Countess Keglevics de Buzin, who started having piano lessons from Beethoven before her marriage in 1801 to Prince Odescalchi. She was the recipient of various compositions for piano by Beethoven, including his set of variations on Salieri's 'La stessa, la stessissima' (WoO.73), the Piano Sonata in E flat, 'Die Verliebte,' op.7, and the Piano Concerto in C, op.15.

Right: Ferdinand, Count von Waldstein (1762-1823), who was in the service of Elector Maximilian Franz in Bonn and was a gifted amateur musician. He was one of the first to recognize Beethoven's genius and gave him the necessary encouragement to go to Vienna. In return, the composer dedicated several works to Waldstein, including the Piano Sonata in C major (op.53) that bears his name.

That first performance of a Beethoven symphony, given in the Burgtheater in Vienna, was of course a landmark, for it showed the composer moving on to yet another plateau as a composer, and it was well received. The program also included a Mozart symphony, an aria and duet from Haydn's *Creation*, as well as Beethoven's own symphony, a piano concerto (very likely the one in C, op.15), his Septet and an improvisation on the piano. In placing himself alongside Mozart and Haydn, Beethoven now laid claim to the succession as their heir and Vienna's leading composer.

During the summer of 1800 Beethoven moved out of the city to Unterdöbling, where he probably wrote the Third Piano Concerto, op.37, and completed the six string quartets of op.18. The concerto, another work in C minor, returns to the more Mozartian idiom of the first two concertos, with many reminiscences of Mozart's own piano concerto in the same key (K.491), which was a particular favorite of Beethoven's. However, the slow movement is in the remote key of E major, and in the central section the soloist again has a dialogue with solo wind instruments – flute and bassoon – supported by pizzicato strings. Apart from an early minuet and two preludes and fugues, the op.18 quartets were Beethoven's first essay in the medium, and he evidently did not feel inspired to continue at that point; apart from arranging the first of the op.14 piano sonatas for string quartet the following year, he did not return to the form until the 'Rasumovsky' Quartets of 1805-6. His main creative energy was still directed towards the piano sonata.

By the autumn of 1801 Beethoven had published two violin sonatas, op.23 and op.24

(the 'Spring' Sonata), a string quintet, op.29, and several more piano sonatas. Op.22 in B flat ranked high in the composer's own estimation, and it is the work of a master who is confident that nothing is beyond his command. The first movement demonstrates how the Beethoven of 1800 was able to create music of compelling power with themes that his contemporaries would have dismissed as mere formulae. The composer wrote of this work to his publisher Hoffmeister: 'Die Sonate hat sich gewaschen, geliebtester Herr Bruder' (This sonata is the tops, my very dear brother).

Preliminary sketches for the Piano Sonata in A flat, op.26, dedicated to Prince Lichnowsky, appear in the same book as those for the violin sonatas just mentioned and for *The Creatures of Prometheus* ballet music (a unique piece of work for Beethoven, and one presaging greater things for the finale of the *Eroica* Symphony). A scribbled note relating to the op.26 sonata indicates that one movement was to be a 'characteristic' piece, that is, something bearing a more or less descriptive title, and the slow movement became famous in several arrangements, including one for full orchestra by the composer. As for the opening theme for variations, the charming melody seemed to invite words, and these were supplied by, among others, Beethoven's close friend Franz Gerhard Wegeler.

While op.26 was published as a 'Grand Sonate,' the two sonatas of op.27 are each labeled 'Sonata quasi una Fantasia,' suggesting that they have an element of improvisation about them. There are many tributes to Beethoven's powers of free improvisation, and several of his contemporaries declared that his written compositions lacked the invention he displayed when following the inspiration of the moment. Amenda – a trustworthy witness – related that at the end of one *Fantasie* (Improvisation) he lamented the fact that such splendid music should be born only to perish at once, whereupon Beethoven contradicted him by proceeding to repeat the whole thing. When the Czech composer Tomášek heard Beethoven improvise in 1798, he was so overwhelmed that for several days he was too discouraged to teach the piano.

Below: A domestic concert at the house of the Malfatti family, who came originally from Lucca. Giovanni, standing behind the piano holding a score, became a popular doctor in Vienna soon after he settled there in 1795; he was Beethoven's doctor for a period and eventually looked after him in his final illness. In between, however, there was a difficult period created by Beethoven's feelings for the doctor's niece. Therese, seated at the piano, inspired deep affection in Beethoven, and he was deeply hurt when in 1810, having asked her family's consent to marry her, that consent was refused.

There certainly is an improvisatory feeling to the openings of both op.27 no.1 in E flat and of its more famous companion piece, op.27 no.2 in C sharp minor. The latter, a measured *adagio sostenuto*, prompted the poet Rellstab to evoke the picture of a moonlight excursion by boat on a Swiss lake – and 'Moonlight' is the name by which the work has been known ever since.

No Romantic association should deprive the opening movement of its Bach-like depth, both in harmonic terms and in the long sustained melodic lines. Neither minuet nor scherzo, the allegretto is astonishingly telling in its brevity, like a great sonnet, and, for all its stormy rhetoric, the finale rises from the eloquent to the sublime in the dialogue of treble and bass that moves from key to key. This movement was without doubt the most tempestuous piece of piano music written up to that time. Competent amateurs who can tackle the first two movements are often completely floored by the third!

The title 'Pastoral' given to the sonata in D, published in August 1802 as op.28, is not Beethoven's own; but it was current on editions published during his lifetime and is not inapposite. As early as the sixteenth century composers had imitated the sustained bass note of the rustic bagpipe when wishing to evoke pastoral images, and the first movement and finale of op.28 begin with a repeated D beneath the theme, a device that also returns at the conclusion in both movements. While we should not make too much of an unauthorized title, there is an undeniable affinity between the peaceful opening of this sonata and the 'Pastoral' Symphony. Although some six years separate the two works, sketches relating to the symphony's 'Scene by the brook' date from 1803. There is also in the sonata a rustic dance, or Ländler, which revolves in the background of the brief scherzo, though it is speeded up beyond the skill of peasants, no matter how merry.

• The onset of deafness •

The year 1801 had certainly seen Beethoven securely provided for financially. Prince Lichnowsky had settled on him the sum of 600 florins annually, and he was now making money from his compositions. Moreover, publishers were even competing for the works. To judge by the amount of music he was composing, there can have been no lack of inspiration. It seemed extremely cruel, then, that Fate chose this moment to make Beethoven realize that there was something wrong with his hearing. From a letter to Wegeler that summer, we learn that the composer had been aware that his hear-

Left: The opening and closing pages of the Heiligenstadt Testament, in which Beethoven expressed all the frustration and agony of realizing that he was going deaf, and so progressively becoming more isolated from society. Written in October 1802, in the form of a letter to his brothers, it came to light only after the composer's death.

ing had been gradually getting weaker over the course of the three previous years – as early as 1798, therefore – but that he had said nothing.

We now know that Beethoven suffered from otosclerosis, or the growth of a spongy bone inside the ear. Today the condition is operable, or may even be alleviated with the help of a hearing-aid. In Beethoven's day, however, there was little that could be done. In fact the doctors believed that his hearing problems were connected with a stomach illness, which apparently dated back to his time in Bonn. The effect on Beethoven was that he withdrew within himself, he told no one, and moved less and less in society. As a feint, he deliberately accentuated his absent-mindedness.

At this point in his life one can only pity Beethoven in his predicament. Just as he seemed on the threshold of success and security, and was enjoying a romance, if we are to believe a letter to Wegeler from late 1801, he was destined to go through the Valley of the Shadow of Death. When he emerged, it was once more into the light of day, but muted with resignation. All of this can be read in the letter known as the Heiligenstadt Testament, which Beethoven dated 6 October 1802, written in the village where he had spent the summer of that year. In it he describes the progress of his deafness and hints at proposed, or at least contemplated suicide, but he had determined to be philosophical, not easy for one still young and 'harder for an artist than for anybody.' His postscript written four days later reads: 'Thus I bid you farewell, and with sadness. Yes, the dear hope which I brought here with me that I might to a certain extent be cured, must now leave me completely. As the autumn leaves have fallen, faded, so too has hope become barren for me. I leave here almost exactly as I came, except that the good courage, which often inspired me in the fine days of summer, has vanished. O Providence, let a pure

day of joy dawn once more for me! It is so long since I felt the warm resonance of true joy. When, when, O God, can I feel it again in the temple of nature and humanity! Never? Oh no, that would be too hard!'

The futility of attempts to relate the music of a great composer too simply to the events and experiences of his personal life is demonstrated by the fact that out of this black period came the radiant Second Symphony in D major, op.36, the strong and dramatic Third Piano Concerto, op.37 (again, significantly, in C minor), the two op.30 violin sonatas and the three piano sonatas published as op.31. About this time Beethoven is reported to have said, 'I am dissatisfied with my past works. Henceforth I shall follow new ways.' Certainly, each of these sonatas presents us with some new aspect of the composer's genius. The best known is the second work of the group. When Anton Schindler once

Below: The house at Heiligenstadt in which the Testament was written. At the time that he was going through this spiritual and emotional turmoil, Beethoven was also composing the Second Symphony (op.36), which is in marked contrast of mood and betrays none of his problems in its music.

asked the composer if the sonata had a special meaning, the latter told him to 'read Shakespeare's *The Tempest*.' On the strength of this passing remark, op.31 no.2, in Beethoven's other dramatic key of D minor, is sometimes called the 'Tempest' Sonata. In its outer movements this great work shows the expansion of harmonic rhythm (in effect, the more deliberate pace of chord changes) characteristic of middle-period Beethoven. Its opening movement, without precedent for somber power, grows out of the plainest figures – a spaced-out chord, a reiterated main note inflected by semitones. As the development moves from key to key it acquires symphonic breadth, though in fact it is remarkably concise. Its modulations to remote keys are so compelling that the return to D minor has to be confirmed by no fewer than twelve measures of the stock device called 'dominant preparation.' The recapitulation thus introduced begins with a stroke of genius that no familiarity can diminish. As in the first measure, the A major chord rises from the deep bass, this time to break into the most articulate form of musical speech, a recitative like those in the Bach Passions. Such extension of its beginning leaves the recapitulation with no space for a coda, so the movement ends with the tonic chord vibrating in the deepest bass of the contemporary pianoforte.

It is strange that although the instrument had developed in tone and sustaining power, the profound, melodic adagio of op.31 no.2 was to be the only full-scale slow movement Beethoven wrote for the piano from 1800 to 1818. The *allegretto* finale is perhaps the most daringly monotonous and certainly the most imaginative *moto perpetuo* ever written, for the rhythmic monotony that gives this movement its haunting quality is countered by a wide range of harmonic changes. It brings to mind a journey by night, and Carl Czerny reported that Beethoven had noted the pervasive motif of four notes when, one night at Heiligenstadt, a horseman at the gallop had passed beneath his window.

• The period of the 'Eroica' •

The new year of 1803 brought Beethoven a step further forward in his career when he was approached by Emanuel Schikaneder to compose an opera. In addition to being the author of *The Magic Flute*, Schikaneder was now manager of the Theater an der Wien, and his proposal was a commission to use his *Vestas Feuer* as the libretto for an opera. With this commission would go free lodgings at the theater, since Beethoven would be a house composer. Quite accustomed to changing his address, Beethoven quickly accepted and obtained permission to hold a concert in the theater. However, the performance was not to be an opera, let alone *Vestas Feuer*. Instead, Beethoven wanted to put on his oratorio *Christus am Ölberge*, op.85. The concert duly took place on 5 April

1803, and in addition to the oratorio, the audience was treated to the First and Second Symphonies as well as the Third Piano Concerto. Ferdinand Ries maintained that Beethoven had contemplated an even longer program, but decided against it at the last minute. No doubt the final rehearsal, which began at eight o'clock in the morning, convinced him. By half-past two in the afternoon tempers were well and truly frayed, and it was only through the timely intervention of Prince Lichnowsky, who sent out for bread and butter, cold meat and wine in large quantities, that spirits were restored.

For the summer of 1803 Beethoven went first to Baden, and then to Oberdöbling, both near Vienna. From this time dates the Violin Sonata in A major, op.47, dedicated to the French violinist Rodolphe Kreutzer, although he never played it. The violin sonatas, as a whole, are not in the same supreme class as the symphonies, concertos, string quartets and

piano sonatas, but this 'Kreutzer' Sonata is a fine example of the maturing 'middle-period' Beethoven. The whole sonata is on a large scale – it lasts well over half an hour – and tests the virtuosity of both players, a work certainly designed for the concert hall rather than the salon. The first movement is a dramatic *presto* framed by an *adagio* introduction and conclusion, and if its grand formal conception is not carried over into the slow movement, a charming and ornamental set of variations, or the dashing *presto* finale, these offer the violinist every opportunity to show off the sweetness and the brilliance of the instrument.

At this same period Beethoven began to work in earnest on the 'Eroica' Symphony, op.55. By the autumn of 1803, when he returned to his rooms in the Theater an der Wien, the work was sufficiently advanced for him to be able to play parts of it on the piano to visitors, and it was certainly finished by May 1804. Its performance was, however, delayed, for, as always with Beethoven, there was suddenly a complete change of plan. He broke with Schikaneder; *Vestas Feuer* never saw the light of day, and

Above: Beethoven tried many ways of overcoming his deafness, among them these aids made by his friend J. N. Mälzel, the inventor of the metronome.

Above: Franz, Count von Brunsvik (1777-1849), the brother of Therese and Josephine. Beethoven was on very intimate terms with the Count, and they addressed each other with the familiar *Du*. The composer dedicated two of his masterpieces to the count, the 'Appassionata' Sonata and the Piano Fantasia, op.77.

when Schikaneder's share of the theater was bought out, Beethoven was dislodged from the building. In the long run some good came out of it, for Joseph Sonnleithner acted as director of the theater for a time, and it was his translation and adaptation of Bouilly's *Léonore, ou L'Amour conjugal* that was Beethoven's libretto for his one completed opera.

If what Beethoven wrote to the publishers Breitkopf & Härtel on 26 August 1804 is correct, then he had by this time not only revised *Christus am Ölberge* and completed the 'Eroica' Symphony, but had also completed the Triple Concerto, op.56, and three new piano sonatas – the 'Waldstein,' op.53, the Sonata in F, op.54, and the 'Appassionata,' op.57. Yet again, out of an atmosphere of upheaval and even unhappiness came a series of superb compositions.

The concerto, for the unusual solo trio of piano, violin and cello, is an unjustly neglected work. True, it does not reach any high peaks of inspiration; but by tackling problems of balance between these soloists and the orchestra, Beethoven was preparing the ground for the other great works in concerto form still to come – the Violin Concerto and the Fourth and Fifth Piano Concertos.

As for the 'Waldstein' and 'Appassionata' sonatas (more unofficial titles), they certainly represent two high peaks in the literature for the piano. From the beginning of his career Beethoven had been interested in exploring the resources of the keyboard, but the 'Waldstein' marked a point of change in the whole concept of the piano sonata, having grown from a series of technical studies which followed the composer's work on the 'Eroica' Symphony. Beethoven had already demonstrated that the true sonata style flourishes on motifs or abstract patterns. In this respect the 'Waldstein' has frequently been misunderstood, even by the greatest musicians. Wagner, for one, found the main theme 'frigid,' and Busoni complained that in the middle-period sonatas Beethoven was too much concerned with what he called the rhetoric of the instrument. Perhaps the repeated chords of the opening did originate as a

writer's exercise, but when the first phrase in C major is restated a tone lower, poetic mystery banishes the prose of technical contrivance. The transition introduces a self-repeating hymn or chorale in E, by which point it should be plain that something strange and wonderful is happening to sonata form. No musical ear, whether trained or not, can miss the unprecedented key changes that, for all their unpredictable range, are still contained within the frame of the Classical style. In the first movement and finale alike key and texture take the place of melodic elaboration; of theme all that is needed is a mere hint to preserve coherence through long stretches of structured sonority. The sustaining pedal is used, perhaps for the first time here, as an essential part of the musical image, most remarkably in the rondo, where, in sovereign disregard of colliding harmonies, each line of the melody is delivered, very softly, over a deep bass note which reverberates all through the instrument. The sonata was much changed in plan during its composition; the original slow movement was a rather diffuse andante in F ('Andante favori'), later published separately. Beethoven replaced the movement with the *Introduzione*, a meditation that says more in a single page than the discarded andante in two hundred measures.

To say that the 'Appassionata' carries keyboard rhetoric to a limit beyond which not even Beethoven could profitably extend it, is not to seek to lessen its greatness as a composition. However, its qualities are not really typical if considered in relation to the sonatas as a whole. For the Romantic era this was the music that went with the frowning Promethean figure of many of the portraits of Beethoven, and this dramatic image is enhanced by the circumstances of its composition and the rain-soaked autograph of the manuscript. However, op.57 in F minor, so far from being rhapsodic, is perhaps the most rigorous in construction of all the major sonatas, both allegros being largely built on the notes of the common chord and making extensive use of the diminished seventh. No lesser composer would have risked the final simplification in the theme for variations, where only a single progression lies outside the most primitive harmony of the basic chords. For the first time in a piano sonata Beethoven abolishes the repeat of the first movement exposition, and its absence enhances the somber splendor of the development, as it moves through a vast expanse of keys. The material is drawn from both the principal themes, and, as these are closely related, the effect combines density and expansiveness in a way unique to Beethoven. The Thirty-two Variations in C minor published in the autumn of 1806 make a kind of appendix to the 'Appassionata,' but this work was not allowed the status conferred by an opus number.

The 'Eroica' received a first private performance in Prince Lobkowitz's palace in December 1804, but the first public performance was not until the following spring, on 7 April 1805. Possibly no similar work in the history of music had made such demands on its listeners, and it is, for that reason alone, a watershed in the history, not only of the symphony, but of the whole of Western music. Contemporary reaction tended to take one of three viewpoints. Beethoven's friends took the view that it was a masterpiece, and that if audiences were unable

to come to terms with it, then they were not sufficiently educated from a musical standpoint. At the opposite pole were those who could find nothing good in the work at all. As far as they were concerned, Beethoven had deliberately set out to be odd and violent. In their opinion, Beethoven was perfectly capable of producing music that was delightful to listen to, so in this work he was merely being perverse. The center group – much smaller than either of the others – found many fine things in the work but were at times perplexed by the changes of direction and certainly found its length difficult. Czerny asserted that one man was heard to shout from the gallery, 'I'll give another *kreuzer* if only the thing will stop.'

There certainly had never been anything quite so long in the history of the symphony, and for this alone one appreciates Beethoven's amazing vision and creative genius. Whatever people might say, he knew instinctively that he was right. And, indeed, he was breaking completely new ground, not only in the history of concerted music, but in the whole function of music in society. Until that time the public went to hear music that delighted and pleased their already formed appetites. In producing his 'Eroica' Symphony, Beethoven established

Below: The damp-stained first page of the autograph of the 'Appassionata' Sonata. Beethoven was working on the sonata while staying as a guest of Prince Lichnowsky at Grätz castle in 1806. After the battle of Austerlitz the castle was occupied by French officers, and to please the French general Lichnowsky asked Beethoven to play at a *soirée*. The composer refused and in a rage left the castle and walked with his precious manuscript through the rainy night to the nearby town of Troppau.

the paramount status of the work of art: its right, and indeed its need, to be considered on its own terms. As a corollary to this, though one which only became evident in its entirety somewhat later, Beethoven ensured the survival of works of art for future generations and the rehabilitation, eventually, of works from the past. Before the public performance Georg August Griesinger had written, in a letter to Breitkopf & Härtel, 'I hear that it is a work of genius, both from those who admire and those who denigrate Beethoven. Some maintain that it has more to it than the music of Haydn or Mozart, that the symphonic poem has been taken to new peaks.'

Below: The poster for *Fidelio,* when given at the Kärntnertor Theater on 23 May 1814. For the revival on this occasion Beethoven wrote a new overture – the fourth connected with the opera and the one most often used in performance.

•*Fidelio*•

From the summit of the 'Eroica,' Beethoven went directly to the challenge of his next peak, *Fidelio.* After his usual summer in the country outside Vienna, he was almost ready with the work by the autumn of 1805. In fact, the opera was originally entitled *Leonore,* so lending its name to the three great overtures that afford us a fascinating insight into Beethoven's creative thinking, in the way that each grows out of the one before. But to avoid confusion, we shall refer to the work as *Fidelio* from the title of its final version. In the circumstances, it was doubly unfortunate that its first night fell on 20 November, only one week after the invading French army arrived in Vienna. Their presence, however, was only a partial explanation of the work's lack of success, and Beethoven rewrote the first act and reduced the original three acts to two during the winter of 1805-6. Even so, the revised version still failed to please when it was heard on 29 March 1806. It is possible that it was Beethoven's own fault on this occasion, for if the audience had had more time to get to know the work, the houses would have improved. Apparently Baron von Braun, in control at the Theater an der Wien, had been quite prepared to let it run, but Beethoven, believing himself to have been cheated out of a percentage of the takings, demanded that his score be returned to him, and the work was taken off. Not until a revival at the Kärntnertor Theater in 1814, after further revisions (when the opera was finally renamed), did it at last meet with success.

Fidelio belongs to the genre of rescue opera, which Cherubini, Méhul and others had already made popular. Florestan has been imprisoned

unjustly by his political enemy Pizarro, and his wife Leonore, disguised as a young man (Fidelio), manages to get work as assistant to his jailer, Rocco. The first act of the final version explores the characters' conflicting emotions: Rocco, torn between natural compassion for his prisoners and the fear of disobeying orders; his daughter, Marzelline, between the devotion of her fiancé, Jaquino, and her new love for her father's young assistant; Pizarro between fear of his cruelty and corruption being discovered and delight at the prospect of having his enemy killed; only Leonore is steadfast in her devotion to her husband. Beethoven expresses this turmoil of passions first in the magical quartet in canon form, in which Marzelline, Leonore, Rocco and Jaquino each respond to the girl's evident love for Fidelio, then in Pizarro's gloating revenge aria, and finally in Leonore's great scene: horrified at Pizarro's plans to kill her husband, she invokes Hope to help her save Florestan. This mood of hope is underlined by the chorus of prisoners whom Rocco has allowed to enjoy a brief respite in the sunlight and open air of the prison garden.

Act II opens in Florestan's dungeon, the deepest in the prison, and his deeply moving scene and aria leads from despair to hope of freedom, then – in the short orchestral epilogue – to final exhaustion. The resolution of emotions inevitably recalls the Heiligenstadt Testament, and Beethoven's struggle is demonstrated by the fact that he made no fewer than sixteen sketches for the opening. The opera now moves swiftly to its climax. Rocco and Fidelio must dig a grave as Pizarro prepares to kill his prisoner, but at the fatal moment Leonore reveals herself and interposes to protect Florestan – 'First kill his wife!' Just then a trumpet signal announces the arrival of the minister come to investigate reports of Pizarro's crimes, and Florestan is saved, the opera ending with general rejoicing and praise of the power of love.

While it is strongly influenced by contemporary French opera, *Fidelio* adopts the conventions of *Singspiel*, performed in German and with spoken dialogue, and it forms a bridge between *The Magic Flute* – which Beethoven once declared to be his favorite of Mozart's operas – and Weber's *Der Freischütz*. Beethoven's dramatic sense undoubtedly found expression more readily in abstract, instrumental forms than in opera, and the theatrical flaws in *Fidelio* have often been pointed out, but it remains one of the great monuments to human nobility and heroism, worthy to stand beside the 'Eroica.'

• 1806 •

Within a matter of weeks of the unsuccessful second run of his opera, Beethoven had turned to something else and, according to his own annotation, began composing the 'Rasumovsky' Quartets on 26 May 1806. He did not go to any of his usual summer haunts that year, but went first with Count von Brunsvik to Hungary, to stay at his country home, and then to Silesia, to stay with Prince Lichnowsky at his castle of Grätz, near Troppau. It was from there that he wrote to Breitkopf & Härtel on 3 September offering all three of the 'Rasumovsky' Quartets, op.59, the Fourth Piano Concerto, op.58, the Fourth Symphony, op.60, *Fidelio* and *Christus am Ölberge*.

Count (later Prince) Rasumovsky commissioned the quartets from Beethoven. He was Russian ambassador in Vienna, and was, in 1808, to form the famous string quartet of Schuppanzigh, Sina, Weiss and Linke, which lasted until 1814, when the Rasumovsky Palace burned down. Of all Beethoven's music, the 'Rasumovsky' Quartets were possibly the least understood by his contemporaries. In fact Czerny maintained that when Schuppanzigh and his colleagues first played them through they merely laughed, and were convinced that Beethoven had played a joke on them. And the violinist Felice Radicati, who fingered the string parts for Beethoven on the manuscript, said that they were simply not music. With no little courage, the composer retorted that they were not for Radicati but for a future age.

Beethoven would have been prepared to stay on at Grätz in the autumn of 1806, but Prince Lichnowsky made the tactical error of trying to arrange a musical *soirée* for the French officers of the army of occupation, inviting Beethoven to play at it. When the time came, however, Beethoven was nowhere to be found. He had left a note in his room for the Prince, in which he said that he was unable to play for the enemies of his country. He may have been telling the plain truth, or he may have retained bitter memories of the French presence in Vienna and the failure of *Fidelio*. He may have been worried about his deafness in such a situation and felt unable to perform. Whatever the reason, it was strong enough to send him off into the night on foot, through the pouring rain, clutching the manuscript of the 'Appassionata' Sonata. As a valedictory on this occasion, Beethoven is said to have written to Prince Lichnowsky: 'Prince, what you are, you are by accident and by birth. What I am, I am through myself. There have been, and will be, thousands of princes. There is only one Beethoven.'

Opposite below left: Scene in the dungeon, where Leonore interposes to prevent Pizarro from murdering her husband; from the 1814 production of *Fidelio*, in which the role of Leonore was taken by Anna Milder (1785-1838) and that of Pizarro by Johann Michael Vogl (1768-1840). Both singers later became friends of Schubert's and interpreters of his songs.

Left: Piano version of *Fidelio* published by Artaria in 1814.

Left: Libretto for the 1805 version of *Fidelio*, published by Anton Pichler, for the performance in the Theater an der Wien. On this occasion the work was not a success.

movement just as thoroughly as the famous 'motto theme' of the Fifth Symphony runs through that work's far more terse and dramatic first movement. The rhapsodic slow movement is followed by a glittering rondo.

• Years of unrest •

Despite the fact that Beethoven's music was heard a good deal in Vienna, both during the winter of 1807-8 and 1808-9, he still let it be known that he was thinking of leaving for a tour, or even for good. Credence was given to this when, at the beginning of November 1808, he received an invitation from Jérôme Bonaparte, King of Westphalia, to go to Kassel as Kapellmeister. Even at the beginning of 1809 he wrote to Breitkopf & Härtel that he was seriously thinking of accepting the offer, and this was only a week or two after he had been given the Theater an der Wien free for a concert on 22 December, consisting entirely of his own

Above: The rooftops of Eisenstadt from the Bergkirche. In 1806 Prince Nicolaus II Esterházy commissioned Beethoven to write a Mass for the nameday of his wife Hermenegild the following year, a task that had fallen to Haydn in the past. Beethoven composed the Mass in C (op.86) and went to Eisenstadt to conduct the first performance in the Bergkirche.

Right: Prince Nicolaus II Esterházy. He was mortified by what he heard in Beethoven's Mass, and bitterly regretted having commissioned the work.

Right below: Hummel, who was the Prince's Kapellmeister. After the performance, Beethoven saw him laughing with his employer and assumed they were mocking his music. In fact Hummel was laughing at the Prince's reaction, but Beethoven was offended and left.

The Fourth Piano Concerto, in G major, shows Beethoven's mature style applied to the most public of his musical forms, and while Mozart is still his model, it is Mozart when he is breaking, rather than keeping, the rules that Beethoven follows. Instead of the concerto opening with the usual orchestral *tutti*, it begins with a brief dialogue, marked *dolce*, sweetly, between soloist and strings before the *tutti* proceeds; while the *andante con moto* middle movement shows the composer at his most theatrical: the threatening unison orchestral opening is progressively 'tamed' by the tender piano phrases, until both unite in a movement of unsurpassed dramatic power, which leads straight into the final rondo, a movement that combines brilliance and reflectiveness in a way that underlines the poetry of the whole concerto.

Within a matter of weeks, Beethoven had completed the Violin Concerto in D major, op.61, which was given its first performance on 23 December 1806 by Franz Clement, for whom it was written. Clement was an old acquaintance and leader of the orchestra at the Theater an der Wien, where he had witnessed the agonies over the reworking of *Fidelio*. The concerto, one of Beethoven's most beautiful works, was a generous offering to an old friend for his benefit concert, though rumor had it that the solo part was only completed shortly before the performance, and that Clement played it at sight. It opens in a most original way, with four soft beats of the kettledrums – a 'motto' that pervades the warm and expansive opening

Above: A portrait of Beethoven about 1805 – the so-called portrait of the Brunsvik House – by Isidor Neugass, who also painted a portrait of Haydn at Eisenstadt.

Fantasy, though not in the same high category as music, is fascinating as a kind of first draft for the great choral finale to the Ninth Symphony, still many years in the future.

The failure of the actual concert may have caused Beethoven to think that he was the victim of intrigue (suspicion of others being one tragic consequence of his deafness) and so strengthened his resolve to leave Vienna. A number of his admirers were sufficiently alarmed to take his threat seriously, meet together, and agree to provide him with an annual income – provided that he remained in Vienna or Austrian territory – for the rest of his life. The contract, agreed with Beethoven on 1 March 1809, was signed by the Princes Lobkowitz and Kinsky and Archduke Rudolph, who was Beethoven's pupil. Although at times the money was not paid promptly, Beethoven was now financially secure for the rest of his life.

The Fifth Piano Concerto, op.73, which Beethoven dedicated to Archduke Rudolph, is by far the grandest of the five piano concertos. Written in E flat, the same key as the 'Eroica,' it does have what one might call a 'Napoleonic' or imperial ring about it. But the title 'Emperor,' though appropriate enough, was certainly not Beethoven's idea. The work has a magisterial introduction for the piano, quite different from the *dolce* introduction to the Fourth Concerto, for here the soloist sets the mood for the first movement proper. Another notable feature is the linking of the second and third movements (one aspect of concerto form that had already interested Beethoven in the Fourth Piano Concerto and the Violin Concerto); this is effected here by a long-held note in the woodwind that drops a semitone, so leading back to the work's tonic key for the triumphant and strongly rhythmic finale. The whole concerto redefines the relationship between soloist and orchestra.

Although Beethoven began to sketch a sixth concerto, he was now too deaf to play in public, and the consequent change in his attitude to the piano is apparent in the Sonata op.78. About the time that it was written J. F. Reichardt reported that the piano-maker Streicher, acting on Beethoven's wish and advice, had given his instruments increased resonance, so that the player might have more command of sustained and expressive sounds. But no piano tone could be beautiful enough for the four-measure *adagio cantabile* introduction and the theme of the *allegro* first movement, which is left 'in the air' without the usual counterstatement. As to the next sonata, op.79 in G, Beethoven instructed his publishers to describe it as 'Sonatine facile' or 'Sonatine,' but though slight in comparison with the true sonatas, it is by no means trivial, and the description 'facile' shows what high standards were expected of Beethoven's friends and pupils.

Of all the masterpieces dedicated to the Archduke Rudolph, the Sonata op.81a, another work in E flat, is the most personal, the three movements being headed 'Farewell,' 'Absence' and 'Return.' The cause of Rudolph's departure, with the rest of the imperial family, was

works. By any standards it was a marathon performance. The program consisted of the 'Pastoral' Symphony, completed in the summer of 1808, the aria 'Ah! perfido,' movements from the Mass commissioned by Prince Nicolaus Esterházy, the Fourth Piano Concerto, the Fifth Symphony, a piano improvisation and the Choral Fantasy, op.80. Beethoven was himself the piano soloist, though when it came to the performance, it was little short of disaster. It was the last time Beethoven performed in public as a soloist on the pianoforte. As for the music itself, no other concert can have introduced so much great music at one time.

The Fifth Symphony in C minor, op.67, is the most celebrated ever written, and its overall character, of struggle leading finally to triumph, has been copied in numerous other symphonies. Its companion piece, the Sixth Symphony in F major, op.68, the 'Pastoral,' is the first example of a fully worked out program symphony, each of its movements headed by a descriptive title. The five movements – the last three being linked together – also represent a big advance in symphonic form. The Choral

the imminent arrival of Napoleon in the Austrian capital. During the French occupation Beethoven, though harassed and fearful of the effect of gunfire on his failing hearing, continued to work, and the sonata was probably completed well before the actual return of his eminent pupil in the following January. Clearly this happy outcome could not have been foreseen at the outset, and the sonata's sequence of sadness, tension, longing and finally joy is purely a product of the creative imagination. The 'motto' figure to the word 'Le-be-wohl' is the ancient cliché associated with horns or trumpets; it dominates the first allegro and, in the coda, makes the overlaps of tonic and dominant harmony which still sound strange. Sentiment in the andante is not tragic; the restless tonality accurately represents the state of someone who, in solitude, finds his thoughts turning to absent friends. The joyous finale wonderfully conveys a happiness free from hint of heroic assertion or showy brilliance.

It was this same turbulent year that Beethoven fell deeply in love with Therese von Malfatti. It was a hopeless passion, but he seriously

contemplated embarking on matrimony. His rejection by the Malfattis was a crippling blow. Fortunately he had made the acquaintance of another woman, Bettina von Brentano, with whom he did not fall in love, and she helped him to get over his disappointment. She also brought Beethoven into contact with Goethe sooner than might otherwise have happened. It was around this time that Beethoven wrote the noble overture and incidental music for a revival of Goethe's drama *Egmont*, a work whose theme is again the heroic fight for freedom from tyranny. For the summer of 1811 Beethoven went to Teplitz, where a new set of people seemed to revive his energy. That winter he was at work on no less than three symphonies. He completed the first of them, the Seventh, op.92, on 13 May 1812, then went on to the Eighth, op.93, and presumably began work on the Ninth, op.125, though it was some time yet before he began to work on it with any degree of consistency. Other compositions of this period reveal Beethoven's amazing capacity for varying the mood and character from one work to the next. The dedication of the Piano Sonata

Below: Johann Andreas Streicher (1761-1833), who married Nanette, the daughter of Johann Andreas Stein, the piano-manufacturer. She was carrying on her father's business at the time of their marriage, and this was taken over by Streicher. In Beethoven's opinion their instruments were excellent. As well as being intimate friends of the composer, the Streichers responded to his vision of what the piano might become in instrumental terms.

Right: The Streicher piano given by Nanette Streicher to Beethoven.

Far right: The Streicher concert-hall and piano showroom as seen in the first half of the nineteenth century.

in E minor, op.90, to Count Moritz Lichnowsky was an acknowledgment of his help in promoting the dedication of *The Battle of Victoria* to the English Prince Regent, but according to Anton Schindler there was a more personal connection. The Count was planning to marry an actress, and Beethoven is said to have explained that the sonata represented, first, an argument between heart and head, and, second, a conversation with the beloved. This second movement is certainly one of the most tender and lyrical of all Beethoven's compositions. The contrast between this sonata and the fierce concentration of the F minor String Quartet, op.95, could hardly be more marked. Contrast between the quartet and the neighboring Trio in B flat, op.97, is just as strong. This 'Archduke' Trio (again dedicated to Rudolph) is Beethoven's last contribution to another instrumental form at which he excelled. The mood of the work moves from a serene beauty to almost rude high spirits.

That autumn, in October, Beethoven completed the Eighth Symphony in Linz, where he had gone in an attempt to prevent his brother

Johann from marrying the woman of his choice. Beethoven himself seems to have had one last romance that summer, which inspired the letter dated early July, found after his death, and addressed to the 'Immortal Beloved.'

· The late period ·

From August 1814 to November 1816 Beethoven completed only three substantial new works, the two powerfully concentrated cello sonatas, op.102, that concluded his small but distinguished output in that instrumental medium, and the first of the last group of five piano sonatas. These are works which herald what is loosely called the 'third' or 'late' period of the composer's creative life. The Sonata in A major, published as op.101, opens quietly. This is nothing new in itself. What is new is the meditative calm that pervades the whole opening movement, apart from the sole *fortissimo* (struck once and fading with the natural *diminuendo* of the instrument) near the end. However, the master of the great 'second period' works has not embraced quietism; after lyric poetry comes a march, lively in rhythm but full of disturbing chromatic harmonies and weird tone colors ranging from the deepest bass to the extreme treble of the piano's compass. Beethoven had written highly successful *marches militaires*, but this piece celebrates no victory, enlivens no parade. If there is humor, it is far from being good humor and has a cutting edge, looking forward almost a century to the nightmarish military music that haunted Gustav Mahler. The adagio that follows the march is to be played longingly. It then returns to the opening of the sonata by way of a cadenza-like flourish. Bitterness, irony, introspective sadness – all these are banished by the recollection. The finale begins in an access of pure joy, while its development section is in the form of a fugue, a musical device that preoccupied Beethoven more and more in his later years.

Meanwhile, in 1813 the victory won by Wellington at Victoria in Spain brought from Beethoven one of his more curious compositions, entitled *Wellington's Victory* or *The Battle of Victoria*, op.91. It was in fact written for an invention called the Panharmonicon, devised by Johann Nepomuk Mälzel (1772-1838), the inventor of the metronome. Some of the composer's admirers were appalled at the thought that he should be involved in such a venture at all, but it was a great success and earned Beethoven a much greater popularity than ever before in Vienna. Its success, coupled with that of a concert on 2 January 1814, during which not only the battle piece but also some items from *The Ruins of Athens*, op.113, were given, now encouraged the composer to think of reviving *Fidelio*. He began work on it in March and continued until the middle of May. The first night was fixed for 23 May at the Kärntnertor Theater. That year Vienna was a place of great excitement. The allied troops had entered the city on 11 April, and in September the delegates to the Congress of Vienna began to arrive. *Fidelio* caught on after its revival in May and was chosen as the first opera to be given before the foreign dignitaries on 26 September. In November Weber conducted it in Prague. Beethoven received 4,000 silver florins as a gift from the nobility at the Congress, which he invested as an inheritance for his nephew Carl. Never again was he to know such popularity and financial security, and although 1815 was, for the most part, spent happily, as autumn drew on it became evident that his brother, Caspar Carl, had not long to live.

Caspar Carl, the father of Carl, appointed his brother sole guardian of the boy, but Ludwig was not content with this and wanted to have

Above: A watercolor portrait of Nanette Streicher, dating from around 1830.

sole custody of the child, in the face of his mother's determined opposition. Indeed, Beethoven's whole approach to the matter was one of almost hysterical obsession, with which he was scarcely equipped to cope. As he fought interminable legal battles with the boy's mother throughout 1816 and 1817, his creativity suffered considerably, and he composed less and less. So convinced was Beethoven that what he wanted was best for the boy, that he never once stopped to ask himself what harm he might be doing to the child.

In the middle of 1818 it was made known that Beethoven's pupil, Archduke Rudolph, was to be created Archbishop of Olmütz (Olomouc), and Beethoven determined to write a Mass for him, which was to be the *Missa Solemnis*, op.123. The enthronement was not due to take place until March 1820, but even so, Beethoven did not complete his Mass in time, largely because of the continuing litigation over Carl. The matter was finally settled in Beethoven's favor on 24 July 1820, but only after the boy's mother had appealed to the Emperor himself.

The winter of 1820-1 was not especially productive, largely because Beethoven was ill, and 1821 itself was little better, though he continued to work on the Mass. It was not until 19 March 1823, however, that he eventually presented a copy to Archduke Rudolph. The *Missa Solemnis* stands alone as Beethoven's only major choral work. The occasionally excessive demands he makes of the singers (as in the choral finale to the Ninth Symphony) are a reflection both of his far greater mastery of purely instrumental and orchestral forms and of his deafness, which sometimes impaired his judgment of what was practical. The visionary power of the Mass, though, places it among his

highest achievements. It is also probable that in the summer of 1822 he began work on the first of the late string quartets, op.127, though it was completed to a commission from Prince Galitzin.

• Last piano works •

Like the *Missa Solemnis*, the Piano Sonata in B flat, op.106, composed between 1815 and 1819, was the largest and greatest of its kind and was also directly associated with the Archduke Rudolph, since the first and second movements were originally intended as a celebration of Rudolph's nameday. Busoni considered that op.106, the 'Hammerklavier,' outweighed any of the symphonies in musical content, and the work may well be thought of as a huge four-movement symphony for the piano. The first two movements are relatively straightforward, if outstanding, examples of Beethoven's art. But the adagio is the most profound slow movement ever written for the instrument. Its great length is sustained by continuous variation and a polyphony as wonderful as that of Bach. When it dies away in a long major chord, it is impossible to imagine how Beethoven is to proceed to the 'large fugato' he had announced to the Archduke. With a unique stroke of genius a repeated isolated note leads to evocations of Bach, in remote keys that gradually swing round to the dominant chord of the long-absent B flat key of the sonata.

The fugue's long subject is related not to Bach but to his predecessors, the German organ masters, though none of them would have risked Beethoven's rigorous adherence to the most pedantic devices of the academic schools

Above left: Miniature on ivory of Baroness Dorothea von Ertmann (1781-1849). She was an accomplished pianist and a frequent interpreter of Beethoven's piano sonatas. The composer dedicated his Piano Sonata in A, op.101, to 'Dorothea Cäcilia.'

Above right: A New Year's card sent from Beethoven to Baroness von Ertmann.

– augmentation, inversion, even cancrizans (in which the theme is made to run backwards). There is nothing free or episodic, no fresh material is introduced to meet the needs of dramatic contrast, yet the most monumental sonata ever written ends, like the Ninth Symphony, with a hymn of joy; here it is the joy of the intellect in its victory over the chaos of the emotions.

The last three sonatas that followed soon after, op.109 in E, op.110 in A flat and op.111 in C minor, do not compare with the 'Hammerklavier' in sheer size and power, but they are, if anything, even finer works of pure music. They demonstrate that the piano remained indispensable to Beethoven for the expression of those elements of fantasy and song that were part of his deepest experience. The indissoluble unity of thought and medium sets them apart, even from the last string quartets.

The beginning of op.109 shows this inseparability of thought and sound. Instead of introducing 'themes' that can be abstracted, as with, say, a Bach fugue, the ideas become the patterns of keyboard figurations: first an elusive sustained melody half hidden within the dialogue of the two hands, then, unprecedented in sonata form, a 'second subject' in a slow tempo with broken chords and scales which range widely over the keyboard. This *adagio* duly returns in the main key to develop the first subject, but the piece sounds quite unlike any possible Classical sonata movement. Its lucidity makes it all the more mysterious; this is a vision that has nothing to do with the Romantic world of half-dreams. Among the concepts that seem to have interested Beethoven in his later music is the unifying of drastic contrasts. So the

prestissimo following the sonata's essentially calm opening, though neither desperate or fate-defying, could scarcely be called good humored. The sonata ends with an *andante* – a sarabande-like theme that introduces five highly contrasted variations and is repeated, unaltered, at the close, the only possible conclusion to this strange and marvelous work.

The remoteness and mystery of op.109 are for the most part excluded from op.110, where personal elements are explicit, and Beethoven finds new depths of meaning in melodic figures and harmonic progressions that look back to much earlier works, particularly in the first movement. In the finale the example of Bach is again in evidence, both in the recitative and 'arioso dolente,' a lament too subdued and introspective for drama, and in the grandly austere three-part fugue.

Op.111 has always seemed the perfect conclusion to the sequence of sonatas, though there is nothing to suggest it was so intended. The unity of its two movements is to be found, not in imaginary thematic relations but in the bringing together of the most intense realizations of the Classical principles, these being action (sonata form) and reflection or contemplation (variations). The theme for variation was no sudden inspiration; it was the result of a long search for the ultimate 'simplification of the idea.' And the variations, while complex in textural elaboration (especially in rhythm), follow closely the melodic and harmonic structure of the theme.

A successful revival of *Fidelio* during the winter of 1822-3 turned Beethoven's thoughts to the possibility of a new opera, and he discussed this idea at some length with Franz Grillparzer, but nothing came of it. Nonetheless, there was a sudden burst of energy, and 16 June 1823 saw the publication of a set of piano variations on a waltz, the 'Diabelli' Variations, op.120. This work had an interesting genesis. In 1819, the music publisher and minor composer

Right: Antonia von Brentano (1780-1869). A close and loyal friend of the composer, Antonia was the dedicatee of Beethoven's 'Diabelli' Variations, op.120.

Below: Giulietta, Countess Guicciardi (1784-1856). Giulietta was a cousin of the Brunsviks, through whom she had got to know Beethoven, and had begun having lessons from him in 1801, when she was seventeen. The composer had fallen passionately in love with her, and the 'Moonlight' Sonata (1802) was dedicated to her. In 1803 she married Count von Gallenberg, a mediocre composer of ballet music.

Right: Carl van Beethoven (1806-58) in his cadet's uniform.

Anton Diabelli had sent a waltz he had written to fifty composers, including Beethoven. Each was invited to contribute a single variation on it for a proposed collection. Beethoven is said to have at first refused (calling the waltz a 'cobbler's patch'), but he then sketched several variations and proposed to another publisher, Simrock, 'some grand variations,' not yet completed. By the spring of 1823 there were thirty-three and the work was finished. Beethoven had produced some impressive variation sets in his youth, but in his mature work, a vastly deepened concept of the variation-principle became increasingly significant. Bach had shown, in the 'Goldberg' Variations, how a masterpiece could be designed on the bass and harmonic structure of a theme without any reference to the initial melody; Beethoven found ways of making coherent and recognizable variations by exploiting every aspect of his theme and by reducing it to an abstraction – an *idea* of a harmonic scheme in which the chords differ while their relations remain identifiable to the attentive ear. So, with Diabelli's prosaic but sturdily constructed waltz he could associate a whole world of marvelous inventions. After its initial statement, the waltz theme is not heard again, but it never ceases to be present, whether as structural foundation, as basic concept, or in the working of some striking detail. In their wealth of creative fantasy and in the deaf composer's marvels of imagined sonorities, the 'Diabelli' Variations contain some of the greatest of all piano music. They were practically Beethoven's last thoughts for the piano.

•The final years •

As early as 1 July 1823 Beethoven had written to Archduke Rudolph to tell him that he hoped that his Ninth Symphony would be finished within two weeks. By this time people had no doubt learned to look upon such claims with a certain amount of skepticism. But by the beginning of 1824 it definitely was finished. The work was being copied, and Beethoven was making arrangements for the concerts in May – the first on the 7th in the Kärntnertor Theater and the second on the 23rd in the Grosser Redoutensaal – which brought to the Viennese public the first performance of the Ninth Symphony and parts of the *Missa Solemnis*, though the latter work had been first heard in its entirety a month earlier in a performance organized in St Petersburg by Prince Galitzin.

Although the first of the two May concerts was well received – apparently the deaf Beethoven had to be turned round to see and to acknowledge the applause at the first performance of the symphony – neither proved the hoped-for financial success. Beethoven moved out of Vienna as usual that summer, but wrote little or no music, though he was overseeing the copying of music prior to publication. He may well have been putting the finishing touches to the op.127 Quartet, and he arranged for its first performance with Schuppanzigh for 6 March 1825.

From now on it was the medium of the string quartet that was to engage most of Beethoven's remaining creative energy. During the following May (1825) he composed the third movement of the op.132 Quartet, which he described as a 'song of thanksgiving in the Lydian mode offered up to the Divinity by a convalescent.' He completed the work by the end of July or the beginning of August, and then got to work on the op.130 Quartet, the third of those – together with op.127 – written to fulfill a commission from Prince Galitzin.

This received its first performance, which was once more undertaken by Schuppanzigh, on 21 March 1826. The last movement caused problems for the players, however, and it was Mathias Artaria's suggestion that Beethoven should write a new closing section. The original was published as a separate piece, the *Grosse Fuge*, op.133. From a letter to Schott dated 20 May 1826, Beethoven also seems to have completed the C sharp minor Quartet, op.131, and there was one more yet to come, op.135, in F. Work may have been well advanced that summer when yet another blow struck the ailing composer.

At the end of July his nephew Carl attempted suicide. Carl always maintained that he had grown worse because his uncle had wanted him to be better. Ever since the boy's father died, he had been almost constantly subjected to his uncle's will and the not inconsiderable force of his personality. Carl spent much of August and September in hospital, and when he came out Beethoven took him to his brother Johann's house at Gneixendorf. They returned to Vienna on 1 December, but Beethoven caught a chill on the way, and when they reached the Schwarzspanierhaus, which was Beethoven's last address in the city, he was obliged to take to his bed.

At first no one seems to have worried too much, including Beethoven himself, assuming

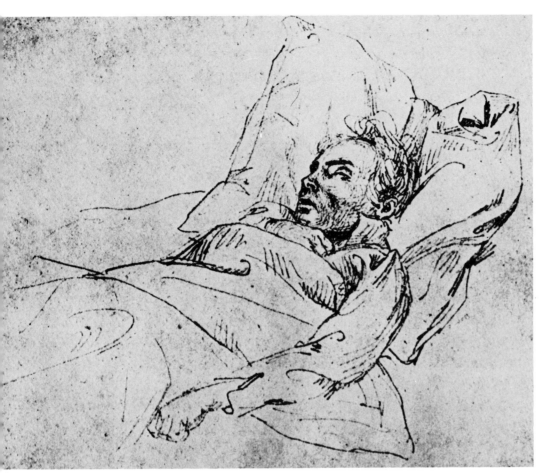

Left: Beethoven in a state of coma during his final illness, as drawn by Josef Teltscher.

Below: The invitation to Beethoven's funeral procession, the wording of which was devised by Stephan von Breuning, a friend of Beethoven since childhood days in Bonn: 'The musical world suffered the irreparable loss of the celebrated composer on 26 March 1827 in the evening towards 6 o'clock. Beethoven died as a result of dropsy, in the 56th year of his life, after receiving the holy sacraments.'

Einladung

zu

Ludwig van Beethoven's

Leichenbegängniss,

welches am 29. März um 3 Uhr Nachmittags Statt finden wird.

Man versammelt sich in der Wohnung des Verstorbenen im Schwarzspanier=Hause Nr. 200, am Glacis vor dem Schottenthore.

Der Zug begibt sich von da nach der Dreyfaltigkeits=Kirche bey den P. P. Minoriten in der Alsergasse.

Die musikalische Welt erlitt den unersetzlichen Verlust des berühmten Tondichters am 26. März 1827 Abends gegen 6 Uhr. Beethoven starb an den Folgen der Wassersucht, im 56. Jahre seines Alters, nach empfangenen heil. Sacramenten.

Der Tag der Exequien wird nachträglich bekannt gemacht von

L. van Beethoven's
Verehrern und Freunden.

that it would be only a temporary state of affairs, but dropsy set in, and after four operations to remove water from his stomach, Beethoven finally passed away on 26 March 1827. His funeral took place three days later and was one of the most impressive ever seen in Vienna. Some 20,000 people are said to have packed the square in front of the Schwarzspanierhaus. There were no less than eight Kapellmeister as pall-bearers, including Seyfried and Hummel, who had come to Vienna from Weimar with his wife as soon as he heard of Beethoven's illness. Among the torch-bearers was Schubert.

Left: A drawing of Beethoven walking in Vienna by J. P. T. Lyser (1803-70), which first appeared in the Hamburg periodical *Cäcilia* in 1833.

From Harpsichord to Pianoforte

For most of the eighteenth century, one of the seemingly most unshakable features of concerted music must have been the position of the harpsichord. In orchestral music it was an essential element of the *fond sonore*, both from an acoustic point of view and also from the point of view of composition. Together with the bass instruments of the orchestra – cello, contrabass and bassoon – the fabric of the music itself rested on the foundation of the *basso continuo*. In the more intimate world of chamber music, too, the *basso continuo* element was of vital importance, and when Mozart and Beethoven began to experiment with composition for string quartet, for example, they found the process difficult from its very novelty of concept.

Whether the development of the pianoforte or musical development caused the demise of the harpsichord is impossible to say. It was one of those fortunate coincidences that the technical development of the pianoforte had reached such a point that, when composers began to feel for new textures and forms in music, the instrument was there, and makers were ready to collaborate in exploring and developing its potential. Above all, it provided scope for the variety of emotional expression that the new music was elaborating. Luckily, in the Vienna of the 1790s, when Beethoven arrived there, there was an established audience for keyboard virtuosity and thus a further source of impulse to the development of the fortepiano and, later, the pianoforte.

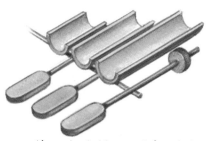

Above: A harpsichord made in 1798 by Jacob Kirckman. This famous maker was the last of a dying breed, and the instrument shown was one of the very last to be made by him – and one of the last made in England until the revival of Baroque music in the present century.

Right: The essential feature of the harpsichord is the fact that its action is one of plucking as opposed to striking, which was to characterize the later piano. Shown here is the jack which, activated by the key from beneath, rises to pluck the string with the quill on its side.

Above: Pietro Longhi, *The Music Lesson*, c.1740.

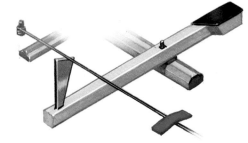

Left: The harpsichord was the most common instrument used to provide the continuo accompaniment for vocal and instrumental music. Longhi's painting (*left*) shows a Venetian instrument.

Above: A primitive xylophone – tuned wooden bars struck by hammers (after a musical treatise of 1637). This shows a simple form of the principle that was applied to the pianoforte mechanism.

Below: Action of the clavichord – closer to the piano than the harpsichord in that the string is not plucked but struck by a brass tangent. Although slight in tone, the clavichord can be very expressive.

As early as 1698 Bartolomeo Cristofori (1655-1731) had produced in Florence an instrument that he called 'gravicembalo col piano e forte' (harpsichord with both soft and loud). The most important innovations were that the strings were struck with hammers and not plucked, and that – unlike in the clavichord, where the simple lever action caused the tangent to remain in contact with the string until the key was released – an escapement action (*see below*) released the hammer immediately after it struck the string. This meant that the volume of sound could be controlled (without the distortions of pitch that would occur in a clavichord) by the force with which the key was struck.

By the mid-eighteenth century, Cristofori's invention (generally known now as a fortepiano) was becoming widely used as an alternative continuo instrument, as it was cheaper and easier to maintain than a harpsichord. In shape fortepianos were modeled either on harpsichords (wing-shaped) or more often on clavichords or virginals, giving the characteristic form of the 'square piano' (*top*). These generally employed the 'mopstick action' (*above and below*), where the angles of the levers were designed to have the same effect as an escapement action, ensuring that the hammer did not remain in contact with the string even if the key was not immediately released; however, this system had the disadvantage that it jammed easily, and it did not survive long after 1800. As with the harpsichord and with other piano actions, the damper remained free of the string as long as the key was depressed.

Above: Cristofori's improved action of 1726. As the key is depressed, the hammer element is raised to strike the string, but the escapement action (working like a trip hammer) immediately releases it. The string resonates until the key is released and the damper (shown in green), which has also been raised, closes on the string and causes the vibration to stop. The independence of the hammer element from the key distinguishes the fortepiano entirely from the direct level action of the clavichord (*opposite below*). The clavichord has, in fact, a very narrow dynamic range, since too great a pressure on the key stretches the string causing distortion of the pitch.

Only two of Cristofori's fortepianos have survived: one, dated 1720, is in the Metropolitan Museum, New York (*see Volume I, p.249*), while the other, dated 1726, is in Leipzig. These instruments had a compass of only four or four and a half octaves (with two strings to each note), but this was increased as the century progressed; Mozart's concert grand, for example, had a compass of five octaves, and by 1794 John Broadwood in London had made an instrument with six.

During the second half of the eighteenth century, composers began to exploit the color and technique of the fortepiano, rather than treating it simply as a substitute for the harpsichord. C. P. E. Bach wrote a double concerto for the two instruments, contrasting their qualities, but the pioneers of piano composition were J. C. Bach and Mozart, whose piano music is unthinkable on a harpsichord, and then Beethoven, whose works laid the foundations for the great age of piano composition.

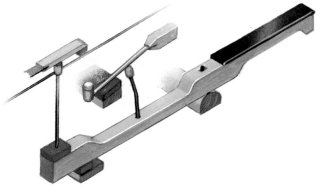

The development of the fortepiano in Germany was due first to Gottfried Silbermann (1683-1753), a celebrated organ-builder and maker of clavichords, who read about Cristofori's invention in 1725 and within a year had produced his own first forte-pianos. Silbermann's instruments, like the piano (*right*) which once belonged to Frederick the Great, generally kept to the familiar harpsichord shape. This derives from the progressively shorter length of the higher pitched strings and still survives, despite all the technical changes, in the modern grand piano.

The square piano (*below*) was made by Johann Zumpe, a pupil of Silbermann who settled in London in the late 1750s and worked at first for the Swiss harpsichord-maker Burkat Shudi. Later he set up his own business and manufactured square pianos – which he had in fact himself invented. J. C. Bach gave a recital on one of these pianos after his arrival in London in 1762, and it soon began to win popularity. Zumpe's piano was greatly improved by Shudi's son-in-law John Broadwood, whose instruments were known for their strength of tone.

Right: Pyramid piano of about 1750, an early version of the upright piano. There was a prototype for this in the clavi-cytherium, a version of the spinet or harpsichord in which the strings were perpendicular to the keyboard. Adapting this for the escapement action which is an essential feature of the fortepiano presented certain challenges, but once they were overcome the way was open for the development of the upright as we know it today, a diagram of which is shown opposite (*top left*).

As to what Beethoven thought of the pianos of his day, three extracts from his letters give us some indication. In 1796, writing to Streicher, for example: 'The day before yesterday I received your fortepiano, which is truly a marvelous instrument. Another person would attempt to keep it for himself, but I would be deceiving you – here you must laugh – unless I told you that as far as I am concerned, it is much too good for me.

Why? Because it deprives me of the liberty to make my own tone. But naturally this must not prevent you from making all your fortepianos in the same way. . . . I hope that . . . you are totally convinced of my genuine desire that the qualities of your instrument should be appreciated in this country and everywhere else.' Then about six years later, in 1802, Beethoven told Nikolaus Zmeskall in a letter that 'the entire tribe of pianoforte-makers have been clustering about me in their concern to be of service to me – and all to no avail. Every one of them wants to make a pianoforte for me precisely as I should like. Reicha, for example, has been besought by the maker of his pianoforte to induce me to allow him to make one for me.' He then set out the effects he required should the maker Anton Walter agree – through Zmeskall – to make one for him. Beethoven particu-larly requested the *una corda* effect, for example, whereby the hammer could be made to strike only one of the strings, as opposed to the three usually fitted to each note at this time. Finally, in 1818, here is Beethoven thanking Broadwood for the gift of a piano sent from London to Vienna: 'I have never known more pleasure than that induced by your telling me of the promised arrival of the piano with which you honor me in offering it to me. I shall consider it an altar on which I shall lay the most beauti-ful offerings of my soul to the divine Apollo. As soon as I receive your splendid instrument, I will send to you the fruit of the inspiration of the initial moments that I spend with it as things by which you may remember me, my dear Broadwood, and I trust that they will be worthy of your instrument.'

Top right: Three developments of the piano action, with different approaches to the escapement mechanism, and, in the lower two diagrams, different solutions to the problem of adapting the mechanism to an upright instrument. The piano action (*top*) developed by Stein and his son-in-law Streicher in Vienna was lighter in touch than that of French or English makers, and the tone had less sonority. This characteristic influenced both styles of playing and the kind of music written for the instrument.

The action of the pyramid piano of 1750 (*lower left*) had the disadvantage that the mechanism involved a weight to pull back the hammer once it had been struck, and it soon became apparent that this was unlikely to be the way for future development. The action of a modern upright piano (*lower right*) made by Hamburger-Brooks places the dampers below the hammers. This 'underdamping' is designed to be more immediately effective, since the vibration of the strings is greatest at that point.

The new instrument dramatically changed the way that composers wrote for the keyboard. The first music example is the opening of a sonata by Domenico Scarlatti (1685-1757), while the other is the start of Beethoven's 'Pathétique' Sonata (1798-9). The texture of the two pieces is strikingly different. The earlier work has a more open quality, relying on a continuous, brilliant sound, with both hands often in unison and with virtually no expressive variation. Beethoven's sonata, on the other hand, shows the stress on chords, changing harmonies, varied rhythm, and much more expression on the part of the player.

BEETHOVEN'S SYMPHONIES

ANTONY HOPKINS

Apart from the first two piano concertos, a form in which Beethoven's own mastery of the keyboard assured him of success, all the works he wrote during the last decade of the eighteenth century were sonatas or chamber music of some kind. This reluctance to embark on a major orchestral composition is surprising. The concept of the symphony as a form had been clarified by such early masters as C. P. E. Bach, Wagenseil, Gassmann and Stamitz; it was subsequently developed with wonderfully inventive powers by Haydn. One would have expected Beethoven to welcome the challenge with enthusiasm, yet even Haydn's tuition failed to give him the necessary confidence. He made some sketches for a symphony in 1795, but they proved abortive. If the lessons with Haydn had planted symbolic seeds, they appear to have lain dormant for some seven years; with apt historical timing they were to flower with the dawn of a new century in the year 1800.

•Symphony no.1 in C•

Following a precept set on many previous occasions by Haydn and his contemporaries, Beethoven begins this symphony (op.21) with a slow introduction. Although the opening measures may seem undramatic to a modern ear, they are sufficiently unorthodox to have elicited a great deal of comment over the years. The standard way of beginning any major work, whether symphony, concerto, sonata or quartet, was to spell out a sequence of notes or harmonies that would establish a 'home' key, or tonal base. The home key, or tonic, to give it its proper name, served both as point of departure and as ultimate destination. At the very start of this symphony Beethoven leads the listener astray by suggesting other 'homes' than the proper one of C major, so that when the music does break into a quick tempo we sense a twofold release. Not only is the sustained tension of the introduction resolved, but also the enigma of uncertain tonality.

If the first main theme of the allegro strikes a slightly military attitude with its crisp precision, the second theme is almost operatic in flavor, with flute and oboe engaging in a delightful dialogue. The ghost of Mozart hovers in the air, soon to be exorcized with peremptory

rhythms that suggest the rapid beat of a side-drum, even though such an instrument had no regular place as yet in the symphony orchestra. Out of this brief clash of arms we are suddenly shifted into a world of shadows and mystery. Cellos and basses lead the way, while the strings above offer an accompaniment of gentle throbbing harmonies that briefly touch on tonal centers as yet unvisited. The air of mystery imparted by this passage is not simply achieved by playing quietly. The music is mysterious because it ventures into tonalities that contradict the basic components of C major, moving far from 'home' into the storm of uncertainty at the center of the movement. This central crisis or climax resolved, the composer reassembles the original material in the third main section, the recapitulation. This is a reassessment of the themes in the light of experience gained during the development. The final bars of the movement emphasize the restoration of the home key of C major, as if to assure us that it is no longer at risk.

The second and third movements give a clear indication of Beethoven's transitional state as a composer, since the slow movement looks back to the formal dance-style of the eighteenth century, while the ensuing 'minuet' totally discards such conventions. Anything less like a minuet could hardly be imagined, and the title must be taken as a joke. The conception is totally original; it is in effect the first symphonic scherzo and is the largest comparable movement that Beethoven was to write for some time.

As for the finale, it begins with an impressive gesture that turns out to be a hoax. Like a bevy of hesitant beginners, the first violins make no less than five abortive attempts to play a scale, progressing one note further each time. It is a characteristic example of Beethoven's musical humor which he would have hated us to take seriously. When at last the movement gets under way, it sparkles with wit and vitality. In particular, the rising scale that initially seemed to frighten the first violins proves a fruitful source of material, whether ascending or descending. Towards the end there are two massive pauses that lead us to expect some great event. Again it is a tease, an amusing exploitation of the effect of anticlimax. The final march, garlanded with scales from the woodwind, is like a children's game. There were no clouds in Beethoven's sky when he wrote this delightful symphony.

•Symphony no.2 in D •

In this symphony (op.36) we again find a slow introduction to the opening movement, but it is very much more elaborate than that of the First Symphony. Although it begins in D major, Beethoven soon plunges into alien keys, taking us into a different world, where eerie horn notes stab through the darkness and rapid ascending scales suggest great winds blowing through echoing caverns. An eloquent phrase on violas and cellos seems like a deep sigh, expressing a sorrow that is singularly absent from the rest of the work, considering that it was written at a time when the onset of deafness plunged the composer into a suicidal mood.

After fluttering trills from flutes and violins, a long sustained A builds the tension until, with a sudden downward swoop, the first movement proper begins. The main theme is given to the cellos, but the swift flurry of notes that flashes through the first-violin part from time to time is an important feature that prevents the music from sounding at all pedestrian. A similar interpolation is to be found in the second subject, an almost Mozartian march to begin with, though subsequently treated in a deliberately rowdy manner. As in the First Symphony, there is something of a storm in the middle of the movement, but it is clearly not to be taken seriously. A more important indication of the direction Beethoven was going to take is the development of the coda, in which cellos and basses share a majestic ascent that recalls 'The Heavens are Telling' from Haydn's *Creation*.

The idyllic larghetto which follows is remarkably relaxed and serene, and, in addition to the wealth of tunes, one of the great delights of the music is its scoring. Trumpets and drums are omitted; clarinets and bassoons in particular lend the movement its special color. Similarly, in the ensuing scherzo, effectively crisp

and compact, the rapid alternation between strings, horns or woodwind is like a practical joke designed to catch the players off guard. A similar trick is played on the audience when, in the central section, the strings come to a complete halt, only to be aroused again by a bellowing unison note on wind and brass, which should take us all by surprise.

The finale too, is full of humor, from its initial hiccup to the tiptoe games in the closing pages. With our instinctive feeling that symphonies are meant to be taken seriously it may be hard to accept that even a substantial outburst of orchestral fury proves to be a hoax, but Beethoven's deflation of his own rhetoric is unmistakable. However, the symphony displays a remarkable unity of themes; it is no longer made up of four independent movements but has become an organic whole.

•Symphony no.3 in E flat •

In the spring of 1804 Beethoven completed his Third Symphony. On the title-page were inscribed two names, Beethoven and Bonaparte. The work was to be dedicated to the great French revolutionary leader, although it is misleading to take it in any way as a portrait. (One does not write a funeral march for someone who is still alive.) However, when news came that Napoleon had assumed the title of Emperor, the composer's republican sentiments

Left: Title-page of Beethoven's First Symphony in C, op.21, dedicated to Baron Gottfried van Swieten. Although the work was completed in 1800 and had its first performance on 2 April that year at the Burgtheater in Vienna, Beethoven had begun it in 1799, using sketches made even earlier.

Below: Maria Casentini, the dancer for whom Beethoven's ballet *Die Geschöpfe des Prometheus*, first performed on 28 March 1801, was given as a benefit. The main theme in the finale of the 'Eroica' was first used in *Prometheus*.

Left: Title-page of the piano version, issued by Steiner in Vienna, of *Wellington's Victory, or The Battle of Victoria*, op.91, written after the French defeats in the Peninsular War in 1813. Like the contemporary Eighth Symphony, it is connected with the inventor J. N. Mälzel, for whose mechanical Panharmonicon it was written, and who was responsible for its programmatic content – it includes 'Rule, Britannia' and 'God Save the King' as well as the sound of gunfire – and even some of the music. In its subsequent orchestral version it became the greatest public success of Beethoven's career.

were so offended that he flew into a rage and tore the title-page in half. In the end the work appeared as the 'Heroic Symphony,' or 'Eroica,' dedicated to His Serene Highness Prince Lobkowitz. It is ironic that a symphony designed to celebrate a man who stood for revolutionary freedom should ultimately be dedicated to a prince.

After two massive chords of E flat major, which proclaim the home key, the most significant theme of the first movement appears in the cellos. The almost pastoral mood of the opening is deceptive; by the twenty-fifth measure we find strongly accented chords that disrupt the even flow of the music, and order is only re-established with a full-blooded repetition of the first theme. The opening movement is particularly rich in material; the mood changes frequently and yet there is a convincing unity to the conception. Ideas that should be mentioned include an elegant 'conversation' between oboe, clarinet, flute and violins based on a three-note phrase, a leisurely rising tune played by clarinets, a strongly rhythmic and athletic passage for strings and a contrastingly gentle theme in the woodwind that begins with no less than nine repetitions of the same note.

During the development section the opening theme is transformed in character, partly by being shifted into a minor key, and partly by being combined with the athletic pattern in the strings. At one point a fugue-like passage emerges, but it is soon engulfed in a violent storm whose dissonances shake the very foundations of harmony. The other really outstanding

moment comes just before the return home to the recapitulation. The orchestral texture is reduced to a mere whisper from the violins and seems for the moment to lose all impetus. Faint and evocative, a distant horn-call reminds us of the original opening theme. The suggestion is accepted joyfully by the full orchestra. Finally, a major structural feature of the movement is the extension of the coda, usually something of a formality. Beethoven launches into it with two strange side-slips in the harmony that must have seemed like a musical earthquake to listeners in 1805. The shock of the unexpected harmonies is emphasized by extreme dynamic contrasts between soft and loud. New light is then shed on the opening theme by a playful counter-melody in the first violins. Only real familiarity can bring a full appreciation of the magnificent architecture of this movement.

The second movement is a funeral march suitable for a mythical hero. Note how Beethoven avoids the use of percussion, the basses supplying a sound comparable to the rumble of muffled drums but musically more interesting. The immense span of the phrases, coupled with the very slow tempo, means that the movement is very long, but for those who are prepared to adjust themselves to its measured tread there are ample rewards. Periodically the feeling of grief is softened by episodes in major keys, like warming rays of sun on a gray afternoon.

The scherzo which follows could hardly be more different, bustling along without a care in the world, its rhythmic vitality unflagging. The

strings set the rhythm ticking with six measures of quiet staccato chords. The oboe then offers us a cheerful little tune beginning with seven repetitions of the same note. This is taken up in turn by a flute, but Beethoven avoids a positive affirmation of the home key of E flat major for no fewer than ninety-two measures, so that when it is finally established it seems an event of great importance. In due course we arrive at the central trio, a term that is particularly appropriate here, since it is mostly scored for three horns, one more than Beethoven uses in any other symphony except the Ninth, where there are four. Although for the most part the exuberant mood is maintained, there is, towards the end of this section, a hushed dialogue between horns and strings that establishes a feeling of twilight different from anything else in the symphony. The quiet ending to the central trio simplifies the transition back to the reprise, but just when we may feel that Beethoven is merely observing an established convention a sudden disruption of the rhythm takes us by surprise.

The theme of the finale must have been a particular favorite of Beethoven's for he used it in several other compositions, including the ballet music for *Prometheus*. The strings pluck out a curiously fragmentary little tune, punctuated by sudden three-note outbursts from wind, brass and timpani. There are two possible interpretations of this enigmatic passage. In the *Prometheus* ballet the hero breathed life into statues, which then took their first faltering

steps. One can imagine such a scene set to this music, but in the absence of any such programmatic explanation it is more likely that Beethoven is once again playing a joke on his audience. What we hear is not in fact the real theme of the movement but the bass of the theme, a servant wearing a master's clothes. When at last the proper tune appears above the enigma, all falls into place. Perhaps the biggest surprise,

Above: Opening of the Fourth Symphony from the autograph score. The work was mainly written down in the late summer and autumn of 1806 while Beethoven was staying at Grätz, with Prince Lichnowksy.

Opposite: The Lobkowitz Palace, near the Augustinerkirche, where the first performance of the 'Eroica' was given in 1804.

Left: Franz Max, Prince Lobkowitz (1772-1816) and his wife Caroline. Lobkowitz, to whom Beethoven dedicated his Fifth and (jointly with his wife's brother-in-law, Count Rasumovsky) Sixth Symphonies, as well as the 'Eroica,' was a lavishly spendthrift patron of music. He was one of the last of the aristocrats to maintain his own orchestra, which he often put at Beethoven's disposal.

in a movement that is full of unexpected developments, shifting from the serious to the frivolous without warning, comes near the end, when there is a fundamental change of tempo. A choir of woodwind instruments initiates a slow variation on the main theme. Gradually the orchestra seems to take on the semblance of a great cathedral organ, with the main theme transferred to the pedals while the organist improvises an elaborate postlude above. Then, with a sudden recollection of the opening flourish, we are whipped into a final *presto* in which the horns present a hunting version of the main theme. The final repetitions of the home chord re-establish security after caprice.

•Symphony no.4 in B flat •

In 1806 Beethoven put aside his work on the C minor symphony we now know as no.5 to write the Fourth (op.60), commissioned by Count Oppersdorf. Thematic relationships between the two symphonies offer clear evidence that both works were in his mind at the same time. The first such clue appears in the very opening measures, despite the great differences in mood and tempo. The same musical concept, two falling thirds, is to be found in the two symphonies – veiled in mystery in the Fourth, defiant and intractable in the Fifth. The two works, in fact, are a world apart in emotional significance, so much so that the Fourth has always tended to be overshadowed by its mighty neighbor. Nevertheless, the Fourth has magical qualities, and is perhaps the best orchestrated of all the nine symphonies.

The opening, in particular, is unforgettable for the beauty of its sound. During the slow introduction the music seems to be feeling its way towards a destination only dimly perceived. At last, after long deferment, a series of brief ascending scale-fragments, crisp and sharp as the crack of a whip, leads us into the

main allegro, where the principal theme alternates swift detached notes on the strings with a smooth *legato* phrase on the woodwind. As a contrast we find a second group of themes, cheerful little tunes allocated almost entirely to the wind and ingeniously interrelated. Many subtle new developments occur in the central section of the movement, of which the most remarkable is the passage leading into the reprise. The violins hover uneasily on two notes for four measures at a time, before an ascending flick evokes a warning grumble from the timpani. This process is repeated, and ultimately opens the way back to the recapitulation.

The second movement begins with an important rhythmic figure against which the violins unfold a deeply expressive melody, later to be elaborately decorated. After a second main theme has been introduced by a solo clarinet and then taken up by the full woodwind choir, the double-basses remind us of the initial rhythmic figure; in due course it comes to dominate the scene, leading to an astonishingly dramatic descent, with each note heavily accented by explosive cannon shots from the timpani. Out of the tumult emerges the gentlest of phrases, coiling sinuously through the violin parts. It has been described by Tovey as 'one of the most imaginative passages anywhere in Beethoven.' Soon a solo bassoon reminds us of the opening rhythm; Beethoven might have preferred a horn here, but the notes would have been unavailable on the instrument used in his time. The closing pages of the movement have a romantic beauty that is virtually unsurpassed.

The ensuing movement is vigorous in its rhythmic drive, alternating strongly accented chords with strange ribbons of unison notes in woodwind and strings. As a contrast, the central trio is mincingly elegant, a parody of the refined conventions with which Beethoven had clearly lost patience. The finale, however, is as exuberant a movement as he ever wrote, almost a study in perpetual motion. Like Mozart and Haydn before him, Beethoven was a competent

Top left: Johann Wolfgang von Goethe in a drawing by Wilhelm Hensel, 1823. Beethoven met Goethe (and later recalled the meeting with great pleasure) in Teplitz in 1812, but Goethe obviously found the composer difficult. He wrote: 'His talent astounded me, but unfortunately he is a quite intractable person, which in fact is not unjustified if he finds the world detestable; but as a result, of course, he does not make things more enjoyable either for himself or for others.'

Top right: Elisabeth (Bettina) von Brentano (1785-1859) in a drawing by Ludwig Emil Grimm of 1809. At about this time Bettina helped Beethoven to surmount his unhappy attachment to Therese von Malfatti. She was also a close friend of Goethe and probably brought about the meeting of the two great men in Teplitz.

violinist, and there are passages in this symphony that suggest that he was recalling hours of technical practice spent in mastering the instrument. There are also notoriously difficult passages for the double-basses as well as a famous bassoon solo. The whole movement bubbles over with good humor and high spirits.

• Symphony no.5 in C minor •

The opening measures of the Fifth Symphony (op.67) have become a musical symbol of the popular image of Beethoven, rugged and uncompromising; yet once the first two phrases have made their dramatic impact, the ensuing passage evokes pathos rather than drama. The falling pattern of each paired interval implies a deep sense of grief, while the driving rhythm seems to forbid such emotional indulgence. There is an almost continuous conflict between a cry for pity and the refusal to grant it. Gradually the rhythm generates more and more force until the battering sounds seem literally to disintegrate in a single explosive chord. Horns in unison announce the imminent arrival of the second subject, a graceful tune whose poise is destroyed by the all-pervading rhythm with which the cellos and basses doggedly persist. Abrupt chords signal the end of the exposition, which should be repeated. The development section is notable for its fierce concentration on the material so far exposed to us. The demonic energy of the rhythm gives a special character to the movement, whose impact is such that it is the most immediately recognizable of all Beethoven's works.

The second movement provides a welcome release from tension. It is a set of variations on a sublimely simple theme, which is presented to us by violas and cellos in unison with a few bass notes sketched in *pizzicato* by the double-basses. The last segment of the tune is lovingly extended by the woodwind, an extension which is at once taken up and amplified by the strings. An unusual feature is the inclusion of a quite independent second theme, a smoothly gliding woodwind tune whose accompaniment in triple figuration makes us assume that it is the start of a variation on the first. The assumption is wrong; the second theme has a clear identity of its own, particularly when trumpets, horns and drums give it a martial air.

In all nine symphonies there is not a scherzo more individual than the one we find here. It suggests an improvisation for orchestra, a prophesy of things to come rather than an extension of dance movements from a previous era. Dark and mysterious, the initial theme seems to grope its way forward, uncertain of its destination. Violins bring the music to a complete halt. A second start by the lower strings progresses a little further, but is again brought to a standstill. In just such a way an improviser will seem to search for an idea. Suddenly Beethoven strikes out boldly in a new direction, hammering out the theme on unison horns supported by chunky chords from the strings. Even though it is confirmed by the full orchestra, this tune also falters, coming to rest on a chord whose waning strength dwindles to nothing. The ghostly opening phrase returns, the music continuing to alternate uncertainty with resolution. In the center we find a section that combines the scholarly pretensions of fugue with an almost impish sense of humor. Cellos and double-basses, filled with a confidence so absent at the start of the movement, briskly set the fugue on its way. Later, as though telling us that such academic devices are no longer valid, Beethoven allows the fugue to come apart. Twice the cellos and basses make false starts in an endeavor to get the music back on course. A return to the opening material seems far from secure, with various woodwind instruments playing tentative fragments of the previously bold horn theme over an almost inaudible accompaniment. Suddenly all movement is stilled, save for the quiet, strangely sinister beat of the drum. In response to its hypnotic throb the violins initiate a weird dance, groping their way upwards step by step. It is an ascent from darkness to light, an ascent that has been hinted at from the very first measures of the movement but which is only accomplished at the last.

The impact of the finale that emerges is enhanced by the addition of three trombones, a piccolo and a contra-bassoon. Perhaps the blaze of sound coming out of a sort of 'aural fog' symbolizes a psychological victory over the composer's deafness. Certainly the pure and straightforward harmonies seem to clarify the harmonic vagueness of the preceding passage. For some time the music continues upon its triumphant way, building towards a climax that surely presages some great event. Instead there is a sudden break, followed by a hollow ticking sound from the violins – as though a ghost has entered, we hear a spectral version of the horn theme from the previous movement. It is an unforgettably dramatic interruption. Order is restored with the return of the majestic march theme with which the movement began.

• Symphony no.6 in F •

The first movement of this symphony is described in the score as 'The cheerful impressions excited by arriving in the country,' the second, 'By the stream,' the third, 'A happy get-together of peasants,' the fourth, 'Storm,' and the fifth, 'The Shepherd's Hymn, gratitude and thanksgiving after the storm.' The title 'Pas-

Above: E. T. A. Hoffmann (1776-1822), in a drawing by Wilhelm Hensel of about 1820. Hoffmann, who was a composer as well as a writer, was one of the most perceptive critics of Beethoven's music. He reviewed the Fifth Symphony in the Leipzig *Allgemeine musikalische Zeitung* in July 1810 and found great beauty in the work.

toral' was sanctioned by Beethoven, though he warned against a too literal interpretation with the phrase, 'more an expression of feeling than a painting' – an admonition probably prompted by the fear that listeners might misinterpret his intentions. Descriptive pieces were much in vogue at the time, but they were mostly trivial and naïve, words that can scarcely be used of this delightful, but major, composition.

Beethoven's 'Pastoral' Symphony (op.68) begins with bare fifth in the bass, the traditional drone-bass of rustic music; above, the violins spell out a simple melody from which much of the material is derived. A notable characteristic of the first movement in particular is the exploitation of repetition, the repetition of pattern that we find throughout nature. After the distraught energy of the Fifth Symphony the mood here is extremely relaxed, a clear symbol of the inner peace the composer found when alone in the country. The harmonies are often sustained over many measures at a time, so that the pace feels slower than the actual pulse of the music would appear to indicate. Long sustained notes in first or second violins shine through the texture like beams of sunlight. The score, like the forest, teems with life, yet the impression we gain is of a great stillness. Towards the end of the movement, clarinet and bassoon anticipate the arrival of the little village band which Beethoven parodies so delightfully in the third movement.

Before the peasants' gathering we spend a lazy afternoon by a meandering stream (second movement), unusually scored with two muted cellos lending depth to the sound. There is an uncharacteristic concession to the purely descriptive on the last page of the movement when

Left: A plaster of Paris medallion of Rahel Levin (1771-1833). She kept a famous literary salon in Berlin, and met Beethoven on his first visit to Teplitz in 1811, where he willingly played her his new compositions and improvised for her.

flute, oboe and clarinet echo the song of nightingale, quail and cuckoo.

Although it contains an amusing parody of a small village band, much of the third movement is scored with a delicacy that would not seem out of place in more aristocratic surroundings. The opening phrase tiptoes its way in, unsupported by harmony; it is answered by a smooth, gentle tune in a contrasting key. Soon a new theme is introduced, rough-hewn, with heavy accents. High horns bellow their approval as swooping figures in the strings suggest the sort of dance where men toss the girls into the air. There is a feeling of robust play far removed from the delicacy of the opening. In due course we hear the little band, depicted with delightful humor, the oboist rhythmically insecure, the clarinetist more accomplished, the horn-player rashly confident in his approach to dizzy heights, the bassoonist cautious and inept. An increase of tempo leads to a second dance tune, accompanied by droningly primitive harmonies. The movement ends in a panic rush as the peasants realize that a storm is about to break.

Without even a final cadence to the preceding music the storm makes its presence felt with a quiet but ominous rumble from cellos and basses. An agitated little figure from the second violins suggests the first drops of rain. Suddenly the storm breaks in its full fury with flickers of lightning in the woodwind and thunderclaps from the timpani. At last it dies away; an oboe sings out a simple melody derived from the first agitated raindrops, now smoothed out into a musical rainbow. An ascending scale on a flute leads without break into the finale. The initial 'hymn' is soon transformed into an ecstatic pean of joy. The movement is part rondo, part variations, culminating in a marvelous climax in which shimmering strings convey an impression of blazing sunlight while the wide-reaching phrases in cellos and basses suggest the trunks of great trees, their branches stretching towards the sky. A long descent leads to a quiet statement of belief, more prayer than hymn. A last whisper of breeze stirs through the strings; a distant horn sounds an almost inaudible curfew.

• Symphony no.7 in A •

After completing the 'Pastoral' Symphony, Beethoven was to wait more than three years before embarking on the Seventh (op.92) in 1811. As in the First, Second and Fourth Symphonies, he begins with a slow introduction, from whose massive first chord a solo oboe tune emerges. Further strong chords mark a gradual accumulation of melodic strands until, in the tenth measure, a rising scale in the strings makes its first appearance. By measure fifteen it has been transformed into an awe-inspiring counterpoint to the initial theme. Soon the woodwind choir presents us with a grave march, almost ritual in character. For some time this and the opening theme seem to compete for our attention until at last the music settles onto the note E natural, which is repeated speculatively more than seventy times within ten measures. Increasingly wide spacing of these repetitions indicates that Beethoven is teasing us, rather as he did at the start of the finale to the First Symphony. At last release comes as flute and oboe delicately mark out the rhythm which is to be the mainspring of the movement. The point made, a solo flute gives us the first subject, a lilting and joyous tune in very different mood from the introduction. The movement is notable for its rhythmic drive, there being few moments of repose.

One of the most striking features of this symphony is the unity of rhythm in the various movements, none more insistent than that of the slow movement. The solemn tread of the opening theme continues for some time until a glowing counter-melody illuminates its dark harmonies from within. One has the image of a grand procession passing by as the full orchestra is increasingly employed. Suddenly the mood changes as clarinet and bassoon introduce a new sustained melody accompanied by gently flowing triplets. It is in the key of A major (after A minor) and seems like a ray of sunshine in a gray sky. Cellos and basses continue to pluck out the initial rhythm, but it is relegated to the background as this radiant theme unfolds. The spell is dissolved by a great descending scale through nearly four octaves, plunging us harshly back into A minor. Soon we find a ghostly little fugue, in which the players seem to grope their way forward uncertainly. An intense crescendo duly leads back to the first theme, which, after a restatement of the lyrical clarinet tune, brings the movement to a strangely disintegrated close.

The scherzo sets a new standard for vitality and humor, excelling all its predecessors in rhythmic vigor. The movement falls into five sections, the brisk opening material being interleaved with a rather more static theme derived from a traditional pilgrims' hymn. Woodwind and horns sustain the tune in organ-like tones, while the violins hold a bagpipe drone that even has to be stoked up from time to time as the imagined 'pipers' run short of breath. After the hectic scramble of the scherzo these long-held notes give a sense of great spaciousness. The last movement displays tremendous energy, with strong accents on the second beat of the measure pounding out the rhythm. There is hardly a moment's respite for the players, Beethoven showing immense intellectual stamina in maintaining such intensity throughout. The final pages must rank as one of Beethoven's most brilliantly conceived passages for orchestra; the notes seem to fly off the page as we are carried on the flood-tide of his inspiration.

• Symphony no.8 in F •

As with the Second Symphony, one would never guess from the musical content that this work was written during a period of emotional disturbance – in this case a family row between

Beethoven and his brother Johann in 1812. To judge from the music one would think that the composer was in an exceptionally good humor. The symphony (op.93) begins without introduction or preamble, although at one time a majestic prelude was contemplated. The first theme is almost old-fashioned, looking back perhaps before venturing on into the unknown. However, its solid confidence is most wittily undermined as the music grinds to a halt. Preceded by a few apologetic chords and some faintly comical bassoon notes, the second subject begins in the distinctly alien tonal center of D major, a key unrelated to the home key of F. As though admitting to an error, the tune falters, turns awkwardly and arrives deviously

Left: Portrait of Beethoven by Joseph Stieler, to whom the composer granted no less than three sittings. The painting was begun in 1819, but not completed until the following year. Beethoven is shown with his *Missa Solemnis*, which he began writing down at this time.

Below: Part of the Credo from the manuscript score of the *Missa Solemnis*, op.123, which the copyist Schlemmer made for Beethoven to present to Archduke Rudolph. Work on the Mass began in 1818, in the long gap in Beethoven's symphonic writing following the Eighth, and continued for some five years, being completed less then a year before the Ninth Symphony.

at the proper key of C. The movement is full of such musical surprises. During the development the character of the opening theme undergoes a considerable change, becoming quite tempestuous. Surrounded by hostile chords in the wind and angry figuration in the violins, a fugue of sorts gets under way, though it is far from academic. The tension increases until at last the reprise of the opening theme blazes out in triumph. There are a number of further surprises, not least the ending itself, which recedes to a mere whisper.

The second movement has a clockwork rhythmic quality that alludes directly to the inventor of the metronome, Beethoven's friend Mälzel. The repeated chords give an impression of mechanical regularity, though the melodic fragments that dance to the rhythm are placed in a wittily capricious fashion. There is even a little phrase to illustrate the winding-up of the clockwork spring. The third movement, on the other hand, pays homage to the spirit of Haydn, a deliberate regression on Beethoven's part that makes a striking change from his whirlwind scherzos. A bland central section is notable for an unusually demanding horn part.

The finale begins with a swift rustling figure from which emerges a nimble dancing tune, beautifully understated. After two brief silences there is a sudden ferocious unison on a wildly unexpected note, not just a joke as it happens but also a seed destined to bear fuit more than 350 measures later, when it is used as a pivot to take the music into a distant tonal center. The whole movement is a brilliant demonstration of how to use a conventional form to prepare traps for the listener.

•Symphony no.9 in D minor •

The idea of setting Schiller's 'Ode to Joy' had come to Beethoven as early as 1793, although the 'Choral' Symphony (op.125) which incorporates it was not to be completed until the winter of 1823-4. Preliminary work on the symphony was spread over a period of years during which a number of major works were written. There were also similar works to the Ninth Symphony born of the French Revolution, among the best of them Méhul's *Chant National du 14 juillet 1800*, which is in D major. At their most grand, these works might involve several choirs and orchestras, with long instrumental introductions, a soloist encouraging the populace, who would be represented by the chorus, and a basic choral melody with variations. One can see here certain ingredients of the Ninth Symphony, and indeed Beethoven himself had, in 1808, composed the Choral Fantasy, a significant pointer towards the symphony.

As we have seen in all the preceding symphonies, the proclamation of a tonal center is of prime importance in the opening measures. Here the music begins as though in a void, the posi-

tive affirmation of D minor not arriving until the seventeenth measure. When it does appear, the main theme is awesome in its rugged grandeur. It is presented in two versions, minor and major. As in the 'Pastoral' Symphony, though to very different effect, the pace of harmonic change is often very slow, giving immense breadth to the music. And, as in the 'Eroica,' the coda here is like an entire new development section. Perhaps most remarkable of all is the closing passage, in effect a funeral march. Its foundation is a chromatic wailing bass, above which brass and wind proclaim funeral fanfares.

The scherzo begins abruptly; note the ingenious use of timpani in the fifth measure, the two drums tuned an octave apart. After two measures of stunned silence a whispering fugue begins, utilizing the dramatic octave leap with which the movement began. For no less than thirty-six measures the volume is kept under tight restraint; then a long sustained note on horns and clarinets signals a crescendo. Within seconds the whole orchestra is playing at full stretch. Suddenly a radiant new theme flowers, bringing a moment of relaxation. The movement is substantially longer than any of the other scherzos, but the material is easy to absorb. Most beguiling is the central section, the so-called trio, which bears an intriguing resemblance to the comparable passage in the Second Symphony.

The elaborate adagio which follows is one of Beethoven's most romantic utterances. Tender sighs begin the movement, leading to the first theme, in which clarinets and bassoons seem to express their approval of each string phrase. These echoes give great spaciousness to the theme which, once it has run its full span, melts into a new tonal center in which we find the second, surely one of the more immediately appealing tunes Beethoven ever wrote. There follow several variations on the first, one of which has a particularly elaborate part for the violins. Brief and distant fanfares fail to disturb the immense calm of this sublime movement.

Above: The timpani part of the original performance material of Beethoven's Eighth Symphony, op.93, showing an alteration in Beethoven's own hand. The symphony was first heard on 27 February 1814 in the Grosser Redoutensaal, Vienna.

The transition from orchestral to choral music in the finale caused the composer much trouble. The actual transition from instruments to voices was facilitated by giving the lower strings a number of quasi-operatic phrases that suggest the inflections of the human voice. The movement begins with a passage of extraordinary violence, a tonal crisis demanding a resolution. Like an operatic hero suddenly appearing on stage, the lower strings declaim their first dramatic phrase. For a second time the orchestral clamor breaks out; for a second time cellos and basses reply. The music then follows exactly the plan Beethoven sketched in a notebook, offering us brief descriptions of the themes of the three preceding movements, each of which is rejected – the first as 'not pleasant enough,' the second as 'merely rather more cheerful,' the third as 'too tender.' At last a semblance of the true theme appears, to be greeted with an orchestral 'shout' of acclamation. Unruffled, smoothly flowing, the tune finally unfolds, duly to be repeated in triumph. Beethoven noted its meaning: 'Now I have found a way to express joy.'

The process is then repeated with a solo baritone taking over phrases comparable to those previously given to the lower strings. As a suitable verbal introduction to Schiller's 'Ode,' Beethoven chose a simple injunction: 'O friends, not these sounds; let us tune our voices more acceptably and more joyfully.' Gradually the chorus is incorporated into the texture, along with a quartet of soloists. From here on the structure of the movement becomes somewhat complex, although it is basically a set of variations on the main theme. One of these is a march, with cymbals and triangle adding the clank of swords and the jingle of spurs. Against its steady tread the tenor soloist sings of 'Brothers like heroes to conquest flying.' It is an essentially operatic passage, which, however, is followed by an orchestral fugue of some complexity, itself a variation on the 'Song to Joy.' After a further affirmation of the main theme there is a silence, out of which emerges a great Hymn of Brotherhood. There follows a vast section of great solemnity, in effect a slow movement within the finale. It ends abruptly with the simultaneous return of the two principal themes, the 'Song of Joy' and the 'Hymn to Brotherhood.' The two are combined in a brilliant fashion. From a huge climax the music suddenly disintegrates. Strangely fragmented phrases express the feeling of awe in the presence of the very Creator of the World.

The start of the final coda suggests the running feet of happy children, and it may well be that Beethoven had a stage presentation in mind. One of his preliminary notes for the baritone's text reads, 'Today is a day of celebration; let it be celebrated in song and dance.' Certainly near the end the solo quartet has an operatic theme whose innocent gaiety recalls Mozart at his most enchanting. Proclaiming the ideal that all men should be brothers, the symphony draws to its close, an epic conclusion to a gigantic conception.

Above: The title-page of Beethoven's Ninth Symphony in D minor, op.125, showing the composer's autograph dedication to Frederick William III, King of Prussia.

Right: Henriette Sontag (1806-54) in about 1824. This famous soprano arrived in Vienna in 1822, and on 7 May 1824 sang the soprano part in the concert in the Kärntnertor Theater which included, amongst other things, sections from the *Missa Solemnis*, as well as the Ninth Symphony.

Below: The orchestra pit of the Kärntnertor Theater.

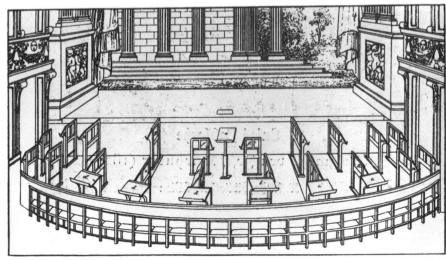

BEETHOVEN AND THE STRING QUARTET

DENIS MATTHEWS

Opposite: The quartet of instruments given to Beethoven by Prince Lichnowsky, now in the Beethovenhaus Museum in Bonn.

Beethoven took up the challenge of the string quartet at three decisive stages in his career, making the rather vague terms 'early,' 'middle' and 'late' especially relevant where the quartets are concerned. The opus numbers, though not always an infallible guide to the order of composition, show this clearly enough: six early quartets, op.18; three quartets, op.59, followed by the two isolated ones, op.74 and op.95; and finally the great works of the last period from op.127 onwards. Though a quartet way of thought was undoubtedly 'in the air' during Beethoven's youth in Bonn, he did not, to our knowledge, produce any string quartets of his own from those early days. Even after his arrival in Vienna, he seemed to hold back deliberately from the string quartet and the symphony until he had consolidated his reputation.

•The op.18 quartets •

Having resolved to begin composing quartets, Beethoven ambitiously planned a group of six. In the case of such sets by Mozart or Haydn, the order of presentation does not necessarily indicate that of composition or conception. With Beethoven's op.18 it is generally agreed on stylistic grounds that no.4 in C minor was the earliest. But whatever may be proved by research, and bearing in mind that Beethoven usually worked at several compositions simultaneously, it would seem most convenient to discuss the op.18 quartets in their printed order.

The F major, op.18 no.1, thus stands proudly as Beethoven's 'first' string quartet, and he had good reasons for placing it where it is. His endless self-criticism, about which the sketches have so much to tell us, did not always finish when a score was complete, and in fact two full versions of op.18 no.1 exist. The earlier score, which he sent to his friend Karl Amenda in the summer of 1799, was painstakingly revised two years later; and though the material and structure remained almost intact, the final version contained countless subtle changes of texture that are object-lessons in true quartet writing.

Most of the changes concerned a lightening of the texture. To write quartets is an infinitely more subtle art than the random distribution of a musical argument between four players, though the argument itself had already cost

Beethoven immense pains. The earlier sketches show him at work on the opening theme in common time, trying out various rhythmic forms before settling on the far more vital and compact 3/4 subject, which was to dominate the first movement with such apparent spontaneity. The scherzo and finale also balance good-humored caprice with intellectual strength, but it is the second movement, the adagio, that is likely to remain longest in the listener's memory. Beethoven was always guarded on the subject of program music, but often admitted external sources of inspiration to his friends. In the case of this intensely tragic D minor movement it was the tomb scene in *Romeo and Juliet*, an influence borne out by the scribbled remark 'les derniers soupirs,' the last sighs, over a sketch for the closing measures.

The G major Quartet, op.18 no.2, makes no attempt to plumb such depths. Much of it, including the first violin's opening flourish, is of an airy lightness, although with Beethoven this never precluded displays of more muscular strength. One such moment comes at the first movement's recapitulation, where the cello asserts a strong repeated-note figure from the transition and then launches the first subject against it in a kind of dramatic counterpoint. The adagio, in its far simpler ternary form, has its own surprise, when the middle section picks up the tail end of its dignified theme in a lively dance rhythm, and on the return of the theme the cello takes over the original violin phrase, opening up a more democratic sharing of interest between the parts. The emancipation of the lower strings had been one of the glories in the later evolution of the quartet, and the soloistic 'concertante' treatment of the cello in Mozart's 'Prussian' Quartets invited increasing rivalry between the players. Beethoven, who visited Berlin in 1796, also wrote two brilliant cello sonatas, op.5, for the same Prussian monarch (though not for the king himself to play). Perhaps significantly, he gave the lead to the cello in the witty and Haydnish finale of op.18 no.2.

The next quartet, in D major, shows how the art of writing quartets 'properly' could yield effects of the utmost economy as well as of brilliant repartee or dramatic force. Its opening is serenely poetic: a long-breathed, ten-measure phrase from the first violin to which the others add the simplest harmonic support. When the first movement awakens by stages to more

63

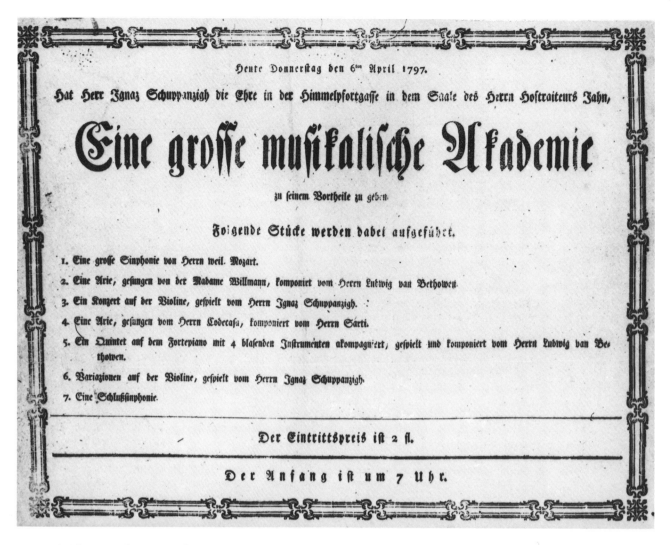

Heute Donnerstag den 6ten April 1797.

Hat Herr Ignaz Schuppanzigh die Ehre in der Himmelpfortgasse in dem Saale des Herrn Hoftraiteurs Jahn,

Eine grosse musikalische Akademie

zu seinem Vortheile zu geben.

Folgende Stücke werden dabei aufgeführt.

1. Eine grosse Sinphonie von Herrn weil. Mozart.

2. Eine Arie, gesungen von der Madame Willmann, komponiert vom Herrn Ludwig van Bethoven.

3. Ein Konzert auf der Violine, gespielt vom Herrn Ignaz Schuppanzigh.

4. Eine Arie, gesungen vom Herrn Codecasa, komponiert vom Herrn Sarti.

5. Ein Quintet auf dem Fortepiano mit 4 blasenden Instrumenten akompagniert, gespielt und komponiert vom Herrn Ludwig van Bethoven.

6. Variazionen auf der Violine, gespielt vom Herrn Ignaz Schuppanzigh.

7. Eine Schlußsinphonie.

Der Eintrittspreis ist 2 fl.

Der Anfang ist um 7 Uhr.

energetic ideas, Beethoven produces surprising key-changes at crucial points that cannot fail to delight even those who know the work well. It does not require a knowledge of harmony to enjoy the rich warmth of the andante, though the 'connoisseur' may note that its sonority is enhanced by its unusual key and by the low-lying scoring of the opening, in which the second violin plays above the first. The third movement, though not so called, is a scherzo, if one accepts the term as meaning capricious rather than merely playful, for there is more than a hint of pathos in its hesitations and leanings towards minor keys. In the finale, beginning with a duet for the violins, Beethoven reverts to the 6/8 rhythm of which Mozart was so fond. The throw-away ending, on the other hand, is more Haydnish, and it was typical of Beethoven to draw such humor out of a mere three-note tag.

Beethoven in C minor was quite another matter, and op.18 no.4 inevitably invites comparison with his other works in that key. In this light the 'Pathétique' Sonata of 1799 seems already more mature, a difference underlined by the similar contours of their opening themes, and which supports the theory that this quartet was the earliest of the set. Neither does the score show any signs of the revisions that had been so copiously bestowed on no.1 in F major.

Much of the writing is orchestral in a rough and ready manner, which is not to deny the attraction of its youthful *Sturm und Drang*. Instead of the expected expressive slow movement Beethoven wrote a 'scherzoso' andante, which pursues its light-footed way with an amusing display of counterpoint, beginning with a fugal exposition. The minuet, however, is the most striking part of this C minor Quartet, illustrating the emotionalization of a dance form to which Mozart had contributed so much, as in his great G minor Quintet (K.516).

In the A major Quartet, op.18 no.5, Beethoven paid a more obvious tribute to Mozart by modeling it on his work in the same key from the set dedicated to Haydn. The likenesses are less of theme than of structure. Beethoven places his minuet second and, like Mozart, follows it with a slow movement in variation form. There is, however, no trace of stylistic plagiarism; Mozart's theme for the variations is graceful and shapely, whereas Beethoven's is alarmingly direct in its march up and down the scale. The finale has more affinity with Mozart's, from which Beethoven inherited the playful effect of antiphony between pairs of instruments, to be offset by a theme in long note-values, whole and half notes, impressively spacious in the neighborhood of quarter and eighth notes.

Above: Advertisement for a concert given in Jahn's concert room on 6 April 1797 as a benefit for the violinist Ignaz Schuppanzigh. In the course of the concert Beethoven played the piano part in the first public performance of his Quintet in E flat, op.16, for piano and wind, which was dedicated to Prince Joseph Schwarzenberg.

The last of this set, no.6 in B flat, has an orderly and epigrammatic first movement, akin to that in the B flat Piano Sonata, op.22, of 1800, a work Beethoven described as 'having washed itself well.' Taken as a whole, the quartet seems to stand at the crossroads, looking back in its adagio to the graceful decorations of a previous generation, but forward in the willfully eccentric cross-rhythms of the scherzo. The finale is disquietingly original, prefacing and interrupting its otherwise cheerful allegretto with a mysterious slow theme marked 'la Malinconia' (Melancholy). It may not be reading too much into it to draw a parallel with the 'Muss es sein?' finale of op.135 that was composed a quarter of a century later.

After completing the op.18 set Beethoven arranged the op.14 no.1 Piano Sonata as a string quartet. He transposed it up a semitone from E major to F, in order to make better use of the lowest notes of the viola and cello, and was obliged to recast the purely pianistic accompaniment to the rondo theme of the finale. This interesting experiment is not normally included in the canon of the Beethoven quartets, but it reminds us that the piano sonatas in particular abound in quartet textures, from the crisp rhythmic opening of the C major op.2 no.3 to the deeply expressive variations in the late sonatas op.109 and op.111.

Below: Portrait of Ignaz Schuppanzigh (1776-1830), dating from about 1825. Schuppanzigh was an excellent violinist and played in the first performances of virtually all Beethoven's string quartets.

• 'Rasumovsky' quartets •

It is out of no lack of respect and affection for the op.18 set that one admits the far greater depth and mastery of Beethoven's next group of three quartets, op.59, called 'Rasumovsky' after the Russian ambassador in Vienna, a keen amateur violinist, who commissioned them. In deference to his patron, Beethoven incorporated a 'thème russe' in the finale of op.59 no.1 and in the third movement of no.2, though not, or not explicitly, in no.3. To complain that he misconstrued the melancholic and modal nature of the first of these folksongs and treated the second with brusque humor and rough counterpoint is beside the point. Once adopted they became Beethoven's property: he did not 'quote' them, but integrated them into the contexts of the complete works.

The three 'Rasumovsky' Quartets, like the last three symphonies of Mozart, are varied enough in character to make a satisfying program in themselves. Op.59 no.1 in F major has, however, acquired a fame of its own through the sheer spaciousness of its opening subject, which passes in mid-theme from its initiation in the cello beneath to the first violin aloft, while the simplest repeated-note accompaniment provides a background of static harmony and suppressed energy. The theme is the proud source of most of the material that follows. Even the Russian tune of the finale seems to derive from it and is announced in the same cello register. Meanwhile, the second movement, substituting for the usual scherzo and trio, thrives on a whole series of epigrams, taking a witty one-note rhythm as a starting-point. The following adagio, which like many other middle-period works leads into the finale without a break, sounds a note of gloom from the drooping contours of its first theme, exploits the higher 'Prussian' register of the cello, and bears the marking *mesto* (sad), which Beethoven had also applied to the tragic slow movement in his early D major Piano Sonata, op.10 no.3.

As though to offset the spacious unfolding of op.59 no.1, the second 'Rasumovsky,' in E minor, plunges us into high drama from the start, the two opening chords playing an important part in the first movement's development. Here the drive of the music is aided by the liveliness of the inner parts, the texture ranging from detailed contrapuntal interplay to strong unison scales and subdued cross-rhythms. The abruptly quiet ending, like that of the much later op.111 Piano Sonata, seems to prepare for the sublimely serene slow movement with its chorale-like first theme. Serene is the word, for Beethoven admitted that he was inspired by a contemplation of the starry heavens and asked that the piece should be treated 'con molto di sentimento.' Compared with this the succeeding 'scherzo' has a minor-key restless quality in its outer sections, dispelled twice by the mock-fugal treatment of its major-key Russian-theme 'trio.' This expansion of the scale of a scherzo by bringing both sections round an extra time occurs in other middle-period works, like the symphonies from the Fourth to the Seventh (including the original version of the Fifth), giving a momentary impression of an eternal perpetual motion.

It is curious that all Beethoven's extended works in E major or minor have all their movements in the home key, instead of moving to a different key for the slow movement or its equivalent. To avoid tonal monotony in the E minor Quartet Beethoven took the drastic (but sublimely humorous) step of basing his finale on an energetic theme that sets out as though in the key of C major. This immediately provokes an invigorating contest of keys that recurs at each return of the theme and is only resolved, with a further increase of energy, when the home key of E minor wins the day on the very last page. The sketchbooks show that the idea of this battle of wits occurred to Beethoven well before the vigorous springing rhythm of the subject.

The third 'Rasumovsky' is, however, definitely *in* C major, which it nevertheless approaches obliquely through a slow and mysterious introduction. One famous precedent for such an opening can be found in Mozart's 'Dissonance' Quartet (K.465), also in C major, and Beethoven himself had prefaced the light-hearted finale of his op.18 no.6 with the darker thoughts of the 'Malinconia.' The eventual allegro seems more conventional than the remarkable first movement of op.59 no.1, its most original features being the soloistic treatment of the first violin at the start and the unsuspected importance of the two simple chords that launch it. Once again the sketches are interesting. A repeated-note idea was written down, apparently in the key of A minor and presumably intended as a slow-movement theme for the quartet. It was shelved, only to turn up six years later as

Below: Andreas Cyrillovich, Prince Rasumovsky (1752-1836), painted in 1820. The prince was Russian ambassador to Austria and was immensely rich. He was also a distinguished musician, and in 1808 instituted a string quartet led by Schuppanzigh in which he himself would sometimes play second violin.

Right: The Rasumovsky Palace in Vienna, built in 1806-7. The palace was totally destroyed when the central heating caught fire on 31 December 1814, during a New Year's Eve ball given by Tsar Alexander for the other delegates to the Congress of Vienna. It was rebuilt, but the Prince never fully recovered from the shock.

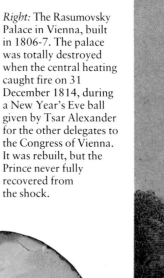

Left: First page of the autograph of the finale of Beethoven's String Quartet in C, op.59 no.3 – the third of the Rasumovsky quartets – composed during 1806 and 1807 and published in 1808 by the Bureau d'Arts et d'Industrie in Vienna.

the haunting allegretto of the Seventh Symphony. Meanwhile, in the quartet and in that same key, a flowing 6/8 movement evolved, memorable for its extended use of cello pizzicato and its pervading melancholy, in which context the grace and charm of its secondary idea come as a surprise.

Perhaps the unrestrained humor and vitality of the fugal finale led Beethoven to abandon his usual scherzo in favor of a real minuet and, what is more, one marked *grazioso*. Yet there is also a unity underlying the contrast between these last two movements of this third 'Rasumovsky,' which Beethoven demonstrated by adding a linking coda to the minuet. An upward scale-figure, reflected in the bass by a downward one, had been the minuet's main topic; and an energized version of the latter sets off the finale's witty and garrulous fugue subject, given out first, as though in mid-air, by the viola. The general exuberance and optimism are unmistakable. It seems that Beethoven had achieved a new philosophy, enabling him to face the world with courage, even with humor. Over a sketch for the finale he scribbled the words, 'Let your deafness no longer be a secret.'

• Op.74 and op.95 •

After having completed the op.59 'Rasumovsky' Quartets in 1806, Beethoven turned his main attention to the orchestra. Not until 1809 did he return to the string quartet, and then he produced a solitary work, op.74, in the same key as two other important works of that time, the 'Lebewohl' Sonata ('Les Adieux') and the so-called 'Emperor' Concerto. In fact, 1809 might well be named Beethoven's 'E flat' year, though the association of that key with grandeur and heroism, as in the 'Emperor' and the earlier 'Eroica,' is belied by the lyrical and intimate character of most of the quartet. As with op.59 no.3, it begins with a slow introduction, though here the mood is tender and exercises a calming influence on the first subject of the main allegro. There are displays of dynamic strength in the development and of 'concertante' virtuosity from the first violin in the coda; on the other hand there is the playful use of pizzicato arpeggios, passed between the players and earning op.74 the nickname of the 'Harp' Quartet. Calmness also prevails in the song-like adagio, and the viola's pizzicato in the last statement of the song may also be thought harp-like.

For the scherzo, however, Beethoven turned to C minor and to an insistent rhythmic pattern recalling the 'fate' motifs of the Fifth Symphony and the 'Appassionata' Sonata. He discouraged a too vehement interpretation by marking the opening both *forte* and *leggieramente* (lightly) and, after the athletic major-key trio, by fining away the dynamics to a mere whisper on its return in preparation for the variations of the finale, which follows without a break. These alternate between rhythmic vigor and lyrical tenderness, epitomized in the two quiet chords that make a surprise ending to the final winding-up. The overriding impression of the 'Harp' Quartet is of a subtle but amiable lyricism, which even subdues the passing defiance of its scherzo.

The all-embracing range of the great composer has always been noted in the vast contrasts between adjacent or in fact contemporaneous works, but the gulf between op.74 and op.95 of the following year is still astonishing. Beethoven described the latter as a 'quartetto serioso,' and the mood is at once apparent from the sternly terse unison opening. Yet if we compare this breakthrough in the quartets with the earlier one of the 'Eroica' among the symphonies, we are bound to observe a reverse process at work: not expansion, but compression. If the tempo marks are taken literally, the F minor is likely to be the shortest of all the quartets by the stop-watch – excluding, of course, the *Grosse Fuge* of op.130, considered as a separate entity – yet it is by far the densest and most concentrated, up to this point, in all four of its movements. F minor was the key of the 'Appassionata' Sonata, and a comparison of the similar harmonic moves in their first subjects only serves to show the Quartet's rapid speed of action. As with the Sonata and the first 'Rasumovsky' Quartet, Beethoven made the unusual departure of omitting the conventional repeat, though with the intense drama of the first movement of op.95 the reason was more obvious: such abrupt changes of mood and brief but ominous silences could hardly bear literal repetition. There are consolatory ideas, certainly, but the movement's obsession with its opening motif is carried through to the bitter end, and although the ending fades away, as in the first movement of the E minor 'Rasumovsky,' there are moments where Beethoven seems to stretch the quartet medium to breaking-point.

This strength of feeling is balanced by the intellectual control of the slow movement. In the key of D major, this moves through fugal counterpoint to a final hushed pause on the mysteriously ambiguous harmony of the diminished seventh. Like the Neapolitan sixth, this chord may have been a stock-in-trade for easy effects of drama or pathos, but the serious composer, as Beethoven once said, still depended on its 'judicious use.' At the end of the slow movements of the 'Appassionata' and the op.95 Quartet it provides a link with the world of action and a cue for a fiery outburst on the same harmony, thus launching the finale of the

Sonata and the scherzo of the Quartet. The scherzo, bearing the marking *ma serioso*, is notable for the abrupt arrival of a beautiful, lyrical phrase in a series of unexpected keys, thereby creating a uniquely integrated 'double' trio section. Despite the concise time scale of the whole, the finale makes room for a brief slow introduction, setting a mood of expressive yearning before the advent of its agitated but tender sonata-rondo. The F minor Quartet also has a coda, but of the most surprising kind in this context – a change of rhythm and a breaking-in of the major key, like a sudden burst of sunlight on an otherwise cloud-covered landscape. As it turned out, the F minor op.95 was Beethoven's farewell to the string quartet for fourteen years.

• Op.127 •

A commission from Prince Galitzin led Beethoven back to the quartet. In 1822 he asked Beethoven to write 'one or two' quartets and left him to fix the fee. Beethoven optimistically promised one in E flat in record time, but with the *Missa Solemnis* and the Ninth Symphony still on the stocks it is not surprising that the first of these new quartets was not ready until the beginning of 1825. Thus op.127 came into being, heralding a series of five great works that were to evoke mixtures of admiration, consternation and bewilderment for generations, though informed opinion has long come to regard the five late quartets as Beethoven's crowning achievement.

Joseph Kerman, in his book on the quartets, chose the same epithet when he described op.127 as Beethoven's 'crowning monument to lyricism.' The main theme of the first allegro is both song-like and lilting. As a tune it sounds simplicity itself and might have been harmonized simply as a waltz or Ländler. But far from

Right: George Polgreen Augustus Bridgetower (1779-1860). A virtuoso violinist in the employ of the Prince of Wales, Bridgetower obtained leave of absence in 1802 to visit his mother in Germany. He went on to Vienna, where he met Beethoven. The Violin Sonata in A, op.47, was written for Bridgetower, though the two men fell out and Beethoven later dedicated the work to Kreutzer.

it: no underlying move is predictable, and yet the whole texture is of the utmost fluidity. The movement is introduced, and punctuated, by a short majestic passage that dissolves into the allegro. At the start, the notes E flat, G and (via B flat) C are emphasized, and it can hardly be accidental that G and C are the keys in which this passage returns. Such things fascinate the musical analyst and also point to a kind of discipline, even when (as may have been the case) they occur subconsciously or instinctively to the composer.

Other unifying devices are obviously conscious: the process of inversion, or turning a theme upside down, is common enough in fugal writing and satisfies the mind with its ingenuity, provided the result is natural and not forced. Inversion adds humor to the grotesquely contrapuntal scherzo, the third movement of op.127, a strangely angular piece that seems to parody the rustic drone-bass pedals of the 'Pastoral' Symphony in its more volatile trio section. Its contrast with the preceding slow movement is drastically complete. Beethoven seldom followed profound ruminations with gradual awakenings or backward glances but preferred to break the spell with an abrupt return-to-earth. The *adagio* theme of the second movement, which cost Beethoven infinite toil in the making, is spacious; and the rapt manner of its introduction must have impressed those Romantics who were able to enter into the spiritual world of late Beethoven. After the lighter two-violin dialogue of the second variation, there is an inspired move to E major for the third, in which the cello is once again elevated in Mozart's 'Prussian' manner.

Even in his deafness Beethoven was well aware of the difference in color when notes of identical pitch are played on the lower strings of the violin and the higher reaches of the cello, and of the homogeneous effect of confining a phrase to a single string. The main finale-theme of op.127 is marked 'sul G' – G string only – for the first violin, giving it a richness that would be lost by the easier course of playing it across the strings. This subject has a faintly modal twist, A flat giving way to A natural, which is pursued in the coda. Many Classical finales increase their pace at this point – the op.95 Quartet is one example of this – but op.127 is unusual in slowing down its lively two-in-a-measure into a leisurely 6/8 with a texture prone to mysterious scurryings and murmurings. For the first and certainly not the last time in the quartets most players must face doubts about the ability to realize the imaginative flights of the deaf Beethoven in actual sound.

• Op.132 •

During his work on op.127 the sketches show Beethoven toying with ideas for the A minor Quartet, op.132, which, in spite of its opus number, pre-dates op.130 and op.131. Going back to Bach, and to essentials, led Beethoven to contrapuntal experiments with a basic four-note motif which he noted down in various canons and inversions. The opening measures of op.132 muse quietly on these permutations before a cadenza-like flurry from the first violin sets a passionate *allegro* in motion. It is not until the development that the unity of these two ideas – the *allegro* theme and the four-note motto – is revealed. Beethoven's particular architectural strength owed more and more to the precise indication and observation of dynamics and other expression marks, details far beyond the notes themselves. Such details, often intensely personal and unpredictable, added to the responsibilities of engravers and performers, and on the subject of the A minor Quartet Beethoven wrote to the violinist Karl Holz in 1825, complaining bitterly about the careless copying of dots and slurs.

erly heard such a ravishing example of quartet texture.

The emotions expressed in the extraordinary slow movement of op.132, which bears the explicit title 'Song of Thanksgiving in the Lydian mode to the Deity from a convalescent,' seem clearly autobiographical, but are somehow elevated into the universal. There is an archaic and Palestrinian feeling about the Lydian sections, which amount to a chorale in slow measured half notes, introduced and interspersed with imitative figures and elaborated in two later variations. With it, we are drawn into the composer's innermost self. Over the first of the two episodes Beethoven wrote 'neue Kraft fühlend' – 'feeling new strength' – and if the superficial impression is of the patient leaping from his sick-bed to dance a lively minuet, the true interpretation is a sudden joyfulness of spirit.

Left and below: Beethoven's music represents two very different aspects, both of the man and his environment. Here (*left*) we have a view of one of the peaceful villages outside Vienna, with a group of musicians at left. Beethoven frequently visited Baden and Mödling, as well as Heiligenstadt, all villages in the Vienna hills. In contrast to the calm of the country, the noble neoclassicism of the Burgtor in Vienna (*below*), opened in October 1824, recalls the more monumental nature of Beethoven's achievement.

Yet the revolutionary qualities in Beethoven – and his manner in the late quartets was in every sense 'new' – neither uprooted traditions nor undermined his respect for the past. So if the first movement of op.132 still shows its allegiance to the principles of sonata form, the second retains the outward shape of a minuet and trio, which one may call, since it is far from being a scherzo, a minuet 'substitute.' Here Beethoven derived the entire 'minuet' section from a pair of clichés, one a counterpoint to the other, yet developed them with endless resource into an extended movement of haunting beauty and tenderness. Then follows the trio section; and here Beethoven used the violin's open A string to evoke an ethereal *musette*, that time-honored imitation of the bagpipes dating back to Baroque music and earlier. It is hard to bear the thought that he never prop-

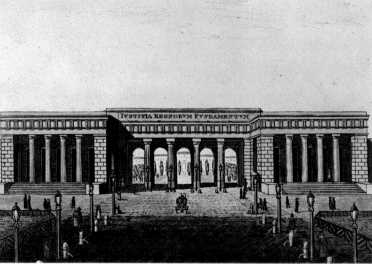

These internal contrasts take some of the shock out of the self-contained little march that Beethoven interposed between the Lydian hymn and the finale. Its sudden burst of A major also serves as a foil to the finale's opening A minor theme, one of Beethoven's most beautiful, passionate and obsessive creations. This theme owes a little to two well-known precedents, the finale of the D minor Piano Sonata, op.31 no.2, and the popular miniature known as 'Für Elise,' but the sketches show that it derived from a rejected idea for an instrumental finale to the Ninth Symphony.

The texture, the maturity and the pathos place the finale-theme in a far higher category than its prototypes, yet it is not, as we feel with some other late Beethoven movements, music of reflection or of passions recollected in tranquillity. The marking *appassionato* is real, though there are moments of mystery and sudden hush just as there are in the jubilant finale of the Ninth. One such passage, a contrapuntal one, occurs shortly before the main theme forces itself upwards, and forwards in tempo, to a goal – the triumph of the major over the minor key – which has a more far-fetched parallel with the Ninth because the context and the means are so different. The writing for quartet makes superhuman demands, with the second violin and viola striving to support the high ecstatic octaves of cello and first violin, and the general intensity of emotion. This sense of stretching the medium almost to breaking-point recurs in parts of the *Grosse Fuge*, so perhaps we should turn our attention to the next quartet, in order of completion, the B flat op.130.

• Op.130 •

With op.130 the most obviously unusual fact is that it is in six movements whichever way we look at it, with the *Grosse Fuge* or with the alternative finale Beethoven composed later. The late quartets continue to expand in their number of movements – op.127 with the customary four, op.132 with five (counting the march and recitative as more than a mere introduction to the finale), op.130 with six, op.131 in seven, which admittedly run on without a break – until op.135, the last of all, returns to the four-movement plan. There were many six-movement predecessors, vaguely covered by the eighteenth-century term 'divertimento,' but Beethoven felt no need to qualify the title of 'Quartet' for op.130, though he included two dance-type movements and two slow (or slowish) movements in the most contrasted styles imaginable.

The innocent ear, listening to this B flat Quartet for the first time, might assume that the opening *adagio* is purely introductory, as in the third 'Rasumovsky,' where an atmosphere of mystery is dispelled for good by the arrival of the main *allegro*. Recurring introductions were not unknown – Haydn's 'Drum-roll' Symphony, Beethoven's 'Pathétique' Sonata and indeed his op.127 Quartet are examples – but in op.130

the returns and the integrations are far subtler, continuing into the coda of the first movement.

For the second movement Beethoven offered a terse scherzo in quick common time, in B flat minor with a major-key trio. In spite of its speed we can marvel at the fantastic interplay of the inner voices, a contrapuntal game that is varied on the return. The trio section is, however, decidedly a showpiece for the first violin, and the added chromatic flourishes that end by turning a 'new' unison figure back into the original opening are a perfect example of drastic but relevant humor. There is also humor of a more leisurely nature in the first of the slow movements, though in answer to the question 'when is a slow movement not really a slow movement?' one might cite this, along with the allegretto of the Eighth Symphony, with the reply 'when Beethoven packs it with scherzo elements and small note-values.' How does this fit into the general scheme of op.130? Since the main theme, low down on the viola, does not

Above: A portrait of Beethoven probably painted from memory after his death by Joseph Stieler. Many who knew the composer felt that the artist captured Beethoven's features most faithfully.

C sharp minor op.131, though there is no evidence that Beethoven regarded these three very different works as a triptych.

The players and listeners who were charmed by the *Danza Tedesca* and moved by the *Cavatina* must have found the *Grosse Fuge* hard to accept in its context, if not completely incomprehensible. Beethoven removed it, probably reluctantly, published it separately as op.133 and reserved the following opus number for his own piano-duet arrangement of this work, which he rightly considered of immense importance. In 1826 he replaced it with a light-weight finale, his last completed movement, showing all the signs of the new and sparer manner that characterizes the F major Quartet, op.135. Both finales of op.130 take the ending of the *Cavatina* as a starting-point and both are in that sense legitimate, representing Beethoven's earlier and later thoughts on the subject.

•Op.131•

Meanwhile, the first half of 1826 had produced the vast single span of the C sharp minor Quartet, op.131. Its seven movements, played as a continuum, might still be traced back to the divertimento, as with the six of op.130, but hardly its range and order of events. It opens with a fugue in slow tempo, imbued with a noble pathos and far removed from the fierce challenges of the *Grosse Fuge*, though its four-note motif reveals a certain kinship. In spirit and outward aspect it harks back to Bach's great fugue in the same key from Book I of the *Forty-eight*, which Beethoven had known since his youth, but there is an episode of two-part writing that suggests a much earlier vocal style. The

begin until the third measure, the first two measures are worth special attention: consciously or not, they stress the three chromatic notes that began the whole work.

The opening phrase of the fourth movement, another minuet 'substitute' marked *Alla Danza Tedesca*, was sketched in A major and B flat before settling in G major, an unusual key in this context. At one point Beethoven creates an astonishingly 'modern' effect by passing the bare notes of the theme, measure by measure and in reverse order, between the four players. It was actually of the *Grosse Fuge* that Stravinsky made his remark about 'contemporary forever': but it applies here too.

There is for most ears a touching simplicity about the song that opens and closes the movement, aptly called *Cavatina* in its honor; but this is offset by a middle section bearing the rare marking *beklemmt*, or 'afflicted,' in which the melodic line becomes fragmented and distorted – even more so than in the disintegrated return of the 'arioso dolente' in the op.110 Piano Sonata. It is impossible not to read an experience of grief and consolation into this music, making the incredible renewal of physical and mental energy in the *Grosse Fuge* the most dramatic continuation possible. The title, 'Great Fugue,' is misleading to the newcomer, for the so-called 'fugue' incorporates an introduction, a double-fugue, a slow movement and a scherzo, followed by extensive developments and afterthoughts. Yet the label is, after all, appropriate. The 'work' – for so it became as op.133 – amounts to an exhaustive survey of a single motif and its rhythmic and fugal propensities. As for the motif, or subject, it is clearly derived from the four-note figure that opens op.132. In a more compressed form it also dominates the first and last sections of the next quartet, the stabbing accent on the fourth note of the subject is pure Beethoven, however, giving strength and poignancy to the climax; it expressed anguish to Wagner, who described the movement as 'surely the saddest thing ever said in notes,' though it closes on a long-held major chord. After this, with the slender link of a rising octave, the second movement appears as if from a vast distance, in a lively but song-like 6/8 time, seemingly improvised and carefree after the serious manner of the fugue. The key is D major, a mere semitone away and yet far distant in harmonic terms – musicians call it a 'Neapolitan' relationship – and after generating a surprisingly heated climax the piece suddenly evaporates. Its place is taken by an imitation of operatic recitative, with mock formality soon yielding to a coloratura display from the first violin; but this brief third 'movement' is content to set the stage for the fourth, an elaborate set of variations that forms the core of the work.

'To set the stage' is the right expression, for it is hard to imagine the serene, innocent variation-theme thriving in the shadow of the opening fugue. Variation form had already been well explored in late Beethoven, and this spacious center-piece is unsurpassed as a compendium of quartet textures. Even the scoring of the theme is notable for its antiphonal sharing between the two violins, enough to dispose of the ill-founded metaphor about 'playing second fiddle.'

The fifth movement is a witty and energetic scherzo in common time, full of epigrams and rustic humor. A recurring tendency to side-slip from its main key is at long last answered by the arrival of a brief but profound and sorrow-laden *adagio*; and the extraordinary cycle of contrasts is completed by the full-scale minor-key finale. Yet its derivation from the very opening is demonstrable, as the serious drama of sonata form balances the seriousness of the fugal first movement, unifying and containing the intervening adventures.

·Op.135·

It seems unbelievable that Beethoven could turn so readily from the vast structure of op.131 to the Mozartian dimensions of the F major Quartet, op.135. But such was the case: Beethoven's last quartet of all was ready in the autumn of 1826, and sketches for it overlapped his work on the C sharp minor. Mentioning Mozart is not irrelevant to our thoughts about op.135, and the one or two critics who found its reversion to Classicism 'retrograde' were surely mistaken. Restraint and economy do not imply lack of depth, and even the language of comedy may express the profoundest emotions, as Mozart so often proved. Beethoven's new-found lightness of touch is apparent in the first ten measures of the opening movement. Then follows an even sparer idea in bare octaves, and when it is later decorated it still remains unharmonized.

This spareness extends, less obviously, to the scherzo that follows. It is more marked when the opening theme is inverted in simple octaves between treble and bass. More unaccountable is the strange out-of-key E flat that upsets both tonality and rhythm, and early listeners (and players) must have been shattered at the wild *ostinato* to which the middle section leads, with the first violin leaping vigorously aloft while the others drum away insistently on a figure fifty times on end. But if op.135 draws attention to the extreme contrast between works, it enjoys its own extremes too. The scherzo is followed by a song, if not of thanksgiving, of 'rest and peace,' as Beethoven called the slow movement in his sketches. It may be analyzed as a theme and four variations, but compared with the opulent sets of variations in op.127 or op.131 the texture is simplicity itself, borne out by the marking *semplice*.

The finale of op.135 is well known for the words Beethoven wrote over the slow introductory figure and the main theme of the *allegro*, 'Muss es sein?' and 'Es muss sein!' – Must it be? It must be! – which are summed up in the overall title, 'The difficult decision.' The musical detective will take note that the one figure is an inversion of the other, and may trace the contours of the second subject to the theme of the previous movement. The total impression is that Beethoven, in his last complete work, also summed up his whole life's struggle, his philosophy and his ultimate faith, in music of disarming lightness. The lightness and simplicity are deceptive, as repeated hearings prove, because they are distilled from the whole gamut of human experience. That is why Beethoven continues to inspire, to amaze and to comfort; and why music lovers stand in lasting awe and gratitude before his final rich testament and legacy: the world of his last string quartets and the medium by which he set such great store.

Above: Beethoven's hands, sketched by C. F. A. von Klober in 1817 as part of the preliminaries for a large painting, now lost, of Beethoven and his nephew Carl at Mödling.

FRANZ SCHUBERT

OTTO BIBA & BRIAN NEWBOULD

Twenty years after Schubert's death, such major instrumental works as the Octet, the G major String Quartet, the String Quintet, and the *Quartettsatz* in C minor remained unpublished. It was nearly twenty years later still that the 'Unfinished' Symphony received its first performance, and when it was published in 1867 it was only the second of his symphonies to appear in print. Imagine that the same fate had befallen Beethoven's instrumental music, and that by unlikely mischance the bulk of it remained undiscovered to this day. What value would we then put upon the greatest works of Schubert, unaware of the rival claims of any major contemporary? The question is designed to provoke thought, not to draw authoritative answers. What place in our esteem, and in the Classical canon, would we accord the 'Unfinished,' the last String Quartet, the last three piano sonatas or the E flat Piano Trio, if the greatest symphonic cycle of all time were not there as a yardstick, nor the awe-inspiring third-period quartets, nor the richest sonata series in keyboard history, nor the 'Archduke,' not to mention its archducal forebears?

It is, of course, the two men's common interests as much as their contemporaneity that pose such problems in the objective assessment of each by later generations. The fates of Berlioz and Chopin are not thus intertwined in modern criticism. Nor are those of Bruckner and Offenbach. Schubert not only lived and worked in the same Vienna as Beethoven, at the same time; he was, like Beethoven, an 'all-medium' composer, as likely to find creative fulfillment in a string quartet as in a symphony, in a piano sonata as in a Mass setting. Moreover, Schubert naturally detaches himself from Spohr, Rossini, Moscheles, Kuhlau, Paganini, Marschner, Onslow, Donizetti, Loewe, Weber and others born in the last twenty years of the eighteenth century, as the originator of the most significant oeuvre by a junior contemporary of Beethoven. Never did historical accident put a composer at greater risk.

Franz Schubert was born on 31 January 1797, at 1.30 in the afternoon, the twelfth child in the family. His father, also called Franz, was a thirty-seven-year-old schoolmaster whose wife Elisabeth was three years older than he. Of the eleven previous offspring only four survived, the rest having died in early infancy. Franz Schubert (senior) had come to Vienna from his native province of Moravia, and his wife originally came from Silesia. The couple met in Vienna and married in 1785. In the following year Franz Schubert senior was appointed to the school in 'Himmelpfortgrund' (the Gates of Heaven!), which was at that time a new suburban district for which development plans had been in operation since 1783. The district was administratively autonomous, but as it was at the very door of the capital of the Empire (if not Heaven), it was socially and culturally dominated by it.

In those days the schoolmaster was generally responsible for the musical life of the community as a whole, primarily as the director of the local choir. He would be in charge of the musical side of things in the church on Sundays and holy days and play the organ. The new community in Himmelpfortgrund, however, did not yet have a church building of its own and was annexed to the adjoining parish of Lichtental. The choirmaster and organist there was Michael Holzer, who had been a pupil of Albrechtsberger, the foremost theoretician of his time, whose pupils included Beethoven; the standards in Holzer's church were accordingly very high. The young Franz Schubert's early musical experience was of church music under Holzer, with whom he studied organ and theory for two years, and in music-making under the parental roof, where he learned the violin.

If you go to Vienna today to get the feeling of these old suburbs of Himmelpfortgrund and Lichtental, you will be disappointed. They have long since been absorbed into the capital, and the old streets have disappeared. The only remnants are the old school building in which Franz Schubert was born and the larger one into which the school, and the schoolmaster's family, moved in 1801, and the parish church in Lichtental. Everything else has completely changed.

When Schubert reached the age of eleven, he auditioned for a place in the Boys' Choir which formed part of the imperial *Kapelle*. The candidates were expected to be good, trained singers, with sound knowledge of musical theory and high academic standards. In return for their service the successful ones received excellent musical and general schooling. Schubert excelled above all his fellow applicants and in 1808 entered the musical establishment as a treble. The main function of the Boys' Choir was the singing of church services in the Chapel of the Imperial Residence, the Hofburgkapelle. The music in the chapel was directed by the Hofkapellmeister himself, or by the sub-director. The difficult, somewhat conservative repertoire consisted in the main of church music of the mid- or later eighteenth century with instrumental accompaniment. For Advent and Lent, when the use of instruments – other than perhaps to double the voices – was not permitted, the music performed dated back to an earlier period, even to the beginning of the seventeenth century.

The boarding school for choristers was in what was known as the Stadtkonvikt, in a building in the old university quarter that was renovated in 1802 and still stands today. They were taught in the same building, in what was called the Academic Gymnasium. The choristers were distinguishable by their special uniform, and they received additional music tuition, both theoretical and practical, given normally by experienced members of the imperial establishment under the aegis of Antonio Salieri, the Hofkapellmeister. Schubert studied organ under Wenzel Ruzicke.

The running of the Gymnasium and the boarding school had been allotted to the Piarists, who were a Roman Catholic teaching order with popular appeal and ideals. They continued to teach Latin, but placed great emphasis on German; they were renowned for their teaching of the natural sciences and for the importance they attached to music. Those entering the Piarist Order first had to undergo thorough musical tuition, and notable composers were always found among its ranks. It was probably for this reason as much as any other that Mozart sent his son to a Piarist school in 1791, by which time there were several to choose from in Vienna.

It is an important factor in Schubert's development that he was educated in one of the finest schools that Vienna had to offer. When the Piarists took the school over in 1802, they reorganized the curriculum and the boarding school in accordance with the most progressive educational thinking of the time. Pater Innozenz Lang, as the headmaster of the Choir School, has also gone down in history as the major reformer of the whole educational system in Austria. The musical education Schubert received was, in short, the finest a gifted child could possibly have received in Vienna. Over and above the formal aspects of their schooling, the boarders were taken on visits to the opera and theater, and one further sociological factor must also be kept in mind: the Academic Gymnasium was considered an élite school, educating not only the choristers but also children from upper-class families. As the son of a suburban schoolmaster Schubert could hardly have mixed in these circles had he not attended the Choir School, and some of his fellow-pupils remained his friends for life.

In the light of all this one should not pay too much attention to the letter that is often quoted, sent by Schubert on 24 November 1812, to an anonymous recipient – possibly his brother Ferdinand – lamenting conditions at the school.

It is a universal fact, as true then as now, that children at boarding establishments wish they had more freedom, a change from institutional food, and money of their own to spend.

In addition to the official music tuition and the necessary rehearsals for public performances with the imperial *Kapelle*, a tremendous amount of chamber music took place, and the choristers formed their own first-rate orchestra. According to Schubert's contemporary schoolfriend, Joseph von Spaun, the orchestra got together after dinner every night to play a symphony and an overture. Schubert played in the second violins. Spaun recalls that he admired the symphonies of Haydn, Mozart and Beethoven (especially nos.2, 5, and 7) as well as those of Kozeluch – who by that time was already regarded as somewhat old-fashioned – and the overtures of Mozart (*The Magic Flute* and *Figaro*) and of Méhul, though he had no time for the fashionable composers of the day, namely Franz Krommer and Abbé Vogler. The choral repertoire to which Schubert was exposed as a chorister of the *Kapelle*, and the instrumental works he encountered in the choristers' orchestra, would have given him a wide musical horizon. He also had one further advantage, in that he was permitted to study under Salieri for a further three years after he left the Choir School, his voice having broken in the autumn of 1813.

On leaving the Choir School, Schubert completed a one-year course in teacher training, involving teaching practice and theory and a knowledge of school legislation. Since a full grammar-school education was at that time not compulsory for teachers, he enjoyed a higher level of education than many of his colleagues, but at the beginning of the new school year in the autumn of 1814 he returned to his childhood surroundings and became his father's assistant at the school in Himmelpfortgrund. Only two years later he was ready to leave teaching for a career as a full-time composer.

Right: Schubert's father, Franz Theodor, in a portrait by one of his sons, the composer's brother Carl. In all Franz Theodor had fourteen children by his first wife Elisabeth, though only five survived childhood. He then married again, and by his second wife Anna he had five children, three of whom survived.

•Early symphonies•

The concentration on larger-scale works such as symphonies and overtures in the repertoire of the Choir School orchestra accounts for the fact that Schubert started composing in these genres early on, and continued to do so throughout his life. In fact, Schubert wrote symphonies rather as Beethoven wrote piano sonatas. Long before he wrote quartets or symphonies, Beethoven gave the world piano sonatas, and the medium exercised him well into his third period. Only at the age of twenty-nine did Beethoven produce a First Symphony. Schubert, at twenty-nine, composed his Ninth, the 'Great' C major.

Sketches have survived for an overture and symphony, both in D major, dated as early as 1811. Schubert was then fourteen, and it is hardly surprising that he had some problems in notating his ideas, as the autograph score of the symphony clearly shows. Nor is it surprising that his admiration for Beethoven's Second Symphony declares itself. Only thirty measures in full score survive, but these suffice to demonstrate a sound harmonic instinct and a precocious understanding of the orchestra. From 1813 to 1818 Schubert produced an average of one symphony a year, all very much in the eighteenth-century tradition, absorbing no less from Haydn and Mozart than from Beethoven. In scale and format they hardly go beyond the latter's first two symphonies: there is nothing so ambitious as the 'Eroica' among them. They have, nonetheless, their own exhilarating charm. Nor are they so hidebound by convention as is sometimes thought. 'The more I study them,' wrote Dvořák, 'the more I marvel.'

The earliest symphony extant, no.1 in D major (D.82), from the year 1813, was probably Schubert's farewell present to the choristers' orchestra. It sprawls somewhat, with youthful garrulity rather than bigness of thought. It also has a slow introduction which is ordinary enough,

Right: Schubert's stepmother Anna, née Kleyenbock, in a drawing by Schubert's friend Moritz von Schwind. Schubert's mother died on 28 March 1812, and his father married again on 25 April 1813.

Below: A view of Schubert's birthplace from the garden of the house, in a watercolor painted about 1880. Schubert's parents had been married in the nearby parish church of Lichtental on 17 January 1785, and he was baptized there on 31 January 1797, the twelfth child born to the couple.

but Schubert is not merely aping his exemplars when in the course of the following allegro vivace he begins the recapitulation by recalling the introduction – twelve measures, almost note for note – without returning to the *adagio* tempo. Instead, he compensates for the difference between the two tempi by doubling the length of each note. This first movement of the first symphony also contains a melody that sounds something like one of Beethoven's sketches for the 'Prometheus' theme used in the 'Eroica,' perhaps an accidental tribute.

Schubert's Symphony no.2 in B flat (D.125), written between December 1814 and March 1815, is dedicated to his old headmaster of the Choir School, Pater Innozenz Lang, with whom he remained in close and friendly contact. Much of this work is propelled by an appealing sense of energy. It is not just a matter of short notes and fast tempi. Well-placed accents contribute, and Schubert becomes increasingly aware of the power of dissonance as an expressive incident as well as an energizing force. An important break with tradition is the choice of a related minor key for the minuet. Several times Schubert was to defy the convention that the minuet or scherzo, like both outer movements, should be in the title key of the symphony.

Symphony no.3 (D.200), again in D major, followed very soon after, during the summer of 1815. Not until the Sixth Symphony did Schubert abandon the title 'minuet' and prefer the Beethovenian 'scherzo,' although all the earlier minuets are fast. When he marks the minuet of the Third Symphony *vivace*, though, a scherzo pace is surely not intended. The heavy, earthy accents must be given their weight, all the more because the foregoing slow movement is not the *andante* found in all the other symphonies but a fairly nimble *allegretto*, while the finale is a headlong *presto* full of the most refined high spirits. The Third Symphony shares with the Fifth an elegance, vitality, and sunny disposition which clearly enshrine, in Schubertian terms, prized qualities of eighteenth-century symphonies.

The Fourth Symphony, in C minor (D.417), of 1816 stands apart from its companions. If the subtitle 'Tragic,' added some time after its completion, exaggerates its character, need we chide the teenage composer? That the issues involved in his only minor-key symphony so far were darker, more intense and more personal, apparently justified the epithet to him. For musical precedents we should look not to Beethoven's Fifth (in the same key) but to Mozart's no.40 in G minor and to the minor-key symphonies of Haydn. Had Schubert lived half a century earlier, we would have called this Fourth his 'Sturm und Drang' Symphony. The minor key here releases, afresh for Schubert, something of the pristine passion of the vintage 'Sturm und Drang' symphonies, and it unlocks a harmonic palette which would serve him with distinction in later symphonic exploits. Remarkable too is the fact that the 'minuet,' which is in a close major key, almost negates its major-key attributes through the tortuous chromaticism and perverse slurring of its theme.

Beside the 'Tragic,' the Fifth Symphony, in B flat (D.485), of the same year displays a winsome lightness of touch. Alone among the symphonies, it dispenses with clarinets, trumpets, drums and second flute – not to mention the second pair of horns enlisted for the 'Tragic.' The dynamic markings are also much more restrained. The work was probably written by Schubert especially for the salon organized by Franz Frischling and Otto Hatwig, which would explain the almost chamber-music scale of the music. The whole emphasis is on melody – melody which pushes itself, memorably, into every corner of the structure. In this respect it comes nearer than any of its forerunners to regenerating the Mozartian ideal.

Different ideals influenced the Sixth Symphony, in C major (D.589), completed in 1818. Rossini's operas had recently found their way to Vienna, to be greeted with enormous enthusiasm. Schubert, perhaps intentionally, conceded to the new taste, espousing the prettiness, the immediacy of effect, the good-humored directness, which were essential to Rossini's instant success. One notices a change in the style of orchestration, among other things. The stringed instruments are less strenuously worked, and the wind gain a new sort of prominence, functioning often as an unaccompanied or lightly accompanied choir. Rossini has little effect on the scherzo and Beethoven not much more, which is perhaps remarkable in Schubert's first so-titled use of the Beethovenian genre. This movement is also longer than the previous

Below: The annotation, in his own hand, reads: 'Schubert Franz croaked this piece for the last time on 26 July' – as his career as a boy chorister came to an end.

Below right: Antonio Salieri (1750-1825), the most celebrated operatic composer of his time and director of the imperial *Kapelle*. He was one of those who auditioned Schubert as a boy soprano in October 1808, and he personally gave him composition lessons, starting in 1812. On the manuscript of some of his early works Schubert described himself as 'pupil of Herr von Salieri.'

third movements, with a suitably extended key-itinerary, and this new enlargement of the least developed of Schubert's movement-types was to have noteworthy consequences in the later works. More prophetic still is the finale, once the pretty Rossinian opening has given way to a truer Schubertian voice: the music gathers a momentum that looks forward to the driving finale of the 'Great' C major Symphony, while numerous other features – a rhythmic figure here, a harmonic juxtaposition or orchestral texture there – point in the same direction.

minor-key work among the early symphonies (no.4), written at about the same time, reveals a side of Schubert's personality not heard in the others, so the A minor (especially) and G minor Sonatinas (D.385 and D.408) are worth the attention that the D major (D.384) already receives.

More than one critic has found the piano writing in the violin sonatinas more truly pianistic and satisfying than in the solo piano sonatas, of which Schubert completed at least six between 1815 and 1819 – the fulfillment of their promise was to come with the second group, written in the years 1823 to 1826. The critical preference in the early works is no doubt an allusion to the more frequent use of patterns and figurations which lie readily under the fingers and fall easily on the ear. The same could, of course, be said with regard to Schubert's songs. An explanation is that the presence of a second instrument (or a voice), which for much of the time will carry a melodic line, frees the keyboard to provide a more pianistic supporting texture, unhampered by the need to

Left: The University square in Vienna in about 1815, showing the University Church and, on the right, the entrance to the school where the choirboys of the imperial *Kapelle* were housed and educated.

Below: The parish church of Lichtental, in which the composer's brother Ferdinand often played the organ. It was for this church that Schubert wrote the Mass in G (D.167) and the Mass in B flat (D.324), which date from 1815. The Mass in C (D.452), dating from 1816, was dedicated to the church's choirmaster, Michael Holzer.

• Early chamber music •

Schubert's attempts at string quartet writing date back at least to 1811, the same year as his first try at a symphony. By 1814 he had already produced a number of quartets or quartet fragments (some now lost). A study of these shows that he needed much time and practice to master the art of quartet composition: a true four-sided discourse did not come naturally or easily to him. One finds here either sound harmonic writing which lacks textural vitality, or counterpoint which is self-consciously stiff. The fusion of harmony and counterpoint in the manner of a Haydnesque *quatuor dialogué* so far eluded him. At least three works, however, deserve the attention of the real enthusiast for juvenile precocity. These are the quartets in B flat (D.112), in G minor (D.173) and in E major (D.353), which are roughly contemporary with, respectively, the Second, Third and Fourth Symphonies. While they do not equal those symphonies in individuality, nor in quality of material, they reveal a new confidence in 'thinking quartet,' and there is little in them that is not either impressive, or enchanting or diverting.

Other early chamber and instrumental works also show great promise. In 1816 Schubert produced three works for violin and piano which he called 'sonatas,' though they were later published by Diabelli as 'sonatinas.' Slender they are, but beautifully wrought. Just as the one

Pfarrkirche im Lichtenthal.

provide a melodic line too. This puts the position over-simply; it is not meant to suggest that all Schubert's music for pianist and one other participant consists of 'tune' and 'accompaniment.' The one major interest of Beethoven that was not shared by Schubert was the concerto. For Beethoven, as for Mozart, 'concerto' had meant, for the most part, 'piano concerto.' Schubert was not the concert pianist that both Mozart and Beethoven were, and this may in part explain his neglect of the concerto. It has been claimed that the Adagio and Rondo Concertante in F major (D.487) for piano, violin, viola and cello (what we call a 'piano quartet') is not real chamber music, but rather a miniature concerto: indeed, it is sometimes played with a string orchestra, not solo strings. But Mozart, too, not infrequently slipped into concerto parlance in a chamber medium. His E flat Piano Quartet (K.493), in particular, is none the worse for that. Schubert in effect borrowed Mozart's license, and having tried it in this Adagio and Rondo of 1816 with more charm than profundity, proceeded in his remaining twelve years to permit himself a degree of concertante abandon in any chamber work he wrote involving the piano, not least in the 'Trout' Quintet.

• The young composer •

It is interesting to consider how Schubert's compositions were affected by circumstance. The earlier symphonies and perhaps the string quartets reflect his continuing association with Salieri and the choristers' orchestra. At about the time that he returned to Himmelpfortgrund

to teach in 1814, his father also organized a string quartet ensemble, which regularly played for its own amusement in the schoolhouse in which the Schuberts lived. Josef Doppler, five years older than Schubert and a friend of the family, became a member of the quartet and one of the most interesting and important patrons of the young composer. Doppler played viola, clarinet and bassoon and also featured in the musical salon (for which Schubert very probably wrote his Fifth Symphony) organized by the merchant Franz Frischling together with Otto Hatwig, a member of the orchestra at the Burgtheater. This was famous because it offered not only song recitals and small-scale vocal and instrumental chamber works, but also large-scale orchestral works such as symphonies and overtures. In fact, several autograph sketches are inscribed by the composer 'for Herr Doppler' – and in later years Doppler was to present to the archive of the Gesellschaft der Musikfreunde manuscript copies of the instrumental parts to Schubert's First, Second and Sixth Symphonies, and a few overtures, that had been used for early performances.

In these early days Schubert also made his mark in the nearest musical center, the parish church in Lichtental. In 1814, in celebration of the centenary of the first Mass to be held in the church, he wrote his Mass in F major, (D.105). This was perhaps the beginning of his emergence in public as a composer who would receive commissions for new works; from his late teens to the very end of his life he was to be a composer of great versatility, able to deliver music suitable for almost any occasion. The offertory motet of 1815, *Totus in corde langueo* (D.136), with its highly unusual scoring for soprano and clarinet, with strings, two horns and two flutes,

Right: The Schubert family, drawn by the composer's brother Carl about 1822. The father is seated; behind him stands his second wife Anna, holding Carl's son, and behind her is the maid Margarethl. In front of his father stands the composer, and behind him one of his brothers.

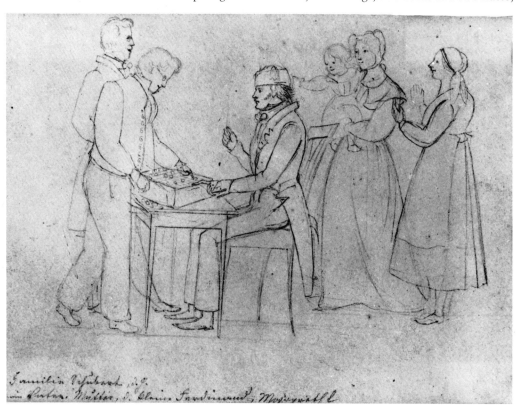

was introduced by his school friend, Joseph von Spaun, to the poet Johann Mayrhofer, and the circle of devotees of the *Lieder* grew. So did the number of songs, for there were an astonishing one hundred and fifty written in 1815, including 'Der Erlkönig' (D.328), and one hundred and ten in 1816. In 1815 Franz von Schober joined this circle, and he it was, unless we are much mistaken, who brought home to Schubert that he was not a schoolteacher who also composed, but a composer first and foremost. In 1817 Schubert set 'An die Musik' (D.547) to words by Schober, who was one of the more widely cultured of his friends. Some of the others regarded Schober as a bad influence, but he was loyal, warm-hearted and always ready to help Schubert, who was devoted to him. By 1816 Schubert had also met Johann Michael Vogl, who became both a close friend and one of the finest interpreters of the songs.

Schubert's early fame was propagated not by publication but by friends, and the number of people impressed by his work was ever on the increase; his music was performed in the most prestigious of places, played from handwritten copies, which represented the simplest, cheapest and most usual means of distributing music. But at that time no one could make a living from composing alone, since royalties and performing rights did not really exist. Furthermore, Schubert had as yet achieved no success

Above: Schubert's room at 380 Innere Stadt (Wipplingerstrasse), as drawn by Moritz von Schwind. This was the first lodging Schubert took on his own in the Inner City. He moved here in 1821, and in this room several of the Goethe poems were set to music, including 'Suleike' (D.720). He also worked on the uncompleted Symphony in E (D.729) here.

Right: Franz von Schober, in a drawing by Moritz von Schwind.

must, like the Mass in F major, have been composed for a particular event. Clearly Schubert was receptive to the needs of church music, and there were two more Masses in 1815 and another in 1816. He later wrote a good deal more choral music in the secular field, for men's, women's or mixed voices, much of it, no doubt, at the behest of Vienna's many musical societies.

Schubert's salon or drawing-room music also flowed from his pen from adolescence on. This is nearly all piano music, for solo piano or for piano duet (a medium, incidentally, which Beethoven hardly touched). It consists in the main of marches (the 'Marche Militaire' is a prime example), dances (waltzes, Ländler, Ecossaises, German dances and the like), and sets of variations. Such music written for social events and even more informal get-togethers, all bears the stamp of Schubert's musical charm, and some of the latest of it lays claim to a good deal more than that. The *Moments Musicaux* (D.780), the two sets of Impromptus (D.899 and D.935) and the *Klavierstücke* (D.946) are as much a mark of the rapid growth of Schubert's creative powers towards the end of his short life as the later chamber works and piano sonatas. Such pieces also point the way forward to the type of composition, in fairly free, improvisatory form, that was soon to become such a feature of Romantic music in the hands of Mendelssohn, Schumann, Chopin and Liszt.

Schubert's many songs, like his other early compositions, appear to have been written to suit circumstance rather than purely for the composer's own pleasure. In 1814, the year of 'Gretchen am Spinnrade' (D.118), Schubert

in what was in those days the most lucrative musical form, the *Singspiel*, or opera. In 1815 alone he wrote no fewer than five stage works that have survived in part or whole, but he made no effort to have these produced at any of the major theaters in Vienna. It is possible that one or another of these *Singspiele* might have been performed in one of the highly ambitious theaters set up in private houses, but we know as little about these as we do about the

Right: Johann Baptist Jenger (1792-1856), Anselm Hüttenbrenner (1794-1868) and Schubert in a watercolor by Josef Teltscher. Hüttenbrenner was a pupil of Salieri, and possibly knew Schubert as early as 1812. Later, he became a friend of Beethoven and often gave financial help to Schubert. Jenger, who was an accomplished pianist, was also a long-standing friend of Schubert. Both he and Hüttenbrenner moved to Graz, where they established a circle of Schubert-admirers. Teltscher's painting was surely done on the occasion of Schubert's visit to Graz in September 1827, when he took part in a charity concert.

Above: Self-portrait of Moritz von Schwind (1804-71) dating from about 1825. Schwind studied at the University of Vienna before turning to painting and enrolling at the Academy. An excellent pianist, he also tried his hand at composition and joined the Schubert circle around 1821.

salons. Such private productions were, in any case, matters of prestige rather than cash. Nonetheless, Schubert's extraordinary rate of production in 1815 alone made a purely musical career seem possible.

Schubert first of all tried to give up the job of schoolmaster and to take up a musical profession in the stricter sense of the term. In February 1816 the post of music-master at a newly opened Music School in Laibach (now Ljubljana in Yugoslavia) was advertised. Schubert applied, but for whatever reasons he did not get the post. Whether or not he was really disappointed we do not know, but he never again applied for any position. However, he was not inclined to stay in the safe job of teaching for which he had been trained. At the end of the academic year in the summer of 1816 he resigned from the post at his father's school to become a freelance composer, concentrating solely on his music.

That this decision was premature is obvious to us now, but the risk must also have been clear both to himself and to his friends. They supported him, however, and for the rest of his life he lived with family or friends, or else as a subtenant with families he had not known before, where he had rights to his own room. His final abode was with his brother Ferdinand. An important milestone in his new career is found in the diary entry for 17 June 1816: 'On this day I composed for the first time for money.' The work was a cantata for the nameday of a professor at the university in Vienna, Heinrich Joseph Watteroth, commissioned by his students and friends and performed in his own home. Schubert received the princely sum of 100 Viennese florins, which represented one fifth of

the annual salary he would have received if he had been appointed to the post at the Music School in Laibach.

• Uncertain success •

The dates inscribed on Schubert's compositions give us some insight into the speed at which he composed, and the amount. Otherwise we know little of how a normal day was spent. One cannot help but wonder whether he would have relished the peace and quiet of a place of his own, and whether with the collapse in 1815 of his love affair with Therese Grob, because her parents disapproved, he gave up forever the idea of marrying.

We likewise have no clue as to his means of existence during the two years from summer 1816 to summer 1818. No commissions for new works are known to us, nor do we know whether, like other composers of that time, he accepted private pupils. He composed and was happy, but he appears to have made no money from his compositions.

On the other hand, he enjoyed increasing prestige and even fame. In 1817 the highly respected *Theaterzeitung* in Vienna published a poem 'To Herr Franz Schubert,' and a year earlier he had even set to music a poem written about him by his friend Johann Mayrhofer. Early in 1818, and probably without his consent, one of his songs – 'Am Erlafsee' (D.586) – first appeared in print as a music supplement to an almanac. In the same year we find for the first time references to performances of his music in the programs of public concerts, but they are all concerts put on by performers, who would themselves have claimed the proceeds.

Again we must ask ourselves why it was that Schubert did not do as other performers and composers did and organize concerts of his own music. We know of only one occasion when he chose to do this, on 26 May 1828. The success and the profit of 800 Viennese florins would certainly have been on a comparable level ten years earlier. However, we should not with hindsight criticize Schubert for being insufficiently ambitious. Even the request to Goethe to allow the settings of the 'Erlkönig' and other poems to be dedicated to him – a request to which Goethe never even replied – did not come from Schubert but, characteristically, from his friend Joseph von Spaun. Such actions were alien to Schubert.

All the more surprising, therefore, was his decision in the summer of 1818 to go to Schloss Zseliz in Hungary (today Czechoslovakia) as music teacher to the court of Count Johann Carl Esterházy. The appointment was only four months long, however, and Schubert's responsibilities were not those of a teacher as such; he was required to make music with the two Countesses, Marie and Caroline, who both sang and played the piano, and to act as their coach. In 1821 Schubert gave further coaching to Caroline as a singer and in 1824 he spent another summer in Zseliz. These sessions, perhaps a pleasant form of patronage, make up the total sum of engagements taken by Schubert in his entire life.

In July and August 1819 we find Schubert in the company of his friend, the singer Johann Michael Vogl, on a journey through Upper Austria to Steyr, Linz and the Benedictine abbey of Kremsmünster. All that we know suggests that Vogl was the initiator, but the artistic highlight of this otherwise musically lightweight journey was the 'Trout' Quintet in A major (D.667), so called because it includes a set of variations based on Schubert's song of that name. The quintet, composed for the active musical community in Steyr, is one of Schubert's best-known works and one that shows his fondness for unconventional instrumentation, since the piano is joined by a quartet of strings made up of violin, viola, cello and double-bass, instead of the normal two violins, viola and cello of the string quartet. Moreover, the piece has five movements instead of the usual four. This, and the instrumentation, makes it closer to a divertimento than to the stricter form that the word 'quintet' implies. The opening movement takes delight in ear-tickling patterned textures, with the pianist frequently having both hands above middle C, well clear of double-bass territory – perhaps Steyr had a particularly powerful bassist. The central scherzo is all infectious vivacity, and the finale is so unconcerned with symphonic or sonata notions of form as something constantly developing and cumulative, that its second half is simply a re-run of its first half at a different pitch. As a mark of the composer's growing maturity (he was still only twenty-two) the modulation between keys is captivating throughout.

Below: Vienna in 1820 seen in the distance from the Vienna woods. Schubert was the only one of the great 'Viennese' composers to have been born in the city and to have spent virtually his entire life there. Unlike many of his contemporaries, who made their living as performers, he never traveled farther afield than Linz, Graz and Zseliz.

•Theater work•

In 1819 Schubert's father made one last attempt to persuade him to return to the economic security of the school. It is possible that when he lived under the parental roof in the winter of 1817-18, and moved with the family to his father's new school in the suburb of Rossau, he did try his hand again at teaching. But if that was the case, it did not last. And in 1819 it seemed to him that he might succeed in the one sphere where a freelance composer might hope to do well – the world of the stage.

Vogl appears again to have been the initiator, for one of Schubert's friends reported, 'He is writing at Vogl's behest, and not just for the sake of it, operettas, operas and other major things. . . .' The fact that Schubert had been commissioned by one of the leading singers of the Vienna Opera promised every success. In fact, Schubert had received from the Kärntnertor Theater a commission to write a *Singspiel*, *Die Zwillingsbrüder* (The Twin Brothers), in which Vogl was to appear in two roles. The extent to which the singer was behind the project and Schubert rather passive about the whole matter may be judged from the fact that an advance payment for the cost of the copyist was not collected by Schubert but withdrawn in his name by Vogl. The first performance took place on 14 June 1820 but was not the hoped-for success. Schubert's devotees in the audience applauded wildly, but from others there were cat-calls. The critics praised a few details, but on the whole they were less than enthusiastic; they had expected something better and more original from Schubert. The composer himself was disappointed, but could console himself with the sum of 500 Viennese florins the venture had brought him.

Two months later, on 19 August 1820, the first performance of his melodrama *Die Zauberharfe* (The Magic Harp) took place in the Theater an der Wien. This time not only was the venture unsuccessful, but the performance itself was bad, though Schubert's music can hardly be blamed for the catastrophe. However, the two works together had brought Schubert a total of 650 florins in one summer, which was more than the annual salary of an instrumentalist in the imperial *Kapelle*.

In 1821 he received a second commission from the Kärntnertor Theater, for two numbers in *Das Zauberglöckchen*, a German version of Hérold's *La Clochette* (1817), a magic opera based on the story of Aladdin, for a fee of 150 Viennese florins. Schubert's contributions were well received, but they were simply occasional pieces that could bring him no lasting prestige. He still needed to write a major work.

In the small town of St Pölten in Lower Austria and in nearby Schloss Ochsenburg he wrote in the autumn of 1821 the greater part of his opera *Alfonso und Estrella*, to a libretto by his friend Franz von Schober, who had arranged the stay. However, we have no evidence of any endeavors by Schubert to have the work put on. The earliest documented performance did not take place until 1854, conducted by Franz Liszt in Weimar.

In April 1823 Schubert completed another *Singspiel*, *Die Verschworenen* (The Conspirators), and in the summer of the same year the opera *Fierabras* was also completed. Schubert's name appeared on a theater program only once more in his lifetime. On 20 September 1823, the play *Rosamunde, Königin von Zypern* (Rosamunde, Queen of Cyprus) by Helmina von Chézy received its first performance, and Schubert had written the incidental music for it. The play went down badly, but Schubert's music was well received at the time and has triumphantly survived, notably the B minor Entr'acte, whose scale and content make it a satisfying concert item. The equally popular 'Rosamunde' over-

Below: Title-page of Schubert's *Valses Sentimentales* for piano (D.779), published as his op.50 by Diabelli. The title was not, in fact, Schubert's own, though the signing and initialing of the cover by the composer indicate his collaboration with the publisher to prevent piracy and so make a profit from his works.

ture, however, is a survival from the earlier theatrical project, *Die Zauberharfe*. Only after *Rosamunde* did Schubert turn his back on the theater and devote himself with renewed vigor to instrumental music. In 1827 he began work again on an opera, *Der Graf Gleichen* (Count Gleichen), but despite making considerable progress, he abandoned it.

•Publication•

Let us return, however, to 1821. For some time Schubert's friends had been disturbed by the fact that although his *Lieder* were in wide circulation as copies or as supplements to almanacs, they were not being published. Schubert himself was not in the least upset at this. His friends had tried to persuade publishing houses in Vienna to rectify the situation, but they met with no success: Schubert's songs were altogether of a much higher quality than the easy songs published by his contemporaries, and they

would have been regarded as a risk by any publisher. However, Leopold Sonnleithner, Anselm Hüttenbrenner and two other friends had Schubert's 'Erlkönig' engraved at their expense and sold on a commission basis by the publishers Cappi & Diabelli in Vienna. Sonnleithner's father held a regular musical salon; the 'Erlkönig' was sold at one of these evenings, and over a hundred copies were bought by members of the audience. We have Sonnleithner's own words on the subject: 'Thus we had the first twelve works engraved at our expense and sold

Above: The title vignette from Joseph Czerny's *Der Wiener Klavier Lehrer*, op.51, published in Vienna in 1826. There was an enormous market for piano-duet music at this time, reflecting the great amount of music-making that went on in the home, but the greater part of it consisted of arrangements of orchestral works, operatic selections, etc. Schubert, however, wrote some outstanding original works for piano duet, several of them on a large scale.

Left: The piano owned by Schubert's brother Ignaz, made by Benignus Seidner in Vienna, on which the composer must certainly have played.

for a commission by Diabelli. From the generous proceeds we were able to meet Schubert's bills for accommodation, at the shoemaker's and the tailor's, at the inn and the coffee-house, and still put a large amount of money into his hand; sadly he needed to be looked after in this way, for he had no idea of domestic thrift and was often persuaded by his friends in the inn (mostly painters or poets and but few musicians) to spend money on useless things, more for their enjoyment than for his.' We need not ask ourselves how Schubert, only six months after earning 650 florins from opera commissions, was in debt to that same amount.

Publishers now began to show an interest in Schubert's music. Cappi & Diabelli bought the rights to the works numbered opps.1-7 and 10-12, which they had previously sold for commission. Sonnleithner felt that Schubert had acted most unwisely in selling the rights in this way, but it is only fair to point out that the fees paid were generous by standards at that time; Schubert was certainly not exploited by his publishers. On the contrary, until 1823 Schubert received from Cappi & Diabelli 100 Viennese florins for a book of songs (normally comprising only three). He was then enticed away to another publisher, Maximilian Leidesdorf, who paid 200 florins for the same. Carl Czerny, to whom we can reasonably point as a fashionable composer at that time, was delighted to receive 125 Viennese florins for his op.2, a piano piece for four hands, and in 1825 Jan Václav Hugo Voříšek, a highly respected composer, was paid 75 florins for a collection of six songs. It is true, of course, that the publishers did well out of Schubert's works, because his music stood the test of time, and reprints and new editions were soon needed.

There is also the fact that more works by Schubert appeared in print than was the case with most of his contemporaries. In the years between 1821 and 1828 eleven different publishers brought out 106 opus numbers, most of them comprising more than one individual work. This means that on average a new work by Schubert was published every month. That represents an enormous amount by prevailing standards. We should also bear in mind that many of these editions had specific dedications, some to friends and colleagues, but others to representatives of the upper classes who were known to be generous patrons.

Over and above all this Schubert continued to write commissioned works that were not published. The largest of these was the Octet in F major (D.803), composed in 1824 for Count Ferdinand Troyer, Master of the Household to that Beethoven pupil and respectable composer, the Archduke Rudolph. As a whole we can ascertain that from 1821 onwards Schubert had a good income solely from the publication of his works, and that this alone should have permitted him to enjoy, as the first freelance composer relying on the financial yield from his works, at least a satisfactory standard of living. The fact that Schubert was sometimes in financial difficulty cannot be blamed on the times or on those with whom he had dealings; the fault lay with Schubert himself, in that he had no idea how to look after his money.

• Personal life •

As far as we can gather, Schubert's daily existence was simple and uncomplicated. His lifestyle appears to have been one of contentment rather than excitement. He was most at home surrounded by his close friends, and these felt themselves to be a group with its own strong sense of identity. His friends provided him with distraction, conversation, discussion and artistic approval, as well as the possibility of going on trips, such as to Schloss Atzenbrugg in Lower Austria or to places just outside Vienna. As a rule the summer months were spent somewhere other than Vienna, but he made no really long journeys, traveling to the west no further than Salzburg and to the south as far as Graz (September 1827), while eastwards he went no further from Vienna than Zseliz.

In addition to this close circle of friends there was a wider acquaintanceship with people who for social or musical reasons were pleased to entertain him. From 1821 – an important year in his life – Schubert became a member of the Gesellschaft der Musikfreunde, actively participating as a viola player and pianist. He seems to have been prepared to forget the unfortunate rejection, for the most inconclusive of reasons, of his first application for membership in 1818. As a member of the orchestra Schubert would have come into contact with all the leading musicians in Vienna. He also enjoyed visits to the theater and the opera and attended concerts. He gave no music lessons and had no other binding commitments, so that he could arrange his time as he wanted, accepting or declining invitations to appear at musical salons as he himself saw fit.

By and large Schubert was a typical member of the middle classes of the country to which he belonged. His satisfaction at the defeat of Napoleon and the hope that this would bring peace to Europe were expressed in musical terms in the song and the canon on a text written presumably by himself in 1813, 'Auf den Sieg der Deutschen' (To the Victory of the Germans, D.81 and D.88). These works are not, however, great nationalistic statements. For Schubert the German victory meant primarily the end of troubled times and French expansionism, as the text makes clear: 'Our pains have disappeared, because the sighs of troubled hearts are no longer heard. Therefore rejoice, Germans!' The same is true of the political song, 'Die Befreier Europas in Paris' (The Liberators of Europe in Paris, D.104) written in 1814. When Emperor Franz I returned from peace negotiations in Paris on 16 June 1814, the streets of Vienna were all decorated and lit up. The schoolhouse, where at that time Schubert was living with his parents, displayed a banner in honor of the Emperor. Subsequently Schubert also showed himself to be a loyal subject of Emperor and country. We see this in his setting of the hymn, 'Am Geburtstage des Kaisers' (On the Emperor's Birthday, D.748), in 1822 – and in the fact that the work was commissioned by the Royal Imperial Theresian College of Knights, a highly traditional and conservative boarding-school.

A potentially troublesome incident in 1820 appears to have done his reputation no harm. One of Schubert's close friends, the Tyrolean

Right: Caricature of the violinist Ignaz Schuppanzigh printed in 1810. The composer dedicated his String Quartet in A minor (D.804) to the violinist, and the performance on 7 March 1824 took place at his house. He also performed Schubert's B flat Trio (D.898) at a public concert in 1828, and played the first violin in the first performances of his Octet (D.803) in 1827.

student and gifted poet Johann Senn, was arrested together with some of his friends, including Schubert. Senn was suspected of taking part in an anti-establishment gathering. Schubert and his friends were released immediately, but Senn was detained in custody for fourteen months and then made to leave Vienna. The fact that Schubert set two of Senn's texts to music in 1823 has led many biographers to see this as a positive act of support for his republican friend. What they have overlooked is that the first edition of these songs omitted the poet's name altogether, perhaps at the publisher's request.

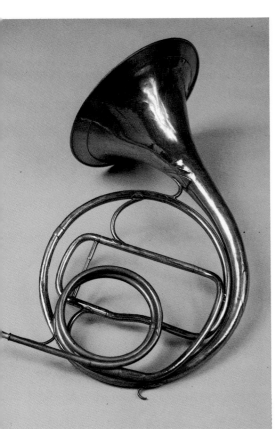

Only in subsequent editions, after Senn's rehabilitation, was his name added.

More difficult is the question of Schubert's religious feelings. He seems to have adopted a lukewarm attitude to the Church as an institution, but not to religion itself, for by all accounts he was a believer. This attitude to the Church may not be totally consistent with the picture of the average member of middle-class society, but it is typical of the early liberalism that is to be discerned elsewhere at this time. He had no difficulty in accepting commissions for religious works, and in 1828 he completed his grand Mass in E flat (D.950), the last of six such works among an impressive output of church music. It was written for the musical society of the parish church of Alservorstadt in Vienna. No restrictions were laid upon him as to length, size or difficulty, conditions of which he took magnificent advantage.

•Orchestral music•

Schubert went through a stage during which he completed no large-scale works. His first six symphonies, as we have noted, were all written between 1813 and 1818, and from the orchestral parts that have survived, we can assume

In his Octet Schubert added clarinet, horn, bassoon and double-bass to the instruments of the string quartet, making full use of their sonorities. Count Ferdinand Troyer, who commissioned the Octet, was an excellent amateur clarinetist, and it was first performed in his house. The wind instruments still had few of the sophisticated mechanical techniques of modern instruments. All those shown date from the first quarter of the nineteenth century: (*above*) a French horn with one crook, but no valve keys; (*far right*) a bassoon; (*right*) an oboe, two flutes and a piccolo, and a boxwood clarinet. The very few keys on the woodwinds made virtuoso passages extremely difficult. Schubert gave prominence to the clarinet in his Octet, particularly in the glorious adagio, without ever taxing his patron too greatly.

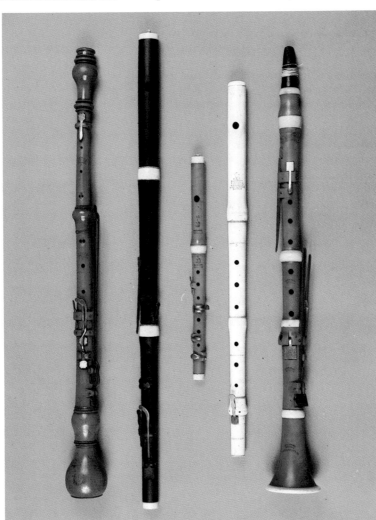

that they were performed at that time, even though we lack more detailed information as to the exact dates or nature of these performances. A manuscript set of parts for the Sixth Symphony reveals that those measures in the first movement that were subsequently crossed out were originally in the parts and then also deleted. In all probability Schubert made this decision on hearing the work performed. When we read of first performances taking place after the composer's death, what is really meant is that these were the first documented performances on public concert platforms. Whether the fragmentary symphonies which followed the Sixth remained unfinished because there was no chance of performing them is not known, but it seems unlikely. A commission for a Rondo Concertante for piano and orchestra in the autumn of 1818 was never fulfilled. In 1819 Schubert wrote two further orchestral works in the form of overtures, and then began a period of search and uncertainty.

His main concern was the symphony, in which he was determined to make his mark. Between 1818 and 1821 he brought three to varying stages of completion. Two of these were in the key of D major. In the first instance, Schubert abandoned the project half way through both a first movement and finale; both fragments (D.615) were left unorchestrated. In the second (D.708A), he made progress on all four movements before setting the work aside, again in 'piano score' only. In both these abortive symphonies the material is attractive and individual, and if they had been completed they might stand alongside the Fifth and Sixth as their natural successors.

A more substantial and fruitful sketch followed in the second half of 1821. Composing straight onto orchestral paper, Schubert fully scored the first 110 measures and continued to write the leading melodic line for the remainder of the work. Sometimes more than one instrument is given, occasionally a bass line, and in a few places up to seven of the fourteen staves are filled. This is the composition now classified as Symphony no.7 in E major (D.729). It goes some way towards bridging the stylistic gulf between the Sixth and the later symphonies. The transitions between themes are moving towards the intense lyricism and rich harmonic color of the Eighth. The Ninth is anticipated in the key change from scherzo to trio, and in the finale, which hints at a new spaciousness and sonority. The inclusion of trombones, absent from the first six symphonies, further cements the connection with the later ones.

• The last symphonies •

The Symphony no.8 in B minor (D.759) was produced in the following year, 1822. This is the one everybody knows as the 'Unfinished,' though, as we have just noted, several others are even more fragmentary. Two movements survive complete. There is a piano sketch of the scherzo with the melody for half of the trio, and two pages of orchestral score for the scherzo have come to light. Of the finale there is nothing. What has never been in question – since the first performance in 1865, that is – is the great beauty of the two surviving movements.

One particular virtue of this symphony, and of its successor, is its song-like quality (not surprising in possibly the greatest of all songwriters). Schubert's tendency to prefer singing melodies to pithy, Beethovenian motifs in a symphonic context here reaches its apogee. The second-subject theme of the first movement, especially, is one of the most perfect melodies ever conceived, although one may, like Copland, find that it defies the 'rules' of melodic con-

Below left: A square piano made by Walter und Sohn, Vienna, about 1820, which belonged to Schubert's friend, the painter W. A. Rieder, and on which the composer must have played; and a lyra guitar made by J. P. Michelot in Paris about the beginning of the nineteenth century. Clementi in London also made lyra guitars, and at one time John Field acted as his salesman for them. There were a number of 'new' instruments at this time, in this case directly influenced by neo-classicism in art, and several composers, including Schubert, wrote pieces for them.

Right: An arpeggione by Vincenz Schuster, taken from a title vignette. The arpeggione was one of the 'new' instruments of the period, and Schubert wrote a magnificent Arpeggione Sonata in A minor (D.821), now generally played on the cello.

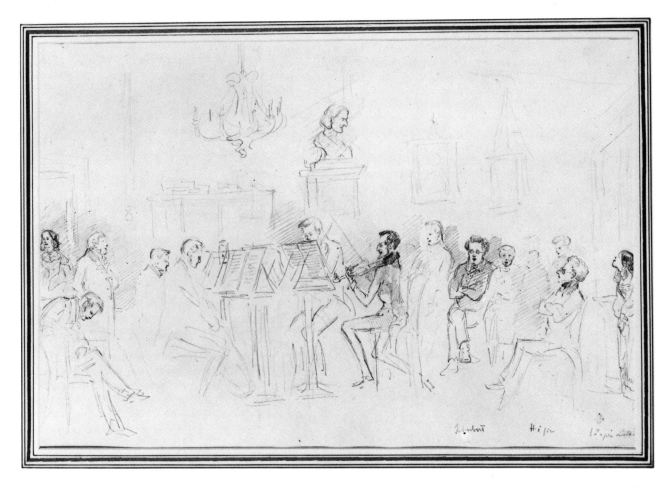

struction. The harmonic transition leading to it, like a sudden shaft of sunlight after the tense and brooding opening, is no less wonderful. Another outstanding feature of the 'Unfinished' Symphony is its measured feeling of space, achieved by focusing at the start on an extreme of the orchestra's pitch-space (that sinuous, ambling line deep in the cellos and basses), by the actual spacing of events with silent or relatively inactive measures (such as the long horn note that splays into the famous second subject), and, at other times, by an awesome bareness of texture. The unhurried tempo of both movements (*allegro moderato* and *andante con moto*) adds to this magical quality. Each is both gentle in pace and triple in time, a fact which conductors tend to see as a test of their ingenuity. There is, of course, contrast enough in the change of key from B minor to E major for the 'slow' movement, and in the musical material itself.

In the early summer of 1823 Schubert contracted a venereal infection which was not cleared until early in the following year. This understandably curtailed his symphonic ambitions for the time being and may well have been the reason why he abandoned the Eighth Symphony and ceased his work for the stage. On 31 March 1824, Schubert wrote in a letter to his friend Leopold Kupelwieser that he was still depressed about the state of his health: 'I feel I am the most unhappy, most wretched person in the world. Think of me as a man whose health will never be really right again, and who in his dejection at it only makes things

worse instead of better.' However, he also mentioned that he was 'paving the way for the great symphony,' in preparation for which he composed several other works.

One of these was the Octet (D.803) mentioned above. The model for this was Beethoven's Septet, for him an exercise leading to his First Symphony. Schubert also wrote six movements and used a similar instrumental ensemble. The Octet is a cheerful work, taking a hedonistic delight in manipulating rhythms, timing harmonic events and sharing out favors among the players. If the clarinet seems to come off particularly well, this may be partly due to the fact that Count Troyer, who was to play clarinet in its first performance, also commissioned the work. But it is, in any case, the obvious instrument to share the limelight with the first violin. The slow movement allots one of Schubert's most eloquent melodies to Troyer's clarinet, the subsequent entry of the first violin reminding us that the song composer knew how to mold an elegant countermelody. Yet the smoothly integrated sonorities of strings and wind are as likely to linger in the mind.

Another work which helped to prepare the way for the new symphony was the Sonata in C major, known as the 'Grand Duo' (D.812) – the finest of a number of important works that Schubert wrote for piano duet. It disposes its harmonies and keys on a broad, symphonic scale and takes every advantage of the span of four hands over the keyboard. For a long time, in fact, scholars believed it was the piano draft

Above: A drawing of a string quartet by Friedrich Gauermann, in which Schubert is depicted at right among those listening to the performance.

89

of a symphony whose full orchestral score had either been lost or, as was too often the case, never completed. The Grand Duo, with its four movements not unsymphonic in type or bearing, gave practice in spacious thinking within extended designs. The Octet gave Schubert the chance to update his treatment of a larger ensemble. It should be remembered that he had not completed a symphony for six years: at this stage in his creative development it was an undertaking not to be lightly embarked upon.

In 1825 Schubert felt ready to begin work on the 'Great C major' itself, long regarded as his seventh symphony but now termed no.9 (D.944). The autograph copy shows that he wrote it down apparently unaided by sketches or rough drafts, but it was not finished until the following year, 1826. As its Deutsch number indicates, it is only recently that these dates have been clarified. Schubert was thought to have written the work in 1828, the last year of his life. There was therefore much confusion between this and a so-called 'Gmunden-Gastein'

Right: Title-page of the autograph of the 'Unfinished' Symphony in B minor, the Eighth (D.759). Schubert worked on the symphony during the fall of 1822, but only the instrumentation of the first two movements was completed.

Below: Bronze bust of Schubert by Josef Alois Dialer, 1829, designed to adorn Schubert's tomb in the Währing Cemetery, Vienna.

Symphony, named after places in the Austrian Tyrol where Schubert was known to have been composing in 1825-6. We know now, as a result of John Reed's close study of the manuscripts, that this long lamented lost masterpiece is the 'Great C major' itself.

As in the 'Unfinished,' a true lyrical impulse prevails, and if there is drama, for instance at the magnificent climax of the second movement, it is but intensified, impassioned lyricism. It may be significant that among the melodic riches of the 'Great' the only theme to remind us of Beethoven resembles that of the only vocal movement of his only vocal symphony, his 'Choral' Ninth, first performed in Vienna in 1825. The 'Great,' however, develops spaciousness very differently from the 'Unfinished,' not through a slow tempo but through multiplication: that is, by repetition, both of whole paragraphs and tiny rhythmic cells; by the reproduction of a passage at higher or lower pitch; by shifting key over the same distance and in the same way two or three times in succession; and by doubling instrumental lines often through as many octaves as the orchestra will allow.

Aiding this proliferation of musical growth is a rhythmic energy that carries all before it, for the work is as much a celebration of rhythm as is Beethoven's Seventh. The activity seems self-perpetuating, and the resulting 'Heavenly length,' to use Schumann's phrase, rightly fills twice as many minutes as the slighter symphonic efforts of Schubert's previous, yet now remote, decade. But the pulsating onward sweep of the music incurs no neglect of detail. In little touches of harmonic and orchestral imagination, the 'Great C major' offers as many riches per page as any score of its time.

The 'Great' is also the culmination of several earlier trends. The massive scherzo continues the enlargement of the form already evident in the Sixth Symphony and the fragmentary D major Symphony (D.708A), from which it adopts its own initial six-note motif. And there

is a glorious solution to the problem of integrating a first movement proper with its slow introduction: as in the Seventh Symphony and the D.615 fragment, leading ideas of both sections are thematically related; and as in the First Symphony, part of the introduction returns in the allegro without reversion to the introductory tempo. In the 'Great C major' this resumption of the opening comes at the very end and forms the perfect climax, driving, with the minimum of musical rhetoric, right into the last cadence.

The year 1825 marks Schubert's maturity in worldly terms as well, for he was then appointed deputy member to the Representative Body, an executive committee of the Gesellschaft der Musikfreunde, and two years later became a full member of that committee. The respect in which this organization was held far beyond its own province brought Schubert musical and social recognition. His widespread acclaim as a composer can also be gathered from his being nominated Honorary Member of the Musical Associations in Graz and in Linz in 1823. In

Below: Trio from the autograph of the 'Great' C major Symphony, the Ninth (D.944). Schubert began work on the symphony as early as March 1825 and spent more than a year on it. Even so, it had to wait until 1839 for its first performance, which was conducted by Mendelssohn with drastic cuts.

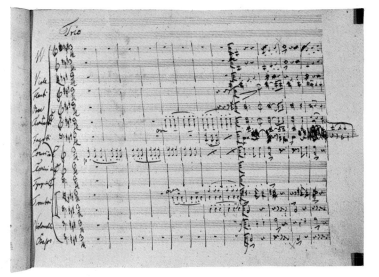

the 'Musical Evening Entertainments' run by the Gesellschaft, Rossini was the only composer to have a greater number of works performed, although the only works by Schubert that appeared on those programs were overtures and vocal works. A performance of the Ninth Symphony, which is dedicated to the Gesellschaft der Musikfreunde, and for which he was paid 100 florins, may have been contemplated but did not take place, one assumes because of the work's great technical difficulties. The score itself was deposited in the archive of the Society, as Schubert's brother Ferdinand noted, as an 'autographed souvenir,' and became part of the collection of autograph scores. The often quoted anecdote that Robert Schumann discovered the Symphony in Ferdinand's house is incorrect. What Ferdinand Schubert possessed was a copy of the work, and in perusing this copy Schumann merely discovered the work for himself. The important consequence of this, however, was that Schumann passed his copy of the score to Mendelssohn, who gave the first performance with the Leipzig Gewandhaus Orchestra in 1839. On that occasion and for many years to come it was regarded as an extremely taxing work.

• Late works •

Schubert's last three string quartets were also fruits of the years 1824 to 1826. They were preceded, in 1820, by an important fragment: the first movement of a Quartet in C minor, known as the *Quartettsatz* (Quartet Movement, D.703). Many facets of anguish seem to be glimpsed in these few pages of music, and one has the distinct impression that an emotional pattern dictates the course of the music. As a result, there evolves a structure which modifies the traditional sonata form perhaps more radically than any other of Schubert's works. The A minor Quartet of 1824 (D.804) seems to inhabit the same spiritual universe and is anxious and unsettled, like an echo of the song 'Gretchen am Spinnrade,' written ten years before. The theme of the second movement, borrowed from the *Rosamunde* music, brings no resolution, and the minuet only yearns for past joys, as did Schiller's words in Schubert's setting of 'Die Götter Griechenlands,' from which the opening is taken. 'Lovely world, where art thou?' asks the singer.

The second movement of the stern and restless D minor Quartet (D.810) consists of variations on the melody of Schubert's song 'Death and the Maiden.' In the case of this melody, as so often with Schubert, it is the harmonies that create the effect rather than the actual progression of notes, and in this quartet they can sound even more poignant than in the original song. With the G major Quartet of 1826 (D.887), the first theme is hardly a melody at all; it is hardly a harmonic progression, merely a change from major to minor, an opposition which comes to dominate the work. Such a stark major/minor conflict looks forward nearly a century to a parallel in Mahler's Sixth Symphony.

Equally remarkable are the Piano Trios in B flat (D.898) and in E flat (D.929). We know that the latter was played late in 1827 by the gifted violinist Ignaz Schuppanzigh, the cellist Joseph Linke, and the pianist Carl Maria von Bocklet, to whom Schubert had dedicated his D major Piano Sonata (D.850) in 1825; he had dedicated the A minor String Quartet (D.804) to Schuppanzigh. The chance to compose with such professional playing in prospect must have been an enormous stimulus, to which we probably owe the last string quartets as well as these two piano trios.

The composer's technique is displayed as confidently as that of the players. In particular, both trios make much of the juxtaposing of distantly related keys. Schubert appears to use this device for the effect produced at the very moment of transition, but the structural consequences cannot be ignored, and indeed he positively enjoys them. In the first movement

Right: The letter in which Schubert dedicated his 'Great' Symphony in C to the Gesellschaft der Musikfreunde in Vienna – for which he received the sum of 100 florins.

Far right: The letter of thanks written by Schubert, dated 12 June 1827, to the Gesellschaft der Musikfreunde for having elected him a member of the Representative Body. He had become a member of the Society in March 1822.

Above: Franz Grillparzer (1791-1872). The poet provided many lyrics for Schubert, whom he first met in 1820. Grillparzer was one of the torchbearers at Beethoven's funeral, along with Schubert.

of the E flat Trio the second subject – to be recognized by its obsession with one five-note rhythm – arrives, after a sharp swerve, in B minor. Schubert has merely deferred the orthodox key (B flat major) and now proceeds to repeat and go on repeating his new tune, with a key-change each time, until that destination is reached. This early shock, with the following waves of color, sets a standard for subsequent wanderlust, which is not lost sight of even in the long finale's extended coda. Schubert attempts cyclic unity in the work by recalling the slow movement in the finale. The cello introduces the theme, made to fit the prevailing tempo and rhythmic climate, in the central development and again in the coda, where the violin joins to extend it into a triumphal last climax.

In 1827 the chance to compose for another professional, the Czech violin virtuoso Josef Slavík, led Schubert to compose two showpieces for violin and piano, the Rondo Brillant in B minor (D.895) and the fine but sadly neglected Fantasy in C major (D.934). Much better known is the String Quintet in C major (D.956) completed within two months of Schubert's death. Like Boccherini, Schubert adds a second cello rather than the second viola of Mozart's five great quintets, but the rich and sonorous texture of Schubert's work is, like Mozart's, wholly in the Viennese tradition. The heart of the quintet is the slow movement, yet another, and possibly the greatest, of the composer's essays in a kind of rapt and sublime inner contemplation. The inner three parts are treated as a continuous core around which the first violin and plucked second cello voice a dialogue potently expressive in its utter simplicity and economy. Once again, the harmonies mean everything – those unique Schubertian progressions that are almost beyond formal analysis.

Like the last string quartets, the second group of piano sonatas was produced between 1823 and 1826. Standing as a kind of prelude to them,

Schubert had composed, the previous year, the 'Wanderer' Fantasy in C major (D.760), a large-scale piano piece whose sonata-like four sections all transform the same thematic idea from his song 'The Wanderer,' written in 1819; Liszt later arranged it for piano and orchestra. Two of the sonatas, like one of the earlier group (D.537), are in A minor. The earlier here (D.784), written in 1823, has a first movement of rock-like grandeur. Its opening, once heard, will not easily be forgotten – it is a peculiarly tense line in hushed bare octaves. The later A minor sonata (D.845) also has a remarkable first movement, unorthodox in relation to Schubert's own as well as to Classical sonata-form practice. At first one does not realize how germane to its argument is the opening confrontation between a curving unison phrase and a chain of six chords, so volatile is the drama that unfolds from it. Yet the illusion of caprice is underpinned by truly organic processes right into the final coda which crowns the piece so magnificently. Sonatas in D major (D.850) and in G major (D.894) complete this group. The second of these is one of Schubert's most successful attempts to conceive a first movement not as something fast, dynamic and incisive, but as a gentler, more serene kind of soliloquy. The second and fourth movements are rondos with some of the composer's most touching and personal thoughts contained in the intervening 'episodes.'

The last three solo piano sonatas were written in September 1828, only two months before Schubert died. Again there is a preceding fantasy, in F minor (D.940), although this is the last in his distinguished output of works for piano duet. Its one long movement falls into four forms of a sort, but the true improvisatory spirit of fantasy is uppermost, control is firm but discreet, and the quality of thought reflects the late date. As a compositional marathon the last sonatas bring to mind Mozart's last three symphonies, and they are as rich in their variety. Beethoven's spirit may seem to speak again in the darkness, the resolute rhythms and even the theme of the Sonata in C minor (D.958), but the work as a whole shows no loss of Schubert's own personality. A brighter light shines through the A major Sonata (D.959). Here we find something of the sunny, lyrical warmth of two earlier works in the same key, the Sonata (D.664) and the 'Trout' Quintet, plus a new depth and majesty of expression. The development makes a long flowing tune, with one variant after another, of a scrap heard only a few moments before. In its unstable middle section the slow movement, by contrast, does not build and develop melody but displaces it with decoration, gesture, and atmosphere. Such passages belie the naïve interpretation of Schubert as a song composer whose instrumental imagination was constrained by the habits, needs or conventions of the song-maker's art. The last sonata of all, in B flat (D.960), is not only the longest, but gives notice of its expansiveness in its opening theme (*molto moderato*), which soon comes to rest with a long bass trill and silent pause. There is no haste, here or later. Time seems almost to stand still in the slow movement, rather as it does in the slow movement of the String Quintet in C, probably written in the same month. Such tracts of self-communion, in which Schubert seems oblivious of art's temporal constraints, expose for many of us the very core of his musical being.

• Last days •

The speed with which Schubert was composing in the last weeks of his life suggests that he may have begun to realize that his end might be near. However, in November he arranged to have music lessons in counterpoint with Simon Sechter, a leading Viennese musical theorist. The first movement of the Quintet in C major uses vigorous counterpoint, but this tuition was in connection with the composition of a Tenth Symphony. The piano sketches for this new symphony in D major, identified in 1977 among a bundle of manuscripts in a Vienna library, are the most difficult of all Schubert's symphonic manuscripts to interpret. Nevertheless, performances of Brian Newbould's realization of the symphony are making it much better known, and we can see that it was intended as a major advance. Of the three movements sketched out, the scherzo is perhaps the most remarkable of all: an amazing display of counterpoint, culminating in a simultaneous presentation of the scherzo and trio main themes. What these tremendous new advances in his thinking might have led to, had he lived, is unimaginable.

The feverish haste with which Schubert seems to have been working (and hence the difficulty in deciphering his writing) may have been due to the fact that at the end of October 1828 the first symptoms of typhus appeared. On 4 November, he went to Sechter for his one and

Below: Schubert's tomb in the Währing Cemetery, Vienna.

only lesson. On 11 November he took to his bed. He was now living with his brother Ferdinand, in the suburb of Wieden. Ferdinand and Schubert's friends called the best doctors to his bedside, and every possible means was tried to improve his deteriorating condition. In his last letter, written on 12 November to Franz von Schober, Schubert described his state: 'I have not eaten or drunk anything for 11 days . . . if I try anything, it comes up again immediately.' He also asked for books to read, if at all possible something by James Fenimore Cooper – he had already read *The Last of the Mohicans*, *The Spy*, *The Pilot* and *The Settlers*. A week later, on 19 November 1828, at 3 p.m., Franz Schubert died, not yet thirty-two years old.

Top left: Page of the orchestral part for first flute in the first movement of the Sixth Symphony. The measures deleted correspond to a deletion in the autograph score, suggesting that the work was in fact performed in Schubert's lifetime, contrary to what has been generally believed.

Above: Invitation to the Requiem Mass held for Schubert.

93

Goethe and Music

German literature has known no more dominant figure than Johann Wolfgang von Goethe (1749-1832), the range of whose work – dramas, novels, poetry, scientific and esthetic works – was extraordinary. He was himself a competent musician, but his importance for musical history lies in his many poems, and his drama *Faust* in particular, that gave inspiration to composers throughout the nineteenth century and beyond. Certainly Goethe understood the power of music, and many of his lyric poems were specifically written to be set to music. However, Schubert, who made so many wonderful settings of the great man's poems, was never able to engage his attention. Beethoven met Goethe in 1812, two years after he had completed his incidental music for the poet's *Egmont*, but while Goethe thought highly of him as a musician, Beethoven's deafness and his abrupt manner prevented any closer contact between them, although their friends, the Brentanos in particular, tried to bring them together. Goethe greatly admired Mozart's music, although Mozart set only one of his poems, 'Das Veilchen' (K.476) from his *Singspiel*, *Erwin und Elmire*; but then Mozart was a great source of inspiration for the Romantic movement, whose writers claimed him as the first Romantic composer.

In 1820-1 Goethe received a new piano from Vienna, made by Beethoven's friend Nanette Streicher. It is seen here (*above*) in his house in Weimar with the stools arranged for duet playing; for throughout the nineteenth century piano arrangements were the main way by which amateur musicians could get to know new orchestral works, almost all of which would be published in this form.

Left: The twelve-year-old Felix Mendelssohn in 1821, the year he was first brought to visit Goethe and played for him on the new Streicher piano.

Above: Goethe as a young man holding a silhouette, painted around 1775.

Above: Goethe's handsome upright piano, in pyramidal form, in the music room of his house at Weimar.

Left: Goethe's own design for the appearance of the Queen of the Night in Mozart's *Zauberflöte*. This was one of a number of sketches he made in 1796 for a planned production of the work at Weimar, including costume designs and a modular set to allow for quick changes of scene. Goethe had also written a sequel to Mozart's opera two years before, and this is a telling indication of the way in which the work was understood at the time. It was in the familiar genre of magic pantomime, and the superficial banalities and inconsistencies of the text, which have often been criticized since then, were overlooked for the symbolic and spiritual values implicit in the drama and expressed so nobly in Mozart's music.

Below: Scene from *Faust* – Gretchen, seduced by Faust, faints in church, taunted by the evil spirit whispering to her as the choir sings the 'Dies Irae.'

Above: Witches' ceremony, drawn by Goethe in 1787, perhaps in connection with his plans for *Faust*, the drama which occupied him throughout his life. He was already working on the material in 1771 at the time of the trial of Susanna Margarete Brandt, a Frankfurt servant-girl who had killed her illegitimate child. The girl's execution in January 1772 deeply shocked Goethe. The first part of *Faust*, completed in its final version in 1807, tells of Faust's pact with Mephistopheles and his seduction of Gretchen, who kills their child. In Part II, completed in 1831, Faust's search for perfection through science and magic leads to a union with Helen of Troy, and to his final redemption.

95

Above: Frontispiece of the textbook of Goethe's *Singspiel, Erwin und Elmire,* written in 1774. This was a time of great creativity for the young poet, whose *Singspiele* and drawings (*below*) showed the influence of Rococo, while the 'Sturm und Drang' movement inspired his passionate novel *The Sorrows of Young Werther,* his Shakespearean drama *Götz von Berlichingen* and the great free-verse hymns 'Prometheus,' 'Ganymed' and 'An Schwager Kronos' – all given wonderful settings by Schubert.

Above: Scene from Goethe's *Singspiel, Die Fischerin* (1782). This was the year of Mozart's *Die Entführung aus dem Serail,* and after Goethe had heard that work he abandoned any further attempts of his own in the genre. However, while in Rome in 1787 he revised both *Erwin und Elmire* and *Claudina von Villa Bella* (1774) with the intention of having them set to music by his friend Philipp Christoph Kayser (1755-1823), who visited him there. Although Kayser did set the first work, Goethe realized his friend's limitations as a composer in comparison to Mozart – nor was he entirely satisfied with the settings of both works made some years later by J. F. Reichardt.

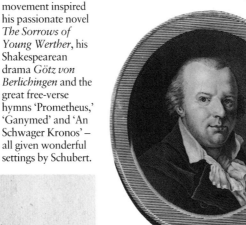

Above: Johann Friedrich Reichardt (1752-1814), Kapellmeister to the court of Prussia and one of Goethe's favored composers. Together with Carl Friedrich Zelter (1758-1832), also a friend of the poet's, Reichardt was a leading member of the North German *Lieder* school, whose work remained much closer to popular folksong than did the more inspired songs of Schubert. Reichardt's setting of *Claudina von Villa Bella* (1789) was the first German opera to be staged successfully at the Prussian court by the local Kapellmeister, but Goethe, no doubt thinking of Mozart and of his own recent stay in Italy, found it lacking in Italian richness. It was later also set by Schubert (1815).

Above: Scene from Goethe's *Egmont* (1787), in which he introduced music at crucial points of the action to convey more effectively than with words alone the nature of a character or situation. Beethoven's setting, written in 1809-10 and first performed at Weimar in 1814, met with Goethe's delighted approval.

Of all Goethe's works, it was *Faust* that continued to attract composers, with its combination of intense human drama and transcendental spiritual striving. There were songs included in the first part of the play, and Schubert's early setting of 'Gretchen am Spinnrade' (1814) brilliantly evokes the unease of Goethe's heroine, while the Walpurgisnacht (witches' sabbath) scene – Cornelius's illustration (*top left*) shows Faust and Mephistopheles led up the mountain to the sabbath by a will-o'-the-wisp – provided a climax to several of the musical settings. Spohr was the first to base an opera on the work, first performed in Prague in 1816, while Adam composed a *Faust* ballet in 1833. Schumann, more ambitiously, worked between 1844 and 1853 on settings of a number of scenes from *Faust* Part II; the score (*top right*) is of the opening, where

Ariel and a choir of spirits sing at dusk to Faust, who, exhausted and restless, seeks sleep. Berlioz wrote *La Damnation de Faust* (1846) for concert rather than stage performance, while Gounod's *Faust* (1859), though it has been hugely popular, is such a travesty of Goethe's work that in Germany it is always known as *Margarete*; Boito's *Mefistofele* (1868-75) is a much finer work. There is also an overture to *Faust* Part I (1839-40) by Wagner, and Liszt, too, wrote a 'Faust' Symphony (1854-7); this ends with the magnificent choral scene in which Faust is redeemed by the 'eternal feminine' and which brings to a close the work completed by Goethe at the end of his life. The portrait of him (*right*) in his last years is by Maclise after Thackeray and Stieler.

No later composer interpreted Goethe's poetry as subtly as Hugo Wolf (1860-93), who made over fifty Goethe settings. These range from the titanic poems 'Prometheus,' 'Ganymed' and 'Grenzen der Menschheit' (though not 'An Schwager Kronos,' since Wolf admired Schubert's setting and never set a text if he felt an adequate version existed), to satirical verses and songs of profound lyricism. 'Anakreons Grab' (*above*), written in 1888 (this orchestral version, 1893), is one of the loveliest, evoking the memory of the ancient Greek pastoral poet.

97

SCHUBERT'S SONGS

PHILIP RADCLIFFE

In the eighteenth century the growth of larger vocal and instrumental forms such as opera and symphony tended to put the separate song into the shade. Handel and J. S. Bach, both great melodists, wrote only a handful of songs, and the same is true of Haydn and Mozart, while all these composers wrote their greatest songs as parts of larger works.

The strongest stimulus to the composition of songs of a more serious and ambitious kind was the poetry of Goethe, which inspired innumerable composers of varying caliber, but it was Schubert who raised the song to a level that enabled it to take its place as one of the most characteristic forms of nineteenth-century music.

Like several other great composers who died young, Schubert developed quickly, but it must be admitted that in his earliest songs there are only fitful gleams of the magical lyricism of his later music. At this stage – not surprisingly in a boy of fourteen – he was attracted by melodramatic and bloodthirsty ballads and clearly influenced by J. R. Zumsteeg and J. F. Reichardt, contemporaries of Mozart who wrote operas as well as songs. An operatic style dominates the young Schubert's settings of long, rambling poems, the music following the moods of the words with no attempt at structural or tonal unity. The lyrical passages are on the whole conventional, but now and then there are striking modulations. One of the most impressive comes at the word 'Jehovah' in 'Hagars Klage' (Hagar's Lament, D.5), Schubert's earliest song, written in 1811. The songs of the following year, 1812, include 'Klaglied' (Lament, D.23), a small strophic song which hints at Schubert's mature style in its deeply appealing pathos. In 'Verklärung' (Transfiguration, D.59), a setting of a translation of Pope's 'Vital Spark of Heavenly Flame,' the operatic manner is more finely under control; there are striking moments, though the dramatic contrasts are too violent for so short a song.

The lyrical and dramatic elements in Schubert's personality were apt to draw him in opposite directions until, by a miracle, they coalesced in his first Goethe song, 'Gretchen am Spinnrade' (Gretchen at the Spinning-Wheel, D.118), written in 1814. The persistent figure in the piano part, suggesting the whirring of the spinning-wheel, gives unity to the song, in which the changing moods are reflected with unfailing sympathy. Particularly characteristic are the varied phrase-lengths and the ease with which the music moves through remote keys. The emotional impact of the song is overwhelming, and it is an astonishing product from a boy of seventeen. He had just read *Faust* for the first time and had obviously been deeply moved by Gretchen's agonized outpouring. She has fallen desperately in love with Faust and longs for death: the description of her emotions culminates in a passionate climax at the mention of his kiss. Of later settings, only that of Berlioz in *La Damnation de Faust* can rival Schubert's depth of emotion.

At this stage it would be idle to expect every song of Schubert's to reach the same high level as 'Gretchen.' He was endlessly enterprising, and his songs ranged from long rambling ballads to small and intimate lyrics. In 1814, he set F. Matthisson's 'Adelaide' (D.95), also set by Beethoven (op.46). Surprisingly, Schubert's is the sparer and more concise of the two. It does not have the luxuriance of Beethoven's setting, but there are some very characteristic touches in the final bars.

In 1815 Schubert wrote no less than 150 songs, including an astonishing number of masterpieces. The longest are the most variable in quality, but in 'Erlkönig' (The Erlking, D.328), the long narrative is handled with complete mastery. The words of Goethe's poem tell of a father who is riding home, carrying his small son; the Erlking casts an evil spell over the child, killing him. The song has a wealth of broad melody and a constant feeling of tension. Particularly subtle is the contrast between the setting of the Erlking's cajoling speeches: in the second speech both the words and the harmony move more quickly. As in 'Gretchen am Spinnrade,' the song is held together by a feature of the piano part, in this case the galloping of the horse. The poem had, of course, inspired many composers before Schubert, but the only setting that approaches his is a later one by Loewe.

During this period Schubert set innumerable poems by Goethe, including many exquisite miniatures such as 'Heidenröslein' (The Wild Rose, D.257), 'Meeres Stille' (Calm Sea, D.216) and 'Erster Verlust' (First Loss, D.226). One of the most striking is the setting of 'Freudvoll und leidvoll' (Joyful or woeful, D.210), the song sung by Klärchen in *Egmont*, which had previously been set by Reichardt. It contains only four lines, and in both settings the last,

Left: Title-page of the first edition of 'Erlkönig' (D.328). Composed in the late autumn of 1815, this song did more than any other to establish Schubert's name during his lifetime, and was the first of his works to appear in print with an opus number, op.1.

'Glücklich allein ist die Seele, die liebt' (Only the loving soul is happy) is repeated. With Reichardt this leads to a pleasant melodic climax, but Schubert produces a singular thrill by first quickening and then broadening the pace of the words, placing a perfectly timed high note towards the end. Another Goethe setting, 'Rastlose Liebe' (Love without Rest, D.138), is an astonishing outburst of passion.

There were other poets of lesser caliber whose work attracted Schubert. L. Kosegarten and L. Hölty inspired him to write small and intimate songs which are often of great charm. Hölty's 'An die Nachtigall' (To the Nightingale, D.196) is best known for Brahms's richly romantic setting, in which the lovesick poet can hardly bear the sweetness of the nightingale's song, but Schubert's version has a gentle and appealing pathos. 'Das Rosenband' (The Rosy Ribbon, D.280), a quiet garden scene, is a very attractive setting of a poem by F. G. Klopstock, later treated in a more ornate style by Richard Strauss. 'Die erste Liebe' (First Love, D.182), to words by Fellinger, is interesting for its continuous structure. It vividly describes the changing emotions of the lover, and has a splendid final climax. Looking back for a moment at Schubert's already voluminous output of songs, the first thing that strikes us is its extraordinary variety. Even so, it is significant that several songs of the period – including 'Erlkönig' – exist in several versions. With all his spontaneity of invention, he was certainly not lacking in self-criticism.

The songs of 1816 include, among fine things like the settings of the Harper's songs from *Wilhelm Meister* (D.325, D.478 and D.479), the magnificent setting of Goethe's 'An Schwager Kronos' (To Time as Postilion, D.369), where the immense energy is controlled by a feeling of endless spaciousness, which results from Schubert's love of modulation. This became an increasingly marked feature of his style. Changes of key that an earlier composer would have reserved for a special moment are used by Schubert as part of his ordinary language. In strong contrast to 'An Schwager Kronos,' is the charm and intimacy of another song of the same year,

Above: First page of the autograph of the song 'Gretchen am Spinnrade' (D.118), which is signed and dated 19 October 1814, when the final copy was made. Early in 1816 Schubert copied it out again and sent it, with a covering letter from Joseph von Spaun, to Goethe. He received no reply.

'An mein Clavier' (To my Piano, D.342), with words by C. F. D. Schubart, who was also responsible for those of 'Die Forelle.'

Songs were less numerous in 1817; the finest range from the floating, ethereal serenity of 'Ganymed' (D.544) to the grim and macabre power of 'Gruppe aus dem Tartarus' (Scene out of Hell, D.583), the most striking of Schubert's settings of Schiller, a poet who did not often inspire him to his highest level. One of the most endearing is 'An die Musik' (To Music, D.547), to words by Franz von Schober, which illustrates well Schubert's gift for writing an interesting bass line under a conventional, repeated chord accompaniment. Equally familiar are 'Die Forelle' (The Trout, D.550) and 'Der Tod und das Mädchen' (Death and the Maiden, D.531), both to be used later in instrumental works. Surpassing these is 'Litanei' (Litany, D.343) with its quiet and tender solemnity.

The year 1818 was unproductive, but in 1819 Schubert became a fellow-lodger of the poet Mayrhofer, which was undoubtedly a stimulus to song-writing. Mayrhofer was a serious and introverted character, and Schubert's settings of his poems often have a deeply thoughtful richness and nobility. On the whole the year was more distinguished for its instrumental music than its songs, but they include the powerful setting of Goethe's 'Prometheus' (D.674), where the declamatory style of some

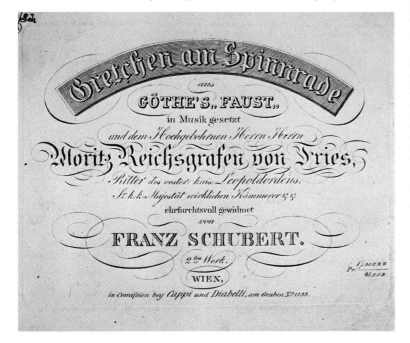

Above: Title-page of 'Gretchen am Spinnrade,' published in April 1821 as op.2 by Cappi & Diabelli. The song was first performed in private by Sophie von Linhart on 2 March 1821, and in public by the same singer on 20 February 1823. Schubert dedicated it to Count Moritz von Fries.

of the more diffuse early songs reappears under greater control, with a superb outburst of defiance at the end.

Schubert had by now made great strides as a song-writer, and his melodies had moved gradually away from the elegant and often operatic inflections of the later eighteenth century. Sometimes they show kinship with the popular Viennese street music of the time, but this influence is counteracted by Schubert's increasing variety of phrase-length, not a characteristic of popular music as a whole. For a composer of the caliber

of Mozart or Schubert the setting of words often leads to great subtlety of phraseology. This can be seen if we compare Schubert's two settings of Goethe's 'An den Mond' (To the Moon, D.259 and D.296), the second perhaps written in 1819 rather than 1815. The first is as symmetrical as a hymn-tune, the same music repeated for each stanza; the second is far more subtle rhythmically and has a very characteristic modulation in the third stanza. Schubert retained his love for chains of modulations through remote keys, but in later songs they are more controlled. Two songs that move through a number of keys in a small space are 'Stimme der Liebe' (Voice of Love, D.412), a passionate love-song to words by F. Stolberg, and 'An die Entfernte' (To the Distant One, D.765), by Goethe. In the Stolberg song, written in 1816, the effect is almost breathless, while in the later one, written in 1822, the modulations come with far greater ease and spontaneity.

• 1820-1823 •

The astonishing fluency in song-writing that came to Schubert in 1815 never returned to quite the same extent, but in quality and in widening emotional range his songs had developed steadily. The dramatic fire of 'Der Erlkönig' has become more flexible and sensitive; the warm lyricism of the best songs of 1815 is now maturer and more sustained, and in the early 1820s there is increasing evidence of the quiet depth and serenity that had first appeared, perhaps, in 'Meeres Stille' of 1815. Schubert's increased maturity as an instrumental composer did not diminish his enthusiasm for song-writing, though it may have affected it in some ways. In his later years he could still on occasion write songs of great length, but as a rule without the violent contrast of mood that appears in the earlier examples; this he reserved mainly for use in instrumental music, often, rather surprisingly, in slow movements.

The year 1820 was not particularly prolific, but its songs include 'Frühlingsglaube' (Belief in Spring, D.686), Schubert's only setting of words by L. Uhland. Its mixture of homeliness and sensitivity is particularly characteristic. The Goethe songs of 1821 include 'Grenzen der Menschheit' (Human Limits, D.716), which is almost Wagnerian in its solemn richness, and the two 'Suleika' poems, although they are in fact by Goethe's lover, Marianne von Willemer, and only 'revised' by the greater poet. Both are vividly evocative in Schubert's most spacious manner. The first is similar in mood to the first movement of the B minor Symphony (the 'Unfinished'), and in both songs the sixteenth notes of the piano part continue for pages on end with no suspicion of monotony. 'Versunken' (Absorbed, D.715), another Goethe song written in 1821, has the same feature, but the extreme instance is the enormously long 'Im Walde' (In the Forest, D.708), to words by Friedrich Schlegel. This is an extraordinary composition,

Right: A portrait of Schubert in watercolor by Wilhelm August Rieder, dating from 1825. According to Schubert's friends, this was one of the best portraits of the composer. Rieder, the son of a composer, knew Schubert very well, and certainly had met him before 1823.

lasting for thirteen pages, in which only twice, for a few measures, do the sixteenth notes in the piano part cease. The interest never flags for a moment, and we can see from such examples that Schubert, though he originally approached composition as a lyricist, could also plan works on a vast epic scale.

The piano parts – it would be unfair to call them accompaniments – of Schubert's songs are endlessly varied in their relationship with the vocal line. Sometimes the texture is spare and economical, as in the first of the two 'Heliopolis' songs (D.753-4): sometimes rich and somber, as in 'Freiwilliges versinken' (Willing Reverie, D.700), where the mysterious figures in the piano part produce a solemn and rather menacing atmosphere; sometimes a single rhythmic figure predominates, as in 'Geheimes' (Secret, D.719), with a charming lightness of touch.

In 1823 Schubert suffered a serious decline in health, but it is dangerous to draw too close a parallel between a composer's creative work and his everyday life. The songs of this year include 'Du bist die Ruh' (You are Rest, D.776), one of the most serene that he ever wrote, and 'Auf dem Wasser zu singen' (To be Sung on the Water, D.774), one of the most sparkling. The piano parts of both are a delight, surrounding the vocal line with a delicate haze.

The same year, he also returned once more to the long narrative ballad in 'Der Zwerg' (The Dwarf, D.771), an impossibly melodramatic poem by M. von Collin, but the music has great power and continuity. It was aptly described by Richard Capell as 'a link between Beethoven and Wagner.' Two long 'flower' ballads to words by Schober, were also composed in 1823,

'Viola' (Violet, D.76) and 'Vergissmeinnicht' (Forget-me-not, D.792). Both contain music of great charm, and 'Viola' is to some extent held together by a recurring refrain that results in a kind of random form, but the inordinate length of both songs has prevented them from achieving much popularity. Several other songs of this period are settings of what Richard Capell described as 'churchyard poetry': 'Schatzgräbers Begehr' (Treasure-seeker's Request, D.761) and 'Schwestergruss' (Sister's Greeting, D.762) are musically very impressive, especially the latter, in which the poet, wandering in the graveyard, meets his sister's ghost. She is living happily in Heaven and warns him that, unless he mends his ways, he will go elsewhere. In these songs Schubert showed himself capable of transcending in his music words of very poor quality.

• *Die schöne Müllerin* •

The autumn of 1823 was occupied mainly with the composition of the song-cycle *Die schöne Müllerin* (The Pretty Miller-Maid, D.795) settings of poems by Wilhelm Müller. Not a poet of great distinction, Müller was a few years senior to Schubert and died a year before him. The poems appear to have been written as a friendly parody of a type of rather self-consciously simple poetry that was beginning to sound old-fashioned, but Schubert took them with perfect seriousness. The cycle was published in 1824 as op.25 and dedicated to Baron Schönstein. Like Schumann's *Dichterliebe* (The Poet's Love), they tell a love-story that, after a happy beginning, turns to tragedy: the miller is eventually supplanted by his rival, the dashing huntsman, and drowns himself in the brook. The words are not great poetry, but their blend of homeliness and deep feeling made an obvious appeal to Schubert. They call mostly for simple and lyrical treatment, and many of the songs make so immediate an appeal that the cycle as a whole is in danger of being dismissed as being merely 'pretty.'

Beneath a deceptively simple exterior, however, it is a work of great subtlety. The plan is admirably balanced: the simple, mainly strophic songs at the beginning lead to two more continuous and extended ones, 'Mein!' (Mine!) and 'Pause' (Pause). After this, the songs become more concentrated as the situation grows more tense, and the cycle ends with the almost hypnotically strophic 'Des Baches Wiegenlied' (The Brook's Lullaby). The brook is constantly referred to throughout the songs, giving Schubert the opportunity to use his boundless inventiveness in the use of appropriate piano parts. In the first song, 'Das Wandern' (A-roving) the water is lively and bubbling; in 'Wohin?' (Whither?) it ripples along more gently; in 'Danksagung an den Bach' (Thanking the Brook) it is very leisurely; and in 'Am Feierabend' (After Work) it rushes feverishly. The first five songs are simple harmonically and do not move far away from their home key; the sixth, 'Der Neugierige' (The Questioner), ranges further afield and is one of the most sensitive. Of the four strophic songs that follow, the impulsive 'Ungeduld' (Impatience) and the gentle 'Morgengruss' (Morning Greeting) are outstanding. After the rapturous 'Mein!' the next song, 'Pause,' is particularly impressive with its deep thoughtfulness and the subtle interweaving of piano and voice.

In 'Der Jäger' (The Hunter) the music suggests the beginning of the young miller's jealousy. It bursts out more vehemently in 'Eifersucht und Stolz' (Jealousy and Pride), with the brook rushing in a mad torrent, and although the conclusion is in the major key, it brings no real hope or comfort. The major–minor antithesis plays an important part in the next four songs. In 'Die liebe Farbe' (The Favored Color) the changes from B major to B minor are angry and bitter. Green, the favorite color of his beloved, is now associated by the miller with the coat worn by his hated rival, and in this song reminiscences of 'Der Jäger' are brilliantly effective. 'Trockne Blumen' (Withered Flowers), in which the miller burns the flowers given to him by his former love, is in the bleakest minor until the last stanza, where a rather half-hearted E major falls back to E minor at the end. 'Der Müller und der Bach' (The Miller and the Brook) is a dialogue between man and nature in which bitterness has turned to gentle resignation. The change from minor to major towards the end is deeply moving.

'Des Baches Wiegenlied' sets a difficult task for the singer, with five stanzas all sung to the same music. But there is a typically Schubertian subtlety whereby an occasional interjection in

Below: Johann Christoph Erhard's *Rastende Künstler im Gebirge* of 1819, showing two artists in the mountains. This was the year that Schubert first visited the mountains of Upper Austria in the company of his friend the singer Johann Michael Vogl. The majesty of mountain scenery, in calm or storm, was a common theme in Romantic painting, poetry and music.

the piano part prevents the phraseology from becoming monotonous. Here the music is firmly rooted in its home key, with only brief glances elsewhere. Apart from the references to 'Der Jäger' in 'Die böse Farbe' (The Hateful Color), Schubert makes no attempt to unify the cycle thematically, as Beethoven had done in *An die ferne Geliebte* and Schumann was to do later. But the fact that the songs are mainly short and concentrated gives the cycle a kind of unity; even the more extended ones are never allowed to expand widely.

Schubert was a compulsive songwriter, and set to music almost any words he could lay hands on. It is true to say, however, that in general the better the quality of the text, the better the setting elicited from him, as with these poets: Heinrich Heine (1797-1856) in a drawing by Wilhelm Hensel dating from 1829 (*top left*); the writing conveys the observation in Heine's handwriting 'Eh bien, c'est moi!' (Well, this man is me!) – Friedrich Rückert (1788-1827), in a drawing by Franz Horny of 1818 (*above*) – Friedrich von Schiller (1759-1827), in a print of about 1794 (*left*) – and (*opposite*) Wilhelm Müller (1794-1827).

• 1824-1826 •

The year 1824 produced only a few songs, but these include 'Auflösung' (Dissolution, D.807), to words by Mayrhofer, in which the voice sings phrases of great breadth against a background of unceasing sixteenth notes. Though it is not long, it gives an impression of extraordinary spaciousness. The following year, 1825, was considerably more prolific, and produced the magnificent 'Die junge Nonne' (The Young Nun, D.828), one of the finest of Schubert's longer songs. The contrast between the tolling of the bell in the convent and the storm outside is vividly portrayed. There are fine variations of pace in the movement of the words, sometimes broad, sometimes pensive, and the final change from minor to major key is overwhelming. The finest of the smaller songs of 1825 is undoubtedly 'Im Abendrot' (Sunset Glow, D.799), with its marvelous stillness and serenity. Also very fine is 'Nacht und Träume' (Night and Dreams, D.827), one of the most quietly beautiful of all Schubert's songs. Particularly characteristic is the way in which the music floats mysteriously from B major to G minor with no intervening steps.

Other songs written in 1825 have affinities with instrumental works. 'Das Heimweh' (Homesickness, D.851), to words by Ladislaus Pyrker, is an extended song which begins in a bleak manner very similar to the opening of the great Piano Sonata in A minor (D.845). 'Die Allmacht' (The Almighty, D.852), a broad and magnificent outpouring, foreshadows in its opening the String Quintet in C major (D.956). The rich warmth of 'Fülle der Liebe' (Fullness of Love, D.856) finds more eloquent expression in the second movement of the Piano Sonata in D (D.850).

Early in 1826 Schubert returned for the last time to Goethe and to *Wilhelm Meister*. This fine group of songs includes his second settings of 'Heiss mich nicht reden' (Bid me not speak, D.877/2) and 'So lasst mich scheinen' (Such let me seem, D.877/3), richer and more polished than the earlier ones written in 1821. The second stanza of this setting of 'So lasst mich scheinen' contains one of Schubert's most startling modulations, suggested by the word 'Schmerz' (pain). Schubert also returned to 'Nur wer die Sehnsucht kennt' (Only he who knows what longing is, D.877/1&4). This poem has produced astonishingly varied reactions from different composers, ranging from the luxuriant sentiment of Tchaikovsky to the feverish intensity of Wolf. Schubert set it four times as a solo song, once as a male-voice part-song, and as a duet for soprano and bass or baritone. The solo settings are very dissimilar, the earliest, written in 1815, being warm and rich, and the latest, written for soprano in 1826, nostalgically melancholy. Of the two 1826 settings the duet is the more impressive, since it is in Schubert's grandest and most tragic manner.

The other songs of 1826 are interesting and varied. The earliest, 'Tiefes Leid' (Deep Sorrow, D.876) is a simple and hauntingly sad little song. 'Fischerweise' (Fisherman's Ditty, D.881), has something of the contented charm of 'Der Einsame' (The Recluse, D.800). Both songs are notable for the way in which a little figure that first appears in the left-hand of the piano part gradually finds its way into the vocal line. The familiar settings of Shakespeare's 'Hark, hark, the lark' ('Ständchen,' D.889) and 'Who is Sylvia?' ('An Silvia,' D.891) are so perfectly suited to the words that it is hard to believe that they were written for German translations. In 'Who is Sylvia?' the movement of the bass under the repeated chords looks ahead to the opening of the Piano Trio in B flat (D.898). Here it makes a particularly effective background for the broad, sustained phrases of the melody. 'Im Freien' (In the Open, D.880), to words by J. G. Seidl, has in its piano part a fluttering figure that reappears in the Impromptu in F minor (D.935/1).

• *Winterreise* •

The songs of 1826 are as remarkable in their variety as the instrumental music, which includes the String Quartet in G (D.887), one of the stormiest of Schubert's works, and the Piano Sonata in the same key (D.894), one of the most serene. On the other hand, although the year 1827 produced little instrumental music,

its most important vocal work was *Winterreise* (Winter Journey, D.911), one of Schubert's quite outstanding achievements.

In *Winterreise* Schubert returned again to the poems of Wilhelm Müller, and he himself said that the composition of these songs gave him more satisfaction than that of any others. The general character of the work can be felt vividly if it is put beside *Die schöne Müllerin*. In the earlier cycle, for all its sadness, the overall impression is of pathos rather than tragedy; in *Winterreise*, despite the great warmth of some of the music, there is a sense of stark despair, sometimes of a chillingly impersonal kind. In *Die schöne Müllerin* there is more narrative interest and a gradual change from happiness to sorrow. In *Winterreise* the poet has already been forsaken by his love, and we see him embarking on a sad and weary journey. The melancholy mood of the first song, 'Gute Nacht' (Good Night), is set by repeated chords similar to those in the opening measures of the slow movement of the 'Great' C major Symphony (D.944) and the Piano Trio in E flat (D.929). This is one of the few strophic songs in the cycle, but there are subtle differences between the stanzas. At the beginning of the last stanza the melody appears, with deeply nostalgic effect, in the major, but the song ends, inevitably, in

the minor. Having said his farewell the wanderer starts on his travels.

The second song, 'Die Wetterfahne' (The Weathervane), is bitterly sardonic in tone; it is in A minor, and the bare octaves at the beginning suggest other works in the same key. Here the glimpses of the major sound harsh and ironic. In 'Gefror'ne Tränen' (Frozen Tears) the mood is gentler, with strange, haunting echo effects in the piano part. 'Erstarrung' (Numbness) is broad and passionate, with a touching reminder of past happiness in its central section. It is followed by 'Der Lindenbaum' (The Linden Tree), the only song to find favor with Schubert's friend Schober when the cycle was first sung. Its simple, homely melody makes an immediate appeal, and its return, after a stormy central section, is particularly beautiful. A fine song in its own right, it is still more moving in its place in the cycle.

The next two songs are both concerned with water, but the atmosphere is far removed from the friendly 'Bächlein' of *Die schöne Müllerin*. 'Wasserflut' (Flood) is short and somber, with a widely sweeping melody: the wanderer senses his own tears as a river. In 'Auf dem Flusse' (On the River), the water is frozen, and the music suitably stark. Although the song is only four pages long, the extraordinary modulations

Above: The opening of Schubert's setting of 'Greisen-Gesang' (Song of the old man, D.778) to words by Friedrich Rückert, completed in the summer of 1822.

Opposite: Title-page of the first edition of the first half of *Die Winterreise* (D.911), published by Tobias Haslinger in January 1828. Schubert died on 19 November that year, and the complete *Winterreise* only appeared the next month.

Opposite above: Early Snow, by Caspar David Friedrich. The sense of winter's menace which pervades Müller's poems and Schubert's music in *Die Winterreise* finds equally strong expression in this work, probably painted in the same year the song-cycle appeared.

to remote keys suggest a vast, almost limitless landscape, especially towards the end. 'Rückblick' (Looking Back), which follows, is perhaps less striking, but its extrovert character is particularly effective in contrast to its somber neighbors.

'Irrlicht' (Will o' the Wisp) is in some ways similar to 'Wasserflut' in its widely sweeping phrases for the voice and the way in which the music sometimes seems to be wrenched back to its key. But its texture is more spare, with phrases that suggest the illusoriness of the phantom gleam. In 'Rast' (Rest) the wanderer describes how he had been given shelter by a charcoal-burner. Here the vocal phrases are still angular and sweeping, very unlike Schubert's more homely and domestic vein. They are sung against a very simple background, suggesting relief from physical weariness but not from unhappiness.

The theme of 'Frühlingstraum' (A Dream of Spring) is familiar: a happy dream followed by disillusionment. Both moods are vividly portrayed. There is something slightly unreal in the graceful melody with which the song opens, and the passage describing the cock-crow has a remarkable bitterness, with suggestions of the whole-tone scale. Like 'Wasserflut' and 'Rast,' it is strophic, and both stanzas end with a passage of great pathos in which a gentle A major subsides into a bleak A minor. The first half of the cycle ends with 'Einsamkeit' (Loneliness), in which the wanderer resents the quiet stillness of the night and longs for a storm. The music is quietly somber, with suggestions of something fiercer.

The second half opens with 'Die Post' (The Mail), in which the wanderer hears the sound of the post-horn, knowing that he will be disappointed. Here, for once, the words call for pathos rather than tragedy, and this is reflected in the music with great charm and sympathy. In 'Der greise Kopf' (The Grey Head) the wan-

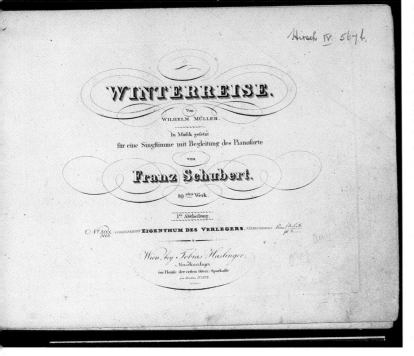

derer, seeing the hoar-frost on his hair, imagines that he has suddenly become old. It opens with a sweeping phrase played by the piano and repeated in a modified form more suited to the limited compass of the human voice. It would be interesting to know which version came first to Schubert. The brief glimpse of C major shortly before the end is deeply moving. Still darker is 'Die Krähe' (The Raven), a song of extraordinary power. The haunting melody, sometimes doubled by the pianist's right hand, and the fluttering figures above it produce a sinister atmosphere which descends to sepulchral gloom in the closing measures.

In 'Letzte Hoffnung' (Last Hope) the realistic suggestions of falling leaves lead to the deep pathos of the words 'Wein, wein, auf meiner Hoffnung Grab' (Weep, weep, on the grave of my hopes), which brings a warmth that is particularly moving after what has gone before it. 'Im Dorfe' (In the Village) is a kind of sinister nocturne, with suggestions of the barking of dogs and the rattling of chains. A beautiful but tantalizingly short lyrical passage in the middle suggests the first movement of the Piano Sonata in G (D.894), and the last page is very characteristic of Schubert in its solemnity and its glances towards a distant key.

The next two songs are very concentrated. In 'Der stürmische Morgen' (The Stormy Morning) the wanderer welcomes the storm that seems to echo his own despair: the ruthless directness of the opening suggests Handel. 'Täuschung' (Delusion) describes a flickering light that may be only a hallucination; the music has a dreamlike charm similar to the opening of 'Frühlingstraum.' In 'Der Wegweiser' (The Signpost) the wanderer sees a sign that appears to him to be pointing to his own grave. This song is one of the greatest of the cycle, similar in shape to 'Auf dem Flusse.' Both songs have a central section in the major key, and explore mysterious and remote tonal regions in their final pages. The repeated notes of the opening phrase of 'Der Wegweiser' sound increasingly sinister and fatalistic towards the end of the song.

The remaining four songs are all on a small scale. In 'Das Wirtshaus' (The Inn) the wanderer sees the graveyard as an inn, but knows that he will find no hospitality there. The music is surprisingly gentle, but with touches of bitterness and disillusionment. The next song, 'Mut' (Courage), is an outburst of defiance, in which passages in the major sound fiercely ironical. In 'Die Nebensonnen' (The False Suns) the wanderer has a hallucination in which he sees three suns. The music is quiet and pathetic, with no

suggestion of sentimentality. The cycle ends with 'Der Leiermann' (The Organ Grinder), in which the wanderer meets an old beggar, making music in a void. It is a dialogue between the voice and the pianist's right hand over an unchanging drone bass. Only towards the end do the two elements of voice and piano coalesce, just before the voice sings its highest note. The song is remarkable not only for its cold and eerie atmosphere, but also for its very skillful construction. It foreshadows the music of many later composers, especially Musorgsky, in its extreme spareness.

• Last songs •

The finest songs of 1828, Schubert's last year, were collected after his death under the title *Schwanengesang* (Swan Song, D.957). In addition to these there is a group to words by Leitner, and two other extended pieces, 'Auf Strom' (On the River, D.943), with horn or cello *obbligato*, and 'Der Hirt auf dem Felsen' (The Shepherd on the Crag, D.965), with clarinet *obbligato*. The latter has great charm, with a magical passage in G major shortly before the quick final section. It was written in October 1828, the same month as 'Die Taubenpost' (The Carrier Pigeon), the last of *Schwanengesang*. It is not known which of these was Schubert's last composition, but in their different ways they show a freshness astonishing in a composer who was desperately ill and not far from his death.

Of the poems of *Schwanengesang* seven are by Rellstab, six by Heine and one by Seidl; they were never intended to be a cycle. Of the songs with words by Rellstab, 'Kriegers Ahnung' (Warrior's Foreboding) is unique in its almost operatic character and contains some powerful and moving music, though the return of the opening mood seems almost too short. With 'Ständchen' (Serenade), which is comparable in popularity to 'Ave Maria' (D.839), Schubert's alterations of major and minor are particularly subtle and sensitive. On the last page the overlappings of the vocal and instrumental phrases produce a remarkable tension. It is a song of great depth, not an elegant drawing-room ballad. 'In der Ferne' (Far from Home), despite fine moments, is less impressive as a whole, perhaps through excessive reiteration of a too familiar rhythm.

It is tantalizing that Schubert only came into contact with the poetry of Heine in the last year of his life. In his six settings of Heine's words he combined his most powerful imagination with the biting terseness that is so characteristic of the poems. Heine attracted other composers; in Schumann's *Dichterliebe* the warmth of the music and the spareness of the words produced something uniquely moving. Brahms's few settings of Heine include 'Der Tod, das ist die kühle Nacht' (Death, that is the cool night, op.96/1), one of his greatest songs. And there is, of course, Mendelssohn's 'Auf flügeln des

Below: Pencil caricature by Franz von Schober entitled 'Michael Vogl and Franz Schubert marching to battle and victory.' Vogl met Schubert in the composer's father's circle of acquaintances, and their relationship was of inestimable benefit for Schubert's development as a song writer.

Gesanges' (On the Wings of Song, op.34/2), of which Heine said, somewhat incredibly, 'it has no melody,' and the brilliant 'Neue Liebe' (New Love, op.19a/4). But in none of these is there the uncanny power of Schubert's settings.

Of these the first is 'Der Atlas' (The Titan Atlas), one of Schubert's grimmest and most powerful songs. Ever since his early years he had been attracted by a dramatic, declamatory style, first in the long, rambling narrative ballads of his boyhood, and later in songs like 'Prometheus.' But never before 'Der Atlas' had he used it with such terrifying directness and concentration. The song occupies only three pages and is dominated by the sinister phrase that first appears under a tremolo. Sometimes, as in 'Der Krähe,' the voice doubles the bass of the piano part, producing a stark, uncompromising effect. The last line contains an agonized cadence. 'Ihr Bild' (Her Picture), with its touching but severely restrained pathos, looks towards Brahms, especially in the unexpected return to the minor in the final bars. 'Das Fischermädchen' (The Fisher Maid), lighter in mood than the other, has a charming, barcarolle-like measure, with very characteristic touches. The three remaining Heine songs show Schubert at his most atmospheric.

In 'Die Stadt' (The City) the poem describes a city by the sea, wrapped in mist, where long ago the poet had lost his love. The most astonishing thing in the song is the persistent use of the diminished seventh; here its effect is wholly impressionistic, giving a suggestion of gray,

unbroken monotony. Towards the end there is a brief climax, but the song ends inconclusively with the mysterious harmony unresolved. In 'Am Meer' (By the Sea) a man and woman sit on the shore and her tears fall on his hand. Here the atmosphere is of an unearthly calm, with the very impressive opening and concluding bars giving a suggestion of the sea. Unusually for so late a song, it is basically strophic, with new and poignant touches in the second stanza. The woman's tears are gently and sensitively suggested at the end of each stanza.

The extraordinary depth of this song reappears in a still more somber mood in 'Der Doppelgänger' (The Double). Here the poet, visiting a house that he had known long ago, is confronted by his own specter. The words are sung to short phrases, eventually rising to a climax of great power, and then dying softly away. The piano part consists mainly of bleak, bare chords; for one moment, towards the end, the music is wrenched violently away from its key, and there is a deeply impressive harmonic touch in the final bars. 'Der Doppelgänger,' like 'Der Leiermann,' suggests many new paths that Schubert might have taken had he lived longer, but the setting of Seidl's 'Die Taubenpost,' which was written after the Heine songs, shows Schubert at his most genial and amiable. After 'Der Doppelgänger' it comes almost as a shock, but in its own right it is a song of much charm. The two together suggest the unbounded range that has assured Schubert's place among the greatest of song-writers.

Above: A ball game during a visit of the Schubertians to Atzenbrugg. The landscape is by Schober, while Schwind is supposed to have drawn the figures. Schubert is on the right of the group of three men sitting in the center foreground, and the violinist is Kraissl, a musician and landscape painter.

ROMANTIC MUSIC

CARL DAHLHAUS

The term 'Romantic' as it is commonly used with reference to music seems to be perfectly straightforward: all music written after that of the first Viennese school and before the modern music of the twentieth century is considered to be Romantic. A more precise definition would be the music composed between 1814-15, the dates of Schubert's 'Erlkönig' and 'Gretchen am Spinnrade,' and 1907, the year in which Schoenberg committed himself to atonality in music. The term was applied to music at an early date, but in the celebrated review by E. T. A. Hoffmann – writer and musician – of Beethoven's instrumental music, written in 1810, it is the work of the Viennese Classical composers which is described as Romantic. Hoffmann wrote: 'Mozart and Haydn, the creators of present-day instrumental music, first showed us Art in her full glory; the one who beheld her full of love and penetrated her inmost being is – Beethoven. The instrumental compositions of all three masters breathe the same romantic spirit, which comes from the same grasp that each has of the actual substance of Art. . . . Haydn interprets the human part of human life in a romantic way. . . . Mozart lays claim to the metaphysical, the wondrous, which dwells in the inner spirit. . . . Beethoven's music moves the lever of fear, of dread, of horror, of pain, and wakens the infinite longing that is the essence of the romantic.'

The idea of a Romantic era in music – as opposed to the 'Classical' era – can, therefore, be extremely confusing, not only because of the literary origins of the term, but also because of doubt as to the period to which it should refer. In the first place, it is generally accepted that an attitude to music which can fairly be described as 'Romantic' was already in existence in the 1790s in discussions on esthetics found in such works as Wackenroder's *Herzensergiessungen eines kunstliebenden Klosterbruders* ('The heartfelt outpourings of an art-loving monk,' 1797), or Wackenroder and Tieck's *Phantasien über die Kunst* ('Fantasies on Art,' 1799). Despite the general belief that theory lags behind practice, we see that in this instance the writers on the subject anticipated the music inspired by the same Romantic spirit by about a decade and a half.

Secondly, the continued existence of musical Romanticism into the second half of the nineteenth century poses further problems. The period that followed the failure of the European Revolutions of 1848-9 and the 'downfall of Hegelianism,' was generally characterized by Positivism – in the field of science – and Realism – in literature and painting. Romantic, or neo-Romantic music, such as we have after 1850 in the music-dramas of Wagner, in Brahms's chamber music and songs, or in Bruckner's symphonies, represents Romanticism in an age of Positivism (which contradicts the idea of a *Zeitgeist* that permeates all manifestations of art and society). Furthermore, it is Romanticism of the highest order, and although Romanticism did also survive in the fields of literature and painting, there it is of poorer quality.

The habit of referring to Schubert, Schumann and Mendelssohn, Weber, Berlioz and Meyerbeer, Wagner and Liszt, as well as Brahms and Bruckner, collectively as Romantic composers is so firmly entrenched that it would be pointless to insist on a change. However, we cannot pretend that there is such a thing as a Romantic era with clearly definable universal characteristics. The historian who takes seriously the names attached to eras, instead of merely using them as convenient though meaningless labels, is inevitably irritated by the question as to whether common or at least similar characteristics allow us to call Schumann and Mendelssohn on the one hand, and Berlioz and Meyerbeer on the other, Romantics. One hesitates to give Verdi, Bizet or Musorgsky the same title, and the term 'late Romantic' to cover Mahler and Strauss is used only for want of a better label to attach to the *fin-de-siècle* atmosphere that typifies the last decade of the nineteenth century, a 'sense of impending modernism,' as Hermann Bahr described it.

However, it is possible to propose solutions to the problems confronting the historian, problems that are posed by the fact that Romantic attitudes towards music were expressed in the 1790s in anticipation of the music itself, by the startling national and individual differences and contradictions found among Romantic composers, and by the historical anomaly of the existence of Romanticism or neo-Romanticism in an age of Positivism. First, we can show that the real origins of Romanticism throughout Europe are to be found in the late eighteenth century; then, that in the Romantic movement at the beginning of the nineteenth century national differences became more marked than before; and finally, that in the music of the later nineteenth century, features associated with Realism also play a significant role alongside the predominant Romantic features. These propositions are reinforced by the fact that the superficially widely divergent national styles of Romanticism in the early nineteenth century – German, French and Italian – can only be understood when they are seen as related manifestations of the same phenomenon with common roots in the eighteenth century.

• Romantic and Classic in Weimar and Vienna •

If we look first at literature, bearing in mind that the musical definition of the term 'Romantic' was always determined by literary definitions, then it is undeniable, taking Europe as a whole, that the history or pre-history of Romanticism begins in about 1770 (unless one chooses to go back as far as Rousseau). The similarities between what in England is called 'early Romanticism' and in Germany is labeled 'Sturm und Drang' are unmistakable, and they cannot be dismissed as mere influences. Nor should we be misled by the fact that in his esthetics – and in a few other works – Goethe was a Classicist; in European terms both his *Werther* and his *Faust* are Romantic works. In Germany, Romanticism is often contrasted with the 'Weimar Classicism' of Goethe, Schiller, Wieland and Herder, partly because of the personal animosity between Schiller, seen as a representative of Classicism, and Friedrich Schlegel, representing the Romantic camp. However, viewed from a European perspective, it is clear that the opposite pole to Romanticism is in reality French Rationalism of the early eighteenth century and French Classicism. These were adapted by the Germans in an eclectic way; indeed the classicistic phase of the Weimar group was only a brief passing one. Furthermore, it is important to understand that although pre-Romantic literature in France in the eighteenth century was stifled by the politically motivated Classicism of the Revolution and the Empire, literature written by French *émigrés* in Germany like Chateaubriand and Madame de Staël had a decidedly Romantic flavor. French literary historians tend always to look upon the furor over Victor Hugo's *Hernani* in 1830 as marking the beginning of Romanticism, instead of seeing this in Sénancour's *Oberman* (1804) or Chateaubriand's *René* (1805). The prejudice inherent in this view, namely that all major literary decisions are to be found in the tragic theater rather than in prose fiction, was dispelled by the Romantic movement itself.

In musical history it was Viennese Classicism (the name having been coined by analogy with Weimar Classicism) that appears to have stood in the way of the extension of the literary concept of the term 'Romantic' to apply to music. When E. T. A. Hoffmann in 1810 labeled Haydn and Mozart as Romantic composers alongside

Opposite: Johann Paul Richter (1763-1825), the German writer who used the pseudonym Jean Paul. His novels, full of irony and sentiment, were very popular in the early years of the century. He was the greatest literary influence on Schumann, who much admired his style and later developed, as did Jean Paul, the idea of the dual personality.

Opposite below: The philosopher Arthur Schopenhauer (1788-1860). He attributed the powerful effect of music to its being the embodiment not of ideas, like the other arts, but of the Will, the active principle itself. The harmonic basis of music is comparable to the structure of nature, and melody to the enlightened life and striving of man.

Herzensergießungen
eines
kunstliebenden Klosterbruders.

von
Wackenroder

Berlin.
Bey Johann Friedrich Unger.
1 7 9 7.

Above: The title-page of the first edition of *The Heartfelt outpourings of an art-loving monk*, 1797, a collection of essays on art by Wilhelm Wackenroder (1773-98). His theory was that intellectual criticism destroys our appreciation of art, and his work became a sort of Bible for the young Romantics of his time.

Right: Ludwig Tieck (1773-1853). A prominent literary figure in Germany, much influenced by Wackenroder, his close friend and collaborator. He completed Friedrich Schlegel's translation of Shakespeare and from 1825 was dramatic adviser to the Dresden Theater.

Beethoven, he was thinking of other criteria than the revolutionary changes in European thought in the late eighteenth century.

To describe the period of Viennese Classicism simply as a phase within the evolution of Romanticism throughout Europe would be little short of revolutionary, in terms both of the layman's musical terminology and of the writing of history. However, there is much to support the idea that our hypothesis of the roots of Romanticism being found in the eighteenth century can also be applied to music. The metaphysical, Romantic approach to instrumental music adopted by Wackenroder, Tieck and Hoffmann was applied to the music of the Viennese Classicists. It is often said that Hoffmann's interpretation of Beethoven's music is merely a Romantic misconception of it. But, given that our understanding of Beethoven's music was governed for a century by it, the historian should hesitate before dismissing it so lightly. In fact, some of the esthetic premises that formed the basis of early Romanticism around 1770 were also shared by the Viennese Classicists (insofar as we can infer implicit musical ideas from their dislike of explicit utterance on musical thought). The idea of originality that guided Haydn, the explanation of a work of art as an organism instead of a mechanism that is crucial to our understanding of Mozart, and the ideal of the sublime work of art that Beethoven made his own, all belong to the history of a Romanticism whose roots are to be found in the later eighteenth century.

This does not mean that Haydn, Mozart and Beethoven were in reality Romantic composers. It is, however, possible to say without exaggeration that the features that the Viennese Classicists and the real Romantic composers had in common – features that developed towards the end of the eighteenth century in opposition to French Classicism and Rationalism – were more significant than those that divided them. If we look upon Romanticism not as the antithesis of Weimar or Viennese Classicism but of French Classicism (in operatic terms the Metastasian form of *opera seria*), then we can discern a common basis, revealing gentle continuity rather than upheaval, in the progression from the eighteenth century to the nineteenth.

• The metaphysics of German Romanticism •

No one will challenge the assertion that the ideas that brought such tremendous change to the European way of thinking towards the end of the eighteenth century have their genesis several centuries earlier. This does not, however, detract from the fact that it was only in their confrontation with French Classicism and Rationalism that they became a tangible force in the evolution of ideas. The concept of a work of art as an organism can be traced back to Aristotle; the esthetic of the sublime can be

Above: Germania et Italia by Friedrich Overbeck (1789-1869). From Goethe onwards Italy signified art and freedom to the German Romantic imagination. Overbeck's ideals were the German and Italian Renaissance painters such as Dürer and Raphael, and he was much influenced by the writers Wackenroder, Tieck and Schlegel.

Left: Pastel by Carl Arnold, *c.*1855, of a quartet evening at the house of Bettina von Arnim (1785-1859), a colorful personality in artistic circles in Germany and a great hostess. In her youth, as Bettina von Brentano, she was a friend of both Goethe and Beethoven.

said to have originated in a tract written probably in the first century AD by an author known as Longinus, which was given currency by the English philosopher Shaftesbury in the early eighteenth century; the ideals of genius and originality can be said to have been expressed in the sixteenth century by Julius Caesar Scaliger in defining the poet as an 'alter deus.' The historical approach to the evolution of ideas is also hinted at by French jurists in the service of the Fronde against Louis XIV during the seventeenth century, who were trying to understand medieval civilization. However, 'prehistory,' in which ideas are conceived, though as yet in isolation and without wide-reaching effect, differs from 'history' itself, in which these same ideas, inextricably interrelated, begin to determine general consciousness.

If the above is true, it implies that the 'organism' concept, the ideal of originality, the esthetic of the sublime and the historical approach (as opposed to a Classicism based on the 'mechanism' concept, the theory of imitation, an esthetic based exclusively on the realization of beauty and a way of thinking that transcends time) together form an interrelated bundle of

Left: Musical Reunion by Wilhelm Ferdinand Bendz. Chamber music plays a role in the Romantic cult of comradeship.

Below: Carl Friedrich Schinkel's design for Hoffmann's opera *Undine*, 1816. Based on La Motte Fouqué's story of the love of a mortal for the water-nymph Undine, this was one of the most important Romantic operas before Weber. Another version was set by Lortzing in 1845 which had more lasting success. Schinkel, whose architecture epitomizes the spirit of German Romantic Classicism, also designed sets for Mozart's *Die Zauber-flöte* (Berlin, 1816).

ideas that began to take effect towards the end of the eighteenth century and were the basis of Romanticism in Europe in the nineteenth century. The question then remains as to what extent and how Romantic musical ideals in Germany, or to be more precise, those of Wackenroder, Tieck and E. T. A. Hoffmann, differed from those prevailing in the rest of Europe. The answer is not hard to find. The Romantic ideals expressed by German writers represent a metaphysical view of instrumental music with two significant features. First, these ideals are expressed in metaphysical and not in psychological terms, and second, it is a theory of instrumental music that does not apply to opera.

Writings on music in the eighteenth century, although referring simply to 'music,' were primarily concerned with opera, whose pre-eminence was practically taken for granted. The French Encyclopedists, whose influence in Europe cannot be underestimated, dismissed instrumental music as an empty though pleasant noise, not fit to be the subject of serious musical discussion. When E. T. A. Hoffmann expressed the view that 'absolute' instrumental music was music in its purest form, he was

making a revolutionary statement – a 'change of paradigm,' as Thomas Kuhn would have said. Ever since Plato, music had been seen as the unity of *Harmonia* (regulated tonal relationships), *Rhythmos* and *Logos*; and *Logos* had always been interpreted as language, the basis of vocal music. In the Romantic era the vocal text was looked upon as an 'extra-musical' feature. Eduard Hanslick, who gave a new positivistic appraisal of the Romantic legacy in the second half of the century, redefined the *Logos* as being the spirit of the music, a spirit that manifested itself in the music independently from any text.

The Romantic claim that instrumental music was the pre-eminent form does, in fact, correspond to the pattern in the output of Haydn, Mozart and, above all, Beethoven. The Viennese school – in spite of Mozart's operas – was regarded throughout Europe as the 'German school of instrumental music.' The string quartet and the symphony joined the opera as its peers. The belief in the pre-eminence and 'paradigmatic' significance of 'absolute' instrumental music (by which is meant non-functional and non-programmatic music) acted as the binding agent between 'Classical' music and 'Romantic' ideals; furthermore, to the rest of Europe it was a specifically 'German school' – to use the term current at the time. It is this European view that helps us discern the national characteristic – the emphasis on instrumental music and its metaphysical significance; it also narrows the gap between German Classical and German Romantic music in a way not possible in a nationally oriented history of music.

There are few who would challenge the view that in terms of compositional techniques the Classical and Romantic periods form a whole, a view succinctly argued by Friedrich Blume in his entries on 'Klassik' and 'Romantik' in the encyclopedia *Musik in Geschichte und Gegenwart*. Between what Hugo Riemann labeled the 'Basso-continuo Era' and the radically new approach to music at the beginning of the twentieth century, the techniques employed – harmonic tonality, periodic structure and the manipulation of thematic material – remained largely unchanged. Although Blume did not perhaps pay enough attention to the emergence of new genres – for example, the development of the *Lied* and of the lyrical piano pieces unknown before the Romantic period, the way in which the string quartet gave way to chamber music involving the piano, and the way the symphonic tone poem (as opposed to the concert overture, from which it grew) deposed the symphony as the pre-eminent form – this does not substantially detract from the pertinence of his argument that compositionally the Classical and Romantic periods do not fundamentally differ.

The fact that German Romantic esthetics are expressed in metaphysical – and not psychological – terms, however, means no less than that the writers saw in 'absolute' instrumental music, freed from functional and programmatic elements, something of the 'essence' behind the mere 'outward appearances' (*Erscheinungen*),

as Schopenhauer would have said. In short, previously downgraded instrumental music became an 'instrument of metaphysics' (Schelling). In the history of ideas the principle of absolute music goes back to the old literary formula that the most crucial thoughts and emotions cannot be expressed in words. Whereas in the eighteenth century the language of instrumental music, because of its non-conceptual nature, had been considered inferior to the language of words, under Wackenroder, Tieck, E. T. A. Hoffmann and Schopenhauer music was elevated above mere words. 'Absolute' music became a language that gave access to thoughts and emotions not capable of formulation in the language of words. The old literary formula was transformed in music to become a new, revolutionary doctrine that was to govern the attitude of the cultured middle classes in Germany towards instrumental music – and above all to the symphonies and late quartets of Beethoven – throughout the nineteenth century into the early twentieth.

If we bear in mind that in Italy and France – forgetting for the moment Berlioz, who managed to create a complex relationship between symphonic and operatic styles – musical history in the nineteenth century was and remained, as in the eighteenth century, the history of opera, and that musical ideals, being operatic ideals, were governed by psychological and literary categories, then we see that the metaphysics of instrumental music, both in the form they took, and in their object (the symphony and the string quartet) are a specifically German phenomenon. Looked at from a European point of view, Viennese Classicism and Romantic musical esthetics in the 1790s grew together to form a whole, the crucial feature being the primacy

Above: An early English edition of the *Marseillaise* composed in 1792 by Rouget de Lisle (*right*). The famous song was propagated with amazing speed. It was several times proscribed, but was always sung at the barricades and was much heard during the July Revolution. In 1830 Berlioz made an arrangement for chorus and orchestra.

Top right: Cartoon by Honoré Daumier, October 1833. The King being crushed in the press was a reminder that the free press should not be stifled again as it had been under the last Bourbon king.

accorded to instrumental music. No one will deny that the metaphysical interpretation derives exclusively from Romantic authors and was by no means intended by the Classical composers themselves. Haydn and Beethoven were governed by the ideal of producing something 'characteristic,' and Beethoven over and above that by a concept of the sublime style that had already formed the basis of the article on the 'Sinfonie' in Sulzer's *Allgemeine Theorie der schönen Künste* (General Theory of the Fine Arts). However, this must be aligned historically with the equally firm fact that Classical instrumental music was received in the nineteenth century in the Romantic spirit. Without wishing to enter into the complex question of the theory and history of the reception of music, it must be said that we cannot know *a priori* whether it is the intentions of the composer or the current mainstream ideas that in the last resort definitely determine the 'spirit' that is embodied in any work of music. Nonetheless, the history of the reception of music represents one further argument why the European view, in which Viennese Classicism and Romantic ideals are brought closer together, must be considered the most convincing.

• French Romanticism: Berlioz and Meyerbeer •

The idea that the *Symphonie fantastique* by Berlioz marks the beginning of Romanticism (or, at all events, of Romanticism proper) in French music, is one of the generally accepted facts of musical history. However, Edward Dent argued that some of the operas of the Revolutionary period, such as *Lodoïska* (1791) and *Elisa* (1794) by Cherubini, deserve to be called Romantic both in terms of the music and the

117

dramatic techniques involved. The problem then becomes a semantic one, because we do not seem to know the criteria on which a work can be definitively described as Romantic or pre-Romantic.

It is, in fact, possible to deem it mere coincidence that the first performance of the *Symphonie fantastique* took place in 1830, the year of the Revolution – the year also in which the furor broke out over Victor Hugo's *Hernani*, the 'official' beginning of Romanticism in French literature. On the other hand, the coincidence of political, literary and musical events makes it extremely difficult for us not to speak of a turning-point in history and describe this epoch-making year in terms of the *Zeitgeist*, a term that became much in vogue in the 1840s.

The July monarchy, which began in 1830, the era of the *juste milieu*, found musical expression in the minds of those living at that time – a perspective that should not be dismissed lightly by the historian – not so much in the music of Berlioz as in that of Meyerbeer. The assertion that Berlioz and Meyerbeer together represented neo-Romanticism in France is clearly a compromise, but one that deserves to be taken seriously, even though it derives from Richard Wagner (*Oper und Drama*, 1851) and was not originally meant as a compliment. The statement challenges us to find a satisfactory category, not just a label such as neo-Romantic, that establishes the affinity between these two – on the face of it – totally different composers.

The works with which Berlioz has made his mark in the repertoire and established himself historically are symphonies (*Symphonie fantastique* and *Harold en Italie*), symphonic cantatas (*Roméo et Juliette*) and scenic oratorios (*Damnation de Faust*). Despite the influence of Beethoven's concept of symphonic style, these works do not belong to the tradition of absolute music but are unmistakably the product of a particular country, or to be more precise, a particular city, where musical thought and ideals – unlike those of Germany – were still primarily oriented to the opera. Although it would be doing Berlioz an injustice to describe him as an operatic composer *manqué*, we must concede that his music always had a quasi-dramatic element. The habit of dividing his output into such categories as 'programmatic symphony,' 'symphonic cantata' and 'scenic oratorio' should not lead us to overlook the fact that Berlioz – whether he was writing for orchestra alone or for orchestra with choir (or even with a speaker) – was invariably guided by the same ideal. His aim was to create, with musical means, a dramatic scenario – what Théophile Gautier would call a *scène idéale* – that was not a poor relation of an opera; on the contrary, the imaginary succession of scenes was intended to transcend the limitations of real opera. We are reminded by this of those dramas by Byron such as *Manfred* that are for reading and not for staging. In *Les Troyens*, Berlioz's attempt at grand opera, we see how he tried to make a compromise between phantasmagoric drama conveyed in symphonic terms

and the realities of the operatic stage, with which he had to come to terms.

The *scène idéale* imagined by Berlioz is related to real opera, of which Giacomo Meyerbeer was the most celebrated representative during the time of the July monarchy, with *Robert le diable* as his first great triumph. This is because both composers, for all the differences in the genres in which they wrote, were governed by a scenic principle in music and as such stood in contradistinction not only to German instrumental music but also to the Italian operatic tradition. Given the existing dichotomy between German symphonic writing and Italian *opera seria* that dominated the esthetic considerations of contemporaries in the early nineteenth century, the principle of 'scenic music' in the French sense has to be seen as a 'third musical culture.' The fundamental principle behind the operas of Meyerbeer is not that of a 'number' performed by a solo singer or an ensemble, in which the scenic element and the dramatic fable are nothing more than the excuse for the music. Instead, he created the *tableau* of music and drama, in which the music has to be justified by the drama and the drama cannot stand without the music.

If the idea of 'scenic music' therefore appears to be one of the characteristic features of French

Above: Freedom or Death – an Allegory on Revolution (1794-5) by Jean-Baptiste Regnault. Painted just after the Reign of Terror, the figure on the left holds aloft the red cap of the French revolutionaries.

Opposite: Manuscript of part of Act I of *La Caverne* by Le Sueur. The opera, based on an episode in *Gil Blas*, the picaresque romance by Lesage, and on Schiller's *Die Räuber*, is about the rescue of Séraphine, abducted by brigands to their hideout in a cave. First performed at the Théâtre Feydeau in Paris in 1793, it was notable for its combination of elements from *opera seria*, *opera buffa* and *opéra comique*. The same theme was also set by Méhul.

Romantic music, it is a valid objection to point out that Meyerbeer is not normally included among the Romantics. The choice of subject-matter by his librettist Eugène Scribe is unmistakably Romantic, with recourse to the demons of the Middle Ages (*Robert le diable*) as well as the preference for historic drama (*Les Huguenots, Le Prophète*) in which history is not merely used as a means of finding names and places for intrigues of love but is real and present, a force capable of moving the masses as depicted on stage. No one will deny all this, but this does not entitle us to label French grand opera *in toto* as Romantic. What led Wagner to join the names of Berlioz and Meyerbeer as French neo-Romantics was the fact that both composers followed the ideal of art as being 'characteristic' – and this in the early nineteenth century, as a precursor of later Realism, was a sign of modernity.

Right: The Entombment of Atala (1808) by Girodet-Trioson, is based on a scene from a story by Chateaubriand. The Indian maiden Atala, a Christian, unable to choose between her love for Chactas whom she has saved, and her vow to her dying mother to take the veil, kills herself and is buried in the forest. *Atala* was originally intended to be part of an epic set among a tribe of American Indians, but was published as part of Chateaubriand's apology for Christianity: *Le Génie du Christianisme* (1802).

Goethe and Humboldt in the 1790s had looked upon that which 'characterizes' as being a sub-compartment of beauty (*das Schöne*). Friedrich Schlegel at the turn of the century, however, in his complex historical and philosophical body of writings, saw that which is 'characteristic' as being the antithesis of beauty and the hallmark of the current Romantic epoch. In music – laying aside some of the scenes from Weber's operas – it was in French Romantic music that this 'esthetic of the characteristic' took its most extreme form.

Classically oriented critics have described the characteristic features of the music of Berlioz and of Meyerbeer as being 'totally fragmented,' They have claimed that melodic lines are broken up unnecessarily simply for the sake of momentary musical effects that are not called for by the music itself, but justified only by the dramatic events – real or imaginary. But the principle of melodic discontinuity, surprise and unpredictability formed an integral part of Berlioz's music, as did the ability to convey a *couleur locale* in musical terms – which for Berlioz and

Meyerbeer meant nothing less than an 'emancipation of timbres.' This descriptive element is one of the salient features of a form that achieved in music the 'characteristic' ideal, as opposed to the traditional ideals of beauty, in the same way as Byron – Berlioz's idol – had achieved it in literature.

• Pre-Romanticism in Italian opera •

Dent's idea that Cherubini's rescue operas *Lodoïska* (1791) and *Elisa* (1794), together with *La Caverne* (1793) by Le Sueur, represent an early form of French Romanticism is supported by the fact that he relates Romantic features in opera with contemporary events in the fields of German and English literature that are universally accepted as being Romantic. These phenomena, as mentioned earlier, find their counterparts in French literature, provided we do not concentrate our gaze solely on the history of tragedy in France and concede that novels such as *René* by Chateaubriand and *Oberman* by Sénancour mark the dawn of a new era. The musical devices employed by Cherubini and Le Sueur (who was Berlioz's teacher) can justifiably be labeled Romantic or at least pre-Romantic. In *La Caverne*, which Le Sueur based on Schiller's play *Die Räuber*, we note an almost excessive use of chromaticism, and in Cherubini's *Elisa* the musical depiction of the mountainous setting is not merely a depiction of the *couleur locale* but is an integral part of the work, musically and dramatically, in much the same way as the forest is treated in Weber's *Der Freischütz*.

If we move to the history of opera in Italy, the controversial era between 1790 and 1830 presents the historian with numerous problems that remain peculiarly difficult to resolve. This is the period that marks the transition from the Metastasian genre of *opera seria* with its succession of 'exit arias' to the innovatory techniques introduced by Bellini and Donizetti. The main obstacle has been the insistence of writers on concentrating on Viennese Classicism, which has stood in the way of a solution to – or even a formulation of – the problems facing the scholar trying to understand the evolution of music throughout Europe. Yet no serious scholar can really be tempted to turn the actual historical situation upside down and deny French and Italian opera the pre-eminence it enjoyed at the time, relegating the operatic composers to the status of mere satellites to the central figures of the Viennese school.

Definitive works on the subject have yet to appear, but it emerges from preliminary investigations that around 1790 many and various changes began to take place that would justify us in talking of 'pre-Romanticism.' In the *opera seria* the most significant structural change was the introduction of ensemble numbers (*pezzi concertati*) and choruses even within an act. The fact that this innovation was taken over from *opera buffa* should not detract from its significance, for in historical terms a borrowing by a pre-eminent art form from elsewhere can ultimately be more significant than the source of the loan.

Libretti, too, were undergoing change, and the Romantic tendencies that were at first semi-latent or isolated anticipations ended up by creating a trend. The fact that Foppa used Shakespeare as the basis of his libretto *Giulietta e Romeo* for Zingarelli in 1796 and that Gaetano Rossi introduced Nordic elements into his choice of subjects (*Ginevra di Scozia* and *Elisa* for Simon Mayr in 1801, and *Emma di Resburgo* in 1819 for Meyerbeer) was hardly noticeable to an age of librettists that was prepared to use any source material that made for an interesting plot. What does emerge strikingly is their deliberate quest for interesting settings that then had to be adequately conveyed in the music. This represented for Friedrich Schlegel the very embodiment of Romanticism, but it is a criterion that had no place whatever in the libretti of Metastasio. In the *opera seria* governed by his influence only vague scenarios are given – a palace, a temple or a pleasant place – without any attempt whatever to paint a genuine *couleur locale*.

In the same spirit of early Romanticism is Sografi's *La Morte di Semiramide* for Nasolini in 1790, which for the first time expressly forsook the traditional happy ending and introduced the new genre of opera with an unmitigated tragic outcome. Metastasio's *Didone abbandonata* also had a tragic end, but this remained an isolated exception in his work. More than any other form, however, it is the *opera semiseria* (the musical counterpart to the *comédie larmoyante*) that has characteristics that allow it to be called, without any strain on the definition, 'pre-Romantic.' Its most successful representative was Paisiello's *Nina* in 1789. The preface to

Above: Dantan the Younger's caricature of Victor Hugo (1802-85), the most revered French writer of his time, whose fight for liberty made him a public figure and member of the National Assembly. The first night of his verse drama *Hernani* in 1830 – his confrontation with the conventions of classical drama – established Hugo as a leader of the French Romantic movement.

Below: The interior of a box at the Académie Royale de Musique, the Paris Opéra, during the performance of a Romantic opera set in the Middle Ages.

Francesco Benincasa's libretto *Il Disertore*, published in 1785 is a kind of manifesto of the *opera semiseria*. It is bourgeois theater in Diderot's sense of the term, characterized by *Empfindsamkeit* (sensitive feeling) – which at its most exaggerated takes the form of madness – but also by a bourgeois element that does not fight shy of outspoken criticism of social conditions. As such, it is a striking expression of a spirit that had been at work throughout Europe since 1770, primarily in literary spheres, but to a lesser extent also in musical contexts.

For all that, it would be overstating the case to refer to such phenomena as 'Romantic.' This would make the term even more confused than it already is, at a time when few historians would shed a tear if the word were to disappear from the vocabulary completely! However, whatever terminology is used, it cannot be denied that around 1790 – that is, at the same time as the French Revolution – sudden changes took place in Italian *opera seria* and *semiseria* which accord with trends visible throughout Europe. These trends, if not themselves part and parcel of Romanticism, share some common bases. It is therefore nonsense to write about the history of opera in Italy between the decline of Metastasian *opera seria* around 1790 and the Romantic operas of Bellini and Donizetti from 1830 onwards as if only the works of Rossini are to be taken seriously. This is seen to be all the more dubious when one bears in mind that in so doing we overemphasize the relative importance of *opera buffa* in comparison with *opera seria* at a time when, despite Rossini's efforts to maintain a balance, comic opera was in decline. Donizetti's *Don Pasquale* is an almost 'extra-territorial' exception, and Verdi's *Falstaff* is clearly a one-off work, written by the composer in his old age, and not an integral part of a continuous evolution of comic opera.

• Politics and Romanticism •

Patriotic and liberal elements relate the heroic operas of Cherubini and Le Sueur – intended in the 1790s as Revolutionary works – to the Italian *Risorgimento*. This is just the opposite of the bias towards a restoration of the political *status quo* that characterizes French and German Romanticism at the beginning of the nineteenth century between the Revolutions of 1789 and 1830. This results in the paradox that, whereas the Italian Romanticism of Bellini, Donizetti and early Verdi has an undeniably political dimension, in Europe in general it cannot be maintained that there is any real correlation between Romanticism and politics. Furthermore, the political element in Italian opera is less apparent in the libretti, where censorship would have suppressed it, than in the overall agitation of the music, which was interpreted as politically motivated.

The Romanticism proclaimed by Victor Hugo in his preface to *Cromwell* in 1827, urging on the Revolution that came in 1830, was felt to be

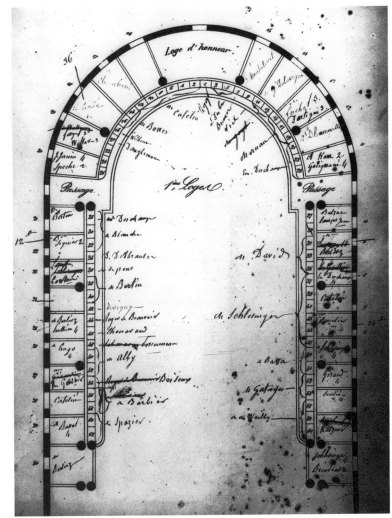

the literary expression of political Liberalism, just like Romanticism in Italy. By way of contrast, the early Romanticism of Chateaubriand (if we may call it that) is the work of an *émigré* seeking not Revolution but Restoration. Apart from some passing revolutionary fervor in the immediate wake of the events of 1789, the same is true of Romanticism in Germany. In the 1830s and 1840s, during the *Vormärz* (the period between the defeat of Napoleon and the Revolutions in March 1848) the devotees of French Romanticism, with its liberal, revolutionary bias, called themselves *Junges Deutschland*, a movement that showed nothing but contempt for German Romanticism, which for them was associated with political reaction.

Again we cannot escape the fact that Romanticism in the nineteenth century took national forms that make overall definition difficult. These national variants grew out of common roots in the 'pre-Romanticism' of the eighteenth century, particular characteristics being singled out and taken to extremes. In Italy the patriotic, revolutionary element was singled out in this way, coupled with the highly charged emotionalism that evolved in bourgeois society in the eighteenth century. Comparison between Romanticism in Italy and in Germany, in literature as in music, is only possible when we understand their earlier common origin.

Above: Part of the seating plan for a concert given by Berlioz at the Conservatoire, 13 December 1840. Among the names can be seen those of Balzac, Gautier, Hugo, De Vigny, August Barbier (who worked on the libretto of *Benvenuto Cellini*) and Jules Janin, the writer and critic. Berlioz received very little official encouragement for his music: for many years none of his works were played by the Société des Concerts, and he was forbidden to use the Hall at the Conservatoire. In order to get his music performed he was therefore forced to organize his own concerts, which involved him in an enormous expenditure of time and energy.

seria from 1830 onwards – an emotionalism found above all in Verdi's duets, and which became the *sine qua non* of the 'music drama' into which 'opera' evolved – and the emotions *in abstracto* that according to Schopenhauer are at the heart of absolute instrumental music, can hardly be considered as variants of the same sentiment behind the whole of Romantic music. We all agree that the quasi-religious primacy of feeling in German Romanticism and the *élan terrible* of grand opera both have their common origin in the *Empfindsamkeit* of the eighteenth century (an enthusiasm for the principle of feeling first articulated by Rousseau); but we are confronted by bewildering divergences caused by differing interpretations and emphases accorded the same common ideas within national trends in the nineteenth century. If the gap between Schumann and Meyerbeer was unbridgeable, the gap between Schumann and Bellini or Donizetti defies even the thought of connecting them.

Above: Fishermen, 1851, by Károly Marko the Elder, who went to Italy from Hungary in 1832 and, inspired, as was Liszt, by the beauty of the landscape, remained there until his death.

Right: The Fountain of the Académie de France in Rome, with St Peter's in the distance, by Corot, *c.*1826-7. The Academy, where Prix de Rome winners stayed, is housed in the Villa Medici on the Pincian Hill; Berlioz called the view from its terraced gardens one of the finest in the world.

Opposite top: Ingres's *Coronation of Pope Pius VII in 1800.* Winner of the Prix de Rome, Ingres lived for many years in Italy, becoming director of the Académie de France in 1834.

Opposite bottom: The Caffè Greco in the Via Condotti, Rome, by Ludwig Passini, 1842. Berlioz described the Caffè Greco as 'the most odious place imaginable – dark, dirty and ill-lit,' but it was much frequented by the inmates of the Villa Medici.

• Feeling as a principle •

The widespread notion that Romantic music is about the expression of feelings and emotions in musical form, and nothing else, is as problematic as it is popular. In the first place, the maxim that to move others a composer must have been moved himself (C. P. E. Bach) goes back well into the eighteenth century, and the general usage of 'Romantic' in relation to music refers to the ideal of *Empfindsamkeit* which was popularized in the nineteenth century but had been evolving since 1750. On the other hand, feeling as an artistic musical principle is so vague and all-embracing that any common ground between German instrumental music and Italian or French opera that we might assume to exist proves on closer scrutiny to be an illusion derived from linguistic imprecision. The highly charged emotionalism that dominated *opera*

The popular notion that in Romantic music we have feelings about to erupt in their search for musical expression is almost inevitably associated with the idea that in the Romantic period considerations of form evolved by the Viennese Classicists were pulled apart or disregarded. In terms of compositional structure Romantic harmony appears to be part and parcel of an amorphous approach towards musical form, whereby excessive chromaticism endangered, or even rejected, the structural principle of major–minor tonality that governed Classical music. Classical sonata form is based on a tonal and harmonic scheme in which, deriving from the contrast of keys in the exposition, the development section produces a modulatory 'slope,' ending in the restoration of the basic key in the recapitulation.

Ernst Kurth, in his book, published in 1920, on the 'crisis of Romantic harmony in Wagner's *Tristan,*' traced the development of mainstream harmony in the nineteenth century and came to the conclusion that a process of increasing chromatic alteration of chords led finally to the dissolution of tonality. This view, however, is one-sided. Kurth failed to understand the significance of the reversion to modal scales which, above all in opera but also in programmatic instrumental works, brought about a form of music that was indubitably modern but also immediately comprehensible. It was modern in that it deviated from cadential formulae of major–minor tonality, but comprehensible in its diatonic base and in the archaic, folkloristic or exotic character associated with modal scales. People 'understood' the music, because it was sufficient to recognize its character without grasping its structure. Although the chromaticism emphasized by Kurth may have led to Schoenberg's atonality, this recourse to modal scales paved the way for the expanded tonality of such twentieth-century composers as Stravinsky, Bartók and Hindemith.

• Romantic form •

The history of form during the Romantic era in the nineteenth century is as ambivalent as that of harmony. Since the influential treatise on composition (1837–47) by the composer and teacher Adolf Bernhard Marx, writers have taken much too simplistic a view of formal development. Even in the Classical era the evolution of form was far more complex than we might be led to believe, and the assertion that any particular established form can be matched by individual treatment of it, in other words that the general rule can always be confirmed and justified by its idiosyncratic variants, is clearly seen to be untenable, even in the case of Beethoven. Starting with his piano sonatas written at the turn of the century (op.27 and op.31), if not earlier, sonata form is seen to be a basis that is not fixed but in a state of permanent reassessment. We see that Beethoven was not composing *in* sonata form but *with* it. If he gives a *cantabile* theme to the modulating 'development' section of a movement in sonata form, while allocating virtuoso passagework to a tonally closed subsidiary-subject section, then we can see that he is taking apart and reassembling the pieces of the model – in which the modulating passages would normally be highly decorated and the subsidiary subjects would be characterized by melodic themes. But he still presupposes that his audience is familiar with the basic form, so that they can recognize the deviations he is deliberately making and can assess their effectiveness.

The form typical of Beethoven stands in contrast to the divided attitude towards form that was shown in the Romantic period, which gave rise to extremes of rigid schematicism and ex-

periment. The fact not only that lyrical piano music in the wake of Schubert showed a preference for song form (A–B–A), whose very simplicity was often in marked contrast to the complex subject-matter it conveyed, but also that sonata form in the works of Chopin and Schumann was achieved by a schematic (often almost mechanical) approach unimaginable in the works of Beethoven, shows that the Romantic composer could well afford to take a highly formalistic approach to composition, because for him the music was about something other than form. Whereas for Beethoven form was still an integral and evolving principle, for the Romantics it was merely the framework that kept the thematic material together. As with a Bach fugue, a lyrical piano piece in the nineteenth century stands or falls by the expressive potential of its basic idea. With Beethoven the thematic material itself is not so crucial to a work as the manner in which the formal considerations (into which thematic material is subsumed) are processed.

If, therefore, in the Romantic period form could sometimes be schematic, because it was of only secondary importance, by way of contrast Liszt's symphonic poems availed themselves of 'experimental' forms as a means of conveying poetic or mythological subject-matter. These forms cannot, however, be explained in simplistic terms as serving the programmatic element of the music. A 'double function form' was developed – on the principle of 'equating' sonata movement and sonata cycle by extending the *cantabile* second subject into the slow movement, the development into the scherzo and the recapitulation into the finale – and this hybrid process fulfilled the technical purpose of constructing a new form from selected features of the symphonic tradition, while fulfilling the artistic purpose of keeping form flexible enough to incorporate the programmatic element, without making Beethoven's mistake in his third *Leonore* overture, criti-

Above: Eugène Lami's print, *c*.1840, of a musical *soirée* – the social context for the majority of Romantic composers.

Opposite top: François-Antoine Habeneck (1781-1849) by Dantan the Younger. Habeneck dominated the musical establishment in Paris for twenty years, as violin teacher at the Conservatoire, conductor at the Opéra and conductor of the Société des Concerts du Conservatoire.

Top left: An autograph song, *Der Maiabend* (1836), by Fanny Mendelssohn, illustrated by her husband Wilhelm Hensel. The first of Fanny's songs were published under her brother's name.

Left: Schumann's first piece of published music criticism, which features his double personality embodied in the characters Florestan and Eusebius. Schumann had acquired a copy of Chopin's 'Là ci darem' Variations and immediately hailed their composer as a genius.

events. The job of the librettist, irrespective of the chosen subject-matter, whether 'Romeo and Juliet,' 'Kabale und Liebe,' 'Hernani' or 'Die Räuber,' was to adapt the text in such a way that one had a natural progression from aria to duet to ensemble; changes of tempo within each number had to be made dramatically as convincing as possible.

In the later works of Verdi this scheme becomes a framework that is concealed but still discernible. Its function is solely to underpin the conflict of emotions in the appropriate musical manner, no matter what changes of mood and situation may occur and no matter how abruptly or frequently they may happen. The stereotyped form that dictated the rules to the librettists became much less conspicuous but remained to some extent in the background to prevent the musical drama devoted to the emotions of the moment from becoming totally amorphous.

Those writing the history of Romantic music have tended to concentrate on individual composers. In fact it is hardly an exaggeration to say that developments in Vienna in the latter half of the nineteenth century have to be pieced together from biographies of Brahms that make no mention of Bruckner, and vice versa. It is true that music in the nineteenth century was formed, in a way that hardly holds true for any other era, by the individual contributions of composers and not by artistic or social norms and ideals. However, the time has come for the history of music based on particular composers – and such an approach is supported by the myth that any particular work is the expression in music of biographical factors – to be complemented by historical accounts primarily concerned with the problems that faced the composers. Such an approach would be guided by the awareness that music represents one of the forms in which the so-called objectified spirit manifests itself – forms that can be understood only if we reconstruct the questions to which they give the answer.

Below: Listening to Beethoven: the Andante of the Seventh Symphony by Eugène Lami. Painted in 1840, this watercolor could have been made after a performance of the symphony at the Conservatoire conducted by Habeneck.

cized by Wagner for trying to make everything fit into a scheme inappropriate to its content.

Liszt's experiments with form represent the other side of the coin of programmatic music that was so conceived as to give music access to the intellectual substance and status of world literature. This does not mean that the musical form itself is unconvincing or merely the vehicle of the subject-matter. Today, Liszt – the great protagonist of program music as representing the spiritual component in music (a component which Eduard Hanslick believed to be a 'pure form') – has been recognized specifically as being an isolated musical structuralist in the nineteenth century and an exponent of techniques belonging to the 'pre-history of modern music.'

The characteristically Romantic concept of form, insofar as it exists at all, must surely be found in the configuration of the extremes – on the one hand the schematic and on the other the experimental. It proves not to be difficult to identify common ground in the dependence on subject-matter – be it the 'poetic' intention of the lyrical piano piece or the 'programmatic' intention of the symphonic poem – that confirms and justifies both the schematic and the experimental approaches. In the schematic approach, form is not the primary object, while the purpose of the experimental approach is to be flexible enough to meet the demands of the subject-matter. Basically the problems, as the composers saw them, were always the same, but it is the diversity of the solutions to them that has served to distort the picture.

The history of form in Italian opera was much less complicated. In broad terms we can describe it as the evolution from a manifest to a latent form. In the first half of the nineteenth century librettists were clearly bound by an established musical theme, namely the alternation of *cantabile (primo tempo)* and *cabaletta (secondo tempo)*. The change from slow to fast had to be motivated by an abrupt change of

CARL MARIA VON WEBER

LUDWIG FINSCHER

Weber is probably the least known of all the great nineteenth-century composers, and he is certainly the only one among them whose reputation rests almost entirely on a single opera – *Der Freischütz*. The remainder of his varied and extensive output has virtually sunk into oblivion, at least in regular concert and opera performances. *Freischütz* apart, Weber's other principal dramatic works – *Euryanthe* and *Oberon*, *Abu Hassan* and the *Die drei Pintos* fragment, which Gustav Mahler completed as a highly effective opera – survive mainly as recordings. In other words, only one work for the stage has outlived a composer who was above all a dramatist, indeed one of the most original and stimulating musical dramatists of the century.

There are many reasons for this, which derive principally from the circumstances of Weber's life. His was a restless existence, bedeviled by the harsh demands of everyday work. His fight against consumption, the artists' disease of the age, together with an almost unrelenting feeling of existential anguish, further overshadowed his life. All this left him little time for creative work and even less for creative reflection, as his output clearly shows. Judged by the standards of *Der Freischütz*, the rest of Weber's output lacks polish and all too often bristles with unresolved problems. Yet the exceptional influence which his work exerted on composers such as Berlioz and Wagner plainly indicates wherein lay Weber's special historical significance: he was, together with Berlioz, the great 'stimulator' of the century, a composer immortalized more through his influence, especially on those younger than himself, than by a series of great, well-polished works.

Weber came from a family which would undoubtedly have been regarded as 'bohemian' in the nineteenth century. His father was a restless and adventurous spirit, quite incapable of holding on to any secure position. For a time he could only keep his head above water by turning his family into a group of traveling players. He tried to make his son, Carl Maria, baptized on 20 November 1786 in Eutin, Holstein, into a child prodigy. The family's nomadic ways, however, did not favor a regular education. As a ten-year-old, Weber received piano lessons and later – but intermittently – tuition in composition from Michael Haydn in Salzburg and the Abbé Vogler in Vienna. The twelve-year-old's op.1, six *Fughetti* for piano, published in Salzburg in 1798, mainly illustrates the conservative nature of Michael Haydn's teaching. Abbé Vogler's influence undoubtedly ran much deeper, not least because of the attraction that his somewhat eccentric ways must have had for the young Weber. The budding composer was introduced to the startling and theatrical effects produced by unusual instrumental registers, combinations of instruments and unorthodox tonal sequences, as well as to ideas for reforms in every possible field of musical life. Vogler may have displayed some features more reminiscent of an eccentric or a mountebank, but he was remarkably knowledgeable, and his tuition very largely consisted of the analysis of Classical works. One may thus assume that Vogler laid the foundation for Weber's literary and musical education, enabling him to become the first 'educated' composer of the nineteenth century in the modern sense.

It was also the Abbé Vogler who secured the position of conductor at Breslau (Wroclaw) for his barely eighteen-year-old pupil and so enabled Weber to acquire a knowledge of the repertory, practice in conducting and all-round experience of theatrical requirements. Weber was also able to start putting into practice his ideas for a more adventurous performing repertory, intensive rehearsing and new seating arrangements for the orchestra. The years spent in Breslau completed the transformation of Weber into an essentially theatrical composer. It was also now that certain characteristic features first came to the fore – a high degree of inflexible consistency and a drive bordering on ruthlessness whenever the assertion of artistic principles was involved. Such an attitude inevitably resulted in conflicts, especially in the realm of the theater. It led to Weber's resignation from his post in Breslau after only three years, in 1806, and the years that followed were as unsettled as those of his childhood had been. Nevertheless, despite all the occasional pieces which he was forced to write during this period, either for his own benefit or for that of others, he doggedly went on composing opera, though the chances of getting a work staged in Germany were very slender.

Following a brief appointment as conductor at the court of the Duke of Württemberg-Öls, at Carlsruhe in Silesia, in 1807 Weber entered the service of Duke Ludwig of Württemberg in

Top: The house in Eutin where Weber was born to Genoveva Brenner, a singer and actress, and Franz Anton Weber, Kapellmeister to the Prince-Bishop of Lübeck and something of an adventurer. Franz Anton's brother, Fridolin, was father of the Weber sisters, Aloysia, with whom Mozart was in love, and Constanze, whom he married in 1782.

Above: A pencil drawing of Weber as a child. Soon after his birth his father moved the family to Hamburg to form the nucleus of a traveling theater company.

Stuttgart, as a secretary rather than a musician. Both the office and the environment had such a fatally stimulating effect on Weber's innate inclination to irresponsibility that 1810 in Stuttgart culminated in catastrophe: he was arrested in connection with a financial scandal which has never been fully clarified and expelled from Württemberg. Nearly three years of restless wandering followed, in the course of which Weber earned high renown as a piano virtuoso, although the bulk of his concert fees went to repay the debts acquired in Breslau and Stuttgart.

Despite his shaky circumstances, it was during this period that Weber began to earn a reputation as a writer of operas. *Silvana*, a Romantic opera composed while he was still living in Stuttgart, which reworked material from an earlier, lost, work, and *Abu Hassan*, a *Singspiel* written in 1810-11, were performed in important opera houses, including those in Frankfurt and Munich, where they achieved a measure of success. Press reports began to make Weber's name known throughout the German-speaking world, even if they did not yet bring him international fame.

In 1813, visiting Prague during a concert-tour, Weber was offered the post of conductor at the Opera there. This provided him with a chance to put into action the plans which he had clearly been working out, despite all the crises and tensions that had afflicted him. He threw himself into his new task with characteristic dedication and vigor. He radically reorganized the theater, introducing a schedule of rehearsals – read-throughs, solo and ensemble rehearsals with piano accompaniment, rehearsals with choir and orchestra, stage rehearsals with piano, dress rehearsals – none of which was in any way taken for granted at that time. He concerned himself with staging, scenery and costumes. He also learned Czech in order to communicate more easily with the theater staff, just as he was later to learn English when he was working on *Oberon*. However, his greatest achievement during three and a half years of work in Prague was the creation of a virtually

new repertory of no less than sixty-two different operas. This replaced the traditional Italian repertory imported via Vienna and destroyed the dominant position of Italian opera and taste.

The way in which the new repertory developed clearly indicates the line adopted by Weber. French opera was the starting-point, mainly *opéra comique*, but also the 'numbers' opera with spoken dialogue and the *drame lyrique*: the work with which he opened his tenure of office in Prague was in fact Spontini's *Fernand Cortez*. This was to lead on to German opera, which, at that time, had little of distinction to show. This development of the repertory was backed up – though not until the opening of Weber's last Prague season, late in 1815 – by a truly revolutionary new departure: the publication of explanatory articles in the *Prager Zeitung*. These essays make it quite clear that from the very start Weber was intent on more than simply replacing one repertory with another, French for Italian. What he was really aiming at was a form of German opera, 'a work of art complete in itself, with all its parts well finished and fused together in beautiful unity,' as he put it in the manifesto addressed to his new Dresden public on 26 January 1817. Such a German opera was to be the product of a peculiarly German quality: 'to attract to themselves the best available to everybody else, because they are eager to learn and dedicated to constant progress.'

• Conductor in Dresden •

A few months later, Weber took up a new post, as the head of the new Deutsche Oper in Dresden, and he set about implementing this program by composing *Der Freischütz*. But even before he started on this crucial task, the organizer in him followed up his manifesto with a practical memorandum, stating the need for a new type of performer, at once singer and actor, not so far produced by either Italian or French opera but essential for the sake of dramatic verisimilitude – a requirement that seemed almost scandalous at the time and had hardly even been suggested since the days of Gluck. He also recommended the recruitment of a permanent operatic choir and choirmaster and, finally, the combination of all these forces, so that the new 'Dresdner Deutsche Oper' – by deliberate contrast with the established Italian Hofoper (Court Opera) there directed by Francesco Morlacchi – might become 'a veritable nursery' for the desired renewal of German opera as a whole.'

Weber was by no means on his own in promoting these ideas and requirements. In fact, his appointment to the post in Dresden in 1816 was part of a general move towards the creation of a specifically German style of opera. This was a direct consequence of political events, above all of the waves of patriotic enthusiasm for the establishment of a unified national German state which swept through German-speaking countries during the final stages of the war of liberation from Napoleon. Weber first encountered these political aspirations in Prague, which had briefly become a sanctuary for the opponents of Napoleon. He had occasion to meet Wilhelm von Humboldt, Ludwig Tieck, Theodor Körner, Bettina von Brentano and Rahel Varnhagen in the house of Liebich, the director of the Opera. The opening of his first Prague season with Spontini's *Fernand Cortez*, an extremely political opera, originally commissioned by Napoleon but equally capable of an anti-Bonaparte interpretation, may also have had political overtones. In Berlin in the summer of 1814, Weber not only discussed with Clemens von Brentano a possible opera about the medieval German hero Tannhaüser, but also became thoroughly involved in the wave of patriotic enthusiasm which followed what appeared to be the final victory over Napoleon. This mood found its expression in the choral settings of poems from Körner's Prussian patriotic collection *Leyer und Schwert* (Lyre and Sword) which Weber composed during the autumn of 1814; he now became overnight a 'bard of freedom,' in whose songs students in particular, but also patriotic intellectuals and solid, freedom-minded citizens, discovered an expression of those national sentiments and aspirations which had been stimulated in them by Prussia's victory. Such people organized themselves into male-voice choral societies, and it is hardly a coincidence that Weber's settings were all written for choral performance.

These songs made Weber tremendously popular, but they also embroiled him in political conflicts and in the resulting cultural confrontations. His appointment in Dresden, as well as a commission to write an opera in German for the inauguration of C. F. Schinkel's newly built Schauspielhaus in Berlin – *Der Freischütz*, which was not in the end performed on this occasion – were both the work of Saxon and Prussian 'political' theater managers who belonged to the German party. They saw the creation of a specifically German theater and opera, and the liberation from the dominance of Italian opera in Dresden and French opera in Berlin, as steps on the road to national self-awareness. Conversely, Weber's role as a 'bard of freedom' and a promoter of German opera aroused suspicions in all those favoring the cause of individual states rather than pan-German patriotic interests. Among these was the King of Saxony, who appointed Weber as conductor for life only with obvious reluctance and after much hesitation, then kept him at arm's length in a way which pained the loyally disposed composer; and another was the King of Prussia, who admittedly did not object to the staging of *Der Freischütz*, but who obdurately opposed the appointment of Weber as Court Composer, or even merely as Court Conductor, long after – and indeed precisely because – this opera had become the 'national opera of the Germans.'

The call to Dresden in 1816, and especially his appointment as conductor for life there on 13 September 1817, provided Weber for the first time in his life with material security and the prospect of an untroubled future. This in turn gave him the inner repose he needed for intensive work. It also allowed him to set about founding a family. Weber began working on *Der Freischütz* early in July 1817, and on 4 November he married Caroline Brandt, an opera singer he had met in Prague. And so the frivolous bohemian, a partner in the innumerable short-lived love affairs of theater life, the reckless spendthrift, finally settled down to become a solid family man.

Weber's years in Dresden proved to be a relatively tranquil and happy period, despite many artistic disappointments and the relentless progress of his consumption. His journeys became shorter and less frequent: he undertook only one more extended tour as a pianist in 1820, going as far as Copenhagen. As a result, he did not need to write so many piano pieces for his own use or undertake as much other occasional work. Official compositions for use at the Saxon Royal Court – cantatas and Masses – did not take up an excessive amount of his time. Despite this, his rate of output slowed down perceptibly. *Der Freischütz* took three years, including many inevitable interruptions for routine theater work; *Euryanthe* a year, with fewer interruptions; and *Oberon*, with a much shorter score, substantially longer; *Die drei Pintos*, the comic opera on which Weber had started to work as soon as he completed *Der Freischütz*, remained unfinished because commissions (first for *Euryanthe*, then for *Oberon*) absorbed all his creative energies.

These commissions were, of course, the direct outcome of the sensational success of *Der Freischütz*. Domenico Barbaia, the manager of the Kärntnertor Theater in Vienna, commissioned from Weber an opera expressly in the manner of *Freischütz*, and the fact that the work, *Euryanthe*, eventually acquired a very different shape contributed to the controversy which has surrounded it ever since. The invitation from Covent Garden in London to write a new opera and conduct it together with *Der Freischütz*,

Below: The Königliche Hoftheater in Dresden in 1843. In 1841 it replaced the Kleine Hoftheater, or Komödienhaus, where Weber was based from 1817 until his death.

Top left: Scenery from a production of *Der Freischütz* in Weimar in 1822: Act II, the scene in the mysterious Wolf's Glen, a sinister and magical spot frequented by supernatural beings. Here at midnight Max meets Caspar, who had called on the evil spirit Samiel to help cast the magic bullets which will put Max in his power. Standing in the magic circle they place the infernal ingredients into the crucible; the casting of each bullet is accompanied by strange and fearsome apparitions.

Above: The autograph of Agathe's aria from Act III of *Der Freischütz*: 'Wie nahte mir der Schlummer' – 'Leise, leise.' Max hopes to win the shooting trial next day and thus win the hand of Agathe in marriage. She has been waiting with anxious foreboding and now in this aria greets his return joyfully.

followed from the popularity which the first had earned for itself in the British capital: no fewer than five adaptations or mutilated versions of the opera were staged there in 1824 alone. In this case it had, however, been made clear in advance that the new work would not be like *Der Freischütz*, even though the material put forward by the manager of Covent Garden, a dramatization of Wieland's epic poem *Oberon*, was extremely Romantic in character.

The triumphant première of *Der Freischütz* at the Berlin Schauspielhaus on 18 June 1821 and its conquering progress to Paris and London had turned Weber into a European celebrity.

The controversial première of *Euryanthe* in Vienna on 25 October 1825 did not substantially jeopardize this reputation, as the work was staged elsewhere, including Dresden, with a greater success, even though the press gave it unfavorable treatment almost everywhere. The opening of *Oberon* on 12 April 1826 in London, together with the eleven performances that followed it, again proved a triumphant success, even though it was a purely local one and was not repeated on the Continent. However, the strain of both rehearsals and performances of *Oberon* dramatically hastened the end, as is recorded in the diaries where Weber painstaking-

the 'national opera,' *Der Freischütz*. It was only later and somewhat hesitantly that a conviction gained ground that he had, on the contrary, been a citizen of the world in musical terms, the first really modern musician, in that he was simultaneously a composer, a writer on musical topics, an organizer and a conductor.

• Virtuosity and drama •

Weber's output is marked by the circumstances in which he grew up and learned his trade. The world of the theater had provided a natural environment for him since he was a child, and he had worked in it himself since the age of eighteen. There was also the equally insecure world of the virtuoso, in which he was forced

Above: Act III of *Der Freischütz*, the morning of the shooting trial. Seated in the background Prince Ottokar, who is to adjudicate, and his retinue wait for the trial to begin and listen to the chorus of huntsmen sing about the pleasures of their life: 'Was gleicht wohl auf Erden.'

Above: Costumes from the opera for a production in Berlin. Max, the forester, and Ännchen, Agathe's confidante, who in her goodness and simplicity brings a sunny, lighter mood to relieve the feeling of menace in this struggle between good and evil.

ly noted the daily course of events and the state of his health. Weber seems to have been aware of the risks, but he wanted to provide financial security for his family. Death came in the night of 4-5 June, and he was buried in London on 21 June.

Eighteen years later Weber's coffin was brought to Dresden, mainly at the instigation of Wagner, who then held his old post of conductor at the court of Saxony: the German musician was to rest in German earth. Wagner's address at the graveside, which culminated in the often quoted – and equally often misapplied – statement that 'there has been no other musician more German than thou,' chimed with a deep feeling prevalent at that time – which was no longer, be it said, Weber's own time – that he had in some special sense been a 'German' composer, the composer of a work regarded as

to earn his living for so many years. Thus drama and virtuosity provide a basic pattern which can be traced in almost all of his important works. Musical drama was just another kind of theater as far as the stage folk among whom Weber grew up were concerned, and music was no more than a means of achieving theatrical effects. Such a point of view must inevitably have inclined the rising composer to French opera, despite all his natural reverence for Mozart, and away from the Italian conception of the genre.

The systematic study of the French repertory, together with that of Mozart's operas, and a demand for actors who really sang – something quite different from the usually low-grade actor–singers and all-round buskers among traditional strolling players – became basic requirements in Weber's program of artistic renewal. All

means used to carry out this program were considered legitimate, provided that the composer concerned did his best to create something new, to move forward along the path of musical progress, even if this involved deliberate extravagance of expression or such eclecticism as the Dresden manifesto claimed: 'To attract to oneself . . . the best available to everybody else.' Such eclecticism is well represented by the score of *Der Freischütz*.

Similarly, Weber's virtuoso writing naturally inclined towards the French model, especially of course in his concertos and concertante chamber music. The combination of sentimentally heroic cadences (usually drawn from opera) with marching rhythms and dramatic outbursts, and the formalization of solo passages into dramatic 'numbers' have much in common with Viotti's French type of concerto. Weber's personal contribution to this style in his piano works included a characteristic brilliance and delight in resolving technical problems (in which he was greatly assisted by his ability to span the interval of a tenth without difficulty); but he also experimented with new tonal effects — chromatic figuring, staccato chords on a sustained note and many other such devices. This handling of the instrument greatly influenced some outstanding piano composers: Hummel in his later years (the link between his A flat and B flat piano concertos and Weber's two piano concertos is particularly close), Mendelssohn and, above all, Chopin.

The fact that Weber was essentially a dramatic composer is most clearly illustrated by those

Above: Helmina von Chézy, whom Weber asked to write the libretto for *Euryanthe*, but whose inexperience undermined the composer's attempt to write a grand opera to follow the success of *Der Freischütz*.

features of his instrumental music which go beyond the boundaries set by the Classical musical categories. One example of this is provided by the mysterious tremolos, quite alien to the piano, which occur in the concertos, another by the two symphonies composed for the Court Orchestra at Schloss Carlsruhe in Silesia in 1807. The latter have little in common with the Classical Viennese conception of the genre, but perhaps more with the contemporary French symphony, in their *al fresco* approach and their theatrical contrasts devoid of any musically logical motivation. The programmatic elements which are embodied in some of Weber's most important instrumental works are equally relevant in this connection: for instance in the E minor Piano Sonata, on the program of which his pupil, Julius Benedict, threw some light; the G minor Piano Trio, Weber's most outstanding chamber music work; and the F minor *Konzertstück* for piano and orchestra, the program of which was outlined by the composer himself. He justified the use of such a program by suggesting that concertos in a minor key were seldom effective if they lacked 'a definite stimulating idea,' a conception which would have been wholly alien to a composer more strongly grounded in the Viennese Classical tradition, such as Hummel. Its outcome, however, was that a regular three-movement piano concerto was turned into a single-movement *Konzertstück*, which, thanks to its popularity and the virtuosity it embodied in both its form and technique, exerted an influence not only on Liszt's piano concertos but on the esthetic theory of Romantic program concertos as a whole.

This conjunction of dramatic quality and virtuosity also underlies that aspect of Weber's instrumental idiom which strikes us as most alive and original today. This is true even of works of relatively minor importance, such as the First Piano Concerto or the two symphonies. Although much in his handling of instrumental

numbers – one of the reasons why Weber's operas are in practice so seldom performed. In the great arias and ensembles of *Euryanthe* and *Oberon* the voices are often treated as though they are virtuoso instruments; meaning and intelligibility are sacrificed to vocal effect and brilliance. Yet it is in just such cases that Weber often relapses into a conventional treatment. Even the finest passages, such as the villain Lysiart's scene of hatred and defiance at the start of the second act of *Euryanthe* or Rezia's 'Ocean Aria' in *Oberon*, are not entirely untainted in this sense.

Above: Euryanthe had its première in Vienna on 25 October 1823. Beethoven had promised to attend, but his deafness deterred him. This entry in Weber's diary records the triumph of the first performance in Dresden in March 1824. Weber's health was failing; after completing *Euryanthe* he wrote only one song in the following year before beginning *Oberon* in 1825.

Right: Wilhelmine Schröder-Devrient (1804-60) as Euryanthe in 1839. Adolar, deceived into thinking that his wife, Euryanthe, has betrayed him, intends to kill her. In the desert they are threatened by a snake; she begs Adolar to escape while she sacrifices herself for him; Adolar kills the snake and spares Euryanthe's life but abandons her to her fate.

Opposite: The autograph score of one of Weber's *Leyer und Schwert* songs written in 1814 for male-voice choir. These settings of Theodor Körner's simple patriotic poems reflected the current wave of nationalist feeling. Their great popularity brought Weber immediate renown and led indirectly to his invitation to develop German opera in Dresden.

parts can be traced back to Mozart, especially in the treatment of woodwind, Weber made the instruments speak, drew out their individual qualities and explored their expressive and technical potential as no other composer had done before him. Yet the purpose of such exploration was seldom merely the pursuit of pure virtuosity – except perhaps in the clarinet works composed for his friend Heinrich Bärmann. It was rather, almost invariably, the virtuoso exploitation of technical possibilities for the sake of more vivid expression, and that almost as much in instrumental works as in operatic ones. It is something more than just Romantic metaphor to say that in Weber's orchestra the instruments 'talk.' But if Weber's instrumental output is permeated by the language of the musical stage, his operatic writing is marked by the effects of instrumental virtuosity, though to a lesser extent. This is the reason for the sheer physical difficulty of singing many of his vocal

• The operas •

It may well be that Weber had tried so hard early on to make an impression as a virtuoso when composing for the piano that he found himself quite unable to avoid the accompanying triteness when he came to write for opera later in life. Of course, his earliest attempts at operatic writing date from his twelfth and his fourteenth years, but it is significant that the surviving fragments of the second of these works, *Das Waldmädchen* (the Forest Maiden) – his first opera has been lost – should be weakest precisely in piling up 'instrumental' coloraturas and effects of virtuosity as ends in themselves, while the underlying style mainly harks back to Mozart. Conventions derived from a variety of sources mark the works that followed. *Peter Schmoll und seine Nachbarn* (Peter Schmoll and his Neighbors), written in 1801-2 in Salzburg while

Weber was receiving tuition from Michael Haydn, is a *Singspiel* in the style of the successful Viennese works by Kauer, Dittersdorf, Weigl and Schenk. *Rübezahl* was written in 1804, after his period of instruction by the Abbé Vogler, and insofar as one can judge from the few surviving numbers, the composer was now attempting to express the crucial influences exerted on him by his teacher, especially in the richly imaginative harmonization and instrumentation.

Silvana marked Weber's first real step forward to independence. It opened up a new source of material – the world of medieval chivalry as seen through Romantic eyes – and, for the first time, displayed his clear affinity with *opéra comique*. The composer continued to think well of this work long after he had completed it in 1808-10, and he later refashioned it several times. As he put it, the composition of *Silvana* in Stuttgart was 'encouraged and stimulated by the kindly interest taken in it by the admirable Danzi.' This Stuttgart conductor, a pupil of Vogler like Weber himself, may perhaps have inspired some of the features which gave a new character to this opera, above all in terms of the *cantabile* treatment of the woodwind and a less 'instrumental' handling of the vocal parts. Historically, the most important aspects of *Silvana*, however, are the Romantic interpretations of chivalry and forest myths combined and Weber's ways of conjuring up descriptive tonal effects for both these aspects, so that both *Freischütz* and *Euryanthe* are foreshadowed in the score. Almost as significant, in view of the future development of Weber's art, is the use of melodrama. Silvana, the title-role, is a mute who conveys what she feels through mime and through the orchestra's expressive way of 'speaking,' chiefly by means of instrumental solos. The need to let instruments act as substitutes for the human voice put Weber on his mettle, and stimulated his imaginative approach to instrumentation.

Weber's first wholly integrated opera in artistic terms, which is still viable today – even though it is hardly ever performed – was *Abu Hassan*, written immediately after *Silvana* in 1810-11 (two further numbers were added in 1812 and in 1823). The ambitious attempt in

Above and right: Designs for a London revival of *Oberon* in 1843: the Garden of the Emir from Act III (*above*) and the Caliph's Harem from Act II (*right*). Made by the Grieve family, these designs were probably based on their scenes for the original production in 1826. Covent Garden was known for the splendor of its sets, but the production of *Oberon* was extremely costly even by their standards. The public was unanimous in its admiration for the scenery and effects. Weber wrote to his wife that it was a complete success, magnificent beyond anything he had ever seen. He was assured that the wild applause for the opera, and particularly for Weber himself, had never been extended to any other composer.

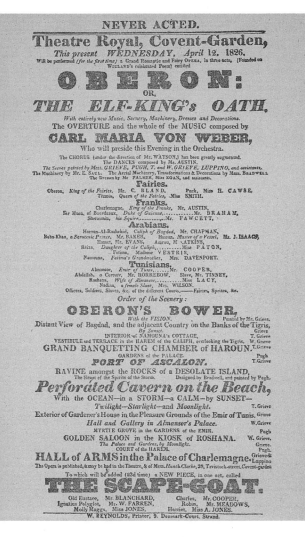

NEVER ACTED.
Theatre Royal, Covent-Garden,
This present WEDNESDAY, *April* 12, 1826,
Will be performed (for the first time) a Grand Romantic and Fairy OPERA, in three acts, (Founded on WIELAND's celebrated Poem) entitled

OBERON:
OR,
THE ELF-KING's OATH,
With entirely new Music, Scenery, Machinery, Dresses and Decorations.
The OVERTURE and the whole of the MUSIC composed by
CARL MARIA VON WEBER,
Who will preside this Evening in the Orchestra.

The CHORUS (under the direction of Mr. WATSON,) has been greatly augmented.
The DANCES composed by Mr. AUSTIN.
The Scenes painted by Mess. GRIEVE, PUGH, T. and W. GRIEVE, LUPPINO, and assistants.
The Machinery by Mr. E. SAUL. The Aerial Machinery, Transformations & Decorations by Mess. BRADWELL.
The Dresses by Mr. PALMER, Miss EGAN, and assistants.

Fairies.
Oberon, *King of the Fairies,* Mr. C. BLAND, Puck, Miss H. CAWSE,
Titania, *Queen of the Fairies,* Miss SMITH.

Franks.
Charlemagne, *King of the Franks,* Mr. AUSTIN,
Sir Huon, *of Bourdeaux, Duke of Guienne,* Mr. BRAHAM,
Sherasmin, *his Squire,* Mr. FAWCETT.

Arabians.
Haroun-Al-Raschied, *Caliph of Bagdad,* Mr. CHAPMAN,
Babe-Khan, *a Saracenic Prince,* Mr. BAKER, Hassan, *Master of a Vessel,* Mr. J. ISAACS,
Hamet, Mr. EVANS, Amrou, M. ATKINS,
Reiza, *Daughter of the Caliph,* Miss PATON,
Fatima, Madame VESTRIS,
Namouna, *Fatima's Grandmother,* Mrs. DAVENPORT.

Tunisians.
Almansor, *Emir of Tunis,* Mr. COOPER,
Abdallah, *a Corsair,* Mr. HORREBOW, Slave, Mr. TINNEY,
Roshana, *Wife of Almansor,* Miss LACY,
Nadina, *a female Slave,* Mrs. WILSON.
Officers, Soldiers, Slaves, &c. of the different Courts, —— Fairies, Sprites, &c.

Order of the Scenery :
OBERON'S BOWER,
With the VISION. Painted by Mr. Grieve.
Distant View of Bagdad, and the adjacent Country on the Banks of the Tigris,
By Sunset. Grieve
INTERIOR of NAMOUNA's COTTAGE, T. Grieve
VESTIBULE and TERRACE in the HAREM of the CALIPH, overlooking the Tigris, T. Grieve
GRAND BANQUETTING CHAMBER of HAROUN. T. Grieve
GARDENS of the PALACE. Pugh
PORT OF ASCALON. T. Grieve
RAVINE amongst the ROCKS of a DESOLATE ISLAND,
The Haunt of the Spirits of the Storm. Designed by Bradwell, and painted by Pugh.
Perforated Cavern on the Beach,
With the OCEAN—a CALM—by SUNSET—
*Twilight—Starlight—*and *Moonlight.* T. Grieve
Exterior of Gardener's House in the Pleasure Grounds of the Emir of Tunis. Grieve
Hall and Gallery in Almansor's Palace. W. Grieve
MYRTLE GROVE in the GARDENS of the EMIR. Pugh
GOLDEN SALOON in the KIOSK of ROSHANA. W. Grieve
The Palace and Gardens, by Moonlight. Grieve.
COURT of the HAREM. Pugh.
HALL of ARMS in the Palace of Charlemagne. Grieve & Luppino
The Opera is published, & may be had in the Theatre, & of Mess. Hunt & Clarke, 38, Tavistock-street, Covent-garden.
To which will be added (23d time) a NEW PIECE, in one act, called
THE SCAPE-GOAT.
Old Eustace, Mr. BLANCHARD, Charles, Mr. COOPER,
Ignatius Polyglot, Mr. W. FARREN, Robin, Mr. MEADOWS,
Molly Maggs, Miss JONES, Harriet, Miss A. JONES.
W. REYNOLDS, Printer, 9, Denmark-Court, Strand.

Above: Playbill for the première of *Oberon* in London, 12 April 1826. Opera in England at this time placed great emphasis on spectacle, and libretto and music were subordinated to amazing stage effects. Weber was forced to try to bring some cohesion to the variety of incident in the libretto of *Oberon* (in Act III alone there were eight scene-changes), and he intended, on his return home, to recast the work completely with added recitatives for production in Germany.

Top right: Pencil drawing of Weber after the portrait by Ferdinand Schimon (1825). Weber became such a popular figure in London at this time that many likenesses were made of him.

Silvana to combine a chivalrous spectacular with folk opera, pantomime, *Singspiel* and *opéra comique* made for a lack of stylistic coherence. In *Abu Hassan*, on the other hand, the composer was able to stick to a single, well-tried formula. The tone of the German *Singspiel* is therefore maintained with a degree of lightness and elegance which Weber had not previously achieved. Moreover, both characters and situations are, for the first time, depicted in an individual, more closely observed and tight-knit way. The piece belongs to the line of 'Turkish' operas which had become popular during the eighteenth century, and it is directly – and sometimes even audibly – modeled on Mozart's *Die Entführung aus dem Serail*. But this is relatively unimportant, for Weber discovered a language of sound in *Abu Hassan* which he developed and diversified in the incidental music for Pius Alexander Wolff's *Preciosa* (1820) and in the unfinished three-act comic opera *Die drei Pintos* (1820-1), but never again significantly altered.

Six years separated *Der Freischütz* from *Abu Hassan*, an unusually long interval for Weber, while the sketching out and elaboration of the new opera occupied three years. That *Der Freischütz* was most carefully planned and prepared is confirmed by its very arrangement, in which traditional elements of the German *Singspiel* and, above all, of *opéra comique* are fused

together to create a new entity. But it is not just the conjunction of these elements – the accurately designed symbolism and dramatic interpretation of the key-signatures, the characterization of individuals and situations by means of different types of musical figures and arias – which represents a new departure. First and foremost, it is the way in which the whole work has been dialectically constructed with a consistent and contrasting emphasis on dramatic conflicts: Heaven and Hell, good and evil are represented as being at once both ethical and natural categories, as good and evil in human terms but also as the demonic and the seductively magical elements in nature. In *Der Freischütz*, nature takes on a Romantically human form, so that what is human becomes inextricably blended with it: man can no longer be distinguished from a nature that is both menacing and protective.

The musical forms that Weber developed to convey this contrast are not only highly effective, but actually bring its dichotomy into the open by musical means for the very first time. Friedrich Kind's libretto was the object of widespread and unjust censure, though Goethe stood up for it. Yet its half-hidden message is brought out on the stage in a uniquely effective way by the music. The actual meaning of the work and its unfailing magic are conveyed in the theater by the pervading mood and character of the opera, which brings to life a set of primeval beliefs about man and nature modified by a Christian outlook.

The way in which Weber used *Singspiel* and *opéra comique*, folkloric naïveté and the pomp of the priests of *Die Zauberflöte* to modulate in musical form the divine power of nature and the abysses of the human spirit with tremendous power and scenic effect – though by no means always with absolute originality – provided a novel factor in the history of music. On the other hand, the emergence of the work as a 'national' opera was mostly a consequence of the historical situation, in which a newly awakened national awareness was in search of an esthetic object with which it could identify.

Weber never succeeded in recapturing the inner and outward consistency of *Freischütz*, though he tried hard and conscientiously to do so in *Euryanthe* and *Oberon*. The choice of basic material for *Euryanthe* and the endless revisions to the libretto indicate that Weber was at least as much to blame as the unskilled author of the text, Helmina von Chézy. There was a clear intention to create a 'grand' opera after the 'popular' *Freischütz*, which had been treated with condescension as 'music for the masses' not only by the conservative and educated section of the public, but also by musicians such as Louis Spohr. It was a matter of bringing the artistic claim implicit in *Der Freischütz* into the open, and doing so by means of the broad and elevated style of grand opera. This clearly appears from the express requests to the author for verse of the highest and most difficult kind. She was able to respond only with the plainest of doggerel. It was even more clearly and radically signaled by the description of the work as a 'Grand Heroic Romantic Opera,' thereby combining in program terms the genres of 'Grand Opera' – a carefully composed form based on mythological or historical material – and 'Romantic Opera' – in other words, opera with spoken dialogue and material drawn from fairytales and ethnic or popular sources. The result was a musical experiment which the conventional and dramatically inept libretto simply failed to support.

In the major scenes of the work, especially at the beginning of Act II, in Lysiart's monologue and his duet with Eglantine, Weber achieved an intensity and refinement of psychological and theatrical characterization as were not to be seen again until Wagner's *Lohengrin*, in those scenes between Ortrud and Telramund which were clearly modeled on the earlier work. The great and unprecedented effect achieved easily surpasses anything in *Der Freischütz* by the power and versatility of its orchestral idiom and its language. It abolishes the frontier between aria and recitative and fully achieves that high degree of integration within a scene that Wagner later aimed at. But the quality is not sustained, and the conventional nature of the libretto rendered relapses into musical convention inevitable.

Conservative critics such as Grillparzer, who firmly held to the ideal of beauty in art, felt that Weber's tendency to 'characterize' was downright criminal: 'Such music is contrary to public order and would generate human monsters if there were any chance that it might eventually become established.' What was involved was the dissolution of traditional forms and Classical periodic formulae in favor of a declamatory melodic approach and a construction of motifs which Schumann, significantly enough in connection with the *Symphonie fantastique* of Berlioz, was to describe soon afterwards as 'musical prose.' Such music has, in fact, not 'become established' even now. Its historical importance lies in its pioneering influence on orchestral style, the construction of scenes, and Wagner's theory of melodic declamation.

Weber had at least set about the composition of *Euryanthe* with certain program conceptions in mind and had retained a considerable say in the elaboration of its text. But *Oberon*, described in the handbill for the first performance as a 'Grand Romantic and Fairy Opera,' turned out to be a matter of adaptation to an alien practice, a form of stage work not in any way viable outside London, with which the composer sought to do his best. The librettist James Robinson Planché, turned *Oberon* into a sort of revue. The specifically English tradition of stage music, which reached back to the masque, had been blended with stage effects from contemporary spectacular shows and elements borrowed from the *opéra comique* and *drame lyrique*, thus producing an utterly disastrous hotchpotch in theatrical terms. Fear that this work as conceived would be suitable only for performance in London and no other operatic center in Europe overshadowed Weber's efforts from the start. With hindsight, it now seems an irony of fate that he should have turned down a simultaneous offer from the Paris Opéra of this commission. This robbed him of his last chance to write an opera within the framework of those French traditions on which he had drawn to a substantial extent in composing both *Der Freischütz* and *Euryanthe*. It would also probably at least have provided him with a theatrically acceptable libretto, possibly like that of Scribe's *La Dame blanche*, based on Sir Walter Scott's novel, which he had seen shortly after its first performance in the setting by Boïeldieu in February 1826 at the Paris Opéra and by which he had been delighted. Nonetheless, in *Oberon* the colorful and exotic sequence of tableaux provided by the action once more released the full splendor of Weber's orchestral color, his genius for generating an exotic background, his ability to convey atmosphere by means of tonal description, and the elegance and lilt characteristic of his use of melody and rhythm.

Right: An anonymous sketch of Weber made while he was in London for the production of *Oberon*. Knowing that he was dying, Weber made the journey in a desperate effort to make some financial provision for his family, but his cheerful, almost daily letters to his wife recorded only the extraordinarily warm and enthusiastic welcome he received everywhere he went.

The score of *Oberon* is undoubtedly the most complex, elaborate and modern that Weber ever wrote. On the other hand, the chaotic nature of the action, innocent of any attempt at sustained logic, put musical characterization and psychological development right out of the question. As part of an ultimately futile attempt to overcome these defects, Weber developed a *leitmotif* technique which went well beyond any earlier use of leading or recall themes. The cipher is Oberon's call on the horn with which the overture starts. It returns in constantly changed and newly modulated forms throughout the opera, always and throughout all its variations as the immutable tone-symbol of the Elvish kingdom and the power of magic, together with their impact on the world of men. Wagner was to learn from this practice. Yet the sweep of the music, which betrays no sense of weariness at all – an extraordinary fact, seeing that the com-

without the example of Weber's virtuoso keyboard technique. Weber, as a theater manager, stage director and writer about music, was Wagner's great model, the prototype of the musician with an all-round education and a philosophical turn of mind. Weber's unrelenting and heroic struggle for professional integrity and self-discipline – despite his nomadic background and scanty education, his materially precarious existence until he had reached the age of thirty and an incurable illness – stands as one of the monuments to the greatness of human nature.

The autobiographical sketch which Weber wrote in 1818 closed with the words ' . . . and when once you come to lay a stone over my remains you may truly write upon it, "He who lies here strove to deal honestly and cleanly with mankind and with art."' His death mask speaks of infinite suffering, but also of repose and release.

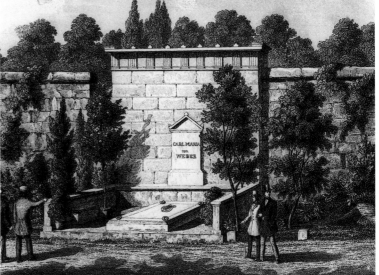

Left: Weber's earnest desire to be reunited with his wife and two small boys was not to be fulfilled; he died on 5 June 1826. Two thousand mourners attended his funeral, and many of London's leading singers took part in Mozart's Requiem. In 1844 Wagner arranged for the body to be brought back to Germany on board the English ship *John Bull*. After a momentous reception in Hamburg (*left*) the coffin was transferred to Dresden for burial (*below*). Music from *Euryanthe* was played, and Wagner, much moved, conducted a chorus he had written for the occasion.

poser was mortally ill – and the attempts to restore some inner unity with the help of *leitmotifs* failed to salvage *Oberon* as a work for the stage – or, at any rate, as an opera in the accepted sense. As a piece of artifice, however, belonging to the theater of total illusion and enchantment, it was not to lack a future.

Weber today survives through modern performances of only a handful of pieces: a single opera, the overtures to *Euryanthe* and *Oberon*, a couple of clarinet concertos and a few piano and chamber-music compositions. This is considerably less than remains of any other of the major nineteenth-century composers, but the new way that he opened up left its mark on the musical history of his century. Berlioz and Wagner learned from Weber what the orchestra could do and the principles of what could be stated through musical drama, while the piano styles of Chopin and Liszt are inconceivable

A Revolution in Wind Instruments

The development of the symphony orchestra, prompted by the growth of public concerts, was accompanied by technical improvements, particularly to wind instruments, as composers made increasing demands on players.

All wind instruments, basically, are tubes in which a column of air is made to vibrate, or pulsate, to produce a sound. In the case of nearly all 'brass' instruments, the biggest limitation had been the range of pitched notes they could play. As long as they consisted of a tube of unvarying length, there was only a handful of notes that could be sounded on them with any degree of ease or reliability: the 'fundamental' or tonic note, and four or five other notes belonging to the same harmonic progression. The trombone overcame this problem with its slide valve mechanism, by which the player could adjust the effective length of the tube, so increasing the range of notes. But the 'natural' trumpet and horn enjoyed no such flexibility. The horn had a wider range of notes, as its greater length and the shape of its tube meant that it was using a higher section of the harmonic series, and although the highest notes would naturally be out of tune, an expert horn-player could make adjustments by skillful blowing or by placing a hand in the instrument's 'bell'; but the average orchestral player could not be relied upon for this kind of expertise. In addition, 'crooks,' additional lengths of tubing, could be attached to the instrument to change its basic tuning, but composers were still faced with the problem of writing for horns that were virtually limited to the harmonic notes of one or two keys. The real breakthrough came around 1820, with the introduction of valves, that shut off, or opened up, sections of tubing at the press of a finger, so dramatically increasing the horn's range of notes. Schumann in his *Konzertstück* of 1849 for four horns was one of the first to demonstrate the tremendous new range and versatility of valve horns.

Improvements to the clarinet took a different path. Keys had been added to woodwind instruments since the Renaissance, to facilitate the opening and closing of the holes by which the effective playing length of the tube is altered, but such arrangements were limited and random in their application. The clarinet had been invented at the end of the seventeenth century, and the wide compass in each of its registers gave it a greater range than the flute or oboe, but also led to difficulties of fingering and problems of correct intonation. However, around 1832, the German flautist Theobald Boehm designed, for the flute, a new and much better system of levers and keys for obtaining a wide range of notes, all of more or less equal tonal quality. His system worked so well that it was soon adapted for other woodwind instruments, none of which benefited more from the Boehm system than the clarinet.

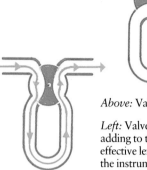

Above: Valve closed.

Left: Valve open, adding to the effective length of the instrument.

Above: Most modern horns have rotary valves, though a few are made with piston valves, like a trumpet or tuba. Rotary valves turn inside the tubing, cutting off or opening up lengths as shown in the two diagrams. The depression of each of the levers controlling the valves alters the basic pitch of the instrument, making it possible to obtain notes outside a single harmonic series, and so allowing it to be played almost equally well in different keys.

Left: A natural horn that could be fitted with crooks to give it a wider range of notes. It was made in Paris, *c.*1826, and was a royal gift to the famous virtuoso Giovanni Puzzi. The beautiful pattern of oak leaves round the bell is a reminder of the horn's traditional use in the hunt. In France, especially, hunting horns were played with skill and panache, which led to their general introduction into the orchestra during the eighteenth century.

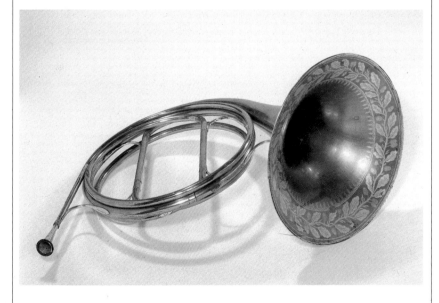

Above: A modern valve horn, showing the keys the player depresses to operate the valves. Such an instrument has a maximum length of tubing of about 5.2 metres (17 feet), and a range of 3½ octaves. Despite its obvious advantages, some musicians have claimed that the valve horn does not have the pure tone of the natural horn. Brahms disliked it for this reason, and in this century Britten specified the use of a natural horn in his *Serenade for Tenor, Horn and Strings*.

Above: An old helical hunting horn (*top*) and two diagrams showing the use of crooks. Each crook added would lower the pitch of the instrument. Though its tightly coiled tube made the hunting horn compact, it was limited to only one or two notes. An improvement was the 'open-hooped' hunting horn (*left*, in Schwind's drawing), which originated in France at the end of the sixteenth century.

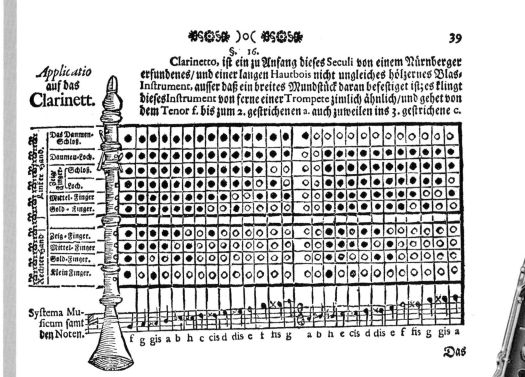

§. 16.

Clarinetto, ist ein zu Anfang dieses Seculi von einem Nürnberger erfundenes/ und einer langen Hautbois nicht ungleiches hölzernes Blas-Instrument, außer daß ein breites Mundstück daran befestiget ist; es klingt dieses Instrument von ferne einer Trompete ziemlich ähnlich/ und gehet von dem Tenor f. bis zum 2. gestrichenen a. auch zuweilen ins 3. gestrichene c.

Applicatio auf das **Clarinett.**

Above: Fingering system for the clarinet, 1732, using black and white circles to represent closed and open holes, with the resultant notes shown beneath. The first clarinets were made around the year 1700 by the Nuremberg instrument-makers, Johann and Jacob Denner. The clarinet's most distinctive features are the wide mouthpiece with a single reed (oboes and bassoons, the other reed instruments to survive from the Middle Ages and Renaissance, have double reeds bound together) and the cylindrical bore.

Far left: Cross-section of a clarinet, showing the cylindrical bore; the tube is of constant diameter from mouthpiece to the start of the bell – again unlike that of the oboe or bassoon, which gradually widens in a conical shape from a narrow opening where the reed is inserted into the top of the tube.

Left: Two early clarinets, showing clearly the simple key systems they were equipped with. The left-hand one was made by the Denners and so represents the instrument – looking quite like a large recorder – in its original form.

Left: A modern clarinet. The clarinet's reed, usually cut and shaped from natural cane, is bound by a metal ligature and covers the aperture in the mouthpiece (*inset*). The player blows against the curved top edge of the reed, which vibrates and sets in motion the column of air in the tube. The system of rings and levers – which has been considerably modified since Boehm's day – enables many of the lower notes in each register to be obtained using the little finger of either hand, and it also permits many other alternative fingerings, allowing the player to execute brilliant passage-work throughout the large compass of the instrument.

140

Almost all wood-wind instruments play in two registers, the lower based on the fundamental note of the harmonic series, and the higher on the second note (one octave above the fundamental); this is usually obtained by 'over-blowing,' altering the pressure of air, or of the lips on the reed, and opening, or part-opening, a hole near the instrument's mouthpiece; some-times notes based on higher harmonics can also be obtained in similar ways. The holes in the body of a recorder, a flute, an oboe or a bassoon are therefore needed to produce inter-mediate notes spanning an octave. However, the cylindrical bore of the clarinet causes it to miss out the register based on the second harmonic, and the upper register obtained by overblowing is based on the third note of the harmonic series, so that it is pitched a twelfth higher than the lower register. While this gives the instrument its com-pass of over three octaves, it also leaves far more intermediate notes to be obtained in each register, and in its early form the clarinet was very difficult to play in tune. Even the modern instrument presents problems in remote keys, and orchestral players normally have a clarinet tuned in B flat, which is suitable for playing music with flats in the key signature, and one in A for music with sharps. The smaller E flat clarinet, used to great effect by Richard Strauss and Janáček among others, still has the shrill sound that originally gave the instrument its name, while the bass clarinet (a member of the orchestra since the time of Wagner), like the older basset-horn, extends down-wards the mellow lower range of the instrument.

Right: Three more eighteenth-century clarinets, each with a slightly different key system and mouth-piece, and (*bottom left*) a picture of a clarinetist of about 1740. A typical clarinet part from the end of the eighteenth century is that in Beethoven's op.11 Trio in B flat for piano, clarinet and cello (*bottom right*). Unlike Mozart's clarinet music, which always exploited the instrument's lowest register, this is almost entirely confined to the upper register.

141

HECTOR BERLIOZ

JULIAN RUSHTON

Opposite: Hector Berlioz (1803-69), winner of the Prix de Rome in 1830, painted by Emile Signol. It was usual for the scholars at the Académie de France in Rome to have their portraits painted to hang in the refectory of the Villa Medici. In the weeks before his premature departure from Rome in 1832 Berlioz sat for this portrait by his fellow-student Signol.

Hector Berlioz belongs to no school, and resists categorization more fiercely, perhaps, than any other major composer. As a result, he has been subjected to an exceptional amount of vilification by critics, academics and fellow-composers; his melodies, his forms, his technical competence have all been savagely attacked. No doubt, his critics were wrong; the originality and vitality of his ideas demanded novel means of expression which affected the fundamental elements of musical language. But the misunderstanding may be partly excused in that Berlioz devised no conventions for his own use. The language he forged depended to an unusual extent upon the subject-matter of his works, all of which are related to a dramatic or poetic theme. This theme determines the manner of each work, so that there is no clearly defined development from an early period, through the middle of his career, to a later style; his works never repeat the inventions, harmonic and melodic or formal, of their predecessors.

Berlioz's proud independence and musical style are ultimately inexplicable phenomena of character. To some extent, however, they can be accounted for by the peculiar circumstances of his upbringing. He was born on 11 December 1803 at La Côte-St-André, a small town in Dauphiné, in south-east France. The nearest large town, Grenoble, was by no means the center of industry and learning that it is today. The savagery of the Revolution was a recent memory; France was generally at war, under the leadership of Napoleon, for whom Berlioz developed an abiding admiration. But he was confined to a province distant from anything like the serious musical activity normally appropriate for the development of a young talent.

Talent he possessed in abundance: he had energy, an excellent ear and the gift of learning quickly how to play musical instruments. What he lacked was experience, which was not to be had. The music of the district consisted of the town band, whose military music is doubtless recalled in Berlioz's admirable marches; the music of the church, usually of a fairly rustic quality, its melodies adapted from old plainchant or, on occasion, from modern comic operas; and the folk music of the region, which certainly affected his melodic idiom. There was amateur music-making in his father's house, but it was not of high quality. Some music circulated in printed form, usually songs in the popular

but hardly complex genre of the 'Romance,' and occasionally selections from operas (but these can have given little idea of what an opera was like). There was no orchestra, nor even a piano. The cultural life of France had been tending to greater centralization ever since the time of Louis XIV, and the destruction of cultural life in the regions during the Revolution had enhanced this tendency.

Berlioz's talent, therefore, was left to derive what nourishment it could from rather feeble fare. He learned the flute and the guitar to a good standard; he studied what music he could and read a couple of books on harmony, but he was not encouraged to regard music as anything other than a hobby. His mother considered the profession barely respectable; his father, a doctor and man of real sensitivity, refused to recognize the force of his son's vocation. He educated the boy as well as he could; he taught him Latin and fostered in him the love of Virgil, which bore fruit, forty years later, in his largest work, *Les Troyens*. Doubtless he smiled on Hector's efforts at composition. The chamber music Berlioz said that he wrote is lost, but a song survives, 'Le Dépit de la bergère,' which may have been written when he was only sixteen. It is a setting of a typically fatuous pastoral plaint, but it has three remarkable features. One is the freshness of its melody, which may refer to folk models but which had sufficient Berliozian character for the composer to remember it and use it again in his last opera, *Béatrice et Bénédict*, in 1862 (it is the delightful 'Sicilienne'). Another is the addition of a coda to the simple structure of repeated music for each poetic strophe; this foreshadows many later examples of Berlioz's extensions to simple, traditional forms. The third is the clumsiness of the piano part. Virtually every composer learns to combine sounds in harmony by using the keyboard instrument. Most have been skilled performers; even those who were not, like Wagner, were brought up to use the instrument. Berlioz stands almost alone in his isolation from this educational aid. He was to argue that he had an advantage of freedom from the ingrained habits, the clichés, which the piano certainly encouraged in many of his contemporaries, but he also suffered from the fact that his music sounds poor, even crude, on the piano – whether it was written for the instrument or transcribed.

143

• Berlioz in Paris •

Thus when Berlioz came to Paris at the age of eighteen, destined for the study of medicine, he was more ignorant than any other great composer at a similar age. He had never heard of Bach and Beethoven; he knew little if anything of Haydn and Mozart. Of Gluck, his life-long idol, and other operatic music, he knew little, although he made up for this rapidly by reading scores in the library of the Conservatoire and by attending the theater as often as he could. In 1823 he made the acquaintance of Jean-François Le Sueur, who was undoubtedly eccentric as a musician and theorist, but was also sensitive enough to perceive that Berlioz had genius, and to encourage him, first by providing him with a teacher of harmony and then by teaching him himself. A couple of modest songs published about 1823 proclaim the composer as 'M. Le Sueur's pupil.'

At the same time, Berlioz got to know the operas of the French tradition. Second only to Gluck in his estimation were the French operas of an *émigré* Italian, Gasparo Spontini. Spontini added to a Gluckian vigor in melody a richness of instrumental color and a grandeur of design in the accumulation of huge musical and dramatic tableaux, which foreshadow the grand opera of Rossini and Meyerbeer; it is by no means an outrageous opinion to regard Act II of Spontini's *La Vestale* as one of the finest operatic acts of the entire school. Then there was Weber, performed in Paris in corrupt versions, but whose sweet and passionate melodies,

electrifying rhythms, masterful instrumentation and evocation of heroism and horror were irrepressible. Gluck made Berlioz a Classicist, apostle of clarity and richness of expression; Weber made him a Romantic, emotionally charged and including in his view of beauty the demonic and the grotesque. Berlioz, like many of his contemporaries (Schubert, Mendelssohn or Schumann, for example), veers between these complementary, and at times contradictory, extremes.

Encouraged by Le Sueur, Berlioz entered for the Prix de Rome in 1826, but the competition for this coveted prize, which guaranteed income for five years as well as requiring the student to travel to Italy and Germany, began with exercises in counterpoint that Berlioz failed dismally. He then formally entered the Conservatoire to study counterpoint with Reicha, who coached him well enough to pass the first stage of the competition thereafter. But Berlioz had to try four times before, in 1830, his entry for the main part of the competition, a dramatic cantata, was awarded the first prize. In 1827 his cantata *La Mort d'Orphée* was declared unplayable, at least on the piano. In 1828 he came second; in 1829 he confidently expected the prize, and in his cantata *La Mort de Cléopâtre* composed with unfettered ardor the scenes where the Egyptian Queen ponders on her unworthiness and meets her death. The result was that no prize was awarded; unfettered Berlioz was too strong meat for the examiners.

In the meantime he suffered several more blows of a different kind. Musical, dramatic and human experiences came thick and fast, particularly in 1827. In that year he encountered the symphonies and overtures of Beethoven in masterly and carefully prepared performances at the Conservatoire under Habeneck; he read Goethe's *Faust* in a new French translation by Gérard de Nerval; he witnessed plays by Shakespeare, given in English (of which he knew little); and he fell in love with the leading actress, Harriet Smithson. Although they did not meet for a few years, he pursued her with his addresses, and her rejection of them inspired him, early in 1830, to complete his best-known work, the *Episode in the Life of an Artist*, subtitled 'Fantastic Symphony in Five Parts.'

Most of Berlioz's earlier works are vocal. In 1824 he completed a Mass: only the 'Resurrexit' survives, a raw piece whose best ideas were used later in various works including the Requiem and *Te Deum*. The following year a cantata on the topical subject of the liberation of Greece shows a marked improvement in the handling of large musical forces, and Berlioz followed it, still before his formal enrolment at the Conservatoire, with an opera, *Les Francs-juges*, which survives in fragmentary form. The overture is well known and makes its points, again, by covering a large canvas with correspondingly huge gestures; lacking subtlety, it nevertheless memorably combines episodes of grandeur, mourning and pulsating excitement, the last in a huge crescendo, outdoing Rossini's, which at the climax bursts into the apotheosis of a pre-

Far right: Study of a dead man by Théodore Géricault, *c*.1818, one of many studies made in Paris hospitals and mortuaries for his painting *The Raft of the Medusa*. In his *Mémoires* Berlioz gives a vivid description of his initial revulsion at the sights of the dissecting-room at the Hospice de la Pitié where he was to pursue his medical studies. When he finally abandoned these, his father cut off his allowance, causing him considerable hardship.

viously gentle melody. The overture is partly based upon a device common in Berlioz's symphonic movements, the use of slow music in the course of a fast movement. The central episode could almost pass as a slow movement; the wind melody is written in huge note-values, so that despite the rapid pulse (repeated in the string accompaniment), it emerges broad and mournful. Near the end, a mighty phrase from the trombones interrupts the music, again in huge note-values, so that the headlong rush to a finish is temporarily halted.

Berlioz's next overture, *Waverley*, is quite different in spirit and form. Prefaced by some lines of Scott ('Dreams of love and Lady's charms/ Give place to honour and to arms'), it makes no attempt to reflect events in the novel but is an exercise of relatively traditional design. It is Berlioz's only independent instrumental work between the early chamber music and the *Fantastique*, and it shows how he could control his invention within a fresh approach to con-

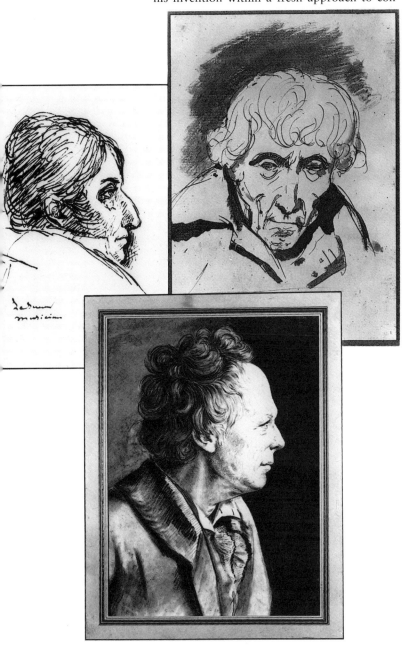

ventions. Nonetheless, his best music of the late 1820s was vocal. In late 1828 he began to set the lyrical scenes from Goethe's *Faust*, Part I, and published the result as *Huit scènes de Faust*, op.1. However, he quickly became dissatisfied with it and withdrew it from circulation, finally bestowing the proud title 'Opus One' upon *Waverley*. Berlioz did not, however, let the music escape into other works, as was his wont; it awaited its hour, which came seventeen years later. Revised and improved in several ways, the music is nevertheless virtually the same when it appears in one of his greatest works, *La Damnation de Faust*.

It is in the prize cantata of 1829, *Cléopâtre*, that the music-dramatist in Berlioz comes into his own. Significantly, it seems to have been inspired by Shakespeare; at its head appears a quotation from the scene in which Juliet ponders her living burial among her dead ancestors. The scene in which Cleopatra addresses the shade of her ancestors inspired accents of a melancholy grandeur, a broadly conceived melodic line over slow-moving, yet restless, harmonies and a persistent yet irregular throb, which Berlioz thought good enough to use, virtually unaltered, in his monodrama *The Return to Life*. The scene in which Cleopatra dies, and the music disintegrates to broken murmurs in the bass instruments after a most realistic imitation of the spasms induced by poison, is possibly more daring than analogous scenes in later works; small wonder the whole thing was too much for the examiners. Also in 1829 Berlioz composed a set of nine songs to words from Thomas Moore, the *Mélodies irlandaises* (later called *Irlande*). These include a few real gems such as 'La Belle voyageuse,' in which his penchant for unusual modulation and irregular phrase-lengths is perfectly balanced in a serene melodic flow. The collection ends with the extraordinary 'Elégie en prose,' in which the voice (a tenor) sings in a declamatory style which never degenerates into the conventional gestures of recitative, while the piano develops a feverish and violently unsettled harmonic background. It was, Berlioz tells us in his memoirs, the outpouring

Above: Cléopâtre et le paysan, 1838, by Delacroix: the asp is brought to Cleopatra and she contemplates death. This was the subject of Berlioz's Prix de Rome cantata in 1829, to which he gave the epigraph from *Romeo and Juliet*, 'How if, when I am laid into the tomb.'

Right: Harriet Smithson as Juliet in the English Theatre Company's production of *Romeo and Juliet* in Paris in 1827.

of his innermost soul, tormented by his love for Harriet; the uniqueness of this song he acknowledged by never performing it, and destroying, to our loss, the beginnings of an attempt to orchestrate it. The piano part is unidiomatic, yet Berlioz thought it best if the singer should accompany himself, a near-impossible demand.

• *Symphonie fantastique* •

Usually the most original works of great artists can be seen, with hindsight, to have been in some sense inevitable, part of the pattern of the artist's development. Berlioz's *Symphonie fantastique* is not quite without precedent, nor is it unrelated to works contemporary with it, or in its recent past. Nevertheless, it must be considered one of the most unforeseeable of all major musical works, and it blazed new paths, filling the ear with novel combinations, to a degree hardly experienced again until Stravinsky scandalized the world with his *Rite of Spring*. Berlioz's symphony created no international stir of that order; but as an artistic gesture it is of comparable force. In the years before it, nothing directly anticipates either its expressive nature or its form. What occurred, early in 1830, was a fusion of experiences as much of life as of music, and this fusion created its own, unprecedented mold.

The symphony is nowhere operatic, but it is dramatic, and the high points of the drama are embodied in expressive instrumental music; the program, integral to the conception, acts, Berlioz said, like the spoken dialogue in an opera, in that it provides the motivation and explains and justifies the mood of the successive movements. It is so important a document, provided by Berlioz himself, that it merits quotation in full:

'Part I: *Reveries – Passions*. The author imagines that a young musician, affected by that malady of the spirit which a celebrated writer has called the 'flux of passion,' sees for the first time a woman in whom all the charms of the ideal being of his imagination are united, and falls distractedly in love. By some strange mechanism of his mind, the image of the beloved always enters his thoughts joined to a musical idea whose character, passionate but noble and reticent, he finds comparable to the character which he believes to be hers. This melodic reflection and the original image pursue him incessantly as a double *idée fixe*. This is the reason for the repeated appearances, in every movement of the symphony, of the melody which begins the first allegro. The passage from this state of melancholy reverie, interrupted by bursts of irrational joy, to that of delirious passion, is the material of the first movement, with its accents of rage and jealousy, its recurrent tenderness, its tears, its religious consolations.

'Part II: *A Ball*. The musician finds himself in the most diverse situations life can offer, in the middle of the tumult of a festival, in the peaceful contemplation of the beauties of nature; but everywhere, in the city, in the fields, the beloved image comes before him and troubles his mind.

'Part III: *Scene in the Fields*. In the country one evening he hears in the distance two herdsmen calling cows; this bucolic duet, the surroundings, the soft rustling of trees gently disturbed by the breeze, and some cause for hopefulness which he has lately discovered, all combine to induce in his heart an unwonted calm and to give his ideas

a more cheerful color. He ponders on his isolation; he hopes soon to be no longer lonely . . . But if she should deceive him! . . . This blend of hope and fear, these thoughts of happiness ruffled by dark forebodings, form the subject of the adagio. At the end, one of the herdsmen takes up the call again; the other does not reply . . . distant rumblings of thunder . . . solitude . . . silence . . .

Above: The rue de la Paix, the fashionable center of Paris in 1830, the year in which Berlioz at last won the Prix de Rome.

Left: Harriet Smithson as Miss Dorillon in a comedy by Elizabeth Inchbald. She was the rage of intellectual (and especially Romantic) Paris, but Berlioz felt for her something more abiding and possessive. They did ultimately marry in 1833, but for several years – without ever meeting her – he worshiped her as an ideal. It was with the hope of bringing his name to her ears that, in spite of opposition from Cherubini, he organized his first – and only partially successful – concert at the Conservatoire in 1828.

'Part IV: *March to Execution*. Having learned for certain that his love is rejected, the composer poisons himself with opium. The dose of the narcotic, too weak to bring death, plunges him into deep sleep accompanied by horrible fantasies. He dreams that he has killed his beloved, that he is condemned, taken to the guillotine, and witnesses his own execution. The procession advances to the sounds of a march which is now somber and wild, now brilliant and stately, in which the dull tread of heavy steps follows without interruption on the liveliest clamor. At the end of the march, the first four bars of the *idée fixe* reappear like a last memory of love, interrupted by the *coup de grâce*.

'Part V: *Dream of a Sabbath Night*. He sees himself at the Sabbath, amidst a troop of horrific ghosts, sorcerers, and monsters of every kind, assembled for his burial. Strange noises, groans, bursts of laughter, distant cries to which other cries seem to respond. The beloved melody comes again, but it has lost its character of nobility and reticence; it is no more than a vulgar dance tune, trivial and grotesque; it is she, coming to the Sabbath. Uproar of delight at her arrival . . . she mingles with the demonic orgy . . . funeral knell, burlesque parody of the *Dies irae*. Round dance of the Sabbath. The Sabbath round and the *Dies irae* combined.'

Various literary precedents can be traced for Berlioz's ideas in this work, which tend to reinforce the importance of the program to the

Below right: The manuscript program for the *Symphonie fantastique: Episode in the Life of an Artist*, which was distributed to the audience at performances. Slight changes were made to different editions which relate to the changing relationship between Berlioz and Harriet Smithson.

Below: Berlioz's listing of the orchestra required to perform the *Symphonie fantastique*. For the first performance of the work in 1830 Berlioz collected an orchestra of 130 players, but at the rehearsal chaos ensued and the concert was canceled.

whole: Victor Hugo's *Last Day of a Condemned Man*, an imaginary monologue; the *Confessions of an Opium Eater* by de Quincey, translated into French by Alfred de Musset; Goethe's 'Walpurgisnacht' in *Faust*, in which Gretchen appears, translated into a witch; and Chateaubriand, the father of French Romanticism, with his 'flux of passions,' to which Berlioz explicitly refers in the program. Such elements distance the work sharply from the obvious musical precedent, Beethoven's symphonies (the 'Scene in the Fields' clearly draws on the second movement of the 'Pastoral'). Rather like Wagner, Berlioz felt that to continue Beethoven required the hidden 'subject' of expressiveness to be brought into the open. He always intended the program to be available to audiences when the symphony was performed. If nothing else, it is needed to explain the *idée fixe*, the recurring melody that seems to belong to no movement except the first. However much we may enjoy the symphony 'purely,' as music, the experience is no more complete without an understanding of the autobiographical-programmatic background

than would be an opera without knowledge of the plot. Nevertheless, Berlioz wrote no more symphonies with programs of this type.

What of the music? Because it embodies what seemed to him the most significant events of his life to date, it incorporates a multiplicity of elements. There is no evidence that any movement apart from the 'March' existed before the symphony was composed, but that a *Faust* ballet had been burning in Berlioz's mind cannot be without significance; the second and last movements are both dances. The 'March' is in fact the instrumental element of an opera – quite literally, as it is taken (apart from the moment of execution) note for note from *Les Francs-juges*. Song appears at the very opening. Berlioz states that he took the melody which begins the symphony from a song he wrote in childhood to a text by Florian from *Estelle et Némorin* (he had also begun work on an opera on this subject in the early 1820s). Estelle was also the name of his first love, and the vernal freshness of the music embodies innocence, anguish and the pangs of young love. With the

allegro come the volcanic passions of a maturer lover, tenderness and jealousy. Berlioz conveys the artist's obsession with the beloved and his alternating moods by a novel structure. The melody representing the beloved – the *idée fixe* – sings freely forth (it too is based on a vocal original, the Prix de Rome cantata *Herminie* of 1828). It makes areas of musical stability, between which the orchestra, barely able to produce another melodic shape but continually obsessed with fragments of the *idée fixe*, engages in vehement, passionate and disturbing developments.

Later it is the *idée fixe* which causes disturbance. In the second movement it is introduced by a sudden lowering of the musical temperature, then integrated fairly closely into the

Right: Engraving after Lami, *c.*1840, of singers receiving an ovation at the Théâtre Italien, scene of another fiasco in the history of the *Symphonie fantastique.* Now married to Miss Smithson, Berlioz arranged a concert at the theater, scene of some of her earlier triumphs. The very long program was to end with the *Symphonie fantastique* and included Mme Dorval in an excerpt from *Antony* by Dumas, Harriet in Act IV of *Hamlet* and Liszt playing Weber's *Konzertstück.* Harriet was outshone by Dorval, who had taken pains to provide tickets for her claque. The concert being prolonged, at midnight, their contracts fulfilled, the theater orchestra walked out, leaving only the handful of extra players Berlioz had engaged himself. His fury can be imagined: the symphony could not take place.

mood of the ball. In the 'Scene in the Fields,' however, the *idée fixe* episode shatters the rural calm; an irruption of passionate recitative in the bass instruments punctuates and finally overwhelms the cool, distant playing of the melody in the woodwind. In the 'March,' the *idée fixe* is part of the added coda, a last memory before the guillotine falls. In the last movement it appears after an introduction of haunting mystery and staggering musical originality (which, contrary to legend, is not just a matter of orchestration, but of the music that is orchestrated). The melody is cruelly burlesqued, as is the *Dies irae.* The 'Sabbath round,' which forms the bulk of the second half of the movement, implies more burlesque through being composed, with much decorum but occasional rude comments from the brass, as an academically correct fugue. This last movement also creates its own form out of the musical material suggested to Berlioz by the scene; indeed the program becomes a sort of elementary musical analysis, with its reference to a procedure of which Berlioz was very fond, the climax through simultaneous playing of two different themes.

That the *Symphonie fantastique* remains an intriguing, and at best a satisfying work, must result from it being a coherent ordering of the composer's disordered passions. It was actually written after his infatuation for Harriet had abated, at least for the time being; he had heard scandalous rumors (quite unfounded) about her, with which he no doubt justified to himself a very natural attachment to a more accessible object. This was the brilliant young pianist Marie Moke, whose affections Berlioz seduced from Ferdinand Hiller. With Berlioz winning the Prix de Rome in 1830 and attracting much attention through the first performance of the *Fantastique,* Camille, as Marie was called, was given permission by her mother to become engaged to him.

Paris, which for years had appeared indifferent to the genius in its midst, and was to be so again, seemed ripe for conquest in 1830. The severe régime of the restored Bourbons was overthrown in the July Revolution; Berlioz, as soon as he escaped from the confinement in which he wrote his Prix de Rome cantata, vigorously embraced the revolutionary cause. The success of Victor Hugo's *Hernani* seemed to have undermined the neoclassical establishment in the theater; there must have seemed every reason, to Berlioz, to suppose that musical bastions of academicism would also fall.

• Italy •

Ironically, Berlioz's success was his undoing. Having won the prize, he was obliged to go forthwith to Rome. He fought against this enforced exile and delayed it as long as he could; both his personal and his artistic life stood to lose ground by it. But his efforts were in vain. His prize had reconciled his family to his musical career, but he could ill afford to lose his pension, and Camille's mother would have broken the engagement if he had defied authority.

Early in 1831 Berlioz arrived at the Villa Medici in Rome, where, as he bitterly pointed out, there was absolutely nothing for a musician to learn. Italian opera interested him very little; and there was plenty of it in Paris. Italian church music was terrible and instrumental music virtually non-existent. So at least it seemed, excusably, to one who had fought artistic battles in Paris. The real disasters, however, were that Berlioz lost touch with vital musical developments in the French capital (which, in turn, was prepared to forget him); and that Camille's mother scarcely waited until he had reached Italy before marrying off her daughter to a safer

Right: Perseus with the head of Medusa by Benvenuto Cellini. Berlioz had long been struck by certain episodes in Cellini's life – perhaps seeing in the frustrations and opposition Cellini had faced similarities to his own – not least in the preparation of the opera *Benvenuto Cellini*, in which the final scene depicts the casting of this statue of Perseus. In his *Mémoires* he wrote: 'I shall never forget the horror of those three months . . . .' The opera's failure was a blow from which his prestige never fully recovered.

Below: Childe Harold's Pilgrimage by Turner, after Byron's poem. Although regarding himself during his time in Italy as a wasted exile, Berlioz was receptive to the beauty and atmosphere of his surroundings. *Harold en Italie* was the fruit of his wanderings in the Abruzzi.

prospect, Camille Pleyel, the manufacturer of pianos. In his memoirs Berlioz relates how he embarked on a return journey, intent on murdering the lot of them and then killing himself, and how at a critical moment his sense of humor got the better of him, and he desisted.

The value of Italy to Berlioz was a fund of experiences on which he later drew as material for art. Like the program of the *Fantastique*, it was an experience of life; the art of Italy made a relatively slight impression. When denying that the Sistine frescoes had inspired him in his Requiem he remarked that he had always been indifferent to conventional beauty. If the art of the Italian Renaissance seemed conventional, the music of nineteenth-century opera was anathema. Berlioz considered opera to be a dramatic form, and he found most Italian examples to be inept or, in the case of the *Romeo and Juliet* opera of Bellini, a defilement of the masterpieces on which they were based. Italian folk music, however, he loved, and it appears from time to time in his works, particularly that of the *pifferari*, the bagpipers of the mountainous region inland from Rome. Whenever he could, he escaped to the hills, usually on foot, carrying his guitar. The Italian sections of his memoirs are among the best; his irritation at his exile competes creatively against his fascination with the light, the scenery and the people (including the bandits).

Berlioz composed relatively little in Italy, and nothing with an Italian theme. The overture *Le Roi Lear* (1831) is his second big Shakespearian piece (it was preceded by a fantasia for orchestra on *The Tempest*). It is his best essay in a

Beethovenian manner. Berlioz did not supply a program, but the music certainly reflects scenes in the play without following their order strictly. The turbulent emotions of various characters represented by musical images – the sonorous bass theme for the King, the plaintive oboe for Cordelia – appear without the tragic framework of, say, Beethoven's *Coriolan*. By contrast the overture *Rob Roy* of the same year is entertaining but loosely made. Berlioz withdrew it after one performance and never returned to Scott for inspiration.

The other main work of the Italian visit was a revision to parts of the *Fantastique* and the composition of its sequel. The complete *Episode in the Life of an Artist* has two parts, the sufferings and near-suicide of the hero in the symphony, and his recovery in the sequel, which Berlioz originally called *The Return to Life*. This piece, usually known by its later title *Lélio*, is hardly a musical work at all. It has six musical numbers, but they were apparently all composed earlier and for quite different contexts. Two come from the 1827 cantata *La Mort d'Orphée* and one from *Cléopâtre*; the last is the 1830 *Tempest* fantasia. What was newly conceived in this was the spoken monologue which introduces each musical number. It acts as a new form of program, motivating the miscellaneous musical items, but it is far more than that. Besides bringing his hero/self back from the edge of the grave into a mental state in which he can work (by attending a rehearsal of his own fantasia on *The Tempest*), Berlioz develops his esthetic credo, proclaiming music's freedom, and vilifying 'academics' (his lines on the despoilers or 'correctors' of masterpieces such as Beethoven's symphonies caused grave offence, for they were a transparent reference to the influential critic F. J. Fétis). He declares his preference for life in the hills (a 'Song of the brigands' follows) and proclaims the gospel of Shakespeare. Despite occasional lapses into forlorn love, the message is remarkably positive. Like the *Huit scènes de Faust*, which range from music for full orchestra and chorus to a song for voice and guitar, *Lélio* is a musical anthology with no pretence at organic unity. Berlioz performed it several times with some success and without apparent fear of the ridicule which has often greeted it since.

The major musical results of Berlioz's visit to Italy appeared after his return to Paris in 1832. His first acts were to arrange for a performance of the revised symphony, with its sequel, and to resume his courtship of Harriet, whom he finally married in 1833. He managed to obtain dispensation from the obligation on him, as a Rome prizewinner, to spend a year in Germany, where his music was later so well received. For the moment to succeed in Paris was of paramount importance. It was normal for a winner of the Prix de Rome to be commissioned to write at least one opera, but Berlioz had difficulty finding an attractive subject; moreover he had acquired such a reputation as a dangerous eccentric that established poets and operatic managers feared to be involved with him. In the

Above: Dance by Night in the Piazza Barberini, Rome, c.1821 by Bartolomeo Pinelli. It was such a carnival scene as this that Berlioz had witnessed in Rome and written into Act II of *Benvenuto Cellini*. It caused him to despair when the conductor, Habeneck, failed to catch the lively pace of the dance, the *saltarello*. Some years later Berlioz reworked the main theme into the *Carnaval romain* overture, which was generally received with great enthusiasm.

Left: The costume from the carnival scene for Gilbert Duprez, who sang the title-role in the original *Benvenuto Cellini*. The first performance in Paris in 1838 was energetically hissed, and only two more were given before Duprez abandoned the role. The opera was taken off while Alexis Dupont – who was furious not to have been given the part in the first place – took five months to learn the role.

event, *Benvenuto Cellini*, which occupied him from about 1834, was not performed until 1838, and its failure ended his chances with the main operatic theaters of Paris. The first fruits of his recollections of Italy were happier. His second symphony, *Harold en Italie*, was begun when Paganini requested him to write a work for solo viola, but then objected to Berlioz's drafts on the grounds that he had not enough to play. Berlioz amicably replied that what Paganini needed was a true concerto, which he would write better himself. Berlioz had absolutely no interest in virtuosity for its own sake, and on converting the work into a symphony with viola solo – a medium which causes considerable problems of balance in the concert-hall – he deleted some of the passagework he had already written. Searching for a subject, he flirted with a plan for a work on the death of Mary Queen of Scots (which may explain the presence in *Harold* of melodies from the rejected *Rob Roy*). He then adopted a title referring to Byron's wandering hero, and, taking no episodes directly from *Childe Harold's Pilgrimage*, created a loose sequence of scenes in which the figure of the lonely wanderer (represented by the viola) is set in contexts reminiscent of his own experiences of Italy.

Harold en Italie is a picturesque symphony where the *Fantastique* is dramatic. It has no program as such, only specific titles for each movement. 'Harold in the mountains: scenes of melancholy, happiness and joy' implies little more than a sequence of moods, like the epigraph to *Waverley*. Marching pilgrims, for instance, were apparently characteristic of Italy, since Mendelssohn evoked a similar scene in the slow movement of his 'Italian' Symphony; this work was not extant when Berlioz composed *Harold*, but the two composers had met in Rome and as they discussed musical topics they might even have invented this idea together. Berlioz's work is less severe in color, but he forms out of a simple melodic germ a vivid scene of the pilgrims' approach, prayer and departure, punctuated by bells and fading into inaudibility. The third movement, the serenade of an Abruzzi mountaineer to his mistress, is a scene Berlioz must have witnessed; he framed the movement and added local color by a lively imitation of the *pifferari*. The finale begins, like Beethoven's Ninth, with reminiscences of the earlier movements, then continues as an 'Orgy of brigands,' which, for an orgy, contains some music of remarkable delicacy and quicksilver modulation between more excitable episodes. Throughout the first three movements there runs a double *idée fixe*: Harold (or Berlioz) represented both by the solo viola and a melody. Berlioz commented that this theme, unlike the *idée fixe* of the *Fantastique*, retains its character in every context. Instead of being transformed in mood, it is ingeniously combined with the music of the March and the Serenade. It is, however, altered to make a magnificent crescendo in the first movement, and after a brief reminiscence it is lost from the finale, as though Harold had fled from, or lost his identity within, the uproarious but witty band of brigands.

Harold begins the series of Berlioz's Italian works which continues with *Benvenuto Cellini*, his first surviving, and first performed, opera. Reading the memoirs of the turbulent artist, Berlioz must have identified with him; in his short story *The First Opera* (in *Les Soirées de l'orchestre*) Cellini appears as the mouthpiece of his own views. In the libretto certain episodes from Cellini's life are rather crudely fused with the obligatory love-interest. It was first intended as a comic opera, with spoken dialogue; it wears with some discomfort its transformation into the semblance of grand opera, and its humor and occasional earthiness displeased its first

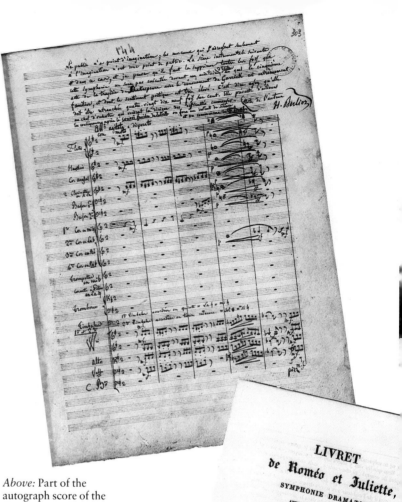

Above: Part of the autograph score of the dramatic symphony *Roméo et Juliette*, 1839. Relieved of his pressing financial worries by a gift of twenty thousand francs from Paganini, Berlioz decided to give up everything and devote himself to the creation of a really important work, 'full of passion and imagination.' Returning to the theme of Romeo and Juliet, which had haunted him since first seeing Harriet in Shakespeare's play twelve years earlier, he spent seven months of 1839 working continuously on the symphony.

audiences. Yet it is a scintillating work. Recent revivals, which tend to revert to something like the 1838 form instead of the revision Berlioz made fifteen years later for Liszt's performances at Weimar, have underlined the truth of what Berlioz wrote in his memoirs after revising it: 'I have just reread my poor score carefully and with the strictest impartiality, and I cannot help recognizing that it contains a variety of ideas, an energy and exuberance, and a brilliance of color such as I may perhaps never find again . . .' Among its marvels are the superb overture, familiar in the concert hall; scenes of farce, executed with remarkable musical inventiveness and timing, such as the opening and the aria of the comic 'villain,' Fieramosca; scenes of tenderness

Above: Romeo and Juliet, a study by Delacroix for the ball scene at the Capulets' house.

Left: The original libretto of *Roméo et Juliette*, dedicated to Paganini. He died in 1840 and never heard the work performed.

Below: The letter from Paganini to Berlioz with the gift of twenty thousand francs: 'Beethoven being dead, only Berlioz can make him live again.' It seems that Paganini wanted to make a public statement of his faith in Berlioz, but the incident provoked a great deal of malicious gossip.

such as the love-duet, made by Fieramosca into a very funny trio; and massive and complex ensembles such as the sextet in the final act and the carnival scene which Berlioz converted in 1844 into an even better known overture, *Le Carnaval romain*. Opinions differ as to how well the opera hangs together; certainly there are severe problems of timing in the later stages. But the casting of the huge statue of Perseus is an outstanding episode, symphonic in technique and at once somber and exalted, forming an unforgettable climax.

The failure of *Benvenuto Cellini* interrupted a period of relative success and happiness for Berlioz, even though he had had to contend with severe financial problems once his pension expired; he was married, with a son, and had to earn his living by journalism. An operatic success, leading to further commissions, while it would certainly have led to a more conventional career and a rather tamer Berlioz than the one we know, would also have relieved him of having to earn his living by words; he might have ended his days as chief conductor of the Paris Opéra. But the pattern of the 1830s was to last; his chief income was journalism, his chief expense producing his own works. His success in Germany, Russia and (to a lesser extent) England; his sinecure as the Conservatoire's deputy librarian; his father's legacy; none of these relieved him of the torment. It is another irony of his life that he hated this profession in which he excelled. He resented not only the time that conscientious discharge of his duties took away from music, but the false image of himself which it fostered, of a literary man who had pretensions as a musician. He hated its hypocrisy and routine, but there was no help for it – and it is a miracle that so much of this writing comes so vividly to life today. The eccentric, the nonconformist of Parisian musical life, is still its most effective mirror, and Berlioz remains the most readable of composer–critics, not excepting Schumann.

• *Roméo et Juliette* •

Although Berlioz's most successful musical works of the later 1830s brought him pitifully little income, he must have enjoyed the sensation of composing swiftly and with such originality and flair, even if it was not properly recognized. The Requiem, a government commission, was written at white heat; its successful performance in 1837 may have made the failure of *Benvenuto Cellini* seem less critical at the time than it proved to be in the long run. Then at the end of 1838 Berlioz conducted *Harold* before an audience which included its first begetter. Afterwards Paganini knelt before Berlioz, declaring him the successor of Beethoven, and next day sent a gift of money which enabled him to reduce his journalistic commitments and devote himself to composition. By the end of 1839 he had composed and performed *Roméo et Juliette*, a dramatic symphony

lasting nearly two hours; and (except financially) it was a real success. Berlioz denied that he had rushed from the performance of *Romeo and Juliet* in 1827 declaring that he would marry Juliet and write his greatest symphony on the play: 'I did both, but I never said anything of the kind . . . I was too overwhelmed to dream of such things.' There is some evidence that the idea of a *Romeo and Juliet* symphony was mooted as early as 1829, the year that saw the citation from the play on a movement of *Cléopâtre*. Later Berlioz let slip to Mendelssohn in Rome the idea of writing an orchestral scherzo on the 'Queen Mab' speech of Mercutio; he lived in terror that Mendelssohn would realize the idea first. But it was only now, during much of 1839, that he could again immerse himself in the play and allow scenes to shape themselves in his mind, then on paper, till they formed one of his most extraordinary conceptions.

Roméo et Juliette is absolutely central to Berlioz's achievement. It represents the furthest stage in his departure from conventional genres of music or music drama. It is also his first large-scale work to be based on an existing major work of art. Later he was to take on *Faust* and the *Aeneid*, but before *Roméo* his large works had had either liturgical or autobiographical origins, or had been adapted very freely from their literary source, like *Benvenuto Cellini*. Berlioz's full-length Shakespearian work also marks the climax of his symphonic decade; thereafter his major undertakings tended even more towards opera. 'The genre of this work,' Berlioz remarked (not without irony) in his preface to *Roméo et Juliette*, 'is surely not open to misunderstanding. Although voices are frequently employed in it, it is neither a concert opera, nor a cantata, but a choral symphony.'

What, however, *is* a choral symphony? In 1839 the answer was by no means obvious. Even today the tally of symphonies based on the dramatic development of a great play is small. The form of *Roméo* is complex and can only be understood in relation to Berlioz's cardinal principle, that the appropriate musical form should arise from the expressive demands of the material. Confronted with his favorite play, he took a synoptic view; it was not about the star-crossed lovers alone, but about the family strife and its resolution. The final scene of reconciliation is integral to his conception, and he saw no way to make it convincing in purely instrumental terms. Berlioz's symphony undoubtedly played its part in the formation of the musical language appropriate to the symphonic poem; it profoundly affected Liszt as well as Wagner, who was present at one of the first performances. But Berlioz could not anticipate the next fifty years of musical development, and to reconcile the warring families in symphonic music would have demanded a complex system of reference by means of *leitmotifs* that might have taxed the ingenuity of Richard Strauss. Accordingly, the finale is frankly operatic; it could be staged. For the first time in the work, a named character is impersonated by a singer; the finale is dominated

by a grandiose conception of Friar Lawrence shaming the families into peace over the bodies of the lovers. This music is good, at times magnificent, but it is related to the conventional gestures of the operatic stage and has been compared, with derogatory intent, to the music of Meyerbeer. It is, however, of a higher caliber than anything in the mainstream of nineteenth-century French grand opera.

The 'problem' of the finale for many listeners and critics results from its nature, not its quality: it is operatic, whereas the whole work is symphonic, and thus it requires a mental gear-change from the earlier unconventional treatment of the heart of the drama, for Berlioz elected that his lovers should not sing. He frankly doubted whether he could render the love of Romeo and Juliet into vocal music without unworthy echoes of his predecessors, and the language of instrumental music seemed to him more suitable to embody the delicate fragrance and subtle agonies of that love – 'a language richer, more varied, less constrained and, by its very vagueness, incomparably more powerful.' Thus at the center of the symphony, after a choral prologue, he placed the three large instrumental movements which are often heard as extracts. The prologue, preceded by an instrumental 'Introduction,' is in effect a sung program with musical illustrations, anticipating the main musical ideas of the symphony. Berlioz handles it with great delicacy and prevents monotony by introducing two movements for solo voices: an invocation to young love and to Shakespeare for contralto, and a setting for tenor of the Queen Mab speech. Nevertheless, the choral recitation is musically somewhat barren, uncharacteristically for Berlioz, and its success has been much disputed. Presumably he felt that a work of such complexity required more than just a printed program, and introducing the voices at the start, by emphasizing the dramatic framework of his

music and the fact of its being a choral symphony, also helped to prepare for the operatic finale.

The first of the main instrumental movements consists of two slow sections leading to a fast dance, but it does not form the usual symphonic introduction and allegro. The first slow section ('Romeo alone') is a tender rhapsody, which still more than the opening of the *Fantastique* suggests that overpowering adolescent heartache which Berlioz had once known so well. It begins with an unaccompanied violin melody of appropriately indeterminate direction and develops into a sighing melody for the whole orchestra whose cadences foreshadow the later love scene. A foretaste of the dance music precedes the second slow section, a long melody for oboe accompanied by a harp-like texture and interspersed with the distant sounds of the ballroom. This section appears to be that meant by Berlioz's heading 'sadness'; it proves to be an integral part of what follows, the 'Feast at the Capulets – Concert and Ball.' The dance is brilliant and frenetic, yet curiously static, suggesting a hollowness behind its whirling brilliance. At its height we hear the oboe melody again, now a unison of wind and brass, and at its original slow tempo combined with the dance in a 'reunion of themes'; Romeo, one may infer, is now at the ball. The subsequent disintegration of the dance music in a curiously sinister chromatic passage represents the quarrel with the affronted Tybalt, but the dance

Left: Sir Walter Scott, *c.*1818, by Andrew Geddes. Berlioz read Scott in translation in the 1820s – 'That giant of English literature' he called him in a letter to his sister Nanci. The *Waverley* overture was composed in 1826/7 and *Rob Roy* in 1831.

Below: Lord Byron in Albanian dress, by Thomas Phillips. Byron spent most of his adult life in Europe, Greece and the Levant – which fascinated Berlioz, who had always longed to travel. The exoticism of Byron's oriental scenery, his romantic heroes and his espousal of the Greek cause gave him wide appeal at this time. Berlioz said he had been much influenced by Byron's poems, most perceptibly in the symphony *Harold en Italie.*

Left: *Scenes from the
Massacre at Chios* by
Delacroix, exhibited at
the Salon of 1824. The
extermination of the
Greek population of
Chios was but one of
the terrible events in
their struggle for
independence from the
Turks. Byron, who died
of fever at Missolonghi,
in Greece, in April
1824, did much to
heighten the wave of
popular enthusiasm for
the fight for liberty by a
small nation with a
heroic past. Berlioz,
moved by the Greek
struggle, composed a
cantata, *La Révolution
grecque*, in 1825.

finally conquers and the movement ends with hectic gaiety. Berlioz has often been roundly abused for his powerful restatement by the full orchestra of the tender melody of the oboe. Exactly such effects, however, are more politely termed 'apotheosis' when they occur in the piano music of Chopin and Liszt, and this writer, at least, cannot see why the one is more vulgar than the other.

There follows the miraculous 'Love scene.' Berlioz begins by setting the atmosphere of a warm spring night whose serenity is tempered by restlessness: the sap rising, the yearning for love. In the main adagio he follows at first the form of Shakespeare's balcony scene. Clarinet and cor anglais suggest Juliet communing with the night, the broader horn and cello melody is Romeo's declaration, the agitated passage, with cello recitative, their first dialogue. Any attempt to trace the sequence of the scene further is probably futile; if Berlioz composed his adagio in that way, he revised it so extensively that the original form of it is lost. Once more the musical form follows no conventional pattern; a recurring refrain which is usually interrupted in order to lead to new developments binds the diverse episodes into a homogeneous whole. Few listeners, however, are likely to be troubled by any difficulty in analyzing this movement, for its formal indeterminacy, its potentially infinite quest for self-prolongation, is so completely convincing as a reflection of its subject.

Before proceeding to the tragic conclusion of the story, Berlioz felt the need to relieve tension, and his most conventionally symphonic gesture in formal terms is the insertion at this point of a scherzo. There is, of course, nothing conventional about the music, which he called 'Queen Mab, or the dream fairy.' Mercutio's speech about this dangerously malicious elf may seem an insignificant element in the play compared to some scenes that Berlioz omits, but he recognized in it the epitome of the midsummer madness that heightens the underlying

Berlioz's adoption of an electric metronome to convey the beat to musicians out of his sight, and his use of huge orchestras were much satirized (*below and bottom left*). In 1845 there were 400 players in a series of concerts he gave in the enormous rotunda of the Cirque Olympique (*bottom right*).

tensions and leads to the catastrophe and composed his scherzo accordingly. Relief, therefore, it may provide; relaxation it does not. It pursues a giddy course, after a series of mysterious 'false starts,' with unnerving switches of harmony and instrumentation. A shadow of the traditional form appears when a slower section acts as a 'trio,' but its melancholic mood and its accompaniment by an eerie sonority of dissonant violin harmonics, and the repeated scratching of a version of the main scherzo theme on the violas, permit no real slackening of the musical tension. The scherzo resumes, with continual variation rather than repetition of its ideas, and new elements are introduced – weird horn-fanfares and tingling antique cymbals accompanying a new melody. In this it is a typically Berliozian instrumental form: unpredictable, and inventive to the last.

After the scherzo, Berlioz plunges into the tragedy, but the next movement, 'Funeral procession of Juliet,' is like a piece of incidental music; it is based on a musical scene inserted into the play by David Garrick in the previous century. An anguished, chromatic theme winds its way around a monotone for chorus; halfway through, the chorus adopts a smoother version of the theme, and the orchestra takes over the monotone, which it transforms into a funeral knell. It is an eloquent piece, but dramatically as static as the scherzo, and it may seem to over-

emphasize a minor element in the play: Juliet, after all, is not yet dead. However, Berlioz had no time for mourning later, since the death of the lovers leads directly to the reconciliation.

The transition to the operatic finale is made in two ways: the return of voices in the 'Funeral procession,' and the return of programmatic music in 'Romeo at the tomb of the Capulets.' This latter music is one of Berlioz's most extraordinary inventions; for once, the critical cliché that his music often sounds years ahead of its time is exactly right. It is purely programmatic, following precisely the events of the version of the tomb scene by Garrick. This was one of very few tamperings with a masterpiece that Berlioz was prepared to acknowledge; what he liked was the final turn of the screw in the plot, whereby, in the Garrick version, Juliet awakens in the tomb before Romeo dies but after he has irrevocably swallowed poison. The movement consists of Romeo's impetuous entry to the tomb, his invocation and taking of poison, Juliet's awakening, delirious joy, despair, last anguish and death of the lovers. The fast music, at the beginning and for the delirious joy, is as volatile as that of the scherzo; the transformation of music from the love scene, there warmly passionate, here hysterical, certainly influenced Wagner's conception of the delirium of Tristan. The melody of the invocation is confided to tenor-register instruments, like Romeo's declaration in the love scene; here, however, there are no cellos, but cor anglais, bassoons and horn, a more hollow sounding and lugubrious combination. Juliet's awakening is fragmentary, halting, but proves to consist of phrases from the love scene; and the anguish and death break the last bonds of musical decorum in gestures of furious, impotent energy. Finally a plaintive oboe seems to embody some dying image of a happier time, and the music ends starkly, with two plucked notes for cellos.

Berlioz was aware that he had taken a risk with this movement, and he revived it only in the context of whole performances. He even appended a note to the effect that, since the

Ein Concert im Jahre 1846!

public had no imagination, it was better omitted unless it could be certain of an audience thoroughly acquainted with Garrick's version of the play. It is not, of course, the conclusion of the work. The symphonic framework of *Roméo et Juliette* is provided by a cross-relation between the beginning and the choral finale; the instrumental opening represents the street fighting of Montagus and Capulets, and the same music is used when the two families begin to dispute over the tomb. Their squabble is quelled by Friar Lawrence, but the musical point is made, and the work ends, like most symphonies, in the key in which it began.

Critics will probably never agree on the success of *Roméo et Juliette* as a whole. Berlioz himself never attempted such a plan again; his next, and final, symphony includes an optional chorus in the last movement, but purely as a reinforcement for the climax. However, Berlioz never rejected one aspect of *Roméo* – its conception for what a modern critic has well called 'the ideal theater of the mind.' Both *La Damnation de Faust* and *L'Enfance du Christ* are dramatic works which were not intended to be staged; their pacing of events, their changes of mood and their occasional instantaneous scene-changes demand a flexibility which the theater does not possess, and which is better left to the imagination.

• The middle years •

Berlioz's final symphony, the *Grande symphonie funèbre et triomphale*, is a magnificent piece of occasional music written to commemorate the tenth anniversary of the Revolution of July 1830. It was originally scored for military band, and some of it was first performed on the march – although Berlioz, who had no illusions about outdoor music, prudently arranged for a concert performance as well. The 'Funeral March' with which it opens consists mainly of two gigantic melodies, of the kind which justify Heine's description of Berlioz in terms of the fabulous or prehistoric, as a nightingale the size of an eagle. Berlioz's music was occasionally accused of being without melody; the charge seems absurd today, but in comparison with most of the music popular in France at the time his melodic style is so far-reaching and complex in its phraseology – superb prose beside jingling verse – that the average member of the public understandably did not grasp that it was melody at all. Yet each of the melodies in this 'Funeral March,' the first austere, the second sweetly lamenting, could serve to illustrate Berlioz's perfect control of organic melodic growth. The second movement ('Funeral oration') is a solo for trombone, transcribed from *Les Francs-juges*; it acts as an interlude before the finale, a triumphal march.

This symphony is drafted on a huge scale, in broad and generous strokes. By contrast, another work of the same period shows Berlioz at his most refined. The song-cycle *Les Nuits* *d'été* (1840-1), to poems by Berlioz's friend and critical champion Théophile Gautier, consists of six love lyrics of admirably varied character. Four of the songs are slow, and elegiac in mood; but they are so different in character that there is no hint of monotony even when, in complete performances, they are heard as the central sequence framed by the two faster songs. The title 'Summer nights' is Berlioz's own and fits some of the songs better than others. Indeed the first, 'Villanelle,' is a spring song, light in texture, fragile as new growth, its essentially three-verse form delicately varied in orchestral and melodic detail. The sumptuous opening of 'Le Spectre de la rose' evokes midsummer warmth, while its more attenuated episodes and its superbly sustained melodic line give the wraith of the flower an almost tragic grandeur. There follow three poems of lost love. 'Sur les lagunes,' the fisherman's song, is the first to strike the note of despair, of total loss, particularly in its haunting refrain: 'Ah, how bitter is my fate, to go to sea unloved.' 'Absence' is less harrowing, for its simple structure and the luminous beauty of its principal idea sound a note of hope. In 'Au cimetière' Berlioz evokes the moonlit, yew-laden churchyard and the sheer misery of the poet's lament by the slightest and most ambiguous changes of harmony. The atmosphere of this song can be so oppressive as to be almost repellent; sensitively performed, it emerges as one of Berlioz's most disturbing and moving pieces. Then 'L'Île inconnue,' in one of those complete contrasts of which the composer was so fond, bursts uninhibitedly forth. Berlioz must have been influenced by Gautier's subtitle 'Barcarolle'; the rhythmical flow of the Venetian song draws

Above left: Letter from Berlioz to the Société des Concerts du Conservatoire asking to be considered for the position of conductor on the retirement of Alexandre Tilmant in 1863. He was unsuccessful; although he had become one of the finest conductors in the world, he was but little honored in Paris.

Above: Pen-and-ink study of the head of Berlioz by J. L. P. Coignet, *c.*1850. Charles Hallé, who knew Berlioz at this time, described him: '. . . with his eagle face, his bushy hair, his air of command, and glowing with enthusiasm. He was the most perfect conductor that I ever set eyes upon. . . .'

the music through a wonderful variety of exotic and humorous touches suggested by the affectionate irony of the text.

Les Nuits d'été consists, therefore, of six individual songs capable of being performed separately. But collectively they form a satisfying whole and deserve to rank with Berlioz's finest achievements. Nor should we forget how original the conception was. At this period French songs, including most of Berlioz's, were simple and conventional in form and sentiment. Even in the original piano version, *Les Nuits d'été* drew French song on to a level of achievement worthy of its German contemporaries (it was composed in Schumann's 'year of song'). It is a matter for regret that Berlioz's later songs, lovely as some of them are, do not follow up this advance in complexity of form and depth of feeling.

Roméo et Juliette was the high tide mark of Berlioz's public success in France. It may have been the domestic upheaval of his separation from an increasingly unhappy Harriet, which came to a head when Berlioz began to tour abroad in the Low Countries and Germany, that caused a somewhat barren spell in his creativity after 1840. He lived with Marie Recio, a singer whom he married after Harriet's death in 1854, but various projects came to nothing. Although the eternally fascinating *Treatise on Orchestration* and his first collection of essays and reminiscences (*Voyage musical*, later incorporated into his memoirs) come from this

Below: Michelangelo in his studio by Delacroix, 1850. For the Romantics, Michelangelo was one of the figures who represented the Faustian struggle in the life of the creative artist. Berlioz had seen Michelangelo's works in Rome – Spontini told him: 'You could never have composed your Requiem unless you had seen Michelangelo's *Last Judgment*.'

time, no major musical work appeared until *La Damnation de Faust* in 1846. The saddest aspect of this is that Berlioz now abandoned his pursuit of original forms of symphonic expression. It is not that the course taken in his later works need be regretted; each is as characteristic, and as original, as anything earlier. But the symphonic drama of the *Fantastique* and *Roméo* represented a new vein in musical expression, one that was absolutely Berlioz's own, and he ceased to mine it.

In 1844 he wrote two overtures, *Le Carnaval romain* (some of which is mere transcription from *Benvenuto Cellini*) and *La Tour de Nice*. The latter was revised and published in 1855, and is thus Berlioz's last independent overture. It shows in its enigmatic and subtly balanced form that he had by no means exhausted his inventiveness in the symphonic medium; and it has no program. Berlioz actually gave it three titles, the final one, by which it is now known, being *Le Corsaire*. In the early 1850s, he tells us that he dreamed a new symphony; he could picture its whole form and was obsessed by the material of the opening. But he prevented himself from composing it; it would cost him too much in lost income from journalism and too much to have it copied and performed; besides, it would have no public. There is nothing despicable in this attitude. Berlioz had suffered real hardship while promoting works which were misunderstood, chief among them *La Damnation de Faust*, which was a major disaster at its first performance. Also, he was an artist who wished to communicate with his fellow beings. He flourished in the public activity of music-making: assembling forces, organizing material, conducting. The shell into which he could retire was no ivory tower, but a private hell.

La Damnation de Faust, 'legend in four parts,' is in many ways a watershed. Although it uses the *Huit scènes de Faust* of 1828-9, they are carefully revised, and sometimes their material is newly developed: the justly famous 'Ballet de sylphes' is a new working of old material. Another significant point is that, after trying a journalist colleague as the versifier of his scenario, Berlioz took over and wrote half the text himself; thereafter he used no other librettist. *La Damnation* has often been compared to *Roméo* as if it were a logical development from the concept of the 'dramatic symphony.' It is, rather, the other side of the coin. Whereas *Roméo* approached opera from a symphonic conception, *La Damnation* reverses the process, and brings the experience and imagination of the dramatic symphonist to bear on a virtually operatic conception: Berlioz's first title for it was one he explicitly rejected for *Roméo*, a 'concert opera.' The result is a little less mixed in genre; there is no narrative, except for a line of epilogue, and everything is dramatically presented, if often in a non-theatrical spirit. The music for the hero is entirely new, and Berlioz's Faust is one of his most interesting creations, the embodiment of a French Romantic conception of the role. Philosophical elaboration is discarded in favor of adventure. There

is no solemn pact with Mephistopheles, only an agreement to sample the delights offered by the devil: Faust is finally damned by a trick. The spirit of this is nearer to the sources of the story, or to Marlowe, than to Goethe, whose words and character of Gretchen (Margaret) Berlioz nevertheless retained.

The music is as richly inventive as in any of Berlioz's works, in both its lyrical and its dramatic passages. Faust has four monologues of wonderful variety and intensity, culminating in the 'Invocation to Nature,' which lays bare the disillusion in the center of his being. The instrumentation of these pieces is fairly light and as subtle as that of *Nuits d'été*. Simpler, but of overpowering lyrical beauty, are the songs of Margaret, 'The King of Thule' and the 'Romance.' These come from the *Huit scènes*, but are touched up with the sensitivity of the mature artist. *La Damnation* is also full of magnificent choral scenes. It might be argued that some of these, and the orchestral Hungarian March, have no very direct or significant bearing on the subject. Many, however, such as the scene with drunken students in Auerbach's cellar, are taken from Goethe; Berlioz merely developed the interpretation of the legend as picaresque adventure, enhancing the vileness of the drunkards by making them sing a perfectly academic fugal 'Amen' for the dead Rat in Brander's song, or developing the soldiers' chorus (from

the *Huit scènes*) by combining it in an exuberant climax, of some technical complexity, with a quite different chorus of students. These roistering scenes are, however, separated by one of ravishing beauty, where Faust is lulled to sleep on the banks of the Elbe and dreams of Margaret. For Berlioz such contrasts had a positive esthetic value. As long ago as the *Huit scènes* he had combined Margaret's 'Romance' and the soldiers' chorus into a single number, pointing out that though they were far apart in Goethe's drama, the juxtaposition might serve to heighten the effect of both movements. This simple trick becomes magical in *La Damnation*, where the 'Romance' is followed by distant reminiscences of the soldiers' chorus; one is not sure if they are real or figments of Margaret's imagination, as they recall to the deserted girl the day when she first saw Faust.

Paris rejected *La Damnation*, but it was applauded in Russia, Germany and England, although usually only excerpts could be given. Ironically, a few years after Berlioz's death it became his most popular work in the French capital. His next substantial piece was a funeral march for the final scene of *Hamlet* (1848); this he never even heard. It is now recognized as being among his most powerful conceptions, a mixture of barbaric splendor and lamentation which reaches a climax when a peal of ordnance is shot off, after which 'the rest is

Above: The Great Day of His Wrath by John Martin (1789-1854). Martin was best known for his vast canvases of apocalyptic landscapes, which had enormous appeal for the Romantic movement. He achieved great fame in Europe, particularly France. His work was known to Berlioz, who rejected some of the comparisons made, by Heine among others, between his compositions and the paintings of Martin – comparisons based largely on his reputation as a composer of music requiring huge orchestras and producing extravagant effects.

silence,' or fragmentation of material so extreme that it represents a silence deeper than the mere absence of sound. This work was published in a miscellany called *Tristia*, with an earlier 'Religious meditation' of unusual serenity, and a very lovely 'Ode on the death of Ophelia' for female voices and small orchestra.

• Religious works •

It is not easy to be sure of the nature of Berlioz's religious feelings, but he does not seem to have shared his father's comparatively assured atheism. His unsolicited interest in religious texts supports the view that his occasional hostility to religion was directed at its worldly face rather than at the very possibility of a Supreme Being. That title was accorded to the unknown God by the revolutionaries in the time of Robespierre; Berlioz's massive religious works are in the tradition of the music of revolutionary ceremony. They deal not with the fears and prayers of an individual but with the fate of humanity at large. One of Berlioz's unrealized conceptions had been for an oratorio on the Last Judgment which would burst forth in earnest in the middle of a profane parody of it. The superimposition of the real thing on a parody is an appetizing musical conception; otherwise it is perhaps a relief that Berlioz never carried through this monstrous project. The liturgical texts he did use, albeit freely, provided a framework to discipline his imagination, and its force is not dissipated by any crude dramatic ideas, or by parody. These works are like rituals, or a musical analogy to the grandest ecclesiastical architecture.

In 1848 the rise of Napoleon III aroused false hopes in Berlioz; he completed in 1849 a *Te Deum* which he originally conceived as part of a gigantic celebration of the first and great Napoleon, but 'Napoleon le petit' lost the opportunity to hear it at his coronation, and it was not performed until 1855. The *Te Deum* is the last of Berlioz's major works to a liturgical text and the greatest of his 'architectural' compositions. It is, however, on the earlier Requiem (1837) that his reputation for musical giganticism largely depends; the popular imagination has been caught by the idea that four brass bands are to be disposed around the hall. Actually they are very small brass groups, and Berlioz intended them to be at the four corners of the orchestral mass, not in galleries or behind the audience, but people have seldom been deterred by facts from forming opinions about Berlioz, and the legend of his dependence on a monster orchestra dies hard. However, it was not unnatural or unprecedented for a composer to see in these great liturgical texts an opportunity to deploy vast forces, and Berlioz's sense of proportion saw to it that he enhanced their effect by contrast with smaller groups. The Requiem uses its brass bands in three movements only: they enter at the top of a crescendo with magnificent effect ('Tuba mi-

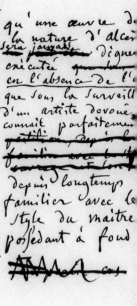

rum'), and appear more briefly in two subsequent movements from the *Prosa* ('Rex tremendae,' 'Lacrymosa'). In between comes a movement so attenuated as to be almost inaudible ('Quid sum miser'), and another ('Quaerens me') scored for unaccompanied voices. The best music in the Requiem is probably in the opening number, a freely fugal and richly expressive prayer, and the Offertory, which anticipates the funeral procession of Juliet in its choral monotone coupled with a winding and expressive fugato based solidly on string tone. In a good performance the Requiem can seem to justify Berlioz's remark that if all his works were to be taken from him but one, he would plead for the Requiem. In a less good one it can seem almost unnervingly varied in scale and inspiration.

The *Te Deum* is a more homogeneous work than the Requiem. The work consists of six large choral movements, alternately designated 'Hymn' and 'Prayer,' whose superficial similarity is overcome, on closer acquaintance, by recognition of the genuine variety in its musical forms and its deployment of the chorus. Berlioz's use of large forces does not merely aim at loudness; the quality of sound in soft passages, quite different with large numbers, was even more important to him. But he certainly aimed to overwhelm with sound and desired a resonant acoustic, composing in broad strokes to accommodate the inevitable reverberation. He performed his Mass, his Requiem and his *Te Deum* in large Paris churches (St Roch, Invalides and St Eustache). He was inspired by the sound and sight, in London's St Paul's, of several thousand schoolchildren singing in unison; after this experience he added to his already

Above: For most of his life Berlioz relied upon the income he gained from journalism and music criticism, much of which he converted into books. But he passionately hated the triviality, the hand-to-mouth existence, and the imposition on his time which kept him from composing. In 1844 Berlioz published his first volume of collected articles: *Voyage musical en Allemagne et en Italie.* This page shows his editing of a newspaper article (on the revival of Gluck's *Alceste* in 1861) for the third volume, *A travers chants,* published in 1862.

complete *Te Deum,* and to the final scene (Margaret's apotheosis) of *La Damnation,* a chorus of children, to be as large as possible. The effect is superb; and it is caused by a weight and depth of sound that have nothing to do with loudness. Berlioz derives an emotional impact from the very discipline needed to control such armies of musicians. He reserved such forces, moreover, for works whose subject seemed to demand them. Another religious subject, the birth and flight into Egypt of the Christ child, is limned unforgettably by the very simplest orchestral means; 'La Fuite en Egypte,' the first part of *L'Enfance du Christ* to be written, requires no more than a handful of woodwind instruments and the strings.

L'Enfance du Christ presents Berlioz as a religious composer as different as possible from the creator of the Requiem and *Te Deum.* In 1844 he had written, in his Three Pieces for 'orgue-melodium' (a kind of harmonium), a 'Rustic serenade to the Madonna' and a fugal 'Hymn for the Elevation' which anticipate both the pastoral and the thoughtfully contrapuntal style of 'La Fuite en Egypte.' This begins with a fugal overture representing the gathering of shepherds around the crib and continues with the well-known 'Shepherds' Farewell,' a tender choral movement framed by gentle strains of the *pifferari.* But the most touching part of this minute triptych is the last, an infinitely tender song for tenor (narrator) and small orchestra, 'Repose of the Holy Family.' In this Berlioz is once more the exquisite miniaturist of *Nuits d'été,* able to compose music of surface beauty and deep emotional penetration with only the slightest instrumental resources.

The remainder of *L'Enfance* was added later (by 1854), to form a larger triptych around the miniature one. The first part, 'Herod's Dream,' is itself divided into three parts: a

short introductory narrative; the scene in Jerusalem; and the scene in Bethlehem. The first two are joined by a Nocturnal March which is the most elaborate instrumental movement of the whole oratorio. Herod's aria is one of Berlioz's most effectively somber pieces; he later has his tyrant rave and rant as he plans the massacre of the innocents, but in the aria he seems almost prepared to sympathize with the king's predicament and concentrates on the uncertainties and miseries of the haunted monarch. These Berlioz represents by the use of ancient scales or modes associated with church and folk music, mingled with the normal modern major and minor scales. Berlioz was influenced in this procedure by his teacher Le Sueur, whose ideals of dramatic religious music he also embraced, but he adopts the old scales without a trace of pedantry or antiquarianism, for their expressive impact alone.

L'Enfance closes with pages of the highest inspiration, whose tone could not be faulted by the most austere critic. A series of sustained notes almost without harmonic connection seems to cut us off in time from the ancient world of the previous events, and the narrator returns to place the whole in its theological framework. The text, a summons to hear the word of Christ's ministry, is strikingly direct, and certainly unexpected from an artist of such equivocal religious opinions. The biblical Christ had a strong appeal to Berlioz, but he kept this quite distinct from Catholic theology and the institution of the Church, and he had at one time flirted with the humanist and socialistic gospel of Saint-Simonism. While his one oratorio does not represent in any sense a conversion, it is a

Above: A setting by Chaperon for the 1863 production of *Les Troyens*. Of the several designs in existence, it is not certain which were used. Although the Opéra was the only theater with the space and resources *Les Troyens* needed, Berlioz was forced to use the ill-equipped Théâtre Lyrique, which could in no way accommodate the spectacle he envisaged.

Opposite bottom: Cartoon of 1891 relating to the first complete Paris production of *Les Troyens* in 1892. It shows Wagner, carrying a document of surrender in his pocket, entering the Paris Opéra from the Trojan horse introduced by Berlioz.

profoundly felt religious statement and seeks to unveil the human aspect of the miracle of the Incarnation. It is as much this directness, even naïveté, of intention, as its unusual form and singularly chaste instrumental color, that mark it off from the main tradition of nineteenth-century oratorio. The closing pages are a prayer from the innermost soul: the orchestra falls silent, and the chorus, with the last echo of a semi-chorus of angels, which also appeared at the ends of Parts i and ii, draws the work to Berlioz's most serene and moving conclusion.

• The last operas •

Berlioz's last two operas are not evidence of any relenting on the part of the musical establishment; neither was staged in complete form in Paris in his lifetime. His composition of the first, *Les Troyens*, is a triumph of will over despair. Even before *L'Enfance* he had considered abandoning composition altogether, and although he had long contemplated an opera on his first literary love, the *Aeneid* of Virgil, he was prevailed upon to write it only by the formidable Princess Wittgenstein. Berlioz's letters to her, giving details of his progress and of his

esthetic views, make compelling reading, and although the opera was finally dedicated 'to the divine Virgil' (*Divo Virgilio*), it is she whom we must thank for its existence. Three acts only of the opera were staged in 1863 at the Théâtre Lyrique, but they brought the composer enough income to free him from journalistic hackwork for the rest of his life. As for *Béatrice et Bénédict*, it was commissioned by a small German theater, and its performance in Baden in 1862 was the culmination of a long and affectionate relationship between Berlioz and the musical towns of Germany (an affection also acknowledged in the setting of his most entertaining collection of articles, *Les Soirées de l'orchestre*, where the civilized musicians of a German town discuss any subject under the sun during the performance of bad Italian operas).

Les Troyens is in some sense a tribute to the operatic tradition in which Berlioz was brought up. Certainly its prime allegiance was to Gluck; and in the late 1850s to compose an opera in that vein was as eccentric as, in 1830, to compose an autobiographical symphony. From the point of view of critical reception of his work, Berlioz was caught in the trap between traditionalism and Wagner. To his French contemporaries he remained dangerously modern, but to a later generation his methods seem out of touch with the liveliest developments in music-drama of the time. Berlioz was aware that Wagner was working on *The Ring*; he did not, however, know a note of it when he wrote *Les Troyens*, nor did he know *Lohengrin*. The most advanced operatic works known to him, in the boldness both of their musical language and of their deployment of the forms of music-drama, were *Tannhäuser* and his own *Benvenuto Cellini*. In this vast work Berlioz seems to look back: to Spontini for the superb organization of large forces in set pieces like the Trojan March, during which the wooden horse is drawn across the stage and the people's rejoicing is pitted against the mournful prophecies of Cassandra; and to Gluck for the mood and placement (if not the musical language) of the arias (Dido's final soliloquy, 'Adieu, fière cité,' has a simplicity and directness of expression which tears the heart, and for which the inspiration lies in such pieces as 'Che farò senza Euridice'). There are also complex groupings of movements like those which Gluck handled so masterfully. The first scene in which Dido appears (in Act III) is founded on three statements of the Carthaginian National Anthem and two statements of Dido's own grateful address to her loyal subjects, 'Chers Tyriens.' Aeneas's great aria in the final act is formed, like certain of Gluck's, out of three different musical sections. The recitative-like first section is very agitated; there follows an agonized slow movement ('Ah, quand viendra l'instant') in which he contemplates the impending farewell; and a fast section in which Berlioz gathers fragmented musical ideas together into a cry of despair (Aeneas is turned from a possible weakening of purpose only by the entry of the Trojan ghosts). The sweep of the music gives it a larger scale than Gluck's arias, but the source of such designs is clear.

Les Troyens is not, of course, broken down into simple recitative and aria; like most pre-Wagnerian nineteenth-century operas, it is a

Below: Aeneas telling Dido of the Misfortunes of Troy by P. N. Guérin, 1815. In a letter to his sister Adèle in 1857, Berlioz wrote that he had finished 'the ring scene,' the idea for which he had borrowed from Guérin's painting, which shows the son of Aeneas taking from Dido's finger the ring given to her by her first husband.

'numbers' opera, but the numbers are frequently complexes of recitative, short arias and chorus, and as the work continues they run into each other without a break. The general trend in the mid-nineteenth century towards continuity in opera, existing in different ways in Verdi and Wagner, is reflected in Berlioz's masterpiece. *Les Troyens* has suffered from an exacerbated form of the critical problem of Verdi's (and to some extent Wagner's) earlier works. Nowadays, happily, we no longer tend to judge these merely as stepping-stones to something greater; but with Berlioz the apparently intermediate type of opera, neither clearly Classical and discontinuous, nor clearly Wagnerian and continuous, is his only operatic essay on the gran-

dest scale. As with all his great works, Berlioz wrote nothing else like it.

A common critical reaction, therefore, was that it is the work of a tired man returning nostalgically to the literary and musical loves of his youth. This view could not be combated for many years because the orchestral score was not available; in piano transcription the music seems impoverished. Performances were rare, yet performance is the only way to demonstrate the beauties of the work. Berlioz himself never heard the first two acts, which take place at Troy; they were for long regarded as a separate opera, *La Prise de Troie*. The last three acts were given at one of Paris's more enterprising theaters, the Théâtre Lyrique, in 1863. There were good aspects to this performance; the Dido, Mme Charton-Demeur, was outstanding. But it was only in 1969 that centenary performances, a complete recording, and the issue of a full score as part of the *New Berlioz Edition* gave the work a fair claim to be considered a part of the normal repertory of operatic masterpieces. For what, in the austere black and white

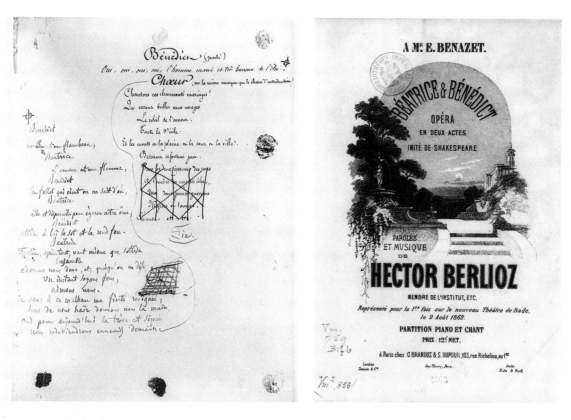

Far left: Béatrice et Bénédict: a copyist's manuscript libretto heavily corrected by Berlioz. He had first considered writing an opera based on Shakespeare's *Much Ado about Nothing* in 1833, and he now wrote the libretto himself from Shakespeare's dialogue. The opera was written for the new theater at Baden, and Berlioz conducted the first performance there in 1862, which was a great success.

Left: An edition of the opera in vocal score.

of a piano score, seems thin, comes vibrantly to life in its orchestration; what may seem constructionally crude on paper proves, in the theater, to have a strength and coherence of dramatic pacing all its own.

Not that *Les Troyens* is without problems. Like all Berlioz's works, it selects the means according to the expressive end and thus allows musical expansion into static tableaux in places where the listener may be expecting a more fluid type of musical-dramatic construction. A good example, because it is musically of unimpeachable quality, is Act IV, preceded by the 'Royal Hunt and Storm,' one of Berlioz's most extraordinary movements. It begins as a pastoral idyll and moves through vivacious hunting scenes to a violent tempest, which Berlioz wanted staged with overflowing streams, trees struck by lightning and rapid comings and goings of people and mythical creatures. Dido and Aeneas are seen entering a cave together. We hear nothing from them of their feelings at this critical point in their relationship; we hear only the savagely dancing satyrs shrieking 'Italy,' to remind the lovesick hero of his destiny. The turbulence is at its height, but it is not the turbulent emotion of the principal characters; perhaps it remotely symbolizes it, but musically it consists of the stark superimposition of several hunting fanfares in different meters with other musical material representing the furious elements. When Dido and Aeneas appear in Act IV, it is in the formal setting of a palace feast. Aeneas is allowed a token fragment of narration of the fall of Troy, before a succession of static ensembles – quintet, septet, duet – explores the more subtle side of the lovers' feelings in an almost oppressively beautiful framework of Mediterranean night (epitomized

in the septet). However, just before the curtain falls on the lovers, now in complete harmony, Berlioz wrenches the music abruptly from its destined cadence for the appearance of the Gods' messenger, Mercury. Striking Aeneas's shield, he emits again the warning cry 'Italy,' whose rhythm has become something of a *leitmotif* since it was first heard from the prophetess Cassandra in the second act, amid the destruction of Troy. The duet is too original for any suspicion to arise of indulgence on Berlioz's part in beauty for its own sake, but the harsh juxtaposition here casts its shadow on what went before, and, besides preparing for the tragic final act, grants even the idyllic fourth the quality of epic.

Few critics would now dissent from the verdict that *Les Troyens* is one of Berlioz's supreme achievements and among the greatest operas of the nineteenth century. Berlioz's last work is never likely to arouse such controversy, yet in its way *Béatrice et Bénédict* is scarcely less surprising than the conclusion of Verdi's career by a comedy, *Falstaff*. In its composer's words, 'a caprice written with the point of a needle,' Berlioz's adaptation of *Much Ado about Nothing* is an *opéra comique* with spoken dialogue. Nothing could be more disconcerting to the German critics who had classified Berlioz as a partner (or, more patronizingly, a forerunner) of Wagner and Liszt in the 'Music of the Future'; the conventions are those of a popular genre which a progressive musician ought to have despised. Indeed, Berlioz did despise popular comic operas; but since he was not dogmatic, he did not despise the genre, only individual works, solely on the basis of the quality of their plots and music. He adopts the convention here because it suits his dramatic purpose.

This purpose, however, is more difficult to grasp, for Berlioz leaves the 'Ado' out of his version. Claudio and Hero appear as contented lovers throughout, simply as a contrast to the eponymous couple who affect discontent to the end (even as they marry they sing, in the last words of the opera, 'we shall be enemies again tomorrow'). There is no Don John, no Dogberry; no plot against Hero's integrity, no version of that eminently operatic scene in which Claudio says 'No' at the altar. Berlioz decided to take one thread from the play to write an intricate but unpretentious opera in which his music serves to explore the feelings which are mostly concealed behind the mask of banter. He thus presents a Beatrice and Benedick whose mercurial spirits modulate smoothly, in the music, to something deeper. In particular Beatrice is fully worthy, in her extended second-act aria, of the passionate girl who in Shakespeare commands Benedick to kill Claudio. She has overheard her cousin speaking of Benedick's love for her; she runs agitatedly on to the stage, in characteristically violent contrast to the frivolous drinking chorus which opens the second act. Dark and dissonant orchestral surges contrast with the limpid melody to paint the confusion of her feelings. Yet she is entirely in the tradition of comic opera in using, at this high point of the drama, the medium of orchestrated recitative, which the convention would normally exclude (compare Mozart's Constanze in *Die Entführung*). Her aria, 'Il m'en souvient,' is Berlioz's invention, a recollection of a dream that had revealed the depth of her feelings for Benedick, but which she had not understood at the time. In a vigorous allegro she proclaims that she loves him; but her pride is nearly too much for her. In the Beatrice of the second act Berlioz, in a few economical strokes, creates a heroine worthy to stand beside his Cleopatra, his Margaret and his Dido.

Elsewhere the work abounds with felicities, showing a variety of high spirits astonishing in a composer by now severely ill. No ugly cynicism lies behind Berlioz's comedy; it is genuinely buoyant, with shadows (Beatrice's aria, or the exquisite Nocturne which ends Act I) placed so as to enrich the prevailing brightness. Benedick is more easily converted to love than Beatrice, but his witty rejection of it is given more space in two brilliant ensembles, a cut-and-thrust duet with Beatrice (in which, in a final aside of more-than-Rossinian electricity, they declare their fascination with each other) and in a trio with Claudio and Pedro. Although nothing happens dramatically during these numbers, in their ingenuity and pace they may be ranked close behind the ensembles of Mozart. As for the overture, which Berlioz constructed with seeming effortlessness from several ideas from the opera, it is among the most brilliant comedy overtures ever composed.

If one can subdivide Berlioz's career, one might take the period from *Harold* to *Roméo* as an Italian period, revisited in *Béatrice*; and the last years, from 1850 and including *Béatrice*, as a period in which Berlioz approached, along his own path, a neoclassical position analogous to that reached in his later years by Schumann. With Berlioz, however, it also represents a return; his two clearest and most traditional overture forms are *Waverley* and *Béatrice*, thirty-five years apart, and the operatic forms of *Les Troyens* and *Béatrice* return to those which might have been expected of him had he continued on the path suggested by his work before the *Symphonie fantastique*.

Berlioz's relationship with his contemporaries and posterity is even more elusive than his relationship with the past. He stands outside all mainstreams, a genuine individualist. The association with Wagner and Liszt is superficial, a rallying cry which Berlioz himself never raised. His sympathies for Wagner were as intermittent and qualified as Wagner's for him. Liszt championed Berlioz in the best way, by numerous carefully prepared performances (including the main revival in the composer's lifetime of *Benvenuto Cellini*), but his art, founded in the piano, developed along totally different lines. Schumann was the first major composer to show understanding of Berlioz, and his 1835 article on the *Fantastique*, as vital a stage in that work's diffusion as Liszt's astounding piano transcription, is still one of the best pieces on Berlioz. But as with Liszt, Schumann demonstrates his extraordinary breadth of sympathy while indicating no parallelism of musical technique. Berlioz stands closer to the Italian and French schools, for all that he was equivocal in his evaluation of them. His melody-dominated style, his dramatic gestures and his forms derive from the vocal styles – song and opera – of Latin Europe, rather than from the symphonic idiom most highly developed in Germany, or the more international language of the great piano composers. Berlioz's lack of interest in and knowledge of the piano in his early years certainly affected the harmonic layout of his music, which has in consequence often been denounced as of doubtful competence; the fastidious distaste of Chopin and Mendelssohn (both of whom Berlioz warmly admired) is an early example of this critical misunderstanding.

Berlioz was that rarity, a genuine lone wolf; and despite the extent of his influence, it is patchy enough for one to say that the development of music would not have been greatly different had he followed his father by settling into medical practice. His importance, therefore, lies primarily and rather obviously in that singularity of his works which is itself a product of his artistic isolation. His music is not, however, to be cherished just because it is different, but because the qualities of feeling that it embodies, and the forms that embody those feelings, are of unique value; their very unconventionality, the risks the music takes with the listener's expectations and fulfillment, is their strength, for they communicate something which no other music can. It is as well to go no further into this esthetic minefield, for if the truth of the last sentence is not felt, even the most thorough musical analysis is unlikely to persuade.

Above: Statue of Berlioz by Alfred Lenoir, unveiled in Paris in 1886. It depicts the composer near the end of his life, when he was, as Gautier said, 'an exasperated eagle deprived of the power to soar.'

FRÉDÉRIC CHOPIN

PHILIP RADCLIFFE

In some of Chopin's critics there has been an element of high-minded puritanism to which the seductive, lyrical charm of his music is suspect, but it is inevitable that not everyone has been able to respond to all of the many facets of his character: the patriotic Polish exile; the fastidious, charming and rather elusive Parisian who loved Italian opera; the melancholy invalid who was at one time the lover of George Sand, the French novelist, and was devotedly nursed by her. The story of his life has often been told. He was born in 1810, of a French father and a Polish mother. Shortly after his birth his parents went to Warsaw, where his father became professor of French at a military academy. At the age of seven he started to take formal piano lessons, focusing on the works of Bach and Mozart, and his first composition, a Polonaise, was published. At eight he played at a charity concert in Warsaw, at twelve he became a composition pupil of Elsner, a distinguished Polish musician. More public appearances followed, and in 1825 he played before Tsar Alexander I, who presented him with a diamond. The climax of this early period came in 1827, with the composition of the Variations for piano and orchestra on 'Là ci darem' from Mozart's *Don Giovanni* and the Sonata in C minor. This early period of Chopin's life was full of hope and promise, with no hint of the unhappiness of later years. He was lively, warm-hearted and obviously had great personal charm.

In 1829 his course at the Warsaw Conservatory ended; Elsner had hoped that Chopin would turn to opera, but it soon became clear that his approach to composition was centered on the piano. He went to Vienna, where he gave two concerts, and from there visited Prague, Teplice and Dresden. Later in the year he returned to Warsaw; a brief love affair with the singer Constantia Gladkowska inspired him to write the Waltz in D flat, later published as op.70, no.3. In March 1830 he played his Piano Concerto in F minor in public, and later in the same year the Concerto in E minor. As a composer he was developing steadily and had already started the first set of twelve Etudes (op.10) before the end of 1829. In November 1830 he left Poland, little knowing that he would never see it again. With Titus Woyciechowski, his closest friend, he went to Vienna, passing through Breslau (Wroclaw), Dresden and Prague. But shortly after his arrival came the disquieting news of an uprising in Warsaw. Woyciechowski immediately returned to Poland, while Chopin remained in Vienna in a state of unhappiness and uncertainty. In July he left for Munich and from there went on to Stuttgart, where he heard the news of the storming of Warsaw by the Russians. Doubt has been cast on the tradition that at this time he wrote the so-called 'Revolutionary' Etude in C minor, but he was certainly thrown into a state of wild despair. He had always been deeply attached to Poland; after 1831 it became a symbol of something unattainable. His music became increasingly somber and passionate, and the elegant grace of the concertos gave place to the fierce intensity of the B minor Scherzo.

In September 1831 Chopin went to Paris, where he was soon plunged into a brilliant whirl of activities, composing, playing and teaching. He made many friends – musicians, artists, aristocrats – but he was happiest in the company of his compatriots in Paris, or elsewhere, and always spoke French with a Polish accent. As a pianist he was also happier when playing to friends, and he became increasingly averse to public appearances. Moscheles wrote that he found certain things in Chopin's music repellent but was completely converted when he heard them played by the composer himself, and on the whole the critics were encouraging. As a composer Chopin had by 1836 become wholly individual and assured, his output including both books of Etudes, the Scherzo in B minor, and the first Ballade, in G minor.

In the summer of 1835 he joined his parents for a holiday in Carlsbad, and in Dresden he renewed his friendship with the Wodzinski family, whom he had known in Warsaw. Their daughter Maria had been Chopin's pupil when a child; now he fell in love with her. For a time they were engaged, but Chopin's health was not good, and there were even rumors of his death; most probably this was the reason for the Wodzinski parents eventually withdrawing their consent. For Chopin this was, temporarily at least, a heavy blow, and the Waltz in A flat, later published as op.69 no.1, is said to have been written as a farewell, although the whole affair may well have been overblown by romantic biographers. About this time he visited the Schumanns at Leipzig; he thoroughly appreciated Clara's playing and declared that she was the only woman in Germany who could

Right: Chopin at the piano, drawn in about 1826 by Elise, elder daughter of Prince Anton Radziwill, a wealthy Polish aristocrat and distinguished amateur musician. Chopin was welcomed into the Radziwill family as a guest; he gave his first concert at a charity fête at the Radziwill's palace in Warsaw as a child in 1818.

Right: Chopin playing at a soirée at the Radziwills, as imagined by the Polish painter Siemiradzki. This was the sort of music-making Chopin preferred to the strain of the concert hall; he would sit at the piano and improvise for hours on end. He spent some idyllic days at the Radziwill country house; in 1818 he wrote a Polonaise for cello and piano (op.3) for the Prince to play with his daughter Wanda.

understand his music. With Schumann, who had given high praise to his 'Là ci darem' Variations, he was on friendly terms, but could not appreciate his music. Chopin's musical tastes, like those of many composers, had marked limitations. Beethoven did not appeal, though it is hard to believe that certain passages in the last sonatas would not have attracted Chopin had he known them. He delighted in the operas of Weber and in Italian opera generally. Schubert he found 'too rough,' but he was devoted to the music of Bach and Mozart; traces of the subtle texture of the one and the flowing lyricism of the other can often be felt in his own work.

In the autumn of 1836 he was introduced by Liszt to George Sand, but they did not meet again until 1837, after Chopin's first visit to London. They became increasingly intimate, and there seems to be little doubt that for some years they were lovers. In the autumn of 1838 they went, with George Sand's children Maurice and Solange, to Majorca. The expedition started happily, but the latter part, spent in the monastery at Valdemosa, must have been a nightmare, with Chopin in very poor health. He was nursed with devoted care by George Sand, and the five years that followed were among the happiest and most productive of his life. Chopin's relations with George Sand continued until 1845, by which time her children had grown up and Maurice resented his presence. Chopin himself was becoming increasingly difficult and neurasthenic, and in the novel *Lucrezia Floriani* that George Sand was writing at the time, one of the characters, Prince Karol, is an obvious and far from flattering portrait of him. George Sand herself denied that this was her intention, but her children maliciously told Chopin that

'Maman had put him into her book.' In 1847 Solange Sand married; this led to trouble between mother and daughter, then, as Solange enlisted Chopin's sympathy, to a complete breach between her mother and Chopin.

There has been a tendency among Chopin's biographers to present George Sand as a possessive and predatory woman, constantly collecting and then discarding lovers. But Chopin cannot have been an easy companion; the Polish poet Mickiewicz went so far as to describe him as George Sand's evil genius. Certainly, the resilience that had brought Chopin back to health after the winter in Majorca seems to have left him after the break with George Sand. In 1848 he gave his last recital in Paris, then, shortly before revolution broke out, he traveled to England. The story of the last year of his life is little but a melancholy record of declining health. He gave recitals in London and in other places, playing with his usual sensibility, but he was too weak physically to play louder than *mezzoforte*. He died in Paris on 17 October 1849.

• Early works •

Of Chopin's earliest works, written before 1832, grace, fluency and brilliance are the most marked characteristics. With a few exceptions, the works for piano with other instruments were written at this time. Of these, one of the most solid is the Piano Trio in G minor, completed in 1829, although the first movement, like that of several other early works, has a curiously lopsided tonal plan, with the first half remaining imperturbably in the home key. What is most lacking is Chopin's very personal

lyricism, though there are glimpses of it in the adagio. The Polonaise for cello and piano, op.3, is more superficial, being concerned mainly with brilliance; the slow introduction, written later than the rest, is more sensitive.

When writing for piano and orchestra in these years Chopin would have had several models, such as Hummel, a very able, if not deeply inspired composer, and Dussek, more erratic but more prophetic and imaginative. The Variations on 'Là ci darem' and the Fantasia on Polish airs give only occasional glimpses of the real Chopin; the former is the more successful of the two, probably because Mozart's exquisitely urbane tune fits more happily into its brilliant surroundings than the Polish folk melodies, which have the air of rustics who have strayed accidentally into a smart salon. The same can be said of the Krakowiak for piano and orchestra, op.14, but the concertos in F minor and E minor, written in 1829 and 1830 respectively, are on a far higher level. They are loosely constructed, and the first movement of the E minor concerto again has a tonal lopsidedness, but in both works there is much really characteristic lyricism, most of all in the slow movement of the F minor concerto. However, the orchestra did not interest Chopin greatly. A third piano concerto, in A major, was begun about the same time; eventually the first movement was published in 1841 in a version for piano solo, entitled 'Allegro de Concert.' The only other work for piano and orchestra is the Polonaise in E flat, completed in 1831. It is a lively and attractive showpiece, but the 'Andante spianato' written several years later as an introduction is on a far higher level, and after it the Polonaise, for all its charm, seems superficial.

Apart from the Sonata in C minor, on the whole a dull and labored composition, the early works for piano solo are either rondos or dances. The Rondo in C minor, op.1, and the 'Rondo à la mazur' in F, op.5, were both written in Poland: the themes of the first, a pleasant if rather diffuse piece, suggest a polka; in the second there is not only the rhythm of a mazurka but also, in the main theme, the suggestion of a modal scale, the Lydian with the fourth note sharpened, that is a common characteristic of Polish folk music. By contrast, the Introduction and Rondo in E flat, op.16, written in Paris in 1832, seems far removed from Poland; it is elegant and well-mannered, with a frivolity which, though rather engaging, strikes a strange note after the solemn gestures of its introduction.

Above: A caricature of a peasant drawn by Chopin as a boy. His school exercise books were filled with sketches and caricatures; he could apparently be relied on to amuse his schoolfriends and had a keen sense of humor which he kept throughout his life. Caricatures of the eccentric English decorated one of his last letters to his friend Grzymala even in 1848.

Left: Polish village musicians: a fiddler and a piper drawn by Elise Radziwill. The story was always told that musicians played in the snow outside the Chopin's house on the night Frédéric was born. Certainly, Polish folk music was part of his inheritance.

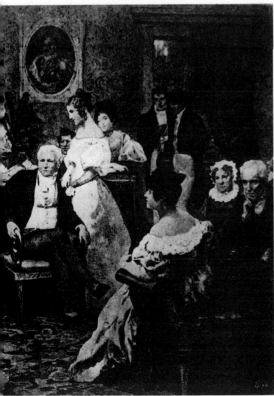

• Dance forms •

Of all Chopin's works his waltzes were the first to achieve wide popularity, and they retain great freshness and charm. He had written several before leaving Poland; mention has already been made of the gentle and unassuming Waltz in D flat, op.70, no.3, written for his first love. The posthumous Waltz in E minor has more character and, unlike the others of this period, a fiery and exciting coda. In the *Grande Valse brillante* in E flat, op.18 (1834), Chopin writes for the first time a large-scale waltz, probably influenced by Weber's *Invitation to the Dance*. It has a fascinatingly unorthodox key system, and in the long and exhilarating coda themes from the earlier part are swept along to a brilliant climax. Of the Waltzes of op.34 (1838) the first is on similar lines; it is less rich in material but more firmly constructed; again there is splendid coda. Chopin was obviously aware of the danger of rhythmic monotony in a waltz: there is a suggestion of cross-rhythm in the opening fanfare of op.18;

op.34 no.3 and op.64 no.1 both have themes in which the phrases of the right hand do their best to contradict the steady pulse of the left hand; and in the main theme of op.42, in A flat (1840), the longest and most brilliant of all, the two hands seem to be playing in different tempi. One of the most beautiful is the unjustly neglected Waltz in A flat from op.64, in which the usual elegance leads to piquant and unexpected digressions.

It was inevitable that Chopin's first published piece should be a polonaise, although the character of the polonaise, or polacca, as used by earlier composers had produced very dissimilar results. Those of Wilhelm Friedemann Bach are slow dances of great beauty, not unlike the sarabandes of his father. Beethoven's, which include the finale of the Triple Concerto, are amiable and elegant, while those by Schubert, for piano duet, are genially Viennese. Of those written by Chopin before leaving Poland, three, in B flat, D minor and F minor, were published posthumously as op.71. They are attractive and quite individual, with touches of the chromatic color that was to become so marked a characteristic of Chopin's later works, but there is none of the flamboyance of Weber's Polaccas or of the finale of Chopin's own 'Là ci darem' Variations.

The Polonaise in E flat for piano and orchestra, already mentioned, was completed before the fall of Warsaw; from this time onwards the polonaise acquired a new, heroic significance. Of the two works in op.26 (1836) the first, in C sharp minor, is a deeply moving piece; the nostalgic central section contains a singularly beautiful duet for the two hands. The Polonaise in E flat minor is somber and menacing in a more impersonal way; there is a strange contrast between the fluctuations of pace in the opening theme and the more formal, processional character of the rest. The processional element is one of the most essential features of the polonaise; it appears almost blatantly in the 'Military' Polonaise in A, op.40 no.1 (1838), a superbly extrovert work which should be a

Below: The Boulevard Poissonière where Chopin lived when he first came to Paris in 1831.

Bottom: A pianist – probably the virtuoso Henri Herz – playing at a fashionable salon.

sufficient answer to those who see Chopin's music as the work of a neurotic invalid. The Polonaise in C minor, op.40 no.2, is mysterious and shadowy; unlike the Polonaise in A, it contains some subtle chromatic digressions.

The three remaining Polonaises are all on a monumental scale. The immensely powerful work in F sharp minor, op.44 (1841), has a main theme which is somber and processional like that of the C minor Polonaise; there is also an extraordinary passage, unlike anything else of Chopin, in which a menacing rhythm is reiterated with hypnotic persistence. This leads, very unexpectedly, to a quiet and courtly mazurka. The return from this to the polonaise theme is highly dramatic, and the final page, with reminiscences of both the polonaise and the mazurka, is one of Chopin's most moving. The Polonaise in A flat, op.53 (1843), is a massive and gorgeously colored work that has often suffered from being treated as a bravura piece; here, if ever, should Chopin's direction *maestoso* be borne in mind. It has something of the forthright quality of the Polonaise in A, but it is far more imaginative. However, splendid though these two polonaises are, the *Polonaise-Fantaisie* in A flat, op.61 (1846), is a deeper and more sensitive work; it is one of Chopin's greatest. The mysterious introduction, during the course of which the main theme is foreshadowed, has a strongly Wagnerian atmosphere. The stately triple measure of the polonaise is maintained throughout, but the actual dance rhythm appears only intermittently. About two-thirds of the way through there is a quiet and deeply thoughtful episode in B major; after this a brief but extraordinarily impressive reference to the introduction is followed by magnificently prepared returns, first of the main theme and then of the melody of the B major episode, in a heroic and triumphant mood. For a long time the unusual structure of the work and the great variety of material led some musicians to regard it as the work of an ailing composer who was losing control over his ideas. Even Liszt, who certainly could not be thought a reactionary, complained of its 'visions déplorables.' But now, from a further distance, it can be seen as one of Chopin's most original and prophetic works.

The mazurka was a less aristocratic dance than the polonaise, more 'racy,' 'of the soil,' and those Chopin wrote before he left Poland have on the whole more character than the early polonaises. The Mazurkas in A minor and F, published many years later in op.68, have a strongly Polish flavor; the latter quotes from a modal folksong, which sounds very exotic in its more humdrum surroundings. Superficially, the mazurkas have points in common with the waltzes; the same triple time and usually the same accompaniment figure. But in the mazurkas there is an almost inexhaustible variety of mood. Sometimes there is a robust energy, as in op.7 no.1 and op.17 no.1, both in B flat. Humor too can be found in some of them, especially in the final measures: op.30 no.3 in D flat ends with a comic juxtaposition of major

and minor; op.33 no.4 in B minor, alternately wistful and aggressive, concludes with a sardonic grimace; and in the final measures of op.41 no.4 in A flat, the music appears to fall asleep in the middle of a sentence. More striking is the emotional depth of many of the pieces, especially those in C sharp minor. Op.30 no.4 has an almost hypnotic intensity, with a passage near the end which could almost have been written by Debussy; in the last page of op.41 no.1 there is a climax of great power followed by a mysterious collapse; op.50 no.3, which opens very unusually with a fugal passage, contains some very Wagnerian chromaticism. Others are more lyrical, especially those in A flat, a key for which Chopin had a particular liking; op.59 no.2 is one of the most attractive, with some fascinating chromatic harmony in the last page. The smaller Mazurkas all have their individuality, their moods ranging from the robust cheerfulness of op.56 no.2, in C major, to the deep melancholy of op.68 no.4, in F minor, a touching and sensitive piece, which is thought to have been Chopin's last composition.

Above: Delacroix's *Liberté devant le peuple*, 1830. Europe was in a state of political upheaval at this time. In France, unrest and disillusion with the reactionary Charles x was smothered by the bringing to power in 1830 of Louis-Philippe, the 'citizen king.' In November that year, an insurrection broke out in Poland, which was brutally suppressed, and Poland's integration into Russia in 1832 brought many exiles to Paris. Chopin's patriotism may have become more intense than it would have been had he been willing or able to return to his native land.

• Preludes, Etudes, Nocturnes and other pieces •

If among the piano works connected with the dance it is the Mazurkas that show most fully the extraordinary variety of content that Chopin could compress into a comparatively small space, this is still more evident in the Preludes. We cannot be certain that he intended his set of twenty-four (op.28, 1838), finished in Majorca, to be played as a continuous cycle, but they do use all the major and minor keys, and it is interesting to put Chopin's first Prelude, in C major, beside the first Prelude of *Das Wohltemperierte Klavier*. Chopin's impetuosity may seem far removed from Bach's serene clarity, but the two pieces are very similar in their persistent use of a single figure, a feature seldom found in any composer between Bach and Chopin. In most of Chopin's Preludes a persistent figure accompanies a more sustained tune, but in other respects they differ widely. One of the most moving of the set is the fourth, in E minor, where, over a background of repeated chords a melody, strangely hesistant at first, gradually expands into widely sweeping curves before a deeply tragic close. Melody of a more ornate character appears in the bass of the equally

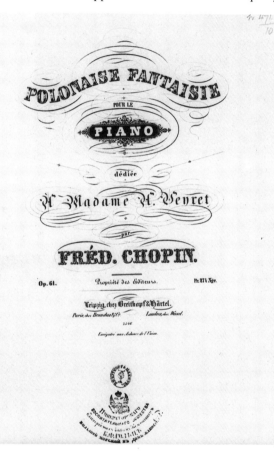

moving Prelude in B minor. There is a great variety of mood; the simple and innocent little Prelude in A is followed by the wildly agitated piece in F sharp minor, in which the melody is surrounded by a haze of grace-notes. Some are outbursts of a startling ferocity: no.18 in F minor is a wild and hectic recitative, and no.24 in D minor exploits the whole compass of the piano with terrifying intensity. As a rule, the pieces do not contain much contrast within themselves, but there is a striking exception, the Prelude in D flat, which, whether or not it was inspired by raindrops, is certainly one of the greatest. Here the repeated notes that are heard under the serene opening melody assume an entirely different character in the central section, when they provide a background to what sounds like a slow and sinister procession. The return to the opening theme is one of the most magical moments in all Chopin's work. In addition to op.28, there is the separate Prelude in C sharp minor, op.45, written some years after the others. It is on a larger scale, but

here again there is a strong kinship in the persistent use of a single figure. The music floats through many keys, with broad melodic phrases coming and going; towards the end there is a fascinating chromatic cadenza.

The Etudes, or 'Studies,' are on a larger scale than most of the preludes and, inevitably, are more concerned with virtuosity, but they have the same power of concentrating on a single idea. In the first set of twelve, op.10, the first Etude, in C, again looks back to the first prelude of *Das Wohltemperierte Klavier* in its persistent treatment of an arpeggio figure, which here gives an effect of great spaciousness. Several of the Etudes deal with some special technical problem: in no.2 in A minor the playing of legato sixteenth-notes and short detached chords in one hand; in the eleventh, in E flat, enormous harp-like chords for both hands. No.3 in E, sometimes called 'Tristesse,' is notable for its serenely beautiful main melody, and for the contrast between the simple harmony of the opening and concluding sections and the hectic chromaticism of the intervening music. Chromaticism of a darker and more tortured kind can be found in the melancholy Etude in E flat minor, no.6. But the climax of the set is the last, the so-called 'Revolutionary' Etude in C minor, a piece of immense power in which the march-like phrases stand out defiantly against a background of surging sixteenth-notes.

The second set of twelve, op.25, completed in 1834, is on the whole more somber and perhaps more varied. In the first Etude, in A flat, the melody is delicately suggested over the rippling sixteenth-notes, and at one stage a counter-melody is suggested with equal delicacy. The next, in F minor, is directed to be played *presto*, but a less than usually precipitate performance can reveal more clearly the extraordinary grace of Chopin's melodic lines and the subtlety of his harmonic details. The same can be said of the formidably difficult Etude in G sharp minor, no.6, in which the per-

Left: Title-page of the *Polonaise-Fantaisie,* op.61 written in 1846 and dedicated to one of his pupils, although her exact relation to Chopin is not clear. It is possible that the question of dedication was not important to Chopin: there are few works dedicated to close friends, and none, for example, to Gryzmala, Delacroix or George Sand.

Below: A Polish bazaar in the drawing-room of the Princess Marcelline Czartoryska in Paris in 1844. The Princess, who had been a pupil of Czerny in Vienna, was one of Chopin's favorite and most talented pupils and became a close friend. She was with him in the last weeks of his life. Chopin was very much part of the Polish community in Paris; bazaars to raise money for the refugees were frequent and he could always be relied upon to help.

sistent thirds in the right hand lead to some surprising clashes. The set contains some charming lightweight pieces, such as the well-known Etude in G flat, but also the magnificent Etude in C sharp minor, no.7, one of Chopin's finest works. Its conception is similar to that of the slow movement of Bach's 'Italian' Concerto; a stream of deeply emotional melody against a background of repeated chords. The last three are all immensely powerful. In the tenth, in B minor, there is an unbroken flow of octaves, gentle and lyrical in the central section, but in the rest of the piece fierce and relentless, with a peculiarly stark conclusion. The slow introductory measures of the next, in A minor (sometimes called 'Winter Wind'), foreshadow the aggressive, march-like rhythm which, surrounded by furiously rushing sixteenth-notes, dominates the music until the wild, rocket-like ascent in the final measures. In the final Etude, in C minor, the energy is more controlled and the harmonic movement broader; the conclusion in C major brings with it a feeling of real triumph. The three Etudes written a few years later for Moscheles are smaller and less brilliant. The first two are both concerned with conflicting duple and triple rhythms; the third, in D flat, with legato and staccato notes played simultaneously by one hand.

Of all Chopin's works the Etudes are the most inseparably connected with the piano; they contain little that could possibly be transferred to another medium. By contrast, the Nocturnes, though beautifully written for the piano, show more than any other branch of his music Chopin's love of flowing and ornate melody, strongly akin to Italian opera. In these works he is endlessly inventive, not only of melodies, but also of distinctive accompanying figures. The early Nocturne in E minor, written in 1827, is already quite characteristic. In Paris he came into contact with John Field and, though Chopin was disappointed by Field's playing and Field found Chopin's music morbid, there are strong affinities between the nocturnes of the two composers. But even in the two sets of three Nocturnes, opp.9 and 15, that Chopin published shortly after he settled in Paris, there are hectic undercurrents far removed from the leisurely and idyllic atmosphere of Field. The second of op.9, in E flat, immediately became very popular. It still retains great charm, and is built on an unusual plan – with two alternating ideas – which reappears in some of the later Nocturnes.

The remaining dozen Nocturnes all appeared in pairs, often strongly contrasted. The two of op.27 (1836) are particularly fine. The first, in C sharp minor, has a strongly defined emotional scheme; the mysterious gloom of the opening eventually leads to a passage of wonderful serenity. The second, in D flat, is more unified in mood; again there are two alternating ideas, both luxuriant with a wealth of subtle detail, and there is a coda of exceptional beauty. In the A flat Nocturne from the next pair, op.32 (1837), the two main themes are remarkably like those of Field's Fifth Nocturne in B flat, but

Right: An anonymous watercolor of Chopin *c.*1829 – the year in which he left the Warsaw Conservatory and started on his travels.

Left: Maria Wodzinska, a self-portrait of 1835. In this year, on a visit to Dresden, Chopin met the Wodzinski family, whom he had known as a child, and fell in love with their daughter Maria. Although they were allowed to become engaged, her family eventually forbade their marriage in 1837, probably because of Chopin's poor health. Her letters, tied up in ribbon, were found in a drawer after his death. He had written on them: 'Moja Bièda' ('My tragedy').

with the important difference that in Chopin's piece the harmonic movement is twice as fast. The first nocturne of op.37 (1838), in G minor, is a gently appealing piece with an impressive, hymn-like central section, but the second, in G major, has greater distinction. The first theme is graceful and rippling, with many thirds and sixths; the second is a simple and haunting melody not unlike that of the second Ballade.

Of op.48 (1841), the first, in C minor, is the finer; it has a deeply pathetic main theme, a solemn and powerful central section, and a surprising return of the first theme against a far more agitated background. Op.55 no.1 in

Above and right: Two fragments of a painting by Delacroix of George Sand listening to Chopin playing the piano. Chopin first met the artist Eugène Delacroix in 1836 through Liszt. Delacroix was also a frequent visitor to Sand's house at Nohant (her son Maurice was to become his pupil), and of the people who surrounded George Sand he was one of the few whom Chopin really liked. The two men had a mutual regard and admiration for one another, and became very close in the last months of Chopin's life.

agitation to the 'Revolutionary' Etude. It contains moments of great pathos, and the reference in the trio to a Polish carol is a reminder of the deep nostalgia for his native land that Chopin must have felt at the time. The second Scherzo, op.31 (1837), is equally fiery, but richer and warmer in coloring. Though opening in B flat minor, it soon moves to D flat for one of Chopin's most inspired lyrical passages. It is in this key that the work ends, but before that there is a gentle, pastoral theme that is never allowed to continue for long, a stormy development, and a long peroration with some thrilling harmonic surprises. The work is remarkable, not only for the variety of its material but for the skill with which it is woven into a convincing structure.

The third Scherzo, in C sharp minor, op.39 (1839), is less lyrical and expansive, and the main theme has a suggestion of Beethoven in its blunt directness; the general impression of the work is of a fierce and uncompromising defiance, especially in the final measures. But in the fourth and last, the Scherzo in E, op.54 (1843), Chopin is in a delightfully relaxed and playful mood. Apart from the broad, rather Mendelssohnian melody of the central section, it is built largely upon short phrases, often taking piquant and unexpected turns, but in the final page, as in the third Ballade, the music becomes grander and more spacious. If more diffuse than the other Scherzos, it is an extremely attractive work which deserves to be more often played.

With their brilliance and energy, the Scherzos are more akin to the Etudes than to any other branch of Chopin's work. The same can be said of the Impromptus, smaller in size and slighter in caliber, with one exception, op.36 in F sharp major (1838), which is one of the subtlest and most thoughtful of all his works. The quiet

F minor (1844), although well-known, is handicapped by a rather commonplace main theme, but its neglected companion, the Nocturne in E flat, is a remarkable work. It has no contrasting central section, but a continuous flow of melody over beautifully spaced arpeggio figures, sometimes accompanied by a second voice, which adds greatly to the harmonic interest. There is a fascinating coda ending with a suggestion of daybreak. The two remaining Nocturnes, op.62 (1846), are quiet, thoughtful pieces, intimate in tone. The broad central melody of the first, in B, and the opening theme of the second, in E, are among Chopin's most inspired; both pieces end with touchingly simple phrases that have no apparent connection with what came before them, yet give a feeling of complete finality. The unfailing lyrical charm of the Nocturnes has sometimes caused them to be dismissed as superficial salon music, but this judgment is itself superficial and does not take into account the power, subtlety and imaginativeness of the finest of them.

Despite their title, Chopin's first three Scherzos contain little that can be described as playful or humorous; they are among his most powerful works. The first, in B minor, composed during his Vienna winter, is similar in its passionate

opening is a beautiful example of Chopin's harmony at its simplest, a suggestion of counterpoint giving it a gentle edge. After a march-like central section the first theme returns, but against a more restless background, eventually breaking out into brilliant but shapely arabesques. After a brief reminder of the serene mood of the opening section, there is an unexpectedly loud and triumphant end. The other Impromptus, in A flat and G flat, and the earlier *Fantaisie-Impromptu* in C sharp minor, though attractive, are less distinguished.

On the other hand the late Berceuse (1844) and Barcarolle (1846) are among Chopin's finest works. The Berceuse is an astonishing *tour de force*. An unbroken stream of melody, sometimes very ornate, is supported by a rocking accompaniment based on two harmonies only; towards the end the melody becomes less ornate and the harmonic movement slower, the music looking for a moment towards another key. This gives an effect of extraordinary serenity, heightened by the final glance at the opening measures of the melody. If the Berceuse has something in common with the Nocturnes, the Barcarolle, with its spacious, outdoor atmosphere, is more akin to the Ballades. This can be felt at once in the magnificent gesture with which it opens. The swaying figure that ac-

companies the melody is as characteristic of Chopin as the melody itself, and in the last three pages all three themes (the third decidedly Italianate) appear in a glowing and triumphant mood, culminating in a brilliant flourish.

• Large-scale works •

The *Fantaisie*, op.49, completed in 1841 is one of Chopin's most masterly structures, built on ideas of remarkable vitality. First there is a solemn, march-like introduction which forms a complete design of its own. After this a passage full of dramatic suspense leads to a procession of themes which follow one another with remarkable continuity, going through various keys and culminating in a brisk and rousing march, very different from that of the introduction. Eventually the themes all return in the same order, but in different keys, as in the first movement of a sonata. But before this there is a quiet interlude of great beauty, the first phrase of which returns for a moment just before the end of the work. The overall plan is very satisfactory and has a robust, almost epic quality for which Chopin has not always been given credit. It is usually described as being in F minor,

Above: Autograph page from the Etude in A minor, the fourth of the second set of twelve, op.25, composed between 1832 and 1834 and dedicated to the Countess Marie d'Agoult, Liszt's mistress. The Countess and Liszt were neighbors and friends of Chopin at this time, and it was at their salon that he first met George Sand. The manuscript shows Chopin's meticulous attention to dynamics, phrasing and pedaling.

Left: A photograph of Chopin a few months before his death in 1849, taken at the house of Maurice Schlesinger, founder of the *Gazette Musicale* and publisher of much of Chopin's music.

Below: For a long time thought to be the last written words of Chopin: a plea for his body to be opened to prevent his being buried alive. His sister Louise took his heart back to Warsaw.

Right: Chopin as Dante by Delacroix. Delacroix had received a commission to decorate the ceiling of the library at the Palais du Luxembourg, where he used Chopin's features to represent Dante. In April 1847 he took Chopin and George Sand to see the finished painting – it must have been almost the last time they were together. Delacroix kept this drawing of Chopin in his room all his life.

but this is applicable only to the introduction. The rest of the work moves more and more towards Chopin's favorite key of A flat, in which it ends triumphantly.

It is a small step from this to Chopin's sonatas. The early Sonata in C minor is, in its outer movements, solidly constructed, but there is a complete absence of the flowing lyricism of Chopin's mature work. It was written in 1828; ten years later Chopin wrote the Funeral March that was eventually to be the slow movement of the Sonata in B flat minor, the rest of which was composed in 1839. This is a work of feverish intensity in which the quieter, more lyrical passages are particularly welcome when they come. The first movement, in which Chopin handles sonata form with great concentration, has remarkable features. The first subject, with its persistent reiterations of a short phrase, suggests a Bach prelude rather than a sonata movement; the second, opening with chorale-like solemnity, gradually increases in fervor. The scherzo rushes wildly through many keys; the opening phrase of the gentle, waltz-like trio recurs with peculiarly touching effect at the end of the movement. After this the first chord of the Funeral March sounds singularly chilling. The juxtaposition of these bleak harmonies and the flowing Italianate melody of the trio is astonishingly effective; the music remains somber and stately, relieved only by the simple pathos of the trio. In the finale, on the other hand, chromaticism runs riot until the persistent triplets, played by both hands in unison, produce a mysterious and ghostly atmosphere, broken only by the sudden explosion at the end. In its own day this finale was considered outrageous; now it can be seen as an astonishingly original piece of music, and a fitting conclusion to one of Chopin's most powerful works.

The Sonata in B minor, written in 1844, is very different. The first movement opens with a splendid theme, but its chief glory is the long, sweeping melody of the second subject. The scherzo is brilliant and light-hearted; the trio, with its rich contrapuntal texture, is one of the most deeply thoughtful passages in Chopin's music. The slow movement, after four solemn and mysterious introductory measures, is a nocturne of extraordinary stillness and serenity; in the central section the repeated figures, in Bachian manner, produce an almost hypnotic effect, and after them the return to the first melody is wonderfully evocative. The finale has a broad and vigorous main theme that stands out vividly against the brilliant episodes by which it is surrounded. Towards the end there is an extraordinary passage in which the two hands go their own ways in complete disregard of harmonic considerations. In the long run there can be little to choose between these two works. The essentially tragic character of the Sonata in B flat minor may make a more immediate impact, but the later B minor Sonata, with its robust energy and rich, glowing lyricism, is hardly inferior.

The Sonata in G minor for cello and piano, one of Chopin's last works, has been generally underrated. The piano part is elaborate, and it is not always easy to maintain a perfect balance, but the slow movement, tantalizingly short, is an exquisitely balanced dialogue for the two instruments, on a theme similar to that of the trio of the Funeral March.

Of Chopin's longer works the four Ballades are his greatest and the most original in independence of design. The word 'ballade' had hitherto been applied only to vocal music, but although there is a vivid suggestion of narrative in the Ballades, it is a narrative concerned with moods rather than with people or events, and they seem not to have been inspired by specific poems. One can imagine whatever 'program' one chooses as the music shifts in mood, freed from the restrictions of traditional forms. Thus the solemn introductory phrase with which the well-known first Ballade (op.23, 1836) opens gives little indication of what is to come, but there is a strong premonition of tragedy in the poignant discord just before the gently elegiac first theme appears; the second is equally lyrical but more serene. When the first reappears it is in a far darker mood and is soon swept aside by an unexpectedly full-blooded and heroic version of the second. The first makes one more appearance, at first subdued and then rising to a passionate climax before being whirled into a stormy coda which has no obvious connection with anything that has gone before it, though there are two fleeting references to the first theme just before the eloquently tragic end. The final bars are almost brutally emphatic.

In the second Ballade (op.38, 1838) there is a contrast not only between two moods but between two keys, the pastoral F major in which it opens and the stormy and tragic A minor in which it ends. The self-contained opening section is remarkable for simple but very beautiful harmony and for the subtlety with which the opening measures anticipate the pastoral rhythm of the main theme. The angry presto breaks violently in on this, but it soon loses its momentum and the first theme returns, wandering restlessly through various keys until the presto returns, seemingly as the result of steadily increasing tension. When the melody of the opening section appears in the bass under a flood of tempestuous sixteenth-notes, it is clear that the music can never return to the calm mood of the opening.

The third Ballade (op.47, 1841), perhaps even more familiar than the first, is a delightful and adventurous comedy. As in the second, the opening section is practically self-contained. Two ideas follow, one with a gently cantering rhythm, the other more solemn. Eventually the opening phrase of the work is heard in a remote key, as though from a distance. It comes gradually nearer, escorted, as it were, by the cantering theme, and finally appears in a grand and triumphant mood. Shortly after this the Ballade ends, brilliantly, with a characteristically unexpected touch in the final chords. The fourth Ballade (op.52, 1842), is arguably the most deeply moving of all Chopin's works. It has points in common with the first; both move from pathos to tragedy, but here there is more

subtlety and continuity. The long and fascinating main theme, a descendant perhaps of Mozart's Rondo in A minor, is constantly varied; at one stage it appears in a surprisingly bare two-part texture, and shortly afterwards with beautifully ornate decorations. The second subject, at first subdued and wistful, eventually appears over a surging background and leads to a tremendous climax. After a very impressive lull there is a stormy coda in which fragments of the first theme occasionally appear, as though swept along by a whirlwind. All Chopin's finest qualities are here; lyrical beauty, subtlety of texture, and a strong dramatic power.

Chopin's output, compared with that of Mendelssohn, Schumann and Liszt, must inevitably seem limited. The orchestra meant little to him, and the choir still less. As a writer for the piano he certainly ranks higher than Mendelssohn; where Schumann is concerned a choice between the two composers will probably be a question of personal temperament. But, without belittling Schumann's great and lovable piano works, it can be said that they are not as unfailingly effective for the instrument as those of Chopin. The texture of Chopin's piano music is always beautifully spaced, with full awareness of the capacity of the pedal. One reason for its continued popularity among pianists is that it is so rewarding to practice. Owing to the wealth of beautiful detail his most exacting passages continue to sound interesting, even when played at a slow pace. As for Liszt, he and Chopin both stood apart from the mainstream of German music of the nineteenth century, but Liszt, with all his enterprise, lacked Chopin's unfailing sense of style; sometimes the widely varied elements of his personality do not seem to be perfectly integrated. Of Chopin this could not be said. Behind his lyrical charm is great strength, and behind his most passionate outpourings there is firm control.

Left: The Countess Delfina Potocka, whom Delacroix called 'the enchantress' – a beautiful, talented and wealthy Polish lady of independent mind who separated from her husband and lived in Paris among both aristocratic and artistic circles. A pupil of Chopin, who had a very high opinion of her as a pianist and singer, she was his close friend for many years and one of the people nearest to him in his last months, often coming to play and sing to him. There is some possibility that the Countess and Chopin were lovers, and it was from this slight evidence – and possibly the existence of some genuine letters – that in 1945 correspondence which proved this relationship was 'discovered.' The letters were found to be fraudulent, and the extent of their friendship remains unknown.

The Traveling Virtuoso: Niccolò Paganini

The dictionary definition of 'virtuoso,' as applied to music, is of somebody skilled in technique. In the nineteenth century, it meant much more than that. A virtuoso performer was a show-business star as much as a musician. The first, and perhaps the most amazing, of this breed was the Genoese-born violinist Niccolò Paganini (1782-1840). He was, without doubt, a superb player. Friedrich Wieck, the composer and Clara Schumann's father, said of him: 'Never did I hear a singer who touched me as deeply as an adagio played by Paganini. Never was there an artist who was equally great and incomparable in so many genres.' While Schubert after hearing him play said that he had 'heard an angel sing.' Paganini himself appreciated some of the greatest music of his time, notably the Beethoven string quartets, which he loved to play with friends.

His own compositions matched his playing in their style and brilliance and were designed to demonstrate his exceptional command of his instrument. The twenty-four Caprices, op.1, were among the few works to be published in his lifetime, and they were composed at the peak of his virtuosic powers. Like Chopin's Etudes, they relate to different aspects of technique, but the imaginative bravura decoration raises them far above the level of mere studies. The last of them, in A minor, inspired works from many other composers, including not only Liszt, whose own virtuoso career was modeled on that of Paganini, but Schumann, Brahms and Rachmaninov.

As with any true-born showman, Paganini's platform manner and appearance counted for a good deal. He was dark complexioned, with a prominent hooked nose, and thin to the point of emaciation; and he adopted an odd, crooked stance while playing. In all he cut a somewhat grotesque figure, and people said he was in league with the Devil – something well in tune with the early nineteenth-century taste for the supernatural. There was another popular rumor, that he had perfected his fantastic technique while in prison for murder. Paganini exploited this diabolic image. One glance from those flashing dark eyes set in the cadaverous face was enough to enthrall the women in his audience.

Right: Eugène Delacroix's oil sketch of Paganini, in about 1832 at the height of the violinist's fame, when he was ceaselessly touring throughout Europe. It captures well his platform stance: right leg thrust forward and the weight of the body thrown onto the left hip, head bent low over the violin, which itself is held at an unusually low angle. One contemporary witness, J. M. Schottky, described him thus: 'His clothes flop loosely about his limbs, and when he takes a bow he moves his body in such a singular way that every instant you expect the upper part to separate from the lower part and both collapse in a heap of bones.'

Above: Adolph von Menzel's painting of the new Potsdam railway in 1847.

Above: Louis Léopold Boilly's painting of the arrival of a diligence at a coaching inn in 1803. The comparison with Menzel's painting (*left*) emphasizes the great advantage that Liszt had over Paganini as a traveling virtuoso. With the coming of the railways (just too late for Paganini), people could travel around Europe or North America in as many days as it had previously taken weeks by coach. Through the rest of the century, Liszt and the parade of concert virtuosos that followed in his footsteps, moved from place to place, living out of a suitcase, much like their 'jet set' counterparts today.

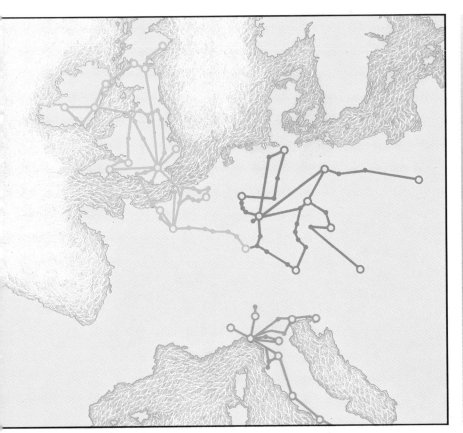

Above: A map of Paganini's major European tours – in Italy in the years 1815-27, always returning to his home town of Genoa; from Vienna to Bohemia, Poland and Germany in 1828-31; in France, Britain and Ireland in 1831-2; and in Belgium in 1834. Given the hardships of coach travel, often bumping along over roads little better than tracks and exposed to all weathers, his tours were an astonishing test of endurance, especially in view of his very poor health.

In one year alone, 1831, during his first tour of the British Isles, he gave eighteen concerts in London and forty-nine in the English provinces, twenty-three in Scotland and a further twenty-two in Ireland. During the great years between 1828 and 1834, he was given a rapturous reception almost everywhere and showered with honors, despite occasional, rather unfair, press accusations of mean-ness and rapacity. After his Paris début, a correspondent wrote of the audience: 'There was a divine, a diabolic enthusiasm. The people have all gone crazy.' A Viennese critic declared: 'Never has an artist caused such a terrific sensation within our walls as this god of the violin.' 'Paganini the incomparable – the matchless Paganini!' raved a critic of the Irish *Cork Constitution*.

Paganini played (*above*) at Covent Garden at the end of his British tour in 1831-2. *The Times* first attacked him for the high prices he demanded, but later conceded: 'It is but justice to say of this extraordinary man, that all the anticipations formed of him, however highly coloured, have fallen short of the reality . . . He forms a class by himself.'

Right: A good example of Paganini's own neat notation: a cadenza for one of his own concertos. In fact, it was unusual for him to write out such passages as precisely as this. He was more often true to the original idea of a cadenza, improvising the music during a performance on the spur of the moment.

Above: Sketch, possibly by George Sand, one of many to show Liszt at the keyboard. Others show whole pianos collapsing under his furious assault!

Below: Bust of Paganini by Dantan. Berlioz described in December 1833 how, after a concert at which his *Symphonie fantastique* had been performed, 'a man stopped me in the passage – a man with long hair, piercing eyes, a strange and haggard face – a genius, a Titan among the giants, whom I had never seen before and at the sight of whom I was deeply moved . . . *It was Paganini.*' The violinist later gave Berlioz 20,000 francs, so he could devote himself to composing.

Left: Paganini as portrayed by Ingres in Rome, 1819. His appearance at this time of his life was much less bizarre than it became later, after he had had all his bottom teeth and part of an infected jaw removed, which changed the whole look of his face, and when his health started seriously to deteriorate from other causes. But he already had his prodigious technique, which was revolutionary and highly unorthodox. It included the use of a low bridge for chordal playing; bowing to produce rapid staccato; and the combination of bowing with left-hand pizzicato. It was the combination of this virtuosity with the sweetness of his tone in lyrical passages that made his playing unique.

Below: In the wake of Paganini's tours publishers flooded the market with arrangements of his music. The grandiose title 'L'Ecole de Paganini' at the head of this London publisher's edition is quite misleading.

Apart from the fact that this music is arranged for the piano, Paganini was, from all accounts, a bad teacher and never established a 'school,' except in the broad sense of creating a new style of playing.

Above: Orchestra, management and guests awaiting Paganini's arrival for a rehearsal. At actual concerts, Paganini always timed his stage entrance very nicely, coming on just when he judged audience expectation to have reached fever pitch. In the picture, one of his violins also awaits him on a chair. He had a superb collection of instruments, including a Guarneri del Gesù that he donated to his home town of Genoa. He also had a Stradivari viola. It was for this instrument that Berlioz specially wrote his symphony *Harold en Italie*. But Paganini never performed it. When Berlioz showed him the score of the first movement, Paganini looked at the rests in the viola part and cried, 'This is not at all what I want. I am silent a great deal too long. I must be playing the whole time.' However, when he finally heard the work he was deeply impressed.

Right: Liszt's hastily sketched notation (without stave lines) for one of his 'Paganini' Studies, dated September 1838. It clearly demonstrates the technical difficulties of music of this kind, and also shows how meticulously Liszt marked phrasing and dynamics in his manuscripts.

Above: If Liszt was the greatest piano virtuoso of his age, it was Carl Czerny (standing, right, beside Berlioz) who laid the foundations for piano virtuosity with his theoretical compositions and his teaching; both Liszt and his great rival Sigismond Thalberg were Czerny's pupils. Listening to Liszt are Joseph Kriehuber, who made the drawing, and the Moravian violin virtuoso Heinrich Ernst (1814-65).

Above: A letter from Paganini, dated April 1830, concerning a canceled concert at the German town of Offenbach, and explaining his poor health. He probably suffered from both syphilis and tuberculosis, ailments aggravated by various drastic treatments, including a very strong purgative.

Right: The 'Casino Paganini,' opened in Paris in 1836, with a ballroom, restaurant, gaming club and concert hall. Its subsequent failure robbed the violinist of much of his fortune. Berlioz later lamented that his example had not been followed, as 'there is not one good public concert-room in the city.'

Above: A well-known print inspired by the story of how the eighteenth-century violinist and composer Giuseppe Tartini came to write his celebrated, and fiendishly difficult, 'Devil's Trill' Sonata. According to Tartini himself, the Devil appeared in a dream and played the piece to him. The notion of there being something 'diabolic' or 'demonic' about the performance of very difficult music was one aspect of that cliché of Romanticism — *Faust* and *Der Freischütz* are but two obvious examples — that superhuman tasks could be performed by making a pact with the Devil.

181

FELIX MENDELSSOHN BARTHOLDY

R. LARRY TODD

Few composers of the nineteenth century enjoyed the almost universal acclaim accorded to Mendelssohn. Esteemed as a composer of the first rank, as a primary advocate for the revival of Bach's and Handel's music, as a distinguished conductor of the Leipzig Gewandhaus orchestra, as a virtuoso pianist and organist, and as a founder of and teacher at the Leipzig Conservatory, Mendelssohn was rightfully admired as a protector of artistic standards in an age when musical values were being assailed and reshaped. Mendelssohn confronted musical Romanticism and struck a balance between tradition and reform. His music evinces a classical purity of structure and emphasis on traditional craft; yet it was not unaffected by the new cult of self-expression which dramatically altered musical esthetics during the first few decades of the nineteenth century.

His childhood coincided with the rebuilding of Prussia after the débâcle at the Battle of Jena. Following the humiliation of the Peace of Tilsit (1807), by which Napoleon imposed upon Prussia severe financial and territorial reparations, ministers such as Stein and Hardenberg saw to it that serfdom was abolished and progress made toward a constitutional monarchy. Meanwhile the philosopher Fichte, returning to an occupied Berlin in 1807, attempted to outline a course for the revitalization of Prussia. In his passionate *Addresses to the German Nation* (1808), intended for all of Germany, he called for a rejection of traditional approaches to education (with their emphasis on learning by rote), and a search for new values nurtured by the imaginative development of the national moral will. Germany would become confident, morally upright, and independent of foreign domination.

In this period of rejuvenation Felix Mendelssohn was raised. He was born in Hamburg on 3 February 1809. (The name Bartholdy was added when the Mendelssohn family converted to the Protestant creed. Felix was baptized on 21 March, 1816.) His father, Abraham Mendelssohn, a well-to-do banker, was soon forced to flee with his family to Berlin on account of his anti-French activities. Abraham's father was the eminent Jewish philosopher of the Enlightenment, Moses Mendelssohn. Dorothea Mendelssohn, the composer's aunt, had in 1804 married Friedrich Schlegel, leader of the Jena school of Romanticism and a powerful force in German literary criticism. A maternal relation, Felix's great-aunt Sarah Levy, had studied with W. F. Bach and collected the works of J. S. and C. P. E. Bach. And at the Mendelssohn residence the children, among them Felix's sister, Fanny, a talented pianist and composer in her own right, enjoyed encounters with the literati of Berlin society.

Felix's precociousness soon became apparent. By the age of ten the boy was reading Caesar and Ovid, and in 1820 he was translating Horace's *Ars Poetica*; other subjects included Euclidean geometry, arithmetic, history and geography. Lessons on the violin and piano probably began as early as 1816, when Felix met in Paris Pierre Baillot and Madame Kiené-Bigot, both acquaintances of Beethoven; piano lessons were continued in Berlin with Ludwig Berger, a highly respected pianist and former pupil of Clementi, and violin lessons with C. W. Henning, court Konzertmeister. A profound influence was exerted on the child by Carl Friedrich Zelter, who undertook to instruct him in theory and composition at some time during 1819. Zelter's background reflected the musical conservatism of eighteenth-century Berlin, and Mendelssohn received a rigorous tuition in figured bass, chorale, double counterpoint, canon and fugue. Zelter's method was largely indebted to J. P. Kirnberger, a pupil of J. S. Bach, and, to a lesser extent, to Marpurg, whose *Treatise on the Fugue* (Berlin, 1754) did much to preserve interest in fugue and other erudite forms of counterpoint. Mendelssohn's workbook from 1819 to 1821, with some seventy folios of exercises, is filled with corrections by Zelter and occasional rather stern remarks.

At about this time Mendelssohn began to compose, first simple piano pieces in binary-dance form or elementary sonata form, but also works for organ, violin and piano, and chorus. His earliest compositions betray a youthful emulation of eighteenth-century composers, above all Bach, but also Mozart and Haydn. By 1821 the boy had completed his studies in three-part fugue; a series of quartet fugues was his next assignment. Then followed in quick succession no fewer than twelve string sinfonias, composed for performance at the Sunday musicales in the Mendelssohn house. One senses in these works the student's striving to achieve greater contrapuntal complexity. In several, the traditional eighteenth-century four-

Above: Mendelssohn at the age of twelve, an oil sketch by Carl Begas, 1821. In this year Mendelssohn was taken by his teacher, Zelter, to visit Goethe, with whom he became a great favorite and who said: 'I am Saul and you are my David.'

part string texture is expanded to five or six parts; in the slow movement of no.9 (1823), Mendelssohn experimented with a division of the orchestra into treble and bass groups and thereby achieved an original antiphonal effect. On the whole, these works, increasingly more ambitious in scope, are an extension of Mendelssohn's studies in counterpoint. They are filled with complex fugues and thick chromatic passagework, as if in response to the music of J. S. Bach. The culmination of this aspect of Mendelssohn's development, though, was postponed until 1825, in the finale of the great Octet, op.20. Here Mendelssohn perfected eight-part fugal writing and triumphantly crowned his study of counterpoint.

In June 1821, Carl Maria von Weber's *Der Freischütz* was premièred in Berlin. This milestone in Romantic opera was carefully studied by the young Mendelssohn, who would imitate the turbulent overture in his Symphony no.1 in C minor (1824). Mendelssohn also began to assimilate stylistic features of Weber's piano music, above all the *Konzertstück* in F minor, the *Invitation to the Dance* (later orchestrated by Berlioz) and the piano sonatas. Mendelssohn's meeting with Weber was followed in November by a momentous trip to Weimar, where he played for Johann Nepomuk Hummel, one of the most renowned piano virtuosi of the day, and, more important, he met Goethe. At the height of his powers in 1821, Goethe had still to produce Part II of *Faust*, with its visions of Hellenic and Byronic worlds. Mendelssohn visited Goethe several times before the poet's death in 1832, and in homage to him he later

created one of his finest compositions, the cantata *Die erste Walpurgisnacht*, op.60.

At about the time of his first visit to Weimar Mendelssohn's musical development entered a new phase. Evidence of his studies with Zelter are still evident, as in his Singspiel *Die beiden Pädagogen* (The Two Pedagogues) of 1821, with its strong hints of Mozart. Nevertheless, Mendelssohn's curiosity about contemporary musical trends now deepened considerably, partly prompted by the première of *Der Freischütz*. The music of Beethoven, however, was most influential on the impressionable youth, particularly the late piano sonatas and, eventually, the symphonies and quartets. Mendelssohn also eagerly studied the music of such virtuosi as Hummel, Field, Moscheles and Dussek. In March 1822 he appeared with the pianist Aloys Schmitt to perform a double concerto by Dussek. The performance probably inspired Mendelssohn to write his two concertos for two pianos, in E and A flat major (1823 and 1824), in which he appropriated pianistic figuration from Beethoven and Field.

By early 1824, Mendelssohn had learned what he could from Zelter. Some doubts, however, still remained for Abraham Mendelssohn Bartholdy about his young son's future. These were partially alleviated by the visit of Ignaz Moscheles to Berlin in November 1824, who was asked by Mendelssohn's mother to provide piano instruction for the young man; a second visit followed in 1826 and secured the lifelong friendship between the two. From Moscheles Mendelssohn acquired a first-hand knowledge of developments in contemporary piano technique, conveniently assembled by Moscheles into two books of Etudes. For his part, Mendelssohn imitated the new advances in such works as the *Allegro vivace*, op.7 no.2, of 1824.

Early in 1825 Mendelssohn accompanied his father on a trip to Paris. Equipped with his new Piano Quartet in B minor, op.3, dedicated to Goethe, he visited the venerable Luigi Cherubini, whose verdict is well-known: 'The boy is rich, he will do well.' Mendelssohn answered by composing a *Kyrie* for orchestra and five-part chorus, as if to outdo some of Cherubini's sacred works. Mendelssohn's other experiences in Paris further confirmed his growing sense of mission as a German composer. He was astonished to find Bach's music confused with that of Monsigny and to discover that Beethoven's *Fidelio*, based upon French rescue opera, was not well known in Paris.

Having returned to Berlin, Mendelssohn prepared to conclude his formal education. He matriculated at the recently founded University of Berlin and attended the lectures of Hegel, Ritter and Humboldt. His reading of literature – above all the works of Goethe, Jean Paul and Shakespeare – quickened his artistic maturity. Like Schumann, he found musical inspiration in Romantic literature. The result was a series of instrumental works, conceived during the period from 1826 to 1829, which are among his most progressive. These include the Quartet in A minor, op.13, in which Mendelssohn broke new ground by incorporating a quotation of his song 'Ist es wahr?' But the principal successes were the three concert overtures: *A Midsummer Night's Dream* (1826), inspired by Shakespeare's play; *Meeresstille und glückliche Fahrt* (Calm Sea and Prosperous Voyage, 1828), based on Goethe's poem, which had also been set by Beethoven as a cantata; and *Die Hebriden* (1830), possibly influenced by Ossianic tales associated with the Hebrides Islands. All three were extensively revised before their final publication in score as a triptych in 1835. In these Romantic works, Mendelssohn refused to tie himself to elaborate programs, as Berlioz would do in his *Symphonie fantastique* of 1830; instead he relied upon the power of suggestion. A few techniques may be mentioned: the use of tonal 'wandering' in the development of *A Midsummer Night's Dream* to depict the entangled lovers in the forest; the use of the piccolo and serpent in *Meeresstille und glückliche Fahrt* to capture the breadth of the ocean as the becalmed ship regains momentum; and the boldly unconventional voice leading at the opening of *Die Hebriden* to suggest an exotic, primitive Ossianic world.

These brushes with Romanticism notwithstanding, Mendelssohn continued to cultivate his study of the traditional masters. In 1827, during a visit to Heidelberg, he met Anton Thibaut, professor of law, who had recently published an eloquent tract arguing for the purification of Church music, in which he praised the music of Palestrina, Handel and others, and called for a revised and corrected Lutheran hymnal. This unabashed historicism deeply impressed Mendelssohn, who began to compose a series of sacred compositions, still largely unknown today. *Tu es Petrus*, op.111 (1827), may well have been inspired by Palestrina's music. *Hora est* (1828), for four four-part choirs, was written in the great baroque polychoral tradition. *Christe, Du Lamm Gottes* (1827), a setting of the Lutheran 'Agnus Dei,' was conceived

Above: Jacob's Ladder: a silhouette made for Mendelssohn (whose first name was Jacob.) However talented and industrious – even his exacting mother felt he worked too hard – Mendelssohn was also a very lively and fun-loving child. At Goethe's house he had a happy time with the poet's grandsons and other guests including Adèle Schopenhauer, sister of the philosopher, who cut this silhouette for him.

Left: The autograph of the overture *A Midsummer Night's Dream*, 1826, inspired by Shakespeare's play. The incidental music to the play was not written until seventeen years later.

Far left: Fanny Mendelssohn (1805-47) by her husband Wilhelm Hensel. Mendelssohn's very talented sister wrote a considerable amount of music, but only some songs, a piano trio and a few piano pieces have been published. Her public life was restricted to occasional appearances as a pianist and the organization of the Sunday concerts at their parents' house in Berlin.

as a cantata in one movement on the Bachian model, with the *cantus firmus* intoned in augmented values and surrounded by a web of orchestral and choral polyphony.

These first attempts to study the choral masterpieces of the past, however, were overshadowed in 1829 by a performance of greater historical consequence: the 'centenary' revival of the *St Matthew Passion*. In 1823 Mendelssohn had received a copy of the work as a Christmas present from his great-aunt, Sarah Levy. At the Singakademie, where the boy had sung as an alto, Zelter had rehearsed several of Bach's motets and part of the B minor Mass but had not dared to revive a work as major as the *St Matthew Passion*. With the assistance of the actor Eduard Devrient, Mendelssohn began

Left: Fingal's Cave by Carl Gustav Carus, 1834. Connections with the legendary Ossian made the cave, 'rediscovered' in 1772, a place of pilgrimage for visitors to Scotland. Scott, in *The Lord of the Isles*, hailed it as 'that wondrous dome, / where, as to shame the temples deck'd / by skill of earthly architect / Nature herself, it seem'd, would raise / a Minster to her Maker's praise!'

Below: A view towards Mull and the Hebrides, drawn by Mendelssohn. This was said to be the moment of inspiration for his overture *Die Hebriden,* later known as *Fingalshöhle* (Fingal's Cave).

cautious rehearsals of the Bach Passion. The performance, given in Berlin on 11 March 1829, was an unqualified success, although the work was presented in a heavily truncated and edited version. It sent shock-waves throughout Europe and prompted many performances, now generally viewed as signaling the beginning of the Bach revival in the nineteenth century.

• Years of travel •

Having determined upon music as his profession, Mendelssohn, now nineteen, decided to visit the major musical centers of England and Europe. He embarked for England in April 1829; in London he was greeted by Moscheles, Klingemann (an emissary at the Hanoverian legation), and other transplanted Berlin friends. At the British Museum he pored over the autographs of Handel and made an inventory for Zelter. He successfully performed his First Symphony (with the scherzo of the Octet substituted for the third movement) and the *Midsummer Night's Dream* overture at the Philharmonic Concerts, and appeared as a soloist as well. He soon established strong ties with English musical circles, which would result in no fewer than nine additional trips to England between 1829 and 1847. Moreover, as if struck by

a Romantic wanderlust, Mendelssohn planned a walking tour of Scotland with Klingemann, and in July the two set out by coach to Edinburgh, with an eye for the Scottish countryside and an ear for Scottish folksongs. At Holyrood Palace in Edinburgh Mendelssohn sketched the opening of his 'Scottish' Symphony, which was not finished, however, until 1842. They visited Sir Walter Scott at Abbotsford, saw the ruins of Melrose Abbey (memorialized by Scott in *The Lay of the Last Minstrel*), and continued to the Trossachs and the Highlands, filling along the way a sketchbook with verses and drawings. The summit of the journey was the trip to Fingal's Cave; looking out on the Hebrides, on 7 August 1829, Mendelssohn sketched the beginning of the overture *Die Hebriden*, which, 'with its bare harmonies and deep scoring in the lower strings,' was an attempt to depict the 'very Ossianic and sweetly sad' quality, as Klingemann described it, of the Hebrides Islands.

The return to Berlin toward the end of 1829 must have been a startling contrast to the experiences in Scotland. As a celebration, Mendelssohn brought with him the score of *Die Heimkehr aus der Fremde* (The Homecoming from Abroad), written for his parents' silver wedding anniversary, though humorously suggestive of his 'campaign' in the wilds of Scotland. His return to the refinement of Berlin society also led to an offer of a chair in music at the University, but he deferred in favor of his friend Adolf Bernhard Marx, editor of the *Berliner allgemeine musikalische Zeitung*. At about this time, Mendelssohn began serious work on his Second Symphony for full orchestra, intended as his contribution to the tercentenary celebration of the Augsburg Confession in June 1830. At first referred to as the *Kirchensinfonie*, the work became known as the 'Reformation' Symphony, because of its use of Luther's chorale 'Ein' feste Burg' as a *cantus firmus* in the finale, and the citation of the

'Dresden Amen' in the first movement. Dissatisfied with the work, Mendelssohn withdrew it; it was printed posthumously, along with many other compositions.

Having recovered from a bout of measles, Mendelssohn set out again; traveling through Leipzig, he reached Weimar on 20 May, 1830. Goethe presented him with an autograph page from *Faust* and encouraged a sojourn in Italy. Mendelssohn continued to Munich, Salzburg and Linz, and arrived in Vienna in August. Heeding Goethe's advice, he then journeyed on to Venice, where, as the poet had done, he marveled at the masterpieces of Titian and Giorgione. Compositionally he busied himself during this period with a series of sacred cantatas. The first of these, *O Haupt voll Blut und Wunden* (O Sacred Head Sore Wounded), was finished in Vienna. Inspired by a painting ascribed to Zurbarán in the art gallery in Munich, the cantata was also indebted to the *St Matthew Passion*, in which Bach cited the same chorale several times. It was followed by other cantatas on Lutheran texts.

Arriving in Rome in November, Mendelssohn furthered his study of sacred music, particularly that written by Italian Renaissance and Baroque masters. He was aided by Fortunato Santini, who had amassed a library of manuscript copies, including a copy of Handel's *Solomon*, and by Giuseppe Baini, who devoted

Above: Watercolor of Durham Cathedral by Mendelssohn, after a drawing he made on his tour of 1829.

Left: Fingal with his Spear, 1805-6, by Philipp Otto Runge. In 1760 James Macpherson, a Scottish literary figure, published *Fingal: An ancient epic poem*, said to be translated from an early Gaelic poet, Ossian. After Macpherson's death these works were found to be largely his own, based on fragments of Gaelic poetry and legend, but also drawing on the epic poetry of Homer and Virgil. However, they enjoyed considerable success for their Romantic spirit and were widely translated.

his efforts to publishing the works of Palestrina. At the Sistine Chapel Mendelssohn heard works by Palestrina, Allegri, Victoria and Baini; he completed a setting of Psalm 115 in its Latin version, 'Non nobis, Domine,' which nevertheless shows Bachian and Handelian influence. Meanwhile, he finished a revision of the overture *Die Hebriden*, which he played for Berlioz (then a recipient of the Prix de Rome), and sketched ideas for *Die erste Walpurgisnacht* and the 'Scottish' and 'Italian' Symphonies.

After an excursion to Naples, Mendelssohn returned to Germany via Switzerland in 1831. In Munich he hastily finished the score of his G minor Piano Concerto for performance and received a commission for an opera. After consulting with the dramatist Karl Immermann in Düsseldorf, he eagerly anticipated writing an opera on *The Tempest*. This was not to be, however; the project was but one in a long series of libretti ultimately rejected by Mendelssohn, who would exhaust his dramatic talents not on opera but on oratorio. While plans for *The Tempest* were still under consideration, Mendelssohn traveled to Paris, appeared in concert at the Conservatoire, wrote a humorous canon for Chopin and, after braving a cholera outbreak, crossed the English Channel in April 1832. *Die Hebriden* was given in London, Mendelssohn appeared as organist at St Paul's, and he composed the virtuoso *Capriccio brillant*, which – complete with a march – was suitably fashioned after Weber's modish *Konzertstück*.

At this time Mendelssohn also finished the first volume of the *Lieder ohne Worte* (Songs without Words), op.19, which he confided to the care of Moscheles for publication. In this novel type of piano miniature, apparently devised as early as 1828, Mendelssohn effectively transposed textless elements of the solo *Lied*, duet and part-song to the keyboard. For some he designated titles, as in the finely crafted 'Venezianisches Gondellied,' no.6, sketched in Italy in 1830. In other, untitled *Lieder*, his intentions were nevertheless clear, as in no.3 in A major, a jubilant hunting song (the buoyant horn calls are brought back in a subtle fashion in the following *Lied*, also in A major). These keyboard pieces, unjustly criticized for their sentimentality, along with the concert overtures, present Mendelssohn in his most Romantic manner. Five more volumes followed, the last in 1845.

The deaths of Zelter and Goethe in 1832 shattered Mendelssohn's well-being, his successes in England notwithstanding. Returning to Berlin, he attempted unsuccessfully to gain Zelter's post at the Singakademie. Another visit to England provided an opportunity to perform the 'Italian' Symphony at a Philharmonic Society concert. A new concert piece was also required, and Mendelssohn obliged with the *Rondo brilant*, op.29; he also collaborated with Moscheles on a series of variations for piano duet, based upon the gypsy music from Weber's *Preciosa*. Then, responding to an invitation to conduct at the Niederrheinische Musikfest, Mendelssohn arrived in Düsseldorf in May 1833. For the three-day festival he programed works by Beethoven, Weber and Mozart, but featured Handel's *Israel in Egypt*, which marked a new effort to revive that master's music. He was soon asked to assume a post as city music director at Düsseldorf; his move there marked the end of the years of travel.

• Düsseldorf and Leipzig •

Mendelssohn's responsibilities at Düsseldorf included the management of the concert subscription series, the revitalization of the theater (in conjunction with Immermann), and performances of sacred music for Catholic services. Though Mendelssohn mounted several operas, among them *Don Giovanni* and Cherubini's *Les deux journées*, his efforts in the theater were largely unsuccessful, and his wish to compose a German opera thwarted. His performances of sacred works were more successful: he introduced (or rather revived) compositions by Palestrina, Allegri, Lotti, Pergolesi, Leo and Lassus, thanks to his researches in Italy. His correspondence with his family, however, indicates that his chief concern during these years was to find time for his own compositions.

Without doubt, the major work of this period was the oratorio *St Paul*, premièred on 22 May 1836 and soon hailed by Schumann as a masterpiece. Mendelssohn had prepared himself by studying and performing the oratorios of Handel; his interpretations of *Messiah*, *Israel in Egypt*, *Alexander's Feast* and *Acis and Galatea* did much to foster a Handelian revival in Germany comparable to the resurgence of

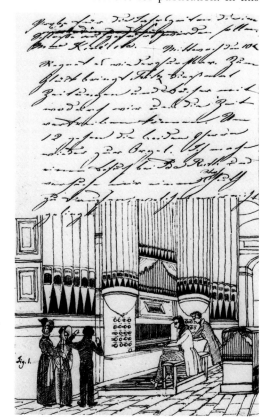

Right: A page from the Mendelssohns' honeymoon diary. From March 1837 Mendelssohn and his wife spent two months on their honeymoon, followed by a month in Frankfurt and a further two months' summer holiday. Together they kept a diary, illustrated with sketches and music; this page, for 10 May 1837, shows Mendelssohn playing the organ in Heidelberg. It was a time of great happiness and relaxation in which he produced a number of compositions. In August they returned home, for Mendelssohn was committed to visit England; Cécile, by now expecting their first child, remained behind.

interest in Bach's music. Based upon a libretto prepared from the scriptures by Julius Schubring, *St Paul* was conceived as a synthesis of Handelian oratorio and Bachian Passion. The dramatic use of the chorus Mendelssohn inherited from Handel; the insertion of chorales he borrowed from Bach. Mendelssohn carefully chose several chorales – including 'Allein Gott in der Höh sei Ehr,' 'Dir Herr, dir will ich mich ergeben,' 'Wachet auf' (also used in the overture to the oratorio to represent Saul's spiritual awakening) and 'O Jesu Christe, wahres Licht' – which convincingly delineate the principal dramatic actions of the text: the stoning of Stephen, the conversion of Saul, the restoration of his sight, and the good works of Paul and Barnabas. Unjustly neglected today, *St Paul* was a major work in the revival of the oratorio, overshadowed only by Mendelssohn's own masterpiece in the genre, *Elijah*.

While working on *St Paul* in 1835, Mendelssohn began negotiations for a position in Leipzig, where he would spend much of the remainder of his life; his arrival there was greeted by Schumann, then editor of the *Neue Zeitschrift für Musik*, who addressed him respectfully as 'Meritis.' As director of the Gewandhaus orchestra Mendelssohn soon made it into one of the finest of the time. Berlioz came to Leipzig in 1843 and was very impressed, and Mendelssohn arranged visits from an impressive list of musicians: Niels Gade (whose *Echoes of Ossian* overture was indebted to *Die Hebriden*), Liszt, Sterndale Bennett, Joachim, Jenny Lind, Clara Novello and, of course, Moscheles. To balance the concert fare, Mendelssohn instituted a series of historical concerts, another expression of his feeling for history: he wished to preserve from the past what he deemed worthy and unhesi-

tatingly rejected the views of those who called for musical revolution in the name of progress.

In March 1837 Mendelssohn married Cécile Jeanrenaud, daughter of a minister of the French Reformed Church. The honeymoon through the Black Forest was one of the happiest times of the composer's life; the couple filled a diary with sketches, drawings and music. Mendelssohn's main work from this time, a large setting of Psalm 42, came in the wake of his Handel studies. Finished in December 1837, the Psalm, op.42, recalls Handel's use of the chorus as a structurally defining unit. Mendelssohn arranged his work symmetrically into seven movements around the central chorus, in which he introduced the motif F–G–B flat–A, one of the psalm intonations which was also traditionally used as a fugal subject. Two other works from this time, the Preludes and Fugues for organ (op.37) and piano (op.35) suggest again a deliberate return to traditional forms, a tendency that culminated in the organ sonatas, op.65, of 1844, Mendelssohn's main act of homage to Bach, which is contemporary with Schumann's own set of fugues on 'B–A–C–H.'

Needless to say, Mendelssohn was not slavishly subservient to the musical past. Some 'progressive' works from this time include the three String Quartets, op.44, and the Piano Trio in D minor, op.49, with their lyrical slow movements taken over from the *Lieder ohne Worte* and their Romantic scherzos. Mendelssohn also finished a new set of *Lieder ohne Worte*, op.38, and *Der erste Frühlingstag* (The First Day of Spring), op.48, a cycle of six part-songs on texts by Lenau, Eichendorff and Uhland. Just how closely Mendelssohn sought to ally the 'absolute' music of the *Lieder ohne Worte* with vocal works is apparent from two pieces from op.38 – no.6, a 'Duett ohne Worte,' and no.4 in A major, which begins as a piano improvisation only to blossom into a homophonic part-song, musically similar to the part-song 'Frühlingsfeier,' op.48 no.3, in E major.

The major work of the early Leipzig period, however, was the *Lobgesang* (Song of Praise) symphony, published as Mendelssohn's Second Symphony. Composed for the celebration in 1840 of the four-hundredth anniversary of the invention of printing, this 'symphony–cantata' was Mendelssohn's response to Beethoven's Ninth Symphony. While Beethoven had reserved Schiller's ode for the finale of his symphony, Mendelssohn expanded the scope of his work considerably: the three movements, linked by transitions, were composed as a large-scale instrumental introduction (sinfonia) to a cantata with no fewer than nine movements. Mendelssohn united the two portions by the sinfonia's powerful opening motif, which is set in the cantata to the text 'Alles was Odem hat, lobe den Herrn' (Let everything that has breath praise the Lord). Very popular in the composer's lifetime, the *Lobgesang* is a felicitous synthesis of vocal and instrumental forces, with elements from Mendelssohn's psalm settings, such as the chorale and choral fugue; the opening of the sinfonia, in fact, recalls that of Psalm 42.

Left: Poster for a subscription concert at the Gewandhaus in March 1839. Included in the program with Mendelssohn's setting of Psalm 42 is the first performance of Schubert's 'Great' C major Symphony, a manuscript copy of which had recently been discovered by Schumann at the house of Schubert's brother.

Above: Title-page of the 'Scottish' Symphony, op.56, first performed in March 1842 at the Gewandhaus. Later that year, Mendelssohn and his wife left for another visit to England, where the work was given an ecstatic reception. The symphony was dedicated to Queen Victoria after she had received him twice with great friendliness and sung 'quite charmingly' to his accompaniment.

Less than two years after the première of the *Lobgesang* (revised by the composer with his customary diligence), Mendelssohn completed his final symphony, the 'Scottish' Symphony, op.56. This work had haunted him since 1829, when he sketched its opening introduction at Holyrood Palace in Edinburgh. Some of its composition overlapped with work on the 'Italian' Symphony and *Die erste Walpurgisnacht* in the 1830s, though the bulk was apparently taken up in 1841 and 1842. The 'Scottish' Symphony is in the tradition of Beethoven's 'Pastoral,' and we can single out some striking passages which in all likelihood reflect programmatic considerations. One such occurs in the coda of the first movement, where Mendelssohn suddenly introduces chromatic scales and bristling diminished-seventh sonorities (did he mean to suggest a storm, as Beethoven had in the 'Pastoral,' or a battle?). The scherzo is filled with hunting calls, while the third movement contains a march-like dirge. The fourth, marked *allegro guerriero*, gives way to a pastoral coda. Moreover, many stylistic features associate the symphony with the overture *Die Hebriden*: scoring for low strings, octave doublings, open-spaced sonorities, an exotic progression by parallel motion at the outset of the development in the first movement, pentatonic turns of phrase (notably in the scherzo, where Mendelssohn simulated a Scottish folksong, just as Dvořák would include pentatonic folk melodies in his Symphony 'From the New World'). In addition, Mendelssohn connected the movements of the symphony without pause, using a cyclical thematic technique reminiscent of Gade's *Echoes of Ossian* overture, premièred in 1840. In the favorable reviews which greeted the symphony, critics commented on its close-knit thematic unity,

which Mendelssohn did not again achieve in an orchestral work. Another attempt at symphonic composition came in 1845, when he began a symphony in C major; the sketches for the exposition indicate an expanded plan for the first movement along the lines of Schubert's 'Great' Symphony in C major. Mendelssohn's busy schedule at this time, however, impeded progress on the work. Perhaps sensing that it would not surpass the formal perfection of the 'Scottish' Symphony, he abandoned the fragment.

• Last years •

By 1842 Mendelssohn was at the height of his powers. He was the recipient of an honorary doctorate from the University of Leipzig and was in constant demand as a conductor at music festivals, and his talents now drew the admiration of Frederick William IV, who as Crown Prince had met Mendelssohn in Düsseldorf several years before. The succession of the new king in 1840 had stimulated a general revaluation of the arts in Berlin. The theater was to be reorganized by Ludwig Tieck, who was brought from Dresden, and Mendelssohn was asked to participate as well. The new king was particularly fond of the Greek tragedies, and Mendelssohn and Tieck began with Sophocles' *Antigone*, which was a success, though it provoked a controversy about the propriety of fitting new music to the choruses. The King now requested a production of Euripides' *Medea*, but Mendelssohn refused the commission. Tieck again collaborated with Mendelssohn in productions of Racine's *Athalie* in 1845 and of *Oedipus at Colonos* the same year.

The new king was also interested in Shakespeare, and here the Mendelssohn–Tieck alliance produced a major triumph. Tieck had contributed to August Wilhelm Schlegel's German translations of Shakespeare; in 1817 he had visited London, studied Elizabethan drama at the British Museum and heard Kemble's performances in several Shakespeare plays. Mendelssohn was now asked to compose incidental music for *A Midsummer Night's Dream*. He could not have hoped for a more favorable assignment. Finally he could return to his programmatic overture of 1826 and place it in a suitable dramatic context. Despite some misunderstandings, the performance was a spectacular success, the high point of Mendelssohn's association with the court of Frederick William IV. From the incidental music we can identify several programmatic motifs in the overture: the four wind chords to suggest the court of Titania and Oberon; the fanfare for the royal hunt; a tetrachordal motive for the elves; the same motif in augmentation and inversion to depict the magic potion administered to Titania and her restoration to consciousness; and the ophicleide to portray Bottom. Mendelssohn brilliantly allied the overture – composed in 1826 without a dramatic sequel in mind – with the play and penned some of his finest music in the score.

In 1843 Mendelssohn was placed in charge of the male-voice cathedral choir in Berlin, for which he composed several psalm settings. His sacred works from this time were written in the spirit of reform instituted by Frederick William III and continued by his son. Lutheran church music, it was thought, should find its ideal expression in *a cappella* music, preferably for male voices, with a discreet use of instruments, and in a declamatory style. Mendelssohn's response can be measured if we compare his setting of Psalm 114, op.51, written in 1839 before the move to Berlin, with works composed for the Berliner Dom. Psalm 114 is Handelian in scope, with a majestic opening chorus

(brought back to conclude the work), complex fugal writing and independent orchestral parts. In Mendelssohn's setting of Psalm 98, on the other hand, written for the New Year's service of 1844 in Berlin, we find a marked contrast. The work begins with an intonation and choral response; the chorus is then split into two four-part choirs in the polychoral tradition. The orchestra, in fact, does not appear until verse 5, where brass and a harp are indicated for 'Lobet den Herrn mit Harfen und mit Psalmen, mit Drommeten und Posaunen' (Praise the Lord with the harp and with psalms, with trumpets and sackbuts). Throughout the psalm the orchestra remains subservient to the chorus. The elimination of instrumental forces altogether

Above: Overbeck's *The Triumph of Religion in the Fine Arts*, painted in Frankfurt in 1847 – the year of Mendelssohn's death. The work of Overbeck and the Nazarenes reflects both the historical conservatism and the strong sense of religion and mysticism to be found in much German Romantic art and literature.

Right: Mendelssohn's drawing of his family at Soden. After his exhausting visit to London in the summer of 1844, Mendelssohn was glad to return to his family at Soden, a spa near Frankfurt. Here he passed a most happy and restful two months delighting in the company of his wife and children. It was here that he finished his Violin Concerto in E minor, which was performed by his friend Ferdinand David the following year.

Above: A performance of *Elijah* at the Cirque de l'Impératrice, Paris, 1887. When in 1845 Mendelssohn was asked to write an oratorio for the Birmingham Festival, there followed a year of frenzied activity and strain, which perhaps contributed to his early death. He conducted the work, to great acclaim, at the Festival in 1846, but many of his English friends found him aged and worn.

was accomplished in the three Psalms, op.78 (1843-4), the *Sechs Sprüche*, op.79 (1843-6, collected for publication, like op.78, posthumously), and the *Deutsche Liturgie* (1846). These *a cappella* works are characterized by a syllabic style, with clear declamation and the use of responsorial and antiphonal effects, and, above all, a stark, forceful manner of expression.

The King was unable to retain Mendelssohn, who was persuaded to return to Leipzig to resume his duties at the Gewandhaus in August 1845. A compelling reason too was the administration of the Leipzig Conservatory, already established under Mendelssohn's leadership in April 1843. Among its faculty were Robert and Clara Schumann, the theorist Moritz Hauptmann and Ignaz Moscheles, who, at Mendelssohn's bidding, came to Leipzig in 1846. Major works written after Mendelssohn's break with the Prussian monarch include the Quintet in

B flat, op.87 (rejected by Mendelssohn because of his dissatisfaction with the finale), the organ sonatas, op.65, and his masterpiece in the concerto genre, the Violin Concerto in E minor, op.64.

In his earlier concertos Mendelssohn had favored the approach developed by Weber in the *Konzertstück*, in which several movements, tonally and structurally 'incomplete' by themselves, are joined by transitions to form a larger work. Mendelssohn then replaced Weber's four-movement scheme with a two-movement plan (a short, lyrical introduction and fast, bravura finale) in the *Capriccio brillant*, *Rondo brillant*, and *Serenade und Allegro gioioso*. In contrast to these quickly written works, a more serious approach is evident in the D minor Piano Concerto (No.2), op.40, written for the Birmingham Music Festival of 1837. The care Mendelssohn lavished upon this work, with its pervasive chromaticism, contrapuntal writing and *Lied-ohne-Worte* middle movement, is reflected by several pages of surviving sketches. Mendelssohn devoted more care, though, to the great Violin Concerto, the composition of which required several years.

As early as 1838 he had begun discussions with the violinist Ferdinand David about plans for the work. By 1842, however, his thoughts had turned to a new piano concerto for England; in 1844 he was still at work on a third piano concerto, the first two movements of which were sketched. Mendelssohn abandoned this project, however, and incorporated some of its ideas into the Violin Concerto, which ranks among his most progressive works. Among the 'reforms' he accomplished in the first movement was a fully-fledged solo at the beginning and the relocation of the cadenza as a structural device to connect the development and reprise. Mendelssohn also thematically related the two transitions between the movements. Like much of the piano music, the Violin Concerto was written in response to the vogue of superficial, mostly pyrotechnical concertos. However, in his op.64 virtuosity is joined with the most rigorous demands of structural integrity.

While at work on the Violin Concerto, Mendelssohn received a request for a new oratorio, to be premièred at the Birmingham Music Festival of 1846. Based largely on the account in I Kings, *Elijah* was created as a companion oratorio to *St Paul*; in many ways it is Mendelssohn's masterpiece. The development of Part I alone reveals his technical mastery. Divided into twenty numbers, Part I recounts the drought announced by Elijah, his exile in the wilderness, his meeting with the widow and his resuscitation of her son, his return to face Ahab, and the trials of fire and water by which the Baal worshipers are refuted. The short opening scene which introduces Elijah presents two motifs that recur throughout the oratorio: a series of brass chords for Elijah, and a sequence of angular melodic tritones, a striking dissonant symbol for the curse of God. This is followed by a substantial overture, a contrapuntal *tour de force* in which a fugue represents the famine, taking over the tritone from the curse motive. The fugue gives way without pause to the precatory chorus of the people, who beg in vain for relief; there follows a poignant choral fugue built upon a tortuous chromatic subject. The opening complex is thus organized symmetrically: Introduction and Overture (fugue); Chorus and Choral fugue. The return of Elijah from the wilderness marks the midpoint of Part I; Mendelssohn fittingly recalls in no.10 the music of no.1. The first ten numbers, in turn, are divided equally by no.5, a chorus which reanimates the curse motive and introduces a chorale in C major with the prophetic text, 'His mercies on thousands fall.' The chorale prepares Elijah's first act, the revival of the widow's dead son (no.8). Similarly, Elijah's encounter with the Baal worshipers and the subsequent trials of fire and water are prepared by no.15, a chorus in which Mendelssohn again inserts a chorale.

Moreover, Mendelssohn succeeded in *Elijah* in devising a more complex approach to tonal structure. Part I unfolds a large-scale progression from D minor to E flat major, a half-step above; it is introduced in Obadiah's aria (no.4), is heard again in nos.14 and 15, and is confirmed in the concluding chorus of no.20. The rise in dramatic tension is reflected by this tonal process; furthermore, the polarity of the two tonalities is increased by a subsidiary system of keys. E flat major is 'challenged' by the Baal worshipers, who exhort their idol first in F minor and then in F sharp minor. The large-scale tonal design, the co-ordinated development of the dramatic events and the subtle use of the chorale place *Elijah* as Mendelssohn's outstanding dramatic work. Its success gave fresh impetus to other composers to return to the oratorio, most notably Hiller, Spohr and, eventually, Liszt.

Mendelssohn composed another major choral work in 1846, a setting of the sequence 'Lauda Sion' for the six hundredth anniversary of the Corpus Christi service in Liège in June. Cantata-like in conception, the work uses a combination of choral movements, solo arias and solo quartets, all with orchestral accompaniment, to set the text by St Thomas Aquinas. *Lauda Sion* is Mendelssohn's most important setting of a Latin sacred text; it is a pity that it was overshadowed by *Elijah*, whose première soon after, on 26 August 1846, was his final major triumph. He immediately busied himself with revisions for the score; during his last visit to England, in April 1847, the oratorio was performed for Queen Victoria and the Prince Consort.

Less than a month later, however, Mendelssohn's sister Fanny Hensel died, a shattering blow from which he never fully recovered; his own end came in Leipzig on 4 November 1847. His anguish for the loss of Fanny is expressed in his final String Quartet in F minor, op.80. The relentless tremolos in the first movement, enharmonic modulations in the slow movement and mannered writing in the finale bear witness to his crisis. Most strange of all is the minuet – with syncopated cross-rhythms which disrupt the meter and a circuitous chromatic approach to the tonic – and the trio, with its curious ostinato bass. Severe contrasts are the rule in this quartet, as if Mendelssohn deliberately sought to display his agonizing struggle to complete it. Among the projects he left unfinished were an opera on the Lorelei legend and a third oratorio, *Christus*.

Mendelssohn's influence on his contemporaries was considerable. He was held in awe by Schumann and respected by Berlioz, but the chief benefactor, perhaps, was Brahms. Mendelssohn's influence appears in such works as Brahms's early piano variations in D, the Piano Quartet in C minor and the Second Symphony. The comparison may be taken further: neither Brahms nor Mendelssohn produced a successful opera; both continued to cultivate the traditional instrumental forms; both were 'academic' in their reverence of traditional counterpoint; just as Mendelssohn withstood the more extreme manifestations of Romanticism, so did Brahms survive the onslaught of *Zukunftsmusik* – Wagner's 'music of the future.' Both cherished their musical heritage as they executed their 'quiet,' though by no means insignificant, musical reforms.

Right: Mendelssohn on his death-bed, a drawing by Eduard Bendemann. In May 1847 Fanny Hensel died while rehearsing her choir in a performance of her brother's *Walpurgisnacht*. Mendelssohn received the news in a letter a few days after returning, completely exhausted, from another visit to London; the shock was so great that he collapsed. He spent some time in Switzerland trying to rest and seemed to be making a slow recovery when he returned to Berlin to organize a performance of *Elijah*. The sight of Fanny's room seemed a severe setback; in October he collapsed again, and died on 4 November 1847.

ROBERT SCHUMANN

BERNARD KEEFFE

On 27 February 1854 Robert Schumann left his house in Düsseldorf and went out into the teeming rain with no coat and only slippers on his feet. It was a day of carnival, and he pushed his way through crowded streets to the bridge over the Rhine. He had no money to pay the toll so he gave the man his handkerchief. When he came to the middle of the bridge, he took off his wedding ring, threw it into the water and jumped after it. Some fishermen hurried to haul him out, but he tried again to jump from the boat and they had to restrain him. They carried him home, and a few days later he was committed to an asylum, where he stayed until his death in July 1856. He was forty-six years old.

We cannot understand Schumann and his music without coming to terms with the age in which he lived. He was born in 1810 in the little town of Zwickau in Saxony. As he grew to manhood, audiences were in raptures over the empty virtuosity of fashionable pianist—composers such as Hünten and Herz. The late compositions of Beethoven were ignored and Schubert was little known; Mozart was treated like a tinkling charmer and Bach was forgotten. The Romantic spirit seemed to exist only in literature. Schumann's father was a bookseller and publisher, and on his shelves young Robert found fuel for his fiery imagination: the poetry of Byron, translated by his father; the poems and novels of Goethe; above all, the outpourings of Jean Paul Richter, the archpriest of what we might call Romantic rapture. These writers taught Schumann the extravagant language of feelings and how to explore his senses and what he later called 'the dark mystery of the unconscious.' They fined down their skin until the slightest touch set off their creative imagination. In such extremes of sensation, it was almost a required fate that an artist should go mad, die young, or both. Schumann risked a double dose of Romantic agony, for he was a writer as well as a musician, and his earliest dream had been to write poetry in the style of Jean Paul, who, he said, 'often brought me near to madness.' For a while he was drunk with words, but soon found in music a more apt intoxicant for his emotions.

Schumann had shown talent for the piano as a boy, but though he had some lessons from a local musician, he seemed unteachable; he had the instinct of an artist but lacked discipline and determination. His father was sympathetic and tried to get his son taught by Carl Maria von Weber, but both had died by the time the boy was seventeen. He became even more dependent on his mother, whom he had always worshiped. But now a stern guardian stood behind her; they wanted nothing to do with music, a profession for paupers, and required the boy to study law. Schumann had little choice; in March 1828 he enrolled as a law student in the University of Leipzig.

Some years later, when Liszt complained of the shortage of countesses and princesses in Leipzig, Schumann retorted, 'We have our aristocracy here: 150 bookshops, 50 printing firms and 30 periodicals.' Leipzig was a city of books and businessmen, prosperous, energetic and forward-looking, but it retained its medieval charm, with many streets looking like Dürer engravings. The Thomaskirche dominated the city, though its former cantor, J. S. Bach, was forgotten. Musical life was sleepy and was to awaken only with the arrival of Mendelssohn in 1834, when he took over the Gewandhaus concerts and later founded the most celebrated conservatory in Europe. But in 1828 Schumann was soon bored with his studies and amused himself with wine and women, spending lavishly, to the constant dismay of his guardian. His tedium was lightened by meeting a kindred spirit, a well-known piano teacher named Friedrich Wieck; he had a few lessons but was soon made aware of his deficiencies: 'I was always a fiery performer, but my technique was full of holes, so I had to take everything slowly and clearly. The consequence was a hesitation which made me doubt my talent.'

After a year at Leipzig, Schumann persuaded his family to allow him to transfer to Heidelberg, ostensibly to sit at the feet of Anton Thibaut, the most admired jurist in Germany. Lawyer he may have been, but he was an amateur musician of equal fame, and Schumann spent many inspiring hours at the house of this 'splendid, God-like man,' until he grew tired of his obsession with the music of the past. Schumann was as dissolute as ever, drinking heavily, and probably at this time he contracted the disease which eventually drove him to madness and death. At Easter 1830 he journeyed to Frankfurt to hear the great Paganini, then at the height of his powers. His Mephistophelean appearance persuaded many people that he had demonic powers, and his sheer virtuosity was, for the time, unrivaled. Schumann placed him above Liszt in his ability to bewitch an audience, and the name of Paganini recurs again and again in Schumann's writings. One of his earliest serious compositions was a set of studies for the piano which were transcriptions of Paganini's for the violin. The experience of the concert in Frankfurt confirmed Schumann's ambition to be a virtuoso; his mother agreed to abide by Wieck's opinion of her son's prospects. This proved frank: 'Taking into account your son's talent and imagination, I undertake to make him one of the greatest living pianists. But he has a lot to learn besides technique. I wonder if our amiable Robert will become more constant, more sober, and may I say, more manly? If your son is to succeed, the will must come from him.' Frau Schumann now agreed that he might become a full-time pupil of Wieck; he returned to Leipzig and took up residence in his master's house at Michaelmas 1830.

It seems unlikely that Schumann ever had the temperament or application to become a concert pianist. Wieck was a teacher of genius, but he often left Schumann to get on alone, because his chief concern was the career of his own ten-year-old daughter Clara. Schumann, though often shy with adults, had a winning way with children and soon established a lively friendship with the girl, but on the piano the young man of twenty could not keep up with the child half his age. In frustration he tried an experiment to speed up his progress and inflicted upon himself a disastrous injury. The evidence is confusing, but he seems to have used a sling to hold up his third finger, so that he could

develop the strength and independence of the fourth. The tendons were damaged and the finger paralyzed; his career as a virtuoso was over before it had started. In this crisis he turned decisively to the two activities which henceforth were to dominate his life, journalism and composition. He started lessons in theory with Heinrich Dorn, music director of the Leipzig theater, and had soon completed his op.1, a set of variations on the name Abegg; he sketched movements of piano concertos and completed three movements of a symphony in G minor. At the same time, by sheer persistence, he persuaded the reluctant editor of the *Allgemeine musikalische Zeitung* to print an article of his about Chopin's early Variations on 'Là ci darem.'

• Florestan and Eusebius •

One can understand the editor's misgivings, because nothing like Schumann's article had ever appeared as music criticism before. Here he penned the famous phrase, 'Hats off, gentlemen, a genius'; here for the first time we meet the imaginary figures that embodied aspects of Schumann's own personality, Florestan, excitable and energetic, and Eusebius, thoughtful and dreamy. They were to be the nucleus of the mythical club of Davidites, the *Davidsbund*, dedicated, like their eponymous patron, to a battle with the Philistines, the musical establishment of the time. In June 1833 Schumann wrote to his mother: 'A group of young cultivated people has formed a circle about me, which I in

Right: Zwickau, in Saxony, in 1840. Here Schumann was born, the youngest of five children, and spent his early life in a happy, prosperous and cultivated home, first attending a private school and from 1820 to 1828 the Zwickau Lyceum. In 1826 his life was marked by tragedy with the death of his only sister and the death of his father shortly afterwards.

Above: The Peterskirche in Heidelberg, 1828/9, by Ernst Fries. Dissatisfied with life at the University of Leipzig, Schumann transferred to Heidelberg, of which he had received vivid reports from a friend. His style of life meant that he made frequent demands on his guardian for more money: 'It would oblige me honored Herr Rudel if you would send me as much as possible as soon as possible.'

Top right: Clara Wieck (1819-96), before her marriage to Robert Schumann.

turn have formed about Wieck's house. We have a plan for a great new journal of music. Its tone and color are to be fresher and more varied than others. In particular, we shall set a dam against the flow of the old time-honored routine.' This was the first hint of a remarkable venture, which was to influence the whole development of musical journalism. The *Neue Zeitschrift für Musik* was launched on 3 April 1834, and within a few months Schumann was running it virtually single-handed. As well as editing, he contributed many reviews of music and imaginative essays, usually signed with the initial F or E. Sometimes they took the form of imaginary discussions between members of the club, now enlarged to include, under pseudonyms, several leading musicians. As well as Florestan and Eusebius, there was Dr Raro, the fount of wisdom, at first perhaps a mask for Wieck, but often an outlet for another aspect of Schumann's personality. Felix Meritis was Mendelssohn, Jeanquirit the pianist Stephen Heller, Vult and Walt were two faces of Jean Paul, and Knif was the unfortunate Fink, editor of the rival *Allgemeine musikalische Zeitung.*

Schumann was undoubtedly one of the greatest of composer–critics. It was as though the fluency of his pen made up for his halting speech, and as far as we can tell, the effort of writing words never brought on the nervous exhaustion he experienced when composing. Perhaps it was because as a writer he could proudly identify with his father, who always wanted him to pursue a literary career. His critical style was evocative and vivid; he described music as a perceptive listener might respond to it. He was never academic and rarely direct; he invented arguments between his pseudonymous personalities with the skill of a dramatist. The targets of his barbed pen were the Philistines, the flashy empty pianist–composers like Herz and Hünten, the time-serving critics and the dead-handed pedants. One particular target was Meyerbeer, the tycoon of French grand opera; on the other hand he greeted with excitement the music of Berlioz, against all expectations, considering his deep-rooted respect for the German tradition. The longest essay that Schumann ever contributed was on Berlioz's *Symphonie fan-*

tastique; this was an astonishingly perceptive analysis in great detail, based solely on a reading of Liszt's piano transcription. He recognized immediately the unique quality of Berlioz's melodic invention.

Inevitably Schumann made some mistakes and lavished praise on musicians of ephemeral interest, such as Ludwig Schunke, 'a God of the Muses,' and Norbert Burgmüller, whose songs he put in the same league as those of Schubert. What is clear is that Schumann responded warmly to honest craft. What he hated was pretension and commercialism. He directed the affairs of the journal for over ten years; it never made great profits, but paid a handsome dividend in its influence on musical journalism everywhere. Schumann's own compositions were rarely mentioned, and he never benefited from the kind of publicity that he lavished on far inferior composers. In fact, until after his death he was better known as a writer on music than as a composer.

In these years a torrent of music as well as words flowed from Schumann's pen. His mastery of the keyboard was immediate; tunes came from his fingers as he improvised, and he noted them down in true Romantic fashion. The originality of his genius was established in his *Papillons,* op.2. 'In many a sleepless night I saw a far-away picture, and while writing down *Papillons* I truly feel a certain independence trying to grow, and now I begin to comprehend my own existence.' From his studies of the music of Bach and Beethoven, rarely heard on the piano in public at this time, he realized that there was more to pianism than flashy brilliance. Above all he was a poet, evoking in music the fantastic imagery of Jean Paul. The very title *Papillons* came from him: a series of brilliant miniatures evokes the revels of a masked ball, ending with the clock striking six, as the revelers steal away in the morning light.

Schumann was treated as one of the family by the Wieck household, admired by his teacher and adored by the children, especially by little Clara – except that she was not so little any more. At the age of fifteen she had developed into one of the leading players of the time; she had toured abroad and astonished everyone, especially with her new-fangled way of playing from memory. Wieck soon noticed with alarm that Clara was taking more than a childish interest in her fellow-pupil; a love affair, let alone marriage, was the last thing he wanted now that she was on the threshold of an international career. Astutely he arranged for Schumann to be thrown into the company of a new pupil, Ernestine von Fricken, and in no time the couple were engaged, almost without a thought. The affair died as quickly as it had begun, but it

gave birth to two masterpieces: the *Symphonic Studies*, op.13, and *Carnaval*, op.9. The studies were in the form of variations on a theme by Ernestine's adoptive father, Baron von Fricken, an amateur flautist. Each variation explored an aspect of pianistic technique, but Schumann originally described them as being 'in orchestral style,' an apt description for music of uncommon richness of texture, which makes terrifying demands on the player. In contrast to this technical *tour de force*, *Carnaval* revealed a bewitching musical imagination. The subtitle is 'Scènes mignonnes sur quatre notes.' The four notes derive from the letters in the name of Ernestine's home town, Asch, and also, as Schumann noticed, the only letters in his own name which were musical notes, read in the German way. In *Carnaval* the intervals are awkward, yet Schumann's themes have such natural grace that they seem spontaneous. Many of the pieces are portraits: of Pierrot, Harlequin, Pantalon and Columbine from the *commedia dell'arte*; of himself and his friends, disguised

as members of the Davidsbund, and indeed the work ends with the 'March of the Davidites.' There are musical sketches of Chopin and Paganini; one portrays Ernestine herself under the name Estrella; another is of someone called Chiarina and is marked *appassionato* – an unspoken, perhaps half-realized, declaration of love for the fifteen-year-old Clara Wieck.

•The battle for Clara•

Just as the lovers were about to sing out to the world their joy in each other, Wieck packed his daughter off to Dresden, forbidding meetings and letters. Two weeks later Schumann's mother died. He was distraught with misery and fear; he could not face the funeral and fled to Dresden and Clara for comfort. Wieck was furious and threatened to shoot Schumann if he tried to see Clara again. He took her away on long tours, and the lovers were separated for months on end in agonies of doubt and loneliness. They corresponded secretly, but sometimes they could communicate only through music. In the

Right: Serenade by Carl Spitzweg (1808-85), the master of Romantic irony in painting.

Below: Musical evening at Anton Thibaut's house in Heidelberg. Schumann wrote in a letter to his mother from Heidelberg that some of his most pleasant hours were spent at the Thibaut house . . . 'When he has a Handel oratorio sung at his home (every Thursday more than seventy singers are present) and accompanies enthusiastically on the pianoforte, two big tears roll down from the fine, large eyes . . . .' Mendelssohn shared Schumann's admiration: '. . . I have learned so much from him and owe him a great deal . . . . What an enthusiasm and glow when he talks.'

summer of 1836 Schumann dedicated to Clara his F sharp minor sonata: 'One single cry of my heart for you,' he called it later, 'in which your theme appears in every possible form.' He attributed it to Florestan and Eusebius, and when she seemed not to respond to it he was in despair. But then in 1837 she played it at a Leipzig concert and she wrote: 'Did you never realize that I played because I knew no other means of showing you what was in my heart?' The great *Fantasie* in C, op.17, which originated as a work to be sold in aid of the Beethoven memorial in Bonn, became 'a deep lament for you.'

Wieck remained deaf to all appeals. He has been cast as one of history's legendary villains, and there is no question that he behaved harshly, but is it any surprise that a father should protect his sixteen-year-old daughter from the attentions of an unstable, neurotic, hard-drinking, somewhat dissolute musician, his career as a pianist shattered by a crippled hand, a struggling journalist at odds with the establishment, an avant-garde composer with little reputation, who paid court to Clara while he was still engaged to Ernestine?

Schumann had to prove his worth. He curbed his drinking in response to appeals from Clara; at her suggestion too he tried to move the office of his magazine to Vienna, though he was forced back to Leipzig by bureaucratic resistance; he contrived to get himself awarded an honorary degree from the University of Jena, but all to no purpose. Wieck was adamant. After two vain

Left: Autograph of the song 'Du bist wie eine Blume,' Schumann's setting of the poem by Heine, from his song-cycle *Myrthen*, his wedding gift to Clara. Several of the songs express Schumann's vision of his future wife: devoted, brave, maternal and, in this song, beautiful as a flower.

Above: Heinrich Heine (1797-1856), many of whose lyric poems Schumann set to music.

Above left: A study by Wilhelm Hensel for Thomas Moore's *Lalla Rookh* (1821), from which Schumann chose *Paradise and the Peri* as 'simply made for music. The whole conception is so poetic and ideal that I was quite carried away by it.' Schumann had intended to write an opera on the story but the work he eventually composed (op.50) was 'an oratorio, but for contented people, not for an oratory.'

attempts at reconciliation the couple resorted to the law; Wieck fought a rearguard action by presenting an impossible list of conditions, followed by scurrilous attacks on Schumann and even an anonymous poison-pen letter to Clara timed to arrive just before she went on to give a recital. Finally the court granted permission, and the marriage took place on 12 September 1840 on the eve of Clara's twenty-first birthday. It was a climax to a remarkable decade, in which Clara had taken her place among the leading pianists in the world and Schumann had revealed his extraordinary genius as a composer for the piano.

Schumann had come to composition as a brilliant improviser; he was by nature taciturn, and it was as if he could speak only through music. As a boy he had delighted his friends with his lightning character-sketches improvised at the keyboard. His fingers, and later his pen, invented phrases, rhythms and patterns of sound that grip the listener like a brilliant con-

versation, witty, poetic, thoughtful, philosophic. This is the poet as hero; Schumann speaks to us man to man, or rather man to woman, for so much of his music is like the excited intimate chatter of a lover. This is the Schumann of *Papillons*, *Carnaval*, the *Intermezzi* and the Impromptus, suites of highly engaging pieces, often quite short, but with an irresistible flow of invention. If, however, they offered no more than catchy phrases strung together with the offhand brilliance of a drawing-room entertainer, the salon star would soon become a salon bore. But right from his op.1, the 'Abegg' Variations, Schumann set his composing genius to work on what for him was fruitful, though it might seem an artificial and sterile system. In part it was a musical cipher, for he derived themes from the letters of names such as Abegg, Asch, Bach, Gade; it was also a musical code, using quotation from Bach's 'Peasant' Cantata, the *Marseillaise*, Schubert's song 'Meine Ruh' ist hin,' Beethoven's song-cycle *An die ferne*

Right: Illustration by Cruikshank for *Peter Schlemihl*, a story by Adalbert Chamisso (1781-1838) which tells how Schlemihl sold his shadow to the Devil for a magic purse but was thereafter an outcast from society. Schumann, with his interest in the bizarre and fantastic, was drawn to Chamisso's strange tale; and he set some of his poems to music in *Frauen-Liebe und Leben.*

Below: E. T. A. Hoffmann's self-portrait as *Kreisler in his madness,* c.1820. Schumann, with his fear that he might himself become insane, identified with Hoffmann's musician, who is so sensitive that he finally goes mad. In 1838 he wrote *Kreisleriana,* (op.16), eight fantasies for the piano.

Geliebte, and above all from the compositions of Clara herself.

If the suites were the excited showing-off of a young lover in front of his girl, the three sonatas and the *Fantasie* in C were the self-revelation that comes from the joy of mutual love and the anguish when that love is threatened. They are partly built on themes by Clara, transformed into a secret language whose significance is only now becoming clear. But if that were all, they would be little more than adolescent effusions, whereas they are of astonishing originality in harmony, rhythm, structure and scale, towering above the routine echoes of Mozart and early Beethoven which passed for piano sonatas in others' hands. What is more remarkable is that Schumann started work on them within two years of the publication of his op.1. Few composers have reached such maturity of style in so short a period of time. And this was not just the spontaneity of genius, but the fruit of many months of thought and revision. Whole movements were rewritten or replaced; he reshaped the songs of a love-sick boy into slow movements which Liszt described as 'some of the most beautiful pages we know.' The challenge to the pianist's technique was unprecedented; even virtuosos found them difficult, and so lacking in glamour that they saw no prospect of reward for their efforts from audiences as baffled as they were. The Sonata in F minor, completed in 1836 and published in 1843 under the absurd title 'Concerto without orchestra,' was given its first public performance by Brahms in 1862, six years after Schumann's death. Even Clara herself, to the end of her career, never played *Carnaval, Kreisleriana* or *Davidsbündlertänze* in full in public for fear of wearying her audience. They were much more in tune with *Scenes from Childhood,* op.15, or the *Arabeske,* op.18, better known because they were much easier to play. Even Schumann's first biographer, the violinist Wasiliewski, writing in 1858, found this music turgid, harsh, and ill-constructed, and Wagner often remarked that Schumann was incapable of writing an inspired melody!

• Leipzig: 1840-44 •

On their wedding-day Schumann presented his wife with the kind of gift she was to know so often – a new composition. It was the song-cycle *Myrthen,* op.25, and it opens with a passionate setting of Rückert's poem 'Widmung': 'You, my soul, my heart; you, my ecstasy and my pain.' The prospect of union with Clara had inspired in Schumann an unparalleled outpouring of music for the voice. In that one year, 1840, he composed no less than 138 songs of the highest quality, including the cycles *Dichterliebe, Liederkreis,* and *Frauen-Liebe und Leben.* He had not written for the voice for twelve years, since the time when, in the first flush of puppy-love for an attractive singer in Zwickau, he had rushed home and poured out his heart at the piano. Those early songs remained unpublished until a few years ago, although two of them had achieved immortality as slow movements in the sonatas. Now again he found exactly the right touch, with a poet's ear for verse. He turned to Rückert, Byron, Goethe, Chamisso, Heine and even Robert Burns. He was gripped by inspiration: 'I shall sing myself to death like a nightingale.'

There is an astonishing range of style, from the ecstatic declamation of 'Waldesgespräch' (Forest Talk) to the hushed magic of 'Mondnacht' (Moonlit Night). The voice part often floats, intoning over a rich melodic accompaniment, or is carried along in the excitement of an accompaniment that only he could have written, as in 'Frühlingsnacht' (Spring Night). The cycles are something new in music, closely integrated, with evocative and extended passages for the piano. He still played with mu-

Top right: Autograph score of *Manfred,* op.115: an overture and incidental music to the dramatic poem by Byron, composed in 1848-9. Schumann, was moved to tears by Byron's poem of Romantic guilt and despair, 'inspired to an extraordinary degree,' wrote Clara.

Right: Poster for the first performance of *Manfred.* Liszt had become interested in the composition of this work – a melodrama, in which the words were spoken to an accompaniment of music – and suggested staging it at Weimar, where the first performance was given on 13 June 1852. The overture, written in a burst of inspired spontaneity, was premièred separately at the Gewandhaus and from the beginning was a complete success; Schumann wrote to Liszt that he considered it 'one of the finest of my brain-children.'

speare, and soon she wrote: 'We enjoy a happiness such as I never knew before. Father has always laughed at so-called domestic bliss, but how I pity those who do not know it – they are only half alive.'

Schumann began to write his first completed symphony, inaugurating the 'year of the symphony' which followed his 'year of song.' During his abortive stay in Vienna in 1839 he had discovered the existence of Schubert's 'Great' C major Symphony. Schumann had arranged for Mendelssohn to conduct the first performance at a Gewandhaus concert in December 1839, when he wrote: 'In rehearsal today I have heard part of the symphony of Franz Schubert. From that point on all my life's ideals unfold.' He expanded on his impression in an article for the magazine, where he referred, unforgettably, to the symphony's 'heavenly length.' The experience set his own creative forces working, and in January 1841 he sketched out in four days a symphony in B flat. The scoring was completed on 20 February, and the first performance, under Mendelssohn, was on 31 March. It was his 'Spring' Symphony, partly inspired by a poem by Adolph Böttger which ended, 'Im Thale blüht der Frühling auf' (Now spring is blooming in the vale), and the main theme of the first movement is an exact setting of the rhythm of those words.

Schumann was inexperienced at orchestral composition, although he had heard a performance in Zwickau of movements from his unfinished Symphony in G minor, which was a

sical ciphers, and in 'Mondnacht' repeats the notes E, B, E, which in German notation read 'Ehe,' marriage. Clara's theme occurs again and again, a distant cry of love, but integrated so naturally into the melodic line that all seems natural and spontaneous. In this single year Schumann established himself as successor to Schubert and forerunner of Brahms and Wolf, a great master of the *Lied.*

After the wedding the Schumanns settled happily into their new home, on the first floor of a house in Leipzig, with their two grand pianos carefully placed in rooms well apart (hers had been a present from Robert a few weeks before). The marriage was in some ways an ideal partnership, with a perfect balance of temperaments. Clara became the lost mother, the protector and comforter, totally dedicated to her husband, who came first in everything. It was completely in the spirit of the Biedermeier age, just like her husband's choice of the poems by Chamisso for his cycle *Frauen-Liebe und Leben.* Their submissive ecstasy jars on our emancipated ears but would have struck an answering chord in Clara, for all that she was, unusually for the time, a successful career woman. She excitedly submitted to Robert's guidance in her education, and within two weeks of their marriage they were studying daily the *Forty-eight preludes and fugues* of J. S. Bach, to Clara's evidently naïve wonder at the contrapuntal skill. Robert made her play Beethoven sonatas and opened her mind to Goethe and Shake-

Above: A late portrait of Schumann by J. B. Laurens, made in 1853. Schumann's health was markedly worse at this time: he suffered from auditory delusions and had difficulty with his speech. He was also troubled by periods of melancholy and vague, disturbing fears. This was the year in which he was forced to resign his post as conductor at Düsseldorf.

Right: A Traveler looking over a Sea of Fog, c.1815, by Caspar David Friedrich. This picture, which dates from the period of Byron's poem, strangely recalls the story of Manfred, who fled society to live in the mountains, invoking the Witch of the Alps in his search for oblivion.

perfectly respectable piece of writing. But he had no first-hand knowledge of the orchestra as player or conductor, and he seriously overestimated the skills even of the famous Gewandhaus orchestra. Things went badly at the first rehearsal, and Mendelssohn advised many changes. This unhappy experience affected Schumann's subsequent writing for the orchestra, which rarely shows the spontaneous freedom in actual scoring that was evident in the original version of the First Symphony. It became an almost automatic response to dismiss Schumann's orchestral skill, and this prejudice is still often encountered. It is possible that it stemmed from the hostility of Mendelssohn's followers, who for years tried to undermine Schumann's reputation. It is significant that the Second Symphony, whose première Mendelssohn mishandled in 1846, was until very re-

cently regarded as the least successful – and was certainly the least played – of the four symphonies, yet opinion today probably places it highest.

Like Beethoven, Berlioz and Wagner, Schumann thought beyond the immediate skills of the orchestras he knew. When he found that even the famous Gewandhaus orchestra could not play what his imagination had dictated, he allowed himself to be guided by Mendelssohn into simplifying and securing his music. He learned to avoid extreme keys, covered awkward entries by doubling, kept to easy registers and often resorted to tremolo to strengthen the sound of the strings. The problem is nearly always in the outer movements of the symphonies, where the vigor and breadth of his conception exceeded the capabilities of the orchestra of his time. He was no Wagner; he did not have the push or the conducting skill to put his ideas across, and merely surrendered. Yet his slow movements are marvels of color and delicacy, and the whole of the Piano Concerto is scored with masterly ease. He uses instruments with unusual imagination, like the solo violin that wreathes its way through the slow movement of the D minor Symphony, or the cello in the Piano Concerto. The handling of the strings in the Second Symphony is masterly, whether in the soaring line of the adagio or in the brilliant toccata of the scherzo. Brahms risked his friendship with Clara by insisting on the publication of the first version of the D minor Symphony, and so demonstrated the lightness and transparency of Schumann's original conception, which he preferred to the later version we now always hear.

In 1841, however, just as with the piano and with song, Schumann's genius now poured out a stream of symphonic works. No sooner was the First Symphony performed than he started on another: at first he thought of calling it a 'sinfonietta' because he wanted only three movements, but settled on *Overture, Scherzo and Finale*, op.52. It is a charming, lightweight work that in a brilliant performance can be very engaging. Then came a *Fantasie* in A minor for piano and orchestra, but he could find no publisher to take an interest in this and he put it aside. Then in May he started on a symphony in D minor in quite a new form, a sort of fantasia, with each movement linked to the next and the whole based on one thematic idea. On Clara's birthday he presented her with the manuscript of this new symphony, the twelve songs of op.37 and the printed parts of the First Symphony. On that day, too, they celebrated the christening of their first child, Marie. It was very heaven to be alive. Schumann immediately started work on yet another symphony, in C minor, but left it with two movements sketched in full. The D minor Symphony was introduced, along with the *Overture, Scherzo and Finale*, at a grand concert in which Liszt and Clara played the piano. The orchestra did badly without Mendelssohn's firm hand, and Schumann's music made a poor impression, overshadowed by the excitement surrounding Liszt's appearance. The symphony was put aside for ten years, and after substantial revision was published as no.4.

Clara was now getting more and more invitations to play in public, and early in 1842 she accepted an invitation to tour north Germany. Schumann dragged himself away from his desk and his duties at the magazine to accompany her. He heard a poor performance of the First Symphony in Bremen, played after just one rehearsal, so this did little to lighten what was for him a miserable trip. He was pushed into the background and often ignored, and when in Oldenburg Clara alone was sent a court invitation, he had had enough. They went on to Hamburg, but there they parted; Clara continued her tour, while Robert returned to Leipzig and threw himself into a study of Classical chamber music, until after five weeks' sepa-

Above: Photograph of Schumann in 1850 at the time he took up the post as conductor at Düsseldorf.

Right: The Schumann children, *c.*1855. From left to right they are Ludwig (1848-99); Marie (1841-1929) and on her lap Felix (1854-79), named after Mendelssohn and born shortly after Schumann entered the asylum at Endenich; Elise (1843-1928); Ferdinand (1849-91); and Eugenie (1851-1938). Missing are Julie (1845-72) and Emil, who lived only a short time (1846-7).

ration, he could take Clara once more in his arms: 'Like a bridegroom, at once happy and anxious.'

Schumann's studies again bore fruit in a typical outpouring of music. In five weeks he had written three string quartets, op.41, and before the year was out he had added the superb Piano Quintet, op.44, the Piano Quartet, op.47, and the Piano Trio, op.88, known as 'Fantasiestücke.' But this manic explosion of creativity took its toll, and Schumann had a breakdown which stopped all work for five weeks. The first shadows were falling across his life.

As with Schumann's orchestration, not long ago it was commonplace to find fault with his handling of the strings in his chamber music;

Above: Title-page of *Lieder für die Jugend*, op.79, the songs written to accompany the *Album for the Young.* Schumann commissioned this title-page especially to appeal to children from the artist Ludwig Richter, who was famous for his fairy-tale illustrations.

Right: Silhouette illustration for 'Träumerei' (Reverie), one of the piano pieces from *Kinderscenen* (Scenes from Childhood), op.15, written in 1838.

after page of the A major, the finest of the three. The Piano Quintet is inevitably the favorite among Schumann's chamber works: the outer movements have a captivating vitality, with passages of Romantic fervor; the ominous C minor march has an unforgettable appeal, setting off the delicate C major section, which Richard Aldrich once so aptly described as 'an aureole of rhythmic enchantment.' As with the piano sonata, song and the symphony, Schumann's genius pounced on chamber music and in a few swift strokes shaped it anew for the Romantic age.

In June 1843 Schumann proudly announced that he had completed 'my longest work, and I think my best.' It was *Paradise and the Peri*, a setting for soloists, chorus and orchestra of a poem by Thomas Moore, taken from a collection with an oriental flavor, *Lalla Rookh.* They had been the theme for a famous performance of *tableaux vivants* in Berlin, and Wagner had contemplated making an opera from them, but put them aside as undramatic. *Paradise and the Peri* is a sentimental tale of an angel cast out of heaven who regains entry to paradise by bringing back the tear of a repentant sinner. Schumann was, as always, original in his approach and abandoned sectional structure and recitative for a flowing, continuous narrative. He handled the orchestra quite idiomatically, and wrote expressive lines for the solo voices, but he was less certain in his writing for the chorus, which is stiff and monotonous in texture. He was delighted to be able to conduct the first performance in Leipzig, which marked his début in this role. He needed to expand his professional activities, because despite their happiness the Schumanns were short of money; they welcomed an invitation from Mendelssohn to teach at his new Conservatory. Clara soon showed that she had inherited her father's gifts and later in life became one of the most sought-after teachers in Europe. Schumann, however, was hopeless; he was so tongue-tied that he would often allow a pupil to play through a lesson without saying a word.

Early in 1844, the Schumanns set out on a much-postponed tour of Russia, which was desperately needed to repair their crumbling finances. The journey, vividly described in Clara's letters home, was a test of endurance beyond our imagining, but they spent four gloriously successful weeks in St Petersburg in March; Clara played before the Tsar and his family, and Robert heard applause for his Quintet and some smaller works. Then they set off on an another exhausting journey to Moscow: 'The sight is indescribable; one feels as if one must be in Constantinople, the city with its countless minarets is so eastern.' They reached Leipzig again on 30 May, after four months of travel. They were exhausted, but their pockets were refreshed, and perhaps because of this Schumann felt able to give up all connection with the magazine and concentrate on composition: 'Happy the man who is comfortable within his four walls, score paper before him, and painting it into splendid compositions.'

but in the second half of the twentieth century we have become accustomed to utter perversity of string technique, so there is little in Schumann's writing to shock listeners or players today. In the past, chamber-music groups did not often choose to play this music, for it needed hard work, audiences were not clamoring to hear it, and life was almost too short to get through all the works of Haydn, Mozart, Beethoven and Brahms, let alone Schumann's. But now that they are recorded, every listener can commune with works which offer some of Schumann's most beautiful thoughts. There are certainly weak pages – sometimes too much fugato, or too frequent repetition of certain rhythmic patterns – but what invention there is: the noble theme of the adagio of the A minor Quartet, the wit and charm of the scherzo of the F major, and the glorious sound of page

Above: Autograph sketch for the *Fantasie* in C major for violin and orchestra, op.131, one of Schumann's late works, which the composer dedicated to Joachim.

Right: Le Fou de peur, ou Le Désespéré (The Despairing Man), a self-portrait by Gustave Courbet, 1843, which touches the Romantic movement's preoccupation with madness and suicide. From an early age Schumann feared that he might go mad, having periods of melancholy interspersed with periods of elation and great creativity.

His euphoria was short-lived. In the middle of August he collapsed with a severe nervous breakdown, made worse by the appointment of Gade to conduct the Gewandhaus concerts in succession to Mendelssohn – a position Schumann had coveted with very little justification, for he was completely inexperienced. And now that Mendelssohn had left, Leipzig seemed artistically dead. Music itself became a torment: 'It cut into my nerves like knives.' Schumann had to stop work on his setting of Goethe's *Faust*, and by the end of the year he was longing to escape from Leipzig. He and Clara were now at last reconciled with Wieck, and partly at his urging they decided to move to Dresden in the hope of finding a new stimulus to their creative lives. On 8 December 1844 they left Leipzig for ever.

• Dresden: 1844-9 •

Dresden was the capital of Saxony, dominated by the stiff and conventional court of King Frederick Augustus. The most exciting aspect of its musical life was the presence of Richard Wagner as conductor at the Royal Opera House. Schumann and Wagner met quite often, but they had little in common, and conversation, predictably, was one-sided. Each thought little of the other's gifts as a conductor and only

grudgingly recognized his quality as a composer, although Wagner used to send composition pupils to Schumann. Far more congenial was Ferdinand Hiller, conductor of the Choral Society, and Schumann joined him in establishing subscription concerts in an attempt to enliven Dresden's dreary musical life, but the public was uninterested and after two seasons they lapsed. Clara was feeling the strain: she was almost continually pregnant, her husband was chronically ill, and she was depressed and frustrated by life in Dresden. Relations with her father had improved for a while, but soon all the old animosity smoldered between them.

One ray of light in this gloom was the realization that her husband was working again after many months of rest in which he had done nothing but pass the time working at fugues. He took up again the *Fantasie* for piano and orchestra that he had put aside in 1841, reshaped it and added two more movements to make a piano concerto in A minor. As with almost everything that he touched, Schumann produced an original masterpiece. Not that it was startling; rather the reverse – it was original because it was so restrained. Concertos were expected to be a species of circus act, a bravura struggle between soloist and orchestra. Perhaps because this was written for Clara, it was more like a conversation between lovers, tender, intimate, but in the end full of joy. Astonishingly, this genial work made slow progress in the public esteem.

Other works were taking shape in Schumann's mind, and at Christmas 1845 he presented Clara with the sketch of a new symphony in C. The work progressed slowly, constantly interrupted by attacks of nervous irritation and weakness, and it was not completed until 19 October. But the first performance took place

Above: Menzel's *The Honoring of the Insurgents Killed in March 1848* – the funeral of those who fell in the Berlin uprising. When the rebellion reached Dresden the following year, Schumann wrote some revolutionary choruses, which he was afraid to publish, and some Marches (op.76), but otherwise his music in no way reflects the political unrest. Clara wrote, 'It seems to me extraordinary how the terrible events without have awakened his poetic feeling in so entirely contrary a manner. All the songs breathe the spirit of perfect peace, they seem to me like spring, and laugh like blossoming flowers.'

just over a fortnight later in Leipzig, which says a lot for the skill of the copyists. The musicians were not so adept, even under Mendelssohn's direction, although obviously he had had little time to study what is still a tricky score. Even Schumann's tongue was loosened by the poor playing, and Mendelssohn took his remarks personally. He was even more annoyed when the local paper criticized him for repeating the whole of Rossini's *William Tell* overture in a concert which ended with the first performance of a new symphony. The differences between Mendelssohn and Schumann were built up by their followers into an absurd artistic squabble in which the principals sat smarting on the sidelines. There is no doubt that it intensified the widespread hostility to Schumann's music, so often described as labored and harsh compared with the smooth perfection of Mendelssohn's. But the squabble was brought to a tragic conclusion when Mendelssohn died suddenly of a stroke on 7 November 1847. Clara wrote: 'Our grief is great for he was dear to us, not only as an artist but as a man and as a friend.'

Schumann's creative power struggled fitfully with the nervous debility that it provoked, but his genius refused to be silenced. He turned again to chamber music and in the summer of 1847 produced a pair of piano trios: in D minor, op.63, and in F, op.80. The first is a warmly Romantic work, rich in harmony and melodic invention, at a level with the best of his chamber music. The second does not sustain this quality, except in the slow movement, which Fanny Davies described as 'one of Schumann's most moving lyric poems.'

For years Schumann had been anxious to get his foot in the door of an opera house, not least because it was the only place where a composer could make any real money. He had thought of many different subjects, from *Till Eulenspiegel* to the *Ring of the Nibelungs*, but in 1847 he settled on *Genoveva*, a medieval story that had been given different literary treatments by Hebbel and Tieck. He asked a friend to prepare a libretto but was dissatisfied, and after consulting Hebbel to no purpose he decided to write it himself. Wagner saw that he was burdening himself with an operatic millstone and tried to warn him off, but Schumann took no notice, and in manic excitement completed the overture before the libretto was finished. Schumann had not the guile or force of personality to manipulate his genius to the make-believe

Top: Menzel's drawing of Clara Schumann with the violinist Joseph Joachim (1831-1907). He and Schumann corresponded from the 1850s, though they did not meet until 1853.

Above: The dedication to Joachim of the *F. A. E.* sonata based on his personal motto 'Frei aber Einsam,' in which Schumann collaborated with his pupil Albert Dietrich and Brahms. Later he replaced their parts with movements of his own to complete his Third Violin Sonata.

Right: Brahms in 1854, the year after he had first met the Schumanns.

adventurous, and he even makes an effect with that most unpromising form, speech with music. It was produced by Liszt at Weimar but doomed to failure, and it is only now, on radio or on records, that this beautiful music can be effectively presented.

Schumann ended 1848 with his *Album for the Young*, op.68, a large collection of simple but exquisite piano pieces for children, which give us an insight into the personality of this shy and lovable man.

By May 1849 the tremors of revolution had reached Dresden, bringing Richard Wagner to the barricades and sending Clara Schumann hither and thither in panic. Her husband kept his eyes on his manuscript paper and effected his own minor artistic revolution by experimenting in many new forms. He added to the *Album for the Young* twelve piano duets and twenty-eight songs for children. For grown-up singers he devised a new form of song-cycle which included duets and quartets as well as solos – *Spanisches Liederspiel*, op.74, *Minnespiel*, op.101 and *Spanische Liebesliederwalzer*, op.138, which was to be a model for Brahms's vocal waltzes. There are songs with harp accompaniment to poems by Byron, hunting songs for male chorus and horns, and for the Goethe centenary he wrote solo settings of nine poems, and the tender *Requiem für Mignon*, his most successful choral work.

He turned to neglected instruments and wrote three *Romances* for oboe and piano and three delightful *Fantasiestücke* for the clarinet, but it was the horn which benefited most from this remarkable year of experiment. The introduction of valves around 1827 had given the instrument complete chromatic freedom. Schumann was the first composer to realize the possibilities this offered the horn as a solo instrument by writing his splendid *Adagio and Allegro* for horn and piano. But he capped this with the superb *Konzertstück* for four solo horns and orchestra. This magnificent work has come into its own only in the last thirty years, when instrumental design and playing technique has caught up with Schumann's visionary style. What in 1945 was still pronounced impossible is now played by young people at school.

1849 was possibly the most productive year in Schumann's life, but in other ways his existence was frustrating and depressing. He was treated with indifference bordering on contempt by the authorities, and although he had taken over a choir, he was ineffective as a conductor and interpreted his singers' discomfort as personal hostility. The production of *Genoveva* promised in Leipzig was put off again and again. Then out of the blue came the suggestion that he succeed Hiller as music director in Düsseldorf: he would be responsible for fourteen concerts a year and a weekly choral practice. Despite his lack of experience, as well as his evident shortcomings as a conductor, Schumann grasped at this in relief and agreed to move to the Rhineland in the fall of 1850.

This prospect raised their spirits, and in the early months of the year they visited Hamburg,

Sturm und Drang of the opera house, and though there are flashes of light they emphasize the surrounding murk. The best thing is the overture, which is still often heard in the concert hall; the opera itself is rarely performed today, and then more out of respect for genius, however misapplied.

As so often, the theater proved a kind of addiction, and Schumann now embarked on another hopeless cause, the composition of elaborate incidental music for Byron's quite untheatrical dramatic poem *Manfred*. This echo of those heady days in his father's bookshop inspired Schumann to an outburst of youthful passion in the overture, one of his finest orchestral works. Many of the other fifteen numbers are imaginative and skillfully written; the choral writing is idiomatic if un-where they were delighted to work once with Jenny Lind, and then Leipzig, where *Genoveva* at last took the stage. It was not a happy début: a stupid accident when one of the singers forgot a crucial prop ruined the first performance, but later, when things were more or less correct, the opera never received more than polite respect. However, it was kept in the repertory, and thirty years later Wagner was annoyed to observe that it received a far better performance than *Lohengrin*. The Schumanns returned to Dresden and packed their bags. On 1 September 1850, after six unhappy years in Dresden, these restless spirits set out for Düsseldorf.

• Düsseldorf: Coda •

Schumann was welcomed with great warmth in Düsseldorf, and within a few days of his arrival was given a concert of his music, followed by a banquet and a ball. Hiller handed over to him an orchestra and chorus of high standard, and initially he worked with enthusiasm and responded to the spirit of his surroundings with several new compositions. He completed a Cello Concerto, and within three months of arriving on the banks of the Rhine had composed a 'Rhenish' Symphony in E flat, which he published as no.3. Here again he struck out in a new direction by giving it five movements and exploiting to the full the possibilities of the chromatic horn. Other orchestral works followed – a series of overtures on literary themes, *Julius Caesar*, *The Bride of Messina*, *Hermann and Dorothea*. He took up again the D minor Symphony which he had withdrawn in 1841, completely rewrote it and published it as no.4. Then he turned again to chamber music, with two violin sonatas and a third piano trio in G minor, but they are uneven works, for already his illness was seriously weakening his mental powers.

Within weeks of Schumann's taking over as conductor, it became evident that he was incapable of directing his forces, and by the end of the first season there was a complaining article in the press. Attendance at choral rehearsals fell away, and discipline collapsed. In the summer of 1852 Schumann became so ill that his assistant had to take the first two subscription concerts. He recovered for a while, but by October 1853 he was incapable of going on and, rather than be dismissed, he resigned. At this very moment the Schumanns' misery was lightened by the arrival from Hamburg of a twenty-year-old pianist and composer. Schumann instantly recognized his genius and for the last time took up his journalist's pen to write in praise: 'He has come, a young man over whose cradle Graces and Heroes have watched. His name is Johannes Brahms.'

Schumann's condition deteriorated badly in the closing weeks of 1853, which are vividly but tragically described in Clara's diary. The nature of his illness is unclear, but opinion now suggests that it was syphilitic in origin. He

suffered terribly from insomnia and aural hallucinations; in February 1854, Clara wrote: 'Robert suffered from so violent an affliction of the hearing that he did not close his eyes all night . . . Every noise, he says, sounds to him like music, a music more wonderful and played by more exquisite instruments than ever sounded on earth.' A few days later, in the middle of the night, he got up and wrote down a theme, which, he said, an angel had sung to him. He was still lucid enough to compose a set of variations on this melody. But on 27 February came the final catastrophe, and a few days later he was taken to the asylum at Endenich.

Clara was distraught with worry, and once again pregnant; on 11 June she gave birth to a son, Felix. Although she was not allowed to visit her husband, they corresponded: 'September 15: A letter from Robert. What can I say? My hand trembles now that I try to write about it. I can only say that I was deeply moved and for a long time I could not read it. "Oh! if I could but see you and speak to you again," runs the letter, "but the distance is too great. I want to know so many things – what your life is like, where you are living, and if you play as magnificently as ever."' Fortunately she did, for by September her money was exhausted, and she took up again her career as a traveling virtuoso. This was to be her life for many years, and it was largely through the unrelenting advocacy of Clara as a pianist that Schumann eventually won recognition as one of the foremost composers for the piano of the nineteenth century. In April 1856 she set out for England, but a week after her arrival came an ominous letter from Brahms – the doctors held out little hope. She returned to Düsseldorf early in July; three weeks later there was a telegram from Endenich: 'I had to go to him, and on Sunday 27 July I traveled there with Johannes. I saw him between 6 and 7 in the evening. He smiled and put his arm round me with great effort, for he can no longer control his limbs. I shall never forget it. Not all the treasures in the world could equal this embrace.' Two days later Schumann died, quite alone, and was buried in Bonn on 31 July.

Above: The private asylum of Dr Richarz at Endenich, near Bonn, where Schumann spent his last two years, his mental condition steadily declining. At his funeral on 31 July 1856 'his dearest friends' Brahms and Joachim walked before the coffin, and Hiller came from Cologne. Clara wrote in her diary: 'All my feelings were of thankfulness to God that he was at last set free . . . if only he had taken me with him.'

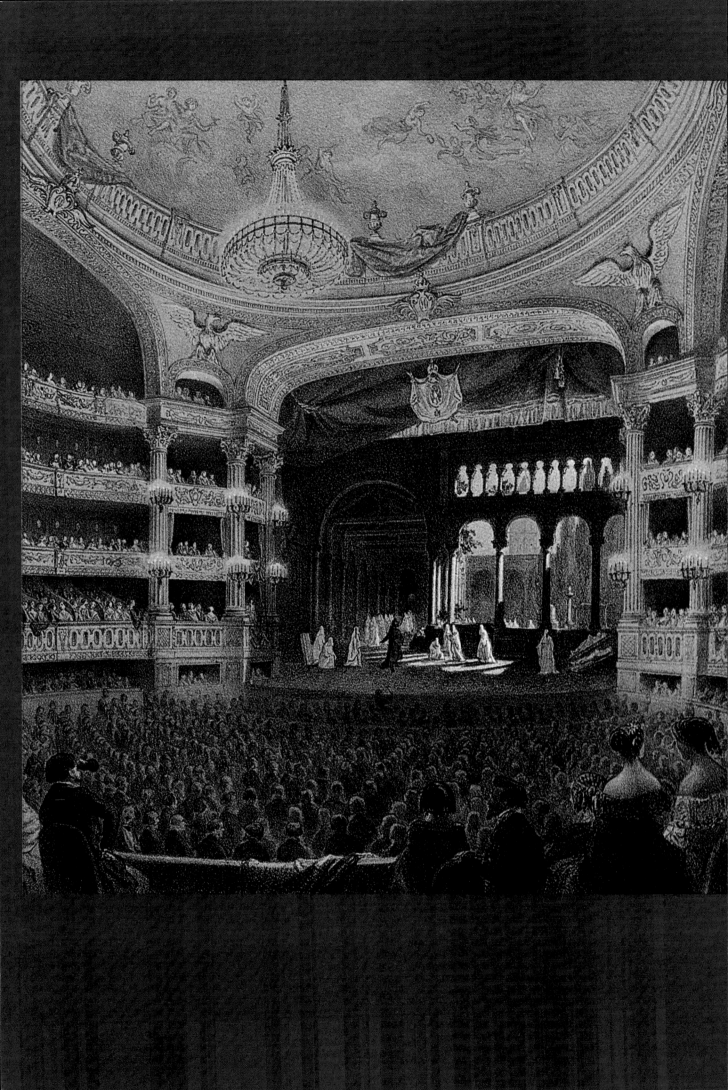

THE OPERATIC TRADITION

ROBERT DONINGTON

Grand opera is a remarkable affair. It stands as an extreme development of a form already somewhat remarkable in the history of music. Drawing as it does upon the resources of at least three contributory arts – words, music and theater – and costing as a consequence notoriously uneconomical sums of money to mount, opera goes the limit for impracticability. But opera goes on. To have survived so actively and tenaciously into our unromantic age, opera must have something of great significance to offer, more than compensating for those extravagant demands.

It is very clearly not the function of opera to reproduce the grim realities of the world outside, and anyone who comes to opera with such an expectation is in for disappointment and disillusion. But that is not how we come. We come partly for escape, perhaps; but, much more positively, we come in order to explore an inside world which opera sets up before our eyes and ears, with as much validity, on its own assumptions, as that workaday world outside with which we are familiar.

One of these assumptions is that feelings and intuitions matter, and that any art which can play upon us as opera does holds value. The mere scenario may come over to us as improbable to the verge of absurdity. But there is nothing either absurd or improbable about those waves of deep emotion and enjoyment which carry us through the great experiences of opera. There we sit, ready for any vicarious adventure and quick to identify with the characters and situations on the stage as they develop through conflict and resolution in the ordinary way of drama. But meanwhile that other influence, the music, goes on as well. Without particularly noticing why, we are being drawn in on a dimension which words do not reach, but music does, with its infinite capacity for shaping our moods and conditioning our fantasies in some sort of quintessential flow. For if this is really opera (and not just incidental music diversifying a play without entering any farther into the dynamics of it), then the drama is developing in the music, too. We could say that opera is drama unfolding as much in the music as in the words and action.

It does not seem to matter much in opera whether the surface story is probable or improbable. What matters is whether an underlying truth of feeling and intuition is getting across.

Here the music is crucial. It can even happen that the singers have words which tell us one thing to music which tells us another, perhaps letting out something quite different about what they are really thinking and planning. That is a resource of dramatic irony which only opera possesses. Or the music may be poignantly recalling something which has already happened, or foretelling something of which the seeds are sown but not yet visible.

Opera so understood did not arise, and perhaps could not have arisen, until the last creative waves of the Italian Renaissance were just about to spend themselves across the threshold of the modern age. The time was the late sixteenth century; the place was Florence, where the Renaissance itself had started some generations earlier. Classical philosophy, classical art and classical mythology had all come flooding back, together with Plato's view that myth has meaning deeper than its surface shows. All those mythological gods and goddesses, heroes and heroines, dragons and dragon-slayers who went into the making of opera were not lay figures for the earliest librettists, but images symbolizing our own human conflicts and passions. And there, perhaps, we are seeing a little farther into that inner world which opera can set up for us, either deliberately as those earliest librettists did, or by some more spontaneous disposition, as happens to any artist whose roots strike deep enough. For even those epic, chivalric, historic or modern characters who tended to replace the mythological ones (until Wagner deliberately brought them back again) get a mythical quality in opera which may be more real than their ostensible reality in the outer world. That is perhaps why we forgive them so readily when they behave improbably, not to say unhistorically. If they offer true images, then they are credible, whatever the cold light of reason might have to say against them. The cold light of reason has very little to do with opera. But 'the heart has its reasons,' as Pascal wrote, 'of which reason knows nothing.' The heart and its reasons have everything to do with opera. Once that point is taken, we know better where we stand with Norma or Tosca, Falstaff or Otello, Siegfried or Brünnhilde or any others whose surface verisimilitude may be much or little, but whose inner reality appeals so plainly to our feelings and our intuitions by way of their music.

• Early opera •

The first opera was *Dafne*, with music by Peri and libretto by Rinuccini. Rinuccini's second libretto, *Euridice*, was set twice. Peri's setting (with insertions by Caccini because he would not otherwise allow his pupils to sing) was given first, in Florence, in 1600; Caccini's was given a month later, but was published first. Yet both of them, and also Cavalieri with his staged morality drama *La rappresentatione di anima e di corpo* (marginally an opera), performed in Rome earlier in 1600, were out-distanced by Monteverdi, whose *Orfeo*, given in Mantua in 1607, is a consummate masterpiece, using an almost equally masterly libretto by Alessandro Striggio the Younger. Public admission to opera began in Venice in 1637, with the opening of the first opera house there, though whether public or courtly, opera was not much different. What had begun with archetypal myth turned now to adventure and intrigue. There was Monteverdi's *Ulysses* of 1640: a very human episode from Homer. There was his *Poppea* of 1642: a much glamorized passage from the life of Nero. The passions shown are not less universal, but they are shown in more ordinary mortals. We can next expect good, eventful storytelling, set to melodious scores of loose construction, with scene after scene making an immediate impact which is sentimental, rousing, comical or harrowing as the moment demands; and if the scenes do not always hang together very lucidly or consistently, at least we can be certain that it will all end happily. Obscure are the disguises

and grievous the misunderstandings; frequent the opportunities for confusion, reckless the artifice and summary the conclusion. What of it? The vitality of the plot and the felicity of the music in the seventeenth-century Italian opera make such good theater of it all; and beneath the pantomime exuberance and the fairytale enchantment, the great human themes glow through perhaps all the more warmly for being so very largely spontaneous.

But meanwhile, quite late in the seventeenth century, French opera had come into being. Its sources were a native tradition of court ballets, having at least some slight plot and often quite

Top: A performance of *Alceste*, Lully's setting of Philippe Quinault's libretto, before Louis XIV at Versailles in 1674.

Above: A Romantic view of the first Paris opera house on rue Vaugirard, which opened in 1671 in a converted tennis court. Many of Lully's *tragédies lyriques* were staged there in its early years.

considerable elements of declamation both spoken and sung, on the one hand and the performances at Paris of a few Italian operas, especially by Cavalli and Luigi Rossi, on the other.

It was Lully who worked with a very competent and classically-minded court poet, Quinault, to produce a most impressive idiom for large-scale drama in music, little altered through Rameau and others for a century to come. Quinault's libretti are mythological or chivalric, still inheriting from the Renaissance poety of Ronsard an air of veiling deeper mysteries than their surface grandeur and romantic adventures wholly reveal, enjoyable as these are on their obvious level as magnificent entertainment. Lully on his side was already practiced in the flexibly melodious recitative which the Italians had brought to Paris. He caused this flexible melody to speak good French by studying, very wisely, the spoken declamation of the best French acting: swift, plastic, passionate, within the boundaries of a highly stylized convention. Lully's declamatory melody, in truly French and very subtle rhythms, carries the drama to a marvel, and while there are also some formal airs for vocal display, these remain relatively simple and of no great length or brilliance, so that drama rather than song is still felt to be the primary aim in view. The dances, too, and the choruses (which might also be danced) usually have a close connection with the drama, in such roles as priests and priestesses, jailers and prisoners, good spirits and bad demons locked in combat in the sway of action. With so much

actual ballet in its background, French opera right through its grandest developments always did include a strong element of dancing and *divertissement*, and as for choruses, Lully both found and developed them, in a style of broad sonority which through its repercussions on Purcell went down to Handel – though in his English oratorios, not his Italian operas.

And so it was that the eighteenth century opened not with one but with two mainstreams

of opera. The French was above all dramatically expressive, in melodious though declamatory recitation (*récit*), with lyrical airs and resonant choruses and altogether plenty of *divertissement*, but appropriate to the action. The Italian was above all vocally expressive, with (by now) relatively compact and unmelodious recitative (*recitativo*) always leading to the big arias, laid out for the greater glory of the singers, in which each emotion in its turn finds musical embodiment. Recitative, once the mainstay of the music, now did little more than sketch in rapid dialogue and action. It was the contrast of emotions as aria succeeds aria which carried the drama forward.

Italian and French opera remained divided until Jommelli, Traetta and Hasse, and Gluck with his thoughtful librettist, Calzabigi, began taking up something of that French emphasis on drama. Artful simplicity, informal construction, swift action and lucid orchestration (sometimes commenting independently on the situation) were the aims successfully, if inconsistently, achieved in Gluck's reforming operas. Their future influence, however, was overtaken by a far greater composer, who by native genius rather than by theory presently fell heir to this reunion of the operatic strands. Mozart began and ended with *opera seria*, giving it a final glory; he assimilated *opera buffa* and *opéra comique*, he made light opera more serious and serious opera more human. He is a classic of classics; nevertheless, he was a prime source of Romantic opera, as in *Don Giovanni* with its

Above: The new Paris opera house at Porte Saint-Martin, opened by Queen Marie-Antoinette in 1781. It became a symbol of the hated régime and was stormed by the revolutionaries in 1789, two days before the fall of the Bastille.

Left: Prison scene from Rameau's tragic opera *Dardanus*, given in Paris in 1739. Rameau reinforced the tradition whereby ballet formed an important element in French opera. Even in the mid-nineteenth century Verdi, Wagner and other visiting composers had to write additional ballet music for Paris productions of their operas.

Above: Scene from the first production of Gounod's *Mireille* in 1864 at the Théâtre Lyrique, one of several centers for opera in nineteenth-century Paris. Gounod's opera was a Romantic love story set in Provence and based on a poem by Frédéric Mistral, who had turned for his sources to old Provençal popular traditions.

eerie statue and its hell-fire ending, and yet more so in *The Magic Flute*, so admired by Weber and Wagner, among many others.

Meanwhile, *opéra comique* in France was growing more sentimental, more sophisticated, more romantic and indeed more operatic. Although traditionally not tragic, it did not have to be literally comic. One example is the 'rescue opera,' where some noble prisoner may be rescued by an equally noble friend from a tyrant of unmitigated villainy. The pattern was set in 1784 by Grétry's *Richard Coeur-de-Lion*, with spoken dialogue, a siege portrayed in full French ballet, and some novel effects of stage lighting made possible by gas. Cherubini, while settled in Paris, deepened both the drama and the music of this highly adaptable species. Perhaps the best of him went into his tragic *Médée* of 1797; but in *opéra comique* he reached his peak in 1800 with *Les deux journées*, one of Beethoven's main inspirations for *Fidelio*.

It had been the genius of Mozart to balance words and music as they had scarcely been balanced since Monteverdi first perfected that original ideal of continuous drama in music. Mozart had learned all there was to learn from Italian fine singing and much of what French opera had to impart about dramatic truth, never more so than when da Ponte gave him libretti poised between laughter and tears. For the best of Mozart is of that supreme order which contrives to carry off the most serious matters with the lightest touch. And there it was that Rossini took up, not so profoundly but with beautiful assurance. He first swept Europe with his inimitable comedy *The Barber of Seville* (1816). This is so deliciously sentimental, so nicely suspended between Romantic impetuosity and Classical restraint, so breathless yet masterly in its pace, its felicity and its orchestration alike, that it did more than any other to set the course for the

Above: The Salle Favart, later the home of the Opéra Comique, housed the Théâtre Italien from 1825 to 1838. Rossini became co-director of the company in 1825, and he did much to form the style and technique of the singers there.

Below: Frontispiece from a score of Gounod's *Roméo et Juliette*, first performed at the Théâtre Lyrique in 1867. His sentimental versions of the great classics gave Gounod an unassailable position as the leading composer of his day in France.

lighter side of nineteenth-century opera. On the more serious side, Rossini did much (especially at Naples between 1815 and 1823) to bind up the dramatic continuity and intensity by interlocking ensembles and choruses with arias through whole scenes, rather than dividing them into distinct numbers. Then in 1824, Rossini was brought to Paris, where he encountered a most curious situation.

• Parisian opera •

Paris in the nineteenth century had become a magnet for international opera. Not many strictly Parisian composers were of the first rank; but many composers working in Paris set the fashions and led the field for just that international manner that we call 'grand opera.' Even *opéra comique* grew more pretentious, so that some specimens were turned into grand operas merely by replacing their spoken dialogue with recitative (and occasionally the other way about). After 1800, Cherubini fell into decline; but in 1803, a not yet very successful Italian appeared on the scene – Spontini – who gained a phenomenal success in 1807 with *La Vestale*. The libretto was offered him by Jouy, next to Scribe the most important literary progenitor of Parisian grand opera. The 'vestal' of the title was an official virgin, found not only to have received a lover into the temple, but in the course of receiving him, to have let the sacred fire go out. When just about to be buried alive by way of punishment, she is rescued by Jupiter in person, who relights the fire with a stroke of his own lightning, thus sanctioning her romantic union and demonstrating that he does not regard her carnal flame as disrespectful to his own pure flame of the spirit. Spontini was inspired by this plot to write the most massive choruses, thrilling ensembles and eloquent vocal melodies, supported by plenty of that most ready of Romantic harmonies, the diminished seventh, some particularly colorful woodwind and altogether an excellent melodramatic handling of both voices and orchestra; while the scenic spectacles

on stage were correspondingly striking. Yet something of classical restraint undoubtedly remains, and Spontini did not altogether desert his declared model, Gluck. It was a splendid new impetus for Parisian opera, and very much a turning-point towards grand opera, without as yet being unreservedly grand or unreservedly Romantic, at least in comparison with what was yet to come. By the time Rossini was sent for in 1824, however, the new impetus had decidedly slowed down, and this he was expected to remedy, besides introducing the best possible representatives of Italian fine singing. Both of these Rossini did.

While settling himself in with brilliant performances of some of his own Italian operas (appropriately revised), Rossini in 1825 brought over, among other Italian works, Meyerbeer's *Il Crociato in Egitto* (1824), of which the success was so resounding that it made Meyerbeer, in Paris and internationally, Rossini's most formidable rival. Then in 1828 Auber, a moderately talented Parisian, hitherto at his best in *opéra comique*, combined with his customary librettist, Scribe, in a most ambitious and lavish production, *La Muette de Portici*, which surpassed all precedents for melodramatic sensation in words, in music and in spectacle. But this in turn was exceeded in 1829 by Jouy and Rossini in an amazing work which did for serious opera rather what *The Barber of Seville* had done for comic opera: *William Tell*, which leans over to grand Romantic opera just about as far as it could without quite losing its classic balance.

Thereafter some strange psychological inability, perhaps, to tolerate great success seems to have silenced Rossini. Donizetti came nearest

Below: Painting (1866) by Fortuny of the visions evoked as the Spanish pianist Pujol plays his *Fantasy on Gounod's Faust*. J. B. Pujol (1835-98) brought many French operas, including Gounod's *Mireille*, to Barcelona in the 1880s.

to his style, though not quite equaling his talent or his spontaneity. Bellini also in certain respects had his limits, but not in felicity or inspiration. In 1831, at the age of thirty, he found a poignancy all his own in *La Sonnambula* and again in *Norma*. The harmony is creamy; the melody flows on and on with unending nostalgic beauty; the orchestration seems simple but gives just the right support and comment. Bellini, too, went to Paris, and was befriended by Rossini, but died in 1835, the year of his less evenly achieved *I Puritani*.

• Weber and Meyerbeer •

Meanwhile in Germany a rather wayward but gifted young Romantic, Weber, was beginning to focus that eminently Romantic aspiration to make of opera, as he put it, 'a work of art complete in itself, of which the several artistic ingredients blend and vanish, and in vanishing, combine to form a new world.' Metastasio or Handel would not have thought much of that, nor da Ponte or Mozart. Wagner, on the other hand, not only thought much of the idea, he seems to have imagined that he invented it, while paying Weber the tribute of calling *Der Freischütz* 'the first German opera' (on other occasions he took the same view of *The Magic Flute*).

Der Freischütz was heard, rather mangled, at Paris in 1824, but a stronger link passed through Weber's (and Rossini's) admirer Meyerbeer, whose long and formidable partnership with

Scribe began in 1831 (the year of Bellini's gentler triumphs) with *Robert le diable*. So typical is this of grand opera in its full development that we should take a good look at it. The Robert of the story is called 'the devil' for a reason which is typically Romantic in its deliberate exploitation of the supernatural. His mother Bertha, now dead, had resisted all suitors until she yielded to a plausible tempter, who was in fact the Devil in disguise. Robert shows the all too human ambivalence of his dual nature. In his better moments he loves the pure Princess Isabella; but there is also a false friend, Bertram, who allures him into mounting follies and disaster, culminating in a most eerie scene in a ruined monastery. All the nuns there have, it seems, become unchaste, with the exception of their pious abbess, whose statue holds a magic branch which will confer power, wealth and immortality on its possessor. But Robert recoils from the blasphemy of stealing this when Bertram lets it out that the abbess was herself called Bertha; and now the statue appears to fix him accusingly with his mother's eyes. But next, a particularly enticing nun, named Helen, overcomes his scruples, and he commits the desperate deed. The nuns, however, prove to be ghostly specters, into whose power Robert now finds that he has delivered himself. Attempting, in this evil mood, to rape Isabella, Robert is prevented by the intensity of her *bel canto* remonstrances, ending up so conscience-smitten that he breaks his magic branch and is only rescued from the avenging courtiers by the further intervention of Bertram, the real villain of the piece. They quarrel, and now Bertram reveals himself as Robert's father, offering him the traditional pact with the Devil, which would finally engulf him; but in a sudden revulsion, Robert prays to high heaven instead, and he is rewarded by one of those astonishing scene-changes for which the Paris Opéra was so justly famous – to a vast cathedral thronged by part of the chorus in a change of costume. There he is united to Isabella with the utmost splendor and to the evident satisfaction of the assembled

and while of course we do not and should not try to understand it in those terms directly, we do respond to the feel of it psychologically, which is indeed the very secret of so much great art. Parisian grand opera of the style of *Robert le diable* is a more profound and genuine artistic achievement than the surface glitter of it might nowadays suggest. Yet even as Meyerbeer was enjoying such unsurpassed esteem, other forces were preparing which put him eventually into exaggerated disrepute. These forces resulted in another of those strange partings of the way which are so interesting historically and can be so creative artistically.

• Verdi and Wagner •

In 1813 both Verdi and Wagner were born. In 1842 Verdi won early fame with *Nabucco* (influenced by Rossini) and Wagner with *Rienzi* (influenced by Meyerbeer). Wagner transcended grand opera with *Lohengrin* in 1850, and Verdi with *Rigoletto* in 1851. Thereafter, Verdi continued to build dramatic power through the vocal intensity of his melody, above an increasingly independent orchestral texture. *Il Trovatore* and *La Traviata* (both 1853) are grand opera, however individually conceived; so are those tailored, like *Un Ballo in maschera* (1859, on a libretto adapted from Scribe), to Parisian expectations. Then came a score of haunting originality, *Aida* (1871), unfolding like some massive symphony into which vocal fragments

congregation, confirmed by other choral voices from unseen angels.

It would be impossible to exaggerate the contemporary success of this most melodramatic of operatic composers. His present reputation is fairly low, attributing to him only the meretricious ability to excite his audiences by ostentatious display. The ostentation is not in doubt, but his work for spectacular grand opera – and indeed the value of such grand opera itself – stands far higher than our subsequent disparagement allows. Meyerbeer's music is composed with the greatest vocal and instrumental skill, and has indeed qualities of judgment and of discretion as well as imagination which raise it far above the obvious. The solo vocal lines are of great inventiveness, and Meyerbeer was always at pains not to cover them with any excesses in the orchestra. Massive orchestration was indulged chiefly in the big choruses, and very masterly it is both there and elsewhere. He is a composer greatly to be reckoned with, and so he was valued in his own day, with an important, if somewhat ambivalent, influence on colleagues as diverse as Verdi and Wagner.

The other outstanding feature of such opera is the remarkable improbability and unashamedly melodramatic quality of the libretti. But this was the Romantic vein; and on another level, it is real enough. The unconscious symbolism of Scribe's text is unintentionally but unmistakably Oedipal in Freud's interpretative sense;

Above: Scene from Act I of *Lohengrin* at its première in Weimar in 1850. In Germany medieval Teutonic epics were another fruitful source of material for opera, and they provided the basis for the great majority of Wagner's libretti.

break, or longer arias, or duets, or ensembles, or choruses, but always spinning the most fateful drama into that orchestral texture. And in old age came *Otello*, reluctantly undertaken at Boito's persuasion, long delayed but triumphant in 1887. Words, action and music have never been more closely interwoven; and opera has nothing finer to show than that thrice-repeated kiss, first given in ecstasy to such music in Act I that it turns our hearts over when Otello finally recalls it at the point of death. But at last, as Verdi approached his eightieth year, he turned from dark tragedy to graceful comedy with *Falstaff* (1893). A still more felicitous Shakespearian libretto from Boito; a miracle of craftsmanship and inspiration from Verdi – how could a great career end better than in this glorious blend of wit and tenderness?

Wagner, on the other hand, though his vocal melody is both expressive and exacting, sought dramatic intensity through symbolic inwardness. Where Verdi was moved by human beings to whom he gave archetypal dimensions in song, Wagner seems to have been possessed by archetypal visions for which he found human or superhuman or subhuman personifications. Only Hans Sachs, perhaps, stands out for quite the rounded humanity in which Falstaff excels.

The Flying Dutchman (1843) could only have been Wagner's – but only in the wake of *Der Freischütz*, on a crest of Romantic freshness and naïve confidence which could not and did not last. By comparison, *Tannhäuser* (1845) falters, but *Lohengrin* (1850) soars like some transformation of grand opera in which everything melts and flows. Yet, in the musically fallow years which followed, Wagner prepared in theory, and began in poetry, that remarkable new idiom, making poetry the end and music the means, which shows to best advantage in *Das Rheingold* and the first act of *Die Walküre*.

The seams in *Lohengrin* are already inconspicuous, but they do exist. Thereafter the Wagnerian melody is seamless, and only the distilled essence of recitative and aria blends into a continuous arioso, of which the modulations follow the most immediate impulses of

the drama, and full cadences are miraculously postponed to the end of acts. *Leitmotifs*, those fragments of musical mosaic attached to characters, situations, objects or ideas, combine as never before into an ongoing symphonic development, a mutual counterpointing of themes and actions, very effectual in binding up the drama. Before he finished *Siegfried* and composed *Götterdämmerung* to complete the *Ring* (1876), Wagner broke off in order to throw in, as he thought, a simpler and more popular work, which turned out to be *Tristan* (1865), followed by *Die Meistersinger* (1868). *Parsifal* came last in 1882. Not since its origins, not even in Mozart, had opera flowed so continuously and flexibly, or set out so deliberately to convey hidden meanings by way of symbolic images.

• Later French opera •

Wagner and Verdi outdistanced most Parisian opera. Berlioz rates in the top league; but so demonic was his genius that even his operatic masterpiece, *Les Troyens* (second part, 1863; first part, posthumously 1890), burns with uneven glory. But it is glory, which cannot altogether be said for the enchanting Offenbach, with *La belle Hélène* (1864) and *The Tales of*

Above: Act I set by E. Bertin for the original production of Bizet's *Carmen* at the Opéra Comique in 1875.

Top: Manet's *Nana*, 1877. Both Nana in Zola's novel and the gypsy Carmen exploit their sexual allure, but while Zola draws a moral from Nana's ugly decline, Carmen's death is seen rather as the work of fate.

Hoffmann (completed by Guiraud, 1881); nor for Gounod with his agreeably sentimental *Faust* (1859). With Bizet we encounter high genius again. Intermittently self-doubting and self-confident, long in finding his true direction but miraculously individual when he did, Bizet transcended the entire tradition of *opéra comique* with his magnificent *Carmen* (1875). So emotionally did Bizet identify himself with the drama that the very force in him which created it may have contributed to his own ending. On the evening of one of the early performances, he had a recurrence of a partly physical but partly psychological illness, and surprised his own much too complacent physician by dying of it. That evening, Célestine Galli-Marié, singing Carmen, almost collapsed on stage during the card scene foretelling death, and did then collapse in the wings, although no news of Bizet's attack had yet come through. The synchronism of this may well be a measure of how much Bizet had poured into this opera of his own inner tension, which the story of his life and of his death shows to have been very severe.

Saint-Saëns with *Samson et Dalila* (1877), Massenet with *Manon* (1884) and Charpentier with *Louise* (1900) do not at all stand up to Bizet's vital achievement; but Debussy does, with his masterpiece of understatement and suggestiveness, *Pelléas et Mélisande* (1902), on a virtually unadapted play by the symbolist poet Maeterlinck. Symbolism was the whole intention here, in the music as in the words, 'dream-like' yet 'more human' (as Debussy described them) than any outward realism. There is some deliberate reaction against Wagner, as well as much unavoidable assimilation from Wagner: there is no perceptible influence from grand opera. Reticence becomes here a creative principle, and only in rare moments for the orchestra does the music blaze out. Yet even this is of the age of grand opera, as if some of its quiet intensity comes by contrast with the grandeur which is *not* happening.

• Russian opera •

Meanwhile, grand opera of both Verdi's and Meyerbeer's varieties combined in Russia with a colorful strain of folk music to produce a national school, in which contrasts of melancholy and humor, sentiment and exuberance, poignancy and awkwardness make up an altogether recognizable and remarkable native style. Glinka, at the start of it, grew up on folksong before he trained conventionally. *A Life for the Tsar* (1836) includes scenes of a dark power which certainly influenced Musorgsky; *Ruslan and Lyudmila* (1842), a charming opera on a fairy-tale by Pushkin, influenced among others Dargomyzhsky, who produced on his own initiative a special brand of austere speech-song, effective in *Rusalka* (1856), somewhat dessicated and overdone in *The Stone Guest* (1872). But this, too, was turned to much better and more powerful effect by Musorgsky, from whom it was transmitted, by another odd twist of the spiral, to Debussy. Borodin's fitful *Prince Igor* (1890) contains among the medley some wonderfully lyrical melody, two very musically funny drunken monks, and those crude but

Left: Georges Bizet (1838-75), from a photograph taken in the year of his death. *Carmen* was based on a story by Prosper Mérimée, and, despite its exotic setting, there is a stark realism in the opera that, like Zola's novels and Manet's paintings, reflects the mood in France after the traumatic events of 1870-1.

Below: Célestine Galli-Marié as Carmen, a role she created. Tchaikovsky praised the way in which she 'managed to combine with the display of unbridled passion an element of mystical fatalism.'

invigorating 'Polovtsian Dances' by which we best know it; but like *Ruslan and Lyudmila* and *Rusalka*, the whole opera stages much better than it looks on paper.

Rimsky-Korsakov was neither amateur nor marginal. The last and best of his long series of attractive operas was *The Golden Cockerel* (1908), a fairytale fantasy with fairytale scoring, hinting, like *The Magic Flute*, at more than its glittering surface spells out. By a further interesting turn of events, Rimsky-Korsakov's uncanny mastery of orchestration helped his great and very different pupil, Stravinsky, to become the master he was of that crucial skill.

Tchaikovsky was a highly professional cosmopolitan, sympathetic to the national school but decreasingly in touch with it. His many operas reflect both Verdi and Meyerbeer. *Eugene Onegin* (1879) centers upon the contrast of two close friends: Lensky, who is sentimental but has a heart; and Onegin, who is sophisticated, but who heartlessly rejects the unsophisticated Tatiana and kills his friend in a duel. When later he finds Tatiana married affectionately to an elderly husband, he desires her now that he can no longer have her – and by his music seems to tell us that his heart is broken. But the poem by Pushkin on which the libretto is based makes the rather different point that such heart as he had died long ago, when he killed the friend who, like the other half of himself, stood for the warmth of feeling which from then on he more than ever lacked. That is the real tragedy of *Eugene Onegin*; and perhaps it was a tragedy particularly disturbing to Tchaikovsky, who loved men and feared women with an almost equal ambivalence. Tatiana seems to have inspired him with a quixotic desire to marry a girl he had himself rejected, and perhaps at the same time to provide himself and the world with an alibi for the homosexuality of which he stood in chronic fear of being exposed. He found it hard to know how to finish the opera, perhaps as a result of not being able to face the full implications for himself of Pushkin's poem. Even so, *Eugene Onegin* is a marvelous work for the warmth of feeling which Tchaikovsky was certainly capable of directing into his music.

Musorgsky, the most Russian, the most chaotic and the most gifted of the national school, moves us in his *Boris Godunov* of 1874 by his sympathy and his compassion for that tyrannical and tormented old Tsar who cannot forgive himself for the murder of the rightful heir. There were grounds enough for fellow-feeling here, since Musorgsky was an alcoholic who must long have been aware that he was destroying himself. Not even *Carmen*, not even *Pelléas et Mélisande* is more splendidly idiosyncratic than this remarkable one-off model.

Smetana was not a Russian, but stands close with his lively comedy *The Bartered Bride* (1866), his powerful *Dalibor* (1868), his more ambivalent comedy *The Kiss* (1876), and his patriotic *Libuše* (1881). Dvořák was most successful with his comic fantasy *The Devil and Kate* (1899) and his folk tale *Rusalka* (1901). Janáček in *Jenůfa* (1904) evoked a rather similar peasant atmosphere, but was already experimenting with a very free and expressive vocal line which grew more severe in *Kátya Kabanová* (1921) – still a warm and human drama – and again in *The Cunning Little Vixen* (1924), where the most human feelings are projected somewhat cynically on to the animals, the least human on to the human characters. *The Makropoulos Case* (1926) is drier still; but *From the House of the Dead* (1930) conveys with strangely convincing sparseness and integrity the desolate appeal of Dostoyevsky's novel. By that time, only Richard Strauss was capable of composing romantic operas successfully in the grand tradition. And that is another story again.

• *Verismo* •

One other grand style crossed into the first quarter of the twentieth century. It is called *verismo* (realism) because of a sort of inverted sentimentality by which harsh subjects, preferably from low life, were regarded as more real than gentle ones. Verdi had kept his greatest intensity of melody, harmony and scoring for moments of inner climax, but in *verismo* opera, the greatest intensity is attempted almost throughout, so that in order to effect any contrast at all, rather artificial strokes of theater are required.

Mascagni's *Cavalleria rusticana* (1890) keeps up a pace of jealous excitement hardly remitted except for the audaciously contrasted Easter hymn: all uncommonly stirring in its blatant fashion. It is habitually billed with Leoncavallo's *I Pagliacci* (1892), where the clown Tonio, in revenge for being spurned by the leading lady, causes her husband to overhear her planning another infidelity, so that he stabs her in earnest during the play within the play: again splendid theater to intoxicating music, if you have no objection to its vulgar streak. But then comes a very much greater and less superficial composer: Puccini. *Manon Lescaut* (1893), having the first of Puccini's impassioned yet foredoomed heroines, swept him to success, while *Tosca* (1900) went all the way into *verismo* and is a violent masterpiece. It is almost flawless in its sustained melodic inspiration and harmonic urgency, swift and cogent in its dramatic planning, potent once more on the unconscious dimensions of fantasy and taboo, improbable only on the literal level where our reason may be taking it but our intuitions are not. Nothing quite so sure-footed as this lurid sortie followed until the surprising and elegant little one-act comedy, *Gianni Schicchi* (1918). Then that fascination with the inscrutable East (or what Puccini imagined as the inscrutable East) which *Madama Butterfly* (1904) revealed, without quite resolving it, touched deeper levels in *Turandot* (completed and performed posthumously, 1926). Puccini adventured wonderfully here into the untried, but anxiously, as if he knew that it was too late for him. It was, and it is in the twilight of grand Romantic opera that we must leave him.

1887 Chabrier: *Le Roi malgré lui*
1888 Lalo: *Le Roi d'Ys*
1900 Charpentier: *Louise*
1902 Debussy: *Pelléas et Mélisande*

Théâtre Italien
1835 Bellini: *I Puritani*
1843 Donizetti: *Don Pasquale*

Théâtre Lyrique
1859 Gounod: *Faust*
1863 Berlioz: *Les Troyens* (part 2)
1864 Gounod: *Mireille*
1867 Gounod: *Roméo et Juliette*
1867 Bizet: *La Jolie Fille de Perth*

Bouffes Parisiens
1858 Offenbach: *Orphée aux enfers*

Théâtre des Variétés
1864 Offenbach: *La belle Hélène*

BERLIN

Schauspielhaus
1816 Hoffmann: *Undine*
1821 Weber: *Der Freischütz*

Oper
1849 Nicolai: *Die lustigen Weiber von Windsor*

DRESDEN

Hofoper
1804 Paer: *Leonora*

1842 Wagner: *Rienzi*
1843 Wagner: *Der fliegende Holländer*
1845 Wagner: *Tannhäuser*
1905 Strauss: *Salome*
1909 Strauss: *Elektra*

LEIPZIG

Stadttheater
1828 Marschner: *Der Vampyr*
1837 Lortzing: *Zar und Zimmermann*
1850 Schumann: *Genoveva*

WEIMAR

Hoftheater
1850 Wagner: *Lohengrin*
1858 Cornelius: *Der Barbier von Bagdad*
1877 Saint-Saëns: *Samson et Dalila*
1893 Humperdinck: *Hänsel und Gretel*

BAYREUTH

Festspielhaus
1876 Wagner: *Der Ring des Nibelungen*
1882 Wagner: *Parsifal*

MUNICH

Hoftheater

1811 Weber: *Abu Hassan*
1865 Wagner: *Tristan und Isolde*
1868 Wagner: *Die Meistersinger von Nürnberg*
1869 Wagner: *Das Rheingold*
1870 Wagner: *Die Walküre*

VIENNA

Burgtheater
1792 Cimarosa: *Il Matrimonio segreto*

Theater auf der Wieden
1791 Mozart: *Die Zauberflöte*

Theater an der Wien

1805 Beethoven: *Leonore (Fidelio)*

Kärntnertor Theater
1820 Schubert: *Die Zwillingsbrüder*
1823 Weber: *Euryanthe*
1842 Donizetti: *Linda di Chamounix*
1847 Flotow: *Martha*

Hofoper
1875 Goldmark: *Die Königin von Saba*
1892 Massenet: *Werther*

PRAGUE

Estates Theater
1791 Mozart: *La Clemenza di Tito*
1816 Spohr: *Faust*

Provisional Theater
1866 Smetana: *The Bartered Bride*

Czech National Theater

1881 Smetana: *Libuše*
1889 Dvořák: *The Devil and Kate*
1901 Dvořák: *Rusalka*

BRNO

German Theater
1904 Janáček: *Jenůfa*

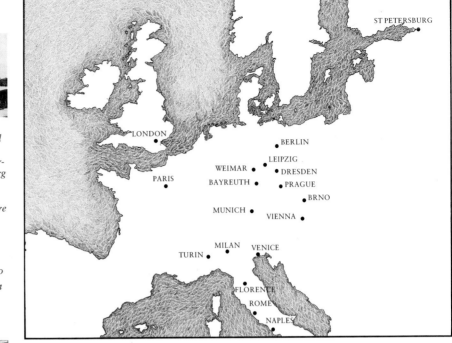

ST PETERSBURG

Imperial Theater

1836 Glinka: *A Life for the Tsar*
1842 Glinka: *Ruslan and Lyudmila*
1862 Verdi: *La Forza del destino*

Maryinsky Theater
1872 Dargomyzhsky: *The Stone Guest*
1874 Musorgsky: *Boris Godunov*
1882 Rimsky-Korsakov: *Snowmaiden*
1890 Borodin: *Prince Igor*
1890 Tchaikovsky: *The Queen of Spades*

Kononov Theater
1886 Musorgsky: *Khovanshchina*

VENICE

Teatro La Fenice

1794 Mayr: *Saffo*
1813 Rossini: *Tancredi*
1823 Rossini: *Semiramide*
1844 Verdi: *Ernani*
1851 Verdi: *Rigoletto*
1853 Verdi: *La Traviata*
1857 Verdi: *Simon Boccanegra*

Teatro San Benedetto
1813 Rossini: *L'Italiana in Algeri*

MILAN

Teatro alla Scala

1814 Rossini: *Il Turco in Italia*
1817 Rossini: *La Gazza ladra*
1827 Bellini: *Il Pirata*
1829 Bellini: *La Straniera*
1831 Bellini: *Norma*
1833 Donizetti: *Lucrezia Borgia*
1842 Verdi: *Nabucco*
1868 Boito: *Mefistofele*
1876 Ponchielli: *La Gioconda*
1887 Verdi: *Otello*
1892 Catalani: *La Wally*
1893 Verdi: *Falstaff*
1896 Giordano: *Andrea Chénier*
1904 Puccini: *Madama Butterfly*

Teatro Carcano
1830 Donizetti: *Anna Bolena*
1831 Bellini: *La Sonnambula*

Teatro della Canobbiana
1832 Donizetti: *L'Elisir d'amore*

Teatro del Verme
1884 Puccini: *Le Villi*
1892 Leoncavallo: *I Pagliacci*

Teatro Lirico
1902 Cilea: *Adriana Lecouvreur*

TURIN

Teatro Regio
1893 Puccini: *Manon Lescaut*
1896 Puccini: *La Bohème*

FLORENCE

Teatro della Pergola
1847 Verdi: *Macbeth*

ROME

Teatro Argentina
1816 Rossini: *Il Barbiere di Siviglia*

Teatro Valle
1817 Rossini: *La Cenerentola*

Teatro Apollo
1853 Verdi: *Il Trovatore*
1859 Verdi: *Un Ballo in maschera*

Teatro Costanzi
1890 Mascagni: *Cavalleria rusticana*
1900 Puccini: *Tosca*

NAPLES

Teatro del Fondo
1816 Rossini: *Otello*

Teatro San Carlo

1835 Donizetti: *Lucia di Lammermoor*
1840 Pacini: *Saffo*
1849 Verdi: *Luisa Miller*

221

The Romantic Ballet

Romantic ballet was a perfect reflection of much of the Romantic movement as a whole: a delight in the beauties of nature; a fascination with faraway places; a concern with the frailties of human life and love; and a taste for the exotic and the supernatural. Its center was Paris, and its real beginnings came in 1831, not with a ballet as such, but with an opera containing a ballet sequence – a French tradition going back to the days of Louis XIV and the *opéra-ballets* of Versailles. This was Meyerbeer's *Robert le diable*, itself a typically Romantic stage work about diabolic possession and ill-fated love; and the ballet sequence, set in a ruined convent, involved a chorus of spectral nuns. The way the dancers hovered amid the moonlit ruins was a far cry from the formal dancing of eighteenth-century ballet, based on themes and characters from classical antiquity.

Nearly all the stars of Romantic ballet were ballerinas (female dancers). The first was Marie Taglioni from Italy. The vision of light-footed grace and beauty she displayed in *Robert le diable* led, the following year, to a ballet created specially for her – *La Sylphide* (not to be confused with the much later *Les Sylphides*). In this she appeared as a sylph, or nature spirit, who lured a young man away from his intended bride. She rose up on her toes, aided by a new kind of dancing shoe, sometimes stuffed with padding at the tip or specially stiffened to support the foot, and her dress was white and of gossamer lightness. Her performance established the definitive style of Romantic ballet all over Europe.

In 1841 came *Giselle*, which once again had all the right ingredients: a rustic background, a strong supernatural element, tragic love. It was associated with two great ballerinas of the period, Carlotta Grisi, for whom

the role was created, and Fanny Elssler. But by 1850 the golden age of Romantic ballet was over, at least in France, where ballet declined into something closer to vaudeville. As a living, growing art form, ballet found a new home, in imperial Russia.

Above: Marie Taglioni (1804-84) as she appeared in *La Sylphide*. The ballet was set in medieval Scotland, a country which had strong Romantic appeal thanks to the novels of Sir Walter Scott.

Left: An outstanding event in the annals of Romantic ballet was the appearance together at London's Her Majesty's Theatre, in 1845, of four of its greatest stars. As pictured here, they were Fanny Cerrito, Lucile Grahn, Marie Taglioni (kneeling) and Carlotta Grisi. Their routine, simply called *Pas de Quatre*, was devised by the choreographer Jules Perrot; and the question of precedence was diplomatically solved by arranging their stage entrances in order of seniority. Queen Victoria and Prince Albert were among the audience entranced by this unique performance.

Marie's father, who was a talented dancer himself, was the force behind her career. Through relentless discipline and instruction he turned her from a thin, ungainly girl into one of the most highly-praised stars of Romantic ballet. The playbill (*below*), for one of her farewell performances (with Grisi and Grahn) shows the mixture of opera and ballet that was typical at the time.

Below: The Neapolitan ballerina Fanny Cerrito (1817-1909), as she appeared, in 1843, in the title-role of *Ondine* (a water sprite). Fanny was choreographed by Jules Perrot to dance with her own shadow in a highly original sequence, revived in our own time by Frederick Ashton and Margot Fonteyn in their version of the ballet.

Fanny made her name in Italy and in London before making her first appearance at the Paris Opéra in 1847. She was then married to the French dancer and choreographer Arthur Saint-Léon. They separated a few years later, and her career ended in 1857. She lived on in Paris until 1909 – the year Diaghilev conquered the city with his Ballets Russes.

Above: Arthur Saint-Léon (1821-70) in *La Esmeralda* by Perrot. Saint-Léon, who started out as a child-prodigy violinist and was also a composer, divided his career between Paris and St Petersburg. His most enduring achieve-ment, right at the end of his life, was his choreography for *Coppélia* (1870), to music by Delibes.

Below: Carlotta Grisi (1819-99) was born near Mantua and danced as a child at La Scala, Milan, where her cousins Giuditta and Giulia were both to become stars of the opera. Carlotta, who was also an excellent singer, nevertheless chose dancing as her profession and at the age of fourteen was seen in Naples by Jules Perrot. He recognized her

remarkable talent and, after promoting her in Milan, London and elsewhere, in 1841 secured her début at the Paris Opéra. They were known as man and wife, although they may never have married. Grisi's greatest role was that of Giselle (in which she is seen *below*), created for her at the Opéra that same year by Perrot, with music by Adolphe Adam.

Right: Claudina Cucci (1834-1913) was of the next generation, but won fame in many of the same ballets. She

made her début in Paris in 1855 in the celebrated 'Ballet of the Four Seasons' in Verdi's *Les Vêpres siciliennes*.

Below: Lucile Grahn (1819-1907) and Perrot in *Catarina* with music by Cesare Pugni. Lucile, born in Copenhagen, was a protégée of the great choreographer and

dancer Auguste Bournonville, though they later quarreled. Hans Christian Andersen called Grahn 'a rosebud born of the northern snows,' and she was the most poetic of the Romantic ballerinas.

Left: Fanny Elssler (1810-84) dancing the Spanish cachucha (with castanets) in the 1836 ballet *Le Diable boiteux* (The Limping Devil). No illustration could convey the fire and passion of the great Viennese dancer, whose much more robust and dramatic style contrasted with the wraith-like dancing of Taglioni. For several years the ballet world was divided in its support for one or other; Théophile Gautier, a true balletomane, described the difference between them as between a

Christian and a pagan dancer. Fanny Elssler was also more adventurous than her contemporaries. In 1840 she toured the United States and then traveled to the Caribbean. In 1848 she crowned her career with a triumphant tour of Russia. Her farewell performance in Moscow, in *La Esmeralda*, brought fifty-two curtain calls and over three hundred bouquets, and half the audience followed her home. Three years later she gave her final performance in her native city of Vienna.

Below: This luscious confection – a cherry or strawberry ice-cream decorated with fresh fruit and spun sugar and surmounted by a silver figure of a ballerina – was created by Alexis Soyer in honor of Fanny Cerrito and Lucile Grahn, both of whom were great favorites with London audiences. Soyer was the chef at London's Reform Club during the 1840s and an ardent balletomane. He named his dessert 'Sultane Sylphe à la Fille de l'Orage,' referring to the ballet scenario he himself devised for Cerrito, *La Fille de l'orage* (The Daughter of the Storm).

Though he was a genuine admirer and friend of the ballerina, Soyer's piece is a parody of a Romantic ballet, set, typically, in a picturesque mountain village and calling for the most elaborate scenic effects and transformation scenes, including a dance of baby cupids with flaming torches as the daughter of Jupiter – the ballet's eponymous heroine – prays for the revival of the lifeless hero. Soyer was not far wide of the mark, for in several of the ballets devised in the 1860s and 70s by Marius Petipa for St Petersburg there were scenes every bit as lavish and absurd.

Above: The Foyer de Danse at the Opéra, shown in a litho-graph of around 1845 from the series *Soirées Parisiennes*. The gentlemen are not interested in the ballet girls for their dancing, while the dancers themselves look suitably provocative. As Mary Clarke and Clement Crisp put it, 'the dancers gained every sort of jewelry except a wedding ring, and the management thereby saved on salaries.' Some of the great dancers, however, married into the nobility; Taglioni became a countess, and Elssler is said to have been married morganatically to King Ferdinand of Saxe-Coburg-Gotha.

The Opéra's Foyer de Danse reached the peak of fashion under the régime of the great Dr Véron (1830-5), which saw the first flowering of Romantic opera and ballet. He had gained immediate popularity by rescinding the ban on access to the foyers imposed by his predecessor, who had also insisted that the dancers' skirts should be lowered to ankle-length. But thirty years later the situation had got out of hand, and when in 1861 Wagner placed the 'Venusberg' ballet in *Tannhäuser* at the start of the opera, the young bloods of the Jockey Club, who arrived too late to see their mistresses dancing, wrecked the performances.

Above: Watching Fanny Cerrito at Her Majesty's Theatre, London, a charming print that may well show her in the title-role of *La Sylphide*, in which she scored a huge success in June 1841, despite the recent memories of Taglioni. Queen Victoria twice went to see Cerrito that season, and this print, with its all-female audience, suggests an idealized image of the Romantic ballerina as an ethereal, chaste young creature, half human, half divine.

The cartoon *(right)* by Honoré Daumier presents a very different image of the ballet audience, but the year is now 1864, when in Paris, at any rate, the heyday of Romantic ballet was past, the last of the great ballerinas, Emma Livry, having died the previous year when her costume caught fire. Says the wife to her husband: 'If you keep staring at the dancers through those glasses in such an indecent way, I'll take you home before the end of the show.'

Right: Jean-Pierre Dantan's caricature of Jules Perrot (1810-92), one of the great male dancers of the Romantic period. Though not blessed with natural grace or good looks, Perrot was a superb athlete and acrobat. His teacher, Auguste Vestris, instructed him 'to turn, spin, fly, and never give the public time to examine your person closely.'

224

Ballet had made a great impression on English audiences since Taglioni's first London season in 1832, but it elicited lampoons as well as stage-struck devotion. W. M. Thackeray's dancer (*below*) leaps overenthusiastically into space off a cliff.

George Cruikshank's cartoon (*above*) may refer to Perrot's lavish *Les Quatre Saisons*, staged in 1848, in which Grisi as Summer competed with Cerrito (Spring), Carolina Rosati (Autumn) and the younger Marie Taglioni (Winter).

The print of a rustic celebration (*bottom*) shows Carlotta Grisi right at the outset of her international career, partnered by Perrot in the ballet *Le Rossignol* (The Nightingale), which was staged at the King's Theatre in London in 1836.

Left: Eliza Forgeot, who created a sensation in 1844 by appearing on stage wearing trousers. She was one of the dancers who brought the achievements of the ballerinas to the popular stage.

Above: Emma Livry (1842-63) as the heroine of *La Sylphide*, a role she danced at the Opéra in 1858 at the age of sixteen. The fact that critics compared her to Taglioni, the ballet's original heroine, brought the great ballerina out of retirement to coach the Opéra ballet, and Emma in particular until her tragic death when she was only twenty-one.

Below: Photographic models adopting dancers' poses for a stereoscopic picture.

GIOACHINO ROSSINI

BENEDICT SARNAKER

Gioachino Rossini was the most important composer of Italian opera during the first half of the nineteenth century. He was recognized by his contemporaries as the greatest of his time, and he enjoyed the widest popular acclaim, wealth, prestige and artistic influence, creating new standards by which other composers were to be judged. It was not until the appearance of Giuseppe Verdi that Rossini ceased to hold the central place in Italian operatic life, and it was only the mature Verdi who achieved a standing more illustrious than Rossini's.

Gioachino Rossini was born in Pesaro, a small city on the Adriatic coast of Italy, on 29 February 1792. Both his parents were musicians – his father, Giuseppe Antonio, was a horn player of good professional repute and his mother, Anna, was a singer – and Gioachino was often left with his grandmother while they toured the opera houses of the region.

By 1802 the family had moved to Lugo, and Gioachino was making good progress in learning the horn from his father. At the same time the boy came under the influence of a local canon, Giuseppe Malerbi, who taught him singing and gave him access to a fine collection of musical scores. So good was Rossini's voice that when the family moved to Bologna, after a throat infection had caused Anna's retirement from the stage, he soon earned himself a place in the Accademia Filarmonica – a singular honor for a boy of fourteen. In Bologna he studied music privately at first, but made such rapid progress that by April 1806 he had been accepted by the famous Liceo Musicale. There he studied singing, piano, cello and (most importantly) counterpoint, under the director of the Liceo, Padre Stanislao Mattei. Although Rossini did not take too kindly to the strict disciplines of traditional teaching, there can be little doubt that the precision of his orchestration, the control he was to display over harmony and the clarity of his part-writing all derive from this early, severe and thorough traditional training.

During these years of study Rossini wrote few works: some sacred music, a few instrumental pieces and a poor (but none the less prizewinning) cantata. His first operatic commission, *Demetrio e Polibio*, came from the tenor Domenico Mombelli in 1807. Lacking knowledge of the complete plot, Rossini had to write number by number until the entire score was complete. Although this was his first opera, it was not performed until 1812, by which time four others had established his name.

Rossini's operatic career began, properly speaking, in 1810 when he was asked by the Teatro San Moisè in Venice (prompted by the singer Rosa Morandi) to compose the music for Gaetano Rossi's one-act *farsa*, *La Cambiale di matrimonio*. The opportunity arose as a result of another composer's failure to fulfill his contract and it proved a golden one, five of Rossini's first nine operas being written for that theater.

With his third opera, *L'Inganno felice*, premièred at the San Moisè in January 1812, Rossini had his first great success – a success which held the Italian stages throughout the next decade. Many commissions followed: his sacred opera *Ciro in Babilonia* was staged in Ferrara during Lent and another success, *La Scala di seta*, was staged at the San Moisè. The greatest achievement of these early years, however, was the première of the two-act *La Pietra del paragone* at the Teatro alla Scala, Milan, on 26 September 1812. This was a total triumph. Rossini hurried back to Venice, where he wrote two more *farse* for the Teatro San Moisè, *L'Occasione fa il ladro* and *Il Signor Bruschino*. In the latter's famous *sinfonia* (overture) he asked the violins to strike their candle shades with their bows. Nowadays this effect is usually produced by striking the metal music-stands – either way it is delightful both for its absurdity and for the logical integration of this unusual device.

Over a period of sixteen months Rossini had written seven operas. Like every composer of that time, he eased the pressures of his task by borrowing material from earlier works, yet despite such short-cuts, these early works contain a remarkable quantity of fine music, and Rossini's *farse* are substantially superior to his earliest efforts at *opera seria*, which are rather stiff and colorless. In the *farse* and *opere buffe* Rossini's musical personality is taking shape. A love of sheer sound and of sharply etched rhythms are the most marked characteristics of his vivacious and happy style, combined with a vein of warm sentiment. Many years were to pass before Rossini reached his full dramatic stature, but already he was proving to be a first-rate orchestrator. The overtures to his first group of operas hold all the rhythmic drive and tuneful vigor of the more mature works, and their appeal is irresistible. Most striking is his treatment of woodwind instruments both as soloists and in ensemble, and such writing (often exposed over a slowly pulsing string accompaniment) displays great expressive flexibility and a richness beyond the scope of his predecessors.

Since there was no effective copyright between the various Italian cities at this time, the only way a composer could make a living was by participating in the performance of his works. A normal contract would stipulate that a work would be written and that the composer would officiate *al cembalo* (at the keyboard). To earn a living Rossini, now in demand, rushed from one Italian city to another, writing, revising and performing frenetically; he soon became Italy's leading composer and his works were everywhere enthusiastically received.

Rossini's first great *opera seria* was *Tancredi*, a setting of a libretto by Gaetano Rossi, which had its first performance at the Teatro La Fenice in Venice on 6 February 1813. The plot was based on a story by Voltaire and concerns the love of Tancredi for Amenaide. Tancredi is unjustly banished by Orbazzano, who himself covets Amenaide. A complex of misunderstandings results in Tancredi thinking that his beloved has betrayed him. Despite this, he defends her honor by provoking a duel with Orbazzano, whom he kills, and then throws himself desperately into battle against his country's enemies, the Saracens. In Voltaire's version Tancredi is mortally wounded before he discovers that Amenaide has in fact been true. In the opera he makes this discovery without fatality, and the story ends with a joyful celebration of love and liberty.

The overture was borrowed from the earlier *La Pietra del paragone*. It starts with a wind-dominated *andante maestoso*, which leads to a proud and vigorous *allegro* employing two contrasted themes. The opening scenes are more lyrical than dramatic and serve to introduce some major characters. The most striking number within this section is Amenaide's 'Più dolce e placido' (accompanied by the chorus). It ranges from the wistful delicacy of the *cavatina* (addressed to peace and her distant beloved) to some of the work's most elaborately decorated passages.

The scene in which Tancredi arrives on the shores of his ungrateful country contains the most famous number in the opera, the *cavatina* 'Tu che accendi' and its companion *cabaletta* 'Di tanti palpiti,' parodied by Wagner in the Tailors' song in Act III of *Die Meistersinger* more than fifty years later. Over a delicate string accompaniment (suggestive of the movement of Tancredi's boat upon the water), an oboe melody articulates the hero's feelings. The pain with which he apostrophizes his homeland gives way to an exquisite tenderness in the aria, which time after time outlines his mixed feelings with unerring accuracy. But *Tancredi* is much more than 'Di tanti palpiti'; it ranges through tenderness, anger, patriotic fervor (in the duet 'Il vivo lampo questa spada'), distress and pain and while it has an infectious freshness and vivacity, its formal power and control are fully mature. There is little in *Semiramide* (his last

Above: Felice Romani (1788-1865). Originally a lawyer, Romani was also an influential critic who championed classical esthetics, but he is now remembered for his opera libretti, of which he wrote over one hundred and twenty. Among the composers he worked with are Bellini (*Norma*, *La Sonnambula*), Donizetti (*Lucrezia Borgia*, *L'Elisir d'amore*), Mayr and Mercadante. For Rossini he wrote *Il Turco in Italia* and *Bianca e Falliero*.

Right: The celebrated leaning towers of Bologna. In 1806 Rossini was accepted by the Liceo Musicale here and studied under Padre Stanislao Mattei. Here he conducted Haydn's *The Seasons*, and his third opera, *L'Equivoco Stravagante*, was first performed at the Teatro del Corso in Bologna in 1811.

opera seria) which does not originate here. Most strikingly, Rossini fused the simple, direct need for lyrical expression with the overall requirements of the drama, and what he did became characteristic of Italian opera as a whole. Whether he created this new fusion remains unproved, but the force of what he did became the reference point for all who followed.

L'Italiana in Algeri (to a libretto by Angelo Anelli and first performed at the Teatro San Benedetto on 22 May 1813) fully shared the success of *Tancredi*, yet could not differ more. It is an *opera buffa* which ranges from the sentimental, through the grossly farcical (the famous, or perhaps notorious, 'Pappataci' trio), via the patriotic, to the hilariously lunatic (the nonsensical patter of 'cra cra, bum bum, din din, tac tac' in the Act I finale). Its silly story concerns Mustafa, the Bey of Algiers, who seeks an Italian wife because he has tired of his own, while Italian lovers attempt to trick him back to fidelity. Its humor is reminiscent of English music hall, but it also features more noble sentiments traditionally reserved for *opera seria* characters. Moreover, Rossini, with the precision and wit of genius, balances one against the other to provide perfect relief and contrast.

Within an orthodox introduction sung by the chorus, Rossini injects true sorrow into the lines 'Ah comprendo me infelice' (sung by Elvira, Mustafa's estranged wife), yet at the same time withholds any shade of tragedy. This fine balance, the very essence of *opera buffa*, leads quickly to an elaborately ornamented virtuoso passage for Mustafa, which portrays his self-opinionated pomposity to perfection. Another mark of Rossini's genius is the hero's first *cavatina* 'Languir per una bella.' This not only portrays his longing for his absent beloved, but also shows real strength and power, yet without being complicated or weighty in manner; in this it merits a place among Rossini's finest tenor numbers. Such qualities extend also to the instrumental treatment epitomized in the Act II number in which the heroine Isabella apostrophizes her beloved with the words 'Per lui che adoro.' This number (which develops into a quartet) is introduced by a flute solo above a bed of pizzicato strings. Although its thematic material is the same as that of the voice, the contrast of color between the two is central to the characterization of Isabella – as becomes clear from the way in which the flute continues to counterpoint the vocal part. The whole section is brief, and a change of instrumental color would completely alter the effect and remove its credibility. It is this kind of nobility and depth of expression which gives *L'Italiana in Algeri* a roundness and memorability which reaches beyond anything previously offered to Italian audiences.

With *Tancredi* and *L'Italiana* Rossini's fame was assured. During late 1813 and 1814 he was in Milan revising his Venetian successes for the Teatro Rè and writing two new operas for La Scala: *Aureliano in Palmira* (26 December 1813, and a successor to *L'Italiana*, *Il Turco in*

Italia (14 August 1814). The latter, to a libretto by Felice Romani, failed miserably. The fault lay not in the work, which is as masterful as *L'Italiana*, but in the fact that the Milanese claimed to hear extensive self-borrowing. They were wrong in their hasty judgment, for *Il Turco* is one of Rossini's finest comic creations and (bar a few short motives) the opera was newly composed. Rossini excels himself particularly in the ensembles, and the quintet 'Oh guardate che accidente!' is one of the funniest and most polished he ever wrote. *Aureliano in Palmira* was only moderately successful with the Milanese, and Rossini's next opera for Venice, *Sigismondo*, was an abject failure.

• Naples and the *opera seria* •

By 1815 Rossini's operas were being performed almost everywhere in Italy, but until then the southern city of Naples had ignored them. Given their city's long operatic heritage, it was understandable that the Neapolitans were suspicious of this brash young northerner's new reputation, and Rossini might never have set foot in Naples but for Domenico Barbaia (1778-1841). Barbaia began his working life as a waiter and ended it as the most powerful operatic impresario in Europe. He was in turn (and at times concurrently) director of the San Carlo and the Teatro Nuovo in Naples (1809-40), of the Kärntnertor Theater and the Theater an der Wien in Vienna (1821-28), and of La Scala and the Canobbiana (1826-32) in Milan. In the composers he encouraged and the works he produced he profoundly influenced the course of Italian opera. Seeking to revitalize operatic life in Naples, Barbaia invited Rossini to write for the two theaters he controlled and to serve as their musical and artistic director. From 1815

Above: In 1814 Rossini composed *Il Turco in Italia* to satisfy the demand for a sequel to *L'Italiana in Algeri*. The new opera was given its first performance at La Scala, Milan, but the audience expressed its displeasure at being fobbed off with music it thought had been taken from Rossini's earlier works. The illustration (from the cover of an early vocal score) shows the poet Prosdocimo in search of inspiration encountering the flirtatious wife Fiorilla in the arms of the Turk.

until 1822 Rossini ruled this domain and, after fierce initial resistance, he became Naples's favorite adopted son.

For his first Neapolitan offering, *Elisabetta, regina d'Inghilterra*, Rossini salvaged much of the music from earlier works, while the remainder offers little that is new. He was much more concerned not to offend a hostile audience than to extend his dramatic or musical ideas. Many claims have been made for *Elisabetta*, but to call it the first opera in which Rossini wrote out all the *coloratura* in order to curb the excesses of singers is an exaggeration. While Rossini's melodies do become more decorative and florid, this is a gradual process and does not appear suddenly in *Elisabetta*. Rather than attempting to discipline singers, Rossini's florid style is a type of musical writing whose development can be traced from *Demetrio e Polibio* to *Semiramide*. The other stylistic feature much commented upon is the fact that all the recitative in *Elisabetta* is accompanied by strings (rather than by a harpsichord and string bass continuo, a texture known as *recitativo secco*). Although this was the first time that Rossini had used this type of accompaniment, he was doing so to please the Neapolitans, who, largely under French influence, were demanding the rejection of *secco* recitative in *opera seria*. Nor was Rossini the first to employ this *recitativo accompagnato*; Simon Mayr had done so two years earlier for these same Neapolitans in his *Medea in Corinto*.

After the première of *Elisabetta* Rossini went to Rome for the production of *Torvaldo e Dorliska* and *Il Barbiere di Siviglia*. During his absence the San Carlo was destroyed by fire, and while Barbaia rapidly rebuilt the opera house Rossini composed two operas for other Neapolitan theaters. *La Gazzetta* was performed at the Teatro dei Fiorentini on 26 September 1816. This theater was the home of traditional Neapolitan *opera buffa*, and Rossini used the Neapolitan dialect for the chief *buffo* role of Don Pomponio, sung by Carlo Casaccia, who specialized in such parts. *La Gazzetta* was even more derivative than *Elisabetta*. Several numbers were transported wholesale from *Il Turco in Italia*, a trio came unchanged from *La Pietra del Paragone*, and several pieces were derived from *Torvaldo e Dorliska*. It was as though Rossini were trying out old numbers on his new audience to see how they would react before committing himself to an original work. After *La Gazzetta* he rarely had to borrow for his Neapolitan operas.

Otello, whose plot is rather loosely based on the Shakespearian play, was first heard at the Teatro del Fondo on 4 December 1816. It is an uneven work, but it marks a major development in Rossini's dramatic achievement. The first two acts are handled fairly traditionally, couched in strict musical forms and projected by a florid vocal line which seems impersonal. Yet it is this very quality which proves so apt an articulation of all the circumstantial forces which keep the lovers apart. When contrasted with the last act's woeful intimacy, the effect of cataclysmic

intensity is profound. Not that the first two acts are musically cold – in fact they contain some of Rossini's most beautiful and expressive music (especially in the ensembles).

Yet without doubt it is in the last act that Rossini excels himself. The somber mood of the opening, in which Desdemona, beside herself with grief at Otello's banishment, is alone with her maid, is richly scored, and the recitative is masterfully written. The sound of a distant gondolier then reminds Desdemona of a friend who has died; she takes up a harp and sings the woeful 'Willow Song' ('Assisa a piè d'un salice'), and has a presentiment of death when a gust of wind shatters a window. The gondolier's song (its text based on the 'Paolo e Francesca' section

of Dante's *Inferno*) is a brilliant interpolation, whose effect is even more powerful than the equivalent point in Verdi's masterpiece, while Desdemona's 'Willow Song' is an accomplished transformation of the traditional strophic framework. The vocal melody and the harp introduction are superb in themselves, yet each strophe modifies or transforms them into precise analogues of Desdemona's mental state: as she becomes more agitated the vocal line becomes more florid; her overflowing pain results in the third stanza's dissonant harmony, leading to a passage of recitative while the orchestra delineates the growing storm which mirrors the dramatic situation. She attempts the final strophe and Rossini gives her a chillingly barren vocal line, shorn of all ornament. An insistent pattern on the clarinet raises the tension until Desdemona, broken in spirit, abandons her singing and the aria is left incomplete. Even the oft-criticized conclusion is essentially right – the blandness for which it is blamed is the only possible background for Otello's abrupt suicide.

Rossini's *Otello* is a work of great and independent merit and was justly famous in its day – indeed until it was overshadowed by Verdi's most mature masterpiece. It was one of the

earliest nineteenth-century Italian operas to accept a tragic ending, a feature which extended opera's dramatic potential and paved the way for Bellini, Donizetti and Verdi. This achievement was hardly diminished when Rossini bowed to commercial pressure and provided a preposterous alternative ending for those delicate audiences that would be offended by the staged death of Desdemona; the important transformation had taken place and others would soon follow. Indeed the third act of *Otello* is the watershed between the spirits of eighteenth- and nineteenth-century Italian opera.

• Comic operas •

Rossini's contract with Barbaia made heavy demands, for he had not only to write the operas for two houses but also to supervise the singers while they learned their parts, to direct the performances and to oversee the productions. The contract did not, however, forbid Rossini writing for other centers, and during the early years of his Neapolitan directorship he produced a number of works for other cities.

Torvaldo e Dorliska was written in Rome for the Carnival season of 1815; it opened the season at the Teatro Valle. This 'rescue opera' has some attractive features, but its reception was mediocre. Eleven days before the première Rossini signed a contract with the rival Teatro Argentina to compose an opera to end the season. Various subjects were tried, and in the end Cesare Sterbini (the librettist of *Torvaldo*) provided a text which they called *Almaviva, ossia L'inutile precauzione* (Almaviva, or the futile precaution) to distinguish it from the exceptionally popular *Il Barbiere di Siviglia* (1782) of

Above: The Spanish soprano Isabella Colbran (1785-1845), painted in 1817 as Saffo in Mayr's opera. She had become Rossini's mistress soon after he arrived in Naples in 1815 (breaking her former attachments to the impresario Barbaia and the King of Naples), and it was for her that Rossini wrote his great dramatic roles, including Desdemona and Semiramide.

Right: The trio from *L'Inganno felice,* which was first performed in Venice in 1812. Stendhal described the opera as 'like the first paintings of Raphael . . . with all the faults and all the diffidence of first youth.'

231

Paisiello. Both works are directly based upon the Beaumarchais comedy in which the Spanish grandee, Count Almaviva (disguised as the poor 'student,' Lindoro – tenor) wins, with the aid of his resourceful servant Figaro (baritone), the young heiress Rosina (soprano) from under the very nose of her elderly guardian Don Bartolo (bass), who secretly plans to marry her himself. The play was the first of a trilogy dealing with the same characters and was itself designed as a comic opera.

The première of *Almaviva* was a disaster, partly because of the great speed at which it was produced and partly because of the hostility of the Paisiello 'fans.' In 1816 it was revived in Bologna under the title *Il Barbiere di Siviglia*, and it is now acknowledged as perhaps the greatest of all comic operas. The libretto is one of the finest Rossini ever set: dramatic situations of perfect effect, characterization which is precise and sharp, and a social breadth and humanity which is as fresh today as it was then.

The opening number, 'Ecco ridente in cielo,' is a serenade sung by Count Almaviva (in his student's disguise) accompanied by a band of hired musicians. It was added by Rossini after the fiasco of the first performance to replace a Spanish melody with guitar accompaniment. Its smooth, flowing lines serve the sentimental situation well – and lead to the first of many deliciously funny situations. Having serenaded his beloved, Almaviva pays his musicians generously and tells them to go away quietly; but his generosity provokes such effusive (and noisy) thanks that all sentiment evaporates in uproar. This intrinsically comic treatment has the dramatic merit of preparing us for the rumbustious entry of Figaro, the local barber and general busybody, singing his glorious patter-song 'Largo al factotum della città,' the most famous bravura aria ever written for the baritone voice.

Scene II gives us an equally famous introduction to the heroine, Rosina, who displays her youthfully joyous personality in the brilliant 'Una voce poco fa' and its companion piece, 'Io sono docile.' Now turning to the 'villains' of the piece, Rossini presents us with another justly famous number, 'La calunnia,' in which Don Basilio, Rosina's singing teacher and friend of her guardian Don Bartolo, advises the latter to spread scandal about Count Almaviva and thus destroy Rosina's love for him. This piece is remarkable for its use of the 'Rossini crescendo,' that steady build-up of orchestral and dynamic force to an overwhelmingly energetic climax. Here it is deployed to describe graphically how calumny spreads from a whisper to a tempest of scandal. The joyous vitality of this work continues to the end with numbers such as the hilarious trio ('Ah! qual dolce inaspettato') between Rosina, Lindoro and Figaro at the moment of elopement: with a ladder poised at the window the lovers insist on going through all the operatic formalities (including a repeat of the *cabaletta*) while their escape ladder disappears and Figaro hopelessly mimics their loving phrases, only to be forced to wait out the demands of the musical form.

After writing *La Gazzetta* and *Otello* for Naples, Rossini returned to Rome, where he produced *La Cenerentola* on 25 January 1817. The opera tells the story of Cinderella, the scullery maid, hated and abused by her stepsisters, who is spirited by magic to a royal ball and ultimately becomes a princess. Here Rossini turned away from the swift, slapstick vein of works like *L'Italiana* and *Il Turco* and further developed that warmth and humanity already displayed in *Il Barbiere*. The heroine, first sung by Geltrude Righetti-Giorgi, starts off cowering and shy but matures into the woman who can (to the exquisitely beautiful melody of 'Ah signor, s'e ver che in petto') forgive all those who have so sorely wronged her. Far removed from the wily, cheeky Rosina, Cenerentola resembles the heroines of later sentimental dramas such as Bellini's *La Sonnambula*.

La Gazza ladra (produced in Milan on 31 May 1817) is a tragi-comedy or *opera semiseria*, an extremely popular genre at this time. The overture is one of Rossini's finest, and in the drama itself he delicately and deftly develops his characters. The heroine Ninetta is the epitome of persecuted innocence. Her father, Fernando, has one of Rossini's finest bass roles, characterizing individual agony in poignant musical detail. Even the pedlar Isacco is beautifully sketched, and only the role of Giannetto, the lover, is blandly and conventionally drawn. Rossini had by now established his own personal style, creating methods and treatments of subject-matter which were to be repeated by his successors because of their popularity, their efficacy and their dramatic vigor.

Above: Rossini's highly lucrative contract for the composition of *Il Barbiere di Siviglia*, which he signed with Duca Francesco Sforza-Cesarini, impresario of the Teatro Argentina in Rome. It has been estimated that Rossini wrote this work in under three weeks, although a lot of the music was simply recycled from earlier operas. The first night in 1816 was a fiasco, partly because of a series of ludicrous accidents and also because Paisiello's version (1782) of the same plot had long been an established favorite, but from the second performance its success was assured, and it soon became Rossini's most popular opera.

Opposite: Geltrude Righetti-Giorgi (1793-1862), a contralto of magnificent technique who created the role of Rosina in *Il Barbiere di Siviglia* and the title role in *La Cenerentola*, 1817. She had been a friend of Rossini's from childhood.

• Rossini's Italian career •

Despite his widespread fame and a constant demand for his services from all over Italy, Rossini's financial security was poor. The traditions and mechanisms of Italian operatic life were such that the composer was paid less for writing the whole of an opera than a leading singer was given for performing one part of it. In addition, the lack of effective copyright meant that only if the composer himself supervised a revival would he receive any payment, and that payment would naturally be much less than he would receive if he were writing a new work – though his labor might be as great, since he would have to revise the work to suit a new group of singers and might have to replace whole numbers to accommodate a singer's individual qualities.

Barbaia affected Rossini's financial position as profoundly as he had affected him artistically. Rather than pay him more for composing (which would merely have angered the singers), Barbaia offered Rossini a share in a company which ran the highly profitable gambling-tables in the foyer of the Teatro San Carlo. It was this, rather than his compositions, which formed the foundation of Rossini's substantial personal fortune, thus contributing to the resources that made it possible for him to retire from the slavery of operatic life at the age of thirty-seven. The remainder of the fortune which made this possible came from productions of his works outside Italy. Here too, Rossini was helped by Barbaia, who as part of his management of the Kärntnertor Theater, introduced Rossini and his works to Vienna, where he was welcomed as a hero.

Barbaia also 'gave' Rossini a wife – or, to be more precise, Rossini took her from Barbaia. When Rossini arrived in Naples the company's *prima donna* was the Spanish soprano Isabella Colbran. She was also at that time Barbaia's mistress. Her exceptional vocal abilities as a dramatic soprano capable of elaborate *fioritura*, combined with her sultry Spanish beauty, completely entranced the young Rossini. Sometime between 1815 and 1822 he replaced Barbaia as Isabella's favorite, and in 1822 they were married. The marriage was not a fortunate one, but the artistic effect they had on each other was considerable. Barbaia's reaction to the loss of

Right: Manuscript of the first measures of 'Largo al factotum,' the famous aria with which the barber Figaro introduces himself in the first Act of *Il Barbiere di Siviglia.*

his mistress is not recorded, but it does not seem to have soured his working relationship with Rossini in any way.

Most people are aware that *Il Barbiere di Siviglia* was written in less than three weeks, and many an anecdote records how quickly and casually Rossini composed; the complete portrait is of laziness, surrender to the whims of impresarios and singers and artistic nonchalance. Yet a closer examination shows that this picture cannot be credited. Rossini's willingness to adapt his works was part of operatic business, and other composers (even Verdi) did the same. The autograph scores are neatly written and carefully organized – hardly evidence of nonchalance – and to accuse a composer of laziness after he had written nearly forty operas within twenty years is patently absurd.

Italian operatic life was organized into seasons, and while a contract might be signed up to a year in advance, it seldom indicated the subject-matter. Often the composer would receive the first installment of the libretto about a month before the première was to take place and would frequently have to start his composition without knowing the plot in detail. With

Above: Luigi Lablache in the role of Figaro, from the 1838 catalogue of Dantan's caricature statuettes. Lablache (1794-1858), a great *buffo* bass, was a member of the Théâtre Italien in Paris while Rossini was its director and became a celebrated Figaro.

Left: Rossini in 1829, the year in which he retired from opera composition.

Above: Sanctuary scene in *Semiramide* by Alessandro Sanquirico (1777-1849), the leading Italian stage designer of his day. He was employed at La Scala for fifteen years and was responsible for the scenery for several other Rossini operas. He was known for his exploitation of the effects of gas lighting, which was introduced into the theater during his time there. *Semiramide* is set in Babylon, and Rossini's opera, one of over sixty versions of the plot, was adapted from a tragedy by Voltaire. It was first performed in 1823 at La Fenice, Venice.

Right: Costume design for Joséphine Fodor (1789-1870) in the role of Semiramide in Paris, where the opera was first performed by the Théâtre Italien in December 1825.

so little time, even moderately complex changes had to be avoided and many scenes (especially opening ones) were written to a pattern. What is remarkable is the variety and dramatic originality of Rossini's works in the face of such conditions. In all probability he created many musical ideas in his head or at the piano before committing anything to paper and then (under the pressure of time) used the autograph score as both the first and final draft. This way of working is hardly unique to Rossini, but in his case the pressure of time was extreme, and each musical gesture had to generate its own momentum if the score were to be copied, learned, rehearsed and produced on schedule.

After the trips to Rome and Milan for *La Cenerentola* and *La Gazza ladra*, Rossini returned to Naples. While he wrote works for other cities during the next five years, only one, *Semiramide*, achieves the level of its Neapolitan counterparts. Although written for Venice (where it was performed on 3 February 1823), it forms a fitting climax to this period, and it also marks the end of Rossini's Italian career. His Neapolitan works of the period were *Armida* (11 November 1817); *Mosè in Egitto* (5 March 1818); *Ricciardo e Zoraide* (3 December 1818); *Ermione* (27 March 1819); *La Donna del lago* (24 September 1819); *Maometto II* (3 December 1820); and *Zelmira* (16 February 1822).

234

Below: Costume design for Moses in *Moïse et Pharaon*, 1827, the Paris version of *Mosè in Egitto*, 1818. The title-role in the première was taken by Nicolas Levasseur (1791-1871), the Opéra's star bass.

Bottom: Sanquirico's Act II set for the première of *La Gazza ladra* at La Scala in 1817.

One of the constant features of these later Neapolitan works is their florid vocal style. At its worst it can be prolix, but its best is dazzling in its splendor. It represents Rossini's response to the team of singers with whom he worked: Isabella Colbran, Rosamunda Pesaroni, Andrea Nozzari and Giovanni David specialized in florid singing, and Rossini rarely failed to exploit the particular qualities of their voices. Solo singing is thus important in these operas, and while the arias present enormous technical difficulties, they also have simpler, more delicately shaded sections which respond to dramatic needs and raise them above mere technical display.

Ensembles increase in both number and length in the later Neapolitan operas. Also vital is the profound shift in the part played by the chorus, which now takes an active dramatic role instead of being a merely passive observer. These changes caused Rossini to create a more dramatic accompanied recitative and to make more prominent use of the orchestra. Even his attitude to the overture changed during these years, and he either transformed the traditional type or abandoned it altogether in favor of a brief orchestral prelude (in which he was much copied by Bellini and Donizetti). An excellent example of the former is the overture to *Ermione*, during which the chorus (from behind the curtain) is heard several times lamenting the fate of Troy.

When the opera starts, these choral interjections are developed into the opening number.

After his successful Viennese visit, Rossini parted company with Barbaia. The Carnival season of 1823 found Rossini at the Teatro La Fenice in Venice, first revising *Maometto II* and then writing *Semiramide*. He and his wife spent the summer of 1823 in Bologna and then departed for Paris. After a brief stay there, during which Rossini started negotiations for future activities there, they went on to London. A Rossini season was staged at the King's Theatre, but did not prosper – mainly because Colbran was by now inadequate for the great vocal demands these roles made. Instead, most of the Rossinis' time was spent growing wealthy at the expense of the English aristocracy, who were willing to spend outrageous sums to have the celebrities present at their musical gatherings or to give lessons to their idle daughters.

• Paris •

By the beginning of August 1824 the couple were back in Paris, where Rossini became the director of the Théâtre Italien. He also agreed to produce existing operas at this theater, to compose new works for it, and to introduce

other Italian operas. In this role, Rossini brought to Paris the finest Italian singers, giving first-rate performances of his most refined Neapolitan operas, including *La Donna del lago*, *Zelmira* and *Semiramide*. He personally supervised these productions and frequently made significant revisions to his works. He also introduced operas by other composers, including *Il Crociato in Egitto*, which launched Meyerbeer's remarkable Parisian career.

Rossini's goal, however, was to compose in French for the bastion of French music drama, the Paris Opéra. He approached this task cautiously, reserving two Neapolitan works for adaptation to the French stage. Thus *Maometto II* became *Le Siège de Corinthe* (9 October 1826) and *Mosè in Egitto* became *Moïse et Pharaon* (26 March 1827). These two reworkings pre-

pared the way for Rossini's great French operas: the *opéra comique Le Comte Ory* (20 August 1828) and *Guillaume Tell* (3 August 1829). In their combination of Italian lyricism with French declamation and demand for spectacle these two operas set an irrevocable course which culminated in grand opera.

Le Comte Ory is, in some ways, an unsatisfactory and problematic work. The plot, often illogical, originates in a medieval ballad which recounts the notorious deeds of Count Ory; Rossini used the ballad's melody in the orchestral prelude and in the drinking chorus in Act II. The work is episodic in nature and polyglot in texture: the librettists, Eugène Scribe and Charles Gaspard Delestre-Poirson, used an earlier *vaudeville* of their own as the basis for Act II and combined this – rather inappropriately – with a first act incorporating music from Rossini's *Il Viaggio a Reims* (a cantata written three years earlier for the coronation of Charles X). Despite such incongruities, *Le Comte Ory* shows us Rossini at his best in his treatment of the orchestra and in the variety and finesse of his vocal writing. A special feature of the latter is his abandonment of the Italian tenor-style which he had employed until then. In this opera (and in its successor *Guillaume Tell*) Rossini used the lighter, clearer and higher-ranged French tenors such as Adolphe Nourrit and Gilbert Duprez, and his writing for their voices deeply affected later composers.

Rossini's last opera was *Guillaume Tell*, based upon the play by Schiller. Here Rossini combined superbly drawn characters with a pastoral setting, an extensive historical panorama and patriotic deeds. The great overture is superbly musical and unashamedly programmatic. With its hauntingly beautiful cello solo, the slow introduction evokes Alpine calm, followed by a storm and a notation of the 'ranz des vaches,' while the final section represents

Right: Title-page of the first edition of the *Petite Messe Solennelle* with a photograph of Rossini in old age.

Bottom: On the dedication page of the *Petite Messe Solennelle* Rossini wrote, addressing God, that 'twelve singers of three sexes, men, women and castrati, will be sufficient for its execution,' and went on to compare these to the twelve apostles in Leonardo's *Last Supper*, but 'there are among your disciples some who sing false notes!! Lord, do not worry, I promise there will not be a Judas at my supper, and that mine will sing in tune and *con amore* your praises and this little composition, which is alas the last mortal sin of my old age.'

Bottom right: Caricature of Rossini by H. Mailly on the occasion of his seventy-fifth birthday in 1867.

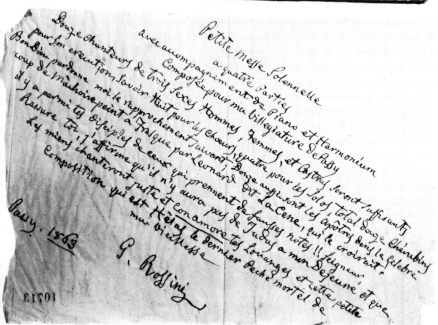

the call to arms and the uprising of the Swiss against their Austrian oppressors. The many spectacular elements such as ballets and processions were written to comply with French operatic tradition, but they are so effectively integrated into the work that we are aware only of the epic scale to which they contribute. Ensembles (rather than solos) dominate the work, and the chorus plays a central role both musically and dramatically, since much of the opera revolves around magnificent choral ensembles such as 'Tout change et grandit en ces lieux,' which ends the work. Among the solo voices the most distinctive change, apart from the treatment of the tenor, can be heard in the bass parts. Gone are the fanciful roulades of a part like Mustafa's in *L'Italiana in Algeri*; the bass is now more declamatory in manner and higher in range, a style which no doubt influenced the great baritone roles of Verdi. Meticulously written, orchestrally magnificent, melodically clear and expressive (yet purged of the excessively florid) and harmonically daring, *Guillaume Tell* is the final purification and apotheosis of Rossini's style.

• The last forty years •

Although all seemed set for furthering Rossini's achievement, fame and fortune, in fact what followed was forty years of virtual silence. Rossini never wrote another opera, despite innumerable attempts to lure him back to the stage. His rate of production had declined over the years and his health was poor. He was also financially secure thanks to a lifetime annuity granted him by the French government. A further factor may have been the change in administration at the Opéra after the 1830 Revolution; Rossini had been so closely associated with the old régime that his influence was now gone.

That there was no decline in Rossini's ability to compose is clear from the *Stabat Mater* and from the set of eight chamber arias and four duets written individually during the 1830s for various society figures and published in 1835 under the title of *Soirées musicales*. But he wrote very little, and a further deterrent to dramatic composition may have been the enormous success of Meyerbeer's first French operas, although the two composers remained on good personal terms until Meyerbeer's death in 1864, for which Rossini wrote a *Chant funèbre*.

It is often said that Rossini's failure to compose seriously and extensively after *Guillaume Tell* was a product of temperamental laziness. Rossini made no effort to dispel this image – indeed he almost fostered it. However, it is more likely and credible that illness, financial security, general exhaustion, the change in artistic and political climate and the final breakdown of his marriage created a personal and artistic climate in which the composition of new operas held little attraction for him. After six years of litigation for the restoration of his pension following the 1830 Revolution, Rossini took a short trip to Germany with an acquaintance, the banker Lionel de Rothschild. Having made friends with both Hiller and Mendelssohn, Rossini returned to Paris late in the summer of 1836 to tidy his affairs and then departed for Italy in October of that year. Some months later he was joined there by Olympe Pélissier, with whom he had begun an affair in Paris during the early 1830s. She nursed him through several illnesses and through his break with Isabella. They now set up a salon in Milan.

The succeeding years (until they returned to Paris in 1855) were depressing ones. Rossini's mother had died in 1827 during the rehearsals for *Moïse*, and the loss of his father in 1839 weakened and saddened him. His health declined further and needed prolonged and painful treatment. One of the few happier events was the immense success of the *Stabat Mater* in performances in Paris and Bologna – the latter under the direction of Donizetti. Although it did not cause him to resume composing, this triumph genuinely pleased Rossini, and he was particularly grateful to the younger *maestro*.

In 1845 Isabella Colbran died, and on 16 August 1846 Rossini married Olympe Pélissier, with whom he had been living for almost fifteen years. Further troubles, however, were in store. The revolutions which swept through Europe in 1848 also reached Italy, and Rossini found himself out of favor because he showed little enthusiasm towards the movement for national unity. There were some demonstrations against the Rossinis and, much embittered by the experience, they moved to Florence. After two miserable years they once again departed for Paris in the hope that French doctors might be able to help where Italian ones had failed.

The move worked wonders; Rossini's health improved dramatically and his famous sense of humor returned. He bought a plot of land in the suburb of Passy, where he built a villa, and rented an apartment in town, where he and Olympe soon ruled one of the most lively and elegant salons of the capital. He also soon returned to composition, calling his late works 'péchés de vieillesse' (the sins of old age). There are no operas among them, but these songs, piano pieces and ensembles combine sophistication with naïveté and are imbued with charm, sentiment, wit and a dash of parody. The most extended piece of these years is the *Petite Messe Solennelle* for twelve voices, two pianos and harmonium (1864). This work is among Rossini's finest achievements and has continued to impress as a deep revelation of the man who, externally, could seem merely witty.

In his last years Rossini lived in honored retirement. His reputation rested on works written forty years before, but he still influenced a younger set of composers with the witty, detached pieces he wrote in his senior years. He fell ill in the autumn of 1868 and soon after, on 13 November, died at his villa in Passy. His will left funds for the founding of a conservatory in his birthplace, Pesaro – a fitting memorial to one of the most creative and refined operatic composers of the nineteenth century.

Above: Statuette of Rossini in the 1830s by the caricaturist Dantan. After Rossini's death in November 1868, at a commemorative performance of *Guillaume Tell* at the Opéra, a bust of Rossini by Dantan was placed in a stage box and covered with wreaths.

VINCENZO BELLINI AND GAETANO DONIZETTI

ROGER PARKER & WILLIAM ASHBROOK

Vincenzo Bellini was born on 3 November 1801 in the Sicilian town of Catania. His family was one which boasted a long-standing musical tradition: his grandfather, Vincenzo Tobia, was an organist, teacher and composer, and his father, Rosario, also earned his living as a musician, if rather more modestly. Given these circumstances, it is perhaps not surprising that the young Bellini showed signs of a precocious musical talent. An anonymous manuscript now preserved in the Bellini Museum at Catania informs us that at eighteen months he had learnt an aria by Fioravanti and could sing it to his father's accompaniment, and that: 'from the age of five, he played [the piano] with considerable ability; at six, when other children had not even begun to exercise their reason, he wrote a musical composition.' Early nineteenth-century Catania, which did not even have a public theater until 1821, two years after Bellini left for good, was clearly a place where music centered primarily around the church service, and the majority of Bellini's surviving compositions from this period are settings of sacred texts. It is likely, however, that the young composer had some opportunities to write secular pieces, both vocal and instrumental, for the private salons of local aristocrats.

From the age of seven, Bellini received musical instruction from his grandfather, but as he moved into adolescence it became increasingly clear that Catania presented too restricted a musical stage for one with such ambitious talents. The Bellini family applied to the city council for a study grant, and eventually one was given. For a Sicilian, indeed for any southern Italian, there was really no decision as to the venue for future musical study: the city of Naples was the unquestionable center of excellence. Laden with compositions and letters of recommendation, Bellini disembarked at Naples on 18 June 1819, no doubt somewhat overawed by the vast range of new musical opportunities available to him.

Although the cultural pre-eminence of Naples in the peninsula had gradually diminished during the second half of the eighteenth century, it was still a focus of musical activity. Its great theater, the San Carlo, was of international standing, while numerous other smaller theaters were flourishing and well attended. But the city was also important for the academic study of music, and the famous Naples Conservatory offered

Bellini the kind of musical and academic training lacking in his provincial beginnings. The rigorous discipline of this institution was notorious, but it did have the reputation of producing some of the finest Italian composers. Bellini's most influential teacher there seems to have been Nicola Zingarelli, a successful opera composer who was also *maestro di cappella* at the Cathedral. Inevitably, much of the young man's time was taken up with academic exercises – strict counterpoint and solfège – but Zingarelli also introduced him to the greatest Neapolitan masters and, perhaps most significantly, to the music of Haydn and Mozart.

Bellini formed two important friendships during this period at the Conservatory. The first was with a fellow-student, Francesco Florimo, who became a lifelong associate and, after Bellini's death, spent a good deal of time chronicling the composer's life. The second friendship was with Maddelena Fumaroli, a young Neapolitan girl with whom Bellini fell in love while giving her singing lessons. Maddelena's parents discovered the attachment and eventually banned the young man from their house. The affair drifted on, however, for some years and ended in circumstances that reveal a rather unpleasant side of the composer's character.

Bellini's music of this period is, for the most part, religious or instrumental, although there are a few operatic pieces and a wedding cantata. But at the end of his period at the Conservatory, as a mark of special distinction, he was offered the opportunity to complete his studies with a 'graduation opera.' To a libretto by Andrea Tottola, Bellini composed his first full-scale dramatic work, *Adelson e Salvini*, which was performed by an all-male cast early in 1825.

Tottola's confused, melodramatic plot, set in a (highly unlikely) seventeenth-century Ireland, concerns a classic triangle of love: Salvini, an Italian painter, falls in love with the orphan Nelly, who is engaged to Salvini's friend Adelson. There is also a villain, Struley, and a frankly comic character, the bass Bonifacio, whose music places in the clearest perspective Bellini's great debt to Rossini. During this period, Rossini was at the height of his fame in Italy and, if we are to believe Florimo, a performance in 1824 of his *Semiramide* was a formative influence on the young Bellini. But in spite of the frequent Rossinian 'fingerprints' in *Adelson* – the florid vocal lines, the orchestral crescendos –

Opposite: Teatro San Carlo, Naples. The impresario of San Carlo, Domenico Barbaia, was instrumental in furthering Bellini's early career: he put on the première of Bellini's second opera, *Bianca e Gernando*, in Naples in 1826 and also arranged for his next two new operas – *Il Pirata*, 1827, and *La Straniera*, 1829 – to have their first performances at La Scala, Milan, where he was also actively involved.

the work also shows considerable originality of melodic writing, with a subtle use of chromaticism quite unprecedented in previous Italian composers, more reminiscent of Chopin and the later Romantics than of Rossini's 'open,' basically simple harmonic style.

The success of *Adelson* was so great that Bellini was quickly offered a commission to write an opera for a gala evening at the Teatro San Carlo, and after a brief holiday in Sicily he settled down to write *Bianca e Gernando*. In sharp contrast to the student cast of *Adelson*, the first performance of *Bianca* on 30 May 1826 boasted some of the greatest singers of the period – among them Méric-Lalande, Rubini and Lablache – and had an unqualified success. The libretto, by Domenico Gilardoni, simpler and less melodramatic than *Adelson*, is based on the popular 'rescue from prison' theme. The music, which was extensively revised some two years later, shows no great stylistic advance on Bellini's first opera, except possibly in its fine portrayal of the heroine Bianca and in some impressive concerted numbers.

But it was Bellini's next opera, *Il Pirata*, which set the seal on his growing reputation within Italy. Aided by the impresario Domenico Barbaia, the composer managed to place *Il Pirata* at La Scala, Milan, where it was first produced on 21 October 1827. Although doubts were voiced in some quarters that Bellini's simple directness of melodic style would be found inappropriate in Milan, which was a far more sophisticated, 'European,' city than Naples, the work was enthusiastically received by both critics and public.

In many senses, *Il Pirata* marks a watershed in the composer's career. Early influences – Rossini in particular – have by now been thoroughly assimilated, synthesized within his primary means of musico-dramatic expression, his richly individual melodic style. Typically moving in the swinging rhythms of Sicilian folk music, with a rudimentary, see-sawing string accompaniment and far less vocal ornamentation than in Rossini's work, Bellini's melodic lines often seem directly inspired by the words which underpin

them. 'Give me good verse, and I will give you good music,' he once said. In this respect it is significant that *Il Pirata* marks the beginning of Bellini's long and fruitful collaboration with the librettist Felice Romani, whose neoclassical restraint and refinement (reminiscent of the famous eighteenth-century librettist Pietro Metastasio) seemed a perfect foil for the composer's delicately balanced, meticulously planned, vocal lines.

The plot of *Il Pirata* again centers upon a 'fatal triangle,' and it culminates in a duel, a death sentence, and a mad scene for the heroine. The work has many fine moments: Imogen's first aria, for example, 'Lo sogno ferito,' which begins hesitantly with a restricted vocal range, but later flows into what one commentator has termed 'pure Belliniana' on the words 'il ciel feriva.' Perhaps the most impressive number is the finale to Act I, in particular its quintet, which is often praised for its unity of conception and perfect balance.

Between 1827 and 1833 Bellini lived for the most part in Milan, taking advantage of the city's rich cultural life by attending several of the most important aristocratic salons. The success of Milan finally encouraged Maddelena Fumaroli's parents to agree to a match between their daughter and the composer, but Bellini had in the meantime changed his sights. The imploring letters which came from Maddelena did not even move him sufficiently to elicit personal replies, and Florimo was enlisted as a go-between, answering the letters as best he could. The constancy of Bellini's operatic heroes seems to have been conspicuously lacking in their creator: Bellini was now poised for the international stage and had fully emancipated himself from his lowly beginnings.

•*La Straniera, Zaira* and *I Capuleti e i Montecchi*•

Very soon after the success of *Il Pirata*, the impresario Bartolomeo Merelli offered Bellini a contract for the Carlo Felice theater in Genoa. Eventually it was agreed that the composer should furnish an extensive revision of *Bianca e Gernando* (now, confusingly, entitled *Bianca e Fernando*), in collaboration with Felice Romani. But the ensuing trip to Genoa was important for another reason, for it was there that Bellini met Giuditta Cantù, the woman with whom he formed perhaps the most intense emotional attachment of his mature life. Giuditta, the daughter of a silk merchant from Pavia, had married Ferdinando Turina in 1819, but the marriage had not been a success, and she spent a good deal of time alone or with relatives. Bellini's account of the beginnings of their affair, which he described at enormous length in a letter to Florimo, and in particular his demands of Giuditta to live only for him, reveal something of his obsessive self-centeredness in his personal dealings with others.

Below: Palazzo dei Gravina Cruylas in Catania, Sicily, where Bellini was born in 1801. The palace now houses a museum of Bellini's life and works.

Meanwhile, Bellini's professional career was continuing its steady rise: *Bianca e Fernando* was a success; revivals of *Il Pirata* were being staged; and Barbaia commissioned yet another new work for La Scala. An anecdote concerning the composition of this opera, entitled *La Straniera*, is revealing. The two men are at work on the final aria of the opera, and Romani finally becomes exasperated because Bellini continues to reject his draft verses: '"Now I must confess to you" [Romani exclaims] "that I don't understand your thoughts about this or what it is that you want." Then Vincenzo, his face animated: "What do I want? I want a thought that will be at one and the same time a prayer, an imprecation, a warning, a delirium," and, running inspired to the pianoforte, he impetuously created his final aria while the other man, staring at him in awed stupor, set to writing. "This is what I want," the Maestro said. "Do you understand now?" "And here are the words," the worthy poet replied, presenting him with them. "Have I entered into your spirit?" Bellini embraced Romani, and that was how the renowned final aria of *La Straniera*, "Or sei pago, o ciel tremendo," was created.'

The plot of *La Straniera*, based on a novel by d'Arlincourt called *L'Etrangère*, has frequently been criticized for its lack of dramatic consistency and, in particular, because it depends more on *coups de théâtre* than on firm character portrayal. Romani felt it necessary to add a long preface to the printed libretto in order to bring the reader 'up to date' with the action which has taken place before the opera begins, and he closed this preface with a note of apology, hoping that the action is clear 'despite the obstacles presented by so fantastic a subject and, above all, despite the necessity placed on me of not departing too far from the novelist's intention.' The action takes place in Brittany in the fourteenth century, with Alaide, the eponymous heroine, married to the King of France but in love with Arturo (tenor). The duet between the two lovers in Act I has been justly praised and even compared to Verdi in the grand scale on which it is conceived. The final aria, 'Or sei pago, o ciel tremendo,' has also suggested Verdian parallels to some; certainly it has the driving Polonaise rhythms and brutal syncopations that we associate with Verdi's early style, but it is significant that, at least in the opening section, there is a restriction of vocal range which is peculiarly Bellinian. Although *La Straniera* is rarely performed today, it marks an important stage in the composer's career. It is also clear from contemporary critical comments that Bellini was by now being regarded as something of a reformer – by some even as a possible 'savior' of Italian musical art.

So far in our chronicle, Bellini could do no wrong in the public's eyes. But, against all expectations, his next work was judged an out-and-out failure. The project, initiated by Merelli, for an opera to open the new Teatro Ducale in Parma, had a confusing inception. The commission was offered to Bellini only after Rossini had turned it down, and there were then some

problems before Romani could be appointed librettist. The idea of setting Voltaire's tragedy *Zaire*, initiated it seems by Florimo, excited some enthusiasm, but matters became delayed and the first night had to be postponed. *Zaira* eventually appeared on 16 May 1829, had a few performances, and then sank virtually without trace; we have evidence of only one revival, and the vocal score was not published. How far this failure is the fault of the music is a matter of some debate. Certainly the Parmesans were not well disposed towards the work (rumors had been circulating that Bellini was indifferent to the project, and local pride seemed at stake). Whatever the case, Bellini followed a time-honored custom and recycled some of the best pieces into his subsequent operas, where they were often highly successful. This cannibalization

Above left: Giuditta Turina. She and her husband greatly helped Bellini after his arrival in Milan in 1827, and for five years she had a passionate love affair with the composer. The portrait dates from around this period.

Above right: Francesco Florimo, a fellow-student with Bellini in Naples and his closest friend. He became librarian of the Naples Conservatory and wrote an admiring life of Bellini after the composer's death.

effectively set the seal on *Zaira*'s downfall, and much of the music became better known in other contexts.

By coincidence, Bellini's next opera, *I Capuleti e i Montecchi* (based on the Italian sources of Shakespeare's *Romeo and Juliet*), also occurred through a series of accidents. The great theater of La Fenice at Venice had commissioned an opera by Pacini, but when the latter failed to appear, the management took advantage of Bellini's presence in the city and switched the assignment to him. By good fortune, Romani was also there, and collaboration began almost immediately. Because of the pressure of time, Romani decided to adapt one of his old libretti, and Bellini used some of the music from *Zaira*.

Below: Giovanni Battista Rubini and Henriette-Clémentine Méric-Lalande in *Il Pirata*. The tenor Rubini (1794-1854) was discovered by Barbaia and spent ten years at the San Carlo in Naples. He created roles in four of Bellini's operas, and it is said that he lived with the composer while he was writing *Il Pirata* and that Bellini made changes to suit his voice and style.

• *La Sonnambula* and *Norma* •

By 1830, after *I Capuleti*, Bellini felt he had reached full maturity. It is ironic that, given these circumstances, 1830 also saw the first serious attack of the complaint which was to cause his tragically premature death five years later. Exhausted after the hurried composition of *I Capuleti*, he succumbed to a violent bout of gastroenteritis and had to convalesce during a summer spent in Como. But his days there were not entirely wasted, as he renewed his acquaintance with the famous soprano Giuditta Pasta, for whom he was to write his three greatest soprano roles.

The first of Bellini's undeniable repertory pieces composed for Pasta was preceded by an unsuccessful attempt to set Victor Hugo's *Hernani*. Again the librettist was Romani, and from the start Pasta showed a keen interest in the project. But eventually the 'revolutionary,' inflammatory nature of Hugo's play proved too great a risk. Five fragments of Bellini's *L'Ernani* survive, some of which were used in later operas.

By the end of 1830, a new subject had replaced *Hernani*, *La Sonnambula*. There is no suggestion of an attempt to preserve the atmosphere of *Hernani* in the new opera, as its melodramatic extravagances have no parallel in *La Sonnambula*, which is a pastoral *opera semiseria*. Romani took the plot from a ballet-pantomime by Eugène Scribe, transferring the action from France to Switzerland, perhaps to enhance the opera's visual aspect. Bellini worked quickly, and *La Sonnambula* was first performed at Milan's Teatro Carcano on 6 March 1831. A fascinating account of the final rehearsals has been left us by Emilia Branca, Romani's wife: 'The orchestra was ready to begin, when the Maestro, very agitated, ran here and there on

In spite of this 'patchwork' quality, the opera was a great success when it first appeared on 11 March 1830 and played until the end of the season. Among the cast were Giuditta Grisi (Romeo) and Lorenzo Bonfigli (Tebaldo).

The plot of *I Capuleti* differs from Shakespeare in several important particulars: Romeo and Juliet know each other before the opera begins; Romeo has already killed one of the Capulets; there is no nurse and no Mercutio. As a tribute to Bellini's skill as a dramatist, many of the most noteworthy passages are ensembles, for example the fine Act I quintet or the final scene of the opera, which many have seen as a fitting prelude to the string of masterpieces that was to follow.

The operas discussed so far are primarily historical documents: none of them has ever had a substantial stage history. Those which follow, however, were all cornerstones of the operatic repertory in the nineteenth century, and one at least has retained this position until the present day.

Above: Medallion of Bellini after a drawing by De Bussy. Bellini's brothers claimed that this portrait was the best likeness of the composer.

Opposite bottom: Set by Sanquirico for the opening scene of *Il Pirata* at its first production at La Scala in 1827.

Below: Giulia Grisi and Giuditta Pasta as Juliet and Romeo in a performance in Florence in 1829 of *Giulietta e Romeo* (1825) by Niccolò Vaccai. Romani adapted the libretto he had written for Vaccai for Bellini's version of the story, *I Capuleti e i Montecchi* (1830), and both singers repeated their roles in the later opera, Pasta singing Romeo in London in 1833 and Grisi Juliet in Paris the same year.

the stage, looking for the poet. Finding him at last, he laid siege to him, clung to him, and for the hundredth time begged him to redo the final strophes, exclaiming: "I want something that will exalt Pasta and raise her to seventh heaven!" Glowing with the flame that lighted his spirit, he was swimming *dans l'embarras de richesses*, and yet was asking for something new. Taken thus by surprise, Romani, who was by then bored, finally lost patience, picked out one of the inconvenient *strette* and, mumbling some words in the direction of the young composer, shook his head, turned his back and hastily left the theater. Bellini, who at times was so subject to painful sensitivity that he found the least contradiction insupportable, gave vent to actions worthy of a vexed boy.'

In spite of these last-minute tensions, the opera was an enormous success, with Pasta and Rubini, the tenor, at the height of their form. In general, one might say that *La Sonnambula* returns to a more florid vocal line (possibly influenced by Pasta, who was principally famous for her interpretations of Rossini); but, in fact, every note is an integral part of the overall melodic shape – there is never decoration simply for its own sake. Added to this is the stimulus of the rustic setting, which drew from Bellini a new, 'pastoral' style to prove very important in the formation of middle-period Verdi operas such as *Luisa Miller*.

It has often been noted that the opera requires something more than the usual 'suspension of disbelief' from its audience. Amina (soprano) is in love with Elvino (tenor) but compromises herself by sleepwalking into another man's room and being discovered there. All ends happily, as a further bout of somnambulism proves the reason for her original predicament, but the success of the piece hinges on the extent to which Amina can present to the audience a dramatically convincing character. In vocal terms, she is surely Bellini's greatest creation so far. From her opening *cavatina*, 'Come per me sereno,' we find

throughout a simple directness of emotion – though this is often achieved through a vocal line of great surface complexity. This seeming paradox is achieved primarily because Bellini's vocal 'decorations' are never merely decorative; they are essential features of the melody, each adding something pertinent to the overall effect. The composer's growing sensitivity to musical characterization can also be seen in his portrayal of Amina. In her sleepwalking scenes, for example, the vocal writing is never such as would demand full-voice treatment and so always allows the interpreter to distinguish these scenes from others by means of tone color.

The case of the tenor (indeed, of all the tenor roles up to *La Sonnambula*) is more difficult. While the capabilities of the soprano voice have changed little in the one hundred and fifty years since Bellini was writing, tenors of today are for the most part quite ill-equipped to tackle Bellini roles. The Bellinian tenor was far lighter in voice than his modern counterpart, but was evidently able to extend his upper range (mostly by judicious shading into *falsetto*) to an extent that would send most of today's tenors apoplectic. It is a problem which, while Verdi, Puccini and Wagner continue to dominate the operatic repertory, remains insoluble.

Yet again, Bellini distinguishes himself in the ensemble music, particularly in the concerted number which closes Act I, 'D'un pensiero e d'un accento.' This in fact became one of the most celebrated pieces of its kind in the nineteenth century and is peculiarly Bellinian in its exclusive concentration on melody. The number starts, as was traditional, at the high point of dramatic confusion – in this case just after Amina has awoken from her first bout of sleepwalking and has been accused of infidelity by her lover. The long opening theme is sung complete no less than three times (first by Amina, then by Elvino, then by the chorus), and although the accompaniment becomes progressively more complex on each repetition, the essential contours are never obscured. In other words, melody reigns supreme throughout the number – as a total and complete expression of the dramatic situation.

After *La Sonnambula*, Bellini planned to relax for the summer with Giuditta Turina, but by July 1831 another project was taking shape to fulfill a commission for a new opera for the forthcoming Carnival season at La Scala. The choice fell on *Norma*, a five-act French play by Alexandre Soumet. Romani had the text ready by August, and by the end of November the music was completed. *Norma* was first performed on 26 December 1831 and was at first rather badly received. But as the season continued the work gradually convinced the Milanese public, and by the end of its run the opera was being proclaimed a triumph.

Today *Norma* is generally considered the composer's masterpiece, and the most famous single number in the opera is also one of the most representative of his mature style. That number is, of course, Norma's first aria, 'Casta Diva,' her prayer for peace to the chaste goddess

Right: Song-sheet from *La Sonnambula, c.* 1849, showing Jenny Lind in the title-role. With its simple plot and fine opportunities for the prima donna, this remained the most popular of Bellini's operas throughout the nineteenth century.

Below: Commemorative print depicting the main personalities associated with the 1830-31 season at the Teatro Carcano in Milan. In its rivalry with La Scala, the Carcano commissioned operas from Donizetti (bottom left) and Bellini (bottom right), whose *La Sonnambula* with libretto by Romani (next to Bellini) was premièred here in 1831, with Giuditta Pasta (center) and Rubini (above Bellini) in the leading roles.

of the moon. 'Casta Diva' is virtually a roll-call of typical Bellinian devices: the simple orchestral sonority; the gentle, arpeggiated string accompaniment; the florid yet directly expressive melodic line; the choral interpolation in swaying parallel thirds; the poignant chromatic notes. The number, and others like it in Bellini's *oeuvre*, bear features which were of considerable influence on later Romantic composers, in particular Chopin, Verdi and Wagner. Perhaps most significant is the positioning of the melodic climax near the very end of the verse, thus creating during the course of the piece a sense of tension and expectation which is acute and, eventually, all-consuming.

But *Norma* has more to offer than beautifully fashioned melodies such as 'Casta Diva.' Though some of the 'martial' scenes perhaps suffer in comparison with Verdi's more dynamic examples of a few years later, there are moments of great drama and energy, in particular towards the end, where Norma confesses her guilt and prepares to meet her death. The writing for the chorus, its stunned interjections punctuating Norma's confession, is most effective, as is the manner in which Bellini manages to harness his expansive melodies to a more kinetic situation.

Perhaps best of all is the duet 'In mia man alfin tu sei,' in which Norma and Pollione (tenor) face one another for the last time: their exchange of short phrases, full of suppressed tension, is set in the form of a long, expressive melody, to which each contributes in turn; but it is as if the individual phrases, perfectly apt in the immediate dramatic context, represent violent argument only on the surface, while on the deepest level the shared melody makes it clear that their intensity and depth of feeling are identical.

The success of *Norma* finally assured, Bellini left Milan on 5 January 1832 to travel back to his homeland in the south. The journey became something of a regal progress: in Naples he heard *I Capuleti* performed in the presence of Ferdinand II, and a further performance of the opera was given in Palermo some time later. Bellini returned to Milan at the end of May,

Above: Wilhelmine Schröder-Devrient as Romeo in a production of *I Capuleti e i Montecchi* in Nuremberg in 1835. Bellini's opera was first performed in Venice in 1830. Male roles were frequently written to be sung by women in the early nineteenth century, after the demise of the castrato, and both Pasta and Malibran also sang the part of Romeo.

Left: Final scene from the first production of *La Sonnambula* designed by Sanquirico. The subject of sleepwalking was popular at the time, and Romani's libretto was based on a ballet-pantomime of Scribe's with the setting changed from the French Camargue to a more picturesque mountain village in Switzerland. Here the villagers show their horror at the sight of the sleepwalking Anina, in peril of her life. In most later productions she walks not on the roof, but along a catwalk above the mill-wheel, as in the illustration of Lind.

and towards the end of the year directed revivals of *Norma* in Bergamo (August) and Venice (December). For the first time since *Adelson e Salvini* in 1825, a complete year passed without a new (or substantially revised) opera.

• *Beatrice di Tenda* and *I Puritani* •

But by the end of 1832, plans were under way to fulfill a long-standing commission for a new work to be performed at Venice's La Fenice. As usual, Romani was the chosen librettist, but this time not with the usual happy results. There was some initial difficulty over the subject (Romani had suggested a plot based on the life of Queen Christina of Sweden) before it was eventually decided to compose *Beatrice di Tenda*, a subject from Italian history. But, the final decision made, Romani became dilatory to an impossible degree, concerning himself with other projects. Eventually Bellini managed to squeeze the libretto out of him, but not before the composer had instigated police proceedings against his one-time friend. Perhaps the creative tensions which existed between the two men made a rift inevitable; although there was a reconciliation some time later, the two never worked together again.

Romani's reluctance to produce *Beatrice* may well have had to do with the considerable structural problems he invented. It was unusual to take a subject directly from history (French plays were by far the most common source), and perhaps it was this that led to the complexities of the plot. Whatever the case, Romani created what is best described as a 'love circle': Filippo,

Duke of Milan (baritone), loves Agnese (mezzo-soprano); Agnese loves Orombello, Count of Ventimiglia (tenor); Orombello loves Beatrice (soprano); but, to bring matters full circle, Beatrice remains the faithful wife of the faithless Filippo. The librettist's diffidence to the entire project is perhaps summed up in the final words of his preface to *Beatrice* '. . . circumstances have altered the plot, the tints, the characters. It has need of the readers' full indulgence.'

When *Beatrice* eventually appeared on 16 March 1833, the Venetian public greeted it with almost unqualified hostility. The extent to which this was justified is still a matter of some debate; the most common feeling these days is that *Beatrice* is less successful than the other mature operas, mainly because its libretto is dramatically rather monochromatic. It has been pointed out, for example, that the eponymous heroine continues to reiterate the same basic feelings throughout the opera, and indeed can do no more than respond to events outside her control; this is in sharp contrast to Norma, whose personality is an important element in the action. Perhaps there is also a sense in which the complex interrelationships of the plot proved too intractable when it came to giving the opera an overall sense of balance and focus: Agnese, for example, who is in some senses the most interesting character, ultimately emerges as a role of only secondary importance.

But before dismissing *Beatrice*, we might recall that during the 1830s and '40s it was possibly Bellini's most successful repertory opera; and that the few revivals it has had recently show clearly that there are many fine musical moments. Filippo's opening aria, 'Come t'adoro e quanto,' while having many of the Bellinian 'fingerprints' mentioned in connection with 'Casta Diva,' has an economy of expression that foreshadows Verdi; much of Beatrice's music uses florid vocal decoration to great effect; the chorus is perhaps more important than in any of Bellini's previous operas, and the grand finale to Act i fully makes up for the absence in *Norma* of a large-scale concerted number.

In February 1833, before the première of *Beatrice*, Bellini signed a contract which took him to London. Traveling by way of Paris and accompanied by Giuditta Pasta, he supervised highly successful revivals of several of his operas in the English capital, and he then returned to Paris in an attempt to secure a contract at the famous Opéra. But France's greatest theater still remained enormously conservative where foreign music was concerned, and eventually Bellini settled for an arrangement with the Théâtre Italien for more revivals and a new work. Negotiations moved rather slowly, it seems, and, nothing loath, the composer indulged freely in Paris's rich social life, meeting among others Chopin and the German poet Heinrich Heine. Perhaps the most important contact from a musical point of view was with Rossini, who had recently retired from the stage after a series of successes at the Opéra and elsewhere. Although, characteristically, Bellini seems to have been suspicious of the older man at first, it is clear that a close relationship was eventually formed, and there is some evidence that Rossini advised his young compatriot both musically and in more practical matters during the Paris years.

In April 1834, after more than six months in the French capital, Bellini finally began work on *I Puritani*. The libretto was by an Italian émigré, Count Carlo Pepoli; the source a French play, *Têtes rondes et Cavaliers*, set during the time of the English Civil War. Finding Paris too hectic an atmosphere in which to write, the composer moved out to the suburb of Puteaux and worked steadily during the summer and autumn. By December rehearsals had begun, and on 24 January 1835 *I Puritani* was first performed at the Théâtre Italien with tremendous success. The triumph of the four principals (Giulia Grisi, Rubini, Tamburini and Lablache) became legendary in years to come.

I Puritani has, perhaps with some justification, been criticized for the dramatic weakness of its libretto; indeed, Bellini himself made it clear in letters that Pepoli was hardly an adequate replacement for Romani. But, while it is certainly true that the opera lacks the dramatic impetus and logic of, say, *Norma*, this should not blind us to the fact that, with its happy ending and historical backcloth, it does not actually attempt to compete on these terms. One thing, however, is certain: writing for the fastidious French audience always tended to put Italian composers on their mettle, and Bellini was no exception. The orchestral writing in *I Puritani* has a level of detail simply not attempted in previous works. Similarly, we gain the vivid impression, particularly in the famous Act II duet 'Suoni la tromba,' that a broader canvas such as patriotism are deliberately juxtaposed with the personal elements of the drama.

One of the many passages in *I Puritani* that deserves special mention is Elvira's *scena e aria* in Act II, 'O rendetemi la speme,' in which the heroine, thinking she has been deserted by her lover, falls into a state of delirium. Although 'mad' scenes were common enough in nineteenth-century opera, Bellini here manages to create added effect by abandoning the vocal decoration which traditionally depicted madness, instead concentrating on simple melodic expressiveness. The impassioned repetition of the scene's opening phrase at the climax of the aria, 'Qui la voce,' is a dramatic master-stroke, with the dictates of formal symmetry and dramatic appropriateness in perfect accord. Finally we should mention the most famous piece in the opera, the quartet 'A te, o cara.' Though perhaps not quite on the level or the grand scale of *La Sonnambula*'s 'D'un pensiero,' this ensemble has much which is typically Bellinian, in particular its long, literally repeated, melody, touching choral interpolations and simple string accompaniment.

After the success of *I Puritani*, negotiations for a new Parisian opera were begun. There was even talk of a fresh collaboration with Romani, but little was settled by the end of August, when Bellini fell seriously ill. On 23 September 1835 he died at Puteaux, isolated from his friends because of suspected cholera (although the true cause of death was revealed at the autopsy to be a recurrence of the dysentery-like illness which had plagued him five years earlier). The composer was buried in Paris on 2 October 1835, with four illustrious composers (Rossini, Paer, Cherubini and Carafa) as pall-bearers. Some forty years later, Italy welcomed back her son with fitting pomp and ceremony when Bellini's remains were transferred from Paris to their final resting-place in the Cathedral of Catania.

Bellini's reputation has ebbed and flowed somewhat since his death. During the nineteenth century there were frequent revivals of his mature works, but in the early years of the twentieth century (paradoxically, in the wake of Wagner, who so much admired his music) performances became something of a rare event. From about the 1950s, however, his popularity has again increased, thanks particularly to the efforts of such interpreters as Maria Callas and Joan Sutherland. His importance in the history of nineteenth-century opera is still difficult to assess precisely. True, in a career which spanned barely ten years, we search in vain for the stylistic developments so prominent in Rossini, Donizetti or Verdi; nor would many make great claims for the composer's powers of musical characterization or rhythmic invention; but through the essence of his musical style, through what Verdi called his 'long, long, long melodies,' Bellini continued to exert an influence on composers as disparate as Berlioz, Chopin, Verdi and Wagner. In this sense, if in no other, he made an original and powerful contribution to the development of the genre.

Above: Sanquirico's set design for the Druid temple in the first *Norma*, produced at La Scala in 1831.

Above right: Donzelli, Grisi and Pasta in a scene from the first production of *Norma*. Pasta found learning the part extremely difficult and doubted her ability to sing Norma's first aria 'Casta Diva', but was ultimately grateful to Bellini for forcing her to persevere.

•Gaetano Donizetti•

Gaetano Donizetti was four years older than Bellini and was a native of northern Italy, born in Bergamo on 29 November 1797. He came from a poor family, his father holding the minor civic post of *concièrge* to the local (state-run) pawnshop. Bergamo was a town with strong musical traditions, boasting of composers and performers of international reputation; among the latter were a whole galaxy of celebrated tenors who were active during the young Donizetti's formative years. As a boy Donizetti must have manifested musical aptitude early, for at the age of eight he was fortunate enough to become a member of the first class to be enrolled in a music school headed by the composer Johannes Simon Mayr (1763-1845).

It is difficult to overestimate Donizetti's good fortune in coming early under the tutelage of a man like Mayr, whose operas and sacred music were at that time performed throughout Italy and beyond. Not only was Mayr a man of great practical experience, but, to judge from Donizetti's lifelong regard for him, he was an excellent and most human teacher. From their earliest days in Mayr's school, Donizetti and his fellow students were exposed to compositions by Gluck, Cherubini, Haydn, Mozart and the young Beethoven, as well as to works by other composers whose names are all but forgotten today. By 1815 he had completed his education under Mayr, who early on had formed sanguine hopes of Donizetti's promise as a composer and who saw to it that his student would be able to go on to Bologna for a two-year course in counterpoint under Padre Mattei, Rossini's teacher.

From his student days Donizetti focused his ambition on making his mark as an opera composer, for only in the theater could a talented young man hope to find fame and fortune in Italy. His only alternatives in the music profession would have been to become a teacher to a group of aristocratic families or to win an appointment as choirmaster in some religious establishment. Such concert life as then existed in Italy depended chiefly on dilettantes or the various royal or ducal courts, and the chief fare to be heard was opera excerpts or transcriptions. To a young man of Donizetti's energy and enthusiasm, and one fortunate enough to have the support of Mayr, there was really no choice at all as to what direction his path should take.

Donizetti returned to Bergamo in the fall of 1817 to await a chance to compose an opera for the stage. In the meantime, he turned out a large number of choral works and instrumental compositions, among the latter some fifteen string quartets written for a local group which included Mayr as violist. The following year he received a contract for his first publicly performed opera, *Enrico di Borgogna*, premièred at Venice in November 1818. This opera was sufficiently well received to earn the fledgling composer a commission to write a one-act farce to be performed the following month, but the most noteworthy thing about *Enrico* is that it contained an aria which Donizetti revised in 1830 for insertion as Anna Bolena's 'Al dolce guidami' – one of the high points in the first of his operas to make his name known in Paris and London. The other operas of this period are of relatively minor significance, offering instances of Donizetti's solid sense of construction, particularly in ensemble passages, and his gift for facile rather than memorable melody. In this area his art was to undergo considerable development and, with *Il Falegname di Livonia* (Venice, 1819), was to show a tendency to absorb some of the external aspects of Rossini's style, then much in vogue. This period of first apprenticeship came to a close when a commission to compose an opera for Rome, almost certainly passed on to Donizetti by Mayr, opened up wider horizons.

• Donizetti in Naples •

This opera for Rome, *Zoraida di Granata* (28 January 1822), turned out to be a resounding, if not durable, success. It served to establish Donizetti's promise, and its most important consequence was to win him an engagement from the impresario Domenico Barbaia in Naples, the city that was to be his home base for the next sixteen years. Fortunately for him, his first opera for Naples, *La Zingara*, a *semiseria* but with spoken dialogue, won a substantial local success, enjoying periodic revivals over the next fifteen years. Another result of the Roman reception of *Zoraida* was a commission to compose his first opera for La Scala in Milan. The result, *Chiara e Serafina*, to a libretto by Felice Romani, was disliked by the audience. More than eight years were to pass before Donizetti would win a resounding success with the Milanese public, a situation that left the composer understandably frustrated.

The early months of 1824 found Donizetti once again in Rome, where, while a revised *Zoraida* failed to repeat its original impact, an *opera buffa*, *L'Ajo nell'imbarazzo*, conclusively demonstrated Donizetti's flair for operatic comedy laced with a touch of pathos. In Naples, meanwhile, Donizetti turned out a variety of operas, while pursuing such activities as preparing operas for production at the Teatro del Fondo and teaching composition. The closing of Italian theaters in 1825, which had been declared a Holy Year by the Pope, temporarily suspended Donizetti's work at Naples, but he was able to find employment at the Teatro Carolino in Palermo for most of that year, since the theater there was allowed to remain open, apparently by special dispensation.

Donizetti returned from Palermo early in 1826, fired with new determination to make his mark. The operas of the years 1826-9 are important to an understanding of his overall development because they reveal his experiments with a wide range of subject-matter and dramatic effects. The most significant in terms of his future is one he wrote without any commission,

Above: Donizetti at eighteen, as a student in Bologna. The accompanying inscription reads: 'Now I shall create wonders from my harmonious pen – let enchanting accents pour forth – To Maestro S. Mayr, in gratitude, offered by Gaetano Donizetti . . . '

Below: Donizetti's parents, Andrea and Domenica. They were married in 1786 and moved into a poor dwelling in Bergamo, in northern Italy, with other members of their families. Donizetti was the fifth of six children and was given little moral support by his father, who urged him to seek regular employment as a village organist rather than aspire to the more hazardous career of composer.

Gabriella di Vergy, his first operatic tragedy. At that time, particularly in Naples, there was an official prejudice against plots with tragic endings, the *lieto fine*, or happy ending, being the preferred form. At this relatively early date, then, Donizetti recognized the direction in which his artistic nature led, that is, towards plots dealing with strong dramatic conflicts and violent action, resulting in death scenes with all their opportunities for pathos and irony. In short, Donizetti in 1826 was a Romantic ahead of his time and not until the next decade would the floodgates of Romanticism open upon the opera stages of Italy.

One of Donizetti's notable accomplishments of 1827 was an opera based upon a popular play of the time, *Otto Mesi in due ore*, requiring elaborate stage machinery and pantomime episodes. The same year he also produced a one-act farce to his own libretto, entitled *Le Convenienze ed inconvenienze teatrali*, a satire on the rehearsal of an old-fashioned *opera seria*, which elicited praise from that stern critic Berlioz. The following year Donizetti's reputation was sufficiently established for him to be invited, along with three other leading composers, to compose a new opera for the opening season of the Teatro Carlo Felice at Genoa. On his return from Naples to Genoa, he stopped off at Rome to marry the twenty-year-old Virginia Vasselli. Of the three children of their union, two were stillborn and one survived less than two weeks.

The next two years saw a continuation of experimentation with various dramatic types, helped along by Donizetti's increasing popularity with Neapolitan audiences, a popularity which attained a higher plateau with his predominantly neoclassical *L'Esule di Roma*, which contains a trio at the end of Act I that attracted much favorable comment. In *Il Paria* Donizetti recognized the value of his score, even though his subject did not rouse much enthusiasm, for he was able to use it as a source for fruitful self-borrowing. In *Il Castello di Kenilworth* he made his first contact with Tudor history – a subject that would later yield such notable

Below: Title-page from Donizetti's copy of the score of a *Stabat Mater* by Pollini, dedicated to the opera composer Zingarelli, whose portrait also appears there. Donizetti wrote a Requiem for Zingarelli, who was a friend of Bellini, while Pollini had lived in Milan with Bellini and assumed a parental role in his development.

Bottom: A lithographed table top given to Donizetti by admirers in 1837. In the center is a portrait of the composer flanked by scenes from his operas in silhouette and biographical details. The three outside bands contain the names of all his operas to date.

results as *Anna Bolena*, *Maria Stuarda*, and *Roberto Devereux* – and this opera also looks towards the future in being the first of Donizetti's scores to contain two important female roles. In imitation of Rossini's *Mosè*, Donizetti even tackled a biblical subject in *Il Diluvio universale*. His last opera before *Anna Bolena*, the almost forgotten *Imelda de' Lambertazzi*, deserves to be remembered because its crudely powerful subject from the Italian Renaissance culminated in on-stage deaths and because Donizetti casts the romantic hero as a baritone rather than as a tenor.

Donizetti's career entered a new phase with the triumph of *Anna Bolena* at the Teatro Carcano, in Milan, on 26 December 1830. This elevated him to the primary rank of Italian operatic composers and opened to him the doors of many theaters. Instead of being principally headquartered in Naples, Donizetti could now expand his horizons, and his year was often to be divided between Naples, Milan and Venice. There was another sort of change, too, for up to this time around half of Donizetti's output had been concerned with operatic

comedies in one form or another; from now on comedies were to occupy a smaller share of his activities, though among them are some of his hardiest successes: *L'Elisir d'amore*, *La Fille du régiment* and *Don Pasquale*. His increasing concern with operatic tragedy and Romantic *melodramma* in particular is indicative of the direction in which popular taste was heading.

The years between *Anna Bolena* and 1838 can be summarized as those in which Donizetti consolidated his popularity. In 1833, for instance, he produced four significant full-length operas: *Il Furioso*, his best-integrated *semiseria*, containing a powerful baritone title role; *Parisina*, Donizetti's own favorite among his operas; *Torquato Tasso*, his one attempt to deal with the artist as hero (again a baritone role); and *Lucrezia Borgia*, his setting of Victor Hugo's recent play, which proved to be one of his enduring successes and a forward-looking score. In 1835 he received a long-awaited invitation

to compose for the Théâtre Italien in the same season that saw the première of Bellini's *I Puritani*. Donizetti's contribution, *Marino Faliero*, although it did not come close to equaling Bellini's success, is a fine serious score, less showily attractive than Bellini's, and one which anticipates the early Verdi.

Written on his return from Paris to Naples, Donizetti's next opera, *Lucia di Lammermoor*, derived from a popular novel by Sir Walter Scott, became such a success wherever it was produced that it had a profound effect on Romantic sensibility. Donizetti's hopes to win an invitation to compose at the Paris Opéra are demonstrated by his *L'Assedio di Calais* (1836), which contains many effects, including a full-scale ballet *divertissement*, that justify the composer's description of it in 1837 'the most congruent to French taste.' In 1837, shortly after the death of his wife at the age of twenty-nine, Donizetti wrote *Roberto Devereux*, which contains a musical portrait of Queen Elizabeth I of England that can take its place beside Bellini's *Norma* as one of the great soprano roles of the period. Donizetti's stay in Naples came to an end following the King of Naples's prohibition of his proposed *Poliuto*, derived from Corneille's *Polyeucte*, as an inappropriate subject because it presented the martyrdom of a Christian saint upon the stage.

• Paris •

The reasons behind Donizetti's leaving Naples were numerous, and the prohibition of *Poliuto* was only one of them. Following the death of his beloved Virginia, Naples became increasingly antipathetic to Donizetti, and his reluctance to stay was aggravated by the King's disinclination to confirm his appointment as director of the Naples Conservatory, a post that an opposing faction worked hard, and ultimately successfully, to gain for Saverio Mercadante. The most important of Donizetti's reasons for abandoning Naples, however, was the arrival of a contract to compose two operas for the Paris Opéra.

For a composer of Donizetti's generation such an invitation set the seal upon his international reputation; he would be following in the footsteps of Gluck, Piccinni, Cherubini and, more recently, Rossini. To a composer Paris also offered practical advantages that no Italian center could match: fees were bigger, rehearsal time more generous, the censorship less restrictive, and the protection of musical copyright more circumspect. Donizetti arrived in Paris in October 1838 to write for the Opéra and to introduce two of his Italian successes (*L'Elisir* and *Roberto Devereux*) to the Théâtre Italien. He must have experienced a sensation of satisfied justification when it was decided that his first score for the Opéra would be the *Poliuto* that had been banned in Naples, but expanded into four acts and retitled *Les Martyrs*.

The first year and a half of this stay in Paris was one of the most productive periods of

Donizetti's career. Besides his labors for the Opéra and for the Théâtre Italien (the latter involving the addition of some new numbers to his existing scores), he made a French version of *Lucia* adapted to the special requirements of the Théâtre de la Renaissance (August 1839) and composed a new three-act opera for that theater, *L'Ange de Nisida*, as well as the two-act *La Fille du régiment* for the Opéra Comique. That *La Fille* came to be regarded as a classic in the repertory of the Comique, the most quintessentially French of all the state-supported theaters, is eloquent testimony to Donizetti's versatility in mastering the French style.

In spite of a most elaborate production, *Les Martyrs* earned only a *succès d'estime* at the Opéra, where it was first given in April 1840. In the summer of that year Donizetti traveled to Milan to arrange *La Fille du régiment* as an Italian *opera buffa*, returning to Paris to put on his next work at the Opéra. For this assignment he had originally intended *Le Duc d'Albe*, half of which he had composed during 1839, but this subject was rejected by the management, with the result that he revised and expanded *L'Ange de Nisida* to a partly new libretto, its title being changed to *La Favorite*. This work had its première in December 1840, and it held

Opposite: Giuditta Pasta as Anna Bolena, a role she created. Pasta sang the part again at her last public appearance in 1850; although her voice was in ruins, her interpretation was still found deeply moving.

Below: The Abdication of Mary Queen of Scots by Joseph Severn, 1850. Artists' interest in depicting scenes with Mary had been renewed by the popularity of Scott's novel *The Abbot*, 1820, although scenes of her life, and in particularly her execution, had been favorite subjects for illustration since the late eighteenth century. Donizetti's opera *Maria Stuarda*, based on the play by Schiller, was first performed in 1835 with Maria Malibran in the title-role.

Below: Giulia Grisi and Maria Caradori in Pacini's *Ivanhoe* in its original production at La Fenice, Venice, in 1832. Giovanni Pacini (1796-1867), who had earlier collaborated with Rossini, was here trying his hand at historical opera based on Sir Walter Scott, but his real success only came after Donizetti and Bellini had left Italy.

Bottom: Sanquirico's set for the Tower of London scene in *Anna Bolena* at its première at the Teatro Carcano in 1830. One of the opera's admirers was Mazzini, hero of the Risorgimento and himself an amateur musician. He wrote: 'The individuality of characters so barbarously neglected by Rossini . . . is celebrated with rare vigor.'

the stage in France throughout the rest of the nineteenth century.

The following year saw Donizetti once more in Milan, where his *Maria Padilla* opened the La Scala Carnival season of 1841-2. At that time he accepted an appointment as music director of the Italian season, April to June of each year, at the Kärntnertor Theater in Vienna, a post he filled throughout 1845. On his way from Milan to Vienna he stopped off at Bologna, where he conducted the first Italian performances of Rossini's *Stabat Mater* at the composer's request. One clause of his contract for Vienna required Donizetti to compose a new opera every year for the Kärntnertor, and his first for that stage was *Linda di Chamounix*, a lasting success. So well received was it, in fact, that the Emperor named Donizetti Hofkapellmeister.

The year 1843 marked the end of Donizetti's career as an active composer, but to it belong three of his most important works: *Don Pasquale* (Théâtre Italien, January), *Maria di Rohan* (Kärntnertor, June) and *Dom Sébastien* (Opéra, November). The first of these is his comic masterpiece; the second, his profoundest penetration into the esthetic of Romantic *melodramma*; the

third, his most massive work, which still has not received the recognition it deserves. In January 1844 his *Caterina Cornaro* was given in Naples, but this had been composed earlier, partly in 1842 and partly in 1843.

• Comedy •

As a young music student Donizetti was trained and encouraged to develop his musical facility. The operatic forms were largely established for him by the examples of Mayr, a major operatic figure at the beginning of the nineteenth century but today largely unknown, and by Rossini. And, although the conservative audiences of that time had, it appears, an insatiable appetite for new works, they remained adamant that these novelties conform to their general expectations, particularly when it came to vocal opportunities for the various singers.

In the course of his career, Donizetti wrote more operas than the combined total of operas by Rossini and Bellini, acting as librettist for three of his works and playing a significant role in the development of several other texts. His versatility as a composer is demonstrated in his mastery of all the operatic genres then current: farce, *opera buffa*, *opera seria* (which he played a very significant part in developing towards the Romantic *melodramma*, which became the dominant form of Italian opera through much of the nineteenth century), *opera semiseria*, French *grand opéra*, and French *opéra comique*.

Donizetti's farces are usually in one act, but sometimes in two. Especially popular in Naples, such works featured one or more comic characters who use Neapolitan dialect, with spoken dialogue, rather than recitative, separating the musical numbers, many of which contain elements of parody and satire. Donizetti composed seven farces between 1818 and 1831, all but one for Naples; further, he adapted one *opera buffa*, *L'Ajo nell'imbarazzo* (first performed in Rome in 1824), as a farce for its Neapolitan première in 1826.

One characteristic of Donizetti's farces is that the opening number (or *introduzione*) is in the form of an extended ensemble, introducing most of the characters and supplying the exposition of the plot. The finales are either aria-ensembles, usually in two tempi, or moralizing vaudevilles (a four-phrase tune repeated by various characters in turn). The most stage-worthy of Donizetti's farces is *Le Convenienze ed inconvenienze teatrali*, which in 1831 the composer expanded to two acts. This work features a good deal of backstage parody, much of it given over to a rehearsal of an inept *opera seria* by a down-at-heel company, and it contains the role of Mamm' Agata, the irrepressible mother of the seconda donna, designed to be sung by a baritone *en travesti*.

The tradition of *opera buffa* which Donizetti inherited from both Mayr and Rossini had evolved from the comic *intermezzi* of the early eighteenth century. These plots characteristically

deal with middle-class characters involved in some sort of imbroglio; musically, they contain prominent roles for a *basso buffo*, a specialist in patter songs, and often have complex mid-point finales. Donizetti composed eleven *opere buffe*, from *Le Nozze in villa* (1819) to the masterly *Don Pasquale* (1843). As a man with a keen sense of humor and fondness for word-play, Donizetti found comic opera particularly congenial. A brief survey of these comedies highlights his development as a theatrical composer: his increasing ability to individualize his characters rather than perpetuate traditional types; his shrewd understanding of the importance of moments of genuine sentiment and pathos to humanize a comic plot; and his growing skill at enriching the traditional patter formulae, rising to such irresistible heights of volubility as Dulcamara's entrance in *L'Elisir d'amore* or the duets for Ernesto and Annibale in *Il Campanello di notte* and for Malatesta and Pasquale in *Don Pasquale*.

L'Ajo nell'imbarazzo was the first substantial success of Donizetti's career, and that this was an *opera buffa* (as it was performed everywhere outside Naples) demonstrates that his ready melodic gift and skillful ensemble-writing matured earlier in this vein. *Alina* (1828) shows a wealth of musical refinement in its varied and extensive choruses and ensembles. *Betly* (1836), with its plot adapted from that used by Adolphe Adam for his *Le Chalet*, is a tender idyll in a Swiss setting, notable for the composer's apt use of touches of local color in his music. *L'Elisir d'amore* and *Don Pasquale* have remained two of Donizetti's most consistently performed scores, their freshness and wit as crisp and beguiling as when they were new.

Opera semiseria is a mixed genre, which inserts a comic (*buffo*) character into what is otherwise a serious plot. Its origins lie within the relatively small companies in which the only available second bass would be the *buffo*, whose vocal abilities were apt to be limited to patter without much sustained singing. *Semiseria* works succeed only to the extent that the comic and serious aspects of a plot reinforce each other – a condition only rarely met. Donizetti composed eleven *semiseria* operas, the earliest being *Enrico di Borgogna*, his first work to be performed publicly; the last, *Linda di Chamounix*, his first opera for Vienna.

Torquato Tasso (1833) exemplifies clearly the problems of this hybrid genre. The serious portion of this opera works very well, but the *buffa* character seems gratuitous to the action and breaks the mood of the piece. Much more successful is *Il Furioso*, from the same year, where the hero Cardenio is driven mad by the thought of his wife's infidelity, while the *buffo* character, Kaidamà, is a natural fool; in their scenes together their misconceptions reinforce one another with powerful irony. Even more successful is *Linda*, where the elderly *buffo* is the tenor's bumbling but charming rival for Linda's affections. Although the plot of *Linda* belongs to the outmoded tradition of the *comédie larmoyante* and seems filled with unabashed

Opposite: Scenes from two productions of *Don Pasquale:* (*top*) at the Théâtre Italien in Paris in 1843, and (*bottom*) in London later the same year, the scene here showing Don Pasquale's final humiliation. The opera was written for the famous cast of Grisi, Mario, Tamburini and, in the title role, Lablache.

Above: Lablache and Mario in *L'Elisir d'amore*. The opera was adapted by Romani from Scribe's libretto for Auber's comic opera *Le Philtre*, with an added element of pathos. Lablache's impersonation of Dulcamara, the quack doctor, helped bring the opera popularity.

Below: Title-page of a vocal score of Donizetti's *Il Furioso all'Isola di San Domingo*, first performed at the Teatro Valle in Rome in 1833. The opera, based loosely on *Don Quixote*, is set on a tropical island and is notable for its insane hero, sung by a baritone rather than the customary tenor.

sentimentality, Donizetti's score contains enough music of elegant finish and proportion to diminish the liability of its libretto.

• *Opera seria* and Romantic *melodramma* •

In the interest of putting Donizetti into a clearer historical perspective, a distinction is made here between *opera seria* (serious works in which the dénouement is resolved happily) and Romantic *melodramma* (serious works with tragic resolutions). *Opera seria*, as Donizetti practiced it in the 1820s, marks the end of what is essentially an eighteenth-century tradition, though it may be viewed as a transitional phase connecting the earlier tradition to the Romantic *melodramma* of the 1830s and after. Although such works with tragic dénouements are not unknown in the first quarter of the nineteenth century, they are relatively uncommon, as the censors, particularly in Naples, preferred plots that reinforced the status quo, especially through the intervention of a beneficent monarch – just the situation that obtains at the end of Donizetti's *Il Castello di Kenilworth*, for example. The transitional aspect of *opera seria* in the 1820s is found in the frequent use of the *musico* (the contralto-hero) as a replacement of the eighteenth-century castrato-hero: the notion that there should be some equivalence between the vocal sound and the sexual characteristics of a given role was

Above: Delacroix's self-portrait of 1821, probably as Ravenswood, the hero of Scott's novel *The Bride of Lamermoor* (though it is often described as Hamlet). Both Delacroix and Donizetti were inspired by Scott; in the latter's opera *Lucia di Lammermoor,* based on the same novel, Ravenswood becomes the more mellifluous Edgardo.

Right: The Bride of Lamermoor, painted in the 1830s by Robert Scott Lauder. It shows Ravenswood's angry intrusion into the wedding ceremony which unites Lucy and Bucklaw. In Donizetti's opera this incident gives rise to the celebrated sextet.

slow in establishing itself. The convention of the *musico* had pretty well disappeared by the end of the 1830s, while, correspondingly, the ascendance of the tenor-hero asserted itself ever more dominantly.

Donizetti wrote eight *opere serie*, from *Zoraida di Granata* to *Il Diluvio universale* (1830), and of all the genres he undertook this seems the most old-fashioned today. His works of the 1820s are important because they show an increasing technical assurance, particularly in his more supple harmony with wider use of modulation in the works from the latter half of that decade. His restless experimentation with a great variety of subjects reflects his dissatisfaction with the dramatic artificiality of the genre and his recognition, after writing the uncommissioned *Gabriella di Vergy* in 1826, that his strongest inclinations lay toward operatic tragedy. His pungent parody of *opera seria* in *Le Convenienze*, to his own libretto, is but one indication that he had ceased to take the genre seriously. Even *Il Paria* for which he expressed a particular fondness, is really a tragedy *manqué* in that the lovers, though still alive at the end, are condemned to death.

Since Donizetti wrote twenty-three operas in the category of Romantic *melodramma*, it ought to be recognized that this is the largest of these various groups and one that contains some of his most important and forward-looking scores. At the same time elements associated with Romanticism are also to be found in Donizetti's

Top: Opening page of the manuscript of *Lucia*, completed on 6 July 1835.

Above: The first French vocal score, showing Fanny Persiani, the original Lucia.

operas in various genres that date from the 1820s: there are storm scenes (*Emilia di Liverpool*), floods (*Otto Mesi in due ore*), mad scenes and prison scenes (both occur in *L'Esule di Roma*). The experimental *Gabriella di Vergy* can be counted as Donizetti's first effort at Romantic *melodramma*, and the pursuit of it was to be his principal occupation during the remainder of his career to *Maria di Rohan* (1843) and *Caterina Cornaro* (1844).

While the vogue for Romantic *melodramma* is usually dated in Italy as stemming from the great success of Bellini's *Il Pirata* (Milan, 1827), Donizetti's first attempt with *Gabriella* was in fact written a year earlier, although in Naples he had no hopes for its performance. The Milanese censors took a less stringent view of tragic endings than did their Neapolitan counterparts, and it is significant that it was in Milan with *Anna Bolena* (1830) and with a north Italian librettist, Felice Romani, that Donizetti was finally able to produce a work that clearly established his high aptitude for Romantic *melodramma*. The pressure of popular favor later caused a slight retrenchment on this front in Naples, but again and again Donizetti found various of his operas in trouble there. For instance, *Maria Stuarda* (1835) was originally composed for Naples, but after it had come as close to production as its dress rehearsal, it was forbidden, although Donizetti was able to put it on the following year in the more favorable climate of Milan. Meanwhile *Lucrezia Borgia* (1833), containing a plot that features a wholesale poisoning, was so offensive to the Neapolitan censors that it was never allowed to be performed there during Donizetti's lifetime.

Several of Donizetti's letters contain passages that shed a good deal of light upon his feelings about Romantic *melodramma*. Discussing a libretto proposed to him in 1835, he told the impresario: 'If I am not in complete sympathy with the libretto I shall send it back. I want love, violent love, without which these subjects are cold.' Another letter, this one to his brother-in-law Antonio Vasselli, reflects his dissatisfaction with the restrictions the censors placed upon Romantic *melodrammi*: 'That the world is a stage and the stage a lesson is an old story. But oh! if only we could show many other truths there, truths that are not permitted in Italy, how much more would be learned, without betraying Christianity or our loyalty as subjects.' Strong emotions and dramatic situations were the traits which Donizetti sought.

In one sense, Romantic *melodrammi* may be regarded as having the happy ending delayed; that is, the lovers who are separated by cruel fate and circumstance, who suffer and die for their love, will find a permanent union in heaven. This idea is clearly expressed, for example, in the final two scenes of *Lucia di Lammermoor* (1835). Lucia, who has been forced into a political marriage and must renounce her beloved Edgardo, goes mad and murders her bridegroom; then in her mad scene she imagines she is going to wed Edgardo, and as her strength fails she envisages herself in heaven praying for him;

later, when Edgardo learns of Lucia's death, he stabs himself so that he may the sooner join her in heaven. Such transcendent love supplied the principal motivation for most of Donizetti's Romantic *melodrammi*, and it moved him to write some of his most persuasive music.

Maria de Rohan contains in its last act the farthest reaches of Donizetti's exploration of the violent world of Romantic *melodramma*. Chevreuse has come into possession of proof that his wife Maria had, before her marriage, been the mistress of Chalais and still loves him. There is a violent scene of confrontation between husband and wife, heightened by Maria's knowledge that Chalais will soon appear. Donizetti's music here is taut with drama and emotion; the old formulas and repetitions are largely discarded in favor of swift, stabbing interchanges, punctuated by the chiming of a clock. When Chalais returns, there is a brief trio, growing immediately out of the preceding duet; then the two men rush off to fight a duel, and in a moment the frustrated Chevreuse returns to announce that Chalais has killed himself. Once more he confronts his guilty wife, who sinks to her knees with a cry. The last interchange is unaccompanied, having all the immediacy of the spoken stage. *Maria di Rohan* is filled with finely wrought music, shot through with irony and rising to moments of great power.

• French operas •

In the French genre of *opéra comique*, which consists of musical numbers separated by spoken dialogue, Donizetti wrote two works: *La Fille du*

Right: Self-portrait of Donizetti in 1841 during his period in Paris, when he lived in the Hotel Manchester on the rue Grammont. This was the year in which he composed the farcical *Rita*, which was not performed until after his death.

régiment and *Rita* (composed 1841, but not performed until 1860). *Rita*, widely performed in recent years, is an unpretentious domestic farce in one act, with a genuinely amusing plot and a witty score. *La Fille du régiment* is a two-act score, filled with charm and characteristic Donizettian moments of pathos, which, in the lesson scene (Act II), contains some of his most hilarious musical parody. So successful was Donizetti in mastering the French forms, such as the *couplet* with its catchy refrain, and in idiomatically setting French texts, that Marie's Act II aria, 'Salut à la France,' became during the latter part of the nineteenth century an unofficial French national anthem.

Right: Donizetti's last letter, to his brother Giuseppe, written in 1846 from the asylum at Ivry to which he had been committed after the final stages of syphilis were affecting his brain. The musical quotation is incoherent.

Below: Daguerrotype of Donizetti with his nephew Andrea, taken in the house in which Donizetti stayed after Andrea had secured his release from the asylum. On the back of the picture is written: 'To the most kind Signora Rosa Basoni, Andrea Donizetti offers this sad souvenir as a testimony of his esteem. Paris 3 August 1847.' Baroness Basoni had been a friend of Donizetti's for some years and was anxious to provide comfort for his last days.

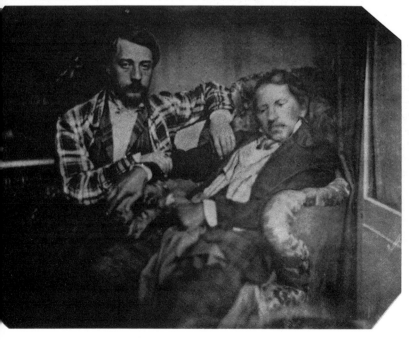

Within the genre of *grand opéra*, the official requirements for the Paris Opéra were that all works presented there had to be set to a French text and had to be composed throughout; that is, without any spoken dialogue. In point of fact, by the time Donizetti came to Paris in 1838 to compose for that theater, a number of other requirements were in force. The theater's great successes of the late 1820s and 1830s – such works as Rossini's *Guillaume Tell* and Meyerbeer's *Robert le diable* and *Les Huguenots* – were massive, spectacular works that contained a ballet *divertissement*. Donizetti wrote three and a half operas for the Opéra. The three are *Les Martyrs*, *La Favorite* and *Dom Sébastien*; the half is *Le Duc d'Albe*, of which he composed most of the first two acts; later this work was completed by other hands to an Italian translation of the libretto and first performed in Rome in 1882 as *Il Duca d'Alba*.

Donizetti's *grand opéra* represents the summit of his achievement as a composer, and his skill at welding together the many varied ingredients required is impressive, although only one of his works in this genre has ever attained the position of a popular favorite, appropriately enough *La Favorite*. Dramatically these works closely resemble the Romantic *melodramma* in their conflicts and dénouements, and it is only their size (both *Les Martyrs* and *La Favorite* are in four good-sized acts; *Dom Sébastien* is in five), their French texts (although all were subsequently translated into Italian for performances there) and their *divertissements* that mark them as *grand opéra*.

Today the original Italian three-act version of *Les Martyrs* – *Poliuto* – is far more frequently revived than its later transformation. *La Favorite* has disappeared from the stages of France, but it circulates in its Italian version, enjoying frequent revivals in many centers. *Dom Sébastien*, the grandest of these works and the one upon which Donizetti pinned his fondest hopes, has, unfortunately, had only one revival in the twentieth century. The expense of mounting it, with its numerous sets and elaborate spectacle, including a full-scale royal funeral, has prevented it from being as well known as it should be. The score contains some interesting local color in Act II, set in Morocco; fine arias that frequently develop into ensembles; and an imposing septet in Act IV. It is a great pity that Donizetti's serious illness did not permit him to pursue the rich vein of *Dom Sébastien*.

In 1844 his health deteriorated markedly, and with it his ability to provide the necessary concentration for extended bouts of composition. His condition had become so grave, owing to progressive paralysis and mental confusion, that he was confined in a sanitorium at Ivry, near Paris. After nearly seventeen months there Donizetti was brought to an apartment in Paris, while his family struggled with the recalcitrant Parisian authorities for permission to bring him back to Italy. He was finally brought back to Bergamo in October 1847 and died there on 8 April 1848. An autopsy confirmed the diagnosis of meningo-vascular syphilis.

Scribe and the Paris Opéra

Eugène Scribe (1791-1861) was the author of over 350 works, including comedies, melodramas in the *style troubadour* and many libretti for both serious and comic operas. His facility led to criticism, but his experience was invaluable to many composers attempting to win success in the operatic capital of the world.

The most prestigious of the Paris opera companies was the Opéra, and Scribe's first success there was with his libretto for Auber's *La Muette de Portici*, 1828. This was followed by Meyerbeer's *Robert le diable* in 1831, the year that Dr Véron took over direction. In five years Véron built up and promoted a team of stars that included Scribe, Auber, Meyerbeer, the designer Cicéri, the tenor Nourrit, the sopranos Cinti-Damoreau and Falcon and the ballerina Taglioni. Scribe provided exactly the right libretti, full of local color, that allowed composers to make best use of the chorus and to include the obligatory ballet.

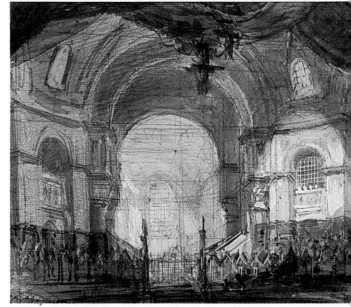

Above: The opening scene of *La Juive*, 1835, the first of many collaborations between Scribe and Fromental Halévy. The leading roles were taken by Cornélie Falcon, Adolphe Nourrit and the bass Nicolas Levasseur.

Right: Set for Meyerbeer's last opera, *L'Africaine*, for which Scribe provided a libretto in 1837, but which was not completed until 1865. The set is designed by Philippe Chaperon, Cicéri's greatest successor at the Opéra.

Left: Scene from *La Dame blanche*, 1825, Boïeldieu's last opera and one of Scribe's earliest triumphs.

Above: Scene from Act IV of Donizetti's French grand opera, *La Favorite*, 1840, with a Scribe libretto.

Right: Set design for the coronation scene in Meyerbeer's *Le Prophète*. The composer, who came to Paris in 1825, was a perfect partner for Scribe, for his talent lay not in building up and resolving dramatic tension over a whole work, but in whipping up emotion in a series of great set pieces. He therefore required from his librettist a succession of scenes that could serve as showpieces for his dramatic choruses, for his ballets and for his star singers. The story of *Le Prophète*,

first performed at the Opéra in 1849 – the first performance there with electric lighting – concerns the revolt of the Anabaptists in Münster and the innkeeper, John of Leyden (sung at the première by Gustave Roger), who poses as a prophet and is crowned Emperor in the Cathedral before his inevitable last-act death. The ballet in the opera is a Dutch skating scene, performed on roller-skates, with music which was later made into the ballet suite *Les Patineurs*.

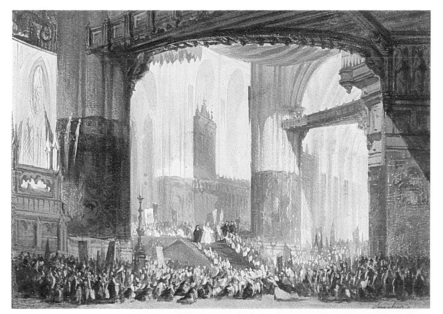

Left: Pauline Garcia-Viardot and Marietta Alboni in a London production of Meyerbeer's *Les Huguenots*. The triumph of the first production in Paris in 1836 quite eclipsed *La Dame blanche*, which had been the great success of the previous year. The story concerns the bloody massacre on St Bartholemew's Day in sixteenth-century Paris, and there are dramatic choruses as well as brilliant numbers for the leading singers. Meyerbeer rewrote the part of Urbain for the contralto Alboni.

Left: Set for Auber's *La Sirène*, 1844 – which had the impresario Domenico Barbaia as one of its characters. Auber's first collaboration with Scribe was an Elizabethan drama, *Leicester*, based on Scott's *Kenilworth*, in 1823, and in all they supplied some thirty operas to the Opéra and Opéra Comique. *La Muette de Portici* ushered in the hey-day of the Opéra, but their greatest success was *Fra Diavolo*, premièred at the Opéra Comique in 1830.

Above: Eugène Lami's lithograph of the Foyer des Acteurs at the Opéra in 1842, with the singers and dancers receiving their admirers.

During the brilliant years of Dr Véron's reign as director of the Opéra and in the following decade, which saw Meyer-beer's great triumphs,

the Opéra became a magnet for society, whether to see and be seen in the audience, or to share in the more Bohemian life of the performers.

Above: Degas's painting of 1872 shows part of the front rows of the audience, the orchestra and the ballet from *Robert le diable*, a scene in which the hero is seduced by the ghosts of nuns damned for their licentiousness. First performed in 1831, the opera was an immediate and lasting success for Scribe and Meyerbeer, although it had taken five months of rehearsals – at the composer's expense – to perfect the score and the performance.

Right: Théophile Gautier (1811-72), the poet and critic whose reports of theater and opera in Paris were extremely influential. In a musical world dominated by grand opera – he himself saw the opera house as 'a sort of secular cathedral of civilization' – he also championed the music of Mozart, Beethoven, Weber and Berlioz. His greatest enthusiasm was for the ballet, and he wrote two famous scenarios for his beloved Carlotta Grisi: *Giselle*, set by Adam in 1841, and *La Péri*, set in 1843 by Burgmüller.

Below: Set design for the final scenes in the original production of *Fra Diavolo* at the Opéra Comique in 1830.

Above: A letter of contract between the English impresario Gye and Scribe and Auber, in which Scribe undertakes to write recitatives and some new numbers for *Fra Diavolo*, which Auber will set to music for a new London production in 1857: 'This recitative, these words will become your exclusive property. They will be written in blank verse and you will arrange to have them translated into Italian. This translation will be done at your cost. Monsieur Auber undertakes to put to music the recitative of the said opera and to arrange the pieces of music agreed between you – in addition he agrees to have finished the said pieces in the 1st Act, 20 April next, the 2nd Act, 10 May next, and the 3rd Act, 30 May next.' Auber was to be paid 4,000 francs and Scribe 3,000 francs. Frederick Gye the Younger (1810-78) ran the Italian Opera House at Covent Garden from 1849 until his death, and in the fifties staged many French operas, including works by Meyerbeer, Gounod and Berlioz. Auber and Scribe kept their bargain: the première at the Lyceum (Covent Garden had burned down) took place on 4 July 1857.

Left: A caricature showing the composers who ruled Paris in the 1840s: on the left are Meyerbeer (with the caged 'Prophète' and 'Africaine,' libretti for which Scribe had provided in 1836 and 1837 but which were not yet completed) and Halévy, 'taking a pinch from Meyerbeer's box of music,' Boïeldieu, crowned with daisies, stands below Berlioz, who writes a letter to the *Journal des Débats*; in the center Adam appears as a postilion on a donkey (his *Postillon de Longjumeau* was first played at the Opéra Comique in 1836), while Auber is mounted on a bronze horse (his *Le Cheval de bronze* opened there a year earlier); behind them Donizetti manufactures popular scores by steam power; on the right, Rossini, god of the river of Harmony, rests in his glory.

Above: After the Académie de Musique at the Porte St Martin had been closed by the revolutionary mob, a new opera house was built on the rue de Richelieu and opened in July 1794. It was demolished in 1820, on orders of the Archbishop of Paris, after the Duc de Berry, heir to the throne, was assassinated there.

Left: The Salle Favart, home of the Opéra Comique from 1840, when it had been rebuilt after a fire, to 1887, when it was again destroyed (and later rebuilt); but its greatest age had been when the Théâtre Italien, at first under Rossini's direction, staged the works of Donizetti, Bellini and Rossini himself, with a team of singers that included Giulia Grisi, Giovanni Rubini (later replaced by Mario), Luigi Lablache and Antonio Tamburini – who exemplified the *bel canto* tradition of the period, developed under Rossini's influence and guidance.

Above: After the demolition of the Académie on the rue de Richelieu a new, supposedly temporary opera house was built on the rue le Peletier; gas lighting was installed in 1822. It was here that the Parisian grand operas were staged, Rossini's *Guillaume Tell*, the colossal spectacles of Auber and Meyerbeer, and, later, Verdi's French operas. It was one of the showplaces of Paris society: a chapter of Dumas's *The Count of Monte Cristo* is devoted to the conversations and intrigues taking place during a performance of *Robert le diable*; when the Count is asked what he thinks of the music, 'What music?' he replies.

In 1860 the competition for a new opera house was won by the young architect Charles Garnier, whose sumptuous building (*below left*) epitomizes the 'Second Empire' style, but was not opened until 1875, when the great days of the Paris Opéra were past. The auditorium seats over 2,000 people and is built in traditional horseshoe style with four tiers of boxes, but the foyers and public rooms occupy a much larger part of the site. The centerpiece is the huge curving staircase, down which (*below*) the architect and his wife are seen walking on opening night, receiving an ovation from fashionable Paris.

GIUSEPPE VERDI

ROGER PARKER

Giuseppe Verdi was born on 10 October 1813 in the tiny village of Le Roncole, then part of the Duchy of Parma. His mother was a spinner, his father an innkeeper. Although detailed information on this early period is rather sparse, one of the few documents we do possess attests to the young Verdi's musical talents. Inside an old spinet preserved from the Verdi household we find the receipt of an instrument repairer. After listing the jobs he has completed, the man adds that the work and additional parts have been given free of charge, 'seeing the good disposition the young boy Giuseppe Verdi has for learning to play this instrument, which is enough to repay me completely.' The year was 1821.

By this time Verdi was certainly taking music lessons from the village organist Pietro Baistrocchi; but it was not long before the pupil outstripped the master, and by 1822, at the age of nine, Verdi assumed Baistrocchi's post. One year later he enrolled at school in the nearest large town, Busseto, to begin a formal training in Italian rhetoric and grammar. The move to Busseto was of crucial importance, as it was there that he came into contact with two men who were to be of considerable influence during the next decade. The first was Ferdinando Provesi, organist at the collegiate church and director of the local music school. Verdi began formal music lessons with him in 1825, and these lasted for at least four years. The other figure was Antonio Barezzi, a rich Bussetan merchant who was to become almost a surrogate father to the young boy. Barezzi was a fanatical amateur musician, joint founder (with Provesi) of the local Philharmonic Society and enthusiastic performer on the flute, clarinet, horn and ophicleide. In 1831 Barezzi took the young boy into his own household, the better to nurture his musical talents; as if providentially to tie up the connection, Verdi fell in love with Barezzi's eldest daughter, Margherita.

We know that during his teens Verdi was already a prolific composer, eager to adapt his talents to local needs. In an autobiographical statement made many years later, he recounted that: 'From my thirteenth to my eighteenth year . . . I wrote an assortment of pieces: marches for brass band by the hundred, perhaps as many little *sinfonie* that were used in church, in the theater or at concerts, five or six concertos and sets of variations for pianoforte, which I played myself at concerts, many serenades, cantatas (arias, duets, very many trios) and various pieces of church music, of which I remember only a *Stabat Mater.*' Unfortunately, none of these early compositions survives, although it is quite possible that some of the marches turn up in revised versions in the early operas. It is significant that, at this stage, there is no special preference for operatic music; we can be sure that Verdi was regarded, indeed regarded himself, less an 'artist' than an 'artisan,' someone willing to turn his hand to religious, instrumental or vocal music as the need arose.

By the time Verdi reached the age of eighteen there were signs that the provincial world of Busseto was growing too small por the young composer. His father, almost certainly encouraged by Barezzi, applied for a local scholarship which would take Verdi to Milan, the undisputed music center of northern Italy. In January 1832 the grant was approved, and in June the young man set out to gain admission to the famous Milan Conservatory. Although the examiners went out of their way to praise the young applicant's composing skills, other factors could not be ignored: Verdi was four years over the usual entrance age; the Conservatory was desperately short of space; his piano-playing was awkward and unconventional. A week after the examination, Verdi approached one of the examiners, Rolla, who advised him to give up the Conservatory and study privately with Negri or Lavigna in the city. Verdi received no official rejection from the Conservatory, a lack of courtesy which left him considerably embittered.

Thanks to the generosity and faith of Barezzi, things did not in the end turn out so badly. The Bussetan merchant offered further financial assistance, and in August 1832 Verdi took Rolla's advice and began private lessons in Milan with Vincenzo Lavigna. Lavigna was himself an opera composer, learned in counterpoint but with considerable practical experience of Milan's famous La Scala theater, where he had been *maestro al cembalo* (a kind of executive *répétiteur*) for over thirty years. Although on the composer's own later admission the two and a half years with Lavigna were spent mostly with dry, academic exercises, 'canons and fugues, fugues and canons of every kind,' some original composition was taught and, most importantly, Verdi was encouraged to learn by example: from nightly attendance at the successes and failures of La Scala and the other Milanese theaters. The

Left: Verdi's application for admission to the Milan Conservatory in 1832. He was turned down without explanation and never discovered why. The refusal always rankled, and he later wrote bitterly on the envelope 'Fui respinto' (I was rejected).

Below: Manuscript of one of Verdi's early compositions, the Nocturne 'Guarda che bianca luna' (See the pale moon), scored for soprano, tenor, bass and flute *obbligato*, to a text by Jacopo Vittorelli, published in 1839.

repertoire of these years, dominated by Donizetti, Bellini and Mercadante, was rather undistinguished, but the staging of Rossini's *Mosè* at the rival Teatro Canobbiana may well have been of some significance to Verdi.

But perhaps Lavigna's greatest contribution was in introducing Verdi to certain influential figures in Milanese musical life. A crucial episode is narrated in what purport to be Verdi's own words in an 'Autobiographical Sketch' which he allowed to be published in 1881. Through Lavigna, Verdi had been invited to attend rehearsals of Haydn's *Creation* by the Milanese Philharmonic Society. The date was April 1834. One day, the conductors failed to appear and Verdi was asked to step in: 'I accepted, I sat down at the piano to begin the rehearsal. I well remember some little ironic smiles from the amateurs, ladies and gentlemen, and it seems that my youthful form, thin and none too elegant in dress, was such as to inspire scant faith. In short we began rehearsing, and little by little, warming and growing excited, I did not limit myself only to accompanying, but began also to conduct with my right hand, playing only with my left: I had a real success, all the greater for being unexpected. When the rehearsal was over, compliments, congratulations on all sides, and especially from Count Pompeo Belgiojoso and Count Renato Borromeo. Finally, whether because the three conductors mentioned above had too many other concerns and could not therefore attend to the job, or whether for other reasons, they entrusted the concert entirely to me. The public performance took place, with such success that it was repeated in the grand salon of the Casino de' Nobili, in the presence of the Archduke and Archduchess Rainer and all the grand society of that time.'

This first public success in Milan was important for two reasons. First, it established a continuing relationship with the Milanese aristocracy which produced at least one important commission – a cantata with words by Renato Borromeo in honor of the Austrian Emperor. Secondly, and more crucially, it brought Verdi into contact with the director of the Philharmonic Society, Pietro Massini, who offered him more conducting tasks – notably a series of performances of Rossini's *Cenerentola* in July 1835 – and whose encouragement of Verdi as a composer was ultimately of greatest importance.

Verdi's prescribed period of study with Lavigna now reached full term and, whether eagerly or reluctantly we cannot tell, the young man returned to the provincial setting of Busseto. He was formally appointed to the post of town music master in March 1836 and, as though to confirm his settled state, in April of that year he married Margherita Barezzi. The next three years must have seemed a depressing turn in his fortunes – a return to the town band, the life of a local celebrity – but Verdi managed to hang on to one Milanese lifeline: his contact with Massini. From several letters in 1836 between Verdi and Massini, it is clear that the young man was writing an opera, originally entitled *Rocester*, which he hoped, with Massini's help, to have performed in Milan. Of course, this ambitious project did not go entirely according to plan: there was an unsuccessful attempt to get the opera staged at Parma in 1837, but eventually they landed something of a coup: the opera, now called *Oberto, Conte di San Bonifacio*, was accepted by La Scala. Resigning his post in Busseto in October 1838, Verdi moved with his wife and their young son back to Milan. His operatic career was about to begin.

• Failure and success •

Oberto was first performed at La Scala in November 1839 and had what the Italians call 'un successo discreto' – a reasonably good reception. The libretto, whose subject is taken from Italian history, is a rather confused affair, perhaps because the opera underwent such a lengthy process of revision. It has, however, one of the stock situations of Romantic *melodramma*: a jealous father, Oberto (bass), whose daughter Leonora (soprano) loves Riccardo (tenor), who in turn loves Cuniza (mezzo-soprano). Verdi's music betrays quite openly the influence of his

most successful predecessors of the last twenty years – Rossini, Donizetti and, perhaps most frequently, Bellini; but there are some passages which hint at the dramatic, new, 'Verdian' voice. Perhaps the best of these is the Act II quartet 'La vergogna ed il dispetto,' which, though by no means as subtle or finished a piece as many that came later, is held together by a powerful rhythmic impetus, that sense of barely restrained energy which was to remain with Verdi throughout his career.

Whatever the opera's failings, the impresario at La Scala, Bartolomeo Merelli, was sufficiently impressed to offer Verdi a contract for three more operas, the first of which was to be, of necessity, a comedy. The composer eventually decided to set an old libretto by Felice Romani, but only because, on his own grudging admission, it seemed 'the least bad' of those offered him. The title was *Un Giorno di regno* (literally, 'King for a Day'). In the meantime, however, Verdi had undergone a series of personal tragedies. His first child, a daughter named Virginia, had died in August 1838, aged less than two; in October 1839 his young son, Icilio Romano, also died; and then, halfway through the composition of *Un Giorno di regno*, his wife Margherita succumbed to encephalitis. In later years the composer made much of the tragic circumstances in which he was forced to write a comic opera, for despite the death of his wife he was held to his contract. When the opera was performed in September 1840 it was an unmitigated disaster: the public was unsympathetic, the singers indifferent, the critics dismissive. *Un Giorno di regno* was immediately removed from the repertoire of La Scala. It was, in many ways, the lowest point in Verdi's long career.

Although even the most dedicated Verdian would hardly place *Un Giorno di regno* on a level with the Rossini and Donizetti comic masterpieces it superficially resembles, several of the comic situations can come off splendidly in performance. In addition, there are at least two characters, Edoardo (tenor) and the Marchesa (soprano), who are treated more in the manner of serious opera and whose arias, though perhaps rather heavily ornamented, give more than glimpses of the operas to come.

But Verdi's real musical breakthrough came with the next opera, *Nabucco*. He himself described in his 'Autobiographical Sketch' how he ran into Merelli some months after his disaster with *Un Giorno di regno*. The impresario, anxious to start him composing again, thrust into his reluctant hands a new libretto by one of the 'resident poets' at La Scala, Temistocle Solera: 'I went home and with an almost violent gesture, I threw the manuscript on the table, stopping, erect in front of it. Falling on the table, the sheaf opened on its own; without knowing how, my eyes stare at the page that lay before me, and this verse appears to me: "Va, pensiero, sull'ali dorate . . . " [Go, thoughts, on golden wings]. I glance over the following verses and I receive a deep impression from them, especially since they were almost a paraphrase of the Bible, which I always found pleasure in reading.

Below: Verdi was born in this farmhouse in the northern Italian village of Le Roncole in 1813. Carlo Verdi and his wife Luigia ran a small tavern and the only local store; they were poor, but not, as some have suggested, illiterate.

Left: Verdi's first spinet, which his father bought him in 1820 and which he kept all his life.

'I read a passage, I read two: then steadfast in my intention of not composing, I make an effort of will and force myself to close the script, and I go off to bed! . . . No good . . . *Nabucco* was trotting about in my head! . . . Sleep would not come: I get up and read the libretto, not once, but two, three times, so often that in the morning you could say I knew Solera's entire libretto by heart.

'All the same I did not feel like going back on my decision, and during the day I return to the theater and give the manuscript back to Merelli . . . He takes the libretto and jams it into the pocket of my overcoat, grabs me by the shoulders, and not only shoves me out of his office, but shuts the door in my face and turns the key. What to do?

'I returned home with *Nabucco* in my pocket: one day a verse, one day another, one time a note, another a phrase . . . little by little the opera was composed.'

Nabucco (originally entitled *Nabucodonosor*) was first performed at La Scala in March 1842 and was a runaway success. At least as far as Milan was concerned, Verdi had definitely 'arrived.'

Nabucco is indeed a remarkable achievement, primarily because its subject-matter and dramatic structure are perfectly matched by Verdi's musical language of that time. The biblical subject tends, in Solera's hands, to be presented in vast, static blocks – what the French call *tableaux vivants* – in which individual characterization is less important than overall scenic effect; the perfect structure for a composer who

Above: The soprano Giuseppina Strepponi (1815-97) with the score of *Nabucco, c.* 1842. She was influential in Verdi's early career and (against his wishes) sang the demanding role of Abigaille in *Nabucco.* She retired in 1846 and began to live with Verdi in 1848. Although the relationship was widely considered scandalous, they did not marry until 1859.

Right: Scene with the witches from the first performance of *Macbeth*, given in Florence in 1847. The originality of Verdi's music required intensive rehearsal, and he took his Macbeth (the baritone Felice Varesi) and Lady Macbeth (the soprano Marianna Barbieri-Nini) through their long duet 'one hundred and fifty times,' while the sleepwalking scene took three months to perfect.

was slow to achieve subtlety but who seemed to have an instinctive grasp of the grand musical gesture. There are aspects of *Nabucco* which owe something to Rossini's *Mosè*, but, particularly in the choral episodes, there is now no suggestion of passive imitation.

The most famous piece is the chorus 'Va, pensiero, sull'ali dorate.' Never before in nineteenth-century Italian opera had the chorus assumed such striking importance within the drama (usually its function was merely scenic and decorative); and never before had it sung in a language so natural and unaffected. But the popularity of 'Va, pensiero' should not eclipse other moments in which massed voices are used with notable originality. During the priest Zaccaria's aria in Part I, for example, the chorus, as if impatient to join the drama, completes the soloist's final phrases: a virtual identification of solo and choral forces. Furthermore, although the opera is best remembered for its grand scenes, there are also advances in individual characterization. There is only an insignificant tenor role, but the baritone (Nabucco) and the soprano (his daughter Abigaille) in some respects set the pattern for Verdi's treatment of these voices in future operas. Nabucco's scene at the end of Part II is a magnificent demonstration of the archetypal Verdian baritone's two opposing emotions: outraged authority and lyrical tenderness, while, as with so many other Verdian heroines, Abigaille's vocal aggression is all the more

effective for being occasionally tempered by contemplative moments (for example, 'Anch'io dischiuso un giorno' at the beginning of Part II).

Nabucco was an important turning-point in Verdi's career. Soon after its first performance he found a new social circle anxious to entertain him. Most important and long-lasting among the friendships he formed was that with Countess Clarina Maffei, wife of the poet and translator Andrea Maffei. The Maffei salon was a meeting-place for many famous artistic figures, as well as an informal debating chamber for social and political issues. In April or May 1842 Verdi began to attend the salon regularly, and his close friendship with the Countess lasted until her death some forty years later.

Verdi's next opera was *I Lombardi alla prima crociata*, first performed at La Scala in November 1843. The urge to repeat the success of *Nabucco*, to write what in modern times we would call a 'sequel,' must have been irresistible, and this work turns out to represent one of the few occasions on which the composer was unable to break much new ground. The libretto, again by Solera, furnishes fine opportunities for grand tableaux, and the Act IV chorus, 'O Signore dal tetto natio,' clearly attempts to produce another 'choral aria' in the style of 'Va, pensiero.' If *I Lombardi* is less successful than *Nabucco*, it is primarily because it lacks the earlier opera's single-minded concentration on grand effects.

Above: Set for the opening scene of *Oberto* designed by Giuseppe Bertoja for a production soon after the opera's première at La Scala in 1839. A critic described the work as 'pleasing in an extraordinary fashion and in a small way epoch-making,' and its mild success led to productions in various other Italian opera houses.

which interrupts Ernani's and Elvira's marriage ceremony, is a dramatic masterstroke, one of the high points in early Verdi opera. It precipitates a final trio (between Ernani, Elvira and Silva), which became one of the most famous set numbers of the work, encored wherever it was performed. This trio encountered a certain amount of opposition from the soprano who created Elvira, Sofie Löwe, who probably wanted a more conventional solo finale for the heroine, but by this stage Verdi was sufficiently sure of himself to refuse any compromise which he considered dramatically inappropriate.

After *Ernani* commissions flooded in, and, after his precarious beginnings, Verdi stepped up his rate of production. *Nabucco*, *I Lombardi* and *Ernani* had appeared at more or less yearly intervals, but in the space of two and a half years from November 1844 to July 1847, six new works were composed. This was the period later dubbed by Verdi his 'anni di galera' (galley years), an unceasing round of premières and revivals. It is no wonder that on occasions, quality was not maintained.

The opera which followed *Ernani* was *I Due Foscari*. Again written to a Piave libretto, it has, like *Ernani*, 'chamber music' proportions. Based on Byron's verse drama *The Two Foscari* and first performed in Rome late in 1844, the opera depicts one of the darker moments of fifteenth-century Venetian history. One particular point of musical interest is Verdi's attempt to supply a direct link between music and character by assigning to each of the major figures an orchestral motif, to be played on each occasion he or she enters the stage. The comparison with Wagner's system of *leitmotifs* is striking, perhaps even more so because there is no possibility of direct influence between the two composers at this stage.

The next opera, *Giovanna d'Arco* (Milan, February 1845), moves back to the 'epic' format

Above: This engraving of Verdi in his early years was frequently used, only the name of the opera engraved on the score being altered to suit the occasion.

Right: Interior of a box at La Scala, 1844. Stendhal described Italian opera boxes as miniature salons, and subscribers would use them as general reception rooms; some even had tiny kitchens. Conversation continued throughout most of the performance, and the house lights were not dimmed. The atmosphere was far closer to a smart night club than to the opera house of today.

• Consolidation •

Verdi's next work, *Ernani* (March 1844), initiated a rather different line of development. For La Fenice in Venice, a smaller, more intimate theater than La Scala, Verdi produced what might in comparison with *Nabucco* be termed a 'chamber opera,' with far less choral participation and an increased emphasis on individual characters. In *Ernani* Verdi worked for the first time with Francesco Maria Piave, who was to become the composer's most frequent librettist. Although less experienced than Solera, Piave was a fluent poet, and perhaps his inexperience was not altogether a bad thing, as it forced Verdi to consider more deeply the dramatic problems he had previously left to Solera.

While *Nabucco* had spread Verdi's fame throughout northern Italy, *Ernani* carried it to other parts of the peninsula, and also to foreign theaters. In the plot, based on the play by Victor Hugo, the heroine, Elvira (soprano), is loved by three men: Ernani (tenor), Don Carlo (baritone) and Silva (bass). Needless to say, she loves only the tenor, but Ernani has made a pact of honor with Silva: when Silva sounds his horn, Ernani must kill himself. The ghostly sound of the horn,

of *Nabucco* and *I Lombardi*, and to Solera as librettist. Though some of the music in this Italianate 'Joan of Arc' barely passes muster (one thinks of the devils' chorus 'Tu sei bella,' more suited to Venetian gondoliers than to other-worldly emissaries), the opera is distinguished by its fine soprano role, written for Erminia Frezzolini, one of the young composer's most distinguished and devoted interpreters. Many would consider Verdian music drama to reach a low ebb with the next work, *Alzira* (Naples, August 1845). Although some of the finale music is effective, Verdi's own later judgment on the opera, that it was 'really poor' (*proprio brutta*), would not be seriously contested by many today. *Attila* (Venice, March 1846) was a further attempt to return to the 'epic' format, although Solera's desertion before completing the final act meant that Piave was called in. The result, as Solera ruefully remarked, is something of a hotch-potch, although certain scenes, particularly those in the first act, are impressively forceful.

Letters of this period from Verdi's pupil, secretary and devoted follower Emanuele Muzio are the nearest we get to personal insights into this shadowy period of his career. We learn of the fame his operas brought him, and of his increasing dislike of petty socializing, no matter how grand the society. We hear how publishers relentlessly pursued him, and of his almost fanatical concern over the first performance of a new work: 'I am going to the rehearsals [of *Giovanna d'Arco* at La Scala] with the signor Maestro [Muzio's respectful term for Verdi] and am sorry to see him tire himself so. He shouts like a madman; beats with his feet so much that he seems to be playing the pedals of an organ; sweats so much that great drops fall on to the score.' Underpinning all this was also a killing schedule of travel and composition, and it is hardly surprising that, after the première of *Attila* in March 1846, Verdi's health broke down seriously; recurring bouts of gastric fever weakened him to the extent that he was advised to take six months complete rest. Already, though, further operas were being planned, in particular a new work for London's Haymarket Theatre. But then, in September 1846, another subject caught Verdi's imagination, a plot taken from the playwright he revered above all others: Shakespeare. This new work, *Macbeth*, was to become a milestone in his career, setting standards of musical and dramatic truth from which he would rarely retreat in subsequent works.

• The period of *Macbeth* •

Macbeth, first performed in Florence on 14 March 1847, marks an important stage in Verdi's career. Its special position seems in large part to derive from one fact: it was the first time that Verdi had taken on a Shakespearian subject. The great English dramatist had been an occasional source earlier in the century (Rossini's *Otello* being perhaps the most celebrated example) but his plays seem to have commanded little of the respectful devotion which characterized Verdi's attitude. Seemingly more concerned than ever before to do justice to his source, the composer took an active part in the creation of the text. Piave, who was again chosen as librettist, had to suffer a storm of critical letters, and eventually Verdi called on Andrea Maffei to assist with various passages. We also come across very definite ideas about the type of singer needed to interpret this precise dramatic conception. Lady Macbeth, for example, obviously far from a conventional operatic heroine, could not be allowed to sing with conventional prettiness: Verdi rejected one famous soprano precisely because she sang 'to perfection,' while he wanted a 'rough, hollow, stifled' voice. Her two showpieces, the aria and duet with Macbeth (Act I) and the sleepwalking scene, 'must not be sung at all: they must be acted and declaimed in a voice that is hollow and veiled.' As if to confirm the opera as a watershed in his progress, Verdi dedicated the score to the man who had assisted him in early life more than any other: Antonio Barezzi. In a letter to his father-in-law, he wrote: 'For many years it has been in my thoughts to dedicate an opera to you, who have been my father, benefactor and friend . . . Now, here is this *Macbeth*, which I love in preference to my other operas and which I thus deem more worthy of being presented to you.'

Indeed, extra care and attention is evident almost everywhere in the score of *Macbeth*. Take Macbeth's first entrance, for example. The conventions of Italian opera would have demanded that the character should sing a full-scale solo aria soon after his first appearance on stage, probably one divided into slow and fast sections (the so-called *cavatina*), but at this point in the drama Macbeth has only a dawning realization of his destiny and so, with much greater dramatic appropriateness, sings a restrained duet

Below: Title-page of the first edition of Victor Hugo's play *Hernani*, 1830. Hugo rejected classical models such as Corneille and Racine to produce a stirring historical melodrama, and he organized a claque of revolutionary long-haired poets to support it. Verdi's *Ernani*, 1844, faithfully reflects the play's violent energies.

HERNANI
OU
L'HONNEUR CASTILLAN,
Drame,
PAR VICTOR HUGO,
REPRÉSENTÉ
SUR LE THÉÂTRE-FRANÇAIS
LE 25 FÉVRIER 1830.

PARIS,
Mame et Delaunay-Vallée, libraires,
RUE GUÉNÉGAUD, Nº 25,
1830.

Left: Antonio Barezzi (1787-1867), the merchant and amateur musician who became Verdi's patron and father-in-law. Even after the death of his daughter, his love and support for Verdi never wavered. Verdi himself was deeply affected by the death of his 'second father' in 1867 and wrote to a friend: 'He died in my arms, and I have the consolation of never having caused him any sorrow.'

Left: Vocal score of *La Traviata*, 1853. Though based on Dumas's recent novel, the opera was staged in the period of Louis XIV to avoid scandalizing the audience with a modern story.

Below: Marie Duplessis at the theater in 1845. She was the model for the courtesan heroine of Dumas's *La Dame aux Camélias* (1845), written shortly after her death at the age of twenty-three.

Above: Set design for the first production of *Il Trovatore* at the Teatro Apollo, Rome, on 19 January 1853, only a few weeks before the première of *La Traviata* at La Fenice, Venice.

with Banquo. The piece, 'Due vaticini compiuto or sono,' is remarkable not only for its lack of vocal ostentation, but also for the manner in which Verdi manages to differentiate the two characters musically: Macbeth's wayward, unresolved line contrasting with Banquo's more down-to-earth expression.

Even when Verdi does follow operatic convention, it is by no means with a passive spirit. Lady Macbeth's opening aria, using the slow/fast aria form mentioned above, has a driving energy which even Verdi had not previously achieved. In the second part, 'Or tutti sorgete,' the intensity of Shakespeare's poetry –

. . . Come, thick night,
And pall thee in the dunnest smoke of hell,
That my keen knife see not the wound it
  makes,
Nor heaven peep through the blanket of the
  dark,
To cry 'Hold, hold!' –

is magnificently recreated, with a vocal line which swoops and rises towards a carefully prepared climax, and with decoration which serves to impel the melodic line relentlessly forward.

Verdi thought highly enough of *Macbeth* to revise it for Paris in 1865; he included several new pieces, one of them a superb new aria for Lady Macbeth in Act II, 'La luce langue.' But without doubt the most celebrated number dates from the original version of 1847, Lady Macbeth's sleepwalking scene, the 'gran scena del sonnambulismo.' We find here an orchestral and vocal detail quite without precedent in the early operas: there is the orchestral introduction, with its delicately muted strings and complex

FIGURINI dell' Opera RIGOLETTO del Maestro G. VERDI

Above: Characters from the first production of *Rigoletto*, which was given at La Fenice in 1851. This guide to the characters and their various costumes was published by Ricordi, the house which, despite many disagreements, published almost all Verdi's work.

Her face is ugly, serious and somewhat Nordic, which I find unpleasant, and she has a very large nose, very large hands and feet... I've looked at her down to the "smallest detail," as they say.'

Muzio's suggestion that Lind was really a singer left over from an earlier age is borne out by the music which Verdi wrote for her: there is a good deal of rather aimless vocal ornamentation, quite different from the dramatically relevant roulades of Lady Macbeth. But, as so often with Verdi's less-than-perfect works, *I Masnadieri* is to some extent saved by its ensembles, where the tensions between opposing factions draw out his qualities as a musical dramatist.

The next opera, *Jérusalem*, is perhaps most important as Verdi's initiation at the Paris Opéra. The introduction was unfortunately somewhat inauspicious: desperately short of time, Verdi had to abandon the idea of writing a completely new work and instead – in the tradition of Rossini – 'adapted' one of his earlier operas, *I Lombardi*, a process which entailed, among other things, a change of venue, the addition of a ballet and a general increase in visual splendor.

Given the hectic circumstances of Verdi's professional life at this period, it was perhaps inevitable that the opera which followed *Jérusalem*, *Il Corsaro*, also showed signs of undue haste. Although the composer was initially enthusiastic about an opera based on Byron's poem *The Corsair*, when he came to compose the music (to another Piave libretto), a certain cynicism and indifference seem to have set in. In contrast to his active participation in the formation of the *Macbeth* libretto, he set this text almost exactly as it was given to him. The first performance of *Il Corsaro* (Trieste, October 1848) was not a success, and the opera has rarely been revived. Certainly a good deal of the music smacks of the ordinary – the opening sequence of chorus, tenor aria, soprano aria, tenor-soprano duet is pure routine – but certain sections rise some way above this level. Best of all, perhaps, is the prison scene from Act III: though the musical design does not quite rise to the heights of *Macbeth*'s Act I duet (whose dramatic situation it partially resembles), there are many striking orchestral details such as the viola and cello solo in the introduction and – always a sign of Verdi's developing skill – a marked absence of literal repetition.

La Battaglia di Legnano followed hard on the heels of *Il Corsaro* but, whatever its eventual failings, certainly did not suffer from any lack of commitment on the composer's part. The revolutionary events which swept through Europe in 1848 had an undeniably inspiring effect on Verdi, as on almost every Italian. The mood is nicely caught in a letter to his mild-mannered librettist Piave, who had joined the Venetian National Guard: 'Just imagine whether I wanted to stay in Paris when I heard of a revolution in Milan. I left as soon as I heard the news, but arrived only in time to see these magnificent barricades. .... You speak of music!! What are

shifting harmonies; the accompaniment, multi-layered and rapidly changing; and finally the vocal line itself, which maintains a perfect sense of overall balance while employing a minimum of literal repetition.

The operas between *Macbeth* and *Rigoletto* (1851) are on the whole superior to the group of works before 1847. *I Masnadieri*, already planned in some detail before *Macbeth*, was written for Her Majesty's Theatre in London and first performed in July 1847. The librettist, Andrea Maffei, based his work on Schiller's play *Die Räuber*. One of the attractions of writing for London appears to have been the opportunity to create a role for the famous Swedish soprano Jenny Lind. Muzio, who came to London to prepare the ground for his master, wrote a detailed report: 'She can read any piece at sight. Her voice is a little harsh in the high register, and a little weak in the low, but by dint of study she has managed to make it so flexible in the high register that she can overcome the most incredible difficulties. Her trills are matchless, she has unequalled agility, and she generally shows off her technical skill with *fioriture*, *gruppetti* and trills: things which went well in the last century, but not in 1847 ...

you thinking of? . . . Do you imagine that I want to be bothered with notes and sounds? . . . There is and must be only one sound pleasing to Italian ears in 1848. The music of the guns! Well done, my Piave, and well done all Venetians; reject every narrow, municipal idea, let us all reach out a fraternal hand and again Italy will become the first nation in the world.'

But in spite of this professed distaste for the 'passive' art of composition, in *Il Battaglia di Legnano* Verdi was contemplating an operatic subject which could give full expression to his patriotic fervor. The librettist was Salvatore Cammarano, already employed for the ill-fated *Alzira*; the settings were Milan and Como during the twelfth century. When the opera was first performed (Rome, January 1849), Rome was on the verge of declaring itself a republic and, given the patriotic subject, an outstanding success was well-nigh inevitable. In one sense, *La Battaglia di Legnano* is the last of Verdi's early 'epic' pieces, and while it is certainly enriched by the composer's experience of the Paris Opéra, there is an occasional feeling that personal and public events are married somewhat uneasily. It has always remained something of a *pièce d'occasion*.

Verdi's next opera, also to a libretto by Cammarano, is undoubtedly one of his best before *Rigoletto*. *Luisa Miller* (first performed in Naples, December 1849) is based on Schiller's play *Kabale und Liebe* and seems at first sight rather an unusual plot for Verdi. It deals with tensions between the aristocracy and bourgeoisie, symbolized by the love of Rodolfo (tenor), son of the local squire, and Luisa (soprano), daughter of a retired soldier. But in fact the greater 'realism' of the plot is matched by a rejection of the grandiose musical elements of the 'epic' tradition. The finale of Act I, justly one of the opera's most celebrated moments, encapsulates perfectly this new approach. The two young lovers encounter their respective fathers in what, from the libretto, seems a typical finale of confrontation. But the manner in which Verdi manages to retain individual musical characterization almost throughout the complex structure is by no means conventional. Significantly, much of the interest lies in the orchestra, with understated chromatic melodies such as that which introduces Walter (bass), Rodolfo's father, serving to keep the atmosphere restrained but nevertheless intense.

The final opera before *Rigoletto* takes place completely in a bourgeois setting. *Stiffelio* (first performed in Trieste, November 1850), with a libretto by Piave, concerns the conflicts and jealousy suffered by a Protestant minister who eventually forgives his unfaithful wife. The opera was seldom revived and was eventually revised extensively, as *Aroldo*. But *Stiffelio* has been praised by many commentators for the originality of its musico-dramatic solutions and in particular for the splendid consistency of its title-role. Although it has never become a repertoire piece, it is in many senses an interesting prelude to the trilogy of masterpieces which were to follow.

• *Rigoletto, Il Trovatore* and *La Traviata* •

Although it might be argued that *Luisa Miller* initiates Verdi's 'second manner' – his final renunciation of the early, 'epic' format – most opera-goers would see *Rigoletto* (first performed in Venice, March 1851) as the great turning-point. The plot, unlike many of the operas which preceded it, has a single-mindedness which makes it easy to summarize. The action takes place in Mantua during the sixteenth century. Rigoletto (baritone) is a hunchbacked jester at the court of the Duke of Mantua (tenor). He protects his daughter Gilda (soprano) from the evil influences of court, but she falls in love with the Duke and is seduced by him. Rigoletto tries to have the Duke murdered, but his plot backfires and Gilda is killed in his place.

This simple tale was not achieved without a struggle. Piave's libretto, which was based on Victor Hugo's play *Le Roi s'amuse*, encountered some determined opposition from the government censors in Venice; among other things, they disliked the 'immorality' of the plot, its melodramatic extravagances (in the final scene, Gilda's body is given to Rigoletto in a sack) and, more fundamentally, the fact that Rigoletto, the ugly hunchback, is the 'hero' of the drama, while the Duke blatantly abuses his position of power. It says much for Verdi's self-confidence and clarity of vision in dramatic matters that he held firm against these criticisms, and ultimately managed to have the libretto passed with only a few minor details altered.

Throughout, the music is of startling originality. Even if many of the new devices had in fact been anticipated in earlier works (in particular in *Luisa Miller*), here they become more

PUBLIÉ PAR EUGÈNE RENDUEL.

M DCCC XXXII.

powerful by being welded into a convincing overall dramatic structure, with no disconcerting lapses into passive tradition. The orchestra, for example, is often liberated from its role as vocal accompanist and in many scenes even supplies the basic musical fabric, over which the singers 'converse' in a naturalistic manner. Recurring motifs, used rather ponderously in *I Due Foscari*, are here much more powerfully handled: the curse which Monterone sets on Rigoletto is depicted by an orchestral phrase, first heard in the opening measures of the Prelude and then recurring at critical moments in the drama. It is also significant that the conventional forms of Italian opera – aria, duet, finale, etc. – are used in *Rigoletto* only when they are appropriate to the dramatic situation. Rigoletto himself, for example, has no set-piece arias; his character is presented in duets and ensembles or, most typically, in *ariosi* like 'Pari siamo' (Act I) and 'Cortigiani, vil razza dannata' (Act II). The *arioso* (best defined as a mixture of aria and recitative, with the expressiveness of the former and the flexibility of the latter) allows this complex character to express his conflicting emotions – paternal love, bitter irony, hatred of the Duke – in close succession to one another, thus enhancing the immediate dramatic effect of the musical contrasts.

But perhaps the virtuosic climax of Verdi's concern for musical characterization comes with the Act III quartet, 'Bella figlia dell'amore.' Although its position in the opera, and the fact that it begins with a long tenor solo, are conventional enough, 'Bella figlia' is remarkable for the manner in which it manages to retain the musical identity of the four soloists. The slight exaggeration of the Duke's ardent love song sets a perfect perspective for the other three characters: Maddalena's wayward, chattering line; Gilda, at times with breathless,

'sobbing' figures, at times rising lyrically above the others; Rigoletto, his insistence on vengeance keeping him firmly rooted to the bass line. It is a further measure of Verdi's gathering integrity as a music dramatist that, even in the climax and coda, these musical personalities are maintained.

Il Trovatore (first performed in Rome, January 1853) seems to reject many of *Rigoletto*'s stylistic advances. The orchestra again takes on a role which is basically accompaniment, the voices express themselves typically in 'closed forms,' all conventional stereotypes, and there is not the subtlety and flexibility of characterization found in the earlier opera. There is also, of course, a problem with the notoriously complicated and unlikely plot, where a great deal of important action happens off-stage (or has occurred in the distant past).

However, the more conservative dramatic structure of *Il Trovatore* (an aspect certainly encouraged by the librettist Cammarano), with its 'cardboard' characters and conventional forms, certainly did not hamper Verdi's musical imagination, and indeed encouraged him to experiment in other directions. For example, however confused the plot may be, the events which occur proceed with a rigorous symmetry quite unlike the natural flow of *Rigoletto*, but equally compelling from a dramatic point of view. The stage action revolves around the two female characters, Azucena (mezzo-soprano) and Leonora (soprano), and their relationships with the two men, Manrico (tenor) and the Count Di Luna (baritone). Acts I and II both open with scenes containing narratives about Azucena and fighting between Manrico and the Count over Leonora. In Act III the Count 'captures' Azucena, and Manrico leaves Leonora (and eventually dies) to save Azucena, while in Act IV the Count 'captures' Leonora, who dies to save Manrico. In this 'monolithic' design, the almost exclusive use of closed forms becomes a dramatic necessity rather than an unfortunate reversion, as their static nature is needed to underline the symmetrically arranged situations.

Top right: The famous quartet, 'Bella figlia dell'amore,' from the last act of *Rigoletto* at its first French performance at the Théâtre Italien, Paris, in 1852.

Above: One of a series of photographs taken of Verdi by Disdéri in Paris in 1850.

Within the closed forms, however, there is immense variety, from the matched sequence of narrations in Acts I and II to the final trio of Act IV. We might cite as an example Leonora's famous 'Miserere' scene from Act III, much performed and recorded as a separate piece. Though the basic form is that of a conventional slow/fast 'double' aria, the addition of a further two musical elements – an offstage chorus of monks chanting the *Miserere* and Manrico singing from his prison window – turns the piece into a dramatic event, with the contrasting musical styles clearly juxtaposed. One might also single out the final trio, 'Ha quest' infame l'amor venduto,' where the three characters' different emotional states – Azucena dreamily recalling the past, Manrico angrily accusing, Leonora weak and imploring – are welded together into a dynamic closed form which nevertheless retains a clear musical identity. Other fine set pieces include Manrico's 'Di quella pira,' the Count's 'Il balen,' Leonora's 'Tacea la notte,' and Azucena's 'Stride la vampa'; each has become a classic example of its respective genre.

With *La Traviata* (first performed in Venice, March 1853), the third opera in this middle-period trilogy, Verdi again took up the challenge of a drama which was 'realistic' and continuously developing. The plot, based on the famous

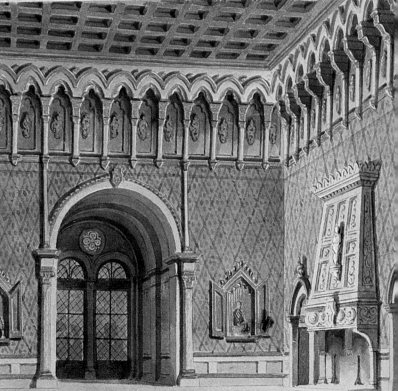

Above: The Sicilian Vespers, 1846, by Hayez. Verdi was asked to write an opera for Paris about this massacre of the French in Palermo in 1282, but was angry at the slovenly libretto by Scribe.

Opposite above: After the masked ball, 1857, by J. L. Gérôme, a painting (based on an actual incident in the Bois de Boulogne) that was the popular success of the 1857 Salon. That October Verdi asked his librettist Somma to prepare a version of Scribe's *Gustave III ou le Bal masqué* (set by Auber in 1833). Despite censorship, *Un Ballo in maschera* was first performed in Rome in February 1859.

Opposite below: Act II set by Bertoja for *Simon Boccanegra*, 1857.

play *La Dame aux camélias* by Alexandre Dumas junior, was certainly rather daring for an opera of the early 1850s, but by this stage Verdi had an unshakable belief in his dramatic intuitions. Although the first performance was one of Verdi's few out-and-out failures, this probably had more to do with inadequacies in the performance (and the lack of conventional showpieces for the singers) than with the subject-matter or the setting. As with *Rigoletto*, the plot is simple and direct. Violetta (soprano), a courtesan, falls in love with Alfredo (tenor), but is persuaded to renounce him by Alfredo's father, Germont (baritone), in order to protect the family honor. She dies of consumption, but not before a deathbed reconciliation with Alfredo.

As the title of the opera (literally, 'The Fallen Woman') suggests, the action centers upon Violetta. While Alfredo and Germont are relatively stereotyped figures – the ardent tenor and the paternal baritone respectively – and are presented musically in this manner, Violetta's musical personality alters with her development through the drama. In Act I her somewhat frenetic gaiety is expressed in light, though brilliant coloratura, even when she is confronted by Alfredo's more directly passionate style (compare, for example, her 'Ah se ciò è ver' with Alfredo's 'Di quell'amor'). By the end of Act II,

however, after her great duet with Germont, her character has blossomed forth in a rich variety of conflicting emotions, from passionate denial to resigned sadness, and the vocal line becomes longer breathed, less highly ornamented, more simply expressive.

In one essential sense, *La Traviata* differs from both *Rigoletto* and *Il Trovatore*: its great moments tend always towards the intimate, towards personal rather than public emotion. This atmosphere of restraint is perfectly introduced by the orchestral prelude to Act I (repeated in a varied form at the beginning of Act III), where the instrumental writing breaks new ground in subtlety (note the unusual register and *divisi* strings of the opening) and delicate chromatic harmony. Similarly, the party scene in Act I is a sophisticated version of the ball in Act I of *Rigoletto*. But, perhaps most important, we find in the opera an increasing melodic expansiveness. Melodies like Alfredo's 'Di quell'amor' (Act I) or Violetta's 'Amami Alfredo' (Act II) make their dramatic effect by arriving at the end of long sections of musical development; they are presented as culminations, as final, distilled statements of emotion. They are strongly prophetic of the later Verdi and are an ultimate illustration of the composer's faith in the voice as the major vehicle of musical expression.

275

Right: Title-page of the Arabic libretto for *Aida*, 1871, first performed at the Khedival opera house. Verdi rehearsed the singers at home but did not go to Cairo, where the first performance was a glittering social occasion, some paying in solid gold for seats.

Far right: Title-page of the cantata *Inno delle Nazioni* (Hymn of the Nations), written for the 1862 Exhibition in London to words by Arrigo Boito. Orchestral pieces had been written for Germany by Meyerbeer and for France by Auber, but Verdi's work became the center of a controversy, whether because the music incorporated two revolutionary songs, 'La Marseillaise' and 'Fratelli d'Italia' or because of jealousy on the part of the musical director of the Exhibition, Michael Costa. In the end its performance was arranged by a rival impresario at Her Majesty's Theatre.

INNO DELLE NAZIONI
COMPOSTO PER LA GRANDE ESPOSIZIONE DI LONDRA
DA
GIUSEPPE VERDI
Gran Cordone dell'Ordine dei SS. Maurizio e Lazzaro, Uffiziale della Legion d'Onore.
POESIA DI ARRIGO BOITO
MILANO, R. STABILIMENTO NAZ. — TITO DI GIO. RICORDI

• Grand opera •

It is time to take up again the story of Verdi's personal life. We left him in 1847 struggling against bouts of ill-health and desperately over-worked. That year Verdi visited Paris in connection with *I Masnadieri* at Her Majesty's Theatre, London, and *Jérusalem* at the Opéra. There he formed an attachment with the woman who was to be his companion for the next fifty years: the famous soprano Giuseppina Strepponi. The couple had met several times, notably when Giuseppina created the role of Abigaille in *Nabucco*; both were now over thirty and had undergone several emotional traumas in the past. By the summer of 1848 they were living together openly in Paris, Verdi having some months earlier returned to Busseto to buy the house and farm lands of Sant'Agata, and in September 1849 they made the bold move of setting up house together in Busseto, where they were to remain for the rest of their lives. But while such free associations (the couple did not choose to marry until 1859) were presumably quite acceptable in Paris, a different moral atmosphere existed in Verdi's home town. In a letter to his father-in-law, Antonio Barezzi, Verdi made his views on the matter clear: 'In my house there lives a free, independent Lady, like me a lover of the solitary life and possessed of a fortune quite sufficient for all her needs. Neither she nor I are accountable to anyone for our actions; but, on the other hand, who knows what our relationship is? Who knows whether or not she is my wife? Who has the right to condemn us? I will definitely say this much: in my house she must command equal or even greater respect than I myself, and no one is permitted to forget this on any pretext; both in

her conduct and character, she has every right to that special consideration she never fails to show towards others.'

Verdi's professional life also underwent a marked change at this point: his next three operas are all, to a degree, influenced by French models, and might be seen as charting his increasing ability to harness this foreign style to his own Italian idiom. As early as 1852 (before the first performances of *Il Trovatore* and *La Traviata*), Verdi had signed a contract in France to produce a full-scale *grand opéra*. The librettist, almost inevitably, was Eugène Scribe, the prolific poet-in-residence at the Opéra during these years, who, with the help of a collaborator, eventually revised an old piece of his own to produce *Les Vêpres siciliennes*, a typical example of the French format with five acts, a generous use of the chorus, an extended ballet in the middle of Act III, and a drama which found its high points in moments of great scenic splendor.

Equally typical was the tendency to interweave private and public concerns. Set in thirteenth-century Sicily, the action centers on an attempt by the Sicilians to overthrow their French oppressors. Guy de Montfort (baritone), is the governor of Palermo. Henri (tenor) is a young Sicilian patriot in love with Hélène (soprano), an Austrian duchess. Jean Procida (bass) is the leader of the Sicilian revolutionaries. The central conflict focuses on Henri, who, it is revealed, is the long-lost son of Montfort; their duet in Act III, 'Quand ma bonté toujours nouvelle,' is one of those dramatic confrontations which brought the best out of Verdi, and stands comparison with the Violetta-Germont duet in Act II of *La Traviata*. But, at least so far as the original audience was concerned, the scenes of visual opulence, planned and executed on an immense scale, were the most impressive.

After *Les Vêpres* Verdi mulled over a number of operatic projects – most important was a setting of Shakespeare's *King Lear*, an idea which had been considered more than once before in his career. But *Lear* was eventually shelved and, in 1856, the composer agreed to write an opera for La Fenice in Venice. The librettist was Piave (with some later help from Giuseppe Montanelli), the source a play by García Gutiérrez, who had earlier provided the composer with *Il Trovatore*. The new opera, entitled *Simon Boccanegra*, was first performed in Venice in March 1857. It was, from the start, never very successful, and when *Un Ballo in maschera* appeared in 1859 was practically ignored in most Italian theaters. Verdi's final acknowledgment that the opera was less than satisfactory came in 1880 when he agreed to revise parts of *Boccanegra* with the help of the librettist Arrigo Boito. Verdi's comments on the original version, made to his publisher and friend Giulio Ricordi, pinpoint the difficulties: 'The score is not possible as it stands. It is too sad, too depressing. There is no need to touch the [prologue] or the last act . . . But I shall redo all the [first] act and give it more contrast and variety, more life.'

A further difficulty with *Boccanegra* is its unusual time-scale, with a lengthy prologue which takes place twenty-five years before the main action. Set in fourteenth-century Genoa, the political action centers on Boccanegra (baritone), the Doge of Genoa, and his political adversary Jacopo Fiesco (bass). Fiesco has brought up Amelia (soprano), not knowing that she is in fact Boccanegra's daughter; Amelia loves Gabriele (tenor), who is in league with Fiesco against Boccanegra. Verdi's principal idea for the revision was a grandiose new scene for Act I which would take place in the Doge's council chamber. Although at first Boito suggested even more radical changes, these were eventually put aside as too time-consuming, and the council chamber scene was composed. This scene (the new Act I finale) is justly regarded as one of Verdi's greatest achievements. We find orchestral subtleties which rival *Otello* or *Aida* (in particular the opening section, with its offstage chorus, and the final moments, where the terrible curse is laid); a slow ensemble with chorus, where Amelia's melodic expansiveness looks forward to Puccini; and, perhaps best of all, Boccanegra's 'Plebe! Patrizi! Popolo!,' one of Verdi's finest baritone solos.

Un Ballo in maschera (first performed in Rome, February 1859) is in many senses a synthesis of Verdi's music of the 1850s. It returns to the classic three-act structure of *Rigoletto* and *La Traviata*, and its action, at least in comparison with the previous two operas, is simple and direct, although it retains certain elements from the tradition of French *grand opéra* which had so influenced the composer during the last five years. Again there were protracted problems with the censor; Antonio Somma's adaptation of Scribe's libretto *Gustave III* had to be moved from its original Swedish setting and placed in seventeenth-century Boston. Riccardo (tenor),

Earl of Warwick, is in love with Amelia (soprano), the wife of Renato (baritone), the secretary and close friend of Riccardo. On the periphery of this classic triangle come two other principals who act as extensions of the two lovers' personalities: Oscar (soprano) is Riccardo's page and underlines the lighter side of that character, while Ulrica (contralto) is a fortune-teller who adds darker shades to Amelia's predominantly tragic figure. A political element is supplied by Sam and Tom (both basses), who plot against Riccardo. They are eventually joined by Renato when he learns of his wife's involvement with the Earl.

In this opera, as with the previous two, there is again a blend of private and political elements, as well as scenes of great visual splendor (notably the 'gallows field' of the Act II love duet and the grand masked ball of the finale). But there is not the slightest sense of strain between these elements. This is partly because the opera has an undeniable center of dramatic and musical attention in Riccardo's love for Amelia, given musical voice in their great Act II love duet. *Un Ballo* is thus unique in mature Verdi in having love interest between the tenor and soprano as a focal point in the drama: while other operas, such as *La Traviata* or *Aida*, may seem similaar from a reading of the libretto, the music changes this emphasis (in the case of *La Traviata* highlighting instead the relationship between Violetta and Germont and thus our sense of Violetta's sacrifice). But also *Un Ballo* is so classically

Above: Photograph of Verdi in St Petersburg for the première of *La Forza del destino* at the Imperial Theater in 1862. Tsar Alexander II was thrilled by the opera, for which Verdi was paid the enormous sum of 20,000 roubles.

Left: Verdi conducting *Aida* in Paris. In the 1870s he traveled widely, conducting many of his works in various European cities.

balanced through the musical flexibility of the major character, Riccardo, and those who surround him – their ability to move freely between comic and serious opera. Many of Riccardo's greatest moments are couched in the language of lyrical comedy (in particular the ensemble he leads off in Act I, 'Ogni cura si doni al diletto,' and his later canzone 'Di tu se fedele il flutto m'aspetta'), while his page Oscar has two delightful arias clearly derived from the lighter

French tradition. Even more surprising, the conspirators Sam and Tom, though they are associated with a characteristically sinister 'plotting motif' in the prelude and the beginning of Act I, also break into ironic laughter at the end of Act II. In this way, far from acting as a distraction to the main business of the drama, they become further integrated into its basic musical expression. The seeming ease with which *Un Ballo* effects the synthesis of styles fought so hard for in the previous two operas should not lead us to underestimate its considerable achievement.

• *La Forza* and *Don Carlos* •

The years immediately following *Un Ballo* were critical for the Italian State, with defeats for the Austrians, the Peace of Villafranca, Garibaldi's southern campaigns and the first meetings of the Italian government. In this last venture Verdi soon found himself actively involved, as he was the elected representative of his home constituency of Borgo San Donnino. But he was always an unwilling politician and probably attended only through the personal insistence of the great Italian statesman Benso Camillo di Cavour, for whom he had great respect. By a happy coincidence, Verdi's name became a focal point for those Italians who wished to unite their country under the rule of King Victor Emanuel: 'Viva Verdi' became a popular slogan, Verdi being an acronym for 'Vittorio Emanuele Re D'Italia.'

We hear very little of new operas until the beginning of 1861, when Verdi agreed to write a work for the Imperial Theater in St Petersburg. The librettist was Piave (his last collaboration with the composer), and the subject, after some discussion, was taken from a Spanish play by Angel de Saavedra, Duke of Rivas (with additional material from Schiller's *Wallensteins Lager*). *La Forza del destino* was eventually performed in St Petersburg in November 1862 and, although revivals took place in Spain, New York, Italy and London during the next few years, was only moderately successful. For a further run of performances at La Scala, Verdi made various revisions, altering the emphasis in the final scene and adding a full-scale overture (in the manner of Rossini's *Guillaume Tell*) to replace the original prelude. This revised version, first performed at La Scala in February 1869, was an unqualified success.

There could hardly be a greater contrast between *La Forza* and *Un Ballo*, at least in respect of their overall dramatic shape. As we have seen, *Un Ballo* is remarkable for the manner in which it manages to offer a coherent, concise focus for the various elements of the plot; *La Forza* was, from the beginning, thought of essentially as a kaleidoscope, making a virtue of its disparateness. Set in eighteenth-century Spain and Italy, the main plot concerns Don Alvaro (tenor) and his love for Leonora (soprano), whose father is accidentally killed by

Right: Set design for the first production of *Otello* at La Scala in 1887. Verdi's librettist Boito cut Shakespeare's first 'Venetian' act, and the opera begins with the storm over Cyprus. After the triumphant first performance the American Blanche Roosevelt, who was present, wrote, 'At seventy-four, this second conqueror may well exclaim: Veni, vidi, vici, Verdi!'

Below: Page from Verdi's full score for *Otello*. The opera had a long and difficult gestation, and at one point Verdi was demoralized by an erroneous newspaper report that Boito wanted to compose his own music for *Otello*.

Alvaro in the opening scene. Revenge is sought by Leonora's brother Don Carlo (baritone). The action ranges far geographically, and it is only by a series of coincidences (improbable even by operatic standards) that this triangle of principals manages to meet up for the final, tragic conclusion. There are also two important subsidiary characters who, unlike Oscar and Ulrica in *Un Ballo*, inhabit musical worlds quite separate from the main drama. Preziosilla (mezzo-soprano), a gypsy camp-follower, enlivens the military scenes, in particular with her Act II 'Rataplan,' which plainly recalls Donizetti's French comic opera *La Fille du régiment*. Melitone (baritone) is, in spite of being associated with the religious elements in the drama, Verdi's first frankly comic character since *Un Giorno di regno* some twenty years earlier.

Although the sheer musical variety of *La Forza* denies it such telling overall effect as *Un Ballo* or *La Traviata*, there are many individual scenes of the highest level, both musical and dramatic. The whole of Act I, for example, is a magnificent single structure, with no distractions from secondary characters and a powerful sequence of dramatic cause-and-effect. There are also scenes in which Verdi's mastery of the *grand opéra* format is again demonstrated. Perhaps the best of these is the finale of Act II, which sets Leonora's decision to take up the life of a hermit against a solemn background of ritual and religion. Preceded as it is by one of Verdi's finest duets (one all the more remarkable for the fact that the relationship between its participants is not as usual one of love or hate, but of confessor and supplicant), it juxtaposes the solemn, threefold injunction and 'epic' style chorus ('Il cielo fulmini, incenerisca') with a

gentle final ensemble ('La Vergine degli angeli') in which Leonora and the monks ask the Virgin to protect her.

The hiatus in operatic activity which occurred between *Un Ballo in maschera* and *La Forza del destino* was to be repeated, at greater length, before Verdi produced a further new work. Admittedly, these were not barren years, as a good deal of time was spent on the revisions of *Macbeth* (in preparation for its first performance at the Paris Opéra) and on further detailed plans for that never-to-be-realized Shakespearian project *King Lear*. But by the middle of 1865, some three years after the première of *La Forza*, and in spite of repeated previous statements that he would do nothing of the sort, Verdi agreed to write again for the Opéra. By November the subject had been decided: he would return to Schiller and write a version of *Don Carlos*. During 1866 he worked hard at the music, putting many scenes through a number of drafts and eventually making some important cuts which were never restored.

When *Don Carlos* was finally performed, it was not a great public success, and Verdi was

Above: Francesco Tamagno (1850-1905), one of the greatest of all Italian dramatic tenors, created the role of Otello. He had written to the composer begging for the honor, but Verdi was initially sceptical. Tamagno was later the first Otello in London and also sang the part in major opera houses throughout Europe and the USA. In this double portrait with Romilda Pantaleone, the first Desdemona, the score of *Otello* is on the table.

accused (not for the last time) of becoming over-influenced by Wagner and not keeping to the tradition of his famous trilogy from the early 1850s. Though the opera's spacious, five-act structure was tailor-made for Paris, an Italian version prepared for Naples in 1872 made it clear that *Don Carlos* (or *Don Carlo* in its Italian version) was simply not a manageable repertoire piece. During 1882 and 1883, after the alterations to *Simon Boccanegra*, Verdi spent considerable time reducing *Don Carlos* to four acts (without the ballet which had been obligatory for Paris). Yet another version (almost certainly carrying the composer's approval) appeared in 1886, restoring some of the 1884 cuts but still leaving out the ballet. It is this version, in Italian, which is most often performed today, and to which we shall refer in the remainder of the discussion.

Verdi's continuing dissatisfaction with *Don Carlos* is of course revealing: it is one of those operas which never really found a 'definitive' form. Each of the versions mentioned above has good and bad points; none is entirely satisfactory from a dramatic point of view. The additions and cuts are almost invariably improvements from a strictly musical viewpoint, but this in itself leads to problems of dramatic imbalance and creates a plot which has to sustain a changed musical equilibrium. In a letter to Camille du Locle (one of the librettists of *Don Carlos*), Verdi writes frankly of the problems Paris created for an Italian musician: '[In Paris] one ultimately finds in one's hands not a unified opera but a *mosaic*; and beautiful as it may be, it is still a *mosaic*. You will argue that the Opéra has produced a string of masterpieces in this manner. You may call them masterpieces all you want, but permit me to say that they would be much more perfect if the *patchwork* and the adjustments were not felt all the time.' The letter, written two years after the première of *Don Carlos* at the Opéra, might with justification be seen as a comment on his own problems with the genre.

The action of *Don Carlos* takes place in France and Spain during the sixteenth century. As with other works conceived for Paris, personal and public tensions are worked out on a grand scale. There is, on the one hand, the love of Don Carlos (tenor), Infante of Spain, for Elisabeth de Valois (soprano), who for reasons of political treaty has to marry Don Carlos's father, King Philip of Spain (bass). There are two other major characters: Rodrigo, Marquis of Posa (baritone), who is a close friend of Carlos and represents the ardent patriotism so common to earlier operas; and Princess Eboli (mezzo-soprano), the *femme fatale* who loves Carlos but becomes involved instead with Philip. The sinister power of the Inquisition is a further important force in the drama and is magnificently represented in one scene by the Grand Inquisitor himself (bass).

As with *La Forza*, this opera presents such a variety of musical events that it is impossible to choose one or two that are representative. There are scenes of great visual grandeur, such as the

Right: First peformance of the *Messa da Requiem* in the church of San Marco, Milan, in 1874. Verdi conducted on this occasion, and the soprano soloist was Teresa Stolz, whose relationship to the composer remains a source of controversy. The German conductor and Wagnerian Hans von Bülow described the work at the time as 'a triumph of Latin barbarism,' but it has always been tremendously popular.

auto da fé in Act III, which recalls the earlier Verdi but also looks forward to *Aida* in the skillful manner by which the various groups on stage are contrasted musically. There are Eboli's two great solos, in particular the renowned 'O don fatale,' which ends with one of those melodic lines so characteristic of late Verdi, in which a character's whole emotional state seems to be summed up in one sweeping phrase. But the opera also has more restrained moments. In Act IV there is a magnificent duet for the two basses, Philip and the Grand Inquisitor: a dark political wrangle, symbolized by an insistently repeated motif in the bass of the orchestra, breaking into passionate declamation for a brief moment. The number which precedes this, Philip's solo 'Ella giammai m'amò,' is similarly suffused with restrained passion. Again, there is one phrase which seems to encapsulate the character's feeling: to the words 'No, amor per me non ha' (No, she has no love for me), a simple cadential phrase is transformed into a statement of universal significance. Such moments triumphantly vindicate Verdi's continual struggle to give *Don Carlos* a convincing dramatic structure.

• *Aida* and the Requiem •

After the première of *Don Carlos* in Paris, Verdi's creative activity ceased: the by now familiar references to his dislike of the public and of theatrical practice reappear. Two projects, however, engaged his professional attention.

One, which we have already discussed, was the refashioning of *La Forza del destino* for La Scala in 1869; the other was the 'Libera me' section of a Requiem Mass to commemorate the anniversary of Rossini's death, the separate movements of which were to be written by leading Italian composers. The music for this Mass was actually completed, but administrative difficulties prevented its performance.

Needless to say, many of Verdi's close associates tried to interest him in operatic subjects, and eventually a breakthrough occurred. Camille du Locle sent Verdi a scenario for an opera set in Egypt, and in May 1870 the composer expressed cautious enthusiasm. Eventually a contract was drawn up for the work, to be called *Aida*, to inaugurate the new Cairo opera house. The making of an Italian libretto was entrusted to Antonio Ghislanzoni (who had assisted Verdi with the revisions to *La Forza*), and elaborate scenery and costumes were ordered from Paris. But then, as the opera was being composed, political events dramatically disrupted the *Aida* timetable. On 19 July 1870, France declared war on Prussia, and exactly two months later Prussian forces began the siege of Paris. Although the siege was eventually lifted in January 1871, it was not until December of that year that *Aida* was first performed in Cairo.

As one might imagine for such a prestigious occasion (Verdi was paid the altogether exceptional fee of 150,000 lire for the score), the work contains many elements of *grand opéra*; but, for a number of reasons, it suffers less than *Don Carlos* or earlier 'French' works from the *mosaic* problems the composer himself had identified. Certainly Verdi controlled the formation of the libretto with a strictness and attention to detail unusual even for him. In many cases, Ghislanzoni was reduced almost to secretarial tasks: the composer would set his own, doggerel

verse and then request his librettist to fashion more respectable poetry to fit the existing music. The eventual result was a drama which brings together personal and grandiose elements in a balance not achieved since *Un Ballo in maschera*, and, like the earlier opera, *Aida* has the additional merit of a musical language which is consistent in the overall atmosphere it creates. Though, as might be expected, the authenticity

of Verdi's Egypt is only notional, his desire to do justice to the unusual setting was obviously an important element which contributed to this increased unity of conception.

Although the setting took Verdi away from convention, the plot has many aspects familiar from earlier works. The action takes place in Memphis and Thebes during the reign of the Pharaohs. Radames (tenor), an Egyptian captain and leader of the troops against Ethiopia, loves and is loved by Aida (soprano), an Ethiopian slave. Amneris (mezzo-soprano), daughter of the King of Egypt, loves Radames and is jealous of Aida. Radames captures Amonasro (baritone), King of Ethiopia, who is revealed as Aida's father. Amonasro tricks Radames into betraying his country, and the two lovers eventually die together in a subterranean vault. As with so many of the operas after *Rigoletto*, religion is an important force in the drama, here represented by Ramfis (bass), chief of the Egyptian priests.

Verdi's musical language is now quite flexible enough to make creative potential out of these different levels of activity. In the opening part of the famous 'triumphal scene' (the finale of

Right: Verdi with Victor Maurel at a Paris performance of *Otello* in 1894. Maurel, a French baritone, was the first Iago, and his relationship with Verdi was at times strained. However, Verdi admired his great interpretative ability and chose him to sing the title-role in the first performances of *Falstaff*.

Below: Verdi and Boito at Sant'Agata. This engraving from *L'Illustrazione Italiana*, 1887, is pure fantasy, and shows Boito as far younger than he actually was at the time.

Below: Special number of *L'Illustrazione Italiana* devoted to Verdi's *Falstaff*. This opera was free of the problems which had beset *Otello*, and this had a rejuvenating effect on the old composer. He wrote to Ricordi: 'In writing *Falstaff* I have given no thought to theaters and singers. I have written it on my own behalf to please myself.' The first performance took place at La Scala, Milan, in 1893, and, like *Otello*, it was a great success.

Bottom: Original set by Hohenstein for the Garter Inn in *Falstaff*. Writing to Emma Zilli, the first Alice Ford, Verdi recalled the rehearsal period as 'a splendid time of enthusiasm, when we all breathed nothing but art.'

looks forward to the freer forms of Verdi's final two masterpieces.

After *Aida*, Verdi wrote no more new operas for some sixteen years; the stream of masterpieces, which had threatened to dry up after *La Forza* and again after *Don Carlos*, finally stopped. One factor was certainly his gathering financial security; another his increasingly critical attitude to the manner in which his ever more precise artistic visions were being realized on the Italian stage. There were also domestic troubles (in part, it seems, caused by his close friendship with the soprano Teresa Stolz, who had created Aida at La Scala) and – an increasing problem of old age – the pain of losing old and close friends. Perhaps also there was the suspicion that, as with Rossini forty years earlier, music history was beginning to overtake him. In 1871, just before the première of *Aida*, Verdi attended Wagner's *Lohengrin* in Bologna. This was the first time Wagner had been staged in Italy (though his theories were well enough known), and the storm of publicity certainly irritated Verdi (his comments on the music were more measured, although not uncritical). At the same time, a generation of young Italian composers, with Arrigo Boito prominent among them, were beginning to reject what they saw as the provincialism of Italian culture, and to look towards Germany as well as France for fresh creative stimulus.

In May 1873, however, a debt of honor stimulated Verdi to take up his pen again. Alessandro Manzoni, the greatest Italian literary figure of the nineteenth century, died in Milan. Manzoni was the author of *I Promessi Sposi* – by far the most famous and respected of nineteenth-century Italian novels – and Verdi had long revered him, at first from afar, later with personal acquaintance. Soon he was proposing to write a Requiem Mass which might be performed on the first anniversary of the great man's death. Part of the work, the 'Libera me,' had already been composed for the abortive Rossini Requiem, and there is some evidence that Verdi had been considering a large-scale religious piece even before Manzoni's death. Whatever the case, the Requiem was finished in

Act II), for example, contrasting musical ideas are immediately identified with the various scenic elements: the massed populace, women with laurels for the victors, the intransigent priests. Later on it is a further musical conflict (Amonasro's plea for mercy countered by the priests' demand of death to the prisoners) which impels the grand ensemble. In between these two sections we have a ballet, in which the subtle 'Egyptian' elements are brought to the fore, and of course the immensely popular trumpet tune which accompanies the arrival of the victorious troops. Such moments of grand scenic display, magnificent as they are, should not cause us to neglect the quieter moments of the score: the beginning of Act III, for example, with its delicate exploration of pure orchestral sonority at the opening; or Aida's unconventionally structured aria 'Oh, patria mia,' which

Three pictures of Verdi's villa at Sant'Agata: a photograph of Verdi's bedroom (*above left*) and two watercolors (*left and above*) by Leopoldo Metlicowitz, who visited the villa in the 1870s, showing the composer with two favorite horses and walking with friends in the park. Verdi purchased Sant'Agata, near his home town of Busseto, in 1848, and lived in the villa until his death.

April 1874, and first performed at the church of San Marco in Milan on 22 May of that year.

At least one distinguished musician (the conductor Hans von Bülow) sneered at the Requiem as being 'Verdi's latest opera, in ecclesiastical dress' (this, it should be noted, before he had heard any of the music), and the statement seems to have remained in currency. There are operatic elements in the piece; it would be strange not to find them in the work of a man who had dedicated himself to the theater. The vocal style of the soloists may be compared quite closely to that of operatic characters of the period – in particular the soprano and mezzo-soprano, who relate to Aida and Amneris respectively; the famous 'Dies Irae' might be seen as the apotheosis of the storm scenes so popular in earlier opera, and so compared to the opening scene of *Otello*, for example; the list could continue. But far more remarkable than these inevitable cross-references is the manner in which Verdi organizes such disparate stylistic material into a coherent whole. Side by side with the operatic elements stand 'classical' forms like the choral fugue and even recollections of Berlioz's *Grande Messe des morts*. It is a tribute to the consistency of his vision that, for many enthusiasts, the Requiem remains one of Verdi's greatest works.

• *Otello* and *Falstaff* •

The sixteen-year gap between *Aida* and *Otello* was in no sense a period of total inactivity. One project was that of assuring the Requiem a

secure European reputation by personally directing foreign performances. In 1874 Verdi conducted it at the Opéra Comique in Paris, and 1875 saw him engaged on a grand tour with the work, first visiting Paris, then London's Albert Hall and Vienna's Hofoper. However, as might be imagined, Verdi's creative silence was a source of great concern to those closest to him, and in particular to his friend and publisher Giulio Ricordi. The latter made several attempts to interest him in new projects, but the composer seems to have become increasingly adept at fencing off any approaches of this kind. Eventually Ricordi engaged Verdi's reluctant interest in a possible collaboration with Arrigo Boito on a version of *Othello*, although when Ricordi appeared at Verdi's hotel with an outline of the libretto, Verdi, still unwilling to compromise himself, advised: 'Now put it into verse. It will come in handy for yourself . . . for me . . . for someone else.'

Partly because of this caution, and partly because of the lengthy discussions between composer and librettist, *Otello* moved along very slowly. The revisions to *Simon Boccanegra* and then *Don Carlos* intervened, and the overall dramatic shape of the opera caused some problems. Here Boito showed himself to be the most sympathetic and dramatically astute of Verdi's many collaborators, always responding to the various demands made upon him, but also willing and able to offer his own suggestions and stimulate new lines of thought. By 1884 most of the difficulties had been ironed out, and Verdi began to compose in earnest. Gradually the opera moved forward, although not without further changes to the libretto, and finally, on 5 February 1887, *Otello* was first performed at La Scala. It was, almost inevitably in the circumstances, a triumphant success, although certain critics saw fit to remark that the composer of *Rigoletto* and *La Traviata* had traveled far since those works and perhaps not entirely carried his audience with him.

One feature of both *Otello* and of Verdi's last opera, deserves immediate emphasis: the extent to which the orchestra becomes emancipated from the vocal lines, often supplying the basic continuity and even developing material in a quasi-symphonic manner. In *Rigoletto* (and even earlier) there had been brief passages of 'orchestral continuity,' but in *Otello* this becomes virtually the norm. Though Verdi never entirely relinquished the idea that the orchestra should accompany the voices, there are many passages where the vocal element is clearly of secondary importance, at least in so far as the central musical argument is concerned. This is important not merely because of the resulting changes in texture, but also because it allowed Verdi to develop material more consciously and freely, in the process giving his work overall unity on a level not previously attempted in Italian nineteenth-century opera.

With hindsight, however, we are probably as inclined to notice traditional elements as we are radical departures. The large-scale finale to Act III, for example, magnificently effective though it is, is an operatic rather than strictly dramatic necessity and had to be invented and then grafted on to Shakespeare's plot. Other moments fitted conveniently into an already existing mold: the prayer scene for the heroine in the final act; the storm scene of the opening of Act I (indeed, all the elements of Act I have a traditional basis, from the drinking song to the final love duet). What has changed is that the connective tissue between and within such numbers has become of far greater importance, and so breaks down any sense of formalism. Iago's famous 'Credo' at the beginning of Act II, for example, is obviously an operatic set-piece, and it was invented by Boito without reference to Shakespeare

Above left: Verdi and Tamagno at the spa of Montecatini. Though *Otello* was the most famous event in their collaboration, Tamagno was also a famous Radames in *Aida* and sang the title-roles in *Ernani* and *Don Carlos*.

Above: Cover of the vocal score of the *Quattro pezzi sacri*, which Ricordi published in January 1898. The four separate pieces were not intended by Verdi to form a whole, and at their first performance in Paris in April of that year the 'Ave Maria' was omitted.

(unless to Iago's speech including the words 'Divinity of Hell' in *Othello*). But the formal flexibility of the piece is quite untraditional. Notice how the tiny motif which begins Act II soon gives rise to lyrical melody, and is later used in the 'Credo' itself; or how the grand full-orchestra melody which initiates the 'Credo' returns at the end (just before 'Vien dopo tanta irrision la Morte') in a richly harmonized, more restrained version. In a sense, techniques like this are the watchword of *Otello*, where the profound sense of naturalism is achieved through a manipulation and enrichment of traditional elements.

If we are to believe Verdi's own statements, he had been looking for a comic opera libretto throughout his later career. We find comic elements, even comic scenes, in several of the operas from *Rigoletto* onwards, but an entirely comic score, with the new methods of organization this would demand, had eluded him. But when, in 1889, Boito eventually presented him with an outline for *Falstaff*, a version of Shakespeare's *The Merry Wives of Windsor* (with additional material from *Henry IV*), he was understandably reluctant. The main objections are set out in a letter to his librettist: 'In outlining *Falstaff* did you never think of the enormous number of my years? I know you will reply exaggerating the state of my health, which is good, excellent, robust . . . so be it, but in spite of that you must agree I could be accused of great foolhardiness in taking on so much! Supposing I couldn't stand the strain? And failed to finish it?' But Boito, to his eternal credit, managed to convince Verdi of the plan's viability, and composition began in the summer of 1889. Needless to say, with a composer well into his seventies, the score progressed rather slowly, with frequent recuperative gaps, the composer insisting that the opera was little more than an old man's diversion: 'I'm enjoying myself writing the music; without plans of any sort and I don't even know whether I'll finish it . . . I repeat . . . I'm enjoying myself.'

On one level Verdi's protestations about *Falstaff* make perfect sense: the opera can indeed be seen as an ironic reflection on a lifetime spent with tragic works, and many 'stock devices' of *melodramma* are overtly lampooned. But this should not lead us to underestimate the piece's profound originality. *Falstaff* has no precedent in Italian opera and influenced many works of the succeeding decades. As with *Otello*, some of the credit for this must go to Boito, who often steered the composer gently towards this or that original solution. For example, it was Boito's idea that the two young lovers, Nannetta and Fenton, be denied a full-scale, 'set piece' love duet and instead be presented in fugitive glimpses during the drama. In his words: 'I would like as one sprinkles sugar on a tart to sprinkle the whole comedy with that happy love without concentrating it at any one point.'

We are immediately made aware that the increase in 'orchestral continuity' mentioned in *Otello* is, in *Falstaff*, developed still further. In the opening scene, for example, the orchestra presents a true symphonic argument: a central theme is introduced and developed, contrasting themes are brought in, the main theme is recapitulated, and so on. However, this not only serves to increase the musical complexity but also aids dramatic verisimilitude in that it liberates the vocal parts, allowing them to converse in a naturalistic manner entirely in keeping with the dramatic context.

As with virtually all Verdi's mature operas, it is impossible to do justice to the embarrassment of riches. One could mention the musical characterization – in particular that of the protagonist, justly regarded as one of the finest baritone parts in the repertory – or the increase (ever since *Otello*) in orchestral and formal emancipation, or the superb manner in which the various scenes are painted musically. But perhaps most noteworthy is the way in which Verdi remained able to experiment musically with such unerring dramatic sense. Perhaps only the trained musician would appreciate that the opening scene of Act I parodies symphonic sonata form, or that the final number of the opera, 'Tutto nel mondo e burla' is an academic fugue which, nevertheless, manages some startling reversals of academic practice; but every opera-goer will instinctively feel the musical aptness of these scenes, their impeccable timing in the dramatic context; and these are qualities which ultimately transcend verbal description.

Falstaff was Verdi's farewell to the stage, but not his last published composition. Between 1890 and 1896 came the *Quattro pezzi sacri*, four sacred compositions in which he made a final attempt to reinterpret religious texts according to his own musical and philosophical stance; Ricordi issued them in 1898. The last years, particularly after Giuseppina's death in 1897, were ones of increasing loneliness. Verdi spent a good deal of time planning and having built a rest home for old and impoverished musicians, the Casa di Riposo; he remained pessimistic about the honors which Italy continued to bestow upon him. On 21 January 1901 he suffered a severe stroke and died six days later. His will distributed lands and possessions among various descendants, with the rights to the operas going to the Casa di Riposo. But Verdi's essential legacy – the operas themselves – he left for all to enjoy. It is difficult to imagine a world in which they will not continue to delight and inspire.

Above: Photograph of Verdi outside La Scala. After his wife's death in 1897 Verdi's loneliness brought him more often to Milan. Much of his remaining energy was taken up by his various charitable interests, especially the Casa di Riposo.

Left: Photograph of Verdi's funeral in Milan in 1901. Toscanini conducted the La Scala orchestra and chorus in 'Va, pensiero' from *Nabucco*, and Verdi was finally laid to rest in the Casa di Riposo. Boito wrote of his deathbed: 'How good and beautiful he was to the last moment . . . The old reaper had to carry off his scythe well battered.'

GIACOMO PUCCINI

WILLIAM ASHBROOK

Few composers have established an abiding popularity with a worldwide public during their lifetimes to the same degree as did Giacomo Puccini. This popularity did not, however, always come easily to Puccini, and it frequently brought upon him harsh criticism both from less successful rivals and from a segment of the audience that found his appeal too unsubtle for their discriminating tastes. Yet it is safe to say that today Puccini's importance both as a composer and as a figure in the history of Italian opera is, quite simply, unassailable.

Puccini belonged to the fifth successive generation of composers forming a musical dynasty based in the Tuscan city of Lucca, where Giacomo was born. Yet the phenomenon that he became cannot be explained merely as the result of genetic inheritance, for none of his respected ancestors, including his father, attracted much attention beyond the walls that ring Lucca. The qualities that set Giacomo apart are based on more than a gift for irresistible melody, deriving too, from his finely developed sense of musical theater and from an equally keen awareness of contemporary trends in music. He kept himself unobtrusively open to changing musical trends during his lifetime, starting with Massenet and the French *théâtre lyrique*, on through Debussy and Richard Strauss, until he had assimilated effects from Musorgsky (revealed outside Russia for the first time in 1908), and even Stravinsky and Schoenberg.

In 1883 Puccini graduated from the Milan Conservatory, where his professor of composition had been Amilcare Ponchielli, the composer of *La Gioconda*, and the student's graduation piece had been a *Capriccio sinfonico*, a purely orchestral work. A constant aspect of Puccini's artistic personality was his desire to appear up to the moment, new-fashioned rather than old-, and to conquer his public with some sort of a *coup*. In the light of this continuing tendency, his student whim of appearing as a symphonist in a country where composers before him had traditionally made their fame in the opera house, clearly indicated his urgent need to stand out somehow from his fellow aspirants for fame.

Puccini's lifelong bent towards Italianizing non-Italian influences is likewise discernible in *Le Villi* (1884), his first opera, which belongs to a genre of stage-work uncommon in Italy, the *opéra-ballet*; and indeed its plot derives from one of the most famous of nineteenth-century ballets, Adam's *Giselle, ou les Willis* (Paris, 1841). The *opéra-ballet* was a quintessentially French form, its provenance stretching back to the elaborate spectacles composed by Lully for the court of Louis xiv. In Italy, on the other hand, the prevailing tendency had been to regard operas and ballets as separate works, presenting them as contrasting portions of a mixed bill. It was not until the 1870s that the French-style *divertissement* became a welcome ingredient in Italian operas, as demonstrated by the *ballabile* in the triumphal scene of *Aida* and the 'Dance of the Hours' in Act iii of Ponchielli's *La Gioconda*. Puccini's *Le Villi*, however, moves beyond the notion of the episodic *divertissement*, for in it the balletic action is central and even provides the final tragic dénouement.

Le Villi was not a notable success; although it aroused both interest and surprise, it could not sustain them. In an attempt to make this opera-ballet seem more substantial, Puccini expanded its original single act to two acts some seven months after its première. Unfortunately, this amplification merely stressed the ineptitude of Ferdinando Fontana's libretto and Puccini's inability yet to sustain a consistent musical personality. The composer soon came to accept *Le Villi* as an aberration, for in his later operas he would confine dancing to such dramatically apposite moments as Manon Lescaut's lesson in the minuet or the horseplay preceding Mimì's entrance in the last act of *La Bohème*.

Puccini's second opera, *Edgar*, first performed in four acts in 1889, reduced to three in 1892 and undergoing still another revision in 1905, also betrayed French influence. Its plot was derived rather crudely by Fontana from Alfred de Musset's closet drama, *La Coupe et la main*, and the character of Tigrana comes across as a not very legitimate descendant of Bizet's Carmen. The weaknesses of *Edgar*, clear from Puccini's subsequent vain efforts to salvage it through revision, stem from Fontana's failure to provide his characters with convincing motivation, which prevented Puccini from achieving sharp musical portraiture. In the long view, however, both *Le Villi* and *Edgar*, for the lessons Puccini learned from them, must be regarded paradoxically as positively negative experience. He became convinced that an opera could not succeed without a strong, clearly motivated plot, encompassing a powerful, self-evident conflict. In the future he would become an active participant with his librettists, ruthlessly shaping his plot to suit his own sense of theatrical viability.

· *Verismo* ·

Right: The medieval towers of Lucca. Though generally unimportant as a center for Italian music, Lucca enjoyed a considerable reputation for its church music, and the cathedral had had a music school since the tenth century. Puccini's ancestors are recorded as having written cantatas for the cathedral, and at the age of ten Giacomo became a choirboy there. Later he played the organ in local churches.

The other principal shaping influence upon Puccini's future came from the *verismo* explosion which followed Pietro Mascagni's success with the one-act *Cavalleria rusticana* (Rome, 1890), a detonation reinforced by the wide acceptance that two years later greeted Ruggero Leoncavallo's *I Pagliacci*. Soon these two operas came to form a practically indissoluble double-bill. Both deal with peasant life, both culminate in crimes of passion, both feature with searing intensity what Zola – one of the sources of literary naturalism – called 'une tranche de vie' (a slice of life).

The usual definition of *verismo* explains it as the operatic equivalent of *naturalism* in literature, a type of intense realism that frequently stresses the sordid and violent aspects of life. The application of naturalism to the unrealistic conventions of opera, however, produced a sense of contradiction. The scores of both *Cavalleria* and *Pagliacci* contain a good deal of material that is not, in any sense, veristic. The first half of the score of *Cavalleria* is given over to a series of expository episodes, none of which would seem out of place in a non-veristic setting: an offstage serenade, an opening chorus, an Easter hymn. Except for Canio's brief outburst, 'Un tal gioco,' much the same point can be made about *Pagliacci*, up through Nedda's 'Ballatella.' One novel feature of *Pagliacci*, however, is that the action is preceded by a 'prologue,' in which Tonio explains the theory of naturalism, rather in the manner of a *raisonneur* in a French play.

The *réclame* which *Cavalleria* and *Pagliacci* aroused tempted a number of other operatic composers, both in Italy and elsewhere, to imitate the subject-matter and intensity of these scores, but few made any lasting impression. Among the exceptions are Massenet's *La Navarraise*, dating from 1894, and *Tiefland* by the German composer, Eugen d'Albert, dating from 1903, but their relative success is pale indeed compared to that of *Cavalleria* and *Pagliacci*. If other composers, in imitating the best-known scores by Mascagni and Leoncavallo, found disillusionment, then so did these two, for none of their succeeding operas produced a comparable splash, and they were tagged, with some slight injustice, as 'one-opera' composers.

The *verismo* movement did not for very long succeed in perpetuating itself in its 'simon-pure' form, although its impulse became transformed and absorbed into something approaching an international style, a style in which veristic ingredients form only one significant strand, but discernible in such varied works as Puccini's *Tosca*, Strauss's *Salome* and Prokofiev's *The Gambler*. The failure of *verismo* as such probably resides in the diminution of esthetic distance between subject and audience. Instead of confronting subjects that dealt with historic or legendary figures, the audience at genuine *verismo* operas faced everyday scenes of ordinary people too close at hand, yet these operas were cast in a basically unrealistic 'sung' convention, which by its very nature implies eloquence and elevation of thought rather than the mundane. That both *Cavalleria rusticana* and *I Pagliacci* were unhampered by this diminution of esthetic distance was due to their leisurely exposition and their skillful deployment of contrasting non-veristic material, as with the tranquil atmosphere of the famous 'Intermezzo' from *Cavalleria* or with the device of the play-within-the-play in *Pagliacci*.

The transformed influence of *verismo*, however, can be detected in a variety of ways. Puccini realized early on that the insertion of realistic details could enhance the sense of immediacy of a work removed from the present in time and place; indeed, of all his operas, only the one-act *Il Tabarro*, his nearest approach to a *verismo* work, is set 'in the present.' Realistic touches, however, are frequently encountered in his operas, as in the embarkation scene in *Manon Lescaut*, where the list of prostitutes to be deported is called off, and as each girl crosses the stage the crowd comments upon her; or the incorporation of street cries in Act II of *La Bohème*, or the details of the poker game in Act II of *La Fanciulla del West*.

The second way in which the veristic influence made itself felt was by hastening the change in vocal style. The kind of vocal virtuosity implicit in the concept of *bel canto*, the notion that even a dramatic singer in such a role as Norma

Above: Franchetti, Mascagni and Puccini as students at the Milan Conservatory. Alberto Franchetti (1860-1942) was a composer whose family fortune made possible the production of several of his early operas, which were in a less realist vein than those of many of his contemporaries.

Right: Puccini (*right*) and Ferdinando Fontana in 1884. Their work together on *Le Villi* (1884) was organized by Puccini's teacher Ponchielli. Fontana was a member of the group calling themselves *Gli Scapigliati* (disheveled ones) and was active in the 1898 uprising.

Below: First edition of Fontana's libretto for Puccini's *Le Villi*.

Libretti also changed after 1890. Instead of the rather abstract poetic diction which had been the norm until well past 1850, a tendency towards a choice of more explicit words, together with a more specific allusiveness, becomes apparent in the wake of *Cavalleria*, as well as a loosening of regular poetic meters.

In Puccini's operas, starting with *Manon Lescaut*, these influences deriving from the veristic impulse are frequently to be discerned. Besides the realistic touches, there are declamatory phrases that demand a singer to recite like an actress – Tosca's famous 'E avanti a lui tremava tutta Roma' is a case in point. The distinctive vocabularies of Madama Butterfly revealing the contents of her sleeves or of the miners in *La Fanciulla* are but a few of the many examples that might be cited to show his acceptance of the changing fashion in libretti.

• *Manon Lescaut* and *La Bohème* •

As long as he lived, Puccini continued to make modifications – some of them slight, occasionally quite drastic – after his operas had been tested by actual performance, but from his first two operas he had learned the advisability of making his major adjustments during the compositional period. None of his operas was to undergo a more painful evolution than did *Manon Lescaut*, a work which saw the contributions of no fewer than seven librettists before it assumed what Puccini regarded as stageworthy form.

A number of special considerations added to the composer's tensions during the years when *Manon Lescaut* was on the drawing-board (1890-2). Not least was the ultimatum delivered by his publisher, Giulio Ricordi, to terminate his monthly allowance to Puccini, which he had continued for nearly ten years, if this third opera did not prove itself decisively successful. At the same time Ricordi was able to exert a positive influence on Puccini's behalf by insisting, as far as he was able, that opera-houses eager to produce Verdi's *Falstaff* would also be required to mount *Manon Lescaut*. Ricordi's influence also enabled him, since he controlled the Italian rights to Massenet's *Manon* (1884), to postpone its introduction to Italy until Puccini's opera had had a chance to establish itself. The very existence of Massenet's opera proved another source of pressure upon Puccini. In spite of the situation, Puccini had insisted upon taking on the same subject, claiming both that its appeal had been proved beyond doubt and that the French novel contained more than enough material to make his opera significantly different from the episodes treated by Massenet. The chief attraction of the subject for Puccini was undoubtedly the figure of Manon herself, a character he felt he could bring to life upon the stage in his own terms.

The project got under way in the months directly following the success of *Cavalleria*

expresses herself in flights of elaborate vocalization, had begun to decline by the 1860s. By then the vocal lines in Italian scores reflect a shift away from embellished song, but still demand poised, essentially lyrical singing to produce their intended effect. With the emergence and spread of operas like *Cavalleria*, the old notions of vocal equilibrium are sharply modified by an increasing emphasis on short passages of great dramatic intensity where the projection of the text, frequently punctuated by sobs, demands an almost declamatory emphasis. Highly charged interjections gain new prominence; or a singer, as in the final pages of Massenet's *La Navarraise*, may be directed to go mad at the sight of her lover's corpse and to collapse in peals of hysterical (and unnotated) laughter.

Right: The last scene of *Cavalleria rusticana* in the original production at the Teatro Costanzi, Rome, in 1890. Written by the unknown Mascagni for a competition, and based on Verga's story of life in a small Sicilian town, it won first prize and started a vogue for one-act operas. Its success overshadowed all of Mascagni's subsequent operas.

Below: Pietro Mascagni (1863-1945). Mascagni's temperamental nature and unwillingness to submit to discipline hindered his progress at first, and after *Cavalleria rusticana* he enjoyed only sporadic success with *L'Amico Fritz* and *Iris*. His last opera, *Nerone*, produced at La Scala in 1935, had marked Fascist connotations, and he died in disgrace in 1945.

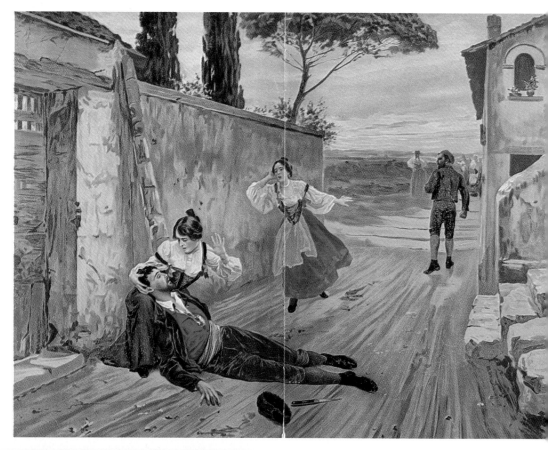

(May 1890), but the impact of *verismo* would modify only the later stages of Puccini's project, as he had already set his heart on his eighteenth-century French subject. The first librettist to whom Puccini and Ricordi entrusted the creation of a text was Leoncavallo, but the two soon proved temperamentally incompatible, and Leoncavallo withdrew from the project to promote his own future. Next, two Milanese dramatists were involved, but since neither of them had much understanding of the special non-literary requirements of a good opera libretto, they soon found Puccini's restless dissatisfaction with their text antipathetic and withdrew in a huff. With the situation seeming desperate, the libretto in limbo as it were, and even Puccini and Ricordi themselves trying their novice hands at producing the effects the composer insisted upon, Ricordi finally enlisted the help of two new figures: Giuseppe Giacosa, a dramatist–poet of high reputation, and Luigi Illica, a skilled contriver of opera texts. In Giacosa and Illica, Puccini discovered a level of comprehension that would sustain their collaboration for more than a decade and yield such fruit as *La Bohème*, *Tosca*, and *Madama Butterfly*. To the libretto of *Manon Lescaut* Illica contributed the idea of the embarkation scene and the realistic touches of the scene of Manon's toilette at the beginning of Act II, while Giacosa was responsible for the revised text of the ardent Act II love duet.

The score of *Manon Lescaut* contains many passages of passionate utterance, an intense lyricism marked by unabashed sensuality, far outstripping anything he had achieved in *Le Villi* or *Edgar*, while trademarks of his style

Left: The comedians on stage in Leoncavallo's *I Pagliacci*, at its première at the Teatro dal Verme, Milan, in 1892. The opera was conducted by Toscanini, and Boito considered it 'a vile spectacle,' but its success was immediate.

Below: Ruggero Leoncavallo (1857-1919) had mixed fortunes in his career, never again matching the success of *I Pagliacci*. His own version of *La Bohème* suffered from comparison with Puccini's, and his high ambitions to write a Wagnerian trilogy later gave way to the mundane necessity of running up operettas.

strikingly apparent for the first time include the concise aria consisting of two varied strophes, a pattern clearly exemplified by the tenor Des Grieux's 'Donna non vidi mai' in Act I, and found in such famous moments in his future work as Cavaradossi's 'E lucevan le stelle' (*Tosca*, Act III), Dick Johnson's 'Ch'ella mi creda libero e lontano' (*Fanciulla*, Act III) and Calaf's 'Nessun dorma' (*Turandot*, Act III). Puccini's use of identifying themes, as exemplified by the phrase by which Manon introduces herself to Des Grieux, 'Manon Lescaut mi chiamo,' which recurs in every act, altered but always recognizable, would remain with him, although later he would tend to vary the instrumentation of such themes rather than their rhythmic shape. His ingenuity in altering, but not in developing, Manon's identifying theme suggests that the lessons learned from his trip to Bayreuth in the summer of 1889 had not been forgotten. The influence of Wagner can also be heard in the chromatic lushness of certain passages in the Act II love duet, where echoes of *Tristan* abound, although Puccini was to use chromaticism of the Wagnerian variety sparingly in the future. Perhaps the most fruitful area for Puccini's future practice is revealed by his predilection for augmented chords and unresolved dissonances, which help to account for a characteristic Puccinian 'color' that pervades much of the score.

After *Manon Lescaut* had demonstrated its hardihood, Puccini having personally supervised its introduction to important theaters in Italy, England, and Germany, the problem of what would be his next opera arose. This posed a dilemma that would beset Puccini severely

between all his succeeding stage works. During his search for a suitable subject, he toyed for a while with *La Lupa*, a play by Giovanni Verga (1840-1922), whose work had been the source of Mascagni's *Cavalleria*. Puccini soon realized that this subject was not for him, but by March 1893 he had discovered Henri Murger's dramatization of *Scènes de la vie de Bohème*, a composite of vignettes dealing with artistic life in Paris's Latin Quarter during the days of Louis-Philippe. This subject appealed to him strongly, not only for the memories it evoked of his own bohemian days as a music student in Milan, but also for its contrast of gaiety and sadness,

Right: Act III of *La Bohème* at its first performance at the Teatro Regio, Turin, in 1896, where it was conducted by the young Arturo Toscanini. The consumptive seamstress Mimi (second from right) was sung by Cesira Ferrani, who had also been the first Manon Lescaut. Critical opinion was mixed: some pointed out the sophistication of the score, while others complained of harmonic malpractice and judged it 'artificial and whimsical.'

Right: It is uncertain how Puccini first came across Murger's *Scènes de la vie de Bohème*, but it may be that he was introduced to it by Luigi Illica, one of the librettists he had used for *Manon Lescaut*. The other, Giuseppe Giacosa (both are shown here flanking Puccini, with Giacosa on the left), was the more talented, an influential writer in his own right and a lecturer on literature at the Milan Conservatory. There was a division of labor between the two librettists: Illica laid out a prose sketch and structure, which Giacosa fleshed out with verse. Illica was the author of many light comedies and had also written libretti for Franchetti and Catalani.

and for the 'luminous' figure of Mimi – just the sort of heroine he had been seeking.

An apparent complication to his choice of this subject was his discovery that Leoncavallo was simultaneously projecting a *Bohème* of his own. That Puccini persevered with his plan, reveals his confidence in his own capacities and the accuracy of his estimate of Leoncavallo's dilatory ways and uncertain sense of theatrical values. Puccini's librettists for *La Bohème* were Giacosa and Illica, and, as before, a considerable revision of the dramatic structure was required before the work took on a shape that satisfied Puccini; in fact, the details of Act IV continued to undergo drastic changes until the end of 1895, just a few months before the première.

The initial reaction to *La Bohème* (Turin, 1 February 1896), exactly three years after the first performance of *Manon Lescaut*, was one of puzzlement. The presentation of characters much like those then encountered in the artists' quarter of any large city seemed a surprising, and not particularly appropriate, novelty; furthermore, the score's mixture of comic and tragic episodes throughout a plot that ended with the death of the heroine seemed confusing to a public accustomed to the clear dominance

of one dramatic genre or the other. Soon, however, the undeniable appeal of the plot coupled with the easily assimilable melodiousness of Puccini's score won the enthusiastic support of the public, even enlarging it to include a broader section of the bourgeoisie, who heretofore had found little to relate to in opera plots.

La Bohème marks a decisive advance over *Manon Lescaut* for the aptness of its proportions, for its unabashed eloquence mixed with light-heartedness and for its more assured, and restrained, orchestration. The minor adjustments that Puccini made to Act II after the première – inserting the little ensemble in which Mimi talks about her bonnet and slightly expanding the orchestral conclusion to the act – demonstrate his keen sense of stage timing. The repetition of thematic ideas has become even more widespread, as in the last half of Act IV, with its frequent quotations of material from Act I, but now, instead of serving the earlier function of identification, Puccini's echoes of material are used for the poignancy of their associations, this last a vein he would rework in both *Tosca* and *Madama Butterfly*.

• *Tosca* •

As early as 1891 Puccini had been attracted to Victorien Sardou's play *La Tosca*, when he had admired Sarah Bernhardt's virtuosity in the title-role, acting in French. Although at the time Puccini barely understood that language, the fact that he could become engrossed in the drama without following it word by word struck him as proof that it was well adapted for the operatic stage. With its strong melodramatic emphasis, including a scene of attempted rape,

Left: The actual Café Momus in the rue des Prêtres in Paris, where Act II of *La Bohème* is set. The drawing, by Thomas Shotter Boys, dates from 1819, a few years before the supposed date of the action of the opera.

with its heroine a temperamental prima donna, and with its action set in actual Roman monuments, *Tosca* offered Puccini just the contrast to the genre scenes more involved with pathos than true tragedy that had recently occupied him. Once again, the librettists were Giacosa and Illica, who labored to compress Sardou's five acts into three, to consolidate the play's large cast of characters into a more manageable number, and to simplify the intricate chain of the play's action so that no loose ends would remain. As had happened with *La Bohème*, the problem of getting the libretto adjusted to Puccini's exacting taste, a problem exacerbated by Giacosa's distaste for the subject – which reduced his versifying of Illica's scenario sometimes to a snail's pace – kept Puccini's nerves on edge. The composition of the score occupied him, in spite of frequent interruptions, for most

of 1898 and 1899. The last part of the score to be completed was the prelude to Act III, with its powerful evocation of the Roman dawn punctuated by the tinkling of sheep's bells and the striking of many church clocks.

Tosca had its première at the Teatro Costanzi in Rome on 14 January 1900. In spite of rumors of bomb-threats in the theater and of the hostility towards the new work from partisans of Puccini's less successful rivals, the audience as a whole was well disposed towards his newest opera, demanding encores of Cavaradossi's two arias, of Scarpia's finale to Act I (the nearest thing to a true ensemble in the score), and of Tosca's 'Vissi d'arte' in Act II. Within the first year of its existence *Tosca* had overcome any resistance raised by certain squeamish sectors of the public, and as the dramatic possibilities of the roles of Tosca and of the villainous Baron

Scarpia came to be generally appreciated, *Tosca*'s place in the repertory was secure.

Tosca offers an interesting example of veristic touches added to a plot that shares features with the older Romantic *melodramma*, and, indeed, the fusion of these traditions, in both text and music, is probably unequaled in its effectiveness. The veristic approach extends to the placing of the action in readily recognizable Roman landmarks, and realistic touches are found in such details as Puccini's musical description of the Sacristan's muscular twitches in Act I, and of Cavaradossi's mixing his paints upon his palette just before he sings his Act I aria, 'Recondita armonia.' Other sure signs of *Tosca*'s *verismo* connection can be found in the frequent use of specific props (the painting of the Marchese Attavanti, the fan, the knife) and in the detailed directions for stage business: Scarpia's offer of holy water to Tosca, his own belated crossing of himself when he finally becomes aware of the *Te Deum* sung at the end of Act I, or Tosca's arranging the candelabra around Scarpia's corpse and her dropping a crucifix on his chest at the end of Act II. The melodramatic aspects of the plot are concerned with Scarpia's pursuit of the escaped prisoner, the torture scene in Act II, and the business of the mock-execution which turns out to be real in Act III.

The opera is noteworthy for what it shows of Puccini's advance in writing for types of voices other than those used in his earlier scores. The title-role calls for a soprano with great dramatic intensity, and in one of his letters Puccini

Milano, 17-2-1904
Première alla Scala
MADAMA BUTTERFLY

explains that he wanted for Tosca the type of voice that could cope with the demands of *La Gioconda*, one with considerable expressive power at both ends of its range. For the role of Scarpia, Puccini experimented with another vocal type new to him. Unlike the more lyric roles of Lescaut or Marcello (in *La Bohème*), Scarpia is the precursor of such powerful roles as Sheriff Rance in *La Fanciulla* and Michele in *Il Tabarro*. The tenor role of Mario is cast rather in the shade by these more vivid vocal and dramatic personalities. Although Puccini gives the tenor much grateful music to sing, he had still to discover how to endow his heroes with a convincing afflatus.

The music of *Tosca* shows many signs of the composer's scrupulous attention to musical characterization. Associated with Scarpia is Puccini's first exploitation of the whole-tone scale, heard in the Scarpia motive which thunders out at the beginning and end of Act I, consisting of a series of three chords featuring the interval of the augmented fourth. The Scarpia motive returns in many guises throughout the

Above: Poster for the première of *Madama Butterfly* at La Scala on 17 February 1904.

Left: Page from the autograph manuscript of *Madama Butterfly*. The failure of the original production was a serious blow to Puccini, who felt it to be 'the most heartfelt and the most expressive opera that I have conceived.' He described the first performance as a 'lynching.' 'Those cannibals didn't listen to a single note – What a terrible orgy of madmen drunk with hate.'

course of the opera, but with its harmony intact, the single exception occuring at the end of Act II, after Scarpia's murder. Puccini is particularly successful at differentiating the lyric expansive forms in Mario's and Tosca's arias and duets, using for them what are essentially closed forms and consistent patterns of tonality, from the more active, dramatic moments associated primarily with Scarpia's evil, which are terse, chromatic and irregular. The progress of the opera gains musical coherence from the relationship of the keys in which the various acts end: Act I in E flat major, Act II in E minor and Act III in E flat minor, offering a harmonic reflection of the various stages of the plot. All in all, *Tosca* offers much fascinating evidence of Puccini's canny resourcefulness as a man of the theater.

• *Madama Butterfly* •

It was while Puccini was in London during the summer of 1900, superintending the introduction of *Tosca* at Covent Garden, that he saw David Belasco's one-act dramatization of John Luther Long's magazine story *Madam Butterfly*. Similar to his experience with Bernhardt in Sardou's *La Tosca* was the emotion he felt watching Blanche Bates in this play, and without understanding much of the English text, he found himself deeply moved by the plight of the abandoned Japanese wife who kills herself. For a few months he restlessly considered other prospects, and it was not until nearly the end of 1900 when he talked to Illica, who had got hold of a copy of Long's original tale, covering the full time-span of Lieutenant Pinkerton's acquaintance and marriage to Cio-Cio-San, that the possibility of a full-length opera on this subject seemed reasonable. At once, Puccini eagerly embraced his newest project.

Not the least of the many features he found attractive in this subject was the opportunity to use a good deal of local color to contrast with his usual musical idiom. Specific Japanese local color had been exploited to some degree in two operas known to Puccini: André Messager's *Madame Chrysanthème* (1893), with its plot derived from Pierre Loti's tale of the same name, which had been one of the sources of Long's *Madam Butterfly* (but with the significant

difference that Chrysanthème survives her abandonment by her French naval lieutenant), and Mascagni's *Iris* (1898). With his subject in hand, Puccini conducted some research into authentic Japanese melodies and instrumental color.

From what has already been said about Puccini and *verismo*, it should be clear that transferring his realistic touches to an alien culture and to a different musical tradition was for him only a logical extension of his earlier practice of introducing a pseudo-eighteenth-century minuet into Act II of *Manon Lescaut* and an authentic bit of French military music at the end of Act II of *La Bohème*. Experts have assured me that most of the Japanese-sounding music in *Butterfly* was concocted by Puccini, rather than adapted by him from pre-existing native material.

The evolution of *Butterfly* proved to be a troublesome time for Puccini. Illica's awkward adaptation of the material caused delays, and it was not until November 1902 that Puccini received a completely versified text. Only then did he realize that the originally projected second act, set in the US consulate at Nagasaki, sadly

Commemorative postcard (*left*) and poster (*below*) for the première of *Tosca* at the Teatro Costanzi, Rome, in 1900. In a year of political strife the news that the Queen of Italy was to attend the performance (she did not in fact arrive until the interval) caused an atmosphere of tension, but the opera emerged a public, if not a critical, success.

defused the cumulative power of the plot and would have to be eliminated, much to Giacosa's and Illica's dismay. The period of *Butterfly*'s composition was further complicated by the composer's low spirits at the time.

The first performance of *Madama Butterfly*, on 17 February 1904 at La Scala, Milan, was one of the great fiascos in the proud history of that theater. Contemporary opinion about this occasion placed the chief blame squarely upon Puccini's rivals and their adherents, claiming that the tumult in the theater that night was as carefully planned and executed as the performance on the stage. Be that as it may, some of the problems were, as Puccini immediately recognized, due to miscalculations in his score. He had long been in the habit of quietly touching up his operas, basing his alterations on his experience of them in the theater: but now, in the wake of the attention focused on this work by its clamorous unsuccess, his modifications would be widely discussed in the press.

Puccini had withdrawn his score after its first performance, returning his fee to Ricordi. The principal changes he would make, before re-exposing it to the public at Brescia (a safe distance from Milan) in May 1904, were to alter one passage that the first audience had shouted down as too closely resembling a phrase from *La Bohème*, to eliminate some material from Act I which slowed down the exposition, and to add several passages to the final scene that would now be preceded by an intermission. Even with this last alteration, however, Puccini insisted on retaining the sense of this scene's close relationship to the one before it (which ends with Butterfly beginning her vigil) by insisting that the final scene be called Act II, Part 2, not Act III. Unlike the première at La Scala, the performances at Brescia enjoyed a warm success, and the future popularity of the score was assured. This did not mean, however, that Puccini's attentions to the score were complete, for over the next half-dozen years he continued to tinker with it: further compressing Act II to keep the focus of attention more squarely on Butterfly, rearranging Butterfly's Act II aria, 'Che tua madre dovra,' to emphasize her fatalistic acceptance of dying, and expanding an orchestral interlude during Butterfly and Suzuki's 'flower duet' to allow more time for the necessary stage business of decorating the house.

One of the changes made for the Brescia production of May 1904 is worth examining in detail because it is a clear illustration of Puccini's sharp sense of theater. In the original La Scala version, Butterfly produces her son, Trouble, showing off to the American consul, but instead of the child being carried off shortly after Sharpless's exit, as he is now, he remained until after the vigil, which kept him on stage for nearly an hour. The uproar at the première had so unnerved the child assigned to this role that Puccini had wisely decided to play down this source of potential trouble. For Brescia he fixed the entrances and exits of the child as we know them today, but doing so required some musical adjustments, one of which is a major improvement.

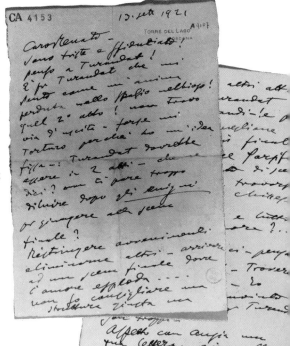

Right: Letter dated 13 September 1921 from Puccini to Renato Simoni about *Turandot*. Simoni, an erudite writer and critic, suggested the eighteenth-century Italian playwright Carlo Gozzi as a possible source for a new opera, and Puccini proposed the play about the cruel Chinese princess, having seen Max Reinhardt's production of it with incidental music by Busoni. Simoni himself worked on the libretto from Schiller's adaptation of Gozzi, collaborating with Giuseppe Adami, the librettist for *Il Tabarro* and *La Rondine*.

For Brescia he wrote Bufferfly's 'Trionfa il mio amor,' one of the great emotional climaxes of the score. Just after Pinkerton's ship has been sighted, Butterfly, believing her faith in his return entirely vindicated, sings an impressive phrase, while the orchestra thunders out the principal theme of her Act I love duet. Originally this passage had been quite different. After recognizing Pinkerton's ship, Butterfly told her son that his name is no longer Dolore, 'Trouble,' but Gioia, 'Joy,' and she gave him an American flag to flourish, while the orchestra proclaimed the opening bars of 'The Star-Spangled Banner.' Here the change serves to throw Butterfly into sharper relief: before she had to share this big moment with the child; now she has it to herself.

After the dramatic intensities of the melodramatic *Tosca*, the score of *Madama Butterfly* is more personal, more poetic, and more pictorial. Many moments seem like musical equivalents of Japanese prints. There is an emphasis on simplicity and clarity of line in the humming chorus that concludes Act II, Part 1. The little fugato tune at the beginning of the opera can be construed as the equivalent of a calligraphic line; its characteristic opening squiggle recurs at many points to emphasize the jocular loquacity of the Japanese characters. The sense of deep space finds its equivalent in the distant voices of the sailors heard in the intermezzo which introduces the final scene. In Act II, Part 1, when Butterfly first regains a little of her composure after Sharpless has asked her frankly what she would do if Pinkerton should not return, she replies 'I believe I should die, but it passes quickly as the clouds pass over the sea.' The last phrase of this passage is set to a rising and falling contour of a whole-tone scale, mirroring the sense of the words, as the muted horns add a mournful color. At such a moment, Puccini's delicate restraint as both poet and painter in tone is admirable.

Above: Photograph of Puccini with Illica, taken after their collaboration had ended with *Madama Butterfly*.

• *La Fanciulla del West* •

Three years were to elapse after the first performance of *Madama Buttterfly* before Puccini found the subject for his next opera. He was in New York, preparing *Butterfly* for its introduction at the Metropolitan, when he saw another play by Belasco, *The Girl of the Golden West*. During those three years he had considered a number of projects, among them an operetta and a series of three one-act operas to be derived from short stories by Maxim Gorky; but each of these ideas had been vetoed by Giulio Ricordi, who insisted that Puccini should aim for a work of major proportions and consequence. At one point Ricordi had pressurized Puccini into signing a contract to compose an opera based on a lurid novel by Pierre Louÿs, but a fastidious streak in the composer's nature made him break this contract because he realized that he was now incapable of composing a work based on a sleazy, sexually explicit *verismo* subject. He had attained a degree of sophistication and understood that the direction of his developing talent would increasingly seek subjects in which the sexual drive is not denied but becomes a stimulus for ennobling love, often attained through suffering and sacrifice.

When Puccini saw Belasco's *Girl*, his command of English was little better than when he had seen the one-act play of *Madam Butterfly* in London, but he was struck by certain non-verbal aspects of Belasco's production. The play had begun with a series of lantern-slides of scenes of the forests and mountains of California, creating a sense of a primeval world, vast and untrammeled by civilization. Further, much of the exposition of *The Girl of the Golden West* had included background music, and at one moment a balladeer had appeared on stage to sing 'Old Dog Tray,' a tune that Puccini would retain in his score.

The Girl of the Golden West lingered in his mind, and several months later an English friend volunteered to make him a translation. In July 1907, now back in Italy, Puccini received this translation and within a week had decided how best to compress the four acts of the play into three for a libretto, and how to move certain episodes from one part of the play to another to increase their significance. An important decision was to move the episode of Dick Johnson's close brush with hanging from the saloon to the outdoors, a change which reveals how important the sense of primitive nature was to Puccini's conception of the subject.

The first librettist to work on *La Fanciulla* was Carlo Zangarini, an experienced dramatist whose mother had been born in the American West, but Zangarini soon tried Puccini's patience because he worked with agonizing slowness and showed no ready understanding of the special requirements of a text designed to be set to music. Before long it became apparent that the services of a collaborator would be needed, and Guelfo Civinini was drafted into service. Later, both men agreed that Puccini's name should be listed with theirs as an equal co-worker on the text, but Puccini refused that designation. With the usual delays, one due to an unfortunate scandal involving Puccini's wife, the composition of *Fanciulla* went forward, and the orchestration of the work was completed during the summer of 1910. The première took place at the Metropolitan in December of that year, the leading roles in the hands of such stars as Destinn, Caruso and Amato, with Toscanini conducting and Belasco co-operating in the staging.

La Fanciulla was promptly put on by the leading opera houses of Europe and the Americas, but once the novelty of the score had worn off a period of disillusionment set in. The principal dissatisfaction seemed to center on the absence of arias, although other sources were found in the crudity of the setting and the drabness of the characters, none of whom appeared to contain the poetic allusiveness that by 1910 seemed to have become Puccini's trademark. The truth of the matter is that Puccini had deliberately eschewed repeating the audience-pleasing effects found in his earlier successes. He had evolved a tighter degree of through-composed musical theater, one whose pacing was principally determined by the unfolding action rather than by moments of musical expansiveness that dilated into immediately recognizable arias. With *La Fanciulla* Puccini had moved ahead of his audience's immediate expectation, and, baffled, they felt disappointed.

To look at *La Fanciulla* from another point of view is to see that Puccini had moved beyond the limitations of *verismo*, a trap which makes Belasco's play today seem far more dated than the opera derived from it. As an Italian, Puccini had been able to view the American West as a mythical place in which certain human verities could be revealed with stark simplicity, a genuine simplicity which originally had been widely mistaken for naïveté. At first glance, the characters seem distinctly unpromising. The 'girl' of the title is Minnie, a barmaid of incredible innocence, but courageous and forthright. The 'hero,' known as Dick Johnson, turns out to be in

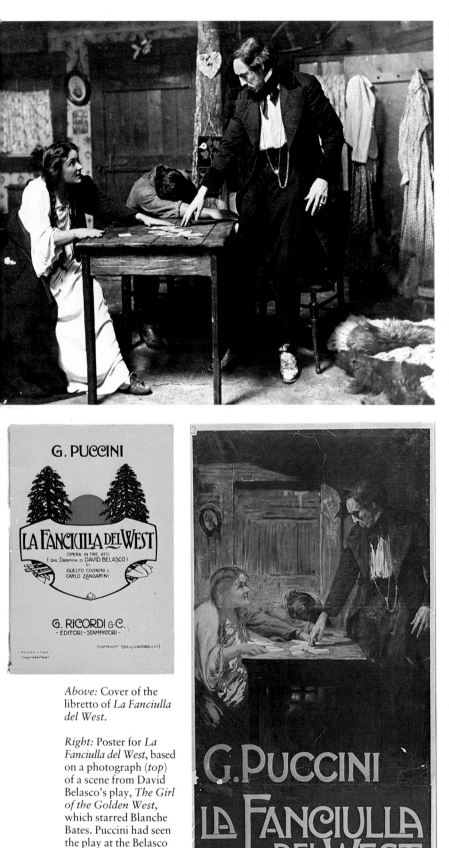

Above: Cover of the libretto of *La Fanciulla del West.*

Right: Poster for *La Fanciulla del West*, based on a photograph *(top)* of a scene from David Belasco's play, *The Girl of the Golden West*, which starred Blanche Bates. Puccini had seen the play at the Belasco Theater when he went to New York for the American première of *Madama Butterfly*, which was based on a play by the same author. The new opera was a triumph in New York.

reality a Mexican hold-up man named Ramerrez, but who is also in search of an ideal to live by. The 'villain' is the sheriff, Jack Rance, who loves Minnie in his sullen fashion, but who proves himself to be a man of his word, even though his integrity condemns him to a life of chilly isolation. Out of this apparently unpromising material Puccini has woven a myth about the redemptive power of love. All the realistic touches of the plot become subordinated and symbolically related to this overriding theme and are ultimately absorbed into it, including even the harrowing *coup de théâtre* in Act II, when Johnson's concealment by Minnie in her cabin is revealed by his blood dripping from the overhead loft on to the sheriff's hand. In the long view, even such an episode as this is more important for what it reveals about the characters involved than as just another shoddy effect of theatrical 'business.'

Writing in 1912, Puccini had some revealing words to say about this score. 'At first hearing the drama can get in the way of listening to the music, but at a second or third hearing the action is familiar and no longer surprises with the same intensity; then the music can be heard. This always happens for operas with exciting libretti.' The score of *La Fanciulla* is one of Puccini's most venturesome, and nowhere is this more apparent than in his virtuosity as an orchestrator. The bassoon *ostinato* that accompanies the poker game near the end of Act II is but one striking example of Puccini's growing expertise in finding an understated way of creating a sense of dramatic tension far exceeding the simple means used to produce it. In *Butterfly* he had used conventional instruments to achieve at times the effect of a miniature Japanese orchestra; in an analogous way in *La Fanciulla* he accompanies the Indian squaw Wowkle's lullaby near the beginning of Act II with a chamber ensemble to create an exotic tone color, which, if it bears no authentic relation to the music of the American Indians, none the less immediately suggests a contrast of cultures. During the atmospheric opening of Act III, set in the redwood forest, the offstage man-hunt for Johnson is suggested by distant shouts and an ominous three-part fanfare, first heard in the bassoons, then the horns and finally the trombones, creating a mood of increasing menace. The variety and richness of Puccini's orchestration in *La Fanciulla* far outstrips anything he had earlier accomplished in this line.

Equally impressive is Puccini's further development in the employment of vocal types in this score. Minnie is a dramatic soprano role, even more demanding than Tosca, calling for a broad range of expressive effects from a simple *cantilena* (as in the Act I Bible-lesson scene) through awakened passionate outpouring (as in the Act II love duet), even to her outburst of hysterical laughter at the end of Act II, when she realizes she has spared Johnson's life by dishonest means. As a heroic figure, Johnson marks an advance over his predecessors, not only in passages with sustained high *tessitura*, more demanding than any Puccini had earlier asked of a tenor, but chiefly because he undergoes a degree of development as a character, something that can scarcely be said of Rodolfo (*La Bohème*) or Pinkerton (*Butterfly*). The baritone role of the sheriff shows Puccini as a more subtle vocal psychologist than he was with the evil Scarpia, the only baritone role of comparable stature. Not that Jack Rance has much grateful music to sing – only in his half-restrained declaration to Minnie do his phrases have strong melodic contour, and even here Puccini suggests the dark impulses of this violent man by a somber *obbligato* for the contrabassoon. Again and again the composer manages to make this dour figure highly communicative, and by the end of the opera Rance elicits a grudging sense of pathos. Viewed from the angle of immediate appeal, *La Fanciulla* may seem at first disappointing, but it is frequently illuminated by esthetic integrity and fundamental nobility – just the traits that Puccini's most vociferous critics over the years were quickest to deny in him.

• *La Rondine* and *Il Trittico* •

Undoubtedly Puccini was deeply disappointed that the general public did not accept *La Fanciulla* as enthusiastically as they had his other operas after *Manon Lescaut*. He went through his by now customary process of briefly con-

sidering and then discarding a number of possible subjects before he became enmeshed in his next project almost without realizing it. In 1913 he went to Vienna to supervise the local première of *La Fanciulla* and was approached by the directors of the Karltheater, the headquarters of Viennese operetta, and offered generous terms and conditions to compose a score for their stage. Temporarily blinded by visions of large sums of money for what seemed only a little effort on his part, and perhaps deluded by his own shaky understanding of the German language, Puccini signed a contract. Almost immediately there were problems, and the full extent of his compromised position became clear in May 1915, when Italy, heretofore neutral, came into the war on the side of the Allies, with the result that Austrian armies invaded northern Italy.

La Rondine eventually had its first performance in Monte Carlo, but it is the most tenuous of all Puccini's post-*Edgar* operas, capable of surviving only infrequent revivals, and, more than any other of his works, dependent upon a glamorous singer-actress for its principal female role. Nevertheless, the score contains many pages of real eloquence and charm, if little of the strength that animates *La Fanciulla*. The sophistication of the harmonic practice in the operetta, which includes even a passage of bitonality, and the subtle understatement of much of the orchestration, testify to Puccini's continuing development in these directions. Nor

Below: Posters for *Suor Angelica* and *Il Tabarro*, which with *Gianni Schicchi* made up *Il Trittico*. In their terseness and compression these operas represent a retreat from the opulence of *Butterfly*, but like *Fanciulla* neither has held a central place in the repertory. Puccini's own favorite was *Suor Angelica*, with its convent setting and climactic vision of the Virgin and Child. *Il Tabarro* is the most veristic of all Puccini's operas: the story of a bargee on the Seine and his unfaithful wife.

has his famed melodic gift deserted him, for Magda's two arias in Act I and much of the dance music in Act II, which also includes a quartet that starts out irresistibly, provide treasurable moments.

As early as 1904 Puccini had toyed with the idea of composing a triple bill of one-act operas, and the novelty of that idea lingered in the back of his mind. Its possibilities of contrast in setting, atmosphere and types of plot appealed to something basic to his nature, and over the years he kept a sharp eye out for potential short plays as well as full-length ones. When he was in Paris in 1912, he had seen a Grand-Guignol play by Didier Gold, entitled *La Houppelande* (The Cloak), about barge life on the Seine. This subject appealed to him so strongly that he acquired the operatic rights to it. The start of the trail that leads to the completed *Trittico* antedates that which led to *La Rondine*, but the latter work had been completed and staged before Puccini found the last two-thirds of his triple bill.

He applied to Illica, but his old collaborator was in no humor to work with Puccini again. Without any indication yet of where the other two one-act plots would come from, he elicited a libretto for *Il Tabarro* from Giuseppe Adami, who had supplied the text for *La Rondine*. When the composition of *La Rondine* was finished in late 1915, Puccini started on *Il Tabarro*, completing it in November 1916.

In spite of being only an hour in duration, *Il Tabarro* can plausibly be ranked as one of Puccini's finest accomplishments. Everything, including even the most minor figures, contributes

to a powerful single impression. The tragic triangle of Giorgetta, the unhappy wife of the bargemaster Michele, whose jealousy becomes aroused at his wife's coldness and who murders her lover, Luigi the stevedore, is revealed step by step, emerging as a cumulative arc of conflicting passion. With this opera Puccini composed his *verismo* masterpiece. The turgid river, the fog-horns, the out-of-tune hurdy-gurdy that plays for Luigi and Giorgetta to dance to, these and all the other accruing details of accurately rendered atmosphere are presented not with the frontal assault of a *Cavalleria* but with a shrewd crescendo of effect, largely supported by a musical vocabulary derived from the French impressionist composers. With *Il Tabarro* Puccini elevates the *verismo* tradition of Italian opera to the highest level it achieved.

Barely two months after he had completed the orchestration of *Il Tabarro*, Puccini had the good fortune to discover the talents of Giovacchino Forzano, the man who would be responsible for rounding out the *Trittico*. The first of the subjects they discussed dealt with a community of nuns in a seventeenth-century Tuscan convent. The subject had particular appeal for Puccini as one of his sisters was a nun; he made a point of reading the libretto to her and her fellow religious to get their reaction to it and was gratified when they wept at the end. The plot deals with Angelica, who, we gradually learn, is an aristocrat banished by her family for bearing an illegitimate son; when she learns from her hard-hearted aunt that the child has died two years previously, the distraught Angelica concocts a poisoned draught. Dying and filled with a sense of having committed a mortal sin, she calls out to the Virgin, who miraculously appears, surrounded by angels and gently motions a little boy towards the expiring nun.

Musically, *Suor Angelica* lacks the compactness that strengthens *Il Tabarro*; the opening

Below left: Salomea Krusceniski. This Ukrainian soprano, who sang Cio-Cio-San in the first revised *Butterfly* in Brescia, had a voice of great power and was also a famous interpreter of Wagner and Richard Strauss.

Below right: Scene from *Gianni Schicchi*, the last of the three one-act operas known as *Il Trittico*, commissioned by the Metropolitan Opera in New York and first given there in April 1918. As the one comedy, it was the most warmly received and was later often taken out of the series and paired with either *Cavalleria rusticana* or *I Pagliacci*, much to Puccini's chagrin.

episodes, in particular, seem somewhat tenuous and disjointed, but they afford a striking contrast to the heightened emotions of the last half of the opera. The high point of this score is the powerful scene between Angelica and her aunt, the Princess (Puccini's most successful contralto role), where the austere older woman's declamatory lines produce a frightening sense of inexorability in opposition to Angelica's frailty and vulnerability.

Less than six months after Forzano had supplied the text for *Suor Angelica*, he delighted Puccini with a comedy set in Florence during the early Renaissance. The occasionally macabre humor arises from the comedy's story, in which the disappointed relatives of Buoso Donati, who has just died, turn to the ingenious Gianni Schicchi, who impersonates the dead man and dictates a new will, leaving the choicest properties to himself and thereby enabling his daughter to have a dowry and to marry one of Buoso's young relatives. Forzano's text is full of acerbic wit, neatly contrasting the grasping relatives with the romantic yearnings of the young lovers, and it inspired Puccini to compose one of his most vivid and delightful scores.

Gianni Schicchi is principally an ensemble opera, although it contains grateful solo moments for the soprano, tenor and baritone. In contrast to the prevailingly slow tempi, minor keys and modal sequences that dominate the scores of *Il Tabarro* and *Suor Angelica*, much of *Gianni Schicchi* moves rapidly to incisive rhythms and bright major keys. There is a brusque, rather abrasive sound to much of the woodwind-dominated orchestration associated with the greedy relatives, while the strings color the love music of the score. Puccini's knack for setting text pointedly reaches its apex here.

Puccini was concerned, and not solely for mercenary reasons, that the *Trittico* be performed intact, rather than dismembered, because he had planned the three works to complement one another. While *Il Tabarro* deals with sensual life, *Suor Angelica* is concerned with the spiritual, leaving *Gianni Schicchi* to make the point that life goes on in the succeeding generation. Viewed in another way, the *Trittico* can be seen as offering three contrasting treatments of love: illicit in *Il Tabarro*, maternal in *Suor Angelica*, and youthful in *Gianni Schicchi*. Further, these operas present three contrasting views of death, for we encounter murder, suicide and death from natural causes leading, with a little help from Schicchi, to its natural consequence, the renewal of the life cycle.

• *Turandot* •

Puccini did not live to complete his final opera, but he supervised its protracted evolution and composed and orchestrated all but the final twenty minutes of his score. Almost two years had elapsed after the première of the *Trittico* at the Metropolitan in New York, and Puccini had canvassed and rejected a number of suggestions. Then, in March 1920 Adami handed him, as a last-minute possibility while his train was pulling out of Milan station, a copy of Andrea Maffei's Italian translation of Schiller's adaptation of Gozzi's *Turandot*, an eighteenth-century Vene-

Below left: Scene from the first production of *La Fanciulla del West* at the Metropolitan Opera, New York, in 1910, with Caruso, Destinn and Amato. The scene shows Minnie's last-minute rescue of the bandit Dick Johnson (Caruso).

Below: Tito Ricordi photographed in cowboy gear around the time of *La Fanciulla del West*, which he produced. He was the eldest son of Puccini's publisher Giulio Ricordi and for a time shared his father's responsibilities in the firm. Tito was an arrogant man, whose relations with Puccini were often strained, but he became important in the raising of production standards in Italian opera, insisting on longer rehearsal periods and more realistic sets.

tian play. It was only some eight months later that Puccini became finally convinced that this Chinese subject, dealing with a princess who asks riddles of her suitors, was really a fruitful one for him and contained a plot that could be developed to meet his demands.

Turandot is a subject entirely different in scope from any that the composer had undertaken previously. It marks his final escape from the *verismo* tradition which had, to some degree, influenced all his operas from *Manon Lescaut* to the *Trittico*. While at first glance the legendary time of *Turandot* and its setting in Peking might seem merely the latest manifestation of Puccini's continuing desire for variety, the point should not be missed that for the first time he is dealing with a fable rather than with a conventional *verismo* drama with traditional characters. The *personae* who appear in *Turandot* are mostly larger-than-life symbols, archetypes who illuminate profound psychological truths. The massive scale of this work, revealed for example by the turbulent crowd scenes in Act I, challenged Puccini to create a sonic world of barbaric splendor and complexity, unlike anything he had previously attempted. This challenge he met insofar as his declining health permitted, and he completed enough of the work to leave convincing evidence that *Turandot* must rank as his finest accomplishment.

The road which led to the plot of *Turandot* in its present form was marked by many false starts, and in retrospect our sense of frustration is increased by our knowledge that Puccini's time was more limited than either he or his librettists appreciated. The original plan was to cast the opera in two massive acts, each divided into two parts. The first was to consist of the present Act I, rounded off by the riddle scene (the present Act II, Scene 2), while the second was to cover what is now the third act, but without the death of the slave-girl Liù. It was not until the end of 1921 that something approaching the present three-act format was finally agreed upon. Two ideas then entered surprisingly late into the project: first, that of the intermezzo of the three masks (Ping, Pang and Pong, an ingenious adaptation of Gozzi's traditional *commedia dell' arte* figures), the episode that now forms the opening part of Act II; and, second, the sacrifice of Liù by means of her suicide in Act III. Both these ideas originated with Puccini – clear evidence of the important role he played in the shaping of this plot.

The slave-girl Liù is the one character in *Turandot* that bears little resemblance to any of the characters in the literary sources. In his correspondence with his librettists, Puccini speaks of developing the role as a *piccola donna*, intending her as a contrast to the icy-hearted Turandot. The notion of making her, through her sacrificial death, the instrument that initiates the thawing of the princess into a woman truly capable of love, is one that unbalances the equilibrium of the rest of this plot, but it provides a needed emotional climax.

The leading tenor role of Calaf in *Turandot* afforded Puccini a chance to achieve a genuinely

heroic note. There is a confidence, a whole-hearted commitment, a readiness to risk all, even his life, in Calaf that makes him seem genuinely and satisfyingly heroic to a degree unmatched by any of his earlier counterparts. And yet he also has warmth and eagerness, as revealed by his Act III aria, 'Nessun dorma.' The soprano role of Turandot contains music with an imperious sweep and grandeur that sets her beyond any of Puccini's previous heroines. In Act I she appears but does not sing a note, and the mere sight of her is enough to inflame Calaf's heart. She introduces herself in Act II, Scene 2, with her aria, 'In questa reggia,' and both her menace and her aura of unaroused passion are revealed by the wide intervals in her propulsive phrases.

By March 1924 Puccini had come to a definite agreement with his librettists about the handling

Above: Gabriele D'Annunzio.

Opposite: Poster for *Francesca da Rimini*, 1914, the opera written to a libretto by D'Annunzio by Riccardo Zandonai (1883-1944).

Below: Cover of the vocal score of *Turandot*, designed by Umberto Brunelleschi, who was the costume designer for the first production of the opera at La Scala under Toscanini in April 1926, seventeen months after Puccini's death.

Right: Brunelleschi's design for the Princess Turandot's costume in Act III. It the first production the role was sung by the Polish soprano Rosa Raïsa, who had sung Francesca in the Italian première of Zandonai's opera in 1916.

of the final scene, but he had to wait until September of that year before they submitted their text to him. Unfortunately, by then Puccini's throat cancer was so far advanced that he managed to make only thirty-six pages of brief musical sketches for the scene before he went to a Brussels clinic for treatment, and there he died on 29 November 1924. It was Toscanini's decision to invite the composer Franco Alfano to perform the thankless task of working up Puccini's sketches so that the opera could be performed in complete form. It was also Toscanini's decision to halt the première (La Scala, 25 April 1926) with the death of Liù, the point where Puccini's orchestration stopped. Alfano's role in the score of *Turandot* was further complicated by Toscanini's dissatisfaction with the first version of the finale he supplied, obliging him to carry out his task a second time.

In retrospect, Puccini appears as the last major figure in the long history of Italian opera that stretches back to Monteverdi and the dawn of opera as a form, and he seems now the final flowering of what was essentially a nineteenth-century tradition, even though he lived well into the first quarter of the twentieth century. It is possible to see today, certainly more clearly than at the time of his death in 1924, that Puccini had a great deal more talent than merely a canny sense of theatrical effect, for he was an artist whose skill increased from work to work; that he moved from the sparse felicities of *Le Villi* to the dazzling splendors of *Turandot* in a progressive development that is not easily matched. His unflagging popularity suggests that he understood, as only the most accomplished composers can, the art of insinuating his complex musical personality into the public's consciousness.

Adam, Adolphe (* Paris, 24 July 1803; † Paris, 3 May 1856). French composer. Adam studied at the Paris Conservatoire with Boïeldieu and initiated a long career at the Paris Opéra Comique with *Pierre et Catherine* (1829). He traveled and worked in London for a time after the 1830 July Revolution, but soon returned to Paris, where his *Le Chalet* (1834) was an outstanding and long-lasting success, as was *Le Postillon de Longjumeau* (1836). In 1847 he founded the Théâtre National as a new operatic stage, but the venture was a financial failure and survived less than a year. Two years later he succeeded his father, Louis Adam, as professor of piano at the Conservatoire.

BIOGRAPHICAL DICTIONARY OF COMPOSERS

Adam's prolific output of some twenty *opéras comiques* shows his sure touch within the genre, but this success hindered him in more serious forms. His most popular work is undoubtedly the music for Coralli and Perrot's Romantic ballet *Giselle* (1841).

Alabiev, Alexander (* Tobolsk, 15 Aug. 1787; † Moscow, 6 Mar. 1851). Russian composer. Born into a rich and influential family, Alabiev was taught to play the piano from the age of ten. In 1812 he joined the army as a cavalry officer and remained in service until 1823. He then lived in Moscow, mixing with the intellectual élite and pursuing a musical career. In 1825, following a murder during a game of cards, he was exiled for six years to Siberia by Tsar Nicholas, during which time he developed enormously as a composer. On his return to Moscow he became a popular success. Among his large-scale works are a symphony, three string quartets and many operas. Alabiev was a fine melodist as is demonstrated by his songs, of which 'The Nightingale' still retains a measure of popularity.

Alfano, Franco (* Posillipo, Naples, 8 Mar. 1875; † San Remo, 27 Oct. 1954). Italian composer. After studies in Naples and Leipzig, and then stays in Berlin and Paris, Alfano became in 1916 professor of composition and subsequently director at the

Bologna Conservatory. He then occupied a similar post in Turin before becoming musical director of the Teatro Massimo in Palermo in 1940. From 1942 to 1947 he worked at the Accademia S. Cecilia in Rome, and finally taught in the Liceo Musicale in Pesaro. Alfano is usually remembered as the composer who completed Puccini's *Turandot*, but in addition to twelve operas, he also produced two symphonies, a triple concerto, ballet music, two string quartets, various piano pieces and a number of songs.

Alkan [Morhange], Charles Valentin (* Paris, 30 Nov. 1813; † Paris, 29 Mar. 1888). French pianist and composer. Alkan joined the Paris Conservatoire as a pupil of Pierre-Joseph Zimmermann when he was six years old and just over a year later made his début at a public concert as a violinist. But his chosen instrument was the piano, and by 1824 he was performing his own compositions. By 1830, he had acquired a reputation as one of the brightest piano-playing stars in Paris, but eight years later he retired from public performance, gaining a reputation as a recluse and an eccentric. In 1848, on the death of Zimmermann, he was rejected for the post of head of the piano department at the Paris Conservatoire in favor of Marmontel, and he withdrew from public life, making his living from private teaching. He maintained

contact with the outside world through his friends, who included Liszt, George Sand and Hiller. He re-emerged in 1873 and for the next four years gave an annual series of six piano recitals at the Salle Erard.

Apart from a symphony, now lost, and a handful of chamber works, all Alkan's music is for the piano and ranges from gem-like miniatures to massive sonata-form movements. It reveals a composer who is original, a complete master of his craft and someone of considerable melodic invention, but who lacks any real passion or emotional intensity. Particularly impressive is the set of piano studies in all the minor keys (op.39), which includes a solo symphony and concerto without orchestra.

Arriaga, Juan (* Bilbao, 27 Jan. 1806; † Paris, 17 Jan. 1826). Spanish composer and violinist. Arriaga began composing without any musical education and at fifteen was sent to the Paris Conservatoire to study composition with Fétis and violin with Baillot. During his time there he composed a symphony and three string quartets, which display astonishing talent and maturity, but he died just before his twentieth birthday. These works remain in the repertory and suggest that, had he lived, he would have developed into a composer of great stature.

Attwood, Thomas (* London, bapt. 23 Nov. 1765; † London, 24 Mar. 1838). English composer and organist. A favorite pupil of Mozart and a close friend of Mendelssohn, Attwood was an important figure in English music during the early nineteenth century. He was known during his lifetime for his stage works but is remembered today as a composer of sacred music. He was a founder-member of the Philharmonic Society, one of the first professors at the Royal Academy of Music, and organist of the Chapel Royal from 1836.

Auber, Daniel (* Caen, 29 Jan. 1782; † Paris, 12 May 1871). French composer. Auber studied with Ladurner, and in 1805 Cherubini took him on as a pupil. After preliminary essays in *opéra comique* in collaboration with Planard, he met the librettist Scribe, with whom he had a long and fruitful association, shaping a new phase in the development of the genre, which now became characterized by more sophisticated libretti and an Italianate melodic style influenced by Rossini. This winning combination is shown to good effect in Auber's first mature *opéra comique*, *Le Maçon* (1825), which was followed by a long line of works including the popular *Fra Diavolo* (1830) and *Le Domino noir* (1837), which show off his characteristically elegant, witty and tuneful French style.

Auber is also significant in the history of French grand opera, and his *La Muette de Portici* (1828) inaugurated the new style of French grand opera taken up by Meyerbeer, Halévy and Rossini, which so influenced Wagner. The mood is serious, with fervent Romantic and patriotic elements, and there is lavish spectacle (such as the eruption of Vesuvius at the climax of the opera), with crowd scenes, huge choruses, ballets and processions.

During his time as director of the Paris Conservatoire (1842-70) Auber's style developed into a lighter lyricism with such works as *Haydée* (1847).

Baillot, Pierre (* Passy, 1 Oct. 1771; † Paris, 15 Sept. 1842). French violinist and composer. Baillot was one of the great violinists of his generation, becoming professor of violin at the Paris Conservatoire in 1795. His compositions include nine violin concertos and a large quantity of chamber music, now seldom performed, including the important *Art du violon* (1834).

Balfe, Michael William (* Dublin, 15 May 1808; † Rowney Abbey, Herts., 20 Oct. 1870). Irish composer and singer. Balfe studied in England and on the Continent. Contact with Cherubini and

Rossini led to singing engagements at the Paris Théâtre Italien, and in 1829/30 he became principal baritone in Palermo, where he produced his first opera. He returned to London in 1833 and had lasting success with the production of *The Siege of Rochelle* (1835), although his attempts to establish English opera on a firm foundation were thwarted by staff quarrels which caused him to return to Paris, where he collaborated with Scribe. Returning later to London, he produced several works, including his greatest triumph, *The Bohemian Girl* (1843), which was performed throughout Europe and North and South America. Balfe continued an active and successful career as composer, conductor and theater manager.

Beethoven, Ludwig van (* Bonn, 16 Dec. 1770; † Vienna, 26 Mar. 1827). German composer. *See pp.23-45, 51-73*

Bellini, Vincenzo (* Catania, Sicily, 3 Nov. 1801; † Puteaux, nr. Paris, 23 Sept. 1835). Italian composer. *See pp.239-246*

Benedict, Sir Julius (* Stuttgart, 27 Nov. 1804; † London, 5 June 1885). English conductor and composer of German birth. A pupil of Hummel and Weber, Benedict moved to England in 1835, where he achieved a reputation as the composer of numerous operas (including *The Gypsy's Warning*, *The Brides of Venice* and *The Crusaders*), cantatas and oratorios. He

accompanied Jenny Lind to America and conducted at Drury Lane, Covent Garden and Her Majesty's Theatre. He was also conductor of the Liverpool Philharmonic Society from 1876 to 1880 and of the Norwich Music Festivals.

Bennett, Sir William Sterndale (* Sheffield, 13 Apr. 1816; † London, 1 Feb. 1875). English composer, pianist, conductor and teacher. Bennett studied under Cipriani Potter at the Royal Academy of Music and by the age of twenty was championed by Mendelssohn and Schumann and was traveling in Europe performing his own piano concertos. He began teaching at the Royal Academy of Music in 1837, became director of the Philharmonic Society (of which he was conductor from 1856-66) in 1842, and in 1849 founded the Bach Society, through which he introduced many of Bach's masterpieces to English audiences, including the *St Matthew Passion* in 1854. He returned to composition in the early 1860s, and from 1866 he was Principal of the Royal Academy of Music.

He made a notable contribution to English musical life, and his works include a symphony, piano concertos, an oratorio and five concert overtures.

Berger, Ludwig (* Berlin, 18 Apr. 1777; † Berlin, 16 Feb. 1839). German composer and pianist. Berger taught himself flute and piano and composed more than 100 pieces before studying composition with Joseph Gürrlich in Berlin from 1799 to 1801. In 1804 he became a pupil of Clementi, and in 1805 they went together to St Petersburg, where they gave concerts with another of Clementi's pupils, John Field. Berger remained in Russia until 1812, when he fled first to Stockholm and then to London, where with Clementi's help he established a reputation as a concert pianist. He returned to Berlin in 1814 to concentrate on composition and teaching, and several of his pupils became leading figures in European music, among them Mendelssohn, Henselt and Nicolai. His songs and piano music were widely

performed during his lifetime, and particularly noteworthy are his setting of Wilhelm Müller's poems *Die schöne Müllerin* (1816, six years before Schubert's version), and his 'Pathétique' Sonata, op.7 (1804).

Berlioz, Hector (* La Côte-Saint-André, Isère, 11 Dec. 1803; † Paris, 9 Mar. 1869). French composer. *See pp.143-165*

Berton, Henri-Montan (* Paris, 17 Sept. 1767; † Paris, 22 Apr. 1844). French composer and teacher. Berton was the most successful of a family of musicians and was a prolific composer of operas. From 1807 to 1809 he was music director at the Opéra Bouffe, then chorus master at the Opéra, and in 1818 he succeeded Méhul as professor of composition at the Paris Conservatoire. His opera *Les Rigueurs du cloître* (1790) is the first example of the 'rescue opera,' of which Beethoven's *Fidelio* was to be the supreme masterpiece.

Berwald, Franz (* Stockholm, 23 July 1796; † Stockholm, 3 Apr. 1868). Swedish composer and violinist. The son of a musician of German origin, who had studied under Benda in Berlin and moved to Stockholm in the 1770s as a violinist in the court orchestra, Berwald had little formal education, but was taught the violin by his father. He was precociously talented and gave public concerts before he was ten. In 1812 he joined his father in the court orchestra, in which he was a violinist until 1824 and violist until he left Stockholm for Berlin in 1828. From 1811 he studied composition under J. B. E. Dupuy; his earliest known works of substance, an orchestral *Fantasie* and a double violin concerto (now lost), date from 1816-17, and during the next decade he composed several important works, particularly chamber music.

Once in Berlin, Berwald was unable to support himself as a musician and by 1835 he was running an orthopedic institute, which kept him occupied until 1841 but then enabled him to return to music without financial worries. He did this first in Vienna and then a year later back in Sweden. Most of the compositions for which Berwald is now known date from the years 1841-5, including the four completed symphonies and several symphonic poems, evocative of Scandinavian landscape and folklore, which are beautifully scored. In 1846, Berwald left Sweden again and for four years traveled extensively. On his return he became the manager of a glass factory in northern Sweden but continued to compose, completing several major chamber works, including two fine piano quintets, and a piano concerto (1855).

Berwald was the first Swedish symphonist of any stature, and he preceded all the great Romantics with the exception of Weber. He was a visionary and experimental composer often far in advance of his time. For a composer whose creative life spanned over half a century, his list of completed works is short, although he composed in most forms – three operas, choral works, songs, solo instrumental music, orchestral and chamber music. It is in the last two categories that his best work was done and the symphony in C, 'Sinfonie singulière,' of 1845 is generally accepted as his masterpiece.

Bishop, Sir Henry (* London, 18 Nov. 1786; † London, 30 Apr. 1855). English composer and conductor. Although Bishop composed many operas and stage works, he is remembered today for his song 'Home, Sweet Home.' He was also a distinguished conductor, was professor of music at both Oxford and Edinburgh, a leading member of the Philharmonic Society and director of music at Covent Garden from 1810 to 1824.

Bizet, Georges (* Paris, 25 Oct. 1838; † Bougival, nr. Paris, 3 June 1875). French composer. Bizet studied at the Paris Conservatoire, where his teachers included Gounod and Halévy, whose daughter he eventually married. His first attempt at the Prix de Rome resulted in a *second prix*; between this and his second (successful) attempt he wrote his first stage work, *Le Docteur Miracle* (1856), for which he shared first prize with Charles Lecocq in a competition organized by Offenbach, the winning entry being produced at the Bouffes Parisiens the following year. Another early opera, *Don Procopio* (1858-9, produced 1906), is in a very competent Italianate *opera buffa* style with traces of the lyrical expressiveness present in his best scores. The last of his early works which deserves mention is the unsuccessful five-act grand opera *Ivan IV* (1862-3, produced 1946), parts of which were used in later works.

Bizet's first mature opera, *Les Pêcheurs de perles* (1863), set in Ceylon, shows the influence of Gounod in its melodic style, while

the enterprising harmonic writing features long pedal notes under chromatic passages, a trait that was to become one of Bizet's harmonic fingerprints. *La Jolie Fille de Perth* (1866), a remote adaptation from Scott with a libretto full of improbabilities, shows a considerable advance in Bizet's dramatic style. Leading themes are used, as in *Les Pêcheurs*, but with far more dramatic effect. *La Coupe du roi de Thulé* (1868-9) seems to advance still further, although only fragments survive.

After completing his father-in-law's opera *Noé*, there followed a period of intense concentration on *opéra comique*; sketches and fragments survive for three projects, and in 1871 he completed *Djamileh*, based on an amorous poem by Alfred de Musset, though this was a failure, due to an undramatic libretto and Bizet's adventurous modal harmony. In *Carmen* (1873-4), Bizet's last and greatest work, he found a near-perfect libretto and also the exotic element with which he worked so well. Adapted from Mérimée's story, it scandalized the straight-laced Paris audience and was initially a failure, even though it has since become one of the most popular operas ever written. In its clarity, freedom from moral restraint, proximity to everyday life and superb characterization, it is one of the finest operas of its age.

Bizet also wrote piano music (including many transcriptions) and songs, and his orchestral works include three that have remained favorites in the concert repertory, the early Symphony in C (1855), the suite taken from his incidental music to Alphonse Daudet's *L'Arlésienne* (1872) – a second suite was assembled by Ernest Guirand – and *Jeux d'enfants* (1871), transcribed from his own suite for piano.

Bochsa, Nicolas Charles (* Montmédy, Meuse, 9 Aug. 1789; † Sydney, 6 Jan. 1856). French harpist and composer. A prolific composer in many forms, including several operas, Bochsa is important today as the man who perfected the modern techniques of harp playing. He composed many works for the instrument, including a teaching method still in use, and his own playing did much to reinstate the harp as a solo instrument.

Boïeldieu, François Adrien (* Rouen, 16 Dec. 1775; † Jarcy, 8 Oct. 1834). French composer. Boïeldieu received his musical training from the cathedral organist, Charles Broche, at Rouen, but the most important influence on him was *opéra comique*. After the successful production in Rouen of his *La Fille coupable* (1793), he moved to Paris and quickly established a reputation as a leading composer in the genre, his most famous work of this period being *Le Calife de Bagdad* (1800). In 1798 he was appointed professor of piano at the newly founded Paris Conservatoire, but in 1803 he left to become composer to the imperial court in St Petersburg.

On his return to Paris in 1811, Boïeldieu's popularity was confirmed with *Jean de Paris* (1812); he was made a member of the Académie des Beaux-Arts in 1817. His masterpiece, *La Dame blanche* (1825), was one of the most notable successes in the history of opera and is the work which represents his position as an upholder of the French as against the Italian school of comic opera. The libretto by Scribe is a romantic story based on a Scottish tale by Sir Walter Scott. The work shows Boïeldieu's great facility of melodic invention, with vocal lines rarely ornamented or virtuosic, orchestration lively and expert, and an individual use of chromatic harmony. Both this work and his next opera, *Les deux nuits* (1829) were admired by Wagner, and Boïeldieu's influence can be clearly traced in *Der fliegende Holländer* and in *Lohengrin*.

Boito, Arrigo [Enrico] (* Padua, 24 Feb. 1842; † Milan, 10 June 1918). Italian librettist, composer, poet and critic. Boito studied at the Milan Conservatory with Mazzucato and there formed a friendship with Franco Faccio. On the completion of their studies, both went to Paris, where Boito met Verdi and wrote a cantata text for him; he also wrote the libretto for Faccio's *Amleto* (1862). He returned to Milan in 1862, and *Mefistofele*, of which Boito was composer, librettist and

conductor, was produced at La Scala in 1868. It was a notorious failure, although a revised version was later highly successful, and Boito turned to writing libretti for other composers, among them Ponchielli's *La Gioconda* (1876).

Despite Boito's enthusiasm for Wagner and the musical avant garde, the publisher Ricordi arranged for him to collaborate with Verdi on the revision of *Simon Boccanegra* for its revival in 1881. Thereafter the friendship between the two composers deepened and led to their collaboration on *Otello* and later *Falstaff*, which Boito regarded as the climax of his artistic career. Meanwhile Verdi encouraged Boito to work on his own opera, *Nerone*, but although the libretto is often judged as one of his greatest achievements, his indecision about the music meant that it was never completed.

Brahms, Johannes (* Hamburg, 7 May 1833; † Vienna, 3 Apr. 1897). German composer. *See Volume III.*

Bruneau, Alfred (* Paris, 3 Mar. 1857; † Paris, 15 June 1934). French critic and composer. Bruneau joined the Paris Conservatoire in 1873 and three years later won a first prize for cello. He then went on to study harmony with Savard (1876-9) and composition with Massenet (1879-81), culminating in a *second prix* in the 1881 Prix de Rome. From 1891 Bruneau collaborated with Emile Zola on a series of operas, which attempted to bring the *vérisme* of the novelist's work onto the operatic stage; but although his music was always well received by the critics and his evocations of nature are particularly fine, he never enjoyed great popular success.

Catalani, Alfredo (* Lucca, 19 June 1854; † Milan, 7 Aug. 1893). Italian composer. Catalani studied in Lucca and Paris and then in Milan with Bazzini, through whom he met Boito, librettist for his first opera, *La Falce* (1875). His most important operas, *Dejanice* (1883) and *La Wally* (1892), exemplify a personal style that – unusually for Italian composers of the time – shows the influence of German music. The vocal writing is essentially Italian, but considerable prominence is given to the orchestra. This together with the interesting harmonic idiom that he employed, demonstrates Catalani's indebtedness to Wagner.

Charpentier, Gustave (* Dieuze, Moselle, 25 June 1860; † Paris, 18 Feb. 1956). French composer. After lessons with Massenet, Charpentier had some success with *Didon*, a *scène lyrique* which won the Prix de Rome in 1887, and with his symphonic suite *Impressions d'Italie* (1887-9).

The opera *Louise* (1900), a colorful, Romantic portrait of Paris, and one of the outstanding works of French *vérisme*, was an immediate success in France and elsewhere and still maintains its place in the repertory. But its success was not repeated in his second opera, *Julien* (1913), based on his earlier symphony drama, *La Vie du poète* (1888). Charpentier also made settings of poems by Baudelaire and Verlaine and composed two sets of *poèmes chantés*.

Cherubini, Luigi (* Florence, 8 or 14 Sept. 1760; † Paris, 15 Mar. 1842). Italian composer, theorist, teacher and administrator. The son of a Florentine musician, Cherubini began to study composition at the age of nine under Bartolomeo Felici and later continued with Bizzarri and Castrucci. By the time he was eighteen he had composed thirty-six works, mainly church music, including a cantata, and in 1778 he went to Venice to study under Giuseppe Sarti.

Cherubini's creative life began in Venice with his first opera, *Il Quinto Fabio* (1779). Thirteen more operas followed over the next eight years, four of which were composed for London, where he spent the years 1784-6. He then spent a year in Paris before returning to Italy to compose his finest work to this date, *Ifigenia in Aulide*, produced in Turin in 1788 with great success. The same year Cherubini returned to Paris, where he composed *Démophon*, in which he abandoned his earlier light

Italian style and developed greater expression through a closer integration of musical and dramatic content. This trend was continued in his next opera, *Lodoïska* (1791), and the period until 1816 saw the completion of a further fourteen operas, including his finest works, *Médée*, *Les deux journées* and *Anacréon*.

In 1805 Cherubini accepted a commission to write an opera for the Burgtheater in Vienna. The opera, *Faniska*, was not a success, and an enforced spell as Napoleon's director of music at Schönbrunn only added to Cherubini's unhappiness. On his return to Paris, he found the popularity of his operas eclipsed by those of Boïeldieu, and his next four operas, produced between 1809 and 1814, did little to restore his position. He composed only two more operas in the last twenty-eight years of his life.

Cherubini's appointment to the Chapelle Royale in 1816 inspired a number of sacred works, including what is arguably his finest composition, the C minor Requiem. A symphony and six string quartets also date from this period. In 1822 Cherubini became director of the Paris Conservatoire, where he exercised an enormous influence on younger French composers and wrote a number of instructional works.

Chopin, Frédéric (* Zelazowa Wola, nr. Warsaw, 22 Feb. 1810; † Paris, 17 Oct. 1849). Polish composer and pianist.
See pp.167-177

Cilea, Francesco (*Palmi, 23 July 1866; † Varazze, 20 Nov. 1950). Italian composer and teacher. Cilea studied with Cesi and Serrao in Naples, where his first opera, *Gina* (1889), was produced. His most successful opera was *Adriana Lecouvreur* (1902), based on a libretto by Scribe set in the age of Louis xv. Influenced by Puccini, Cilea's style is charming and ingenious but has little lasting distinction.

Clementi, Muzio (* Rome, 23 Jan. 1752; † Evesham, Worcs., 10 Mar. 1832). English composer, keyboard player and teacher, music publisher and piano manufacturer of Italian birth. Clementi's father, a silversmith and capable amateur musician, was quick to recognize the talent displayed by his son, who by the age of twelve was a proficient organist well versed in counterpoint. In January 1766, at the age of fourteen, Clementi secured the post of organist at his home church, S. Lorenzo in Damaso, and in the same year Peter Beckford, an English Member of Parliament, heard him play the piano and took him to his estate in Dorset to complete his education. Apart from the time spent traveling on concert tours, England was Clementi's home for the rest of his life.

Clementi's first public concerts as a pianist in London in 1774 were greeted with unprecedented critical acclaim. In 1780, he made his first concert tour of Europe, remembered for the piano contest with Mozart in Vienna, in which Clementi was considered superior in mechanical virtuosity, while Mozart excelled in beauty of touch and musicianship. On his return to England in 1783, Clementi accepted the young J. B. Cramer as his pupil, and the following spring began a full schedule of concerts as keyboard soloist at the newly organized Hanover Square Concerts. At the height of the season, however, he departed abruptly for Lyons, where he attempted unsuccessfully to elope with a former pupil, Mlle Imbert-Colomés. By May 1785 he was back in London, where he remained for many years, achieving great eminence.

In 1802 Clementi began his third European tour, and he remained abroad until 1810. These years were devoted to the promotion of Clementi pianos, developed and manufactured in collaboration with F. W. Collard, and to negotiations with composers and publishers for rights to new music, including a contract for five major compositions from Beethoven.

Clementi's own compositions fall into three categories; piano music, chamber music and symphonies. Many of the 64 piano sonatas have remained constantly in the repertory, while the 100 studies of the *Gradus ad Parnassum* (1817-26) make up the most important scholastic work in the development of modern piano playing. Clementi's chamber music has never gained a great response and his symphonies, some twenty of which were composed after 1813, have, until recently, remained unknown. But there can be little doubt that Clementi saw them as his most important work, and the reconstruction of four of them in the 1970s shows him to have been a master of symphonic form and orchestration in addition to his established reputation as a composer and pedagogue for the piano.

Cornelius, Peter (* Mainz, 24 Dec. 1824; † Mainz, 26 Oct. 1874). German composer. His parents were actors, and it was as an actor that he first trained. At the age of twenty he began to study music with Siegfried Dehn in Berlin and in 1852 moved to Weimar, where he became part of the Liszt circle and championed the ideas of Liszt, Wagner and the 'New German School' – as opposed to those of the critic Hanslick exemplified in the music of Brahms – in a series of articles in the *Neue Zeitschift für Musik*.

Cornelius's first works were *Lieder*, for many of which he also wrote the verses, and his six *Weihnachtslieder*, op.8, are particularly fine. His first opera was *Der Barbier von Bagdad* (1858), whose première, under Liszt's direction, created a scandal. Cornelius moved to Vienna the following year, where he wrote his second opera, *Der Cid*, under the influence of Wagner. At the latter's instigation he moved to Munich, where he was appointed to a post at the Royal School of Music. His teaching duties (and his ceaseless efforts on Wagner's behalf) interfered with composition, and his third opera, *Gunlöd*, remained unfinished.

Cramer, Johann Baptist (* Mannheim, 24 Feb. 1771; † London, 16 Apr. 1858). English composer, pianist and publisher of German birth. Son of the violinist and part-time composer, Wilhelm Cramer, Johann spent most of his life from the age of three in London, apart from

European concert tours. He learned the rudiments of music from his father and later was a pupil of Clementi for piano and C. F. Abel for composition. His first public performance as a pianist was at the age of ten, and he was later recognized by both Beethoven and Ries as one of the foremost pianists of his time.

Cramer's compositions comprise chamber works and numerous piano works, including over a hundred sonatas. He was also founder of an important music publishing company.

Czerny, Carl (* Vienna, 21 Feb. 1791; † Vienna, 15 July, 1857). Austrian piano teacher, composer, pianist and writer on music. Czerny learned to play the piano from his father and by the age of ten was accepted by Beethoven as one of his few pupils. He decided early in his life not to pursue a career as a traveling virtuoso and devoted himself to composition and teaching, counting among his pupils many of the finest pianists of the nineteenth century, including Liszt and Thalberg. Czerny's many sets of studies for the piano, which covered every known problem of pianistic technique, are the most important compositions for advanced teaching in the history of the instrument.

Czerny's published compositions extend beyond op.1000, several of them containing up to fifty individual pieces. They embrace almost every known musical form from church music to symphonies, from stage works to chamber music, in addition to many hundreds of piano pieces.

Dargomyzhsky, Alexander Sergeyevich (* Troitskaye, Tula district, 14 Feb. 1813; † St Petersburg, 17 Jan. 1869). Russian composer. *See Volume III.*

David, Félicien (* Cadenet, Vaucluse, 13 Apr. 1810; † St-Germain-en-Laye, 29 Aug. 1876). French composer. An orphan from the age of five, David began his musical career as a chorister in the church of Saint-Sauveur at Aix-en-Provence, where he became director of music in 1829. The following year he was admitted to the Paris Conservatoire. He then joined the Saint-Simonians, with whom he traveled as a missionary in the Middle East in 1833-5. His early interest in church music gave way to oriental subjects, and through his *ode-symphonie*, *Le Désert* (1844), and his *opéra-comique*, *Lalla-Roukh* (1862), he influenced many French composers, including Gounod, Thomas, Lalo, Saint-Saëns, Massenet and Delibes. In many respects he was second only to Berlioz among contemporary French composers.

Delibes, Léo (* Saint-Germain-du-Val, Sarthe, 21 Feb. 1836; † Paris, 16 Jan. 1891). French composer. *See Volume III.*

Donizetti, Gaetano (* Bergamo, 29 Nov. 1797; † Bergamo, 8 Apr. 1848). Italian composer. *See pp.247-257*

Dragonetti, Domenico (* Venice, 10 Apr. 1763; † London, 16 Apr. 1846). Italian double-bass player and composer. Outstandingly the best double-bass player of his time, Dragonetti did much to promote interest in the instrument. His compositions were almost exclusively for his own instrument and include concertos, more than 30 string quintets with double bass, and some duets and songs. During his long life he was a friend of Haydn, Beethoven and Berlioz and was much admired by each of them. He lived and worked in London from 1794.

Dussek, Jan Ladislav (* Čáslav, Bohemia, 12 Feb. 1760; † Saint-Germain-en-Laye or Paris, 20 Mar. 1812). Bohemian pianist and composer. The son of a celebrated Bohemian organist and music teacher, Dussek began to learn the piano when he was five and in 1779 embarked on a career as a virtuoso pianist, traveling during the next five years throughout Europe. In 1786 he settled in Paris and in 1789 fled to London, where with Haydn and Salomon as his friends, he became the most fashionable pianist and teacher in England. He encouraged the firm of Broadwood to extend the range of the piano – in 1791 from five to five and a half octaves, and in 1794 to six octaves. In 1799 Dussek left London for Hamburg to escape the creditors of his bankrupt music-publishing business, and from 1804 to 1806 he was Kapellmeister to Prince Louis Ferdinand of Prussia. These were the most prolific years for Dussek as a composer and a time when he began to display his remarkable originality. After the Prince's death, Dussek withdrew from public performance and devoted his periods of sobriety to composition. He spent the last few years of his life near Paris in the service of Talleyrand.

Dussek composed a large quantity of music: fifteen piano concertos, more than a hundred extended chamber works, forty piano sonatas and many smaller piano pieces, two stage works, a solemn Mass and many songs. While his earlier Classical works are very much products of their time, his later music, and in particular the Piano Sonata in F minor, op.77, completed in the last year of his life, was moving boldly towards the world of the great Romantic composers.

Field, John (* Dublin, 26 July 1782; † Moscow, 23 Jan. 1837). Irish composer, pianist and teacher. The son of a violinist, Field was forced by his father to practice his piano playing incessantly from the age of five, and he began to perform in public at the age of nine. In 1793 the Field family moved to London, where John worked in Clementi's piano warehouse in exchange for lessons, soon becoming Clementi's most brilliant pupil. In 1802, he accompanied Clementi on a concert tour of Europe, which ended in St Petersburg, where Field decided to remain for the rest of his life.

Field was in almost every sense a Romantic, and he was the originator of a school of pianism which culminated in Chopin. He was the originator of the Nocturne, composing eighteen pieces with this title, as well as seven piano concertos and some chamber music. He was the most important piano teacher in Russia before Rubinstein.

Flotow, Friedrich, Freiherr von (* Teutendorf, Mecklenburg-Schwerin, 27 Apr. 1812; † Darmstadt, 24 Jan. 1883). German composer. Flotow showed talent at an early age and was sent to study with Rejcha in Paris, where he stayed until the July Revolution of 1830. His first opera, *Peter und Kathinka*, was performed at the court theater in Schwerin in 1835. He returned to Paris, but struggled to make an impression with his operas, although they were produced at the Opéra and also in Vienna, Hamburg, Berlin and elsewhere.

His lasting fame rests on the works on which he collaborated with the writer Friedrich Wilhelm Riese, including *Die Matrosen* (a reworking of an earlier opera, *Le Naufrage de la Méduse*, 1839), *Alessandro Stradella* (Hamburg, 1844) and *Martha, oder Der Markt zu Richmond* (Vienna, 1847) which had a remarkable triumph and is still in the repertory.

Förster, Emanuel Aloys (* Niederstein, 26 Jan. 1748; † Vienna, 12 Nov. 1823). Austrian composer, theorist and teacher. One of the most distinguished teachers in Vienna from 1776 until his death, Förster knew Haydn, Mozart and Beethoven, who recommended him highly and whose op.18 may have been influenced by Förster's quartets. As a composer, Förster was an important link between the mature Haydn and Mozart and the early Beethoven. His experiments with form and tonality helped to undermine the equilibrium of the High Classical period.

Gade, Niels (* Copenhagen, 22 Feb. 1817; † Copenhagen, 21 Dec. 1890). Danish composer, conductor, violinist, educator and administrator. *See Volume III.*

Giordano, Umberto (* Foggia, 27 Aug. 1867; † Milan, 12 Nov. 1948). Italian composer. He studied at the Naples Conservatory with Serrao and made his mark as a composer of *verismo* opera with *Mala vita*, produced in Rome in 1892. His great success came with *Andrea Chénier*, written to a libretto by Illica and first performed at La Scala, Milan, in 1896; this was followed by *Fedora* (1898), based, like Puccini's *Tosca* of 1900, on a melodrama by Sardou designed for Sarah Beinhardt, and notable for Caruso's early triumph in the tenor role.

None of Giordano's finely or-chestrated operas, which include *Siberia* (1903), *Madame Sans-Gêne* (1915), *La Cena delle beffe* (1924) and *Il Rè* (1929), achieved comparable success, but *Andrea Chénier* and *Fedora* have held their place in the repertory, chiefly because his fresh, if unsubtle, lyric style offers splendid opportunities for powerfully dramatic performances from soprano, tenor and baritone.

Glinka, Mikhail Ivanovich (* Novospasskoye [now Glinka], nr. Smolensk, 1 June 1804; † Berlin, 15 Feb. 1857). Russian composer. *See Volume III.*

Gounod, Charles (* Paris, 18 June 1818; † Saint-Cloud, 18 Oct. 1893). French composer. He studied at the Conservatoire with Rejcha, Paer, Halévy and Le Sueur, and after winning the Prix de Rome, in 1839, he undertook the usual studies abroad, taking a particular interest in German music and literature. He returned to Paris in 1845, took up a post as an organist, and in 1847 began to study for the priesthood. He was soon to change his mind, and in 1851 his first opera, *Sapho*, was performed; Adam suggested the clarity and classicism of Gluck rather than Rossini or Meyerbeer as the main influence. This was followed by *La Nonne sanglante* (1854), a work in the melo-dramatic vein, but Gounod's gifts of lyricism, elegance of expression and wit are better displayed in his light comic operas such as *Le Médecin malgré lui* (1858), a perfect adaptation of Molière, and *Philémon et Baucis* (1860). The work which sealed Gounod's reputation as the foremost opera composer of his day, however, was *Faust* (1859), which became the most popular French opera ever written. *Faust* displays a profundity which was lacking in the usual fare of the theater of the day, coupled with Gounod's characteristic sensitivity to the text, lyrical melodic style and feeling for harmonic and orchestral color. Staged originally as an *opéra comique*, the spoken dialogue was later changed to recitative.

After *Faust*, Gounod attempted to continue with its grand manner, and in *La Reine de Saba* (1862) and *Roméo et Juliette* (1867) he tried to conquer the Opéra by bowing to its musical conventions, but without the same success. The light simplicity and charm of *Mireille* (1864) was no better received, even though it was the most natural outlet for Gounod's particular talents. He then occupied himself with religious music until 1876, after which came three more rather grandiose works: *Cinq Mars*

(1877), *Polyeucte* (1878) and *Le Tribut de Zamora* (1881).

Gounod holds an important place in the history of nineteenth-century French music as a precursor of the musical renewal of the 1880s, retaining characteristically French qualities in serious music drama.

Halévy, Fromental [Lévy, Elias] (* Paris, 27 May 1799; † Nice, 17 Mar. 1862). French composer. Halévy studied in Paris with Berton and Cherubini and won the Prix de Rome in 1819. One of the most distinguished composers of French grand opera, his most important work is *La Juive* (1835), with libretto by Scribe, a masterpiece in the genre greatly admired by Wagner. Halévy's other operas include *La Reine de Chypre* (1841) and the comedy *L'Eclair* (1835).

Halévy was the most influential teacher at the Paris Conservatoire in the mid-century, becoming professor of harmony in 1827 and of composition in 1840; his pupils included Massé, Gounod, Bizet and Saint-Saëns.

Hartmann, Johann Peter (* Copenhagen, 14 May 1805; † Copenhagen, 10 Mar. 1900). Danish composer and organist. *See Volume III.*

Heller, Stephen [István] (* Pest, 15 May, 1813; † Paris, 14 Jan. 1888). French pianist and composer of Hungarian birth. Heller was launched on his career as a virtuoso pianist when he was fourteen, but after two years suffered a nervous breakdown

and seldom again appeared in public. In 1838 he traveled to Paris, to study with Kalkbrenner, but was unable to afford his fees. However, he was to remain there for the rest of his life.

From the time of his arrival, Heller began to make his name as a composer of piano music, and his work was held in particular esteem by the more critically discriminating of his contemporaries – Schumann, Berlioz and Hallé among them. His most original works, such as the evocative miniatures *Rêveries* (op.58), *Nuits blanches* (op.82) and *Feuilles volantes* (op.123), look forward to the impressionism of Debussy and Fauré.

Henselt, Adolf von (* Schwabach, nr. Nuremberg, 9 May 1814; † Warmbrunn [Cieplice Sl. Zdroj], Silesia, 10 Oct. 1889). German pianist and composer. A pupil of Hummel, Henselt had almost given up public performance by the age of thirty, and his reputation as one of the great pianists of his time was largely created by a few privileged composers, Mendelssohn and Schumann among them, who heard him play when he was at his peak. In 1838 he settled in Russia, where he became responsible for a school of piano-playing that, through his pupil Zverov, was to produce such eminent and influential players as Skriabin, Rachmaninov and Lhévinne.

Unlike many of his contemporaries among pianist–composers, Henselt was not inclined to write showpieces for his own performance and was not over-prolific. Worthy of mention are his Piano Trio in A minor, op.24, a fine example of Romantic chamber music, and the Piano Concerto in F minor, op.16, which is full of memorable melodies and bravura pianism.

Hérold, Ferdinand (* Paris, 28 Jan. 1791; † Thernes, nr. Paris, 19 Jan. 1833). French composer. He studied first with his father, who had been a pupil of C. P. E. Bach, then at the Conservatoire, where his teachers included Louis Adam

and Méhul. After winning the Prix de Rome (1812), he studied in Rome and Naples, where his first opera was produced in 1815. He returned to Paris that year, but, though he tried both serious and comic operas, he had little success until *Marie* (1826). This was followed by the two *opéras comiques* for which Hérold is still remembered, the romantically ghoulish *Zampa* (1831) and the more lighthearted *Le Pré aux clercs* (1832), works which stand comparison with Weber's operas.

Hérold was extremely prolific in his short life and, in addition to his operas, produced symphonic and chamber works and several ballets, including *La Somnambule*, which was the inspiration for Bellini's opera, and *La Fille mal gardée* (1828), which still retains its place in the repertory.

Hiller, Ferdinand von (* Frankfurt-am-Main, 24 Oct. 1811; † Cologne, 12 May 1885). German composer, conductor and critic. He came from a wealthy Jewish family and showed exceptional brilliance as a child. From 1825 he studied with Hummel, going with him to Vienna in 1827, where he met Beethoven and Schubert and published a Piano Quartet as his op.1. A period in Paris (1828-35) brought him into contact with many leading musicians, including Berlioz, Chopin, Liszt, Rossini and Meyerbeer, and in 1840 he studied church music in Rome with Baini. Later he was active in Leipzig and Dresden, and, from 1850 until his death, in Cologne, where he founded and directed the Conservatory.

Hiller's compositions embrace operas, oratorios, concert overtures and symphonies, though it is his piano works that show the Mendelssohnian purity of his style to best advantage.

Himmel, Friedrich Heinrich (* Treuenbrietzen, Brandenburg, 20 Nov. 1765; † Berlin, 8 June, 1814). German composer. Through his piano playing Himmel was recognized as a musician of promise by Frederick William II of Prussia and was sent to Dresden to study at the King's expense. His early compositions – cantatas and operas – were Italianate in style, but after settling in Berlin in 1795, he turned to the German *Singspiel* with great success. His stage works seem largely products of their time, but his instrumental and chamber works have been undeservedly neglected despite Beethoven's praise of them.

Hoffmann, Ernst Theodor Armadeus (* Königsberg [Kaliningrad], 24 Jan. 1776; † Berlin, 25 June, 1822). German writer, composer and lawyer. Better known as a Romantic literary figure, E. T. A. Hoffmann made his living for many years as

a composer, holding the post of musical director of the theater in Bamberg from 1808 to 1813. He composed several operas, including the archetypal Romantic opera *Undine*, produced in Berlin in 1816 with sets by C. F. Schinkel, and also wrote sacred and chamber music and five appealing piano sonatas.

However, his own music never matched the brilliant and progressive tendencies of his critical writings, which were notable particularly for their elaboration of a Romantic musical theory based on the works of Gluck, Haydn, Mozart and Beethoven. Music also played a key role in Hoffmann's imaginative writing, and he is chiefly remembered today as the author who inspired Schumann's *Kreisleriana* (for piano), Offenbach's *Contes d'Hoffmann* and Tchaikovsky's ballet *The Nutcracker*.

Hummel, Johann Nepomuk (* Pressburg [Bratislava], 14 Nov. 1778; † Weimar, 17 Oct. 1837). Austrian pianist, composer and conductor. The son of an able professional musician, Hummel became a pupil of Mozart at the age of eight and after two years of residence in the Mozart household was taken by his father on a triumphant concert tour of Europe. On reaching London, he became a pupil of Clementi, and on his return to Vienna in 1793 he studied composition under Haydn and Albrechtsberger.

Having completed his education with Salieri, Hummel set out on a series of concert tours, which brought him fame as both pianist and composer. He returned to Vienna in 1803 to take up an appointment at the court theater, but left after a year to succeed Haydn as Kapellmeister to Prince Nicolaus Esterházy at Eisenstadt. He held this post until 1811, when he was dismissed for neglecting his duties. He later held similar appointments at Stuttgart, from 1816 to 1818, and at Weimar, from 1819 until his death.

As a pianist, Hummel was considered one of the greatest of his time, and for many he was the equal of Beethoven and Clementi. As a teacher he was of paramount

importance as one of the great developers of pianistic technique, and among his many pupils were Czerny, Henselt and Thalberg. While Hummel was highly regarded as a composer during his lifetime, his music now inevitably appears superficial in comparison with his contemporary Beethoven. However, by developing the more ornamental aspects of Mozart's music and exploring the expressive quality of minor keys he provided an important link between Viennese Classicism and the Romantic piano style. Almost half of Hummel's published works, numbered up to op.127, are for his own instrument, but the range of his compositions is broadly based and includes operas, ballets, concertos (among them the enjoyable Trumpet Concerto), chamber music and church music.

Kalkbrenner, Frédéric (* between Kassel and Berlin, early Nov. 1785; h Deuil, nr. Paris, 10 June 1849). French pianist and composer of German extraction. Among the many pianists who became famous at the beginning of the nineteenth century, Kalkbrenner was unusual in that he succeeded as both a Classically trained contemporary of Beethoven and later as one of the popular Romantic pianists in Paris, when Liszt and Thalberg were at their peak. His greatest success in the first half of his career was in London, where he settled in 1814, taking over from Cramer as the most fashionable performer and teacher. In 1824 he moved to Paris, where he lived for the rest of his life.

Despite the fact that he had studied under both Haydn and Albrechtsberger, Kalkbrenner's own compositions – which include concertos, chamber music and sonatas – appear to have been merely display pieces for his own virtuosity.

Kreutzer, Rodolphe (* Versailles, 16 Nov. 1766; † Geneva, 6 Jan. 1831). French violinist, composer and teacher. Kreutzer has been immortalized by the Beethoven violin sonata that bears his name, but during his lifetime he was considered a worthy rival as a composer to Cherubini and a violinist the equal of Rode, Baillot and Spohr. He composed many concertos and chamber works for his own use as well as numerous operas and ballets, performed in Paris with great success between 1790 and 1820. Violin students continue to appreciate the *42 Etudes ou caprices pour le violon* (originally 40), published in 1796.

Kullak, Theodor (* Krotoszyn, 12 Sept. 1818; † Berlin, 1 Mar. 1882). Polish pianist, teacher and composer. A protégé of Prince Radziwill, he studied with Dehn, Czerny, Sechter and Nicolai and became piano-teacher to the Prussian royal family. In 1850, with Julius Stern and Adolf Bernhard Marx, he founded the Berlin (later Stern) Conservatory, but five years later left to found his own Neue Akademie der Tonkunst. In addition to pedagogical works he contributed some brilliant works to the piano repertory, including a concerto and a sonata.

Leoncavallo, Ruggero (* Naples, 8 Mar. 1857; † Montecatini, 9 Aug. 1919). Italian composer and librettist. Leoncavallo was admitted to the Naples Conservatory in 1866 and graduated in 1876. Literary studies followed at Bologna University and he then worked as an itinerant café pianist throughout Europe and the Near East. An introduction to Giulio Ricordi led to musical and literary work, but Ricordi concentrated on his literary talents and did little to further his operatic aims. Thus frustrated, Leoncavallo deliberately set out to write an opera in the *verismo* idiom to compete with the current favorite – Mascagni's *Cavalleria rusticana* – and over a period of five months he wrote the poem and music of *I Pagliacci*. He took this to the rival publishing firm of Sonzogno, and a performance was arranged at the Teatro dal Verme, Milan on 21 May 1892 under Toscanini, which made Leoncavallo a celebrity overnight. Sonzogno sought other works, and Leoncavallo offered *I Medici*, which he had written before *Pagliacci* and which Ricordi had already rejected. *I Medici* was an abject failure, and its undigested mixture of Meyerbeer and Wagner was ruthlessly criticized. Further

unhappiness followed when both Leoncavallo and Puccini set the same subject, *La Bohème*, since Leoncavallo's version rapidly lost ground to Puccini's. Only one further opera, *Zazà* (1900), achieved real stature, and the rest of Leoncavallo's career is a catalogue of minor works and extensive travel.

Le Sueur, Jean-François (* Drucat-Plessiel, Somme, 15 Feb. 1760; † Paris, 6 Oct. 1837). His early career was as a church musician, and after a number of appointments he was made director of music at Notre Dame, Paris, in 1786. Here he caused controversy and drew crowds by introducing programmatic symphonic music for the great church festivals, a practice he defended in pamphlets on the use of 'dramatic and descriptive' music in church. In 1793 his first opera, *La Caverne*, a story of brigands, was produced at the Théâtre Feydeau, and in 1795 he was named as one of the commissioners of the newly established Conservatoire. However, the Opéra shied away from the lavish production effects he demanded, and it was not until 1804, after Napoleon had made him court composer, that *Ossian ou les Bardes* was produced there, with great success. Other grand neoclassical operas followed, but few were actually put on.

In 1818 Le Sueur was appointed professor of composition at the Conservatoire, and through his teaching, particularly of Berlioz, but also of Gounod, Marmontel and Ambroise Thomas, he became one of the founders of the grand French style of the nineteenth century.

Liszt, Franz (Ferenc) (* Doborján [Raiding], 22 Oct. 1811; † Bayreuth, 31 July 1886). Hungarian composer and pianist. *See Volume III.*

Loewe, Carl (* Löbejün, nr. Halle, 30 Nov. 1796; † Kiel, 20 Apr. 1869). German composer and singer. The twelfth child of a schoolmaster and cantor, Loewe was trained to sing by his father.

When only thirteen, he was granted an annuity by Napoleon's brother, Jérôme, King of Westphalia, which enabled him to continue his piano and composition studies. In 1820 he became organist and cantor of the Jakobikirche, Stettin, where he remained for most of his life.

Loewe wrote more than 350 songs, of which the ballads, much influenced by Zumsteeg, are the most successful. Among the best are his settings of 'Edward,' 'Erlkönig' and 'Odins Meeres-Ritt.' He also composed much other music, including symphonies, concertos, five operas and seventeen oratorios.

Lortzing, Albert (* Berlin, 23 Oct. 1801; † Berlin, 21 Jan. 1851). German composer, conductor, singer and actor. The son of an actor, Lortzing began singing and acting at an early age. He made his reputation with the comedies *Die beiden Schützen* (1837) and *Zar und Zimmermann* (1837), both of which are characterized by their breezy tunefulness and a particular theatrical flair.

Hans Sachs (1840) anticipates Wagner's *Die Meistersinger* not only in its text but also in its portrayal of the main character, while Lortzing had his greatest success with *Der Wildschütz* (1842), which, drawing on the German countryside for inspiration, is strongly reminiscent of Weber. The Romantic magic opera *Undine*, for which he wrote his own libretto, was produced in 1845 in Leipzig, where Lortzing worked as Kapellmeister. He also worked in Vienna and Berlin.

Louis Ferdinand, Prince of Prussia (* Friedrichsfelde, nr. Berlin, 18 Nov. 1772; † Saalfeld, 13 Oct. 1806). German composer and pianist. There is no account of Louis Ferdinand's musical education or evidence of unusual ability until in 1793 he is reported to have played a piano sonata in public with great distinction. Three years later his playing made a lasting impression on Beethoven, with whom he formed a close friendship and whose C minor Piano Concerto (no.3) was dedicated to the Prince in 1804.

Louis Ferdinand's development as a composer was much influenced by his friendship with Dussek, who as Kapellmeister at Magdeburg from 1804 to 1806 gave him the only professional advice on composition that he received. By the time of his death at the Battle of Saalfeld, Louis Ferdinand had completed about fifteen compositions, mainly for chamber ensembles or solo piano. The most outstanding of these works is the Piano Quartet in F minor, a fine work by any standards and an amazing achievement for an amateur.

Marschner, Heinrich (* Zittau, 16 Aug. 1795; † Hanover, 14 Dec. 1861). German composer. Marschner studied in Bautzen and Leipzig and later in life held appointments in Dresden, Leipzig and Hanover. The operas which brought his first success, *Der Vampyr* (1828) and *Der Templer und die Jüdin* (1829), both clearly show the influence of Weber and, while considerably extending it,

do not succeed in departing from the *Singspiel* structure. However, their sophisticated approach to characterization, in which the main characters contain both good and evil traits, attracted Wagner, as did Marschner's orchestration, chromatic harmony and tendency towards more fluency between set numbers. Lines of similarity have been traced between these operas and Wagner's *Lohengrin*; in particular, the central character in Marschner's most successful opera *Hans Heiling* (1833) is a prototype for Wagner's *Der fliegende Holländer*. *Hans Heiling* established Marschner as one of the foremost German nationalist composers.

Mascagni, Pietro (* Livorno, 7 Dec. 1863; † Rome, 2 Aug. 1945). Italian composer and conductor. Mascagni's father, a baker, expected him to follow in his footsteps, but pressure from an uncle made it possible for him to have music lessons. In 1882 he was admitted to the Milan Conservatory, where he studied with Ponchielli and Saladino, but he was dismissed for lack of application after two years. He then earned his living as a double-bass player and conductor. In 1888 his wife submitted the recently completed *Cavalleria rusticana* to the publisher Sonzogno's second competition for one-act operas. It won one of the three prizes, and within a year Mascagni was world-famous and had established *verismo* as the vanguard of operatic style.

The success of *Cavalleria rusticana* proved crippling. Mascagni tried to diversify his style, but the expectations imprinted on the public mind by *Cavalleria rusticana* proved stronger than his desires and talents. Of his fifteen operas, only *Il piccolo Marat* (Rome, 1921), based on an exciting plot from the time of the French Revolution, had some substantial success, but after this Mascagni's career slid rapidly away, and by allowing himself to become the official composer of Mussolini's Fascist régime he added opprobrium to his lack of success. As a conductor he was capable and did much for his own works by his direction.

Massenet, Jules (* Montaud, nr. Saint-Etienne, 12 May 1842; † Paris, 13 Aug. 1912). French composer. Massenet studied at the Paris Conservatoire with Thomas, winning the Prix de Rome in 1863. His position on the French operatic scene was established with *Le Roi de Lahore* in 1877, and during the 1880s and after he held a position of unfailing popularity with French audiences. Certain characteristically French traits can be traced throughout his extremely prolific output, among them a gift for appealing and charming melody and smoothness of craft in the harmonic background and orchestral coloring. His sensitivity to popular taste can be seen both in the variety of his operatic subjects and styles (for example, oriental in *Le Roi de Lahore*, grand opera in *Le Cid*) and in the ease with which he could assume and digest various contemporary idioms, from Wagner to Italian *verismo*.

Massenet's first two operas of the decade 1880-90, *Hérodiade* (1881) and *Manon* (1884), both have female characters who are vividly characterized in the sensual vein which is almost his stock-in-trade. Although comprised of separate numbers, the musical structure of *Manon* recalls Wagnerian practice in the association of motifs with different characters and in the role of the orchestra as a commentator on the stage action.

The last decade of the century saw the outstanding successes of *Werther* (1892) and *Thaïs* (1894). In *Werther* there is the same Wagnerian orchestral prominence already seen in *Manon*, but there is also a tendency towards freer, more open-ended aria forms. Although Massenet continued to produce a string of operas in a similar mold up until his death, he never managed to regain the huge successes of his earlier works.

Mayr, Johannes Simon (* Mendorf, nr. Ingolstadt, 14 June 1763; † Bergamo, 2 Dec. 1845). Italian composer of German birth. Taught music by his father, Mayr became a capable performer on many instruments and was soon noticed

by a Swiss patron, who took him to Italy, where his formal musical studies began in Bergamo and continued in Venice. Following some early compositions in 1786, he made his mark with an oratorio and in 1791 was commissioned to write three more. At the same time, Piccinni encouraged him to turn his attention to opera, and the success of *Saffo* (Venice, 1794) led to an illustrious operatic career with over eighty operas including *Lodoïska* (Venice, 1796), *Ginevra di Scozia* (Trieste, 1801), *Tamerlano* (Milan, 1813), *La rosa bianca e la rosa rossa* (Genoa, 1813) and *Medea in Corinto* (Naples, 1813).

In 1802 Mayr succeeded his teacher Lenzi as *maestro di cappella* in Bergamo, and in 1805 he became the director of the cathedral choir school. He remained at these posts for the rest of his life and was renowned and much loved a teacher; his most famous pupil was Donizetti, whom he did much to encourage. Mayr was the central figure of Italian opera in the generation before Rossini.

Méhul, Etienne-Nicolas (* Givet, Ardennes, 22 June 1763; † Paris, 18 Oct. 1817). French composer. Born into a poor family, Méhul became organist at the Franciscan convent at Givet at the age of ten, and when Wilhelm Hanser became organist at the monastery at Lavaldieu, he became his pupil. He was placed with Edelmann in Paris for lessons in composition by a rich patron and subsequently contrived a meeting with Gluck, who accepted him as a part-time pupil.

Méhul was slow to succeed as an opera composer, and it was not until 1790 that his ninth attempt at an opera, *Euphrosine et Coradin*, was staged. From this time on, however, he enjoyed almost uninterrupted success and composed a further thirty-two *opéras comiques* in the next twenty-seven years. *Uthal* (1806) and *Joseph* (1807) probably represent the high point in his career. He was also an accomplished symphonist, and his command of this medium enabled him to use orchestral color, and often the most unusual scoring, to enhance the sense of drama in his operas and, especially, in his overtures. Méhul was associated with the Paris Conservatoire from its foundation in 1795 until his death.

Mendelssohn Bartholdy, Felix (* Hamburg, 3 Feb. 1809; † Leipzig, 4 Nov. 1847). German composer. *See pp.183-193*

Mercadante, Saverio (* Altamura, nr. Bari, bapt. 17 Sept. 1795; † Naples, 17 Dec. 1870). Italian composer and teacher. In 1818 he entered the Royal Conservatory in Naples, where his teachers included Zingarelli. Some early ballet music achieved a marked success, and this led to an invitation from Rossini to compose his first opera, *L'Apoteosi d'Ercole*, for the San Carlo opera house. This was enthusiastically received, and thereafter Mercadante concentrated principally on operatic composition. His seventh opera, *Elisa e Claudio* (La Scala, 1821), established his European reputation in London, Barcelona and Paris in 1823 and in Vienna a year later. Among his most successful later operas were *I Normanni a Parigi* (1836), *Il Giuramento* (1837), *Il Bravo* (1839), *La Vestale* (1840) and *Virginia* (1866).

Mercadante traveled widely, spending lengthy spells in Spain and Portugal. In 1833 he was appointed director of music at Novara Cathedral, a post he held for seven years, during which time he wrote much church music, although this did not interrupt his operatic career. In 1840 he succeeded Zingarelli as head of the Naples Conservatory, a post he held, despite the blindness that

overtook him in 1862, until his death thirty years later. His instrumental works include two symphonies and numerous concertos as well as chamber music.

Messager, André (* Montluçon, Allier, 30 Dec. 1853; † Paris, 24 Feb. 1929). French composer, conductor, critic, opera administrator, pianist and organist. Messager studied with Gigout and Loret at the Ecole Niedermeyer and became a friend of Saint-Saëns, who gave him guidance. At the age of twenty-one he obtained an organist's post at Saint-Sulpice in Paris, but despite other church posts, he felt more and more drawn to the theater, and eventually his ballet *Les deux pigeons* was given at the Opéra in 1886. This was followed by a series of *opéras comiques* and operettas, which kept alive the French lyric tradition at the period of Puccini's reign over Italian opera, among the most famous being *Véronique* (1898) and *Fortunio* (1907).

Messager was an outstanding conductor and held posts at the Opéra Comique – where he conducted the première of Debussy's *Pelléas et Mélisande* – Covent Garden and the Opéra and as conductor of the Conservatoire concerts.

Meyerbeer, Giacomo [Jakob Liebmann Meyer Beer] (* Vogelsdorf, nr. Berlin, 5 Sept. 1791; † Paris, 2 May 1864). German composer. Meyerbeer came of a wealthy Jewish family, and after studies with Zelter and the Abbé Vogler – Weber was his fellow-pupil – he traveled widely and became renowned as a pianist. In 1816, on the advice of Salieri, he started a study tour in Italy, which extended to nine years. The outstanding success of his sixth Italian opera, *Il Crociato in Egitto* (1824), led to its being staged in London and Paris, the latter performance making Meyerbeer a composer of European renown.
He settled in Paris in 1825 and, after six years of planning, his first French grand opera, *Robert le diable*, with libretto by Scribe, was staged at the Paris Opéra in 1831; its success was the greatest that either Meyerbeer or the

Opéra had ever seen and put the composer unchallenged at the head of his profession. More than any other work, it also established the form and conventions of *grand opéra* in Paris, which were to have a strong influence on both Verdi and Wagner. Another collaboration with Scribe, *Les Huguenots* was produced in 1836, but despite its overwhelming success their next work did not appear until 1849 – *Le Prophète*, followed by an equally successful comic opera, *L'Etoile du nord* (1854). Work on *L'Africaine*, which had been planned since 1837, was threatened by the death of Scribe, and although it was finished, the composer died during the rehearsal period. Its première on 28 April 1865 proved a brilliant posthumous tribute to Meyerbeer. From 1842 he had also held posts in Berlin, and he wrote a number of works by royal command, as well as sacred and patriotic compositions, but it was in France that he was best appreciated.
Meyerbeer's operatic successes did not just depend on the lavish productions and stirring subject-matter. His operas were put together with immense care, and he made notable developments in instrumentation and orchestral technique and in the use of the chorus. Above all, he always ensured that the singers themselves were the focus of the work, requiring the highest level of vocal skill, but offering them parts that were always rewarding to perform.

Moniuszko, Stanislaw (* Ubiel, Lithuania, 5 May 1819; † Warsaw, 4 Jun. 1872). Polish composer. He studied in Warsaw and Berlin, then became a music-teacher and church organist in Wilno (Vilnius). Of his fifteen operas, *Halka* (1847), a tragedy of peasant life, is a cornerstone of Polish national culture. It was first performed in Wilno, and its success in Warsaw in 1858 led to Moniuszko's appointment as conductor at the Opera and professor at the Conservatory there.
Moniuszko's other works include church music, cantatas and over 400 songs, which, like the operas, represent a conscious attempt to develop a specifically Polish idiom.

Monsigny, Pierre-Alexandre (* Fauquembergues, nr. St Omer, 17 Oct. 1729; † Paris, 14 Jan. 1817). French composer. *See Volume I.*

Morlacchi, Francesco (* Perugia, 14 June, 1784; † Innsbruck, 28 Oct. 1841). Italian composer and conductor. A pupil of his uncle, a cathedral organist, Morlacchi studied at Loreto with Zingarelli and with Padre Mattei in Bologna. He produced his first opera in 1804, and in 1810 his *Le Danaidi* made him famous throughout Italy. In 1811 he was appointed Kapellmeister at the Italian Opera in Dresden, a post which he held for the rest of his life. Morlacchi was not an innovator and was content to compose in the Italian style long popular in Dresden, ignoring Weber's activity at the German theater there in the decade from 1816. Like his older contemporaries Mayr and Paer, he was duly eclipsed by the meteoric rise of Rossini.

Moscheles, Ignaz (* Prague, 23 May, 1794; † Leipzig, 10 Mar. 1870). German pianist, conductor and composer of Bohemian birth. The son of a Jewish merchant, Moscheles showed early musical ability and from the age of ten studied under Dyonis Weber, head of the Prague Conservatory. By the time he was fifteen he had already performed his own compositions in public, including a piano concerto. On Weber's recommendation, he went to Vienna to complete his studies under Albrechtsberger and Salieri, supporting himself by teaching and serving as assistant Kapellmeister to Salieri at the Vienna Opera. His career as a pianist also prospered in Vienna, and he was soon regarded as one of the leading virtuosi of the time.

Moscheles admired Beethoven above all other composers and in 1814 worked with him on a piano reduction of *Fidelio*. From 1816 to 1821 he traveled around Europe as a concert pianist, then settled for twenty-five years in London, where he was appointed professor at the Royal Academy of Music and conductor of the Royal Philharmonic Society. When the Leipzig Conservatory was founded in 1846, Mendelssohn prevailed upon

Moscheles to move there as principal professor of piano, a post he held until his death.

As a composer, Moscheles was highly regarded during his lifetime, though few of his works have held a place in the repertory. From 142 published works, including many long sets of piano pieces, the early Romantic Piano Concerto in G minor, op.60, the Etudes, opp.70 and 95, and the *Concerto pathétique*, op.93, are especially worthy of revival.

Müller, Wenzel (* Tyrnau [Trnava], Moravia, 1767; † Baden, nr. Vienna, 1835). Austrian composer. He studied with Gassmann and Dittersdorf and was engaged as conductor at the Leopoldstadt Theater in 1786, by which time he had begun his remarkably prolific career as a composer of *Singspiele*; he was to write some 300 in all. His *Sonnenfest der Brahminen* (1790) won the approval of Mozart and Haydn and was staged by Goethe in Weimar, and one of his songs was used by Beethoven as the theme in his op.121a Variations for piano trio. But although Müller's pieces provoke interesting comparisons with *Die Zauberflöte* or *Der Freischütz*, they are firmly rooted in the tradition of Viennese popular comedy, and many of his songs have the same instantly familiar ring as the contemporary Ländler and waltzes of Lanner and Strauss. Müller's finest scores are those he composed for the plays of the great poet of magic comedy, Ferdinand Raimund.

Nicolai, Otto (* Königsberg [Kaliningrad], 9 June 1810; † Berlin, 11 May 1849). German composer and conductor. He studied in Berlin with Berger and Zelter, and in 1833 became organist of the Prussian Embassy chapel in Rome, where he continued his studies under Baini. Four years later he went to Vienna as a singing-teacher and Kapellmeister at the Kärntnertor Theater, returning to Rome in 1838.

Nicolai's first opera, *Rosmonda d'Inghilterra*, was written for Turin in 1838 but given in Trieste as *Enrico II* the following year. After three more operas were successfully produced, he returned to

Vienna as Hofkapellmeister. Here he initiated the Philharmonic Concerts (thus founding the Vienna Philharmonic Orchestra), earning a reputation as an exemplary orchestral trainer and conductor. In 1847 he went back to Berlin to direct the Royal Opera, and it was there that he produced his most famous work, *Die lustigen Weiber von Windsor* (1849), based on Shakespeare's *Merry Wives*, which combines his German flair for comic opera with the melodic fluency of his Italian training.

Offenbach, Jacques [Jacob] (* Cologne, 20 June 1819; † Paris, 5 Oct. 1880). French composer and conductor of German birth. Offenbach studied first with Joseph Alexander and Bernhard Breuer, and later in Paris with Vaslin and Halévy. He began his theatrical career as a cellist at the Opéra Comique and there began to write light pieces for the stage.

Offenbach's operettas, particularly those of the 1860s, are the best reflection of the frivolity and froth of Parisian taste during that period and symbolize the musical spirit of the age. In 1850 he became conductor at the Théâtre Français, then at the Théâtre Marigny, which he opened as the Bouffes Parisiens in 1855. A string of successes through the 1860s, from *Orphée aux enfers* (1858) to *La belle Hélène* (1864), *Barbe-bleue* (1866), *La Grande-Duchesse de Gérolstein* (1867) and *La Périchole* (1868), was only abated by the new, more somber mood of Paris after the war of 1871. Offenbach continued to compose, however, and his attempt at a full-length serious work, *Les Contes d'Hoffmann*, was completed by Guiraud after his death.

The prevailing tone of his operettas is one of sparkling wit: satire of the manners and politics of the day and parody of familiar music are coupled with absurd situations and words.

Onslow, Georges (* Clermont-Ferrand, 27 July 1784; † Clermont-Ferrand, 3 Oct. 1853). French composer of English descent. Although he studied the piano under Dussek and Cramer, Onslow did not start

to compose until he was well into his twenties. He then wrote a few chamber works for performance with friends, before going to study with Antonín Rejcha. Onslow became a considerable composer, particularly of chamber music, and was highly esteemed by his contemporaries. His best work is in his quintets, of which he wrote more than thirty.

Pacini, Giovanni (* Catania, 17 Feb. 1796; † Pescia, 6 Dec. 1867). Italian composer. Pacini became music director of the San Carlo opera house in Naples in 1825, and by 1830 he was at the height of his success, producing during the next sixteen years some forty operas in all the main centers of Italy. His star waned as Bellini and Donizetti rose to fame, and he devoted himself increasingly to the music school he established in Viareggio. In 1837 he was appointed director of the ducal chapel at Lucca. After the death of Bellini, Pacini returned to the stage and achieved an immense (and justified) success with *Saffo* (1840), his masterpiece. Despite further successes, rivalry with Verdi embittered his later years.

Paer, Ferdinando (* Parma, 1 June 1771; † Paris, 3 May 1839). Italian composer. Paer's operatic career started with *Circe* (Venice, 1792), and many commissions followed, his most important early work being *Griselda, ossia La virtù al cimento* (Parma, 1798), a treatment of the Boccaccio story in the *semiserio* style in which Paer made his greatest mark. In 1797 he assumed the musical direction

of the Kärntnertor Theater in Vienna, where he came to know Beethoven. His finest opera, *Camilla*, was produced there in 1799, while *Leonora* (anticipating Beethoven's *Leonore–Fidelio*) was produced in 1804 in Dresden, where he had gone as Kapellmeister the previous year.

Paer was much admired by Napoleon, who made him his *maître de chapelle* in 1807, and Paris was to remain his home. Many other accolades followed, which, combined with his earnings as a singing-master in high society, kept him wealthy and influential even after Napoleon's downfall. Gifted melodically and commanding a fluent technique, he was prolific in many fields of composition and occupies an important place in operatic history.

Paganini, Niccolò (* Genoa, 27 Oct. 1782; † Nice, 27 May 1840). Italian violinist and composer. Violin lessons began with his father when he was seven, and continued with Giacomo Costa. Such was his progress that he was playing in public by the time he was nine. He also started to compose and took advice rather than offical lessons from the operatic composer Francesco Gnecco. In 1795 his father arranged for the violinist Alessandro Rolla to take him on as a pupil. But by this time the young Paganini had already made a name for himself, and after six months Rolla decided that there was no more that he could teach him and recommended serious study of composition. Accordingly, he studied counterpoint with Ghiretti and composition with Paer. Still under the watchful eye of his tyrannical father, Paganini made his first concert tour in 1797. It was a brilliant success, and the triumph led Paganini to the realization that he could support himself financially, and he contrived to escape the restraints of his father and set out on his own.

Whether as a reaction to home life without pleasures or relaxation, or whether by natural inclination, Paganini's life of gambling and debauchery began as soon as he was on his own. Rumors started of his being in league with the devil. His outrageous behavior merely added fuel to the fire, and Paganini, who realized that there was financial profit in this infamy, did nothing to discourage the fast-spreading gossip. But his performances were, by all accounts, wonderful.

The greatest testimony to Paganini's playing is in his compositions. The two aspects of his work are inextricably linked: he set himself extraordinary technical problems, which he overcame with dramatic effect in performance; but there are many lasting qualities in his music, and he was capable of inspired melodies and moments of great poetry within the framework of the most dazzling virtuoso music. In addition to the celebrated *Caprices* and other pieces for solo violin, Paganini composed six concertos, a set of quartets and two sets of duos for violin and guitar. *See also pp.178-181.*

Paisiello, Giovanni (* Rocca-forzata, nr. Taranto, 9 May, 1740; † Naples, 5 June 1816). Italian composer. *See Volume I.*

Pixis, Johann Peter (* Mannheim, 10 Feb. 1788; † Baden-Baden, 22 Dec. 1874). German pianist, composer and teacher. Pixis was the most celebrated of a family of musicians, his father a composer at Mannheim and his brother, Friedrich, one of the most successful violinists of the Viotti school. Johann Peter made his name as a virtuoso pianist and was much in demand as a teacher. His greatest period of success was in Paris at the same time as Liszt, Chopin and Thalberg (1830-45). As a composer, his output was large, but only a few piano pieces are ever heard today.

Pleyel, Ignaz Joseph (* Ruppers-thal, 18 June 1757; † Paris, 14 Nov. 1831). Austrian composer, music publisher and piano-maker, active in France. *See Volume I.*

Ponchielli, Amilcare (* Paderno Fasolaro [now Paderno Ponchielli], nr. Cremona, 31 Aug. 1834; † Milan, 17 Jan. 1886). Italian composer. He was the chief figure in a group of conservative Italian composers who found their ideal in the middle-period works of Verdi.

His first operas, *I Promessi Sposi* (1856), *La Savoiarda* (1861) and *Roderico, rè dei goti* (1863) had moderate success, but his most famous work is *La Gioconda* (1876), with libretto by Boito, which mixes elements of French grand opera with Italian Romantic *melodramma*.

Puccini, Giacomo (* Lucca, 23 Dec. 1858; † Brussels, 29 Nov. 1924). Italian composer. *See pp.287-303*

Radicati, Felice (* Turin, 1775; † Bologna, 19 Mar. 1820). Italian violinist and composer. A pupil of Pugnani, Radicati became one of

the most celebrated violinists of his time. He composed nine operas, a violin concerto, chamber music and songs, but his best work is to be found in his string quartets, some of which are worthy of comparison with those of Boccherini.

Reichardt, Johann Friedrich (* Königsberg [Kaliningrad], 25 Nov. 1752; † Giebichenstein, nr. Halle, 27 June 1814). German composer and writer on music. After studying at Königsberg University, Reichardt journeyed through Germany and Bohemia, meeting some of the major composers of his day. After a year in government service he became conductor of the Royal Opera in Berlin, but was dismissed in 1794 when he supported the French Republican cause. He settled at Giebichenstein, which he made a haven for protagonists of the new Romanticism. After its bombardment by Napoleon's troops in 1806, he went for a short time to Kassel in the service of Jérôme Bonaparte, but returned to Giebichenstein in 1809.

Reichardt composed in most of the major genres, including symphony, concerto and opera, but is above all important as a composer of *Singspiele*, three written by Goethe, and of songs.

Rejcha, Antonín [Antoine Reicha] (* Prague, 26 Feb. 1770; † Paris, 28 May, 1836). Czech, later French, composer, theorist and teacher. Rejcha's father died when he was ten months old and he was adopted by his uncle, Joseph Rejcha, a distinguished cellist and composer who was appointed leader of the electoral court orchestra in Bonn in 1785. There Antonín played the violin and the flute in the *Hofkapelle*, alongside Beethoven and C. G. Neefe, and started to compose in earnest, with several of his works being successfully performed under his uncle's direction. In 1794 he set out for Hamburg, where he earned his living as a teacher and composed two operas, but without any real success. He went to Vienna in 1802, renewing his friendship with Beethoven and Haydn and enjoying the patronage of the Empress, who commissioned an opera from him. In 1808, he left for Paris, where he lived for the rest of his life. He succeeded

Méhul as professor of counterpoint at the Conservatoire in 1818, counting Berlioz, Gounod, Franck and Liszt among his pupils.

Rejcha was a prolific composer, particularly of chamber music. His work is unfailingly well crafted and demonstrates an unusual melodic gift. Although Classically based, his later works, like those of his Bohemian contemporaries Dussek and Voříšek, contain certain emergent elements of Romanticism.

Ries, Ferdinand (* Bonn, bapt. 28 Nov. 1784; † Frankfurt-am-Main, 13 Jan. 1838). Pianist, composer and copyist. The most celebrated member of a German family of musicians, Ries was one of Beethoven's few pupils and was also befriended by Clementi. He made his reputation as a pianist and soon successfully introduced his own compositions at his concerts. He composed six symphonies, nine piano concertos, a large quantity of chamber and instrumental music and two operas. He is remembered today as co-author (with F. G. Wegeler) of *Biographical Notices of Ludwig van Beethoven.*

Rietz, Julius (* Berlin, 28 Dec. 1812; † Dresden, 12 Sept. 1877). German composer, cellist, conductor and editor. Rietz was a most influential musician and a skilled composer. He was admired by Mendelssohn, whom he succeeded in 1835 as director of the Opera at Düsseldorf. In 1847 he moved to Leipzig, where he later became conductor of the Gewandhaus Orchestra and professor of composition at the Conservatory. He moved to Dresden as court conductor in 1860.

Rietz's compositions – operas, Masses and orchestral music – show mastery but lack inspiration,

although his Second Symphony is still occasionally performed.

Rode, Pierre (* Bordeaux, 16 Feb. 1774; † Château de Bourbon, Lot-et-Garonne, 25 Nov. 1830). French violinist and composer. A favorite pupil of Viotti, Rode became one of the best and most influential violinists of his time, and his style had a material effect on the playing of Louis Spohr. Both Beethoven and Boccherini dedicated compositions to him. Of his own music, the 24 *Caprices* for solo violin are still played, but the concertos and chamber music are now of only passing interest.

Rossini, Gioachino (* Pesaro, 29 Feb. 1792; † Passy, nr. Paris, 13 Nov. 1868). Italian composer. *See pp.227-237.*

Saint-Saëns, Camille (* Paris, 9 Oct. 1835; † Algiers, 16 Dec. 1921). French composer. *See Volume III.*

Salieri, Antonio (* Legnago, 18 Aug. 1750; † Vienna, 7 May 1825). Italian composer and teacher. *See Volume I.*

Schubert, Franz (* Vienna, 31 Jan. 1797; † Vienna, 19 Nov. 1828). Austrian composer. *See pp.75-93, 99-109.*

Schumann, Robert (* Zwickau, 8 June 1810; † Endenich, nr. Bonn, 29 July 1856). German composer. *See pp.195-209.*

Sechter, Simon (* Friedberg, Bohemia, 11 Oct. 1788; † Vienna, 10 Sept. 1867). Austrian theorist, composer, conductor and organist. He received all-round training in education and worked as a tutor in Vienna. From 1810 to 1825 he taught piano and singing at the Institute for the Blind, and he was appointed second, then first court organist in 1824 and 1825 respectively. Sechter soon established his reputation as an expert in musical theory and later counted Bruckner among his pupils. He was universally respected and admired, even though he took up a markedly conservative position, founded on Rameau's thorough bass, rather than point the way forward.

Sechter left innumerable compositions – the figure of 8,000 works has been mentioned – but only some fugues, preludes, organ pieces and string quartets, mostly semi-compositional routine exercises, have appeared in print.

Silcher, Friedrich (* Schnait, Württemberg, 27 June 1789; † Tübingen, 26 Aug. 1860). German composer, conductor and collector of folksongs. After spending nine years as a teacher, Silcher moved to Stuttgart in 1815 and studied piano and composition with Konradin Kreutzer and Hummel. From 1817 to 1860 he was director of Tübingen

University, and he also taught at the Evangelical College there.

Silcher composed exclusively for the voice, and many of his choral works and songs are of great beauty, including a set based on themes from Beethoven's symphonies and sonatas. He also collected and arranged folksongs from Germany and elsewhere, and, inspired by Pestalozzi, became a leading promoter of popular musical education.

Sor, Fernando (* Barcelona, 14 Feb. 1778; † Paris, 10 July 1839). Spanish composer and guitarist. Although he wrote music in various forms, including an opera and several ballets, Sor is chiefly known for his guitar compositions.

Considered the finest player of his time, his sonatas and studies for his instrument remain a fundamental part of the classical guitarist's repertoire.

Spohr, Louis (* Brunswick, 5 Apr. 1784; † Kassel, 22 Oct. 1859). German composer, violinist, conductor and teacher. He studied the violin from the age of five, and at fourteen played a concerto of his own at the Brunswick court, where he joined the ducal orchestra. During the first twenty years of the new century he toured extensively throughout Europe as a virtuoso, while holding appointments with the court orchestra at Gotha (1805-12), at the Theater an der Wien in Vienna (1813-16) and at the Frankfurt Opera (1817-19). In 1822, on Weber's recommendation, he became court conductor in Kassel, where he remained until his death.

Spohr was a prolific composer, and although his symphonies are

rarely heard, several of his violin concertos (notably no.8 in A minor), the four clarinet concertos, the nonet (op.31) and octet (op.32) and other chamber works have remained in the repertory. His oratorios and cantatas were in their time extremely popular in England, and he was a notable operatic composer, making stylistic developments which profoundly affected the course of operatic history; he anticipated Wagner's music dramas in his use of through-composition (rather than separated numbers) and by introducing *leitmotifs*. *Faust* (1816), *Zemire und Azor* (1818-19) and *Jessonda* (1823) are of particular interest.

Spontini, Gaspare (* Maiolati, nr. Iesi, 14 Nov. 1774; † Maiolati, 24 Jan. 1851). Italian composer and conductor. Spontini studied in Naples and, after the successful productions of several Italian operas, moved to Paris where he established his name with *Milton* (1804). His reputation as one of the leading composers of the day was sealed with *La Vestale* (1807), the success of which was due in part to the skillful libretto by Etienne de Jouy and in part to Spontini's ability to pace large-scale dramatic effects and exploit opportunities for striking *coups de théâtre*. His next opera, *Fernand Cortez* (1809), equals *La Vestale* in its grand scale and spectacular effects, although the music is less even in quality.

In 1819 Spontini was appointed to the Berlin Court Opera and soon had to compete with the new style of German Romantic opera. This caused divisions of opinion between public and court (which favored Spontini's grandiose Italianate works), and his attempt to regain his hold on audiences with a German opera, *Agnes von Hohenstaufen* (1827, revised 1837), was unsuccessful. His operas are usually regarded as the starting-point of French grand opera, although his style is still rooted in the Classical tradition of Gluck.

Steibelt, Daniel (* Berlin, 22 Oct. 1765; † St Petersburg, 20 Sept. 1823). German composer and pianist. The son of a harpsichord

and piano manufacturer, he was sent under royal patronage to study piano and composition with Kirnberger. After a spell in the Prussian army, he deserted in 1784 and fled the country. In 1790 he went to Paris, where he prospered as a pianist and composer and in 1796 moved to London. The last years of his life were spent in St Petersburg, where he succeeded Boïeldieu as director of the Opera.

Steibelt showed considerable originality in his scoring and harmonic practice, but generally for instant appeal; among his compositions, which include operas, ballets and many brilliant piano works, his eight piano concertos stand out for their grand effects, notably the 'Storm' Rondo of no.3 in E.

Thomas, Ambroise (* Metz, 5 Aug. 1811; † Paris 12 Feb. 1896). French composer. Thomas studied with Le Sueur in Paris and began his operatic career with a marked success, the *opéra comique La Double échelle* (1837). His subsequent works in this genre were not so favorably received until *Le Songe d'une nuit d'été* (1850), which was a triumph. Thomas tended to follow the lead of other composers rather than produce original and innovative works of his own: both *Psyché* (1857) and his greatest success, *Mignon* (1866), owed much to Gounod. However, his elegant and expressive style and melodious lyricism were responsible for the success of his next work, *Hamlet* (1868). Thomas was a distinguished professor at the Paris Conservatoire and its director from 1871.

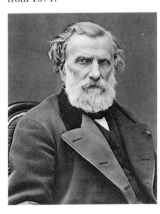

Tomášek, Václav Jan Křtitel (* Skuteč, 17 Apr. 1774; † Prague, 2 June 1850). Bohemian composer, pianist and teacher. Tomášek was taught the violin and later the organ and piano, but he learned to compose only from dedicated study of the works of others, most notably Kirnberger, Vogler, Mozart and Beethoven. Without ever becoming a great virtuoso, he was able to earn a living teaching the piano in Prague, while slowly making a reputation with his compositions. In 1806 he accepted a post as music tutor and composer to the household of Count Georg Buquoy, which gave him financial security and allowed him to continue his teaching and composition.

Tomášek composed a symphony, a piano concerto and chamber music, but his most original work was in his small piano pieces, the *Eclogues* and *Dithyrambs*, which are exquisite early Romantic miniatures of the same kind as the Impromptus of Voříšek and Schubert. His songs, many of which are settings of Goethe, are also of great beauty.

Verdi, Giuseppe (* Le Roncole, nr. Busseto, 9 Oct. 1813; † Milan, 27 Jan. 1901). Italian composer. *See pp.263-285.*

Verstovsky, Alexei Nikolayevich (* Seliverstovo, Tambov district, 1 Mar. 1799; † Moscow, 17 Nov. 1862). Russian composer. He studied with Field and Steibelt in St Petersburg, and for many years he held administrative posts in the Imperial Theaters in Moscow,

where he was highly respected. Verstovsky composed, apart from songs and ballads, almost exclusively for the theater, including incidental music, melodramas, dramatic cantatas, vaudevilles, and operas. His first vaudeville, *Grandma's Parrot* (1819), was followed by several which enjoyed some success, including *Quarantine*, while his first opera, *Pan Twardowski* (1828), clearly showed the influence of Weber, as did his greatest success, *Askold's Tomb* (1835), which ran for some 600 performances in Moscow and St Petersburg. Verstovsky's songs are acknowledged to be landmarks in the history of the Russian ballad.

Viotti, Giovanni Battista
(* Fontanetto da Po, 12 May 1755; † London, 3 Mar. 1824). Italian composer and violinist. He became a pupil of the famous Italian violinist Gaetano Pugnani in 1770, and joined the court orchestra at Turin in 1775. In 1780-81 he toured Europe with his teacher and then went alone to Paris, where he quickly established himself as a violin virtuoso. In 1788 he set up an opera company, but after the Revolution was forced to leave France and went to London, where he again appeared on the concert platform. After some years in the wine trade, in 1818 he successfully applied for the post of director at the Paris Opéra, but ran into misfortune when the Duke of Berry was murdered at the theater and patrons began to fall away.

Viotti is remembered as the founded of an influential school of French violinists which included his pupils and disciples, Rode, Baillot and Kreutzer. His own compositions center on the violin as a solo, chamber and concerto instrument. Most important are his twenty-nine concertos, heirs to the Classical tradition but also showing certain progressive features later developed by Spohr and others.

Voříšek, Jan Václav (* Vamberk, 11 May, 1791; † Vienna, 19 Nov. 1825). Bohemian composer and pianist. Having shown prodigious talent as a pianist and organist by the age of eight, Voříšek became a pupil of Tomášek in Prague and then Hummel in Vienna, where his success soon gained him the

friendship of Beethoven, Meyerbeer and Moscheles. As a pianist Voříšek was considered the equal of both Beethoven and Hummel, while as a composer a high proportion of his comparatively small output is music of inspiration and originality. Especially worthy of attention are the Violin Sonata, op.5, the Symphony in D, op.24, the B minor Piano Sonata, op.20, and the Impromptus, op.7 – the first examples of a form later followed by Schubert and Chopin.

Weber, Carl Maria von (* Eutin, nr. Lübeck, 18 Dec. 1786; † London, 4 June 1826). German composer and pianist. *See pp.127-137.*

Weigl, Joseph (* Eisenstadt, 28 Mar. 1766; † Vienna, 3 Feb. 1846). Austrian composer and conductor. Son of the composer and cellist Joseph Franz Weigl (1740-1820), he studied with Albrechtsberger from the age of ten and at sixteen composed his first opera, which gained him the approval of Gluck and Salieri. After his appointment in 1792 as Kapellmeister and composer to the Vienna Court, Weigl composed a long list of operas and ballets, many of which – *Die Schweizerfamilie* above all – became popular favorites, as well as instrumental works, several church cantatas and two oratorios. After 1827 he concentrated his efforts on a series of Grand Masses.

Wesley, Samuel (* Bristol, 24 Feb. 1766; † London, 11 Oct. 1837). English composer and organist. The more talented of the two sons of the Rev. Charles Wesley, he was the most distinguished English-born musician of his time. He was successful as a child prodigy and became an extremely fine organist, while his own music displays qualities of craft and originality.

Apart from a huge quantity of church music and other vocal works, Wesley composed symphonies, concertos, chamber music and many instrumental pieces. His brother, Charles Wesley (1757-1834), wrote a number of organ concertos and anthems; his illegitimate son, Samuel Sebastian

Wesley (1810-76), who became organist of Winchester Cathedral, was the well-known composer of church music who is now the best remembered member of the family.

Zandonai, Riccardo (* Sacco di Rovereto, Trentino, 30 May 1883; † Pesaro, 5 June 1944). Italian composer and conductor. Zandonai studied with Mascagni at the Liceo Musicale in Pesaro and embarked on a career as a successful composer of operas and famous conductor. He was the last exponent of *verismo*, although his harmonic language and orchestration betray the influence of Debussy and Ravel. His first success, *Grillo del focolare* (Turin, 1908), was followed by another seven operas, including *Conchita* (Milan, 1911), based on a story by Pierre Louÿs, and his finest work, *Francesca da Rimini* (Turin, 1914), with a libretto by Tito Ricordi after D'Annunzio's tragedy. Zandonai also composed instrumental and vocal works as well as ballet and film music. He was director of the Conservatory in Pesaro from 1940 until his death.

Zelter, Carl Friedrich (* Berlin, 11 Dec. 1758; † Berlin, 15 May 1832). German composer, conductor and teacher. A friend of Goethe, many of whose poems he set, Zelter was a pioneer of the German *Lied*. His ideas on musical education and organization formed the basis for Berlin musical life for much of the nineteenth century, and he was himself one of the most significant teachers of the age, counting Mendelssohn, Nicolai, Loewe and Meyerbeer among his pupils.

Zelter also devoted time to reviving interest in the music of Bach, editing several of his works and organizing the centenary performance of the *St Matthew Passion* in 1829, which was conducted by Mendelssohn. Apart from his *Lieder*, many of which are still performed, Zelter composed a quantity of church music, and many male-voice choruses for the Liedertafel he founded in 1809.

Zingarelli, Niccolò (* Naples, 4 Apr. 1752; † Torre del Greco, nr. Naples, 5 May 1837). Italian composer and teacher. Zingarelli

was an opera composer of almost unprecedented success throughout Europe from the production of his second opera, *Montezuma* in 1781, until his last, *Berenice*, of 1811, when he was eclipsed by Rossini's rising star; his best known work was *Giulietta e Romeo* (1796). Zingarelli achieved nearly as great a reputation as a teacher, becoming director of the Naples Conservatory in 1813, where he numbered among his pupils some of the most famous of the next generation of opera composers, including Bellini and Mercadante, and continued to battle against Rossini's influence. He spent his last years composing oratorios and church music.

Zumsteeg, Johann Rudolf (* Sachsenflur, nr. Mergentheim, 10 Jan. 1760; † Stuttgart, 27 Jan. 1802). German composer and conductor. A once successful composer of operas, church music and several works for his own instrument, the cello, Zumsteeg holds his place in history for his development of the ballad and for his strong influence on Schubert. He had a close boyhood friendship with Schiller, whose words he later frequently set to music, one of his finest works being his setting of the choruses for the poet's *Die Räuber* (1782).

INDEX

Works are normally listed under composers; institutions are listed under place. Figures in **bold** type refer to principal discussion of a composer and his work; figures in *italics* refer to subjects or authors of illustrations.

PICTURE CREDITS